"On a wide-ranging canvas and with bold strokes, J. V. Fesko gives us a study of baptism which joins a treasury of theological citations with strong theological insights. After a survey of the history of the doctrine, Fesko focuses on the Reformed tradition and its important figures and confessions. He indicates the biblical dimensions of the meanings of baptism and provides a positive and constructive statement of its theological truth. This is a valuable work for its mastery of primary sources as well as its clear articulation of the covenantal dimensions which give a Reformed theology of baptism such power and purpose for Christian believers."

—Donald K. McKim, Editor, *Encyclopedia of the Reformed Faith*

"This book represents a substantial accomplishment, one that provides a useful resource for those wanting to deepen their understanding of the sacraments, particularly baptism. Reflecting a massive amount of research against the background of an in-depth survey of various views of baptism in church history, Fesko provides an extensive exegetical and biblical-theological study of the covenantal and eschatological significance of baptism followed by systematic theological reflections on key issues like baptism as a means of grace, the efficacy of baptism, the biblical warrant for infant baptism (and against paedocommunion), and the importance of baptism for the church. One need not agree with Dr. Fesko's reflections at every point to benefit from his considerable labors."

—Richard B. Gaffin, Jr., Emeritus Professor of Biblical and Systematic Theology, Westminster Theological Seminary

"Wonderfully Reformed...John Fesko shows the fruitfulness of reflecting on baptism as a marvelously robust doctrinal statement. He is to be commended for his first rate, deep theological thought on a core sacrament of our faith."

—William H. Willimon, Presiding Bishop, The United Methodist Church, Birmingham Area, North Alabama Conference

"J. V. Fesko's *Word, Water, and Spirit* is a major work that both models how to do theology by moving from historical theology to biblical and systematic theology and, most importantly, presents fresh insights for a Reformed understanding of baptism. Fesko's fair-minded, page-turning history of the doctrine of baptism is itself worth the price of the book. Most enlightening, however, is his biblical-theological survey of baptism as new creation, covenant judgment, and eschatological judgment. The book's emphasis on God's judgment in baptism is particularly innovative and helpful. These insights pave the way for treating baptism systematically as a means of grace and as a sacrament in relation to its recipients and ecclesiology. Highly recommended for all who wish to grapple seriously with the doctrine of baptism and its implications."

—JOEL R. BEEKE, President and Professor of Systematic Theology, Puritan Reformed Theological Seminary

Word, Water, and Spirit

A Reformed Perspective on Baptism

OTHER BOOKS BY THE AUTHOR

Diversity within the Reformed Tradition: Supra- and Infralapsarianism in Calvin, Dort, and Westminster

Last Things First: Unlocking Genesis 1–3 with the Christ of Eschatology

What Is Justification by Faith Alone?

Justification: Understanding the Classic Reformed Doctrine

The Law Is Not of Faith: Essays on Grace and Works in the Mosaic Covenant (co-editor and contributor)

The Rule of Love: Broken, Fulfilled, and Applied

Where Wisdom Is Found: Christ in Ecclesiastes

Word, Water, and Spirit

A Reformed Perspective on Baptism

J. V. Fesko

REFORMATION HERITAGE BOOKS
Grand Rapids, Michigan

Word, Water, and Spirit: A Reformed Perspective on Baptism
© 2010 by J. V. Fesko

Published by
Reformation Heritage Books
2965 Leonard St., NE,
Grand Rapids, MI 49525
616-977-0889 / Fax 616-285-3246
orders@heritagebooks.org
www.heritagebooks.org

Printed in the United States of America
10 11 12 13 14 15/10 9 8 7 6 5 4 3 2 1

Library of Congress Cataloging-in-Publication Data

Fesko, J. V., 1970-
  Word, water, and Spirit : a Reformed perspective on baptism / J.V. Fesko.
    p. cm.
  Includes bibliographical references (p.   ) and indexes.
    ISBN 978-1-60178-101-7 (hardback : alk. paper)   1.   Baptism—Reformed Church. 2. Reformed Church—Doctrines. I. Title.
  BX9427.5.B36F47 2010
  234'.161—dc22
                                        2010029699

---

*For additional Reformed literature, both new and used, request a free
book list from Reformation Heritage Books at the above address.*

For my grandfather
Ismael Alatorre Valero
(June 1, 1923–March 8, 1987)
Me enseñaste a ser un hombre de Dios más de lo que supiste.

————————————

You taught me to be a man of God more than you knew.

Table of Contents

Preface

This book represents the conclusion of a long journey. When I went to seminary in the early 1990s, I arrived with my TULIP (the five points of Calvinism[1]) in hand. Many of my professors sought to pluck the petals off my TULIP. But the more my professors challenged me, the more I studied and read, the more my TULIP grew into an entire garden. Through the works of John Calvin, Francis Turretin, Jonathan Edwards, Louis Berkhof, and the like, I realized that there were far more than five points of Calvinism in the Reformed faith.

One of the points with which I initially struggled was infant baptism. As I studied the doctrine, it was in reading an anti-paedobaptist work by Baptist theologian Paul Jewett that I became convinced of one of the more crucial points of the Reformed faith: the indispensability of covenant theology. From that point onward, I studied and sought to understand the doctrine of the covenant and especially its signs. Over the years, I have become more and more convinced, steeled, and encouraged by God's covenant dealings with His people and especially the signs of the covenants.

In my decade-plus ministry in the pastorate, however, I found that people often were not as convinced as I was of the doctrine of the covenants and their attending signs. I ministered in the Baptist-dominated South, where visitors and even some church members looked with a high degree of suspicion on the Presbyterian practice of baptism. Why was so little water used? Why were infants baptized? I also encountered those who were in full retreat from the Reformed doctrine of baptism. Even though they had had some of their children baptized as infants, they were stepping back and refraining from having their newborns baptized out of a fear they had committed a grave error. I also found many students who were skeptical

---

1. The five doctrines that make up the acrostic TULIP are total depravity, unconditional election, limited atonement, irresistible grace, and the perseverance of the saints.

of the Reformed doctrine of baptism. Like a guest invited to a meal, they would gladly eat the main portion but politely leave that part untouched.

My hope is that people with all sorts of questions will be able to profit from this book. For those who want to learn about the doctrine of baptism, I hope the book is informative and edifying. For those of a Baptist persuasion, my prayer is that they will see that their Presbyterian brothers and sisters have a biblical understanding of baptism. For those who have retreated from the Reformed doctrine of baptism, my hope is that they will see and understand why baptism is so important and why, as the sign of the covenant, it should be administered to their children. Even if it is only in a small way, I want the church to know that God has spoken and said so much through water and the Word as He applies it by the Spirit.

There are a number of people to whom I owe a great deal of appreciation: Bryan Estelle, John Muether, Darryl Hart, Lane Keister, Mike Horton, and Will Willimon. I am especially thankful to both Dave VanDrunen and Jay Collier. Dave read through an early draft and really helped me clean it up. Jay was especially helpful, not only in his encouragement to pursue the book and have it published with Reformation Heritage Books, but with his editorial comments and key research tips at points. I am also thankful to Joel Beeke for reading the manuscript and his willingness to publish it. Many thanks are also due to the publishing staff at Reformation Heritage, without whom this book would not have seen the light of day.

I owe a great deal of thanks especially to my wife, Anneke. Our Lord has blessed me through you in so many ways. You have shared in my joys, challenges, and times of laughter and sorrow. Most important, especially as it relates to this book, we have both been able to receive a life-enduring blessing through our respective baptisms and have together heard the gospel promises preached audibly and seen them visibly poured out on our son, Val. I look forward to baptizing our second child with the visible Word of God in the sacrament of baptism. My prayer is that both of our children will lay hold of the gospel promises by faith alone in Christ alone by His grace alone.

My grandfather, Ismael Alatorre Valero, was a godly man, one for whom I continue to have a great deal of respect. He was very humble, had a diligent work ethic, loved his family, and was a Baptist deacon. But most of all, he loved Christ. I can remember as a small child listening to his prayers before dinner. He loved to pray. My grandmother would remind him as he started to give thanks, "Solamente por la comida, Ismael!" (Only for the food, Ismael!) Sadly, my grandfather died when I was seventeen years old. As painful as his death was for my family, our hope lies continually with the grace and mercy of our covenant-keeping Lord. In more ways than you ever knew, Papa, you taught me to be a man of God—a man of my word. It is to your memory that I dedicate this book. I look forward one day to breaking bread with you, the church, and our Lord at the marriage feast of the Lamb on that glorious eternal Sabbath-day rest.

Soli Deo Gloria

Abbreviations

General Abbreviations

ca.	*circa*, about
cf.	*confer*, compare
e.g.	*exempli gratia*, for example
i.e.	*id est*, that is
LXX	Septuagint
MT	Masoretic text (of the Old Testament)
NT	New Testament
OT	Old Testament
OPC	Orthodox Presbyterian Church
PCA	Presbyterian Church in America
q.v.	*quod vide*, which see
RCC	Roman Catholic Church
vol.	Volume
v., vv.	verse, verses

Commonly Used Abbreviations

ANE 1&2	Pritchard, *Ancient Near East*, vols. 1&2
ANF	Ante-Nicene Fathers
BDAG	Bauer-Danker-Ardnt-Gingrich, *A Greek-English Lexicon of the New Testament*, 3rd ed.
BDB	Brown-Driver-Briggs, *Hebrew and English Lexicon*
BECNT	Baker Exegetical Commentary on the New Testament
BBR	*Bulletin of Biblical Research*
BC	*Book of Concord*
BNTC	Black's New Testament Commentary
CD	Karl Barth, *Church Dogmatics*
CH	*Church History*

CNTC	*Calvin's New Testament Commentaries*
CTJ	*Calvin Theological Journal*
CTS	Calvin Translation Society
CTQ	*Concordia Theological Quarterly*
EBC	Expositor's Bible Commentary
EQ	*Evangelical Quarterly*
HALOT	*Hebrew and Aramaic Lexicon of the Old Testament*
ICC	International Critical Commentary
IJST	*International Journal of Systematic Theology*
JETS	*Journal of the Evangelical Theological Society*
JPSTC	Jewish Publication Society Torah Commentary
JSNT	*Journal for the Study of the New Testament*
LC	Larger Catechism
LCC	Library of Christian Classics
LQ	*Lutheran Quarterly*
LW	Luther's Works
MAJT	*Mid-America Journal of Theology*
Mid Rabb	*Midrash Rabbah*
NCB	New Century Bible
NIB	New Interpreter's Bible
NICNT	New International Commentary on the New Testament
NICOT	New International Commentary on the Old Testament
NIDNTT	*New International Dictionary of New Testament Theology*
NIDOTTE	*New International Dictionary of Old Testament Theology and Exegesis*
NIGTC	New International Greek Testament Commentary
NIVAC	NIV Application Commentary
NPNF[1 and 2]	Nicene and Post-Nicene Fathers, First and Second Series
NSBT	New Studies in Biblical Theology
NTC	New Testament Commentary
NTS	*New Testament Studies*
PNTC	Pillar New Testament Commentary
PR	*Princeton Review*
PTR	*Princeton Theological Review*
SC	Shorter Catechism
SJT	*Scottish Journal of Theology*
TDNT	*Theological Dictionary of the New Testament*
TNTC	Tyndale New Testament Commentary

TOTC	Tyndale Old Testament Commentary
TynBul	*Tyndale Bulletin*
WBC	Word Biblical Commentary
WCF	Westminster Confession of Faith
WTJ	*Westminster Theological Journal*
ZAW	*Zeitschrift für die alttestamentliche Wissenschaft*
ZNW	*Zeitschrift für die neutestamentliche Wissenschaft*

Introduction

Most professing Christians have passed through the waters of baptism. Whether one is a Baptist, a Roman Catholic, a Presbyterian, a Methodist, or a member of one of any number of denominations large or small, he likely has been baptized at some point. But this is only the tip of the iceberg. Above the surface of the waters there is apparent harmony, but below lurk jagged and sharp edges of differing opinions regarding what baptism actually means, how it should be defined, and to whom it should be administered.

There are some for whom baptism is a remembrance of the work of Christ. For others, it is a means by which God cleanses a person from sin. Others believe it is a sign of the covenant. For still others, it is a token of the believer's faith and commitment to God. But despite these doctrinal differences, all denominations can be classified into two groups—those who baptize *only adults* who make a profession of faith (the Baptist tradition) and those who practice *both adult and infant* baptism.

When opinions on a doctrine multiply and flood the theological scene, requiring proponents of various views to build little theological boats in which to escape the rising waters, it is necessary to return to first principles and re-examine the doctrine afresh. We find ourselves in such a time of floods and boat-building today; hence, this study.

METHODOLOGICAL PRESUPPOSITIONS: COVENANT AND CANON

The goal of this study is to explain what baptism means, define it, and identify to whom it should be administered. The underlying methodological commitment of this study is that God reveals Himself to His people through Christ and covenant. In one sense, this may not seem all that significant, as all relate baptism to Jesus in some fashion and many make reference to the covenant concept to some degree. Often, though, that reference to the doctrine of the covenant is nominal and does not undergird the explanation of the doctrine of baptism. Such a reference appears in a recent book written by Baptist theologians titled *Believer's Baptism: Sign of the New Covenant in Christ*. The term *covenant* appears in the subtitle, but there is little effort to set forth the doctrine of the covenant in the book. The largest interaction with the doctrine is directed more at correcting paedobaptist understandings of covenant rather than setting forth a positive exposition of the doctrine as it relates to baptism. Moreover, the doctrine of covenant does not permeate the various essays in the book.[1]

A similar trend appears in Stanley Grenz's (1950–2005) summary statement regarding baptism and the Lord's Supper, which he calls "community acts of commitment":

> As symbols of his story which is now our story, baptism and the Lord's Supper form the practice of commitment within the community of faith. Through these two acts we enact our faith as we symbolically reenact the story of redemption. We memorialize the events of Jesus' passion and resurrection, we bear testimony to the experience of union with Christ which we all share in the community, and we lift our sights to the grand future awaiting us as participants in the covenant community of God.[2]

In one respect, it is commendable that Grenz mentions the covenant. However, all biblical covenants involve two parties. After all, a covenant is an agreement.[3] Grenz's statement explains what the community enacts: its faith, its remembrance, its testimony, its experience, and its hope for the future. What, however, is God saying through these "acts of commitment"? God has given His covenant to His people through Christ; man has not

---

1. Thomas R. Schreiner and Shawn D. Wright, *Believer's Baptism: Sign of the New Covenant in Christ* (Nashville: Broadman & Holman, 2006), 97–162, 257–84. There are some exceptions to this trend, such as Paul K. Jewett, *Infant Baptism and the Covenant of Grace* (Grand Rapids: Eerdmans, 1978), 219–50; also Fred A. Malone, *The Baptism of Disciples Alone: A Covenantal Argument for Credobaptism Versus Paedobaptism* (2003; Cape Coral, Fla.: Founders Press, 2007).

2. Stanley Grenz, *Theology for the Community of God* (Nashville: Broadman & Holman, 1994), 677.

3. Michael Horton, *God of Promise: Introducing Covenant Theology* (Grand Rapids: Baker, 2006), 10, 23–34; Meredith G. Kline, *Kingdom Prologue: Genesis Foundations for a Covenantal Worldview* (Overland Park, Kan.: Two Age Press, 2000), 1–8; cf. John Murray, *The Covenant of Grace: A Biblico-Theological Study* (Phillipsburg, N.J.: P & R, 1987).

scaled the heights, knocked on heaven's door, and offered a man-made rite to Him. So many theologians focus on what the covenant servant does, but what about the covenant Lord?

The absence of the doctrine of the covenant is even sharper in the Roman Catholic doctrine of baptism. Roman Catholic theologians historically have conceived of their soteriology largely in terms of ontology rather than covenant. Roman Catholic theologian Edward Schillebeeckx (1914–2009) explains that the "peculiarly Protestant theology of the Covenant" leads to a "spirituality that is entirely different." He writes that though John Calvin (1509–1564) spoke of the sacraments containing and really giving grace, nevertheless there was a world of difference between the Calvinist and Roman Catholic interpretations of the sacraments.[4]

Michael Horton has adapted Paul Tillich's (1886–1965) typology of the various kinds of philosophy of religion to explain the differences between Roman Catholic and Reformation soteriologies: overcoming estrangement, meeting a stranger, and the stranger never met. The stranger never met is the totally transcendent and therefore unknowable God, such as in the philosophy of Immanuel Kant (1724–1804). Then there is the idea of overcoming estrangement. According to Roman Catholic doctrine, for example, in baptism man receives the infused righteousness of Christ and the created grace of God, a *habitus* (habit), a disposition or inclination toward spiritual good. Through this infusion of created grace man cooperates with God and overcomes his fallen estate. As it was in the creation before the fall, so it is after the fall in baptism and beyond—grace perfects nature. On the other hand, Reformation theology historically has argued that man's sin is not an ontological but a moral-ethical problem. Man is a covenant breaker. He is redeemed by meeting a stranger—Christ, who redeems him. Grace redeems nature. The difference is not between nature and grace but sin and grace.[5] Moreover, man encounters this stranger within a context, namely, that of covenant.

The difference between an ontological and a covenantal approach appears in Francis Turretin's (1623–1687) interaction with Thomas Aqui-

---

4. Edward Schillebeeckx, *Christ the Sacrament of the Encounter with God* (New York: Sheed and Ward, 1963), 185.

5. Michael Horton, *Lord and Servant: A Covenant Christology* (Louisville: Westminster John Knox, 2005), 3–21; also idem, "Meeting a Stranger: A Covenantal Epistemology," *WTJ* 66.2 (2004): 259–73; cf. Paul Tillich, "The Two Types of Philosophy of Religion," in *Theology of Culture* (New York: Oxford University Press, 1959), 10–29.

nas (1225–1274) regarding *prolegomena*. Turretin argues that when God is
set forth as the object of theology, He cannot be known as God is in Himself. In such an ontological approach, God is incomprehensible. Instead,
God as the object of theology must be approached in terms of how He
has revealed Himself in the Word. In the Word, God comes to sinful man
as He has covenanted in Christ. All good theology must embrace these
two points: Christ and covenant.[6] Turretin's point is simple. God does not
nakedly reveal Himself, but comes clothed in Christ and covenant. This
produces two important correlates.

Covenant

First, it means that a believer cannot have a mystical salvation experience
based in some sort of unique private event that is divorced from Christ
and the Word, such as it is captured in the C. Austin Miles (1868–1946)
hymn "In the Garden," which speaks of an experience that "none other has
ever known." It is not that man overcomes his estrangement as his soul
deals directly with God in some sort of mystical experience.[7] Rather, Jesus
the stranger condescends to fallen man. This means that man's redemption is inextricably bound with redemptive history, as God has progressively
revealed Himself in covenant to His corporate people, culminating in His
revelation in Christ. Knowledge of God is openly revealed in the concrete
events of redemptive history in God's condescension to His fallen creatures. Beginning in the Old Testament, God covenanted with historical
flesh-and-blood people, and He gave the new covenant through the God-
man, Jesus. Theologians, therefore, cannot merely start with the advent of
Christ and the individual's profession of faith, but must account for God's
covenantal dealings with His people from the very beginning in the garden-temple of Eden.

    The fact that God reveals Himself in covenant also means that indi-
viduals cannot isolate themselves. All individuals are redeemed as part of
the covenant community, the body of Christ, the church. This is not a new
observation, as to be a part of the new covenant is to be joined to Christ

---

    6. Francis Turretin, *Institutes of Elenctic Theology*, ed. James T. Dennison, trans. George
Musgrave Giger (Phillipsburg, N.J.: P & R, 1992–97), 1.5.4; cf. Thomas Aquinas, *Summa
Theologica* (Allen, Texas: Christian Classics, 1948), 1a qq. 12–13, 1.58–59.

    7. For analysis of these individualistic mystical trends, see Harold Bloom, *The American
Religion* (1994; New York: Chu Hartley, 2006), 54, 236, 220, 250–58; cf. E. Y. Mullins,
The Axioms of Religion, eds. Timothy and Denise George (1908; Nashville: Broadman &
Holman, 1997), 1–26, 60.

Himself. It is interesting that Justin Martyr (100–165) once wrote that $\not\times$ Christ Himself is the new covenant.[8]

Canon

The commitment to the principle that God reveals Himself in Christ and covenant brings a second correlate, namely, that doctrine is canonical; doctrine must be built on the whole of Scripture, not merely the New Testament. This is a point that even those not normally associated with conservative evangelicalism have noted. Walther Eichrodt (1890–1978) explains that the encounter with Christ in the Gospels is inseparably bound up with the Old Testament past, a history that points into the future. That which indivisibly binds the two testaments is the irruption of the kingdom of God into this world. This irruption is the unifying principle because the same God builds His kingdom in both testaments. This is why the central message of the New Testament leads back to the message of God in the Old Testament.[9] Eichrodt saw the need to look at the whole of Scripture to understand any one part.

Eichrodt's observation echoes in the writings of others, such as Gerhard von Rad (1900–1971): "The student of the New Testament also works with the Old Testament material which has been absorbed into the New by typological means. It is therefore the two Testaments which are our instructors, bidding us give more serious consideration to this element which is obviously typical of the Biblical understanding of history." Von Rad explains that it is only when the student of Scripture is able to make people believe that the two testaments belong together that he has the right to term his pursuit a theological undertaking, and therefore a truly biblical theology.[10]

Leonhard Goppelt (1911–1973) has observed this pattern in the hermeneutics of the apostle Paul. Goppelt explains: "So far as we can tell, Paul was the first to use the Greek word *typos* (adj. *typikos*) as a term for the prefiguring of the future in prior history. God dealt in a typical way (*typikos*) with Israel in the wilderness, in a manner that is a pattern for his dealing with the church in the last days. The fortunes of Israel are types (*typoi*) of the experiences of the church (1 Cor. 10:11, 6; cf. Rom. 5:14)."[11]

---

8. Justin Martyr, *Dialogue with Trypho*, chap. 51, in ANF 1.221.

9. Walther Eichrodt, *Theology of the Old Testament*, trans. J. A. Baker (Louisville: Westminster John Knox, 1961), 1.26.

10. Gerhard von Rad, *Old Testament Theology*, trans. D. M. G. Stalker (Louisville: Westminster John Knox, 1960–65), 2.410–29, esp. 428–29.

11. Leonhard Goppelt, *Typos: The Typological Interpretation of the Old Testament in the*

Other theologians have noted the necessary unity of the Scriptures. Roman Catholic theologian Hans Urs von Balthasar (1905–1988), in his five-volume presentation of doctrine as theo-drama, begins his study with a survey of the relationship between the theater and Christian theology. In his survey of the history of religious-themed theater, he explains that Easter plays in the Middle Ages naïvely portrayed Christ's descent into the underworld. Von Balthasar then explains the characteristics of the typical Easter play:

> Its perspective was centered in the Eucharistic mystery and at the same time in the whole drama of salvation. The consequences for theology of a genuinely dramatic grasp of the *descensus* are immeasurable; we shall continually be coming across them. It is from this center, insofar as they remain in contact with it, that the other episodes of the Old and New Testaments have their dramatic relevance; wherever they become independent units they are in danger of being merely episodic, moralistic or simply entertaining.[12]

Here von Balthasar sees that to isolate any one part of the dramatic narrative neutralizes its meaning, which can be derived only from its connection to Christ. Therefore, it is not merely Reformed theologians who see the need to argue doctrine from the basis of the whole canon; they are joined by a number of voices from different portions of the international theological spectrum, including Brevard Childs (1923–2007), Pope Benedict XVI, and Francis Watson.[13]

To construct theology on the basis of the canon takes into account the whole of God's revelation in Christ, but also adds a fullness and depth of understanding to the church's reading of Scripture. This practice also recognizes the plain and simple fact that for Jesus, Paul, and every other first-century theologian, the Old Testament was the Bible.[14] This means

---

New (1939; Grand Rapids: Eerdmans, 1982), 4–5; contra Malone, *The Baptism of Disciples Alone*, 138–39.

12. Hans Urs von Balthasar, *Theo-Drama: Theological Dramatic Theory* (San Francisco: Ignatius Press, 1988), 1.114.

13. See Brevard S. Childs, *Biblical Theology of the Old and New Testaments: Theological Reflections on the Christian Bible* (Minneapolis: Fortress, 1992), 70–79; Scott W. Hahn, "The Authority of Mystery: The Biblical Theology of Benedict XVI," *Letter & Spirit* 2 (2006): 97–140; Francis Watson, *Text and Truth: Redefining Biblical Theology* (Grand Rapids: Eerdmans, 1997), 127–78.

14. Richard Hays, *Echoes of Scripture in the Letters of Paul* (New Haven: Yale University Press, 1989), x–xi, 21–24; see also Watson, *Text and Truth*, 216–19.

that the church must learn to read the Old Testament as Paul read it and not according to created hermeneutical systems, such as the literalism of dispensationalism or any other theological explanation of the Bible that fails to take into account the necessity of explaining any doctrine from both testaments.[15] Nineteenth-century German universities first granted institutional recognition to the idea that the New Testament should be studied separately from the Old Testament and *a fortiori* in isolation from theology and history.[16] To study the isolated New Testament, therefore, and derive doctrinal conclusions from it is a relatively recent and novel development in the context of church history. Readers must understand the grammar and immediate historical context of a passage, but also must relate any New Testament passage under consideration to the rest of the canon, especially if there is an allusion, echo, or quotation of an Old Testament passage.[17]

The necessity of a commitment to canonical theology is illustrated briefly in John the Baptist's statement to the crowds gathered at the Jordan River: "I did not know Him, but He who sent me to baptize with water said to me, 'Upon whom you see the Spirit descending, and remaining on Him, this is He who baptizes with the Holy Spirit'" (John 1:33; cf. Matt. 3:11; Mark 1:8; Luke 3:16). What many do not realize is that English translations of this verse do not translate the word βαπτίζω. Translators merely transliterate the Greek term. Clearly, John's baptism is literal, but Christ's is of a different nature. A normal reading of the verb βαπτίζω means immersion in water, but its metaphorical meaning is that of being overwhelmed by something.[18] If analysis were to stop here, perhaps it would have done

---

15. See Herbert W. Bateman IV, "Dispensationalism Yesterday and Today," in *Three Central Issues in Contemporary Dispensationalism: A Comparison of Traditional and Progressive Views*, ed. Herbert W. Bateman IV (Grand Rapids: Kregel, 1999), 31; Charles Ryrie, *Dispensationalism Today* (Chicago: Moody, 1970), 37, 131; idem, *Basic Theology: A Popular Systematic Guide to Understanding Biblical Truth* (Wheaton: Victor Books, 1986), 525–32; 539–41; cf. Friedrich Schleiermacher, *The Christian Faith* (London: T & T Clark, 1999), 62, 611.

16. Markus Bockmuehl, *Seeing the Word: Refocusing New Testament Study* (Grand Rapids: Baker, 2006), 38.

17. See G. K. Beale and D. A. Carson, *Commentary on the New Testament Use of the Old Testament* (Grand Rapids: Baker, 2007), xxiii–xxviii. There has been a flowering of literature exploring the interconnected relationship between the Old and New Testaments. See, e.g., Steve Moyise, *The Old Testament in the New* (London: T & T Clark, 2001); Craig A. Evans, ed., *From Prophecy to Testament: The Function of the Old Testament in the New* (Peabody, Mass.: Hendrickson, 2004).

18. I. Howard Marshall, "The Meaning of the Verb 'to Baptize,'" *EQ* 45/3 (1973): 131, 137; also idem, "The Meaning of the Verb 'Baptize,'" in *Dimensions of Baptism*, JSNT Sup 234, eds. Stanley Porter and Anthony R. Cross (Sheffield: Sheffield Academic Press, 2003): 8–24.

justice to the grammar and immediate historical context, but what about the greater context of redemptive history? John refers to the promise of the outpouring of the Holy Spirit, and various Old Testament passages state that the Spirit is "poured out" or "sprinkled" (Isa. 32:15; 44:3–5; Zech. 12:10; Ezek. 36:25–27; 39:39). From this broader redemptive-historical context, it is evident that the outpouring of the Holy Spirit is the same thing as the baptism of the Spirit.

Based on this type of canonical contextualization, it is evident that John had in mind the descent of the Spirit from above like an outpoured stream of water. This baptism would be one of Spirit and fire in the sense that it would purify and purge the recipient by an agency more powerful than water. But if the verb βαπτίζω is to be coordinated with the Holy Spirit, then what is said of it also must be true of water baptism. For John the Baptist, βαπτίζω cannot have referred only to dipping and plunging in water. Rather, the verb must imply being drenched with water from above as well as from below.[19]

Good theology cannot rely merely on lexicons and grammars, but ultimately must grow organically from the canonical context; theologians must define and employ terms in the manner in which the Scriptures define and employ them. This canonical method simply recognizes the tried and true hermeneutical axiom: words mean nothing apart from a context. This aphorism can be modified: biblical words mean nothing apart from their immediate historical and broader redemptive-historical contexts. This redemptive-historical hermeneutical principle will be used in this essay to explain the doctrine of baptism.[20]

PLAN OF THE PRESENT ESSAY

Given the observations made above, this essay will proceed along the following lines. Part I will survey the history of the doctrine. Ordinarily, a chapter or two on this subject might suffice, but given the scarcity of standard historical works on the doctrine of baptism, a greater amount of space must be employed.[21] Any serious study of a doctrine must be done with an

---

19. Marshall, "The Meaning of the Verb 'To Baptize,'" 139.

20. This is a decidedly different approach than Malone's commitment to the grammatical-historical hermeneutic, one that eschews connections to the Old Testament (*Baptism of Disciples Only*, 28–29, 138–39, 219).

21. See Bryan Spinks, *Early and Medieval Rituals and Theologies of Baptism: From the*

awareness of its antecedent history. As J. Gresham Machen (1881–1937) observed, "A man cannot be original in his treatment of a subject unless he knows what the subject is; true originality is preceded by patient attention to the facts which, in application of modern pedagogic theory, is being neglected by the youth of the present day."[22] The historical study of baptism is a sorely missed element in recent treatments of the doctrine—in the hands of some writers, their cup of cappuccino has become all froth and no coffee.[23] Therefore, this part will survey the understanding of baptism from the post-apostolic church and trace it through the Middle Ages, the Counter-Reformation, the Reformation, the post-Reformation, and modern periods, examining key documents and theologians.

Part II will consist of a biblical-theological survey of the doctrine of baptism covering main themes connected with it, namely, baptism as new creation, covenant judgment, and eschatological judgment. This portion of the study will identify key concepts connected with the doctrine of baptism. In other words, it will show how the Bible itself unfolds the doctrine of baptism by exploring the three above-mentioned themes from the canon of Scripture. In terms of Geerhardus Vos's (1862–1949) explanation of biblical theology, this section will trace these themes through the Scriptures with a line—the progressive unfolding of baptism from Genesis to Revelation.[24]

Part III will employ the same biblical-theological data gathered in Part II, the straight line, in order to draw a systematic-theological circle.[25] In other words, there is the need to systematize the biblical-theological data to show how it all coheres. At the same time, this section will keep an eye to the historical issues and questions that were raised in Part I and provide

---

New Testament to the Council of Trent (Aldershot: Ashgate, 2006); and idem, *Reformation and Modern Rituals and Theologies of Baptism: From Luther to Contemporary Practices* (Aldershot: Ashgate, 2006).

22. J. Gresham Machen, *What is Faith?* (1937; Edinburgh: Banner of Truth, 1991), 19.

23. Bockmuehl notes this trend among New Testament scholars vis-à-vis Martin Luther's reading of the Pauline corpus (*Seeing the Word*, 37). The ignorance of the history of the doctrine of baptism is especially true of treatments coming from proponents of the so-called Federal Vision. See Douglas Wilson, *"Reformed" Is Not Enough: Recovering the Objectivity of the Covenant* (Moscow, Idaho: Canon Press, 2002), 85–108; E. Calvin Beisner, ed., *The Auburn Avenue Theology Pros and Cons: Debating the Federal Vision* (Fort Lauderdale, Fla.: Knox Theological Seminary, 2004), 233–44, 254–269; Steve Wilkins and Duane Garner, eds., *The Federal Vision* (Monroe, La.: Athanasius Press, 2004), 47–126.

24. Geerhardus Vos, "The Idea of Biblical Theology as a Science and as a Theological Discipline," in *Redemptive History and Biblical Interpretation: The Shorter Writings of Geerhardus Vos*, ed. Richard B. Gaffin, Jr. (Phillipsburg, N.J.: P & R, 1980), 23.

25. Vos, "Biblical Theology," 23–24.

answers to them. Part III therefore will survey baptism as a means of grace, as a sacrament, and as a formal doctrine, and in terms of the recipients and the relationship of baptism to ecclesiology. Following Part III, the essay will conclude with some observations regarding the importance of the doctrine of baptism for the church.

THE ULTIMATE AIM OF THE STUDY

The overall goal of this book is to validate the exegetical and theological conclusions of the Westminster Confession of Faith on baptism: "Baptism is a sacrament of the new testament, ordained by Jesus Christ, not only for the solemn admission of the party baptized into the visible church; but also, to be unto him a sign and seal of the covenant of grace, of his engrafting into Christ, of regeneration, of remission of sins, and of his giving up unto God, through Jesus Christ, to walk in newness of life" (WCF 28.1). However, understanding such a statement involves the idea that the sacraments are God's visible revelation—what the Word is to the ear, the sacraments are to the other senses, but chiefly to the eyes. Recognizing that the sacraments are divine revelation means not only that they are signs of the covenant, but that they can be means either of covenant blessing or sanction.

There are no neutral encounters with God and His revelation, whether in Word or sacrament. Whether man receives Word and sacrament as covenant blessing or sanction depends on the presence or absence in the recipient of faith in the incarnate, crucified, risen, and ascended Messiah. Moreover, despite the insistence of some on one exclusive mode of baptism, all three modes—immersion, sprinkling, and pouring—are biblical, as all are connected in some way with the promised baptism of the Spirit.

Paul Tillich (1888–1965) once wrote of the "death of the sacraments."[26] He believed that a complete disappearance of the sacramental element would lead to the disappearance of the cultus, and eventually to the dissolution of the visible church itself. This stinging observation is true of many churches. In some churches, the sacraments have been relegated to the museum of faith as relics and trappings of a bygone era. One Baptist church, which shall remain nameless, placed the administration of baptism in the "traditional" worship service, which was held in the evening for those who liked "old-time religion." Baptism, apparently, was not considered

---

26. Paul Tillich, *The Protestant Era* (Chicago: University of Chicago Press, 1948), 94.

contemporary enough to be celebrated during the "contemporary" worship service. In other quarters, baptism is treated as a quaint sentimental observance dedicated to what P. T. Forsyth (1848–1921) called the "cult of the child."[27] The cult of the child cuts across denominational lines, whether in the baptism of an infant in a Presbyterian church as congregants fawn over a newborn, or in the efforts of a small child to "swim" out of the baptismal pool in a Baptist church to the sound of muffled laughter. In the Roman Catholic setting, there seems to be no shortage of those who rarely darken the door of the church, but when a child is born they want to have him or her baptized, "just to be safe," as if baptism were a "fire insurance policy."

Surprisingly enough, Tillich believed that finding "the solution of the problem of 'nature and sacrament' is today a task on which the very destiny of Protestantism depends."[28] In many ways, this is certainly a true statement, as not only are Protestants leaving Geneva for Rome or Constantinople, but an unawareness of exactly what the sacraments are has so relativized them that many Protestants see no difference between their own practice and that of the Roman Catholic Church.[29] Yet if the sacraments are objective revelation of God, then the church must recapture an understanding of their significance.

Would sentimentalism and saccharine emotions dominate congregations if they realized that a person is baptized into the death of Christ? Would characterizations of baptism solely as man's pledge to God dominate if churches realized that baptism is God's visible covenant promise when accompanied by the Word? Would as many languish in their struggles with a lack of assurance were their baptisms to echo throughout their lives—the echo of the sign and seal of the covenant promises of God in Christ? Would so many flippantly approach baptism or disregard it if they recognized that it is the objective, double-edged, blessing-and-sanction revelation of God? A biblical doctrine of baptism is crucial for the edification of the church and the glory of the triune Lord.

---

27. P. T. Forsyth, *The Church and Sacraments* (1917; London: Independent Press Ltd., 1955), 172.

28. Tillich, *Protestant Era*, 112.

29. See, e.g., Scott and Kimberly Hahn, *Rome Sweet Home: Our Journey to Catholicism* (San Francisco: Ignatius Press, 1993); Roger Beckwith, *Return to Rome: Confessions of an Evangelical Catholic* (Grand Rapids: Baker, 2009).

PART I

The History of the Doctrine

CHAPTER 1

Baptism in the Patristic Age, Middle Ages, and Counter Reformation

Any study of a doctrine ideally should begin with a survey of its history. This is important not only so that the investigator can stand on the shoulders of giants and learn from great theological minds, but also so he can trace the development of the doctrine. As noted in the introduction, while all Christian denominations practice baptism, and while the external rite looks identical in many respects from one church to the next, radically different theologies often inform the practice. This chapter therefore begins with a survey of the Patristic Age and the Middle Ages. This survey is not in any way exhaustive, as the subject easily could fill several monographs. Nevertheless, important features of the development of the doctrine must be observed by exploring key documents and a cross-section of theologians.

Therefore, the survey of the Patristic Age will examine the *Didache*, the *Shepherd of Hermas*, and the writings of Justin Martyr, Tertullian, and Augustine. For the Middle Ages, the chapter will explore the works of Peter Lombard, Bonaventure, and Thomas Aquinas. The chapter will conclude with a survey of the Counter Reformation in both the dogmatic decrees and the catechism of the Council of Trent. Though the views expressed by Trent were promulgated after a number of views from the Reformation, it is fair to say that Trent crystallized the views largely of Augustine, though they had been refined by a number of medieval theologians.

THE PATRISTIC PERIOD

The *Didache*

One of the earliest extant documents to give a glance into baptismal theology and practice in the early Patristic period is the *Didache*, or the *Teaching of the Twelve Apostles*. Scholars date the *Didache* to 100–120 AD and believe that it likely reflected the beliefs and practices of a Jewish-Christian community, one that was dominated by Torah observance. Scholars believe, however, that the first half of the document was intended as a pre-baptismal catechism.[1]

There is not much in the *Didache* that gives an investigator great insight into an early theology of baptism, though some things suggest general contours. The document begins by explaining that there are two ways, "One of life and one of death" (§ 1).[2] Those who are marked by the way of life obey the two great commandments, and those who are not so marked disobey them. Beyond the moral parenesis, there is a hint of realized eschatology in the conclusion of the document when it states that in the last days false prophets will multiply and sheep will turn into wolves. Deception will reach its pinnacle when a "world-deceiver" will appear as "Son of God" and "do iniquitous things which have never yet come to pass since the beginning." On the heels of these events, the *Didache* explains, "Then shall the creation of men come into the fire of trial and many shall be made to stumble and shall perish; but they that endure in their faith shall be saved from under the curse itself" (§ 16).

It is within this context of the two ways that culminate in judgment and salvation that instructions for baptism appear. The seventh chapter states that converts are to be baptized into the triune name of God, Father, Son, and Holy Spirit, and this is to be done in "living water" (ὕδατος ζῶντος), that is, running water. If living water is not available, then "other water" is to be used. Cold water is preferred over warm, though if the former is not available, the latter is acceptable. If "living" or "other" water is not available, it is acceptable to pour out water three times in the triune name of God. In addition, baptismal candidates are to fast one or two days before their baptisms.

From these sketchy details, some basic observations can be made. First, it is evident that the mode of baptism was not of great concern, though there was certainly a tiered preference, beginning with immersion in cold living water. Second, it seems that those who were baptized were those who would be saved on the last day, which means that there was some awareness of a connection between baptism and eschatology. Third, there is an insistence on baptism in the triune name of God, which echoes the Great Commission (Matt. 28:18–20). Fourth, given that baptismal candidates

---

1. Bryan D. Spinks, *Early and Medieval Rituals and Theologies of Baptism: From the New Testament to the Council of Trent* (Aldershot: Ashgate, 2006), 14–16.

2. All subsequent citations come from *The Teaching of the Twelve*, in ANF 7.377–82.

were supposed to fast in anticipation of their baptisms, it is safe to assume that these instructions were for adult converts. The baptism of infants was not in view.

Beyond these basic observations, few conclusions can be drawn from the *Didache*, such as how the document's author(s) understood the water to function in baptism. Did the water cleanse the baptismal candidate from sin, as in later views, or was it symbolic for the work of the Holy Spirit? We must turn to other Patristic documents to find some answers.

The *Shepherd of Hermas*

The *Shepherd of Hermas*, which probably dates from the early to middle second century, is a series of visions, followed by twelve commandments and ten parables, purportedly written by one Hermas. In the ninth parable, the longest, the author receives a vision of a tower made of stones, which is supposed to be imagery representing the church, consisting of the faithful. In this parable, the author makes a number of statements concerning baptism. In particular, he writes: "Before a man bears the name of the Son of God he is dead; but when he receives the seal he lays aside his deadness, and obtains life. The seal, then, is the water: they descend into the water dead, and they arise alive. And to them, accordingly, was this seal preached, and they made use of it that they might enter into the kingdom of God."[3]

It appears from this statement that the author ascribes certain consequences to baptism that are not found in the Scriptures. In particular, this statement appears to echo Paul's teaching in Romans 6, the idea of being buried with Christ in baptism and being raised with him to walk in newness of life (Rom. 6:3–4). Yet, there is a significant difference between Hermas and Paul. The apostle attributes saving efficacy not to the water but to the believer's union with Christ (Rom. 6:5). By contrast, Hermas states that when a person descends into the waters of baptism, he arises alive. In other words, saving efficacy is tied to the waters of baptism.[4]

Justin Martyr

A similar pattern emerges in the writings of Justin Martyr (110–165), an early Christian apologist from whom a number of writings have survived

---

3. *The Pastor of Hermas*, Similitude 9.16, in ANF 2.49.
4. Cf. Spinks, *Theologies of Baptism*, 26; Everett Ferguson, *Baptism in the Early Church: History, Theology, and Liturgy in the First Five Centuries* (Grand Rapids: Eerdmans, 2009), 214–20.

to the present day. One of his more famous works is his *First Apology*, in which he defends the Christian faith and addresses a number of theological topics, including baptism. In this brief chapter (as in the *Didache*), Justin explains that when a person is persuaded of the Christian faith, he is to fast, pray, and seek God for the forgiveness of his sins. Once this is completed, the candidate is then baptized: "Then they are brought by us where there is water, and are regenerated in the same manner in which we were ourselves regenerated. For, in the name of God, the Father and Lord of the universe, and of our Savior Jesus Christ, and of the Holy Spirit, they then receive the washing with water."[5] There is a clear connection here between the water and regeneration. In support of this claim, Justin cites John 3:5 and Isaiah 1:16–20, passages that speak of new birth and the forgiveness of sins. Therefore, in the water of baptism a person is illuminated in his understanding and obtains the remission of sins.[6]

Tertullian

It is important to examine the writings of Tertullian of Carthage (ca. 160–225) about baptism, not only because he was an apologist and a founding father of Western theology, but because his work *On Baptism* (ca. 200–206) is the only extant treatise on the doctrine that antedates the Council of Nicea (325 AD).[7] Tertullian begins his treatise by explaining why God chose water as a vehicle of divine operation. He argues that water was one of the shapeless substances with which God originally created the world (§ 3).[8] It should come as no surprise, then, that Tertullian argues that the waters of the primeval creation typify baptism, though he also identifies the Red Sea crossing and the water that flowed from the rock as other types.[9] In addition, he states that God used water and made it a channel of sanctification in that the outward sign resembled the inward grace that was communicated in the rite. Combining the ideas of the waters of creation and baptism, Tertullian writes:

---

5. Justin Martyr, *The First Apology*, § 61, in ANF v. 1.

6. Martyr, *First Apology*, § 61, in ANF v. 1; cf. similar comments in idem, *Dialogue with Trypho*, § 138, in ANF 1.

7. Steven A. McKinion, "Baptism in the Patristic Writings," in *Believer's Baptism: Sign of the New Covenant in Christ*, eds. Thomas R. Schreiner and Shawn D. Wright (Nashville: B & H Academic, 2006), 173.

8. Tertullian, *On Baptism*, § 3, in ANF v. 3.

9. Tertullian, *On Baptism*, § 9.

All waters, therefore, in virtue of the pristine privilege of their origin, do, after invocation of God, attain the sacramental power of sanctification; for the Spirit immediately supervenes from the heavens, and rests over the waters, sanctifying them from Himself; and being thus sanctified, they imbibe at the same time the power of sanctifying.

Tertullian goes on to explain, "Therefore, after the waters have been in a manner endued with medicinal virtue through the intervention of the angel, the spirit is corporeally washed in the waters, and the flesh is in the same spiritually cleansed."[10]

From these statements it is apparent that, for Tertullian, God through the Holy Spirit uses the water of baptism as an instrumental means of cleansing a person from his sin. Tertullian did not believe, though, that the Holy Spirit is given through the water of baptism, but that the one baptized is cleansed from sin and prepared for the indwelling of the Holy Spirit.[11] According to Tertullian, then, baptism is a necessary element in a person's salvation.[12] If this is so, how were believers in the Old Testament saved if they were not recipients of the sacrament? Tertullian answers this question by arguing that in the Old Testament, salvation was granted through a bare faith, but in the wake of the passion and resurrection of Christ, an amplification has been added to the sacrament, which he calls "the sealing act of baptism." He explains that baptism is "the clothing, in some sense, of the faith which before was bare, and which cannot exist now without its proper law." When Tertullian mentions the "law," he means the Great Commission and the command to baptize.[13]

Though Tertullian believed that baptism is necessary for salvation, as it cleanses a person from sin and prepares him to receive the Holy Spirit, this does not mean he automatically assumed the necessity of baptizing infants. Tertullian believed that baptism should be delayed until the child completely understood the commitment involved in becoming a Christian. He believed that when baptism was administered to small children or infants, the child and the one(s) who brought the child were assuming the responsibility of being a Christian for the child. Parents had little evidence

10. Tertullian, *On Baptism*, § 4.

11. Tertullian, *On Baptism*, § 7.

12. Tertullian, *On Baptism*, § 12; J. N. D. Kelly, *Early Christian Doctrines* (San Francisco: Harper Collins, 1978), 209.

13. Tertullian, *On Baptism*, § 13.

from small children that they would live obediently, and therefore Tertullian believed that baptizing small children or infants was dangerous.

We must keep in mind that Tertullian's understanding of baptism was informed by his soteriology. He believed that infants are innocent of sin and therefore not immediately in need of baptism: "Why does the innocent period of life hasten to the 'remission of sins'? More caution will be exercised in worldly matters: so that one who is *not* trusted with earthly substance *is* trusted with divine! Let them know how to 'ask' for salvation, that you may seem (at least) to have given 'to him that asks.'"[14] In other words, since an infant is innocent of sin, he has no need for baptism, so why needlessly encumber a child with the obligation to obedience when it is quite possible the child will grow up only to reject the Christian faith?

In addition to these theological points, Tertullian makes some liturgical observations concerning the timing, practice, and preparation for baptism. He opines that Passover is the most preferential day for baptism, as it was the time when Christ was crucified. A second choice is Pentecost, on which day the resurrection of Christ was repeatedly proved among the disciples. Tertullian concludes, however, that every day belongs to the Lord and therefore every time is suitable for baptism. While there may be greater solemnity for the administration of baptism on Passover or Pentecost, there is no difference in terms of the grace a person receives if he or she is baptized on any other day.[15] Tertullian also advises, as do the *Didache* and Justin Martyr, that the baptismal candidate should pray and fast prior to his reception of the sacrament.[16]

Though Tertullian opposed infant baptism, other Patristic witnesses testify to its practice. Origen (ca. 185–ca. 254) states, "Little children are baptized 'for the remission of sins.'"[17] Origen believed every person was born polluted by sin and therefore required baptism: "The baptism of the Church is given for the forgiveness of sins, that, according to the observance of the Church, that baptism also be given to infants; since, certainly, if there were nothing in infants that ought to pertain to forgiveness and indulgence, then the grace of baptism would appear superfluous."[18] There

---

14. Tertullian, *On Baptism*, § 18.

15. Tertullian, *On Baptism*, § 19.

16. Tertullian, *On Baptism*, § 20.

17. Origen, *Homilies on Luke: Fragments on Luke*, trans. Joseph T. Lienhard (Washington: Catholic University Press of America, 1996), homily 14 on Luke 2:21–24 (58).

18. Origen, *Homilies on Leviticus: 1–16*, trans. Gary Wayne Barkley (Washington: Catholic University Press of America, 1990), 8.3.5 (158).

are similar statements in Cyprian (d. 258), Hippolytus of Rome (170–236), and Chrysostom (347–407).[19]

Augustine

Augustine (354–430) was arguably the greatest theologian of the first millennium of the church. Augustine is known for many things, such as the priority of divine grace in salvation and his debates with Pelagius (ca. 354–420/40), but also for his writings on the doctrine of the church. In his writings from the Donatist controversy, he devotes great attention to ecclesiology, specifically to the doctrine of baptism (though not everything Augustine wrote on the subject comes from his anti-Donatist writings).

The Donatist controversy was sparked by the Diocletian persecution of the church. The specific issue was whether a sacrament, such as baptism, was invalidated if the minister who administered it later apostatized under the pressure of persecution.[20] Did the minister's defection from the faith nullify the baptism? Those who followed the teachings of Donatism believed that serious sin by the one who administered the sacrament did indeed negate it. This meant that a person who received baptism from a minister who later apostatized needed to be rebaptized.[21] Augustine countered by stating that the efficacy of the sacrament does not depend on the minister but on Christ, as it is He who ultimately administers the rite. Augustine states, "If 'the conscience, then, of him who gives in holiness is what we look for to cleanse the conscience of the recipient,' what means are to be found for cleansing the conscience of the recipient when the conscience of the giver is stained with guilt, without the knowledge of him who is to receive the sacrament at his hands?"[22] The efficacy of the sacraments, and more specifically baptism, therefore depends on God and not man, according to Augustine.

The Donatists held a view that has been called *ex opere operantis* ("on account of the work of the one who works"). In other words, the efficacy

---

19. Cyprian, *The Epistles of Cyprian*, epist. 68.2, in ANF 5.353–54; Hippolytus, *The Treatise on the Apostolic Tradition of St. Hippolytus of Rome, Bishop and Martyr*. (London: Alban Press, 1992), 21.3; Chrysostom, *Baptismal Catecheses*, in Augustine, *Against Julian* 1.6.21, in *Fathers of the Church*, vol. 35, trans. Michael Schumacher (Washington: Catholic University of America Press, 1957). For other citations and references, see Joachim Jeremias, *Infant Baptism in the First Four Centuries* (1960; Eugene, Ore.: Wipf & Stock, 2004), esp. 11–18.

20. See B. B. Price, *Medieval Thought: An Introduction* (Oxford: Blackwell, 1996), 38–40.

21. Jaroslav Pelikan, *The Christian Tradition: A History of the Development of Doctrine* (Chicago: University of Chicago Press, 1971), 1.308.

22. Augustine, *The Letters of Petilian, The Donatist*, 3.15.18 in NPNF[1] 4.603.

of the sacrament depends on the personal qualities of the minister. By contrast, Augustine's position has been called *ex opere operato* ("by the work performed"). This term reflects the idea that the sacrament is dependent not on man but on the grace of Christ, which the sacraments represent and convey. A modified Donatist position (one that rejected baptismal regeneration) was eventually taken up by sections of the Radical Reformation and continues to be significant within sections of Protestantism, especially those that stress the importance of holiness or charismatic gifts. Augustine's position became normative within the Western church, especially in the Roman Catholic Church, and was maintained, albeit in a modified form, by the sixteenth-century Reformers.[23]

Beyond the ecclesiological connections that Augustine drew to baptism, there are important connections to his soteriology. Augustine, in contrast to Pelagius, believed in what later theologians would call the total depravity of man. Like Pelagius, he believed that all men imitate Adam in his sin and transgress the commandment of God. However, unlike Pelagius, he believed that God holds all men accountable for the sin of Adam and that they carry about a fallen nature because of Adam's sin. Augustine based his understanding of original sin on his exegesis of Romans 5:12.[24]

That all people, including infants, are guilty of sin means that both adults and infants need the sacrament of baptism to be saved.[25] This is because, according to Augustine, it is "the sacrament of regeneration." Augustine bases this theological conclusion on his understanding of John 3:3: "Even an infant, therefore, must be imbued with the sacrament of regeneration, lest without it his would be an unhappy exit out of this life; and this baptism is not administered except for the remission of sins."[26] The great African theologian believed, then, that baptism frees an infant from the serpent's poisonous bite, the guilt of original sin, and conforms him to the image of Christ. More broadly, Augustine also explains: "Inasmuch as the generation of sinful flesh through the one man, Adam, draws into condemnation all who are born of such generation, so the generation of the Spirit of grace through the one man Jesus Christ, draws to the justification

23. Alister E. McGrath, *Historical Theology: An Introduction to the History of Christian Thought* (Oxford: Blackwell, 1998), 77–79.

24. Augustine, *On the Merits and Forgiveness of Sins, and On the Baptism of Infants*, 1.10 in NPNF[1] 5.18–19.

25. Augustine, *On the Baptism of Infants*, 1.63 in NPNF[1] 5.40.

26. Augustine, *On the Baptism of Infants* 2.43 in NPNF[1] 5.62.

of eternal life all who, because predestinated, partake of this regeneration."[27] Here there is a nexus of doctrines that funnel into Augustine's understanding of baptism. Yes, an adult must place his faith in Jesus, and this is a result of the prevenient grace of God in predestination, but at the same time the water of baptism is necessary to change, cleanse, and regenerate the one who was baptized. The regenerative power of baptism is also effective on baptized infants, who, though they have not committed actual sins, are guilty of original sin, and therefore liable to condemnation.

Augustine, however, did not base his understanding of baptism, especially of infants, solely on Romans 5 and John 3 and the need for regeneration. He also gave his doctrine of baptism a covenantal cast, something that was absent in the theology of Justin Martyr and Tertullian, for example. First, Augustine believed that infants were to receive baptism because its Old Testament counterpart, circumcision, was given to infants: "As therefore in Abraham the justification of faith came first, and circumcision was added afterwards as the seal of faith; so in Cornelius the spiritual sanctification came first in the gift of the Holy Spirit, and the sacrament of regeneration was added afterwards in the laver of baptism." Augustine also draws on the example of Isaac, "Who was circumcised on the eighth day after his birth, the seal of this righteousness of faith was given first, and afterwards, as he imitated the faith of his father, the righteousness itself followed as he grew up, of which the seal had been given before when he was an infant."[28] Augustine then draws the parallel to baptism: "So in infants, who are baptized, the sacrament of regeneration is given first, and if they maintain a Christian piety, conversion also in the heart will follow, of which the mysterious sign had gone before in the outward body."[29]

Some questions naturally arise. How can an infant be regenerated but not converted? How does this process work with an adult who ostensibly is first converted and then regenerated in baptism? Augustine answers, "The sacrament of baptism is one thing, the conversion of the heart another; but that man's salvation is made complete through the two together." He believed that the sacrament could be administered to an infant without the child being converted. On the other hand, using the thief on the cross as an example, he believed that one could be saved apart from the sacrament. In both cases, if a child is baptized but not converted, or an adult is converted

---

27. Augustine, *On the Baptism of Infants* 2.43 in NPNF[1] 5.62.
28. Augustine, *On Baptism, Against the Donatists*, 4.24 in NPNF[1] 4.461–62.
29. Augustine, *On Baptism, Against the Donatists*, 4.24 in NPNF[1] 4.461–62.

but not baptized, God will fill up what is involuntarily lacking for a person's salvation. Augustine stipulates, however, that if one of these elements is voluntarily lacking, the person is liable for the omission. So, for example, if a person claims to be saved but refuses to be baptized, such a person's profession is invalid: "Nor can there be said in any way to be a turning of the heart to God when the sacrament of God is treated with contempt." Likewise, a person can be baptized, but if he never responds with faith, he too will be held accountable for his contempt.[30]

SUMMARY AND ANALYSIS

At this point, the chapter has surveyed the *Didache*, the *Shepherd of Hermas*, and the views of Justin Martyr, Tertullian, and Augustine. From this cross-section of documents and views, the following points should be noted.

First, earlier documents, such as the *Didache*, seem to say little about the theology of baptism and place a greater emphasis on liturgical practice, the mode, and the required preparation to receive the sacrament. There is flexibility in terms of the mode, whether running or standing water, cold or warm, or, if none of these is available, water poured from a vessel three times on the recipient.

Second, as time passed there was greater theological reflection on baptism, primarily the idea that the water was not merely symbolic but that, by divine ordination, it actually had the power to regenerate a person and cleanse him of his sins. This development was present, however seminal, as early as the second century in the *Shepherd of Hermas*, and developed quite clearly in the later expressions of Justin Martyr, Tertullian, and Augustine.

Third, there was less emphasis in the third and fourth centuries on questions of mode and more attention given to the theology of baptism, particularly as the rite relates to ecclesiology, as well as discussion concerning the proper recipients of the sacrament. Baptist theologians appeal to Tertullian, who preferred that infants and young children not be baptized. Yet it seems little if any attention is given to the theology of Tertullian's view, namely, his belief that infants are innocent of sin and therefore do not need to be baptized. Moreover, Baptists who appeal to Tertullian ignore his statements concerning the regenerative powers of the water.[31]

---

30. Augustine, *On Baptism, Against the Donatists*, 4.25 in NPNF[1] 4.462.
31. See, e.g., McKinion, "Baptism in the Patristic Writings," 173–77.

When asking questions of historical theology, one should be cautious and not appeal to one aspect of a theologian's views to claim evidence for one particular position apart from an examination of the whole. In this case, one should not merely investigate whether infants were or were not baptized, but also, when they were, seek the theological reason. While there might be a parallel between current Baptist practice and that of Tertullian, the two practices seem worlds apart theologically. Equating the two positions is like saying that Baptists and Roman Catholics believe the same thing about the baptism of adults. The same must be said about historical defenses of Protestant paedobaptism. Investigators should stipulate the very different theological assumptions underlying early expressions on infant baptism. It is therefore important to observe the characteristics and theologies of an expressed view of baptism, but also to offer some analysis as to why a view was expressed in the manner it was.

For example, why was there an apparent shift from Paul's view that salvation is by faith alone in Christ alone to the idea that the water of baptism plays an instrumental role in salvation by regenerating a person and cleansing him of sin? The answer to this question lies in the theological-philosophical development of the time, particularly the realism in the theology of the Patristics. If the question of infant baptism is set aside and attention is given to the broader issue of the cleansing power of the water, it is evident that Justin Martyr, Tertullian, and Augustine believed there was miraculous power in the water itself. In the same way, Justin believed that those who partake of the Lord's Supper eat the literal flesh and blood of Christ. He writes in his *First Apology*:

> For not as common bread and common drink do we receive these; but in like manner as Jesus Christ our Savior, having been made flesh by the Word of God, had both flesh and blood for our salvation, so likewise have we been taught that the food which is blessed by the prayer of His word, and from which our blood and flesh by transmutation are nourished, is the flesh and blood of that Jesus who was made flesh.[32]

Long before views on transubstantiation developed, Justin expressed a realistic view of the supper. Naturally, he had a similarly realistic view of baptism, seeing power in the water to regenerate man.

There is a similar pattern in Tertullian. Based on his commitment to certain tenets of Stoicism (the idea that the universe consists of cause and

---

32. Justin Martyr, *First Apology*, 66.2 in ANF 1.185.

matter, and that matter lies sluggish and ready for any use by the first cause), Tertullian believed that both the soul and God are corporeal beings, and this in turn led him to believe that the soul of a person is derived from the souls of his parents, just as the body is so derived.[33] For example, when Tertullian explains his views on the transmission of original sin, he does so using realistic language: "Every soul, then, by reason of its birth, has its nature in Adam until it is born again in Christ; moreover, it is unclean all the while that it remains without this regeneration; and because unclean, it is actively sinful, and suffuses even the flesh (by reason of their conjunction) with its own shame."[34] According to Tertullian, sin flows substantively from the soul to man's body. Tertullian, though, rejects the dualistic view of man, which teaches that anything material is inherently evil. Nevertheless, if original sin is substantival, it should be no surprise that the cure is also substantival. For example, Paul Tillich explains: "It was easy for Tertullian, with his Stoic background, to think of the Spirit as a material force in the water. This force somehow physically extinguishes the former sins and physically gives the Spirit. Here we see what has been called Tertullian's 'materialism.'"[35]

This realistic view of sin is even more pronounced in the theology of Augustine. Like Tertullian, Augustine believed in the realistic view of the transmission of original sin. He believed that all men were seminally present in Adam. Man therefore requires the infused grace of God to counteract the effects of original sin.[36] For example, Augustine writes:

> For by this grace He engrafts into His body even baptized infants, who certainly have not yet become able to imitate anyone. As therefore He, in whom all are made alive, besides offering Himself as an example of righteousness to those who imitate Him, gives also to those who believe on Him the hidden grace of His Spirit, which He secretly infuses even into infants.[37]

In support of his understanding of infant baptism, Augustine cites 1 Peter 3:20: "'And by the like figure baptism saves you.' Now infants are

---

33. Justo L. González, *A History of Christian Thought* (Nashville: Abingdon, 1987), 1.183; see Tertullian, *The Soul's Testimony*, § 3 in ANF 3.176–77; cf. Seneca, *Ad Lucilium Epistulae Morales*, Loeb Classical Library, trans. Richard M. Gummere, (1917; Cambridge: Harvard University Press, 1967), LXV.2 (1.445).

34. Tertullian, *A Treatise on the Soul*, 40 in ANF 3.220.

35. Paul Tillich, *A History of Christian Thought: From Its Hellenistic Origins to Existentialism* (New York: Simon & Schuster, 1968), 49.

36. Augustine, *On the Baptism of Infants*, 1.19–20 in NPNF¹ 5.22–23.

37. Augustine, *On the Baptism of Infants*, 1.10 in NPNF¹ 5.18–19.

strangers to this salvation and light, and will remain in perdition and darkness, unless they are joined to the people of God by adoption, holding to Christ who suffered, the just for the unjust, to bring them unto God."[38] It seems clear that Augustine interprets this passage quite literally, and therefore concludes that infants are unsaved, indeed damned, if they remain unbaptized. However, Augustine conceded that unbaptized infants did not suffer the same penalty as one guilty of grievous sin: "It may therefore be correctly affirmed, that such infants as quit the body without being baptized will be involved in the mildest condemnation of all."[39]

We must keep this realistic view of sin and grace in mind. True, the aforementioned authors believed that water is not intrinsically miraculous and that God through Christ and the Holy Spirit ultimately saves a person from his sins. Nevertheless, they believed that the water of baptism is a channel or instrument for the grace of God, and they viewed grace in a substantival manner. When this material view of grace and baptism was combined with later views on the role and authority of church tradition, naturally these Patristic views, especially those of Augustine, became authoritative in the Middle Ages.

THE MIDDLE AGES

In the Middle Ages, there was a definite development in terms of the systematic expression of doctrine in the scholastic works of a number of theologians. For example, though the term *sacrament* was used in Western Christianity from the time of Tertullian and was defined by Augustine, an organized and systematic theology of the sacraments first appeared in the theological works of a number of medieval theologians.[40] This section will survey the views of Peter Lombard, Bonaventure, and Thomas Aquinas.

Peter Lombard

Peter Lombard (1100–1160) was one of the key theologians of the Middle Ages who explained and defined the sacraments. In the *Sentences*, Lombard defines a sacrament in the following way:

---

38. Augustine, *On the Baptism of Infants*, 1.41 in NPNF[1] 5.31.
39. Augustine, *On the Baptism of Infants*, 1.21in NPNF[1] 5.22–23.
40. Spinks, *Theologies of Baptism*, 141.

"A Sacrament is a sign of a sacred thing." However a sacrament is also said to be a sacred secret, just as there is said to be a sacrament of the Divinity, so that a sacrament is a sacred thing signifying and the sacred thing signified; but now one deals with the sacrament, according to which it is a sign—Likewise, "A Sacrament is the visible form of an invisible grace."[41]

Lombard relies on Augustine's earlier definition of a sacrament as a sign of a sacred thing.[42] He concludes his definition by once again citing Augustine, who elsewhere defined a sacrament as a visible form of an invisible grace.[43] Beyond this, Lombard distinguishes between a sacrament and a sign. A sign is, "The thing beside the species, which it bears upon the senses, causing something else out of itself to come into one's thinking."[44] Again, Lombard draws this definition from Augustine.[45] He goes on to amplify the difference between a sign and a sacrament by explaining: "Therefore not only for the grace of signifying have the Sacraments been instituted, but also for that of sanctifying. For those things which have only been instituted for the grace of signifying, are solely signs, and not Sacraments."[46] In other words, a sign can point to the grace of God, but not all signs have been ordained to convey sanctifying grace. Hence, while all sacraments are signs, not all signs are sacraments.

Lest one think that Lombard drifts too far into bald theological construction grounded merely on church tradition, note what he says regarding the nature of baptism as a sacrament. Again, relying on the statements of Augustine, Lombard compares baptism and circumcision:

However, there was among those Sacraments a certain Sacrament, that is of circumcision, conferring the same remedy against sin, which Baptism now does. Whence Augustine says: "For which purpose circumcision has been instituted among the people of God, which was then a mark of the justice of faith, and which prevailed for the purgation of the original and old sin from great and small; just as Baptism

41. Petri Lombardi, *Sententiae in IV Libris Distinctae*, 2 vols. (Grottaferrata: Collegii S. Bonaventurae ad Claras Aquas, 1981), 4.1.2. Translation cited from http://franciscan-archive.org.

42. See Augustine, *City of God*, 10.5 in NPNF[1] 2.183.

43. Lombard cites Augustine, *Questions on the Pentateuch*, 3.84.

44. Lombard, *Sentences*, 4.1.3.

45. Augustine, *On Christian Doctrine*, 2.1 in NPNF[1] 2.535.

46. Lombard, *Sentences*, 4.1.4.

took over from it to prevail for the renewal of man, for which purpose it has been instituted."[47]

Based on Augustine's explanation, Lombard agrees that circumcision and baptism operated in parallel fashion, which implies a covenantal cast to his understanding of baptism, though it is not developed explicitly. This is not to say, however, that Lombard believed there was a one-to-one correspondence between the two rites.

Lombard explains that faith and good works justified women in the Old Testament, since they could not be circumcised:

> But better is it to say, that they who went forth from Abraham, were justified through circumcision, but their women through faith and good work, their own, if they were adults, and/or that of their parents, if they were little ones; but they who were before circumcision little ones were justified in the faith of their parents, but the parents through the virtue of the sacrifices, that is through the virtue which they understood spiritually in those sacrifices.[48]

Lombard assigns an instrumental role to circumcision in Abraham's justification, something that goes against Paul's intention in his explanation of the Old Testament rite. Nevertheless, Lombard's point is in line with the Patristic understanding of baptism. That Lombard believed circumcision played a role in Abraham's justification is evident when he writes, "Moreover circumcision had been given for very many causes, that is so that through obedience to the mandate Abraham might placate God, whom Adam through prevarication had displeased."[49]

A question naturally arises, namely, Why replace circumcision if it was more or less able to accomplish that which baptism does? Lombard explains that baptism is better because a fuller grace accompanies the New Testament rite. Circumcision merely brought the forgiveness of sins. However, in baptism, the recipient receives not only the forgiveness of sins but also attending grace that augments his or her virtues. Lombard writes:

> Whence it is said to be a water of refection, which makes the arid fecund and grants in a more ample abundance to those already fruitful; because, howsoever much through faith and charity had beforehand

47. Lombard, *Sentences*, 4.1.7; Lombard cites Augustine, *On Nuptials and Concupiscence*, 2.11.
48. Lombard, *Sentences*, 4.1.8.
49. Lombard, *Sentences*, 4.1.9.

someone just approaches to Baptism, he receives there a more abundant grace, but not thus in circumcision. Whence to Abraham, having
already been justified through faith, it was only a mark, it conferred
nothing upon him interiorly.[50]

As in Patristic expressions, the water of baptism brings the grace of
God, grace that not only cleanses from sin but assists a person in his sanctification. However, Lombard makes no mention of baptismal regeneration,
though it seems to be assumed.

Bonaventure

Bonaventure (1221–1274) was a contemporary of Thomas Aquinas (ca.
1225–1274). Following the practice of most theologians in his day, he
wrote a commentary on Lombard's *Sentences*. In many respects, Bonaventure's views have great similarity to those of Lombard, though Bonaventure
clarifies and emphasizes certain points. For example, Bonaventure states
that the sacraments are divinely instituted signs through which "beneath
the cloak of material species God's power operates in a hidden manner."[51]
Bonaventure further explains:

> In themselves the sensible signs cannot produce any effect in the order of
> grace, although they are by nature distant representations of grace, it was
> necessary that the Author of grace institute them for the sake of signify-
> ing and bless them for the sake of sanctifying; so that through natural
> similitude they would represent, through conjoined institution they
> would signify and through superadded benediction they would sanctify
> and prepare for grace, by which our souls are healed and cured.[52]

Bonaventure makes some distinction between the nature of the sacraments and the way in which they bring grace. Like Lombard before him,
Bonaventure therefore believed that sacraments are vessels of grace, though
grace is not substantially present in them, as grace dwells only in the soul
and can be infused only by God.[53]

Bonaventure is careful to distinguish the various causes of grace in the
sacraments: the efficient cause is God's institution, the material cause is
the representation through sensible signs, the formal cause is sanctifica-

---

50. Lombard, *Sentences*, 4.1.9.
51. Bonaventure, *The Works of Bonaventure: Breviloquium*, ed. Jose de Vinck (Paterson,
N.J.: St. Anthony Guild Press, 1963), 2:223.
52. Bonaventure, *Breviloquium*, 6.1.3 (224).
53. Bonaventure, *Breviloquium*, 6.1.5 (225); also Spinks, *Theologies of Baptism*, 144.

tion through grace, and the final cause is the healing of mankind through a proper medicine.[54] He argues that Christ instituted the rite of baptism by first being baptized Himself; then, by determining the form of the rite, He made it universal.[55] In this way, Bonaventure connects the baptism of Jesus with the Great Commission.[56] Beyond this, Bonaventure explains how baptism should be administered:

> For anyone to be validly and fully baptized, the form established by the Lord must be said aloud: "I baptize thee in the name of the Father, and of the Son, and of the Holy Spirit. Amen." No word should be omitted, none added, nor should the order given here be changed, nor should the word "name" in the beginning be altered. There must also be immersion or ablution of the whole body, or at least of its most noble part, by means of the element of water, in such a way that the immersion and the vocal expression are performed simultaneously by one and the same minister.[57]

Bonaventure prefers immersion, and shortly after this statement he stipulates that threefold immersion represents the death, burial, and resurrection of Christ.[58]

Like his Patristic and medieval predecessors, Bonaventure also believed that baptism causes regeneration, which is effected by the grace annexed to the rite.[59] He echoes this idea when he concludes his explanation of baptism:

> And because the purpose of Baptism is to deliver both children and adults from the power of the prince of darkness, both should be exorcized, that the hostile spirits may be expelled, and both instructed, that the adults may be delivered from the darkness of error and formed to the faith, and that the godparents representing the children may learn what to teach them; lest the sacrament of Baptism be prevented by human default from achieving its intended end.[60]

Here it is evident that Bonaventure sees baptism as regenerating the recipient. However, other soteriological elements are present, in that

---

54. Bonaventure, *Breviloquium*, 6.1.6 (225); also Spinks, *Theologies of Baptism*, 144.
55. Bonaventure, *Breviloquium*, 6.4.4 (236).
56. Spinks, *Theologies of Baptism*, 144.
57. Bonaventure, *Breviloquium*, 6.7.2 (245).
58. Bonaventure, *Breviloquium*, 6.7.4 (246).
59. Bonaventure, *Breviloquium*, 6.7.4–5 (247).
60. Bonaventure, *Breviloquium*, 6.7.6 (248).

while the grace in baptism cleanses, forgives, and regenerates, nevertheless because of human default, whether the individual's failures post-baptism or the godparents' failures to instruct a baptized child properly, the goal of baptism (i.e., salvation) may not be reached in some cases.

Thomas Aquinas

Aquinas in many ways represents the pinnacle of medieval theology. He unfolds his understanding of baptism most famously in his *Summa Theologiae*, where he explains not just baptism but the broader rubric of the sacraments. Like his predecessors and contemporaries, Aquinas bases his definition of a sacrament on Augustine's, namely, that a sacrament is a visible sign of invisible grace. However, like Bonaventure, Thomas states that a sacrament is not an efficient cause of grace, but rather a formal or final cause,[61] though he later explains that the sacraments also function instrumentally.[62] A sacrament has no inherent power but receives its power only through divine institution.[63]

Thomas argues that there were sacraments in the Old Testament just as there are in the New Testament, though the sacraments of the "old law" foretold the coming of Christ and therefore did not manifest Jesus as clearly as the sacraments of the "new law."[64] Also, like Augustine and Lombard, Thomas believed there was a parallel between circumcision and baptism, though the two rites did not function in precisely the same manner.[65] Thomas writes:

> The protecting pillar of cloud and the crossing of the Red Sea were indeed figures of our Baptism, whereby we are born again of water, signified by the Red Sea; and of the Holy Ghost, signified by the pillar of cloud: yet man did not make, by means of these, a profession of faith, as by circumcision: so that these two things were figures but not sacraments. But circumcision was a sacrament and a preparation for Baptism; although less clearly figurative of Baptism, as to externals, than the aforesaid.[66]

---

61. Thomas Aquinas, *Summa Theologica*, (Allen, Texas: Christian Classics, 1948), IIIa q. 60 art. 1.

62. Aquinas, *Summa*, IIIa q. 62 arts. 1–3.

63. Aquinas, *Summa*, IIIa q. 60 art. 5.

64. Aquinas, *Summa*, IIIa q. 60 art. 6; cf. q. 61 art. 3.

65. Aquinas, *Summa*, IIIa q. 62 art. 6.

66. Aquinas, *Summa*, IIIa q. 70 art. 1.

So there is some connection between the Old and New Testament rites, but Thomas places greater power in baptism because it looks back on the completed passion of Christ, whereas circumcision looked forward to an event that had not yet transpired.[67]

Aquinas explains that baptism derives its justifying power from Christ Himself, and specifically from the power of His passion.[68] Thomas bases the cleansing, regenerating, and justifying power of baptism on his understanding of John 3:5. In this vein, he approvingly cites a passage from a sermon by John Chrysostom: "When we dip our heads under the water as in a kind of tomb, our old man is buried, and being submerged is hidden below, and thence he rises again renewed."[69] This positive quotation of Chrysostom means that Thomas did not believe that baptism could be repeated, because "baptism is a spiritual regeneration; inasmuch as a man dies to the old life, and begins to lead the new life."[70]

Aquinas also believed that both adults and infants should receive baptism because it is a remedy against both original and actual sin. Adult converts are therefore supposed to be baptized, though if the person lacks the intention to receive the sacrament, his baptism is not valid.[71] However, the person who is baptized "is freed from the debt of all punishment due to him for his sins, just as if he himself had offered sufficient satisfaction for all his sins."[72] The baptized person receives not only the forgiveness of sins, but grace and virtues as well.[73] Aquinas further explains: "The baptized are enlightened by Christ as to the knowledge of truth, and made fruitful by Him with the fruitfulness of good works by the infusion of grace."[74] Concerning the baptism of infants and young children, Thomas writes: "Consequently it became necessary to baptize children, that, as in birth they incurred damnation through Adam, so in a second birth they might obtain salvation through Christ." Thomas believed that through baptism a child receives a good conscience, or habit (*habitus*), which enables him to live as a Christian.[75]

---

67. Aquinas, *Summa*, IIIa q. 70 art. 4.
68. Aquinas, *Summa*, IIIa q. 66 art. 2.
69. Aquinas, *Summa*, IIIa q. 66 art. 3.
70. Aquinas, *Summa*, IIIa q. 66 art. 9.
71. Aquinas, *Summa*, IIIa q. 68 art. 8.
72. Aquinas, *Summa*, IIIa q. 69 art. 2.
73. Aquinas, *Summa*, IIIa q. 69 art. 4.
74. Aquinas, *Summa*, IIIa q. 69 art. 5.
75. Aquinas, *Summa*, IIIa q. 68 art. 9.

Regarding baptismal practice, Aquinas believed it could be performed through immersion, sprinkling, or pouring. He based the latter two modes on his reading of Hebrews 10:22 and Ezekiel 36:25, which speak respectively of the hearts of believers being sprinkled and the outpouring of water to cleanse the heart. Aquinas also held that baptism by immersion more clearly represents the burial of Christ, and therefore this mode is more frequently employed and more commendable.[76] Additionally, Aquinas believed that either threefold immersion or single immersion is acceptable, as the former points to the Trinity and the latter represents the unity in the Godhead.[77]

SUMMARY AND ANALYSIS

In the Middle Ages, there was a refinement of the theology of baptism couched in a systematic expression of a theology of the sacraments. In a sense, there was a move away from the substantival view of grace, such as in the theology of Tertullian, and a refined expression of how grace and baptism relate. The refinement came in the acknowledgement that the water of baptism functions instrumentally in a person's redemption. So while theologians of the Middle Ages might have demurred from saying that grace is substantively present in the water, they nonetheless would have been comfortable saying that the water is a vessel of divine grace, in that the power of God comes instrumentally through the water. This distinction would remain in later Roman Catholic expressions and would be connected specifically to the doctrine of justification, not just soteriology in general, in the formal declarations of the Council of Trent. Eventually the sacraments received the designations of created and uncreated grace (*gratia creata et increata*) by Roman Catholic theologians. The idea is that the uncreated grace of God is His uncreated power that belongs to the Godhead alone. Created grace, on the other hand, is grace that is infused into a person through the sacraments and creates a *habitus gratiae* (habit of grace)—a disposition toward righteousness.[78]

Another observable feature of the medieval theologians is their deliberate effort to construct a theology of the sacraments, and more specifically

---

76. Aquinas, *Summa*, IIIa q. 66 art. 7.

77. Aquinas, *Summa*, IIIa q. 66 art. 8.

78. Richard A. Muller, *Dictionary of Latin and Greek Theological Terms: Drawn Principally from Protestant Scholastic Theology* (Grand Rapids: Baker, 1985), 134, q. v. *habitus gratiae*.

baptism, on the whole canon of Scripture. While some statements identify types of baptism, such as Tertullian's identification of the Genesis 1:1 waters as such, given the systematic attention to the sacraments, theologians of the Middle Ages looked to both testaments and explicitly explained the relationship between circumcision and baptism. Aquinas also identified the Red Sea crossing as a type of baptism. This implies a covenantal cast to the theology of baptism, though it is important to note that this thread lies undeveloped, as neither Lombard nor Aquinas identify circumcision or baptism as the sign of the covenant.

This raises a related and important observation, namely, that medieval theologians approached their soteriology largely in terms of ontology rather than in terms of covenant. For Lombard, Bonaventure, and Aquinas, the water of baptism functions instrumentally to create an ontological change in the one who is baptized. The recipient of baptism is regenerated. Moreover, in a sense, baptism conveys an impersonal force or power. This is evident in a number of places in Aquinas, who believed that in baptism a person receives the power of the passion of Christ.[79] Additionally, sin is not viewed so much in forensic terms, but largely in ontological categories, so that a person—adult or infant—is cleansed from both original and actual sin and infused with grace, virtues, and habits that enable him to live the Christian life. In this way, Aquinas believed, baptism "opens the gates of the heavenly kingdom to the baptized as it incorporates them in the Passion of Christ, by applying its power to man."[80] In other words, baptism secures a person's entry into the kingdom, but it does not secure his permanent place. Alternatively, according to Thomas, baptism "gets you in" but obedience "keeps you in."

These trends—a refined theology of the sacraments, baptism as the instrumental means of grace, and an ontological conception of redemption—informed the declarations of the Council of Trent.

THE COUNTER-REFORMATION

Subsequent chapters will investigate the views of the Reformers and figures from the post-Reformation period, but this section will focus on the Counter-Reformation, specifically the dogmatic decrees of the Council of

79. Aquinas, *Summa*, IIIa q. 66 art. 2.
80. Aquinas, *Summa*, IIIa q. 69 art. 7.

Trent and the Tridentine catechism. The Council of Trent represents not only the response to the Reformation, but also largely the crystallization and systematic presentation of the views of Augustine.

Council of Trent (1546–1547)

The council deals with the doctrine of original sin in session five. Like Augustine, the council rejects the views of Pelagius.[81] The council goes on to specify that man cannot remove original sin except by the merit of Jesus Christ, though this merit is applied through baptism: "If anyone denies that the actual merit of Christ Jesus is applied to both adults and infants through the sacrament of baptism duly administered in the form of the church: let him be anathema."[82] Furthermore, the council states: "If anyone says that the guilt of original sin is not remitted through the grace of our Lord Jesus Christ which is given in baptism, or even asserts that all which pertains to the true essence of sin is not removed, but declares it is only erased and not attributed: let him be anathema."[83]

In the sixth session, on the doctrine of justification, the council elaborates on its causes, explaining that the final cause is the glory of God, Christ, and eternal life. The efficient cause of justification is the God of mercy, who of His free will washes and sanctifies His people, placing His seal on them and anointing them with the promised Holy Spirit. The meritorious cause is God's Son, who merited justification for God's people. The one formal cause is the righteousness of God. Baptism, however, is the instrumental cause, "which is the sacrament of faith, without which justification comes to no one."[84]

In the seventh session, the sacraments and baptism are specifically addressed in a number of key statements. For example, in line with Augustine and medieval theologians, in its "Canons on the Sacraments in General," Trent rejects the idea that the sacraments of the new law are no different from those of the old law, except by reason of external rites.[85] The council also states: "If anyone says that the sacraments of the new law do not con-

---

81. Dogmatic Decrees of the Council of Trent, in *Creeds and Confessions of Faith in the Christian Tradition*, eds. Jaroslav Pelikan and Valerie Hotchkiss (New Haven: Yale University Press, 2003), 2.819–71; sess. 5, §§ 1–2. All subsequent quotations are drawn from this edition.

82. Council of Trent, sess. 5, § 3.

83. Council of Trent, sess. 5, § 5.

84. Council of Trent, sess. 6, § 7.

85. Council of Trent, sess. 7, § 4.

tain the grace which they signify; or do not confer that grace on those who place no obstacle in the way, as if they were only external signs of grace or justice received by faith, and some kind of mark of the Christian profession by which believers are distinguished from unbelievers in the eyes of people: let him be anathema."[86] Here it appears Trent has a basic Zwinglian Protestant view of the sacraments in its crosshairs. Yet, once again, Trent simply repeats the teachings of Augustine and Aquinas on these points, echoing an *ex opere operato* view of baptism.

In addition to these statements, the "Canons on the Sacrament of Baptism" contain a number of statements that echo Augustinian teaching, such as the necessity of baptism for salvation.[87] However, beyond this there are declarations that appear to be aimed at the theology of the Radical Reformation. Trent rejects the idea that one must be the age of Christ, presumably some thirty years old, or at the point of death before he can be baptized.[88] Trent also defends infant baptism:

> If anyone says that little children, because they make no act of faith, should not after the reception of baptism be numbered among the faithful; and that, therefore, when they reach the age of discretion, they should be rebaptized; or that it is better that their baptism be omitted than that they be baptized while believing not by their own faith but by the faith of the church alone: let him be anathema.[89]

If one takes note of Roman Catholic soteriology, as well as the role baptism is seen to play in terms of the removal of sin and regeneration, it naturally follows, as it did for Augustine, Aquinas, and others, that infant baptism is necessary.

Catechism of the Council of Trent

During the fourth session of the Council of Trent in 1546, it was suggested that the council create a basic catechism, not only to present the formulations of the council in a simplified form for catechumens, but also to serve as a response to Reformation catechisms. The catechism did not appear until 1566.[90] The catechism's treatment of the sacraments in general relies once again on the definitions of Augustine:

---

86. Council of Trent, sess. 7, § 6.
87. Council of Trent, sess. 7, § 5.
88. Council of Trent, sess. 7, § 12.
89. Council of Trent, sess. 7, § 13.
90. Spinks, *Theologies of Baptism*, 154.

Of the many definitions, each of them sufficiently appropriate, which may serve to explain the nature of a Sacrament, there is none more comprehensive, none more perspicuous, than the definition given by St. Augustine and adopted by all scholastic writers. A Sacrament, he says, is a sign of a sacred thing; or, as it has been expressed in other words of the same import: A Sacrament is a visible sign of an invisible grace, instituted for our justification.[91]

Augustine's definition of a sacrament lies at the foundation of the Roman Catholic view, and all other statements and definitions appear merely as footnotes. Note, though, that the catechism reflects the developments of the Council of Trent in terms of the coordination of the sacraments with justification:

With regard to the definition of Baptism although many can be given from sacred writers, nevertheless that which may be gathered from the words of our Lord recorded in John, and of the Apostle to the Ephesians, appears the most appropriate and suitable. Unless, says our Lord, a man be born again of water and the Holy Ghost, he cannot enter into the kingdom of God; and, speaking of the Church, the Apostle says, cleansing it by the laver of water in the word of life. Thus it follows that Baptism may be rightly and accurately defined: The Sacrament of regeneration by water in the word. By nature we are born from Adam children of wrath, but by Baptism we are regenerated in Christ, children of mercy. For He gave power to men to be made the sons of God, to them that believe in His name, who are born, not of blood, nor of the will of the flesh, nor of the will of man, but of God.[92]

Here there is the continuing exegetical reliance on John 3:5 and the belief that baptism is the water of regeneration and union with Christ. For this reason, the catechism also states that baptism is necessary for salvation.

As in previous explanations (Augustine, Bonaventure, or Aquinas), infants are to be baptized not only because they require cleansing to remove the effects of original sin, but because it was practiced in the Old Testament through its analog, circumcision:

Circumcision, too, which was a figure of Baptism, affords strong argument in proof of this practice. That children were circumcised on the

---

91. *The Catechism of the Council of Trent: Ordered by the Council of Trent*, ed. St. Charles Borromeo (1566; Rockford: Tan Books and Publishers, 1982), 143.

92. *Catechism of Trent*, 163.

eighth day is universally known. If then circumcision, made by hand, in despoiling of the body of the flesh, was profitable to children, it is clear that Baptism, which is the circumcision of Christ, not made by hand, is also profitable to them.[93]

The catechism helpfully summarizes the Tridentine teaching when it spells out six effects of baptism: the remission of sin, the remission of all punishment due to sin, the grace of regeneration, infused virtues and union with Christ, the donation of Christian character, and the opening of the gates of heaven. It is especially noteworthy that the catechism states,

> This grace is accompanied by a most splendid train of all virtues, which are divinely infused into the soul along with grace. Hence, when writing to Titus, the Apostle says: He saved us by the laver of regeneration and renovation of the Holy Ghost, whom he has poured forth upon us abundantly, through Jesus Christ our Savior. St. Augustine, in explanation of the words, poured forth abundantly, says: that is, for the remission of sins and for abundance of virtues.[94]

According to the catechism, baptism brings the infusion of grace and virtues, which also explains why baptism is necessary for salvation. How can one be justified if he is not cleansed from sin? How can one progress in his justification if he has not received the infused grace of God, as well as virtues to assist him? It is important to see that the definitive Roman Catholic understanding of baptism is inextricably intertwined with its soteriology.

CONCLUSION

In this survey of the Patristic Age and Middle Ages with the culmination in Trent, we see an unbroken line of development from the earliest days of the church, especially from Augustine to the Counter-Reformation. Some have noted that the Council of Trent codified Augustine's view of justification. It also may be said that the council codified Augustine's doctrine of baptism. However, this does not mean that Trent authoritatively represents the teaching of Scripture. Trent arguably represents the teaching of a number of church fathers and theologians of the Middle Ages.

Nevertheless, in the sixteenth-century Reformation, there was a decided break from this line of development on a number of doctrines. There was

---

93. *Catechism of Trent*, 172.
94. *Catechism of Trent*, 188.

significant development in the understanding of the sacraments in general, but also in the doctrine of baptism. Specifically, there was a break from the ontologically shaped understanding of baptism to an explicit covenantal understanding.

CHAPTER 2

Baptism in Luther and Lutheranism

Martin Luther (1483–1546) is known without question as the great theologian of the doctrine of justification by faith alone. Luther's view was a stark contrast to existing Roman Catholic doctrine and revealed the great differences between the early Protestant and Roman Catholic soteriologies. Given that Patristic and medieval views on salvation were inextricably intertwined with their views on baptism, it is only natural that with Luther's formation of a different soteriology, his view of baptism also differed from that of the Roman Catholic Church.[1] For this reason, it is necessary to survey Luther's view on baptism, as it represents a unique contribution to the development of the doctrine.

It is important to note that Luther is one of the chief fountainheads of confessional Lutheran theology. However, given that others contributed to the Lutheran confessional corpus, there is both overlap and some divergence between Luther and confessional Lutheranism.[2] Therefore, this chapter will explore the views of Luther and confessional Lutheranism, but at the same time identify some unique features of Luther's understanding of the rite. The chapter will survey Luther's basic understanding of the sacraments and the nature of baptism, examine his defense of infant baptism, and conclude with some hermeneutical and liturgical observations.

---

1. Bernhard Lohse, *Martin Luther's Theology: Its Historical and Systematic Development* (Minneapolis: Fortress, 1999), 298.

2. For Luther's status as the fountainhead of the Lutheran tradition (unlike John Calvin, who was one among many influential theologians in the Calvinist—or, more properly, Reformed—tradition), see Carl R. Trueman, "Is the Finnish Line a New Beginning? A Critical Assessment of the Reading of Luther Offered by the Helsinki Circle," *WTJ* 65 (2003): 232; Robert Kolb, *Martin Luther as Prophet, Teacher, and Hero: Images of the Reformer, 1520–1620* (Grand Rapids: Baker, 1999); Richard A. Muller, *After Calvin: Studies in the Development of a Theological Tradition* (Oxford: Oxford University Press, 2003), 63–104; R. Scott Clark, "*Iustitia Imputata Christi*: Alien or Proper to Luther's Doctrine of Justification?" *CTQ* 70 (2006): 269–310.

THE SACRAMENTS

As observed in the previous chapter, theologians in the Middle Ages defined a sacrament as a sign of a sacred thing. Medieval theologians were fond of citing Augustine: "A sacrament is the visible form of an invisible grace."[3] Luther had a similar definition that also relied on Augustine, but it is fair to say that his definition had a different orbit from those of medieval theologians. Luther defined the sacraments as "promises which have signs attached to them."[4] In other words, medieval theologians focused on the grace of God (a substance infused), whereas Luther focused on the Word of God (a promised declared).

Differing soteriologies inform the respective views of baptism here. Given the medieval emphasis on the necessity of infused grace, it is to be expected that they would put an accent on water as an instrumental cause of justification. With his doctrine of justification by faith alone, Luther naturally stresses the Word. To this end, Paul Althaus (1888–1966) explains, "For Luther, a sacrament consists in the combination of the word of promise with a sign, that is, it is a promise accompanied by a sign instituted by God and a sign accompanied by a promise."[5]

This same emphasis on the sacraments as visible promises is present in the writings of Philip Melanchthon (1497–1560), Luther's co-reformer and lieutenant, who had a large part in shaping confessional Lutheran theology. In his late definition Melanchthon states that a sacrament is "a ceremony established in the Gospel to be a testimony to the promise which belongs to the Gospel, that is, the promise of reconciliation or grace."[6] This definition is largely consistent with how Melanchthon defined the term in the first edition of his *Loci Communes*: "We have said that the gospel is the promise of grace. This section on signs is very closely related to the prom-

---

3. See Petri Lombardi, *Senentiae in IV Libris Distinctae*, (Grottaferrata: Collegii S. Bonaventurae ad Claras Aquas, 1981), 4.1.2; cf. Augustine, *City of God*, 10.5, in NPNF[1] 2.183. See also Thomas Aquinas, *Summa Theologiae* (Allen, Texas: Christian Classics, 1948), IIIa, q. 60 art. 2; Bonaventure, *The Works of Bonaventure: Breviloquium*, ed. Jose de Vinck (Paterson, N.J.: St. Anthony Guild Press, 1963), 2.223.

4. Martin Luther, *The Babylonian Captivity of the Church*, LW 36.124.

5. Paul Althaus, *The Theology of Martin Luther* (Philadelphia: Fortress, 1966), 25; cf. LW 36.65; 36.124.

6. Philip Melanchthon, *Loci Communes (1543)*, trans. J. A. O. Preus (St. Louis: Concordia Publishing House, 1992), loc. 13, (139).

ises. The Scriptures add these signs to the promises as seals which remind us of the promises, and definitely testify of the divine will toward us."[7]

This same emphasis appears in the *Apology of the Augsburg Confession* (1531), which was written by Melanchthon. The *Apology* defines the sacraments as "rites, which have the command of God and to which the promise of grace has been added." The *Apology* explains:

> For just as the Word enters through the ear in order to strike the heart, so also the rite enters through the eye in order to move the heart. The Word and the rite have the same effect. Augustine put it well when he said that the sacrament is a "visible word," because the rite is received by the eyes and is, as it were, a picture of the Word, signifying the same thing as the Word. Therefore both have the same effect.[8]

Once again, there is reliance on Augustine, but in a decidedly different direction from the views of the Middle Ages.

Given this emphasis on the Word, one that fits with Luther's understanding of justification by faith, it is not surprising that he rejected the Roman Catholic *ex opere operato* view of the sacraments. Luther argued that it was heresy to hold that the sacraments give grace to the recipients simply by the performance of the rites.[9] In similar fashion, the *Apology* states:

> Here we condemn the entire crowd of scholastic doctors who teach that the sacraments confer grace *ex opere operato* without a good disposition in those receiving them, as long as the recipients do not place an obstacle in the way. It is simply a Judaistic opinion to think that we are justified through ceremonies without a proper disposition in the heart, that is, apart from faith.

The *Apology* goes on to explain: "The reason for this is plain and well established. A promise is useless unless it is received by faith. But the sacraments are the signs of the promises. Therefore, in their use faith needs to be present." Faith is instrumental in justification, not the sacrament.[10]

At this stage, it is evident how Luther's understanding of justification by faith alone informed his understanding of the sacraments in general. Luther and confessional Lutheranism recognized the importance of the

---

7. Philip Melanchthon, *Common Places (1521)*, LCC (Philadelphia: Westminster, 1969), 133.

8. *Apology of the Augsburg Confession*, art. 13, in BC, 219–20; cf. Augustine, *Tractates on John*, 80.3, on John 15:3, in NPNF¹ 7.344.

9. LW 31.106–12; cf. LW 32.12–18.

10. *Apology*, art. 13, in BC, 221–22.

Word and promise of the gospel. This is something that surfaces in Lutheran expressions on baptism.

THE NATURE OF BAPTISM

Luther's understanding of baptism features the same emphases as his view of the sacraments. In the *Smalcald Articles* (1537), Luther writes, "Baptism is nothing other than God's Word in the water, commanded by God's institution, or as Paul says, 'washing by the Word'" (§ 5; cf. Eph 5:25).[11]

In his Small Catechism, Luther asks four questions that explain the nature of baptism. Luther explains in the first question that the water of baptism is not plain water, but is "water enclosed in God's command and connected with God's word." In the second question, he states that baptism brings about the forgiveness of sins, redeems from death and the devil, and gives eternal salvation to all who believe. In the third question, Luther qualifies his answer to the second question, which could be misread as affirming baptismal regeneration, by stating that the water clearly does not bring about the benefits, but that they come by the Word of God, which is "with and alongside the water, and faith, which trusts this Word of God in the water." In the fourth question, Luther explains the significance of baptism: "It signifies that the Old Adam in us with all sins and evil desires is to be drowned and die through daily contrition and repentance, and on the other hand that daily a new person is to come forth and rise up to live before God in righteousness and purity forever."[12]

Considering that Luther intended the Small Catechism to be a simple way in which the head of a household could instruct his family in theology, the questions and answers seem fairly straightforward. Yet the fourth question and answer contain one of the more important points regarding Luther's theology of baptism, one that is easily misunderstood, but one that is crucial to differentiating Luther's view from that of the Roman Catholic Church.

Lutheran scholars have long noted an apparent contradiction between Luther's doctrine of justification by faith alone and some of the statements the German Reformer made concerning baptism. For example, in Luther's lecture on Psalm 110, given in 1535, there is a statement that appears to be no different from the Roman Catholic position:

---

11. BC, 319.
12. Small Catechism, "The Sacrament of Holy Baptism," in BC, 359.

You can see the water of baptism as you can see the dew, and you can hear the external or spoken Word; but you cannot see or hear or understand the Spirit, or what he accomplishes thereby: that a human being is cleansed in baptism and becomes a saint in the hands of the priest so that from a child of hell he is changed into a child of God. Nevertheless this is truly and actually accomplished. One has to say, in view of the power which attends it, that the Holy Spirit was present at the event and was making believers by means of water and the word.[13]

How can such a statement be reconciled with Luther's understanding of justification by faith alone and his rejection of an *ex opere operato* view of the sacraments?[14] The answer comes in reflecting on Luther's answer to the fourth question in his Small Catechism, particularly the idea that the sacrament is basically equivalent to the promise of the gospel—it is the visible Word.

There is a peculiar characteristic in Luther's explanation of the significance of baptism: "It signifies that the Old Adam in us with all sins and evil desires is to be drowned and die through *daily* contrition and repentance, and on the other hand that *daily* a new person is to come forth and rise up to live before God in righteousness and purity forever."[15] Note the emphasis on the idea that although baptism is a definitive event at a specific point in a person's life, it is also something that is daily.

Scholars have noted this point, especially in contrast to the apostle Paul, who states, "Or do you not know that as many of us as were baptized into Christ Jesus were baptized into His death?" (Rom. 6:3). Paul's use of an aorist passive ἐβαπτίσθημεν, which denotes an event in the past, differs from Luther's emphasis that baptism signifies a daily event. Bernhard Lohse (1928–1997) explains the difference between Paul and Luther: "For Paul, then, the old man is already killed in the baptism, and the new has already arisen. Baptism is thus an event that is complete in itself and that the Christian should confess ever anew. In his reflection, however, Luther depicted baptism as something to be accomplished ever anew."[16]

Setting aside the question of the exegetical and theological viability of Luther's position, this difference between Paul and Luther provides the necessary information to enable us to understand Luther's statements on

---

13. LW 13.303, on Ps. 110:3.
14. Jonathan D. Trigg, *Baptism in the Theology of Martin Luther* (Leiden: Brill, 2001), 77.
15. Small Catechism, "The Sacrament of Holy Baptism," in BC, 359, emphasis added.
16. Lohse, *Luther's Theology*, 302; cf. Althaus, *Theology of Luther*, 357–58.

baptism that appear to reflect the very *ex opere operato* view of the sacraments he roundly condemns. Unlike his Roman Catholic contemporaries, Luther did not view baptism as one distinct and definite event, but rather as lifelong, as stated in his Small Catechism.[17] In other words, not everything Luther attributes to baptism is brought about at the precise moment of the administration of the rite. Unlike the Roman Catholic view, which held that a person was regenerated at the moment of baptism, as the sacrament functioned *ex opere operato*, Luther believed that the effects of baptism and the moment of administration are not necessarily linked.[18]

This did not mean that Luther believed a person is to be baptized on a daily basis. Rather, because baptism is the visible Word of God, its effects are supposed to echo throughout a person's life. Luther writes:

> We must therefore beware of those who have reduced the power of baptism to such small and slender dimensions that, while they say grace is indeed inpoured by it, they maintain that afterwards it is poured out again through sin, and that then one must reach heaven by another way, as if baptism had now become entirely useless. Do not hold such a view, but understand that this is the significance of baptism, that through it you die and live again. Therefore, whether by penance or by any other way, you can only return to the power of your baptism, and do again that which you were baptized to do and which your baptism signified. Baptism never becomes useless, unless you despair and refuse to return to its salvation. You may indeed wander away from the sign for a time, but the sign is not therefore useless. Thus, you have been once baptized in the sacrament, but you need continually to be baptized by faith, continually to die and continually to live. Baptism swallowed up your whole body and gave it forth again; in the same way that which baptism signifies should swallow up your whole life, body and soul, and give it forth again at the last day, clad in the robe of glory and immortality. We are therefore never without the sign of baptism nor without the thing it signifies. Indeed, we need continually to be baptized more and more, until we fulfill the sign perfectly at the last day.[19]

---

17. Mark D. Tranvik, "Luther on Baptism," in *Harvesting Martin Luther's Reflections on Theology, Ethics, and the Church*, ed. Timothy J. Wengert (Grand Rapids: Eerdmans, 2004), 23–24; also idem, "Luther on Baptism," *LQ* 13/1 (1999): 75–90.

18. Trigg, *Baptism*, 78–79.

19. LW 36.69.

Jonathan Trigg explains Luther's comment: "The present tense of baptism arises from the fundamental principle of Luther's theology—the word of the Lord on which baptism is predicated, 'He who believes and is baptized shall be saved.' This word is always to be heard in baptism; it is never silenced."[20]

In one sense, Luther's view coheres with the broader contours of his theology, especially vis-à-vis his doctrine of justification by faith alone. Just as a person hears the gospel and believes, and the Word through the application of the Spirit justifies and saves him by faith alone, so the water, the visible Word, functions alongside but never apart from the audible Word to bring about the promise. In an interesting statement from one of Luther's sermons, his Word-centered understanding of the sacrament appears quite clearly:

> How does this (creation) happen? Through the words "Let it come into being." Through this word everything was created and conceived. Even humanity was created by this word. If you or I were to speak thusly nothing would happen. But when God says, "Let it come into being," the world is full of people, children and animals.... Thus you can reason: If God is able by the word to create heaven and earth and fill the world, that is everything we see with our eyes, why is it not possible to take water and baptize, saying "In the name..." and so be washed from all sins in body and soul?[21]

For Luther, the sacrament apart from the Word is useless and is no better than the water a cow drinks.[22] The apprehension of the Word made visible in baptism by a God-given faith brings about salvation.

This explanation can account for an adult who makes a profession of faith. What, however, of infants who are baptized? How did Luther maintain his understanding of justification by faith alone alongside his doctrine of infant baptism?

DEFENSE OF INFANT BAPTISM

In addition to facing the Roman Catholic view of *ex opere operato* on one side, Luther had to open a second battlefront against the views of the Radical Reformation, particularly its rejection of infant baptism. In contrast

---

20. Trigg, *Baptism*, 202–203.

21. "Predigt am Freitag nach Dionisii in der Schlosskirche" (1537), as quoted in and translated by Tranvik, "Luther on Baptism," 26.

22. LW 1.228.

to Roman Catholic views on infant baptism, which stretched back to the Patristic era, Luther defended the practice largely on the basis of four chief arguments that can be found in his *Concerning Rebaptism* (1528): the divine command, the argument from tradition, the parallel between circumcision and baptism, and the doctrine of *fides infantium*, or infant faith.

The divine command

The first pillar on which Luther based the practice of infant baptism was the divine command to baptize in the Great Commission (Matt. 28:18–19). Luther also based his argument on Mark 16:16: "He who believes and is baptized will be saved; but he who does not believe will be condemned." Luther's point was that baptism is not of human but divine origin. Echoing the teaching of Augustine in his writings against the Donatists, Luther states that man does not baptize, but that God Himself ultimately performs the rite.[23] Luther believed that since the command to baptize is universal, it therefore includes children, as they are a part of the people of God.

In response to the Anabaptist claim that Mark 16:16 presumes that a person must have faith in order to be baptized, Luther argues: "This they interpret to mean that no man should be baptized before he believes. I must say that they are guilty of a great presumption. For if they follow this principle they cannot venture to baptize before they are certain that the one to be baptized believes. How and when can they ever know that for certain?"[24] Luther declared that there is no way of being absolutely sure of a person's faith; even in the case of an adult, the church has to make a best-case evaluation of a person's profession. However, in distinction from the Anabaptists, who argued for the necessity of faith, Luther affirmed that baptism could in no way be based on faith. Luther writes, "There is quite a difference between having faith, on the one hand, and depending on one's faith and making baptism depend on faith, on the other."[25] For Luther, baptism is not based on a person's profession of faith but on the promise of God in the gospel, to which the external sign of baptism is added.

---

23. "Fourth Part: Concerning Baptism," BC, 457–58; see also David C. Steinmetz, *Luther in Context* (Grand Rapids: Baker, 1995), 95–96.

24. LW 40.239.

25. LW 40.252.

Church tradition

The second pillar on which Luther made his case for the legitimacy of infant baptism was church tradition. While Luther was known for basing his theology on the Word, he was not reticent to point out that the church had baptized infants from the earliest days, and he was unwilling to change an ancient practice apart from solid biblical argumentation because of what he deemed to be "weak arguments" from his Anabaptist opponents.[26] Luther could not conceive that God would allow the church to practice heresy unchecked for hundreds of years. Moreover, he said, if the Anabaptist position was correct, given that adult baptisms had been practiced hardly at all for hundreds of years because the vast majority of people in the church had been born within it, then the church did not truly exist. Luther writes:

> If the first, or child, baptism were not right it would follow that for more than a thousand years there was no baptism or any Christendom, which is impossible. For in that case the article of the creed, I believe in one holy Christian church, would be false. For over a thousand years there were hardly any other but child baptisms. If this baptism is wrong then for that long period Christendom would have been without baptism, and if it were without baptism it would not be Christendom.[27]

The sign of the covenant

Luther's third pillar was the parallel he drew between circumcision and baptism. This, of course, was not a unique argument, as other theologians going back to Augustine had drawn this parallel. However, unlike medieval theologians, who merely drew on the parallel to make an implicit covenantal argument for the practice, Luther explicitly drew out the connections between circumcision and baptism, something for which he is not well known.

Luther observed that in the Old Testament, God accepted both male and female infants through the covenant of circumcision.[28] This is not to say that Luther believed that female infants received circumcision, but rather that circumcision was the sign of the covenant that pointed to the promise of redemption, which was effectual for female as well as male infants.

---

26. LW 40.241.
27. LW 40.255–57.
28. LW 40.244.

Again, the promise is primary—the promise to which the sign of circumcision was connected.

From the covenant sign of circumcision, Luther then argued for the
same principle regarding the covenant sign of baptism. He writes:

> Our baptism, thus, is a strong and sure foundation, affirming that God
> has made a covenant with all the world to be a God of the heathen
> in all the world, as the gospel says. Also, that Christ has commanded
> the gospel to be preached in all the world, as also the prophets have
> declared in many ways. As a sign of this covenant he has instituted
> baptism, commanded and enjoined upon all heathen.... In the same
> manner he had made a covenant with Abraham and his descendants
> to be their God, and made circumcision a sign of this covenant. Here,
> namely, that we are baptized; not because we are certain of our faith
> but because it is the command and will of God.[29]

True, Luther did not greatly employ the covenant theme in his theology
as his Reformed contemporaries did. Nevertheless, at this point Luther's
argumentation is thoroughly covenantal, in marked contrast to his medieval
predecessors—though it arguably echoes the teaching of Augustine.[30]

Luther elsewhere devoted significant space to the exposition of a covenantally framed understanding of baptism. In his lectures on Genesis 17,
he argues for the covenantal connections between circumcision and baptism to substantiate the practice of infant baptism. According to Trigg's
analysis, the themes of covenant and the signs thereof are not marginalia
but dominate the Reformer's lectures page after page.[31] In fact, though the
occurrences are not abundant, Luther calls baptism a covenant in his Genesis lectures, which date from 1535 (there is also a reference where he made
the same connection that dates to 1519).[32] For example, Luther employs
the covenant concept in his exegesis of Genesis 17:3–6:

> If [inclusion in the kingdom, justification] was brought about with
> the Jews in the Old Testament through the medium of circumcision,
> why would God not do the same thing with the Gentiles through
> the medium of the new covenant of baptism? The command pertains
> to all.... Hence whereas circumcision was commanded only to the

---

29. LW 40.252.

30. See Augustine, *On Baptism, Against the Donatists*, 4.24, in NPNF[1] 4.461–62.

31. Trigg, *Baptism*, 45; cf. Heinrich Bornkamm, *Luther and the Old Testament*
(Philadelphia: Fortress, 1969), 182–83.

32. See LW 1.228; 3.103; 35.29–43; cf. Trigg, *Baptism*, 45.

descendants of Abraham, baptism is commanded to all the nations, with the promise of salvation if they believe.[33]

Luther's argument for infant baptism on the basis of the parallel between the covenant signs of circumcision and baptism was ultimately based on his doctrine of justification by faith alone. In other words, the signs of circumcision in the Old Testament and baptism in the New Testament both were annexed to the one promise of redemption.

Fides infantium

The connection between baptism and justification by faith leads to Luther's fourth pillar. He articulated a doctrine of *fides infantium* ("infant faith") to support the practice of infant baptism, though the degree to which Luther employed this concept varied throughout his career.[34] For example, from 1518 to 1521, Luther held to an idea long practiced in the medieval church, namely, baptizing a child into the *fides aliena* ("faith of another").[35] The "faith of another" referred to the faith of the church and the parents. Around 1525–26, Luther began to speak of *fides infantium* and rejected the idea of *fides aliena*. In 1528–29, however, Luther developed a full-fledged defense of infant baptism based on *fides infantium*.[36] In his later years, Luther employed *fides infantium* as a main pillar for his defense of the practice of infant baptism, but he considered it something of a hypothesis.[37] He writes: "Because child baptism derives from the apostles and has been practiced since the days of the apostles, we cannot oppose it, but must let it continue, since no one has yet been able to prove that in baptism children do not believe or that such baptism is wrong." He goes on to state, "For even if I were not sure that they believed, yet for my conscience's sake I would have to let them be baptized."[38]

Beyond arguments from reason, Luther deduced *fides infantium* biblically from the divine command to circumcise on the eighth day.[39] He also

---

33. LW 3.104.

34. On *fides infantium*, see Trigg, *Baptism*, 103–104.

35. LW 32.14; cf. Althaus, *Theology of Luther*, 364; Lohse, *Luther's Theology*, 304; John W. Riggs, *Baptism in the Reformation Tradition: An Historical and Practical Theology* (Louisville: Westminster John Knox, 2002), 28; Roland Bainton, *Here I Stand: A Life of Martin Luther* (Nashville: Abingdon, 1978), 109–10.

36. Riggs, *Baptism*, 28.

37. Trigg, *Baptism*, 104; see also Tranvik, "Luther on Baptism," 34.

38. LW 40.254.

39. LW 3.102.

argued that the burden of proof was on his detractors to demonstrate biblically that infants could not possess faith. To argue for the possibility of *fides
infantium*, Luther pointed to the instances of innocent blood shed in the
offering of children to idols by the Jews, the slaughter of the innocents in
the days of Christ (martyrdom was considered a "baptism in blood"), and
John leaping in the womb of his mother in the presence of Christ.[40]

Luther adduced two other scriptural proofs for *fides infantium*. The first
was the fact that Christ bade little children to come to Him and said of
them, "Of such is the kingdom of heaven" (Matt. 19:14). The second was
the idea that since baptism was the visible Word of God, and the Word of
God does not return void, through the Spirit baptism would bring about
faith in the heart of an infant who was baptized (cf. Isa. 55:11).[41]

Keep in mind that Luther did not believe that regeneration was tied
to the moment of administration. Also, remember his belief that baptism
was the visible Word. While there may appear to be similarities between
his view and a Roman Catholic *ex opere operato* view of baptism, Luther's
understanding was quite different, even when it came to the baptism of
infants. Baptism for Luther is not a visible manifestation of invisible grace
or power that effects regeneration at the moment the water is poured, but is
the visible promise of the gospel, which, like the audible Word, and through
the power of the Holy Spirit, brings about what it promises throughout the
life of the infant who is baptized.

The basic contours of Luther's view on infant baptism can be found in the
writings of other Lutheran theologians. Melanchthon, for example, largely
repeats three of Luther's arguments for infant baptism in his *Loci Communes*.
However, it appears that he goes beyond Luther's concept of *fides infantium*.
Luther argued that it was possible that an infant could have faith. However,
Melanchthon writes: "It is certainly true that in all adults repentance and
faith are required. But it is sufficient to hold this regarding infants, that the
Holy Spirit is given to them through Baptism, and effects in them new affections, new inclinations toward God in proportion to their condition."[42] It
seems that Melanchthon tied regeneration to the baptism of infants.

Other Lutheran theologians appear to have latched onto this Melanchthonian stream. For example, Johann Baier (1647–1695), in his *Compendium
Theologiae Positivae* (1685), writes: "For faith is at first *conferred upon* and

---

40. LW 40.241–42.
41. LW 40.243.
42. Melanchthon, *Loci Communes (1543)*, loc. 13, 145.

sealed to all infants alike by Baptism, and by this faith the merit of Christ is applied to them. But adults, who receive faith from hearing the Word before their baptism, are only sealed and confirmed in their faith by it." Similarly, John Gerhard (1582–1637), in his *Loci Theologici*, states: "To infants Baptism is, *primarily*, the ordinary means of regeneration and purification from sin;…*secondarily*, it is the seal of righteousness and the confirmation of faith. To adult believers it serves principally as a seal and testimony of the grace of God."[43]

Others, however, did not write with such certainty on the relationship between baptism and infant faith. Martin Chemnitz (1522–1586) was willing to embrace the idea of *fides aliena* in a qualified manner, arguing that it was the faith of the parents who brought the child forward for baptism. The parents would pray by faith alone that the baptized child would receive faith. However, Chemnitz writes: "Through the washing of water in the Word there is no doubt that Christ works and is efficacious by His Spirit in the infants who are baptized, so that they may receive the kingdom of God, even though we do not understand how this takes place."[44]

The baptismal regeneration views of Melanchthon, Baier, Gerhard, and Luther's *fides infantium*, however, do not appear in the Lutheran confessional corpus. Instead, there is a much more modest statement concerning infant baptism. In Luther's Large Catechism, the Reformer states: "We bring the child with the intent and hope that it may believe, and we pray God to grant it faith. But we do not baptize on this basis, but solely on the command of God. Why? Because we know that God does not lie. My neighbor and I—in short, all people, may deceive and mislead, but God's word cannot deceive."[45]

Hence, though Luther was willing to argue for *fides infantium* at various places and times in his writings, he thought of it only as a possibility, and when pressed, he retreated to the bedrock of the dominical command and the promise of the gospel, not relying on the possibility that an infant might have faith.[46]

---

43. As quoted in Heinrich Schmid, *The Doctrinal Theology of the Evangelical Lutheran Church* (Philadelphia: Lutheran Publication Society, 1899), 546–47.

44. Martin Chemnitz, *Loci Theologici*, trans. J. A. O. Preus (St. Louis: Concordia Publishing House, 1989), loc. 19, 2.729.

45. "Fourth part: Concerning Baptism," BC, 464.

46. Contra Timothy George, "The Reformed Doctrine of Believer's Baptism," *Interp* 47 (1993): 247.

TYPOLOGICAL AND LITURGICAL OBSERVATIONS

Before concluding the survey of Luther and Lutheranism on baptism, there are two hermeneutical and liturgical observations. First, like his patristic and medieval predecessors, Luther saw that there were Old Testament types that pointed forward to baptism. For example, Luther interpreted the Red Sea crossing as pointing to baptism, as did the apostle Paul (1 Cor. 10:2). In his exegesis of Psalm 78:13, Luther writes, "He has led also us through and leads us through in this way in baptism."[47]

There are similar connections in his lectures on Genesis 9, where he writes:

> In accordance with the meaning, the Red Sea is truly a baptism, that is, death and the wrath of God, as is manifest in the case of Pharaoh. Nevertheless, Israel, which is baptized with such a baptism, passes through unharmed. Similarly, the Flood is truly death and the wrath of God. Nevertheless, the believers are saved in the midst of the Flood. Thus death engulfs and swallows up the entire human race; for without distinction the wrath of God goes over the good, and the evil, over the godly and the ungodly. The Flood that Noah experienced was not different from the one which the world experienced. The Red Sea, which both Pharaoh and Israel entered, was not different. Later on, however, the difference became apparent in this: those who believe are preserved in the very death to which they are subjected together with the ungodly, and the ungodly perish. Noah, accordingly, is preserved because he has the ark, that is, God's promise and Word, in which he is living; but the ungodly, who do not believe the Word, are left to their fate.[48]

Luther therefore saw connections of both the flood and the Red Sea crossing to baptism. It was the presence or absence of faith that made the waters of the flood or the Red Sea crossing a blessing or curse.

Melanchthon saw the same connection between the Old Testament type and the New Testament antitype. He writes, "Just as the passage of the Israelites through the Red Sea was a figure of the afflictions of the church and its deliverance, so the immersion in baptism is a figure of afflictions and deliverance."[49] Both Luther and Melanchthon saw a redemptive-historical cast to the Scriptures and saw the unity between the testaments, which is illustrated in the connections they drew between the Red Sea crossing and baptism.

---

47. LW 11.53; also Trigg, *Baptism*, 118.
48. LW 2.153.
49. Melanchthon, *Loci Communes (1543)*, loc. 13, 143.

This brings a second observation: in the previous quote, Melanchthon mentions "immersion in baptism." As did their predecessors, it appears that Luther and Melanchthon looked at questions concerning the mode of baptism with a degree of flexibility. For example, the editors of the critical edition of the *Book of Concord* note that the original published Latin and German versions of the Small Catechism included a woodcut picturing the baptism of an infant. The editors describe the woodcut as showing a pastor holding a naked infant face down over the water of a large font with one hand while scooping water on the child with the other hand.[50] However, as early as 1519, Luther expressed his preference for total immersion, not as essential to the validity of the rite, but as the optimal expression of it.[51] So, then, it appears that questions of mode were not considered absolutely essential to the rite for the Lutherans.

CONCLUSION

In this survey of the views of Luther and Lutheranism on baptism, we see a decided break with the Roman Catholic theology of the day. This break was driven, of course, by competing views of soteriology. For the Roman Catholic Church, salvation was, in large part, the ontological transformation of an individual, which was accomplished through the administration of the sacraments. In the water of baptism, a person was justified, regenerated, and infused with grace, habits, and virtues, thereby equipping him to live the Christian life in the hope of not merely seeing the gates of heaven open, but of entering and remaining. Luther, however, saw things differently. He believed that a person's justification was by faith alone, which ruled out the possibility of the water of baptism serving in an instrumental role.

Rather than looking at redemption in ontological terms, Luther looked at it more in terms of God's promise and the power of the gospel, and to a certain degree as the outworking of God's covenant with His people.[52] Baptism most certainly brought the grace of God, but baptism was not limited to the moment of administration but accompanied a person throughout his life as the Word made visible. In this way, baptism was a perpetual tes-

---

50. BC 359, n. 77.

51. LW 35.29; Trigg, *Baptism*, 93, n. 142.

52. See Daphne Hampson, *Christian Contradictions: The Structures of Lutheran and Catholic Thought* (Cambridge: Cambridge University Press, 2001), 25, 47.

timony to the believer, and like the Word of God, it brought God's grace and its effects.

There was also an eschatological cast to Luther's doctrine of baptism. As in his doctrine of justification and the concept of *simul iustus et peccator* ("at the same time a sinner and righteous"), Luther saw the already/not yet tension in baptism. A person is righteous by faith alone, which secures his eschatological standing before God (the already), but he still struggles with the abiding presence of sin throughout his life, awaiting the completion of his sanctification (the not yet).[53] So baptism, though definitively and in one moment declaring a person's justification through a visible sign of death, burial, and resurrection to new life, nevertheless echoes throughout the person's life, signaling his ongoing need for sanctification and the power of baptism, the fulfillment of the visible promise of the gospel.[54] For Rome, it was the power of the water; for Luther, it was the power of God's promise.

---

53. Hampson, *Christian Contradictions*, 27.
54. Tranvik, "Luther on Baptism," 37.

CHAPTER 3

Baptism in Zwingli and the Anabaptists

In this survey of the history of the doctrine of baptism, it is important to examine the views of other voices during the sixteenth-century Reformation. Martin Luther and John Calvin feature prominently in most studies of the Reformation, as they should, given their influence. However, it is equally important to explore the views of other first-generation Reformers, such as Ulrich Zwingli (1484–1531). Zwingli contributed in a unique way to the theology of the Reformation, especially as it pertains to the sacraments. His position on the sacraments in general, and baptism specifically, was quite different from those of Luther and Roman Catholicism. His understanding of baptism largely hinged on his understanding and definition of the term *sacrament.*

In addition to Zwingli, it is important to survey the views of the Radical Reformation, or the Anabaptists. Anabaptist theologians, while ultimately charting a distinct course, started their theological journeys by working with the German and Swiss Reformers, such as Luther and Zwingli. While baptism was not the only doctrine for which the Anabaptists were known, it has been called a touchstone of their theology.[1]

In surveying the views of Zwingli and the Anabaptists, this chapter will showcase two contrasting views on baptism that can be compared with the broader stream of sixteenth-century thought, whether Roman Catholic, Lutheran, or Reformed.

---

1. William R. Estep, *The Anabaptist Story: An Introduction to Sixteenth-Century Anabaptism* (1963; Grand Rapids: Eerdmans, 1996), 235.

ZWINGLI

The definition of *sacrament*

For many theologians, the definition of a sacrament drives the nature and understanding of baptism, and Zwingli is no exception. In many ways, Zwingli echoed the antecedent tradition concerning the nature of the sacraments. In his *Reckoning of the Faith* (*Fidei Ratio*), written in 1530 over three or four days to present to Charles V around the time of the Diet of Augsburg, he explains: "A sacrament is a sign of a sacred thing—that is, of grace that has been given. I believe that it is a visible figure or form of invisible grace which has been provided and given by God's bounty; that is, a visible example which presents an analogy to something done by the Spirit." Zwingli further explains that the sacraments are "a public testimony," and he illustrates the relationship between the sign and the thing signified when he writes, "As when we are baptized the body is washed with the purest element, but by this it is signified that by the grace of divine goodness we have been drawn into the assembly of the church and God's people, wherein we ought to live pure and guiltless."[2]

Zwingli's reliance on the historic definition of Augustine in this statement is evident. However, two elements stand out as unique to Zwingli's theology. The first is the relationship between the sacrament and the grace that it represents. In the Roman Catholic view, the grace or power of God comes instrumentally through the water. The water is a vehicle or conduit for God's grace. For Zwingli, however, the water of baptism is an analogy to what occurs by God's work through the Spirit. Therefore, the sacrament and God's grace are not intertwined as they are in Roman Catholic theology. To this end, Zwingli writes: "I believe, yea, I know, that all the sacraments are so far from conferring grace that they do not even convey or distribute it." Instead, "Grace is produced or given by the Divine Spirit (for when I use the term 'grace' I am speaking the Latin for pardon, that is, indulgence and gratuitous kindness), so this gift pertains to the Spirit alone."[3]

Though Zwingli does not mention the Roman Catholic position at this point, he nevertheless rejects what lies behind an *ex opere operato* view: "A channel or vehicle is not necessary to the Sprit, for he himself is the virtue

---

2. Ulrich Zwingli, *Reckoning of the Faith*, in *Creeds and Confessions of Faith in the Christian Tradition,* eds. Jaroslav Pelikan and Valerie Hotchkiss (New Haven: Yale University Press, 2003), 2.262.

3. Zwingli, *Reckoning of the Faith*, in Pelikan and Hotchkiss, *Creeds*, 2.260.

and energy whereby all things are born, and has no need of being borne."[4] A number of scholars have noted that Zwingli's rejection of the common Roman Catholic view was not rooted exclusively in his understanding of Scripture but also in his Neoplatonic commitments. Zwingli had a profound suspicion of outward things, which was derived in part from Augustine's Neoplatonism, with its emphasis on the inward versus the outward and the spiritual over the material.[5] Zwingli's view of sacramental efficacy, therefore, also goes beyond Luther's view. Luther and later Lutheranism believed that the sacraments were the visible promise of God and, when combined with Word and Spirit, accomplished what was visibly proclaimed through them. For Zwingli, the sacraments were analogous to the grace of God rather than in any way directly connected to it.

The second unique quality of Zwingli's view of the sacraments is their status as public testimonies. For Luther and Lutheranism, the sacraments were primarily the visible promise of God. However, Zwingli placed a great deal of emphasis on the pledge or oath-nature of the sacraments. This aspect of the sacraments originated from Zwingli's understanding of the definition of the Latin term *sacramentum*, which was an oath that a soldier took in allegiance to his commanding general. Zwingli explains: "The sacraments act as an oath of allegiance. For in Latin the word *sacramentum* is used of an oath. And those who use the same oaths are made one race and alliance, coming together as one body and one people, to betray which is perjury."[6]

In a famous passage from his *Of Baptism* (1525), a work aimed not only at explaining the sacrament but also at refuting the views of Anabaptists, Zwingli writes:

> As used in this context the word sacrament means a covenant sign or pledge. If a man sews on a white cross, he proclaims that he is a Confederate. And if he makes the pilgrimage to Nähenfels and gives God praise and thanksgiving for the victory vouchsafed to our forefathers, he testifies that he is a Confederate indeed. Similarly the man who receives the mark of baptism is the one who is resolved to hear what

---

4. Zwingli, *Reckoning of the Faith*, in Pelikan and Hotchkiss, *Creeds*, 2.260.

5. See W. P. Stephens, "Zwingli's Sacramental Views," in *Prophet, Pastor, Protestant: The Work of Huldrych Zwingli After Five Hundred Years*, eds. E. J. Furcha and H. Wayne Pipkin (Allison Park, Pa.: Pickwick, 1984), 161; idem, *The Theology of Huldrych Zwingli* (Oxford: Clarendon, 1986), 187–88. Also see, Timothy George, "The Presuppositions of Zwingli's Baptismal Theology," in *Prophet, Pastor, Protestant*, 73.

6. Ulrich Zwingli, *An Exposition of the Faith*, in *Zwingli and Bullinger*, LCC, ed. G. W. Bromiley (Philadelphia: Westminster, 1953), 264–65.

God says to him, to learn the divine precepts and to live his life in accordance with them.[7]

In this quotation, Zwingli uses the Swiss confederation of thirteen cantons, which had a white cross as its identifying badge, as an illustration of how the sacraments, specifically baptism, function. He also draws on a famous Swiss victory in 1388 over the Austrians near Nähenfels in Glarus. Each year Swiss citizens would make pilgrimages to the battlefield to pay tribute to the soldiers who had fallen in the engagement.[8] From these points, it is evident that Zwingli neglected the idea that the sacraments convey grace, whether in a Roman Catholic or Lutheran sense.

On baptism

In Zwingli's explanation of baptism, he begins by noting four senses the term bears.[9] He argues first that the term means immersion in water, when a person individually pledges to live the Christian life; according to Zwingli, this was the subject matter of Jesus' teaching in John 3. Second, it refers to inward enlightenment and calling, the baptism of the Spirit, the subject Christ addressed in Acts 1. Third, it denotes the external teaching of salvation and immersion in water, such as in John 1, when John the Baptist said he baptized with water. Fourth, it is used for external baptism and internal faith, that is, for Christian salvation and God's gift of grace as a whole.[10] Zwingli believed the term *baptism* could be used as a metonymy, as in 1 Peter 3: "For neither as water nor as external teaching does baptism save us, but faith." Stressing the Protestant teaching on justification, Zwingli affirms, "Christ himself did not connect salvation with baptism: it is always by faith alone."[11]

In terms of justification by faith alone, Zwingli believed that the church fathers erred in their exegesis of John 3:5. Zwingli states, "These

---

7. Ulrich Zwingli, *Of Baptism*, in *Zwingli and Bullinger*, 131. There was some variation, however, in how Zwingli could express his definition of a sacrament. In his *Exposition and Basis of the Conclusions* (1523), Zwingli states: "When I call the body and blood of Christ a sacrament, I mean by sacrament what was first said of it, namely that which has been instituted by the unerring sure word of God" (Ulrich Zwingli, *Huldrych Zwingli: Writings*, eds. E. J. Furcha and H. Wayne Pipken [Allison Park, Pa.: Pickwick, 1984], 1.102). Cf. Stephens, "Sacramental Views," 155, 165; idem, *Theology*, 180, 192; George, "Baptismal Theology," 79–80.

8. Bromiley, ed., *Zwingli and Bullinger*, 334.

9. George, "Baptismal Theology," 76.

10. Zwingli, *Of Baptism*, in Bromiley, *Zwingli and Bullinger*, 132.

11. Zwingli, *Of Baptism*, 133–34.

doctors thought that by water he meant material water, and consequently they ascribed more to the water than was justified."[12] One of the points that Zwingli reiterates throughout his treatise on baptism is that material water cannot give birth to anything but material things: "Material water cannot contribute in any way to the cleansing of the soul."[13] Instead, Zwingli held that when a person was baptized, he was publicly received into the church, and his baptism was a testimony that he already had received the grace of redemption. Baptism, therefore, does not bring grace, but instead testifies to the church that grace has been given to the one receiving the rite.[14]

The passage on which Zwingli rested much of his understanding of baptism was Romans 6:1–4. Zwingli argued that Paul was not writing about external baptism but the internal baptism of the Spirit.[15] Paul, however, used external baptism to explain, by way of analogy or illustration, what was true about baptism itself, the spiritual realities to which water baptism pointed. Zwingli explains that immersion signifies death, in parallel with the death and burial of Christ. Likewise, emergence from the water signifies the resurrection of Christ and the spiritual resurrection of the individual to walk in newness of life. Zwingli summarizes by writing: "For when you were plunged into the external water, it signified that you were plunged into the death of Christ, that is, as Christ died for you, so you too died to the old man. And when you re-emerged, it signified the resurrection of Christ, that in him you were raised up again and now walk in the newness of life."[16]

Given the strong emphasis Zwingli placed on the centrality of faith, and his idea that baptism merely testifies to the grace a person already has received, it seems only natural to assume that Zwingli rejected infant baptism. This, however, would be a hasty conclusion.

Early in Zwingli's career, in 1523, he expressed hesitance on infant baptism.[17] Zwingli acknowledged that infants were baptized in the early church, but he said that the practice was not as widespread as it was in his own day. Nevertheless, apart from a cited historical source, Zwingli argued that children were first catechized and then later baptized. Zwingli then states:

---

12. Zwingli, *Of Baptism*, 154.
13. Zwingli, *Of Baptism*, 154.
14. Zwingli, *Reckoning of the Faith*, in Pelikan and Hotchkiss, *Creeds*, 2.261.
15. Cf. Ulrich Zwingli, *Friendly Exegesis* (1527), in *Writings*, 2.292.
16. Zwingli, *Of Baptism*, in Bromiley, *Zwingli and Bullinger*, 150–51.
17. David C. Steinmetz, *Reformers in the Wings* (1971; Grand Rapids: Baker, 1981), 200–201.

This manner of instruction I should like to see adopted again in our own day, namely that inasmuch as children are baptized so early, we undertake to instruct them when they reach that degree of understanding at which they are capable of hearing the word of God. Otherwise they might be at a great disadvantage which could be harmful to them, should they not be well instructed in the word of God right after baptism, as the young were instructed in times past, before baptism.[18]

Statements such as these arguably fueled the Swiss Anabaptist movement.[19] Zwingli even shared these reservations with several well-known theologians of his day, including Desiderius Erasmus (ca. 1466–1536), Guillaume Farel (1489–1565), and Johannes Oecolampadius (1482–1531).

Whatever reservations Zwingli had, the following year, in 1524, he wrote his first defense of infant baptism, claiming that he had been deceived into denying the legitimacy of the rite.[20] However, Zwingli did not retain infant baptism for exactly the same reasons as his Roman Catholic or Lutheran counterparts.[21] Like Patristic writers, medieval theologians, and Luther, Zwingli argued for the legitimacy of infant baptism based on the parallel between circumcision and baptism. Zwingli first acknowledged the broader point that both circumcision and baptism are signs of the covenant. He stipulated, though, that just as circumcision did not justify Abraham, neither does baptism justify the recipient. However, he explained that baptism as a covenant sign originated from God, the one who draws His people into the covenant.[22] Therefore, Zwingli did not view baptism purely and only as the pledge-oath of the believer because it is initiated by God, though it is fair to say that his emphasis fell on its role as a pledge-oath.[23]

Based on the parallel between the two rites, Zwingli notes that baptism is an initiatory rite. He then goes to the Great Commission to demonstrate to his Anabaptist critics that infants can receive the rite because Christ's statement begins with the command to baptize and is followed by the command to instruct: "This, then, is the literal sense: 'Go ye and make disciples of all nations'; then there follows the initiation with which they are to make disciples: 'baptizing them in the name of the Father, and of the Son, and of the Holy Ghost'; and after the initiation the instruction: 'teaching them

---

18. Zwingli, *Writings*, 1.100–101.
19. Stephens, *Theology*, 194; cf. George, "Baptismal Theology," 86, n. 47.
20. Stephens, *Theology*, 196; George, "Baptismal Theology," 79–80.
21. George, "Baptismal Theology," 75.
22. Zwingli, *Of Baptism*, in Bromiley, *Zwingli and Bullinger*, 138.
23. Stephens, *Theology*, 205.

to observe all things whatsoever I have entrusted to you.'"[24] This means that not only can an adult receive baptism and then instruction, but because baptism is the New Testament rite of initiation and sign of the covenant, so can infants.

Zwingli also believed that the parallel between circumcision and baptism legitimized infant baptism—as infant males were circumcised in the Old Testament, infants were to be baptized in the New Testament. Zwingli writes: "Baptism is just as much the symbol of the Christian people that has received from God the covenant that his son should be ours, as circumcision was once the symbol of that covenant the Lord should be their God and they should be his people." He goes on to explain:

> They, therefore, that trust in God through Christ and lead their own to this trust (to say this at the same time) are themselves circumcised just as Abraham and his seed were of old, but with the circumcision of Christ, which is baptism, Colossians 2.11. Our baptism, then, looks altogether to the same thing as circumcision did of old. It is a sign of the covenant which God has struck with us through his Son.[25]

This means Zwingli saw an underlying covenantal unity that began with Adam and continues into the present. Like other theologians before him, he saw the unity of the covenant supporting the practice of infant baptism.[26] Just as infants were included in the people of God in the Old Testament, in the New Testament infants were not to be denied baptism, as it was the replacement sign for circumcision.[27]

Elsewhere, Zwingli emphasized the continuity of the covenant and the connection between the two signs, circumcision and baptism. He writes:

> For there is one Church, one faith, and God is not more angry with us and our children than he was with the Jews, whose children were just as much in the covenant and in the Church as their fathers were. Here also there is an analogy: circumcision was given to the children of the Hebrews. Therefore baptism ought not to be refused the children of Christians.[28]

---

24. Zwingli, *Of Baptism*, in Bromiley, *Zwingli and Bullinger*, 142.

25. Zwingli, *Writings*, 2.224; cf. Stephens, *Theology*, 206.

26. Zwingli, *Of Baptism*, in Bromiley, *Zwingli and Bullinger*, 131, 138; cf. Stephens, "Sacramental Views," 160; idem, *Theology*, 186; also John W. Riggs, *Baptism in the Reformed Tradition: An Historical and Practical Theology* (Louisville: Westminster John Knox, 2002), 25.

27. Scott A. Gillies, "Zwingli and the Origin of the Reformed Covenant 1524–27," *SJT* 54 (2001): 43, 46.

28. Zwingli, *Friendly Exegesis*, in *Writings*, 2.353.

However, unlike his Roman Catholic or Lutheran counterparts, Zwingli wanted to be explicit that baptism did not convey grace to the baptized infant. Zwingli writes: "Circumcision, then, which formerly occupied the place of baptism, was only an external act of ceremony, and the Holy Spirit was not given in that act any more than in baptism."[29] In what way would the baptism of an infant be of benefit to one who might not yet possess faith?

As explained above, Zwingli believed that in the case of an infant, baptism as the initiatory rite could precede a profession of faith. Nevertheless, it is important to note that Zwingli believed that even in the absence of faith in the infant, two things were operative. First, there was the antecedent promise of God that undergirded the administration of the rite.[30] Second, there was the faith of the parents who brought the child for baptism. Concerning the baptism of adults, Zwingli writes:

> This baptism is administered in the presence of the church to one who before receiving it either confessed the religion of Christ, or has the word of promise whereby he is known to belong to the church. Hence it is that when we baptize an adult we ask him whether he believes. If he answers yes, then at length he receives baptism. Faith, therefore, has been present before he receives baptism. Faith, then, is not given in baptism.

Concerning infants, on the other hand, Zwingli explains:

> But when an infant is offered the question is asked whether its parents offer it for baptism. When they reply through witnesses that they wish it baptized, the infant is baptized. Here also God's promise precedes, that he regards our infants as belonging to the church no less than those of the Hebrews. For when they who are of the church offer it, the infant is baptized under the law that since it has been born of Christians it is regarded by the divine promise among the members of the church. By baptism, therefore, the church publicly receives one who had previously been received through grace.[31]

Unlike Luther, Zwingli was willing to base infant baptism on a *fides aliena*, a faith of another, namely, the faith of the parents. Of course, this was not the only basis, as there were also the pillars of the divine promise and the underlying covenantal unity between the Old Testament and New Testament.

---

29. Zwingli, *Friendly Exegesis*, in *Writings*, 2.353.
30. George, "Baptismal Theology," 78.
31. Zwingli, *Reckoning of the Faith*, in Pelikan and Hotchkiss, *Creeds*, 2.261.

As to how the sacrament of baptism was beneficial for infants, Zwingli believed that though the sacraments did not bring or confer grace (in contrast to Roman Catholic and Lutheran views), they assisted the contemplation of faith. Zwingli writes: "In baptism sight and hearing and touch are all claimed for the work of faith. For whether the faith be that of the Church or of the person baptized, it perceives that Christ endured death for the sake of his Church and that he rose again victorious. And that is what we hear and see and feel in baptism."[32] There is a corporate aspect to Zwingli's view of baptism, especially as it relates to infants. In the Roman Catholic understanding, for example, it was the recipient, infant or adult, who alone received the grace offered in the sacrament. In Zwingli's understanding, however, it was not only the adult who was baptized who could see, hear, and feel the death and resurrection of Christ; this visible symbol was also present for the whole church to observe, serving to "augment faith" and "be an aid to it."[33] The baptized infant would receive catechetical instruction as he grew up in the church, come to faith, and observe the baptism of others, thereby having his own faith augmented and assisted.[34]

THE ANABAPTISTS

There were those from within the Protestant Reformation who believed that the Reformers had not gone far enough. One of their main points of concern was infant baptism. This circle of theologians, who were later called Anabaptists, or "re-baptizers," believed that only a person who had undergone a radical conversion experience could and should be baptized.[35] The Anabaptists therefore believed that the key to the reformation of the church was their program of baptismal reform.[36]

No one Anabaptist theologian was dominant, but a survey of key figures and documents can serve to paint a general portrait of the Anabaptist theology of baptism.[37]

---

32. Zwingli, *Exposition of the Faith*, in Bromiley, *Zwingli and Bullinger*, 264; see also Zwingli, *Exposition and Basis*, in *Writings*, 1.115.

33. Zwingli, *Exposition of the Faith*, in Bromiley, *Zwingli and Bullinger*, 263.

34. Steinmetz, *Reformers*, 204.

35. Justo L. González, *A History of Christian Thought* (1975; Nashville: Abingdon, 1993), 3.89.

36. Hughes Oliphant Old, *The Shaping of the Reformed Baptismal Rite in the Sixteenth Century* (Grand Rapids: Eerdmans, 1992), 77.

37. Estep, *Anabaptist Story*, 177.

Conrad Grebel

Conrad Grebel (ca. 1498–1526) was an influential theologian of the Anabaptist movement. In a letter dated September 5, 1524, to another Anabaptist theologian, Thomas Müntzer (ca. 1488–1525), Grebel addressed the subject of baptism. He stated that baptism for adults was supposed to be administered with the person's consent to "Christ's rule" (Matt 18:15–17), or the willingness to be subject to church discipline. "Christ's rule" was a common theme in Anabaptist theology. Thus, Anabaptists rejected the idea that a person could be born into the church. Rather, the church was a voluntary association of believers who committed to live in obedience to the gospel. Those who did not live holy lives were subject to church discipline, or "the ban."[38] Grebel therefore rejected patristic formulations of baptism, saying Augustine, Tertullian, Theophylact, and Cyprian dishonored the faith and suffering of Christ. Grebel went as far as to say, "Infant baptism is a senseless, blasphemous abomination, contrary to all Scripture, contrary even to the papacy."[39]

Concerning baptism itself, Grebel, like other Anabaptist theologians, believed that it was representative of the believer's *imitatio Christi* (imitation of Christ). Grebel explains: "True Christian believers are sheep among wolves, sheep for the slaughter; they must be baptized in anguish and affliction, tribulation, persecution, suffering and death." He goes on to state:

> The Scripture describes for us thus, that it signifies that, by faith and the blood of Christ, sins have been washed away for him who is baptized, changes his mind, and believes before and after; that it signifies that a man is dead and ought to be dead to sin and walks in the newness of life and spirit, and that he shall certainly be saved if, according to this meaning, by inner baptism he lives his faith.[40]

The writings of other Anabaptist theologians also express the primacy of the decision to believe, the *imitatio Christi*, and the idea that baptism is connected to the believer's profession of faith, not the promise or covenant of God.

---

38. See, e.g., Menno Simons, *On the Ban: Questions and Answers*, in *Spiritual and Anabaptist Writers*, LCC, vol. 25, ed. George Hunston Williams (Philadelphia: Westminster, 1957), 261–71.

39. Conrad Grebel, "Letters to Thomas Müntzer by Conrad Grebel and Friends," in Williams, *Spiritual and Anabaptist Writers*, 80–81; see also idem, *The Sources of Swiss Anabaptism: The Grebel Letters and Related Documents*, ed. Leland Harder (Scottdale, Pa.: Herald Press, 1985), 290–91.

40. Grebel, "Letters," in Williams, *Spiritual and Anabaptist Writers*, 80; idem, *Sources*, 290; cf. Old, *Baptismal Rite*, 90.

Hans Denck

Hans Denck (ca. 1500–1527) initially embraced the Lutheran Reformation, but later joined the fledgling Anabaptist movement. Denck was later associated with Anabaptist theologians such as Müntzer.[41] Denck devoted a third of his *Confession Before the Nuremburg Council* (1525), a document that the ministers of Nuremburg required him to submit so they could evaluate his beliefs, to the subject of baptism.[42] In the second chapter, he states that just as it is useless to try to wash the red color off a brick or the black off a piece of coal, it is pointless to try externally to wash sin from a man. Rather, it is necessary for God alone to descend and penetrate the abyss of man's uncleanness to cleanse his heart. Denck argues that it is not baptism with water that is key but the baptism of Christ by the Spirit.

Denck explains that when a person struggles in the crisis of belief, which Denck likens to a flood or a life of despair, he enters into a covenant with God, who therefore cleanses him of his sin. Denck writes: "Where this covenant is, there the Spirit of Christ also comes hither and ignites the fire of love which consumes fully what infirmity remains and completes the work of Christ." He goes on to explain: "Where baptism transpires in the previously mentioned covenant, it is good. Where not, it serves no purpose for the reason indicated."[43] This means that baptism, according to Denck, is not necessary for salvation. Rather, internal baptism is necessary.

In Denck's understanding of baptism, there are several important factors. First, for Denck, it appears that water baptism is something of a meaningless rite and that the inner baptism is key. Second, Denck's view of the inner baptism is very similar to another aspect of his theology that appears in his *Confession*, namely, his doctrine of Scripture. Denck believed that the Scriptures were merely a human document that could not be profitable except by the Spirit of God: "I hold the Scriptures dear above all of man's treasures, but not as high as the Word of God which is living, strong, eternal and free of all elements of this world."[44] In other words, Scripture is not identical with the Word of God. He calls the Scriptures "a lantern which shines

---

41. González, *Christian Thought*, 89.

42. Hans Denck, *Confession Before the Nuremberg Council*, in Pelikan and Hotchkiss, *Creeds*, 2.669–70.

43. Denck, *Confession*, in Pelikan and Hotchkiss, *Creeds*, 2.670

44. Hans Denck, "Recantation," in *Selected Writings of Hans Denck*, ed. and trans. Edward J. Furcha and Ford Lewis Battles (Pittsburgh: Pickwick, 1976), 123.

in the dark…but it cannot of itself…entirely remove the darkness."[45] The inward illumination of the Spirit for hearing the Word of God in Scripture and the inner baptism are in parallel. Third, given these two emphases in Denck's understanding of baptism, it is important to note how divergent his soteriology was from that of the Protestant Reformers. In the works of Luther or the Lutheran confessions, or in Zwingli's writings, justification by faith alone features prominently, but Denck's *Confession* starts with faith but then moves in broad strokes to explain how a person ultimately must live by love.[46]

The following statement evidences that Denck believed that the Christian life had to be marked by a daily struggle in order for it to be authentic: "Indeed, if I say today, I believe, I might, nevertheless, tomorrow reprove myself for lying, yet not I, but the truth reproves which I perceive imperfectly in me."[47] This statement reflects an idea in Denck's soteriology, namely, that a person is saved through his *imitatio Christi*.[48] As David Steinmetz notes, "To be sure, Jesus plays an important role as an example to be imitated in man's struggle to attain perfect surrender to the will of God."[49] Denck's understanding of soteriology as the *imitatio Christi* opposed the teaching of the Reformers on justification by faith alone, a doctrine that he believed clouded the moral imperatives that lie at the heart of the gospel. In contrast to many Reformed expressions of the period, Denck did not define faith as that which relies on, trusts, rests on, or accepts the obedience of Christ, but as obedience itself: "Faith is godly obedience."[50] He also believed that Reformation doctrines such as original sin and predestination, and the Reformed emphasis on preaching and the sacraments, weakened the Christian's resolve to yield himself fully to the will of God. Denck believed, therefore, that inner spirituality was more important than the performance of ritual acts.[51]

This brief survey shows that a personal conversion marked by lifelong despair was central to Denck's understanding of salvation and, by extension, baptism. A person could not be baptized apart from this existential angst,

---

45. Denck, *Confession*, in Pelikan and Hotchkiss, *Creeds*, 2.668; cf. Steinmetz, *Reformers*, 212, 216; Estep, *Anabaptist Story*, 191–92.

46. Old, *Baptismal Rite*, 107.

47. Denck, *Confession*, in Pelikan and Hotchkiss, *Creeds*, 2.667.

48. Steinmetz, *Reformers*, 210.

49. Steinmetz, *Reformers*, 216.

50. Denck, "Recantation," in Furcha and Battles, *Selected Writings*, 125.

51. Steinmetz, *Reformers*, 217.

and the external baptism was not key but the internal baptism of the Spirit. For Denck, baptism was a sign of the covenant of sorts, in that it was an external sign that represented the covenant of belief initiated by the believer. In Luther or in Zwingli, there was the idea that baptism represented the promise of God's grace, or the gospel, and that in this way baptism was a sign of the covenant. Luther explained baptism in terms of the promise of God, and Zwingli placed a far greater emphasis on the person's oath-pledge. For Denck, however, baptism was exclusively the man-initiated covenant with God. He was not the only Anabaptist theologian to articulate such a view on baptism.

Balthasar Hübmaier

Balthasar Hübmaier (1480–1528) was initially associated with Zwingli's Swiss reform movement but quickly became disenchanted with the slow pace. Hübmaier eventually struck out on his own by departing from Zurich, taking up residence in Waldshut, and associating with the Anabaptist movement.

One of Hübmaier's chief desires was to see the church reject the practice of infant baptism. He began to preach against infant baptism and persuaded a number of people to postpone the baptism of their children and have them dedicated instead. Later, in 1525, another Anabaptist leader arrived in Waldshut and convinced Hübmaier and sixty others to be rebaptized—or, in their eyes, to be baptized properly for the first time—in the public fountain, with Hübmaier using a bucket to pour water over the people.[52]

Hübmaier produced two major documents that deal with baptism: *On the Christian Baptism of Believers* and *Christian Catechism* (1526), in which there is a large portion devoted to the subject of baptism.[53]

Hübmaier did not believe that infant baptism was a legitimate practice. When asked what he thought of the rite, he responded, "Nothing, other

---

52. Old, *Baptismal Rite*, 93; also Bryan D. Spinks, *Reformation and Modern Rituals and Theologies of Baptism: From Luther to Contemporary Practices* (Aldershot: Ashgate, 2006), 86.

53. Hübmaier wrote other works, including *Dialogue with Zwingli's Baptism Book*, in which he interacted with Zwingli's views on baptism; *Old and New Teachers on Believers' Baptism*, which was a collection of quotations of Patristic and contemporary theologians; and another dialogue with the views of Oecolampadius in the crosshairs (see *Balthasar Hübmaier*, eds. and trans. H. Wayne Pipkin and John H. Yoder [Scottdale, Pa.: Herald Press, 1989]; H. Wayne Pipkin, "The Baptismal Theology of Balthasar Hübmaier," *MQR* 65 [1991]: 34–53).

than that the adult child gives a bath to the young child, thereby depriving it of the real water baptism of Christ" (q. 39).[54]

Why did Hübmaier reject infant baptism, whether in its Roman Catholic, Lutheran, or Zwinglian forms? The answer stems from Hübmaier's soteriology. In the broader structure of Hübmaier's catechism, there is a basic *ordo salutis*, which shows why he rejected infant baptism. In question 21, Hübmaier explains what the gospel is: "Christ died for the sake of our sins, and arose for the sake of our justification, Romans 4." In the following question, he states, "What follows from this message," to which he answers, "Faith." Subsequent to these questions, Hübmaier explains the difference between a dead and living faith, citing James 2 to define dead faith. He then explains that a living faith produces the fruits of the Spirit and works through love (qq. 24–28). Quite discernibly, Hübmaier places faith in the chief place in his *ordo salutis*.[55] What follows from faith is not only good works but the desire for water baptism (q. 31).

Hübmaier explains that there are three types of baptism: Spirit, blood, and water (qq. 32–33). Spirit baptism is the inner illumination of the heart that takes place by the operation of the Holy Spirit through the living Word of God (q. 34). Baptism of blood is the daily mortification of the flesh until death (q. 36). Hübmaier's explanation of water baptism showcases how his soteriology informs his understanding of the rite:

> It is an outward and public testimony of the inner baptism in the Spirit, which a person gives by receiving water, with which one confesses one's sins before all people. One also testifies thereby that one believes in the forgiveness of his sins through the death and resurrection of our Lord Jesus Christ. Thereupon one also has himself outwardly enrolled, inscribed, and by water baptism incorporated into the fellowship of the church according to the institution of Christ, before which church the person also publicly and orally vows to God and agrees in the strength of God the Father, Son, and Holy Spirit that he will henceforth believe and live according to his divine word. And if he should trespass herein he will accept brotherly admonition, according to Christ's order, Matthew 18. This precisely is the true baptism vow, which we have lost for a thousand years (q. 35).

---

54. Balthasar Hübmaier, *Christian Catechism*, in Pelikan and Hotchkiss, *Creeds*, 2.676–93. All subsequent quotations are taken from this edition.

55. See also Balthasar Hübmaier, *On the Christian Baptism of Believers*, in *Balthasar Hübmaier*, eds. and trans. H. Wayne Pipkin and John H. Yoder (Scottdale, Pa.: Herald Press, 1989), 143–47.

From this statement, the contours of Hübmaier's *ordo salutis* surface. Baptism is not a means of grace, nor does it have the power to regenerate the one who is baptized. Rather, it is the outward public testimony of the inner baptism. While there appear to be echoes of the views of Zwingli in the idea that baptism is a public pledge (which is not surprising, as Hübmaier worked with Zwingli for some time), what has completely disappeared is any reference to the covenant or promise of God. Baptism completely revolves around the profession of the individual, though this profession is the result of the prior inner working of the Holy Spirit, the inner baptism.[56]

Hübmaier's emphasis on the profession of faith in his explanation of the baptismal pledge is evident in the following:

> It is a commitment made to God publicly and orally before the congregation in which the baptized person renounces Satan and all his imaginations and works. He also vows that he will henceforth set his faith, hope, and trust solely in God and regulate his life according to the divine word, in the strength of Jesus Christ our Lord, and if he should fail to do so, he thereby promises the church that he would dutifully accept brotherly discipline from it and its members, as has been said above (q. 41).

Baptism is the believer's pledge to God as well as to the church. Since it is for believers, it is immediately evident why infant baptism is invalid.

Hübmaier believed it was absolutely essential that a person profess his faith prior to baptism. If baptism was the pledge of a person's faith, then apart from that faith there could be no pledge, hence no baptism. Hübmaier colorfully explains: "There must be wine in the cellar before one hangs out the sign or the hoop of the keg, or it is a falsehood. Thus one must believe before one hangs out the sign of faith, or it will be hypocrisy."[57] Hence, summarizing Hübmaier's *ordo salutis*, it is first the hearing of the Word; second, faith in Christ; third, baptism; and fourth, following Christ and performing good works. What should be noted is how prominent a role the act of the will, the decision to believe, plays in Hübmaier's understanding of the rite.

---

56. Steinmetz, *Reformers*, 205.

57. Balthasar Hübmaier, *Dialogue with Zwingli's Baptism Book*, in *Balthasar Hübmaier*, eds. and trans. H. Wayne Pipkin and John H. Yoder (Scottdale, Pa.: Herald Press, 1989), 212, also 196.

Many Anabaptists were voluntarists through and through.[58] Hübmaier's voluntarism is especially evident in a treatise he wrote on the freedom of the will, one that is marked by his trichotomous view of man.[59] Hübmaier believed that man consisted of body, soul, and spirit.[60] Prior to the fall, these three substances were entirely free to choose good or evil, life or death, heaven or hell.[61] In the fall, man's body and soul were affected by sin, but his spirit was not. Hübmaier writes: "But the spirit of man has remained utterly upright and intact before, during and after the Fall, for it took part, neither by counsel nor by action, yea it did not in any way consent to or approve of the eating of the forbidden fruit by the flesh. But it was forced, against its will, as a prisoner in the body, to participate in the eating."[62] Hübmaier sets forth an inherently Neoplatonic view of man, in that there is a spirit-matter antithesis that sees the spirit as imprisoned in the body. This is one of the reasons Hübmaier emphasized inner baptism over and against the external rite.

Moreover, his anthropology was quite semi-Pelagian, in contrast with Protestant views vis-à-vis man's total depravity. Hübmaier's anthropology mirrors that of Roman Catholicism when he states that even after the fall, "Only the spirit has maintained its inherited righteousness, in which it was first created." He further states that the spirit "has the same form before and after the Fall of Adam, our forefather, whatever proud thinkers may say about the higher and lower faculties of man."[63] In man's salvation, "The soul is free and can follow either the spirit or the flesh. If it follows Eve, that is the flesh, it becomes an Eve and carnal. But if it is obedient to the Spirit, it becomes a Spirit."[64] It is not that either the law or the gospel

---

58. Old, *Baptismal Rite*, 100; see Steinmetz, *Reformers*, 200; also idem, "Scholasticism and Radical Reform: Nominalist Motifs in the Theology of Balthasar Hübmaier," *MQR* 45 (1971): 123–44, esp. 130.

59. Cf. *Luther and Erasmus on Free Will and Salvation*, LCC, vol. 17, ed. E. Gordon Rupp (Philadelphia: Westminster, 1957); Thor Hall, "The Possibilities of Erasmian Influence on Denck and Hübmaier in Their Views on the Freedom of the Will," *MQR* 35 (1961): 149–70; John Calvin, *The Bondage and Liberation of the Will: A Defense of the Orthodox Doctrine of Human Choice against Pighius*, ed. A. N. S. Davies, trans. G. I. Davies (Grand Rapids: Baker, 1996).

60. Balthasar Hübmaier, *On Free Will*, in Williams, *Spiritual and Anabaptist Writers*, 116.

61. Hübmaier, *On Free Will*, 118.

62. Hübmaier, *On Free Will*, 120.

63. Hübmaier, *On Free Will*, 124; cf. Steinmetz, *Reformers*, 202–203.

64. Hübmaier, *On Free Will*, 125.

assists man in his salvation, but both law and gospel mixed together provide a "wholesome plaster for our souls."[65] In this way, then, when man, through his un-fallen spirit, chooses to take the medicine of the gospel, his soul is regenerated and he is justified.[66]

Hübmaier provides exegetical support for his doctrine of baptism by arguing that adults who were baptized as infants must submit to rebaptism because of what Matthew 28:18–20 and Mark 16:15–16 teach. These are the same texts to which Luther and Zwingli appealed, but Hübmaier quite obviously explains them differently. Hübmaier writes: "Since Christ commanded his disciples to preach and baptize, that very command orders us to hear the preaching and to be baptized." Hübmaier further explains that baptism is a command to which a person must assent, and infants cannot do so because "the infant knows neither good nor evil and cannot consent or vow either to the church or to God" (q. 40).

What is interesting about Hübmaier's appeal to these two passages is that he ignores Zwingli's explanation, one with which Hübmaier was familiar. Zwingli had explained Matthew 28:18–20 in his *Of Baptism* (1525), which was a specific refutation of the Anabaptist exegesis of the passage. Yet, in Hübmaier's catechism, there is no attempt to work with the Greek text or interact with the specific exegetical questions.

Zwingli argued that the Greek does not say, "teach all the nations," but rather, "make disciples of all the nations." This statement is then followed by two participles that tell how the apostles were supposed to make disciples, namely, through baptism and instruction.[67] Hübmaier never attempts to interact at this level with the Greek text, but simply appeals to it with the assumption that one must first believe and then be baptized.[68] Some have suggested that Hübmaier was ignorant of the intricacies of Greek grammar, which is a distinct possibility. He rejected the historical-grammatical exegesis that the Reformers had learned from Christian humanists. He believed that the average Christian could understand the message of the Scriptures apart from the assistance of learned pastors.[69] Regardless of the degree of Hübmaier's knowledge of Greek, he was alone neither in his

---

65. Hübmaier, *On Free Will*, 130.
66. Steinmetz, *Reformers*, 206; cf. Estep, *Anabaptist Story*, 196–99.
67. Zwingli, *Of Baptism*, in Bromiley, *Zwingli and Bullinger*, 141–43.
68. See also Hübmaier, *Dialogue with Zwingli*, 198–201.
69. Old, *Baptismal Rite*, 96–97, 100–101.

rejection of infant baptism nor in his conception of baptism as the believer's pledge to God.

One thing is clear: Hübmaier based his understanding of baptism largely on the New Testament; he had only a very limited interaction with the Old Testament, and this interaction was usually only on points raised by opponents.[70] When Hübmaier did interact with the Old Testament, he came to distinctly different conclusions than his opponents. For example, in his understanding of 1 Peter 3:20, Hübmaier argued that the ark, not the flood, was the type for baptism: "From this passage you can obviously see that Noah's ark is a figure or shadow of baptism." This fit Hübmaier's understanding of baptism, as the ark was Noah's response of faith to the instruction of the Lord to build the ark.[71]

Hübmaier rejected the common appeal to Colossians 2:11–12 to support infant baptism, a passage that notes the parallel between circumcision and baptism. He writes: "When Paul writes there on circumcision which is done without hand, and of baptism in which we are resurrected by faith, it refers to the inward baptism and not to the outward water baptism, as you say."[72] Hübmaier believed that there was no parallel between circumcision and baptism, nor one between the Passover and the Lord's Supper, as was commonly argued. Rather, he believed that the New Testament rites represented the destruction of the old and the institution of completely new, unprecedented rites.[73]

The Schleitheim Confession (1527)

The Schleitheim Confession was known as the first Anabaptist confession of faith written by the Swiss Brethren, who were led by Grebel and Felix Mantz (1498–1527).[74] Various Anabaptist movements were condemned by Roman Catholic, Lutheran, and Reformed churches alike, and Anabaptism was made a crime punishable by death. Hübmaier, for example, was burned at the stake in Vienna on March 10, 1528.[75] It would be hasty to conclude that Anabaptists were persecuted for their views on baptism alone, though

---

70. E.g., Hübmaier cites Rom. 6:4; Acts 8:12; 10:47; 16:15, 31–33; 18:8; Ezek. 44; Deut. 17:11; Ex. 18: 28; John 12:48 (*Dialogue with Zwingli*, 224).

71. Hübmaier, *On Christian Baptism*, 134, see also 117; *Dialogue with Zwingli*, 228.

72. Hübmaier, *Dialogue with Zwingli*, 186. This was also Hübmaier's understanding of Rom. 6:4, namely, that Paul spoke of inward baptism (*Dialogue with Zwingli*, 206).

73. Hübmaier, *Dialogue with Zwingli*, 188.

74. Pelikan and Hotchkiss, *Creeds*, 2.694.

75. Spinks, *Theologies of Baptism*, 84.

many Reformers rejected their views and thought them heretical. The different Anabaptist movements also supported the Peasants' War, rejected civil authority, advocated the idea of communal property, and, in some cases, even promoted polygamy. Roman Catholic, Lutheran, and Reformed theologians saw not only theological but societal implications that could arise from such beliefs, and therefore persecuted Anabaptists. However, in some locations, such as in Strasbourg, Anabaptist congregations were openly tolerated.

Grebel died of the plague in 1526 and Mantz was executed in January 1527. Other leaders were forced to flee Switzerland. In February 1527, the remnants of the Swiss Brethren, led by Michael Sattler (ca. 1490–1527), met in Schleitheim to compose their confession.[76] Sattler was later apprehended and tried by Roman Catholic authorities. While his rejection of infant baptism played a role in his trial, so did his denial of the real presence of Christ in the Lord's Supper, refusal to ascribe to Mary the role of mediatrix or advocate, unwillingness to swear an oath, and pacifism. Moreover, the Roman Catholic authorities identified him as a Lutheran, seeing no difference from the Protestants in his Anabaptist views. Sadly, Sattler was burned at the stake. His associates were executed by sword, and his wife and female followers were all drowned.[77] It was in this context of persecution that the Schleitheim Confession was drafted.[78]

The confession states the following regarding baptism:

> Baptism shall be given to all those who have been taught repentance and the amendment of life and who believe truly that their sins are taken away through Christ, and to all those who desire to walk in the resurrection of Jesus Christ and be buried with him in death so that they might rise with him; to all those who with such an understanding themselves desire and request it from us; hereby is excluded all infant baptism, the greatest and first abomination of the pope. For this you have the reasons and the testimony of the writings and the practice of the apostles (Matt. 28:19; Mark 16:6; Acts 2:38; 8:36; 16:31–33; and 19:4). We wish simply yet resolutely and with assurance to hold to the same (§ 1).[79]

---

76. See Harder, *Sources*, 443–48.

77. See *The Trial and Martyrdom of Michael Sattler*, in Williams, *Spiritual and Anabaptist Writers*, 136–44.

78. Spinks, *Theologies of Baptism*, 84; Pelikan and Hotchkiss, *Creeds*, 2.694.

79. Schleitheim Confession, in Pelikan and Hotchkiss, *Creeds*, 2.697.

This brief statement demonstrates several representative characteristics of an Anabaptist view of baptism.

First, a person must exhibit repentance and good works, and must profess his faith in Christ, before he can be baptized. The person must request to be baptized, which automatically precludes infants from the rite. Second, there is no discussion or mention of the idea of covenant. Though it is unstated, this article reflects the idea that baptism is the pledge of the one who is baptized and nothing more. Third, the article states the belief that infant baptism was a practice started by the pope and does not mention that many of the church fathers approved of the practice. Moreover, in bringing scriptural support for the baptism of adults exclusively, there is appeal solely to the New Testament and the practice of the apostles. No attempt is made to relate baptism to the Old Testament in any way. In fact, in the fifty-plus Scripture citations or allusions in the confession, there are only two from the Old Testament. This reflects the fact that Anabaptist theology as a whole, not simply for the doctrine of baptism, was built on the New Testament almost exclusively.[80] Fourth, there is no mention of the proper mode of baptism.

CONCLUSION

This survey of Zwingli and the Anabaptists shows that there are some important points to note before proceeding in the study. First, Zwingli's views vis-à-vis the Reformed tradition are somewhat unique, as he placed a greater emphasis on the idea of baptism as a pledge-oath than one finds in the views of the second-generation Reformers. With good reason Karl Barth (1886–1968) writes: "Among his contemporaries he was a lonely figure."[81] This is not to say that Zwingli was terribly out of the mainstream, as he affirmed infant baptism based on the covenantal unity of redemption in both the Old Testament and New Testament, and he had a covenantal understanding of the rite.

Zwingli's view of the pledge-oath nature of baptism, however, likely contributed to the development of Anabaptist views on baptism. Their views were similar to Zwingli's in some respects, but only in terms of the

---

80. Cf. Steinmetz, *Reformers*, 221, 225–26; Estep, *Anabaptist Story*, 193–96, 206–07; González, *Christian Thought*, 92; Harder, *Sources*, 427–28.
81. Barth, CD IV.4, 128.

most basic points, such as baptism as the pledge-oath of the believer, indifference on the mode of baptism, and the influence of Neoplatonic ideas in their understandings of the sacraments. Zwingli and the Anabaptists saw baptism primarily as the believer's pledge, but Zwingli also emphasized the covenant and God's antecedent promise, unlike the Anabaptists. This is especially evident in the hermeneutical differences between the two and in the virtual absence of the use of the Old Testament in the Anabaptist doctrine of baptism. Neither Zwingli nor the Anabaptists debated at all over the mode. Zwingli, in fact, showed a preference for immersion. Immersion only later became an issue in Anabaptist theology.[82] Zwingli and the Anabaptists had similar emphases on the importance of inner spiritual baptism, but there were some differences regarding the external elements, ranging from a de-emphasis of the external elements in Zwingli to the complete superfluity of the external elements in an Anabaptist like Denck.

Though there are these similarities between Zwingli and Anabaptists, the differences were driven by Anabaptist soteriology and anthropology. In contrast to the Reformers, Anabaptists saw the freedom of the will as definitive in their soteriology. In this respect, it is important to note the irony and inaccuracy of labels. The Anabaptists are called "radical reformers" because of their rejection of a number of common theological views, chief among them infant baptism. Yet, the soteriology and anthropology of many of the Anabaptist theologians, such as Grebel or especially Hübmaier, were decidedly traditional, that is, very similar to Roman Catholic views. On questions such as grace and nature, free will, and predestination, the Anabaptists reflected the views of medieval theology. By contrast, Reformers such as Luther and Zwingli were decidedly radical in their soteriology and anthropology, which is manifest in their doctrine of justification by faith alone, their views departing from the contemporary Roman Catholic tradition. In this sense, the Reformers were the flaming radicals.[83]

This is an important point to note, as the radical reformers saw their movement as restoring New Testament Christianity, as a return to the *radix*, or root—hence, the Radical Reformation. In their eyes, they were taking the Protestant Reformation to the next logical step by rejecting infant baptism and reformulating the doctrine of the church around the idea that it was exclusively a voluntary community. But the radical reformers failed

---

82. González, *Christian Thought*, 92.

83. Steinmetz, *Reformers*, 198, 207; idem, "Scholasticism and Radical Reform," 137; cf. Estep, *Anabaptist Story*, 197.

to grasp the fundamental issue of *sola fide*, which represented a renaissance of the Pauline understanding of the gospel. In other words, it is not proper to argue that the Anabaptists made the necessary reforms to the doctrine of the church, as they operated with what was basically a Roman Catholic soteriology and anthropology. Therefore, Anabaptist views on baptism fall short. Soteriology and ecclesiology are interconnected, part of the organic body of doctrine contained in the Scriptures. Anabaptist ecclesiology is arguably built on a Roman Catholic soteriology, though Anabaptists do come to some different conclusions regarding the nature of the church.

CHAPTER 4

Baptism in the Reformed Tradition

Moving forward in the investigation, it is necessary to survey the Reformed wing of the Reformation. One of the chief figures is John Calvin (1509–1564). Calvin was a prominent second-generation Reformer, but this is not to say that he is regulative for the tradition. The second portion of this chapter will show that other Reformed theologians played a key role in the development of the doctrine of baptism.[1] Hence, this chapter will survey Calvin's writings to identify the key points of his doctrines of the sacraments and baptism. The second portion of the chapter will survey two major Reformation documents, the Belgic Confession (1561) and the Heidelberg Catechism (1563). These documents not only were important in the formation of the Reformed confessional and theological identity during the closing years of the Reformation, they were foundational for the Dutch Reformed tradition and endure into the present. Hence, surveying these documents on the sacraments and baptism will aid the investigation into the development of the doctrine of baptism.

JOHN CALVIN

On the sacraments

Calvin defines a sacrament as "an outward sign by which the Lord seals on our consciences the promises of his good will toward us in order to sustain the weakness of our faith; and we in turn attest our piety toward him in the presence of the Lord and of his angels before men."[2] Below the surface

---

1. See Richard A. Muller, *After Calvin: Studies in the Development of a Theological Tradition* (Oxford: Oxford University Press, 2003), 63–104.

2. John Calvin, *Institutes of the Christian Religion*, LCC, vols. 20–21, ed. John T. McNeill, trans. Ford Lewis Battles (Philadelphia: Westminster, 1960), 4.14.1.

of this definition are three important strands that reflect the thought of Augustine, Martin Luther, and Ulrich Zwingli.[3]

First, Calvin explains that his definition does not differ greatly from Augustine's classic definition of a sacrament, namely, "a visible sign of a sacred thing" or "a visible form of an invisible grace."[4]

Second, it appears that Calvin's definition at this point also echoes Luther's understanding of a sacrament as the visible Word or promise of God.[5] This theme surfaces periodically in Calvin's writings. For example, Calvin writes in his Genesis commentary: "It is common to all sacraments to have the word of God annexed to them, by which he testifies that he is propitious to us, and calls us to the hope of salvation; yea, a sacrament is nothing else than a visible word, or sculpture and image of that grace of God, which the word more fully illustrates."[6] Elsewhere, Calvin writes: "Just as men are known by their appearance and speech, so God utters His voice to us by the voice of the prophets, and in the Sacraments puts on, as it were, a visible form, from which He can be known according to our small capacity."[7] Luther's influence on Calvin seems to be evident in that his definition dates to the 1536 edition of the *Institutes*, in which Calvin was indebted to Luther on a number of points.[8] This is not to say that Calvin does not develop the idea in his own way, which is evident in a number of places throughout his locus on the sacraments in the 1559 edition of the *Institutes*.

Third, there seems to be an echo of Zwingli when Calvin states that the sacraments are the event by which the recipient attests his piety toward God and men.

So in one sense, it seems that Calvin took the best elements of Augustine's, Luther's, and Zwingli's definitions of the sacraments and incorporated

---

3. To trace the evolution of the development of Calvin's understanding of the sacraments, see B. A. Gerrish, *Grace and Gratitude: The Eucharistic Theology of John Calvin* (Edinburgh: T & T Clark, 1993), 109–16.

4. Calvin, *Institutes*, 4.14.1; Alister McGrath, *Reformation Thought: An Introduction* (1988; Grand Rapids: Baker, 1993), 182; François Wendel, *Calvin: Origins and Development of His Religious Thought* (1950; Grand Rapids: Baker, 1997), 313; Ronald S. Wallace, *Calvin's Doctrine of the Word and Sacrament* (Edinburgh: Scottish Academic Press, 1995), 133.

5. So Gerrish, *Grace and Gratitude*, 104.

6. John Calvin, *Genesis*, CTS, vol. 1 (rep.; Grand Rapids: Baker, 1993), 451.

7. John Calvin, *John 1–10*, CNTC (1961; Grand Rapids: Eerdmans, 1995), 138.

8. Some have pointed out that the outline of the 1536 edition of the *Institutes* follows Luther's Small Catechism. For the parallels between the two, see Alexandre Ganoczy, *The Young Calvin* (Philadelphia: Westminster, 1987), 137–45.

them in his own understanding of the term.[9] This tells the investigator what Calvin implicitly approved from these other theologians.

However, further exploration reveals that Calvin disapproved of a number of things from the formulations of other theologians. For example, Calvin disagreed with Zwingli's understanding of the Latin term *sacramentum* as an oath-pledge by a soldier to his commanding officer, though he did not mention Zwingli by name. He argued that Zwingli had taken the classical Latin definition of the term rather than look to see how the term had been used by the Patristics.[10] According to Calvin, the Patristics used the term to denote sacred signs.[11]

In addition, Calvin rejected the Roman Catholic understanding of the sacraments, particularly the doctrine of *ex opere operato*. This rejection is evident in Calvin's explanation of the nature and function of the sacraments. He believed that the sacraments are never without a preceding promise, and that the sacraments function as an appendix for the purpose of sealing the promise itself.[12]

From this general trajectory, three important elements of Calvin's understanding of the sacraments emerge. First, there must be an antecedent promise, which Calvin believed came through the preaching of the Word. Hence, Calvin writes: "A sacrament consists of the word and the outward sign."[13] Elsewhere, Calvin makes evident the importance of both Word and sacrament when he writes: "The preaching of the gospel is called the kingdom of heaven, and the sacraments may be called the gate of heaven, because they admit us into the presence of God."[14]

However, Calvin is careful to stipulate the difference between the Roman Catholic and Protestant ideas of what is meant by "the Word." Calvin writes: "For we ought to understand the word not as one whispered without meaning and without faith, a mere noise, like a magic incantation, which has the force to consecrate the element. Rather, it should, when preached, make us understand what the visible sign means."[15] In other words, Calvin believed that the Word must be preached in conjunction with the sacrament; the mere recitation of the baptismal formula of Matthew 28:18–20 or the *hoc*

---

9. McGrath, *Reformation Thought*, 182–83.
10. Wendel, *Calvin*, 314.
11. Calvin, *Institutes*, 4.14.13.
12. Calvin, *Institutes*, 4.14.3.
13. Calvin, *Institutes*, 4.14.4.
14. Calvin, *Genesis*, 118.
15. Calvin, *Institutes*, 4.14.4.

est corpus meum is not enough: "The sacrament requires preaching to beget faith."[16] In this sense, there is an inherent priority of preaching over the sacraments, in that there can be preaching without the sacraments, but the sacraments cannot be administered without preaching. In fact, without the preaching of the Word, Calvin says, the sacraments have "no effect," are "pure corruptions," and are "empty and delusive signs."[17]

Second, the preceding promise of which Calvin writes must be understood as covenantal. Calvin explains, "Since the Lord calls his promises 'covenants' and his sacraments 'tokens' of the covenants, a simile can be taken from the covenants of men."[18] In contrast to Roman Catholic theology, Calvin did not believe that the Old Testament sacraments, such as circumcision, merely foreshadowed the grace that would come through Christ in the New Testament. Rather, Calvin believed that the Scriptures placed Christ as the substance of both Old Testament and New Testament sacraments.[19] Calvin identified circumcision, purifications, sacrifices, and rites from the law of Moses as Old Testament sacraments, but in the wake of the ministry of Christ there are now only two, baptism and the Lord's Supper.[20] True, the sacraments of the New Testament more clearly reveal Christ, but Calvin nevertheless believed the sacraments of both testaments were equal. "They," writes Calvin, referring to Old Testament saints, "felt the same power in their sacraments as do we in ours; these were seals of divine good will toward them looking to eternal salvation."[21]

Third, the sacraments are seals. Calvin likened the sacraments to the seals that are attached to government documents and other public acts that are nothing taken by themselves, but, when seals are added, confirm what has been written. With this illustration, Calvin explains the relationship between circumcision and justification as it related to Abraham. He writes: "There Paul expressly argues that Abraham's circumcision was not for his justification but for the seal of that covenant by faith in which he had

---

16. Calvin, *Institutes*, 4.14.4; Wilhelm Niesel, *The Theology of Calvin* (1956; Cambridge: James Clarke, 2002), 213; Wendel, *Calvin*, 314.

17. John Calvin, *A Harmony of the Gospels: Matthew, Mark & Luke*, CNTC (1963; Grand Rapids: Baker, 1995), 252; idem, *Isaiah 1–32*, CTS, vol. 7 (rep., Grand Rapids: Baker, 1993), 212; idem, *Harmony of Exodus, Leviticus, Numbers, and Deuteronomy*, CTS, vol. 3 (rep., Grand Rapids: Baker, 1993), 321; cf. Wendel, *Calvin*, 312; Wallace, *Calvin's Doctrine*, 135–36.

18. Calvin, *Institutes*, 4.14.6; Niesel, *Theology of Calvin*, 214.

19. Calvin, *Institutes*, 4.14.23.

20. Calvin, *Institutes*, 4.14.20.

21. Calvin, *Institutes*, 4.14.23.

already been justified."[22] So the sacraments are visible covenantal promises that are an authoritative seal to God's Word.[23]

Beyond this, Calvin is explicit in his insistence that the sacraments must be founded on the promise (or Word) of God, but also that they have a christological and pneumatological cast to them. Calvin believed that in order for the sacraments to be effectual, a person must use them with faith in Christ. He did not think that people can place their confidence or trust in the sacraments per se, but rather in the One who is the author of the sacraments.[24] Likewise, the sacraments do not merely point to or convey a bald power or grace, but rather set forth Christ: "Therefore, let it be regarded as a settled principle that the sacraments have the same office as the Word of God: to offer and set forth Christ to us, and in him the treasures of heavenly grace. But they avail and profit nothing unless received in faith."[25] Through faith, the Holy Spirit makes the sacraments effectual for the recipient.[26] Calvin, rejecting an *ex opere operato* view, did not believe that there was any inherent power in the sacraments themselves.

Calvin argued that unless the Holy Spirit accompanies the administration of the sacraments, they are of no benefit to the recipient.[27] For the unbeliever, for example, the sacraments are "nothing more than cold and empty figures."[28] Commenting on Galatians 3:27, Calvin explains Paul's understanding of this point:

> Baptism is far from being efficacious in all. It is absurd to say that the grace of the Holy Spirit should be so bound to the external sign. Both the uniform doctrine of Scripture and also experience seem to be able to confute this statement. I reply that it is customary for Paul to speak of the sacraments in a twofold way. When he is dealing with hypocrites who boast in the bare sign, he then proclaims the emptiness and worthlessness of the outward sign and strongly attacks their foolish confidence. Why? Because he considers, not the ordinance of God, but the corruption of the ungodly. When, however, he addresses

---

22. Calvin, *Institutes*, 4.14.5.
23. Niesel, *Theology of Calvin*, 214–15.
24. Calvin, *Institutes*, 4.14.12.
25. Calvin, *Institutes*, 4.14.17.
26. Wendel, *Calvin*, 316.
27. Calvin, *Institutes*, 4.14.17.
28. Calvin, *Institutes*, 4.14.8.

believers, who use the signs properly, he then connects them with the truth which they figure.[29]

Just as the Holy Spirit makes the preaching of the Word effectual, He enables the believer to see that the sacraments attest of God's good will to him, and that they sustain, nourish, confirm, and increase his faith. Calvin writes: "It is therefore certain that the Lord offers us mercy and the pledge of his grace both in his Sacred Word and in his sacraments. But it is understood only by those who take Word and sacraments with sure faith, just as Christ is offered and held forth by the Father to all unto salvation, yet not all acknowledge and receive him."[30]

Before we survey Calvin's understanding of baptism, one last subject deserves attention: his understanding of the sacramental union. Calvin wanted to explain the relationship between the sacrament and that which it sealed, or, in later theological nomenclature, the sign and the thing signified. When he explains the nature of Paul's language in Romans 6:4 and Galatians 3:27, Calvin states that it is proper to say that Christians who have been baptized have "put on Christ." He writes: "We must always use these terms while the institution of the Lord and the faith of believers correspond, for we never have naked and empty symbols, except when our ingratitude and wickedness hinder the working of the divine beneficence."[31] Calvin therefore sees the sign and the thing signified as inseparable. However, Calvin is careful to explain that the sign and the thing signified must not be confused. In his commentary on 1 Corinthians 10:4, Calvin writes: "In the old sacraments the reality was united with the signs and conveyed to the people. Therefore, since they were figures of Christ, it follows that Christ was tied to them, not locally indeed, and not in a union of nature or substance, but sacramentally."[32]

Within the broader context of Calvin's comments, it is the Roman Catholic, and perhaps Lutheran, understanding of the Supper that is in view. Calvin goes on to write: "That is why the apostle says that the rock was Christ, for metonymy is very commonly used when speaking about the sacraments. Therefore the name of the reality is transferred to the sign

---

29. John Calvin, *Galatians, Ephesians, Philippians & Colossians*, CNTC (1963; Grand Rapids: Eerdmans, 1995), 68.

30. Calvin, *Institutes*, 4.14.7.

31. John Calvin, *Romans and Thessalonians*, CNTC (1963; Grand Rapids: Eerdmans, 1995), 123.

32. John Calvin, *1 Corinthians*, CNTC (1963; Grand Rapids: Eerdmans, 1995), 205.

here, because it applies to it, not properly, but figuratively, because of that union about which I have already spoken."[33] To emphasize the point of the connection but not confusion of the sign and the thing signified, Calvin explains: "The sacraments of the Lord should not and cannot be at all separated from their reality and substance. To distinguish, in order to guard against confounding them, is not only good and reasonable, but altogether necessary; but to divide them, so as to make the one exist without the other, is absurd."[34] Calvin employs the common theological aphorism that the sign and the thing signified are *distinctio sed non separatio* ("distinct but not separate").[35] However, there is one caveat to this principle on which Calvin bases the sacramental union of the sign and the thing signified: the recipient must possess faith. As explained above, if a person does not have faith, the sacraments are empty symbols.

With this basic understanding of Calvin's view of the sacraments in general, the chapter can now turn to the specific issue of his understanding of baptism.

On baptism

Calvin begins his locus on baptism by giving a definition of the rite: "Baptism is the sign of the initiation by which we are received into the society of the church, in order that, engrafted in Christ, we may be reckoned among God's children."[36] This definition contains several important themes connected with Calvin's doctrine of baptism: the nature of the visible promise from God, what it represents for the one who is baptized, and the fact that it is given not to individuals but to the church.

As noted above, Calvin defines a sacrament as a visible seal to the promise of God. What exactly does God promise in baptism, according to Calvin? He connects two primary things to baptism: righteousness and the forgiveness of sins.

In baptism, believers are assured that the condemnation that once hung over them has been removed and that God's wrath has been withdrawn. The righteousness of God in justification is exhibited in the sacrament, but

---

33. Calvin, *1 Corinthians*, 205.

34. John Calvin, *Short Treatise on The Supper of Our Lord*, in *Selected Works of John Calvin: Tracts and Letters*, eds. Henry Beveridge and Jules Bonnet, trans. Henry Beveridge (1849; Grand Rapids: Baker, 1983), 2.172; cf. Wallace, *Calvin's Doctrine*, 167–69.

35. See Jill Raitt, "Three Inter-related Principles in Calvin's Unique Doctrine of Infant Baptism," *SCJ* 11/1 (1980): 51–61.

36. Calvin, *Institutes*, 4.15.1.

Calvin clearly stipulates that this righteousness is received through imputation, which, as Calvin argues in the rest of his corpus, comes through faith alone.[37] Calvin's rejection of baptism as a cause of salvation is evident in his explanation of 1 Peter 3:21 and Titus 3:5, when he writes: "For Paul did not mean to signify that our cleansing and salvation are accomplished by water, or that water contains in itself the power to cleanse, regenerate, and renew; nor that here is the cause of salvation, but only that in this sacrament are received the knowledge and certainty of such gifts."[38]

Calvin's rejection of baptismal regeneration is especially evident in his response to the Council of Trent: "I neither can nor ought to let pass the very great absurdity of calling baptism alone the instrumental cause. What then will become of the gospel? Will it not even be allowed to occupy the smallest corner? But baptism is the sacrament of faith."[39]

Calvin also states that in baptism God promises the believer the forgiveness of sins, and this promise is a sure thing; for this reason, believers should embrace the promise by faith.[40] Hence, Calvin puts a strong emphasis on what God promises in baptism to the believer, which is couched in terms of covenant.

It should be no surprise, then, given that baptism represents first and foremost the promise of God, that Calvin rejects the Donatist understanding of baptism—in other words, baptism does not depend on the faith or piety of the one who administers it, as it ultimately is administered by God. Calvin writes that because a person is initiated by baptism into the name of the triune Lord, baptism is not of man but of God. He goes on to explain: "Ignorant or even contemptuous as those who baptized us were of God and all piety [the priests of the Roman Catholic Church], they did not baptize us into the fellowship of either their ignorance or sacrilege, but into faith in Jesus Christ, because it was not their own name but God's that they invoked, and they baptized into no other name."[41]

Baptism, on the other hand, is not only God's promise to the believer, according to Calvin, but also represents the believer's pledge to God: "Baptism serves as our confession before men. Indeed, it is the mark by which

---

37 Calvin, *Institutes*, 4.15.10.

38. Calvin, *Institutes*, 4.15.2.

39. John Calvin, *Canons and Decrees of the Council of Trent with the Antidote (1547)*, in Beveridge and Bonnet, *Selected Works*, 3.116–17.

40. Calvin, *Institutes*, 4.15.17.

41. Calvin, *Institutes*, 4.15.16.

we publicly profess that we wish to be reckoned God's people; by which we testify that we agree in worshipping the same God, in one religion with all Christians; by which finally we openly affirm our faith."[42] Baptism vis-à-vis the believer, however, is not merely a pledge but also the visible sign of the believer's union with Christ: "We are children of God from the fact that we put on Christ in baptism."[43] Elsewhere, Calvin succinctly states that baptism is "the symbol of our engrafting into Christ."[44] The believer is visibly engrafted into Christ through baptism, yet since he struggles with sin throughout his life, baptism is also the entrance to the battle of the mortification of the flesh, a battle that endures for the entire life of the believer.[45]

Calvin believed that the mortification aspect of baptism was foreshadowed in the Old Testament, particularly in the Red Sea crossing. He writes that God "promises us in baptism and shows us by a sign given that by his power we have been led out and delivered from bondage in Egypt, that is, from bondage of sin; that our Pharaoh, that is, the devil, has been drowned, although he does not cease to harry us and weary us."[46] However, Calvin also turns the judgment-image of drowning on the recipient of baptism: "Baptism indeed promises to us the drowning of our Pharaoh and the mortification of our sin."[47] This did not mean that a person is totally cleansed from sin in baptism. Rather, Calvin writes: "For so long as we live cooped up in this prison of our body, traces of sin will dwell in us; but if we faithfully hold fast to the promise given us by God in baptism, they shall not dominate or rule."[48] Note that the efficacy of baptism lies not in the water but in what the water points to: the promise of God.

One can trace the idea of the supremacy of the promise of God in Calvin's commentary on Titus 3:5 and then in a sermon on the same passage. Calvin begins his comments by noting, "I have no doubt that there is at least an allusion here to baptism and, I have no objection to the explanation of the whole passage in terms of baptism; not that salvation is obtained in the external symbol of water, but because baptism seals to us the salvation obtained by Christ." He goes on to explain:

---

42. Calvin, *Institutes*, 4.15.13; Wendel, *Calvin*, 319, 322.

43. Calvin, *Institutes*, 4.15.6; cf. 3.11.9; idem, *Romans*, 122–23.

44. John Calvin, *2 Corinthians and Timothy, Titus, and Philemon*, CNTC, eds. David W. Torrance and T. F. Torrance, trans. T. A. Smail (1964; Grand Rapids: Eerdmans, 1996), 382.

45. Calvin, *Institutes*, 4.15.11.

46. Calvin, *Institutes*, 4.15.9.

47. Calvin, *Institutes*, 4.15.9.

48. Calvin, *Institutes*, 4.15.11.

Although he mentions the sign to exhibit God's grace clearly to us, yet to prevent us from fixing our whole attention upon it, he soon reminds us of the Sprit, that we know that we are not washed by water but by His power.... It is God's Spirit that regenerates us and makes us new creatures, but since His grace is invisible and hidden, a visible symbol of it is given to us in baptism.[49]

In a sermon on the same passage, Calvin makes the same point to a different audience. In Calvin's commentaries, his primary audience is pastors and other scholars, whereas in his sermons, his target is the common man. Calvin preaches:

No doubt but that in this place saint Paul had an eye to baptism, and meant to set forth this doctrine unto us as it were to be seen in a glass. For inasmuch as we are rude, God is not contented only to witness to us by his gospel that we are washed and made clean in the blood of our Lord Jesus Christ: but also he has given us a figure thereof, so that when we are baptized it is as much as if God had shown to the eye, that we ourselves bring nothing to him but utter filthiness, and that it is his office to make us clean.

Calvin goes on to explain the relationship between the sign and the thing signified in the sacrament of baptism:

How is it he shows us therewithal, that the said washing consists not in the visible water: for what a thing were it, if our souls should be cleansed by an earthly and corruptible element? The water then has not that power. Yet notwithstanding because of our infirmity it behooves us to begin at the water, that we may be lifted up higher. Yes, I say, we must begin at the water, but we must not tarry at it. For the sign that is offered to our eyes, serves to lead us to the Holy Ghost, to the end we may know how it is from him that the power of baptism proceeds.[50]

Both Calvin's commentary and sermon carefully make the distinction between baptism and what it signifies without separating them. This structure (the sign and the thing signified) sets Calvin's view apart from the Roman Catholic position.[51]

Calvin also believed, in similar fashion to Luther, who looked at baptism as a lifelong event, that baptism is of great importance for the believer's

49. Calvin, *Titus*, 382–83.

50. John Calvin, *John Calvin's Sermons on Timothy and Titus* (1579; Edinburgh: Banner of Truth, 1983), ser. 16, 1225–26.

51. Egil Grislis, "Calvin's Doctrine of Baptism," *CH* 31 (1962): 47.

sanctification. The one who is baptized undoubtedly will struggle with sin throughout his life; such a one "ought to recall the memory of [his] baptism and fortify [his] mind with it, that [he] may always be sure and confident of the forgiveness of sins."[52] In this way, baptism confirms the faith of the believer. Calvin wanted his readers to understand that there is a strong connection between the sacrament and the reality to which the sign of baptism points, for God, according to Calvin, works through outward means, in this case the water of baptism. He also stipulated, in contrast to an *ex opere operato* understanding, that the grace a person receives in baptism is received only by faith. Lack of such faith, Calvin believed, renders a person liable before God, because he has failed to believe the promise of the gospel set forth in baptism.

The last point to note is that Calvin believed that baptism is connected to the church.[53] He did not believe that baptism is given to individuals in the church, thereby permitting the rite to be administered by anyone.[54] Rather, he argued that the Great Commission was given to those who had been appointed apostles. Therefore, as with the Lord's Supper, the apostles—and, in his own day, duly ordained ministers—are the only ones who are allowed to administer the rite, as they are the stewards of Christ.[55] Hence, baptism is a sacrament of the church. As to how the church administers the rite, through pouring, sprinkling, or immersion, and once or thrice, Calvin was indifferent. He writes: "These details are of no importance, but ought to be optional to churches according to the diversity of countries."[56]

On infant baptism

Given what Calvin writes on baptism, and especially the centrality and importance of faith, a typical Baptist response might be to wonder how Calvin can affirm and promote the practice of infant baptism. Calvin argued on several grounds that infant baptism was necessary and that it was sinful to withhold the sign of the covenant from children.[57] He believed the doctrine was of great importance and added a separate locus to the subject in the second edition of his *Institutes* (1539) in response to Anabaptism.[58] He

---

52. Calvin, *Institutes*, 4.15.3.
53. See Wallace, *Calvin's Doctrine*, 234–53.
54. Niesel, *Theology of Calvin*, 211–12.
55. Calvin, *Institutes*, 4.15.20.
56. Calvin, *Institutes*, 4.15.19.
57. Calvin, *Institutes*, 4.16.9.
58. Calvin, *Institutes*, 4.16.1; McGrath, *Reformation Thought*, 184.

based his case on several pillars: the differences between adult and infant baptism, the unity of the covenant in the Old Testament and New Testament, and the truth that children are legitimately members of the church and should not be denied the sign of initiation.

Calvin explained that adult and infant baptism were not identical; perhaps he might have said they are different species of the same genus. He argued that the Scriptures present adults as those who require faith and repentance before they can be baptized. Calvin illustrated this point by appealing to Old Testament Israel, where a Gentile who desired to become part of the covenant people had to be instructed in the Lord's covenant and the law before he could be marked by circumcision.[59] He further illustrated the point by the example of Abraham, noting that God did not adopt Abraham and begin with circumcision, but first declared His covenant, and then, after Abraham professed his faith, made him a partaker of the sacrament. Infants, however, are in another category. Abraham first professed his faith, whereas Isaac received the sign before he professed his faith. Calvin succinctly states the principle: "If the children of believers are partakers in the covenant without the help of understanding, there is no reason why they should be barred from the sign merely because they cannot swear to the provisions of the covenant."[60]

Calvin made this argument on the basis of the second pillar of his defense, namely, the covenantal unity between the Old Testament and New Testament. He believed that salvation was the same in the Old Testament as it is in the New Testament, namely, justification by faith alone in Christ alone. He thought the patriarchs received the same spiritual promise that New Testament believers receive, though they received it in circumcision and New Testament believers receive it in baptism, since both rites represent the mortification of the flesh and the forgiveness of sins. Moreover, he taught that Christ was the foundation of both circumcision and baptism.[61] Calvin supported this claim by exploring the parallel between the two rites. He writes that though there are visible differences in the practices, whatever belongs to circumcision also belongs to baptism. Both circumcision and baptism were "tokens" or signs of the covenant, by which people were initiated into the covenant and assured of their adoption as the people and

---

59. Calvin, *Institutes*, 4.16.23.
60. Calvin, *Institutes*, 4.16.24.
61. Calvin, *Institutes*, 4.16.3.

household of God.[62] Like other theologians before him, Calvin found exegetical support for seeing the two rites as parallel in Colossians 2:11–12, where Calvin identifies both as spiritual rites. Paul argues that believers are circumcised with a circumcision made without hands, which is symbolic for laying aside the body of sin. Likewise, believers are buried with Christ in baptism. Calvin writes, "What do these words mean except that the fulfillment and truth of baptism are also the truth and fulfillment of circumcision, since they signify one and the same thing."[63]

Calvin's third pillar was that since infants belong to the covenant and are members of the church, they should not be denied the sign of membership. Arguing from the covenantal unity between the Old Testament and New Testament, Calvin believed that if children of the Jews in the Old Testament were members of the covenant, the same is true of the children of Christians: "If they grasp the truth, why shall they be driven away from the figure?"[64] Calvin held that as members of the church, children should not be torn from the body of Christ by being denied baptism.[65] He illustrated this point by appealing to Christ's reception of children. He argues:

> If it is right for infants to be brought to Christ, why not also to be received into baptism, the symbol of our communion and fellowship with Christ? If the Kingdom of Heaven belongs to them, why is the sign denied which, so to speak, opens to them a door into the church, that adopted into it, they may be enrolled among the heirs of the Kingdom of Heaven.[66]

Calvin also believed that Christian parents are to bring their children forward as members of the church and offer them to God by having them baptized.[67] This did not mean that Calvin overturned his belief in *sola fide*. Early in his 1536 *Institutes*, Calvin without hesitation affirms *fides infantium* like Luther before him: "Therefore the opinion stands firm, that no men are saved except by faith, whether they are children or adults. For this reason, baptism also rightly applies to infants, who possess faith in common with adults." Calvin did not assert this point without qualification; he writes:

---

62. Calvin, *Institutes*, 4.16.4.
63. Calvin, *Institutes*, 4.16.11; Wendel, *Calvin*, 325–26. Cf. Calvin, *Genesis*, 456; Calvin, *Colossians*, 331–33.
64. Calvin, *Institutes*, 4.16.5.
65. Calvin, *Institutes*, 4.16.22.
66. Calvin, *Institutes*, 4.16.7.
67. Calvin, *Institutes*, 4.16.32.

Nor ought anyone to take this in a sense that I am saying faith always begins from the mother's womb, when the Lord calls even on adults themselves sometimes later, sometimes sooner. But I am saying that all God's elect enter into eternal life through faith, at whatever point in age they are released from this prison house of corruption.

However, like Luther, he did not place the weight of infant baptism on this point alone, but rested it on his understanding of the teaching of Christ: "But if this reason were to fail us, we would still have abundant proof that in baptizing infants we are obeying the Lord's will: who willed that they be allowed to come to him."[68]

By 1559, Calvin had moderated his position on *fides infantium* and affirmed that, though it is beyond human ability to understand how God accomplishes it, infants can be regenerated at the earliest of ages. Calvin readily acknowledged that all people are born with original sin and the pollution that it brings, but he nonetheless believed that an infant either is unpleasing and hateful to God or that it is justified in His sight. In support of this claim, Calvin offers John the Baptist as one who was "sanctified in his mother's womb—something he could do in others." Calvin points out that since John could be filled with the Holy Spirit while yet unborn, "let us not attempt, then, to impose a law upon God to keep him from sanctifying whom he pleases, just as he sanctified this child."[69]

Critics of this argument countered that it was impossible for an infant to have either faith or repentance. Calvin responded: "Infants are baptized into future repentance and faith, even though these have not yet been formed in them, the seed of both lies hidden within them by the secret working of the Spirit."[70] Calvin based this argument, once again, on the unity of the testaments, specifically the idea that if infants received circumcision, "a sacrament of repentance and of faith, it does not seem absurd if they are now made participants in baptism—unless men choose to rage openly at God's institution."[71]

There are two important points to note regarding Calvin's argument concerning the seeds of faith and repentance in infants. First, though Cal-

---

68. John Calvin, *Institutes of the Christian Religion: 1536 Edition*, trans. Ford Lewis Battles (1975; Grand Rapids: Eerdmans, 1995), 101–102; see also Grislis, "Calvin's Doctrine of Baptism," 53–54; Wendel, *Calvin*, 324.

69. Calvin, *Institutes*, 4.16.17.

70. Calvin, *Institutes*, 4.16.20. Cf. Wallace, *Calvin's Doctrine*, 190; Gerrish, *Grace and Gratitude*, 119.

71. Calvin, *Institutes*, 4.16.20.

vin retained the practice of infant baptism, his understanding of the rite was decidedly different from his Roman Catholic counterparts. Roman Catholics practiced the rite because they believed the water was instrumental in removing the corruption of original sin and in justification. The corollary was that if an infant was not baptized, he was subject to hell, or at least *limbus infantium*. Calvin completely rejected such notions, as he believed that faith alone saves, not baptism.[72] On the other hand, Calvin acknowledged that just because infants born to Christian parents have the seed of faith and repentance does not automatically admit them to all of the privileges of church membership. Calvin held that Scripture set no limitations concerning the age of a child to be baptized, but that all who partake of the Lord's Supper have to be able to discern the body and blood of the Lord; they have to examine their consciences. Calvin writes: "A self-examination ought, therefore, to come first, and it is vain to expect this of infants."[73]

Basing his argument on the unity of the covenant, Calvin admitted that circumcision corresponds to baptism, and the Lord's Supper replaces the Passover. However, he notes that people were not allowed to take the Passover indiscriminately, but it was eaten only by those who were old enough to inquire into its meaning.[74] In response to Michael Servetus (1511–1553), who rejected infant baptism and argued that if infants were baptized they also should receive the Lord's Supper, Calvin writes: "By baptism they are admitted into Christ's flock, and the symbol of their adoption suffices them until as adults they are able to bear solid food. Therefore, we should wait for the time of examination, which God expressly requires in the Sacred Supper."[75]

Clearly Calvin did not base infant baptism merely on a logical deduction, but on what Scripture says in passages such as Colossians 2:11–12. Hence, where Scripture expressly states a point, such as the need for self-examination before partaking of the Supper, he yields to its authority.

---

72. Calvin, *Institutes*, 4.16.26; cf. idem, *Genesis*, 458; Calvin, *Acts 1–13*, CNTC (1965; Grand Rapids: Eerdmans, 1995), 107; Grislis, "Calvin's Doctrine of Baptism," 55–56.

73. Calvin, *Institutes*, 4.16.30.

74. Calvin, *Institutes*, 4.16.30.

75. Calvin, *Institutes*, 4.16.31.

THE BELGIC CONFESSION AND THE HEIDELBERG CATECHISM

The Belgic Confession (1561) and the Heidelberg Catechism (1563) were composed toward the close of the Reformation (1565) in different parts of Europe by different groups of theologians. Nevertheless, it stands to reason that they can be treated together since they comprise, along with the Canons of Dort, two-thirds of the Three Forms of Unity, the doctrinal standards of many Reformed churches, particularly those in the Dutch Reformed tradition.[76] In other words, historically the Dutch Reformed churches have seen that the two documents are compatible. So in view of this long-standing tradition, this section will explore these documents jointly. To amplify what is found in the Heidelberg Catechism, we will draw on the commentary and writings of one of its chief contributors and authors, Zacharias Ursinus (1534–1583).[77]

On the sacraments

Chapter 33 of the Belgic Confession treats the subject of the sacraments. It begins by stating that the sacraments were instituted by the goodness of God because of man's "crudeness and weakness."[78] He gave the sacraments "to seal his promises in us, to pledge his good will and grace toward us, and also to nourish and sustain our faith." These points echo common Protestant themes, especially those of Luther, in that the sacraments are God's visible promises. At the same time, Calvin influenced the author of the confession, Guido de Brès (ca. 1522–1567). De Brès employed as a source document the Gallican Confession, which was authored partially by Calvin. Therefore, it should come as no surprise to find similar themes and

---

76. On the history of the Belgic Confession and Heidelberg Catechism, see Nicolaas H. Gootjes, *The Belgic Confession: Its History and Sources* (Grand Rapids: Baker, 2007), 13–32, 133–60; Lyle D. Bierma, et al., *An Introduction to the Heidelberg Catechism: Sources, History, and Theology* (Grand Rapids: Baker, 2005), 15–48.

77. This is not to say that Ursinus was alone, as many others worked on the Heidelberg Catechism. Another prominent figure was Caspar Olevianus (1536–1587). For Olevianus's views on the sacraments and baptism, see R. Scott Clark, *Caspar Olevian and the Substance of the Covenant: The Double Benefit of Christ* (Edinburgh: Rutherford House, 2005), 193, 198–205; Lyle D. Bierma, *German Calvinism in the Confessional Age: The Covenant Theology of Caspar Olevianus* (Grand Rapids: Baker, 1996), 66–67, 86–87.

78. All quotations of the Belgic Confession and Heidelberg Catechism, unless otherwise noted, are from *Creeds and Confessions of Faith in the Christian Tradition*, eds. Jaroslav Pelikan and Valerie Hotchkiss (New Haven: Yale University Press, 2003), 2.405–57.

emphases in the Gallican Confession.[79] However, at certain points de Brès also used the work of Theodore Beza (1519–1605) in the composition of the Belgic Confession.[80]

All of these influences led de Brès to emphasize the importance of the Word: "He has added these to the word of the gospel to represent better to our external sense both what he enables us to understand by his word and what he does inwardly in our hearts, confirming in us the salvation he imparts to us."[81] The paragraph goes on to state: "For they are visible signs and seals of something internal and invisible, by means of which God works in us through the power of the Holy Spirit. So they are not empty and hollow signs to fool and deceive us, for their truth is Jesus Christ, without whom they would be nothing" (§ 33).[82] In these statements on the sacraments, there is no direct reference to God's covenant, though the sacraments are nevertheless signs and seals of God's promises, the truth of which is Christ. This is, of course, distinct from Roman Catholic conceptions of the sacraments, which see them as merely visible signs of God's invisible grace. Significantly, there is no employment of Augustine's traditional definition here in the Belgic Confession.

By way of contrast, the Heidelberg Catechism, in roughly the same amount of space, gives a slightly fuller statement concerning the nature of the sacraments. In a sense, though obviously not intentionally, it amplifies what is implicit in the Belgic Confession. The catechism asks, "Since, then, faith alone makes us share in Christ and all his benefits, where does such faith originate?" The catechism responds: "The Holy Spirit creates it in our hearts by the preaching of the holy gospel, and confirms it by the use of the holy sacraments" (q. 65). Unlike in Roman Catholic doctrine, salvation is seen as by faith alone in Christ alone. The Holy Spirit uses the Word to bring about

---

79. See Gootjes, *Belgic Confession*, 48–70, esp. 70. On the pan-Protestant characteristics of the Heidelberg Catechism on the sacraments, see Lyle D. Bierma, *The Doctrine of the Sacraments in the Heidelberg Catechism: Melanchthonian, Calvinist, or Zwinglian*, Studies in Reformed Theology and History, no. 4 (Princeton: Princeton Theological Seminary, 1999).

80. See Gootjes, *Belgic Confession*, 71–91, esp. 86–87; cf. Theodore Beza, *The Christian Faith*, trans. James Clark (1558; Sussex: Focus Christian Ministries Trust, 1992), 51–63.

81. Note the similar theme from the Gallican Confession § 34: "We believe that the sacraments are added to the Word for more ample confirmation, that they be to us pledges and seals of the grace of God, and by this means aid and comfort our faith" (all quotations taken from *The Creeds of Christendom*, ed. Philip Schaff [1931; Grand Rapids: Baker, 1990], 3.356–82).

82. This point also is echoed by the Gallican Confession: "Yet we hold that their substance and truth is in Jesus Christ, and that of themselves they are only smoke and shadow" (§ 34).

faith and confirms that Word through the sacraments. The Belgic Confession makes the same point with its emphasis on the promises of God.

The catechism defines the sacraments in the following manner: "They are visible, holy signs and seals instituted by God in order that by their use he may the more fully disclose and seal to us the promise of the gospel" (q. 66). Ursinus amplifies the covenantal nature of the sacraments in his commentary when he writes: "Sacraments are rites, or ceremonies instituted by God to the end, that they may be signs of the covenant, or of God's good will towards us, and of the obligation of the church to repentance and faith; and that they may be marks by which the true church may be known and distinguished from all other religions."[83]

The Heidelberg Catechism and the Belgic Confession both view the sacraments as means of grace, though it is important to stipulate that they do not function *ex opere operato*, as in Roman Catholicism. Rather, the sacraments are the means by which the Holy Spirit confirms that the whole of salvation is rooted in the one sacrifice of Jesus Christ given on the cross (q. 67).

Ursinus explains that in every sacrament there are two things, the sign and the thing signified: "The sign includes the element which is used, together with the whole external transaction. The thing signified is Christ, with all his benefits; or, it is the communion, and participation of Christ, and his benefits." Ursinus then goes on to show the nature of the sacramental union. He writes: "The signs are material, visible and earthly; the things signified are spiritual, invisible and heavenly." Ursinus stipulates, however, that when he writes that the thing signified is "spiritual," he is not invoking a Greek dualism. Rather, "The things signified are here called spiritual, not as it respects their substance; but as it respects the manner in which they are received, because they are received through the working of the Holy Ghost, by faith alone, and not by any of the members of our body."[84] This statement shows that Ursinus definitely gives a pneumatological cast to the sacraments.

Ursinus goes into great detail to explain the nature of the sacramental union, which he likens to the hypostatic union of the two natures of Christ, though he makes some important caveats regarding the difference. Ursinus writes: "A sacramental union, therefore, is not corporal, nor does it consist in the presence of the sign and the thing signified in the same place; much less in tran, or con-substantiation; but it is relative." Ursinus clearly rejects

---

83. Zacharias Ursinus, *The Commentary of Dr. Zacharias Ursinus on the Heidelberg Catechism* (1852; Phillipsburg, N.J.: P & R, n.d.), 342.

84. Ursinus, *Commentary*, 347.

the Roman Catholic and Lutheran understanding of the Lord's Supper, though the same general principles apply to baptism. In what way is the relationship between the sign and the thing signified relative? Ursinus gives two answers: (1) in terms of likeness or correspondence between the sign and the thing signified; and (2) in terms of the joint exhibition and reception of the signs and the things signified, which must be properly used (i.e., they are of no benefit apart from faith).[85]

In the conclusion of Ursinus's treatment of the sacraments in general, among eighteen points of summary he includes the following helpful statement concerning the sacramental union and the proper use of the sacraments:

> The union between the signs and the things signified is in like manner not natural or local; but relative, by the appointment of God, by which things invisible and spiritual are represented by those that are visible and corporal, as by visible words, and are exhibited and received in connection with the signs in their lawful use.

Ursinus also writes:

> The names and properties of the things signified are attributed to the signs; and, on the other hand, the names of the signs are attributed to the things signified, on account of their analogy, or on account of the signification of the things through the signs, and on account of the joint exhibition and reception of the things with the signs in their lawful use.[86]

What if the sacraments are not lawfully used? Are they merely empty and naked signs, as Luther and Calvin expressed? No. Ursinus writes: "The godly receive the signs to salvation; the ungodly to condemnation. It is, however, only the things signified, which the godly can receive to salvation."[87]

On baptism

Concerning baptism, the Belgic Confession, article 34, has a statement that is rich in typology and that spans redemptive history. The confession begins straightaway by making the connection between baptism and circumcision: "We believe and confess that Jesus Christ, in whom the law is fulfilled,

---

85. Ursinus, *Commentary*, 348.
86. Ursinus, *Commentary*, 355.
87. Ursinus, *Commentary*, 355.

has by his shed blood put an end to every other shedding of blood, which anyone might do or wish to do in order to atone or satisfy for sins. Having abolished circumcision, which was done with blood, he established in its place the sacrament of baptism." Several things are immediately noticeable in this statement. First, the Reformation hermeneutic is at work, in that the confession sees a Christ-centered cast to the Scriptures, with both circumcision and baptism pointing to Him. Moreover, though the confession does not explicitly say so, it implicitly recognizes baptism as the sign of the covenant because it connects it with circumcision. The confession also sees baptism, like circumcision, as an initiatory rite, as by baptism people "are received into God's church and set apart from all other people and alien religions," and so in this way bear God's "mark and sign." In contrast to Anabaptist understandings of baptism, the confession sees baptism, therefore, primarily as God's sign to His people.

The confession does not make an explicit statement concerning the relationship between the sign and the thing signified, something that developed with greater clarity in the theology of Early and High Orthodoxy, but the sacramental union is present. The confession states that the water of baptism washes away the dirt of the body when it is poured or sprinkled on the one who is baptized (note the mode of baptism). However, this external sign points to the inner cleansing that is accomplished by the blood of Christ by the Holy Spirit: "It washes and cleanses it from its sins and transforms us from being the children of wrath into the children of God." This statement does not promote baptismal regeneration. The statement must be read not only in the immediate context but also in the broader context of the confession. Recall that the sacraments seal and confirm God's promises to the church, and that salvation is by faith alone in Christ alone (cf. §§ 22–23).

The confession clarifies the nature of baptism and employs typology not frequently found in confessional statements. Addressing the transformation that occurs in the believer, the confession states:

> This does not happen by the physical water but by the sprinkling of the precious blood of the Son of God, who is our Red Sea, through which we must pass to escape the tyranny of Pharaoh, who is the devil, and to enter the spiritual land of Canaan. So ministers, as far as their work is concerned, give us the sacrament and what is visible, but our Lord gives what the sacrament signifies—namely the invisible gifts and graces.

Here the confession weds the *ordo* and *historia salutis* by seeing the Red Sea crossing as a foreshadow of the outpouring and regenerative work of the Holy Spirit, all of which is signified and confirmed visibly in baptism. This regeneration does not occur *ex opere operato* through baptism.

In line with previous church tradition and the rest of the first and second generation Reformers, the confession argues for the legitimacy of infant baptism. In a statement aimed at Anabaptist practice, the confession first says that re-baptism is erroneous and that the rite should be performed only once. Echoing Luther's teaching, the confession states: "Yet this baptism is profitable not only when the water is on us and when we receive it but throughout our entire lives." A similar statement appears in the Gallican Confession as it addresses the error of Anabaptism: "We hold, also, that although we are baptized only once, yet the gain that it symbolizes to us reaches over our whole lives and to our death, so that we have a lasting witness that Jesus Christ will always be our justification and sanctification" (§ 35).

The idea of baptism as a lifelong echo of God's promise shows how baptism is employed for infants who have yet to profess faith. At this point, the confession brings out what has been implicit, namely, baptism as the sign of the covenant: "We believe our children ought to be baptized and sealed with the sign of the covenant, as little children were circumcised in Israel on the basis of the same promises made to our children." The confession states that Christ shed His blood no less for the cleansing of little children of believers than for adults. It continues: "Baptism does for our children what circumcision did for the Jewish people. That is why Paul calls baptism the 'circumcision of Christ' (Col. 2:11)."

In the Heidelberg Catechism, there is a similar emphasis on these themes. A contrast between the two documents, however, is the catechism's emphasis on the comfort, assurance, and incentive to obedience to which baptism contributes. For example, the catechism states that in baptism the believer sees the promise of God (cf. q. 71) and is assured that he has been washed with the blood and Spirit from his sinfulness (q. 69). In light of the forgiveness of sins through grace by the work of Christ, which is pictured in baptism, the believer is supposed to "more and more die unto sin and live in a consecrated and blameless way" (q. 70).

Elaborating on the theme of assurance, Ursinus employs a redemptive-historical hermeneutic to demonstrate how baptism brings comfort concerning the preservation and deliverance of the church from all of her afflictions. Ursinus writes:

Those who are baptized are plunged, as it were, in affliction; but with
the full assurance of deliverance. It is for this reason that Christ speaks
of afflictions under the name of baptism, saying, "Are you able to be
baptized with the baptism that I am baptized with?" (Matt 20:22).
The ceremony connected with baptism intimates deliverance from our
varied afflictions. We are immersed, but not drowned, or suffocated.
It is in respect to this end that baptism is compared to the flood;
for as in the flood, Noah and his family who were shut upon the ark
were saved, yet not without much anxiety and peril, whilst the rest
of mankind who were without the ark perished; so, those who are in
the church, and who cleave to Christ, will most certainly be delivered at the proper time, although they may be pressed with afflictions
and dangers from every side; whilst those who are out of the church
will be overwhelmed with the deluge of sin and destruction. We may
here appropriately refer to the passage of Paul, where he compares the
passage of the Israelites through the Red Sea to baptism: "All were
baptized unto Moses in the cloud and in the sea" (1 Cor. 10:2).[88]

This statement does not harmonize precisely with what Ursinus said
regarding the unlawful use of the sacraments. In this statement, the wicked
are flooded with sin and destruction, which seems not to be related to the
administration of baptism. Nevertheless, the point stands that Ursinus,
unlike Luther and Calvin, saw the sacraments generally, and baptism specifically, as double-edged. For the one who looked on baptism by faith, it
was a source of comfort and assurance, but not so for the ungodly.

The catechism explicitly states that the water of baptism does not bring
about the fulfillment of the promises: "Does merely the outward washing
with water itself wash away sins? No; for only the blood of Jesus Christ
and the Holy Spirit cleans us from all sins" (q. 72). The following question
seems to be making a summary statement concerning baptism when it asks,
"Why does the Holy Spirit call baptism the water of rebirth and the washing away of sins?" To this question the catechism responds:

> God does not speak in this way except for a strong reason. Not only
> does he teach us by baptism that just as the dirt of the body is taken
> away by water, so our sins are removed by the blood and Spirit of
> Christ; but more important still, by the divine pledge and sign he
> wishes to assure us that we are just as truly washed from our sins
> spiritually as our bodies are washed with water (q. 73).

---

88. Ursinus, *Commentary*, 360–61.

Note once again the role that the sign of baptism plays in assuring the believer of the promises of the gospel.

Ursinus amplifies the catechism at this point by explaining that in baptism there is "a double washing: an external washing with water, and an internal washing with the blood and Spirit of Christ. The internal is signified and sealed by that which is external, and is always joined with it in the proper use of baptism." Ursinus further subdivides the internal washing into another twofold washing, one with the blood of Christ and the other with the Spirit. He explains that to be washed in the blood of Christ is to receive the forgiveness of sins or to be justified on account of His shed blood. To be washed with the Spirit of Christ consists in regeneration, which consists in a changing of the will and heart, so as to produce a hatred of sin and a desire to live according to the will of God.[89]

Lastly, the catechism defends the practice of infant baptism by bringing forward what has been implicitly argued thus far—that infants, as well as their parents, are included in the covenant and belong to the people of God. Since redemption by Christ through the Spirit is promised to these children no less than their parents, infants by baptism receive the sign of the covenant, and are incorporated into the church and set apart from the children of unbelievers. The catechism bases this argument largely on the Old Testament precedent, declaring that what was done through circumcision in the Old is now done through baptism in the New (q. 74).

Ursinus expands on the teaching of the catechism and offers four basic arguments to support infant baptism:

1. Baptism should be given to all of those who belong to the covenant and church of God, which includes infants.

2. Those to whom belong the benefit of the remission of sins and regeneration should not be excluded from baptism, which, again, includes infants.

3. A sacrament is a solemn rite of initiation into the church, which distinguishes the church from various sects, and means that whatever age one may be, all who are a part of the church should receive the sign of the covenant.

4. Infants as well as adults were circumcised in the Old Testament.[90]

---

89. Ursinus, *Commentary*, 361.
90. Ursinus, *Commentary*, 366–67.

In the rest of his explanation of infant baptism, Ursinus answers objections and denies the legitimacy of infant communion, as Calvin did in his treatment of the subject.[91] In these respects, Ursinus's explanation and defense of infant baptism are somewhat commonplace.

However, Ursinus's defense of the rite is made unique by the separate treatment he gives to the subject of circumcision. He treats circumcision under six headings: what circumcision is, why it was instituted, why it was abolished, what has replaced it, where circumcision and baptism differ, and why Christ was circumcised.[92] In his explanation of why circumcision was instituted, he makes some noteworthy points, such as that circumcision was "the sacrament of initiation and reception into the visible church."[93] Ursinus saw a parallel between circumcision and baptism, in that baptism identifies those who "ought to be regarded as members of the visible church, whether they be adults professing repentance and faith, or infants born in the church."[94] This is an important distinction, one that does not explicitly surface in the catechism and is not present in Calvin. This distinction was carried forward by others in the Reformed church in the subsequent development of the doctrine.

Another important point that Ursinus explains is the spiritual aspect of circumcision. Ursinus understood that circumcision had a temporal and typological character to it, in that it was connected to the temporal blessings of the land of Canaan and signified that the future redemption from sin would be through Christ, the seed of Abraham. However, he also recognized that circumcision reminded the Israelites of their natural uncleanness and the importance of guarding against all sin, especially sexual immorality. However, on the spiritual side, circumcision was not merely to show the recipient his sinfulness, but was also a sign of regeneration, which bound the person to faith and obedience.[95]

These are just highlights of the points that Ursinus explains regarding the nature of circumcision, but they represent not only the unity of salvation in Ursinus's theology, but also the idea that there has been only one church throughout redemptive history. Therefore, Ursinus believed it was necessary

---

91. Ursinus, *Commentary*, 368–71.
92. Ursinus, *Commentary*, 374.
93. Ursinus, *Commentary*, 375.
94. Ursinus, *Commentary*, 366.
95. Ursinus, *Commentary*, 375–76.

to show how circumcision was indeed a sacrament, one that was replaced by baptism, which thereby validated the practice of infant baptism.

CONCLUSION

In this survey of Calvin, the Belgic Confession, and the Heidelberg Catechism, we see that a number of theological headwaters feed into the stream of Reformed thought. Augustine, Luther, and Zwingli influenced Calvin in his formulation of the doctrine of the sacraments and baptism specifically. Calvin then influenced Guido de Brès, especially through the Gallican Confession, which served as a starting point for the Belgic Confession. Moreover, Ursinus incorporated a number of these streams into the Heidelberg Catechism. This is not to say that the Reformed formulations of the sacraments and baptism were flattened out, as there are a number of unique features or emphases in each expression. What was often implicit in one expression became explicit in another, such as Ursinus's point that baptism was an initiation rite into the visible church. However, there is also a great degree of harmony between the confessional statements and the explanations of the sacramental union in both Calvin and Ursinus.

CHAPTER 5

Baptism in Early Orthodox Reformed Theology

At the close of the Reformation in 1565, the first and some second generation Reformers were dead: Martin Luther, Philip Melanchthon, John Calvin, Wolfang Musculus (1497–1563), Martin Bucer (1491–1551), and Peter Martyr Vermigli (1499–1562). During the periods of Early (1565–1630/40) and High Orthodoxy (1630/40–1700), there was further development and refinement of the doctrines of the sacraments and baptism.[1] At the opening of the Early Orthodox period, a number of second generation Reformers, such as Zacharias Ursinus and Caspar Olevianus, continued to contribute to the development of Reformed theology. In many respects, the theologians of the Early and High Orthodox periods did not innovate, but codified and refined the substance of the Reformation. This was possible not only due to the appropriation of the scholastic method, but because of continued polemics with other theological camps, such as the Roman Catholics, Lutherans, Anabaptists, and Socinians.

Amandus Polanus (1561–1610), Johannes Wollebius (1586–1629), and William Ames (1576–1633) stand out as representative theologians of the Early Orthodox period. Polanus studied at the universities of Tübingen, Basel, and Geneva. He was appointed professor of Old Testament at Basel in 1596 and served as dean of the theology faculty from 1598 to 1609.[2] Wollebius also studied at the University of Basel and was appointed professor of Old Testament there in 1607. Wollebius based his major theological work on the work of Polanus.[3] Ames is noteworthy because he worked

---

1. Richard A. Muller, *Post-Reformation Reformed Dogmatics*, (Grand Rapids: Baker, 1987), 1.40–52. Muller relies on the brief but well-balanced survey of Reformed Orthodoxy by Otto Weber, *Foundations of Dogmatics* (Grand Rapids: Eerdmans, 1981), 1.112–27.

2. Muller, *Reformed Dogmatics*, 1.44. For a brief but excellent survey of the life and work of Polanus, see Robert Letham, "Amandus Polanus: A Neglected Theologian?" *SCJ* 21/3 (1990): 463–76.

3. Muller, *Reformed Dogmatics*, 1.46.

both in England and on the Continent. He studied at Christ's College, Cambridge, and went to the University of Leiden in 1611. In 1618–19, he participated in the Synod of Dort as the assistant to the president, Johannes Bogerman. He became a professor of theology at the University of Franecker in 1622 and the rector of the university in 1626.[4] Given that Ames worked in both the English and Continental contexts, he serves as something of a bridge between the two groups, one who cross-pollinated the English and Continental Reformed traditions that would later flower in the Westminster Standards.

In addition to considering the views of these three theologians, this chapter will explore the Thirty-Nine Articles and the Irish Articles. These two confessions are important in connection with the work of James Ussher (1581–1656). Ussher was the Anglican archbishop of Armagh, Ireland, and likely was the sole author of the Irish Articles (1615).[5] The work and theology of Ussher are important because the Irish Articles served as a source document for the Westminster Standards. In fact, Ussher twice was offered a seat at the Westminster Assembly, but he declined.[6] The Irish Articles contain Reformation themes that also are found in the work of other Reformed theologians. The Thirty-Nine Articles (1563) are also important, though, because Ussher used many of its statements in the Irish Articles; indeed, the Thirty-Nine Articles not only were used by the Church of England, but were adopted in 1560 by the Irish Anglican church.[7] The Thirty-Nine Articles also served, in a sense, as a source document for the Westminster Standards, as the Westminster divines originally were given the task of revising the articles before they were called upon to write a new confession of faith and catechisms.

AMANDUS POLANUS

There is a unique feature to the theological expressions of Polanus and Wollebius on the sacraments, namely, the Ramist method. Ramism developed from the thought of Peter Ramus (1515–1572), who modified the use

---

4. Muller, *Reformed Dogmatics*, 1.42.

5. Philip Schaff, *Creeds of Christendom* (1931; Grand Rapids: Baker, 1996), 1.663; Charles Richard Elrington, *Life of Archbishop Ussher*, in James Ussher, *The Whole Works of the Most Rev. James Ussher* (Dublin: Hodges and Smith, 1847–64), 1.43–44.

6. Muller, *Reformed Dogmatics*, 1.44.

7. Schaff, *Creeds*, 1.663.

of Aristotelian logic in his theology. One of his chief complaints was that Aristotelian logic was far too complex. Ramus therefore opted for what he believed was an easier method of doing theology.

Ramism is not a philosophy per se, but rather a method of dividing a subject into two parts.[8] Ramus explains: "The form and method which is kept in this art, commands that the thing which is absolutely most clear, be first placed: and secondly that which is next clear, and so forth with the rest. And therefore it continually proceeds from the general to the special and singular."[9] For example, Ramus writes: "Dialectic otherwise called Logic is an art which teaches to dispute well. It is divided into two parts: *Invention*, and *judgment*.... An argument is either *artificial* or *without art*.... The first is that which has the beginning of itself is either *simple* or *compared*."[10]

In the following survey of Polanus and Wollebius, this bifurcation method surfaces in their explanations of the sacraments and baptism. However, there are no great differences between their explanations of the sacraments and baptism and those of their more Aristotelian-minded colleagues.

On the sacraments

Polanus begins declaring his doctrine of the sacraments by unpacking the connection to the covenant. He explains, in a manner reminiscent of Calvin's understanding, that God gives divine signs with His covenants that present truth to the senses. These signs are either natural or given. Polanus identifies a natural sign as one that is self-referential, such as a rainbow, which signifies either rain or fair weather. By contrast, a given sign is one that God has appointed to a specific end, such as when He appointed the rainbow as the sign of the Noahic covenant. Polanus divides the category of given signs into miracles and sacraments. The former is a demonstration of God's power, such as the Red Sea crossing, whereas the latter is a seal by which God confirms true doctrine.[11] Polanus further defines a sacrament

---

8. See R. Scott Clark, *Caspar Olevian and the Substance of the Covenant: The Double Benefit of Christ* (Edinburgh: Rutherford House, 2005), 58–63.

9. Peter Ramus, *The Logike* (1574; Leeds: The Scholars Press, 1966), 11–12; edited spelling.

10. Ramus, *The Logike*, 17. Cf. Frank Pierrepont Graves, *Peter Ramus and the Education Reformation of the Sixteenth Century* (New York: MacMillan, 1912), 130. See also Walter J. Ong, *Ramus, Method, and the Decay of Dialogue: From the Art of Discourse to the Art of Reason* (Cambridge: Harvard University Press, 1958).

11. Amandus Polanus, *The Substance of Christian Religion, Soundly Set Forth in Two Books* (London: 1595), 114. All quotations have updated spelling in lieu of archaic English spelling. Cf. John Calvin, *Institutes of the Christian Religion*, LCC, vols. 20–21, ed. John T. McNeill,

as "an outward sign, which God joins to his covenant, which he has made with men."[12] There are two types of covenants, temporal and eternal (note the twofold Ramist bifurcation). By a sacrament of an eternal covenant, God confirms the promise of eternal life, and there are only two such covenants in the Bible: the covenants of works and grace.[13]

Polanus explains that there were two sacraments for the covenant of works, the trees of knowledge and life. The tree of life signified the eternal life man would have received if he had remained obedient to the divine command. The tree of knowledge, on the other hand, signified the consequences of obedience and disobedience to the divine command.[14] The covenant of grace also has its sacraments, which, according to Polanus, are seals of the righteousness of faith. Polanus writes: "The Sacrament of the covenant of grace is a sacrament by which the faithful are both admonished, and also are made sure that the covenant of grace, and all the benefits of God which are promised in this covenant, do not only belong to others, but severally to every one of them, who do use the Sacrament according to God's ordinance."[15] Polanus is careful to stipulate, though, that the sacraments do not save, but rather point our faith to Christ, the only foundation for salvation.[16]

Polanus explains that both Word and sacrament point to the gospel of Christ: "The receiving of Christ in the word and sacraments do not differ indeed: for in both there is the same thing and the same substance, to wit, Christ with his benefits. It does not differ in the manner, for it is spiritual in them both. The difference is not in the instrument by which we receive it, for in them both faith is the instrument to receive it by." What then is the difference between Word and sacrament? Polanus states that the difference lies in the outward form; the Word is heard only by the ears, whereas the sacraments are experienced by all the other senses: touch, taste, smell, and sight.[17]

In a move that had become standard in the Reformed explanation of the sacraments, Polanus stated that there are two parts to a sacrament of the covenant of grace, the earthly and heavenly matter, or what later would be called the outward sign and the inward spiritual grace. He believed that

---

trans. Ford Lewis Battles (Philadelphia: Westminster, 1960), 4.14.18.

12. Polanus, *Christian Religion*, 116.
13. Polanus, *Christian Religion*, 116.
14. Polanus, *Christian Religion*, 116–17.
15. Polanus, *Christian Religion*, 117.
16. Polanus, *Christian Religion*, 118.
17. Polanus, *Christian Religion*, 118–19.

a sacrament had an outward action or ceremony appointed by Christ. He writes: "The earthly matter in the sacrament, is a sign or token, by which under a certain promised similitude, a heavenly matter is signified and represented to the faithful, that so they might be assured, that the heavenly matter is as certain spiritually present, as they do certainly see the earthly matter, to be bodily present before their eyes." The heavenly matter, Polanus argued, is the covenant of grace in the blood of Christ.[18] Echoing Augustine and his conclusions from the Donatist controversy, Polanus believed that recipients are not supposed to respect the earthly elements or the minister who offers the sacrament, but ultimately Christ.[19] He held that there is a sacramental union between the earthly and heavenly matter, in that the minister offers the earthly matter, which is the sign, but the thing signified is spiritual and is received by faith from the hand of Christ.[20]

Polanus identifies seven ends of a sacrament:

1.   That it might be a remembrance of God's benefits, both already offered, and hereafter to be offered, that is to say, that it might put the faithful in mind of Christ's benefits.

2.   That our faith might thereby be increased, exercised and strengthened.

3.   That by it we might be stirred up to thanksgiving for the benefit of our redemption.

4.   That it might be a bond of mutual love and concord in the church.

5.   That it might be the bond of public meetings, and of the preserving of the ecclesiastical ministry.

6.   That it might be a note of our profession, whereby as by a cognizance, the Church is discerned from infidels. So by circumcision the Jews were discerned from the Gentiles.

7.   That it might be a witness of our confession and society with the church.[21]

---

18. Polanus, *Christian Religion*, 119–20.

19. Polanus, *Christian Religion*, 120, 122–23; cf. Augustine, *The Letters of Petilian, The Donatist*, 3.15.18 in NPNF[1] 4.603.

20. Polanus, *Christian Religion*, 125.

21. Polanus, *Christian Religion*, 126–27.

In these seven ends, Polanus firmly grounded the sacraments in his doctrine of the church. The sacraments are not merely for the individual, he said, but for the corporate body. In contrast to Anabaptist views, the sacraments are first and foremost supposed to draw the minds of the faithful to the benefits of Christ, to the covenant promises of God.[22]

Polanus went on to identify the sacraments of the covenant of grace in the Old Testament, which is the way he explains the covenantal unity of the church in both testaments. He identified two Old Testament sacraments, circumcision and Passover. Polanus explained that circumcision was the sacrament by which all of the Israelite males were engrafted into the covenant God had made with Abraham. Polanus recognized two parts of the sacrament of circumcision: the foreskin and the outward action of circumcision.[23] He writes: "The foreskin, was a sign that our nature is corrupted, that men are born guilty in this carnal generation: and therefore stand in need of the regeneration and renewing which was to come by the blessed seed, who should bruise the head of the serpent, and in whom all the nations should be blessed." The heavenly matter of circumcision was the need for redemption through Christ. Polanus writes: "Circumcision of the foreskin, was a sign of the circumcision of the heart, that is to say, of justification by faith, of forgiveness of sins, and of regeneration." The outward matter was the minister cutting away the foreskin and the faithful Israelite submitting to the rite. In addition, the one who was circumcised was to be thankful, because not only did his circumcision signify that he had put off the sins of the flesh but that he had received this blessing from God. Therefore, he would give thanks for this blessing, though in the case of infants the thanksgiving would come from parents and relatives.[24]

On baptism

With this understanding of the sacraments in general and more specifically the sacrament of circumcision, we now have a basis to understand how Polanus unfolds his doctrine of baptism. Polanus explains that the sacraments of the New Testament are rites that have been instituted by Christ Himself: baptism and the Lord's Supper. Polanus then defines baptism as

---

22. Cf., e.g., Balthasar Hübmaier, *Christian Catechism*, in *Creeds and Confessions of Faith in the Christian Tradition*, eds. Jaroslav Pelikan and Valerie Hotchkiss (New Haven: Yale University Press, 2003), 2.676–93, esp. 680–81, qq. 35, 41.

23. Polanus, *Christian Religion*, 128–29.

24. Polanus, *Christian Religion*, 129–30.

"A sacrament of the New Testament, whereby is signified and sealed up to us, that we are as certainly washed in the blood of Christ from sins, as our body is certainly washed through water in the name of the Father, the Son, and the Holy Ghost."[25] Polanus believed that baptism replaced circumcision, as both are initiatory rites by which people enter the church and seals of regeneration. Moreover, just as the Israelites were circumcised only once, so Christians are to be baptized only once. Polanus explains the sacraments in general and circumcision in a twofold Ramist manner, and he identifies the two parts of baptism: water and the outward action of the rite. The water, according to Polanus, signifies the cleansing of sin by the blood of Christ on the cross, and the action of the rite consists of the sanctification of the water and the outward washing.[26]

Polanus explains that the outward washing of baptism, the sign signifies the "sure pledge of the inward washing, whereby we with the blood of Christ are washed from sins." For this reason, he argues, the outward washing of baptism is called "the washing of regeneration." Polanus affirmed that regeneration and adoption, which are signified in baptism, are according to the form of the covenant in which God promised to be the God of Abraham and of his seed after him. Though the minister washes outwardly with water, Christ ultimately washes the recipient inwardly by His blood.

As with the sacrament of circumcision, baptism also has two parts for the recipient, the reception of the rite and subsequent thanksgiving.[27] Polanus explains that in the reception of the rite, the recipient is made a partaker of the covenant of grace and reconciled, justified, regenerated, adopted by God, and given the freedom of the sons of God. This is not to say that Polanus believed in an *ex opere operato* view of baptism. Rather, Polanus's rejection of baptismal regeneration must be suspended on the context of his concept of the sacraments, namely, that a person's regeneration and justification are outwardly signified in baptism. Moreover, it is not the water that accomplishes these soteric blessings, but Christ working on the heart of man: "The outward man feels the force of the water: but the inward man feels the powerful working of the blood of Christ." Polanus is careful to stipulate that though infidels might be baptized, only believers receive the benefits of the rite.[28] Though Polanus does not explicitly say so,

---

25. Polanus, *Christian Religion*, 132.
26. Polanus, *Christian Religion*, 133.
27. Polanus, *Christian Religion*, 134.
28. Polanus, *Christian Religion*, 135.

it is evident that his doctrine of election undergirds his understanding of baptism at this point, namely, that it is only the elect who benefit from the sacrament of baptism.[29]

Beyond these points, Polanus lists seven reasons why infants should be baptized:

1. They also do pertain to the covenant of the grace of God.

2. To them also belongs the promise of the forgiveness of sins through the blood of Christ.

3. They belong to the church of God. *Children or the elected Children*

4. They are redeemed by the blood of Christ.

5. To them is promised the Holy Spirit.

6. They are to be discerned from the children of infidels.

7. Also in the Old Testament infants were circumcised.[30]

He closes his treatment of baptism in the same way he closed his explanation of circumcision, writing that an adult who is baptized, or the parents who bring a child for baptism, should be marked by thanksgiving. Even one baptized as an infant should be marked by thanksgiving: "When he comes to ripe years, [he] ought afterward in the whole course of his life to be thankful to God for this benefit."[31] Polanus here reflects the Reformation idea of the lifelong echo of baptism found not only in Calvin but also in Luther.[32]

JOHANNES WOLLEBIUS

There are some similarities between Polanus and Wollebius, as the latter based his theological work on the writings of the former. Moreover, Wollebius was a Ramist like his predecessor. However, Wollebius had distinct emphases.

On the sacraments

Wollebius sets forth his doctrine of the sacraments on the heels of his explanation of the covenant of grace. He explains that the covenant of grace is sealed by sacraments. He defines a sacrament as "A divinely instituted

---

29. Cf. Polanus, *Christian Religion*, 16–18.

30. Polanus, *Christian Religion*, 135.

31. Polanus, *Christian Religion*, 136.

32. LW 36.69; Calvin, *Institutes*, 4.15.3, 11.

act of worship, in which the grace promised by God to the people of the covenant is sealed by visible signs, and the people of the covenant are at the same time bound to obedience to him."[33] From this definition, Wollebius presents a doctrine that, in many ways, takes the best of the Reformed tradition and distills it into a number of succinct propositions.

For example, in his elaboration of the origins of the term, Wollebius incorporates Zwingli's understanding of the Latin *sacramentum*.[34] He states that a sacrament is an oath by which a person swears his allegiance to the covenant of God, but at the same time, it is God's pledge to bring about what He promises by His grace.[35] However, Wollebius also favorably cites the famous Augustinian definition that a sacrament is a visible sign of an invisible grace.[36] Again, relying on Augustine's response to the Donatists, he affirms that a sacrament does not depend on the intention of the minister but on the institution of God.[37]

Wollebius, like Polanus before him, goes on to explain that a sacrament has two parts, the earthly and heavenly matter. The earthly matter of the sacrament is the visible sign or element. The internal or heavenly matter is the thing signified, namely, Christ and His benefits.[38] Wollebius places emphasis on Christ as the object of the sacraments, not merely the power of God, as in the Roman Catholic understanding.[39] As far as the relationship between the sign and the thing signified, Wollebius explains that they are united, not naturally or locally, but relationally. In other words, Wollebius did not believe that the sacraments are the actual grace. For example, in terms of the Lord's Supper, he did not believe that the bread and wine are the literal body and blood of Christ. Wollebius writes: "We do not deny the presence of Christ, and of his body and blood, in the sacramental action; in addition to his being present by his divine person and his Holy Spirit, he is also present by his body and blood, not locally but sacramentally."[40]

---

33. Johannes Wollebius, *Compendium Theologiae Christianae*, in *Reformed Dogmatics*, ed. and trans. John W. Beardslee, III (New York: Oxford University Press, 1965), 22.1.2.

34. Cf. Ulrich Zwingli, *Of Baptism*, in *Zwingli and Bullinger*, LCC, ed. G. W. Bromiley (Philadelphia: Westminster, 1953), 131.

35. Wollebius, *Compendium*, 22.1.1.

36. Wollebius, *Compendium*, 22.1.4.

37. Wollebius, *Compendium*, 22.1.9; cf. Augustine, *Letters of Petilian*, 3.15.18 in NPNF¹ 4.603.

38. Wollebius, *Compendium*, 22.1.11–12.

39. See e.g., *Catechism of the Council of Trent: Ordered by the Council of Trent*, ed. St. Charles Borromeo (1566; Rockford: Tan Books and Publishers, 1982), 143.

40. Wollebius, *Compendium*, 22.1.1–16.

Wollebius did not hold that the relational union between the sign and the thing signified empties the sacraments of their significance. Rather, he sets forth four reasons to refute the claim that the sign and thing signified have to be locally united: (1) signs reveal the truth; (2) they confer grace; (3) signs apply grace; and (4) signs seal grace. Wollebius then expands and illustrates these four points. He writes:

> Sacraments reveal truth in the same way that a picture shows what a man looks like; they confer grace in the same manner as a scepter or keys and the like, which, when they are given, confer the royal power or the ability of entering a house; they are application of the promise, like the promise of God to preserve the one hundred forty-four thousand on whose foreheads the sign marked by the angel was placed (Rev. 7:3); and finally, they are confirmation, as are money deposited in escrow, seals, and the like. All these four are found in a sacrament.[41]

From the sacramental union, Wollebius explains how and why the Scriptures sometimes speak of the sacraments actually bringing about soteric blessings. He carefully distinguishes between the function of the sign and the thing signified by stating that sometimes the effect of the thing signified is attributed to the sign. He explains, though, that the sign has not brought about the effect, but that this is simply sacramental language, or a metonymy. A metonymy is a figure of speech that employs a word to refer to something else with which the word is associated, as the effect for the cause, the cause for the effect, or the sign for the thing signified.[42] For example, Wollebius writes: "The bread is the body of Christ; that is, the sacrament of the body of Christ. Circumcision is the covenant of God; that is, the sign or sacrament of the covenant. The seven cows are seven years; that is, the symbols of seven years. So we are said, sacramentally, to be cleansed by water, because baptism or washing is the sacrament of cleansing."[43]

Wollebius further expands on the difference between the sign and the thing signified by explaining how the sacraments relate to soteriology: "The effects of sacraments are not justification and sanctification through the performance of the rites, but the confirmation and sealing of both benefits."[44] Wollebius rejects an *ex opere operato* view of the sacraments. He

---

41. Wollebius, *Compendium*, 22.1.17.
42. See F. B. Huey, Jr. and Bruce Corley, *A Student's Dictionary for Biblical and Theological Studies* (Grand Rapids: Academie Books, 1983), 125.
43. Wollebius, *Compendium*, 22.1.19.
44. Wollebius, *Compendium*, 22.1.21.

supports this claim by appeal to Romans 4:11, which affirms that Abraham was justified before he was circumcised. Wollebius also explains that though "the sacraments as signs are the common possession of all the people of the covenant, with regard to the thing signified, they belong only to the elect alone."[45] Though he does not state it explicitly, this is an important distinction, one that lies implicit in the theology of other reformers, but becomes explicit here. In short, the sacraments are given to the visible church and all who are a part of it, but they are effectual only for the invisible church.

Wollebius concludes his treatment of the sacraments in general by setting forth the sacraments of the Old Testament and New Testament: under the former, they were circumcision and the Passover, and under the latter they are baptism and the Lord's Supper.[46] He explains, "The sacraments of the Old and New Testaments are one in the thing signified and in substance; namely, Christ and his benefits, which are the heart of every sacrament."[47] Once again, Wollebius sees a covenantal unity between the testaments that is a hallmark of Reformed theology and hermeneutics. More specifically, Wollebius goes on to write that just as circumcision was the rite of initiation, engrafting into the covenant, and of spiritual rebirth or spiritual circumcision, so is baptism.[48] This is not to say that Wollebius believed that the Old Testament and New Testament sacraments were exactly identical. He acknowledges six differences:[49]

1. The external signs.

2. The mode of representation, namely in the Old Testament it was Christ to come, whereas in the New Testament, it is Christ already come.

3. Number, in that besides circumcision and the Passover, in the Old Testament there were also others, such as the sacrifices and Levitical rites.

4. Extent, in that the New Covenant extends beyond the nation of Israel.

---

45. Wollebius, *Compendium*, 22.1.22.
46. Wollebius, *Compendium*, 22.2.1–3.
47. Wollebius, *Compendium*, 22.2.1.
48. Wollebius, *Compendium*, 22.2.2.
49. Wollebius, *Compendium*, 22.2.3.

5. Duration, those of the Old Testament were good until the advent of Christ, and those of the New Testament until the end of the world.

6. The clarity.

Beyond these general points, Wollebius polemicizes against the Roman Catholic understanding of the sacraments, particularly the relationship between the Old Testament and New Testament sacraments and the number. In other words, he gives the reasons why the Reformed churches reject the seven Roman Catholic sacraments.[50]

On baptism

Wollebius then moves on to discuss the sacrament of baptism. He defines baptism as the means by which "the elect are received into the family of God, and sealed to the remission of sins and rebirth through the blood of Christ, and through the Holy Spirit, by external sprinkling with water." Wollebius then explains that the term *baptism* means both immersion and sprinkling, and consequently washing.[51] He states that the external matter of baptism is water, and the internal matter is Christ with the benefits of His death, burial, and resurrection.[52] In terms of the external form of the rite, he shows his preference for sprinkling, though on practical and not theological grounds. Given the colder climate in his region, it was potentially harmful and even deadly to immerse an infant completely in water. Nevertheless, Wollebius believed that immersion was an excellent representation of the death and resurrection of Christ. He did not express a preference for single or triple sprinkling, so long as no superstition was attached to the specific mode of administration. Wollebius stated his desire that baptism be administered not merely by one finger but by the whole hand so that it more clearly corresponded to a genuine sprinkling or washing.[53]

Wollebius explained that the purpose of baptism is to confirm both a person's reception and engrafting into the family of God and his regeneration.[54] Additionally, both professing adults and their children, who are reckoned among the covenant people, are the proper recipients of baptism. Wollebius supported the practice of infant baptism based on a number of

---

50. Wollebius, *Compendium*, 22.2.4–6.
51. Wollebius, *Compendium*, 23.1.1.
52. Wollebius, *Compendium*, 23.1.5–6.
53. Wollebius, *Compendium*, 23.1.89.
54. Wollebius, *Compendium*, 23.1.13.

exegetical arguments. First, he cited Matthew 19:4 and Jesus' dominical command to allow the children to come to Him. Wollebius did not think it proper to exclude from baptism those whom Christ wanted brought to Him. Second, he cited the reason added by Christ in Matthew 19:14: that children are part of the kingdom of heaven. The sign of the covenant rightly belongs to everyone to whom the kingdom of heaven and the covenant of grace are given. In this vein, Wollebius also cited Genesis 17:7 and Acts 2:39, arguing that the covenant promise was given both to believers and their children. Third, he pointed to the analogy between circumcision and baptism. Fourth, he noted that the apostles are recorded as having baptized entire families or households (Acts 16:15, 33).[55]

In addition to these arguments, Wollebius explained that infants are not without faith and reason. In a similar fashion to Calvin, Wollebius writes: "Although they do not have those things fully developed, yet they have them in seed and root; although not in the second act, yet in the first, although not with the evidence of external work, yet by the inner power of the Holy Spirit."[56] Wollebius also stipulates, however, "As in the order of nature one is first born and then fed, so baptism precedes the Lord's supper."[57] In other words, like Calvin, Wollebius rejected paedocommunion.[58] Wollebius did note that in order for a child to be baptized, he must have at least one Christian parent. The children of unbelieving parents are not to be baptized, and can receive the rite only when they have reached years of discretion and have professed their faith in Christ.[59]

WILLIAM AMES

On the sacraments

Ames defines a sacrament as "a sign sealing the covenant of God," and cites Romans 4:11.[60] He further explains, "A sacrament of the new covenant, therefore, is a divine institution in which the blessings of the new covenant are represented, presented, and applied through signs perceptible to the

---

55. Wollebius, *Compendium*, 23.1.14.
56. Wollebius, *Compendium*, 23.1.15; cf. Calvin, *Institutes*, 4.16.20.
57. Wollebius, *Compendium*, 23.1.18.
58. Cf. Calvin, *Institutes*, 4.16.30–31.
59. Wollebius, *Compendium*, 23.1.16.
60. William Ames, *The Marrow of Theology*, trans. John Dykstra Eusden (1968; Grand ʾids: Baker, 1997), 36.2.

sense."[61] Ames stated that the sacraments are a secondary testimony based on the primary divine testimony of the covenant, and therefore God's favor and grace that arise from true faith are confirmed and furthered by the sacraments.[62] Ames, however, carefully explains: "The sacraments do not include the spiritual thing to which they refer in any physically inherent or adherent sense for then the signs and the things signified would be the same."[63] On the other hand: "Neither are they bare signs which merely indicate and represent. They communicate and testify to the thing itself; indeed, they present the thing to be communicated."[64]

Ames gives some important clarifications that help the reader understand the difference between the sign and the thing signified, saying that the union "is neither physical nor yet imaginary; it is rather a spiritual relation by which the things signified are really communicated to those who rightly use the signs."[65] Ames then expands on this point:

> From this union follows a communication of predicates. First, the sign is predicated of the thing signified, as when sanctification of the heart is called circumcision; second, the thing signified is predicated of the sign, as when circumcision is called the covenant and bread the body; third, the effect of the thing signified is predicated of the sign, as when baptism is said to regenerate; fourth, a property of the sign is predicated of the thing signified, as when breaking, which is applicable to bread, is attributed to Christ; fifth, a property of the thing signified is attributed to the sign, as when sacramental eating and drinking is called spiritual.[66]

Though Ames did not say so explicitly, he echoed the Reformed principle of the sacramental union, affirming that the sign and the thing signified are *distinctio sed non separatio*.[67]

Lastly, it is important to note how Ames understood the sacraments as having a primary end as a seal of the covenant, though he stipulated that the sealing of the covenant "occurs not on God's part only but secondarily

---

61. Ames, *Marrow*, 36.12.
62. Ames, *Marrow*, 36.13–14.
63. Ames, *Marrow*, 36.18.
64. Ames, *Marrow*, 36.19.
65. Ames, *Marrow*, 36.27.
66. Ames, *Marrow*, 36.29.
67. Cf. John Calvin, *Short Treatise on The Supper of Our Lord*, in *Selected Works of John Calvin: Tracts and Letters*, eds. Henry Beveridge and Jules Bonnet, trans. Henry Beveridge (1849; Grand Rapids: Baker, 1983), 2.172.

on ours."[68] He identifies a secondary end as the "profession of faith and love." Ames further writes: "Taking the sacraments symbolizes the union we have with God in Christ and the communion we hold with all those who are partakers of the same union, especially with those who are members of the same church."[69] Ames therefore believed that baptism should be administered only by lawful ministers of the church and could be done by immersion or sprinkling.[70]

On baptism

Of first importance is how Ames's treatment of baptism relates to the other loci in his work. Most Reformed theologians, whether of the Reformation or post-Reformation periods, begin with a locus on the sacraments and then segue to baptism and the Lord's Supper.[71] In contrast to many of his predecessors and contemporaries, Ames instead moved from a locus on the sacraments to church discipline.[72] This was not so much a substantive change as an organizational move that reflected an emphasis on ecclesiology: "Discipline is usually associated by the best theologians with the word and sacraments in the marks of the church."[73] Ames explains:

> In the preaching of the word, the will of God is set forth and really applied to beget and increase faith and obedience. In the administration of the sacraments the will of God is applied to persons through the seals to confirm faith and obedience. In the exercise of discipline the will of God is also applied to persons in censure to remove the vices contrary to true faith and obedience.[74]

Ames believed that discipline is related to the sacraments, as it pertains only to those who have the right to partake of the sacraments.[75] In other words, only those who have been baptized can come under the discipline of the church, including suspension from the Lord's Supper for impenitence.[76]

---

68. Ames, *Marrow*, 36.31.
69. Ames, *Marrow*, 36.34.
70. Ames, *Marrow*, 40.4, 14.
71. Cf., e.g., Calvin, *Institutes*, 4.14.1–4.17.50; Theodore Beza, *The Christian Faith*, trans. James Clark (1558; East Sussex: Focus Christian Ministries Trust, 1992), 4.31–52, 51–68; Belgic Confession, §§ 33–35; Heidelberg Catechism, qq. 66–82.
72. Ames, *Marrow*, 37.
73. Ames, *Marrow*, 37.3.
74. Ames, *Marrow*, 37.2.
75. Ames, *Marrow*, 37.6.
76. Ames, *Marrow*, 37.21.

One should keep in mind this ecclesiastical cast to Ames's understanding of the sacraments, and of baptism more specifically.

In his treatment of baptism, Ames did not spend a great amount of space.[77] He explained in typical fashion that Christ instituted baptism, thereby rejecting the Roman Catholic number of the sacraments because only the Lord can institute a sacrament, not man.[78] Ames then writes, "Baptism is the sacrament of initiation or regeneration…[and] represents and confirms our very engrafting into Christ."[79] Ames carefully distinguishes, however, between the sign and the thing signified: "From the time of our first engrafting into Christ by faith a relationship of justification and adoption is entered into." For Ames, soteriology hinges on faith, not on the sacrament. He further explains: "As the sacrament of that engrafting [namely, justification by faith alone], baptism stands for the remission of sins (Mark 1:4). And it stands, also, for adoption in that we are consecrated by it to the Father, Son, and Holy Spirit, whose names are pronounced over the baptized."[80] Baptism, therefore, is not instrumental in a person's justification, as it is in Roman Catholicism, but the benefits of redemption "are sealed by initiation in baptism."[81]

On infant baptism

With the rest of the Reformed tradition, Ames argued for the propriety of infant baptism. He writes that all who are part of the covenant of grace should be baptized.[82] Ames then gives five reasons for infant baptism:

1. Because if infants are partakers of any grace, it is by virtue of the covenant of grace and so both the covenant and the first seal belong to them.

2. The covenant in which the faithful are now included is clearly the same as the covenant made with Abraham (Rom. 4:11; Gal. 3:7–9).

3. The covenant as now administered to believers brings greater and fuller consolation. If it once pertained to adults and their infants,

---

77. Ames, *Marrow*, 40.
78. Ames, *Marrow*, 40.2–4.
79. Ames, *Marrow*, 40.5–6.
80. Ames, *Marrow*, 40.7.
81. Ames, *Marrow*, 40.10; cf. 27.8; Dogmatic Decrees of the Council of Trent, session 6, § 7, in Pelikan and Hotchkiss, *Creeds*, 2.829–30.
82. Ames, *Marrow*, 40.11.

the consolation would be narrower if it now only pertained to adults to the exclusion of their infants.

4. Baptism supplants circumcision (Col. 2:11–12).

5. From the very beginning of regeneration, whereof baptism is a seal, man is merely passive.

In many respects, these five arguments had become common in Reformed explanations of the covenant. However, Ames offered a unique statement and clarification.

Ames explains the ground of baptism: "Faith and repentance no more constitute the covenant of God now than in the time of Abraham, who was the father of the faithful. Therefore, the lack of these ought not to prevent infants from being baptized any more than it prevented them from being circumcised then."[83] This is an important difference from theologians such as Luther, Calvin, or Wollebius, who partly based infant baptism on the presumption of a seminal faith in the infant. Ames made the point that for baptism, like circumcision, the administrative ground of the covenant sign is first and foremost the covenant, the promise of God, not the faith of the person. God initiated the covenant and its sign, not man. If this is so, infants can receive the sign of the covenant because they have been born within the visible church, the visible covenant community. Ames did not rely on the concept of *fides infantium* or a seminal faith, but solely on the covenant promise of God.

THE THIRTY-NINE ARTICLES AND THE IRISH ARTICLES

This survey now moves from the theological constructions of individual theologians such as Polanus, Wollebius, and Ames to examine two important Early Orthodox confessions of faith, the Thirty-Nine Articles and the Irish Articles. Rather than treat the two confessions separately, it will be helpful to see them side by side. This not only will facilitate a comparison of the documents, but will help highlight what emphases were eventually appropriated into the Westminster Confession of Faith or bypassed.

---

83. Ames, *Marrow*, 40.13.

On the sacraments

Given the convergent streams of the Thirty-Nine Articles and the Irish Articles, there is a great degree of similarity between the documents on the doctrines of the sacraments and baptism. In fact, the opening statements on the sacraments from both confessions are nearly identical:

Thirty-Nine Articles	Irish Articles
Sacraments ordained of Christ be not only badges or tokens of Christian men's profession, but rather they be certain sure witnesses, and effectual signs of grace, and God's good will towards us, by the which he does work invisibly in us, and does not only quicken, but also strengthen and confirm our faith in him (§ 25).	The Sacraments ordained by Christ be not only badges or tokens of Christian men's profession, but rather certain sure witnesses, and effectual or powerful signs of grace and God's good will towards us, by which he does work invisibly in us, and not only quicken, but also strengthen and confirm our faith in him (§ 85).

Both documents, in parallel fashion, have statements on the number of the sacraments, rejections of the other five Roman Catholic sacraments, and rejections of the veneration of the elements. Both confessions also affirm that the efficacy of the sacrament does not depend on the worthiness of the minister, following Augustine's formulations from the Donatist controversy.

On baptism

In both confessions, there are brief statements on baptism, though it is here that there is a distinct difference between the two:

Thirty-Nine Articles	Irish Articles
Baptism is not only a sign of profession, and mark of difference, whereby Christian men are discerned from other that be not christened; but it is also a sign of regeneration or new birth, whereby, as by an instrument, they that receive baptism rightly, are grafted into the Church; the promises of the forgiveness of sin, and our adoption to be the sons of God by the Holy Ghost, are visibly signed and sealed; faith is confirmed, and grace increased by virtue of prayer unto God (§ 27).	Baptism is not only an outward sign of our profession, and a note of difference, whereby Christians are discerned from such as are no Christians; but much more a Sacrament of our admission into the Church, sealing unto us our new birth (and consequently our justification, adoption, and sanctification) by the communion which we have with Jesus Christ (§ 89).

There are some conceptual similarities between the statements, such as when the Thirty-Nine Articles state that baptism distinguishes Christians from non-Christians, or those who "be not christened," which the Irish Articles call "such as are no Christians."

The biggest difference is that Ussher eliminates any reference to the idea that baptism is "an instrument" by which people are grafted into the church. Instead, he states that baptism is a seal of the new birth. This difference in nomenclature is arguably significant; calling baptism an instrument of engrafting into the church is not common to the Reformed explanations of the sacrament. Does this represent a more Roman Catholic emphasis, one reflecting a view of baptismal regeneration? The short answer to this question is no. But this does not mean that the difference is insignificant. There are several important points to note.

First, the Thirty-Nine Articles affirm that a person is justified by faith alone, *sola fide* (§ 11), indicating that the articles do not positively set forth a view of baptismal regeneration. Second, in correspondence with Samuel Ward (1577–1643), an Anglican bishop, Ussher indicates his approval of the Thirty-Nine Articles, which shows that Ussher approved the articles on this point.[84] Third, there were Anglicans who read the Thirty-Nine Articles in such a manner as to permit a limited view of baptismal regeneration. Ward, for example, held that baptism removed the stain of original sin from infants. He was fully aware that his position was in the minority.[85] Ward's admission is evidence that the use of the term *instrument* did not demand a view of baptismal regeneration, but it seemed to allow for such a reading. Both Ward and Ussher approved of the Thirty-Nine Articles despite their theological differences on baptismal efficacy. Fourth, Ussher's correspondence with Ward presents a reasonable explanation as to why Ussher did not repeat the language of the Thirty-Nine Articles in the Irish Articles.[86]

This conclusion seems warranted, especially in contrast with Ussher's modifications. Not only did he delete the reference to baptism as an instrument, he emphasized that it is a seal of the new birth. Moreover, in his statement on the sacraments, he qualified the language of the Thirty-Nine Articles by writing that sacraments are "effectual *or powerful signs* of grace and God's good will towards us" (§ 85; emphasis added). It seems that Ussher and the Irish Articles back away from some of the nomenclature employed by the Thirty-Nine Articles to emphasize the traditional Reformed understanding.

There is confirmation of these conclusions in Ussher's chief theological work, *A Body of Divinity*. Ussher explains that sacraments are seals of the promise of God in Christ: "Wherein by certain outward signs, (and sacramental actions concerning the same) commanded by God, and delivered by his minister, Christ Jesus with all his saving graces is signified, conveyed, and sealed unto the heart of a Christian. For Sacraments are seals annexed by God to the word of the Covenant of grace."[87] There is a repeated emphasis on the sacraments as seals in this definition. When Ussher defines baptism, he makes the same point. In answer to the question, "What is Baptism?" Ussher replies:

> It is the first Sacrament of the New Testament by the washing of water (Eph. 5:26) representing the powerful washing of the blood and

---

84. "Letter CCI: Ussher to Ward," in Ussher, *Works of Ussher*, 15.9.

85. "Letter CLXX: Ward to Ussher," in *Works of Ussher*, 15.505.

86. For a fuller picture of the interaction between Ussher, Ward, and Revs. George Downame and William Bedell, see correspondence in *Works of Ussher*, 46–47, 144–45, 480–83, 493, 499–507, 508–20, 538. I am grateful to Jay Collier for drawing my attention to this important correspondence and helping me clarify my analysis of the Thirty-Nine Articles.

87. James Ussher, *A Body of Divinity: Being the Sum and Substance of the Christian Religion*, ed. Michael Navarr (1648; Birmingham: Solid Ground Books, 2007), 364.

spirit of Christ; (1 Cor. 9:11; Heb 10:22) and so sealing our regeneration or new birth, our entrance into the Covenant of Grace, and our engrafting into Christ, and into the body of Christ, which is his Church (John 3:5; Tit. 3:5; Acts 8:27). The word Baptism signifies in general any washing: but here is specially taken for that sacramental washing which seals unto those that are within God's covenant, their birth in Christ and entrance into Christianity.[88]

Once again, Ussher states that baptism "represents" and seals a person's regeneration, and that baptism is a "sacramental" washing, which reflects the common Reformed emphasis on the sign and the thing signified.

Further along in his treatment of baptism, Ussher specifies: "The inward things are really exhibited to the believer as well as the outward; there is that sacramental union between them, that the one is conveyed and sealed up by the others." However, Ussher adds, "The sacraments being rightly received, do effect that which they do represent."[89] However, we must not miss his emphasis that the sacraments must be *rightly received*, which means they must be received by faith. In other words, for Ussher, the sacraments do not function *ex opere operato*. He believed that not all who receive the sacraments benefit from them: "The inward grace of the Sacrament is not communicated to all, but to those only who are heirs of those promises whereof the Sacraments are seals." Ussher explains that in the Old Testament, circumcision not only was a seal of the righteousness of faith but a boundary marker between Jew and Gentile. Likewise, baptism is an outward badge of the member of the church, which distinguishes the Christian from the unbelieving world. However, Ussher writes: "This is but the porch, the shell, and outside: all that are outwardly received into the visible Church, are not spiritually engrafted into the mystical body of Christ. Baptism always is attended upon by the general grace, but not always with the special."[90] Hence, though baptism effects what it communicates, it hinges on the faith of the recipient.

What, however, of infants? Both the Thirty-Nine Articles and the Irish Articles affirm infant baptism:

---

88. Ussher, *Body of Divinity*, 372.
89. Ussher, *Body of Divinity*, 375.
90. Ussher, *Body of Divinity*, 375.

Thirty-Nine Articles	**Irish Articles**
The Baptism of young children is in any wise to be retained in the Church, as most agreeable with the institution of Christ (§ 27).	The Baptism of Infants is to be retained in the Church, as agreeable to the Word of God (§ 90).

Within the framework of his theology, Ussher explains what happens regarding the sign and the thing signified in infant baptism. To the question, "But what say you of Infants baptized that are born in the Church; does the inward grace in their baptism always attend upon the outward sign?" Ussher responds: "Surely no: the Sacrament of baptism is effectual in Infants, only to those and to all those who belong unto the election of grace. Which thing though we (in judgment of charity) do judge of every particular Infant, yet we have no ground to judge so of all in general: or if we should judge so, yet it is not any judgment of certainty; we may be mistaken."[91] Ussher first ties the grace of redemption to election, then later explains, "Baptism is not actually effectual to justify and sanctify, until the party do believe and embrace the promises."[92]

In a somewhat lengthy explanation, Ussher goes into greater detail as to how an infant benefits from baptism:

> We know that an estate may be made unto an Infant, and in his infancy he has right unto it, though not actual possession of it until such years. Now the time of the child's incapability, the use and comfort of this estate is lost indeed; but the right and title is not vain and empty, but true and real, and stands firmly secured unto the child to be claimed what time soever he is capable of it. Even so Infants elect have Christ and all his benefits sealed up unto them in the Sacrament of Baptism; yet through their incapableness they have not actual fruition of them, until God give them actual faith to apprehend them. Is Baptism lost then which is administered in our infancy? Was it a vain and an empty Ceremony? No, it was a complete and effectual Sacrament; and God's invisible graces were truly sealed up under visible signs. And though the use and the comfort of Baptism be not for the present enjoyed by the Infant; yet by the parent it is, who believes God's promises for himself and for his seed, and so by the whole Congregation: and the

---

91. Ussher, *Body of Divinity*, 376.
92. Ussher, *Body of Divinity*, 377.

things then done shall be actually effectual to the Infant, when ever it shall be capable to make use of them.[93]

Ussher is clear that baptism is not effectual until the infant is capable, until the infant possesses faith. There are no soteric events tied to the moment of the administration of baptism.

One has to wonder whether Ussher's statement on baptism lies behind the Westminster Confession's similar point:

> The efficacy of baptism is not tied to that moment of the time wherein it is administered; yet, notwithstanding, by the right use of this ordinance, the grace promised is not only offered, but really exhibited, and conferred, by the Holy Ghost, to such (whether of age or infants) as that grace belongs unto, according to the counsel of God's own will, in his appointed time. (28:6)

This connection between Ussher and the Westminster Assembly certainly seems plausible, especially given the use of the Irish Articles by the divines, as well as the personal interaction between Ussher and one of the Scottish advisors, Samuel Rutherford (1600–1661).[94] While Ussher's *Body of Divinity* was not published until 1648, it is possible that there was knowledge of Ussher's theology from his other writings. Nevertheless, regardless of the lines of influence, direct or indirect, there is an uncanny degree of substantive similarity between the two statements.

In addition, there is another observation to make about Ussher's statement, namely, the ecclesiological focus he places on infant baptism when he writes, "And though the use and the comfort of Baptism be not for the present enjoyed by the Infant; yet by the parent it is, who believes God's promises for himself and for his seed, and so by the whole Congregation."[95] Ussher later comments: "Every one that is present at Baptism should consider, that being a public action of the Congregation, every particular person ought reverently to join in it. Shall the whole Trinity be present at Baptism (Matt. 3) and we be gone?" Ussher exhorted the church to pray for the infant who is baptized and encouraged each individual to renew the covenant with God.[96]

---

93. Ussher, *Body of Divinity*, 377.
94. See the editor's introduction, *Body of Divinity*, ix–x.
95. Ussher, *Body of Divinity*, 377.
96. Ussher, *Body of Divinity*, 381.

Beyond this, Ussher made a series of pastoral observations. As to why some have a low view of baptism, he cited private baptisms, the fact that the rite was performed on days other than the Lord's Day, the fact that people in the church would leave immediately after the sermon and would not stay to observe the baptism, and that parents would bring their children forward for the rite but then never instruct them in the faith: "Baptism is not made use of, as it ought, in the whole course of men's lives."[97] Ussher explains:

> Baptism should of continual use through a Christian's whole life. It is administered but once, but it is always lasting in the virtue and efficacy of it. Baptism loses not its strength by time. In all your fears and doubts look back to your Baptism, and the promises of God sealed up unto you there; lay hold on them by faith, and you shall have the actual comfort of your Baptism, and feel the effect of it, though you never saw it. In your failings, slips, and revolts, to recover yourself have recourse to your Baptism: new baptism you shall not need; the Covenant and seal of God stands firm, he changes not: only renew your repentance, renew your faith in those blessed promises of grace which were sealed up unto you in your Baptism.[98]

Ussher, then, has a very pastoral cast to his doctrine of baptism, one not often found in theological works.

There are other features of Ussher's understanding of baptism and infant baptism. However, enough has been unearthed to show why Ussher demurs from the nomenclature of the Thirty-Nine Articles concerning baptismal efficacy. Ussher also arguably gives greater power to the sacraments, displaying what seems to be a Lutheran emphasis, in that the sacraments effect the promises represented as they function in a parallel fashion to the Word. However, the person must have faith in order to benefit from baptism. Additionally, Ussher's formula is different from Roman Catholicism, which holds to an *ex opere operato* view of the sacrament and baptismal regeneration at the moment of administration. Regeneration does not occur at the moment of baptism and the sacrament is efficacious only if the recipient looks upon it by faith. Who is it that believes? Only the elect.

---

97. Ussher, *Body of Divinity*, 380.
98. Ussher, *Body of Divinity*, 381.

CONCLUSION

In this survey of Early Orthodox Reformed theology, we see a continuation of trends and themes that began with the Reformation. There is still an emphasis on the sacraments as signs and seals, on the covenant, and on the rejection of an *ex opere operato* view of the sacraments. There is an emphasis on defining the relationship between the sign and the thing signified, or the sacramental union. However, other important distinctions are refined, such as when Wollebius carefully connects baptism with initiation into the *visible* church. This point was briefly mentioned by Ursinus in his explanation of infant baptism, but it will continue to feature directly in future discussions of baptism.[99] Two other important contributions come from Ames, who explicitly coordinated baptism with church discipline and the covenant promise as the ground of administration. These trends continue in the theology of High Orthodoxy and therefore merit exploration.

---

99. See Zacharias Ursinus, *The Commentary of Dr. Zacharias Ursinus on the Heidelberg Catechism* (1852; Phillipsburg, N.J.: P & R, n.d.), 366.

CHAPTER 6

Baptism in High Orthodox Reformed Theology

In High Orthodoxy, the Westminster Standards represent the high–water mark of confessional and catechetical writing. In addition to these documents, the formulations of Francis Turretin (1623–1687) and Herman Witsius (1637–1708) are worthy of examination, as they are two of the better-known Continental Reformed theologians. This is especially the case with Turretin, as his work was later employed as a textbook by Charles Hodge (1797–1878) at Princeton Seminary and therefore influenced several generations of theological students.

Turretin studied at the universities of Geneva, Leiden, Utrecht, Paris, Saumur, Montauban, and Nimes. He was initially called to be the pastor of the Italian congregation in Geneva in 1648 and was later appointed professor of theology at the university in 1653. He is one of the best-known Reformed Scholastics. Witsius studied at the universities of Utrecht and Groningen. After his studies, he served as a pastor at Westwoud, Wormer, Goes, and Leeuwarden from 1656–1675. In 1675, he was appointed professor of theology at the University of Franeker, and then, in 1680, he was called to a post at the University of Utrecht. Witsius ended his career at the University of Leiden (1698–1707). He retired due to his failing health one year before his death.[1]

The last document meriting exploration from the High Orthodox period is the Second London Confession (1689). This document serves as an important foil against which to contrast a traditional Reformed understanding of the sacraments and baptism. The Second London Confession is unique because it is a modified version of the Westminster Confession of Faith (1647), giving a historical example of how a Calvinistic soteriology is wedded to a Baptist understanding of the sacraments and baptism.

---

1. Richard A. Muller, *Post-Reformation Reformed Dogmatics* (Grand Rapids: Baker, 1987), 1.49.

THE WESTMINSTER STANDARDS

On the sacraments

The Westminster divines' explanation of the sacraments appears in chapter 27 of the Westminster Confession. In many respects, several antecedent streams of theological thought are codified in this chapter. For example, like John Calvin before them, the divines explain that the sacraments are "holy signs and seals of the covenant of grace" (27.1). Whereas Roman Catholicism sees the sacraments as instruments of divine grace, which is the created power (an infused habit) of God, the confession states that the sacraments "represent Christ, and his benefits" (27.1). It is important to correlate the Westminster conception of the sacraments with its doctrine of the visible church: "Unto this catholic visible church Christ has given the ministry, oracles, and ordinances of God, for the gathering and perfecting of the saints, in this life, to the end of the world: and does, by his own presence and Spirit, according to his promise, make them effectual thereunto" (25.3).

There are two key things to note. First, the sacraments do not represent merely an invisible grace, a common aphoristic statement regarding the nature of the sacraments going all the way back to Augustine and also employed by Ulrich Zwingli and Calvin.[2] In fact, it is curious that this Augustinian aphorism does not appear in the chapter on the sacraments or in the Westminster catechisms. The closest that the Standards come to the Augustinian definition is in the explanation of the parts of a sacrament: "The parts of a sacrament are two; the one an outward and sensible sign, used according to Christ's own appointment; the other an inward and spiritual grace thereby signified" (LC q. 163). The omission of Augustine's aphoristic definition is especially evident when the divines define a sacrament in the Shorter Catechism: "A sacrament is a holy ordinance instituted by Christ; wherein by sensible signs, Christ, and the benefits of the new covenant, are represented, sealed, and applied" (q. 92; LC q. 162). For the Roman Catholic Church, the sacraments are visible forms of invisible grace, whereas in the Westminster Standards, the sacraments are visible signs that represent Christ first and foremost.[3]

---

2. Augustine, *City of God*, 10.5, in NPNF[1] 2; Ulrich Zwingli, *Reckoning of the Faith*, in *Creeds and Confessions in the Christian Tradition*, eds. Jaroslav Pelikan and Valerie Hotchkiss (New Haven: Yale University Press, 2003), 2.262; John Calvin, *Institutes of the Christian Religion*, LCC, vols. 20–21, ed. John T. McNeill, trans. Ford Lewis Battles (Philadelphia: Westminster, 1960), 4.14.1.

3. Cf. *Catechism of the Council of Trent: Ordered by the Council of Trent*, ed. St. Charles Borromeo (1566; Rockford: Tan Books and Publishers,1982), 143.

The second point to note is that the Standards explain that the sacraments are for the "gathering and perfecting of the saints" (25.3). Elsewhere, the Standards appear to embrace a sacramental efficacy that is closer to Rome than Geneva when they state: "The sacraments become effectual means of salvation, not by any power in themselves, or any virtue derived from the piety or intention of him by whom they are administered, but only by the working of the Holy Ghost, and the blessing of Christ, by whom they are instituted" (LC q. 161). At first blush, this seems very similar to a Roman Catholic understanding of the sacraments. In fact, some have drawn that conclusion, arguing, for example, that the Westminster Confession teaches baptismal regeneration for infants and adults. David Wright claims, "The Westminster divines viewed baptism as the instrument and occasion of regeneration by the Spirit, of the remission of sins, of engrafting into Christ (cf. 28:1). The Confession teaches baptismal regeneration."[4] However, this is a misreading of the Westminster Standards, because such a conclusion fails to define baptismal regeneration properly.

Nowhere do the Standards state that a person is regenerated by baptism. In fact, a key tenet of the Roman Catholic understanding of baptism is that it *ex opere operato* regenerates both adult and infant alike, and cleanses them of original sin at the moment of administration. A related aspect of the Roman Catholic understanding of baptism that should be noted is that baptism is the instrument of justification, whereas for the divines, justification is by faith alone.[5] This difference between the confession and Roman Catholicism is especially evident when the documentary-source history of the confession is taken into account. The divines were first called to amend the Thirty-Nine Articles (1571), and they also used James Ussher's Irish Articles (1615) as a starting point for their own confession. The statements of both the Thirty-Nine Articles and Irish Articles were clearly available and well known, yet the divines chose to steer away from specific phrases:[6]

---

4. David F. Wright, *What Has Infant Baptism Done to Baptism? An Enquiry at the End of Christendom* (Milton Keynes: Paternoster, 2005), 99; also, idem, "Baptism at the Westminster Assembly," in *The Westminster Confession into the 21st Century*, vol. 1, ed. J. Ligon Duncan III (Fearn: Mentor, 2003), 161–85, esp. 168–70.

5. Dogmatic Decrees of the Council of Trent, session 6, § 7, in Pelikan and Hotchkiss, *Creeds*, 2.829–30.

6. Philip Schaff, *Creeds of Christendom* (1931; Grand Rapids: Baker, 1996), 3.504–505, 542.

Thirty-Nine Articles	Irish Articles	Westminster Confession
Baptism is not only a sign of profession, and mark of difference, whereby Christian men are discerned from other that be not christened; but it is also a sign of regeneration or new birth, whereby, *as by an instrument, they that receive baptism rightly*, are grafted into the Church; the promises of the forgiveness of sin, and our adoption to be the sons of God by the Holy Ghost, are visibly signed and sealed; faith is confirmed, and grace increased by virtue of prayer unto God (§ 27; emphasis added).	Baptism is not only an outward sign of our profession, and a note of difference, whereby Christians are discerned from such as are no Christians; *but much more a Sacrament of our admission into the Church, sealing unto us our new birth (and consequently our justification, adoption, and sanctification)* by the communion which we have with Jesus Christ (§ 89; emphasis added).	Baptism is a sacrament of the new testament, ordained by Jesus Christ, not only for the solemn admission of the party baptized *into the visible church*; but also, to be unto him *a sign and seal of the covenant of grace*, of his engrafting into Christ, of regeneration, of remission of sins, and of his giving up unto God through Jesus Christ, to walk in newness of life. Which sacrament is, by Christ's own appointment, to be continued in his church until the end of the world (28.1; emphasis added).

Manifestly the divines did not employ the term *instrument*, as do the Thirty-Nine Articles. In contrast to the Irish Articles, the divines specify that baptism is entrance into the *visible* church, and they make no mention of justification, which further distances them from anything resembling baptismal regeneration and the views of the Council of Trent.

To say that baptism regenerates and justifies is entirely different from saying the sacraments are effectual means of salvation. The sacraments (note the plural, i.e., not just baptism), *and* the preaching of the Word and prayer, are effectual means of salvation (LC q. 154). *Salvation* is a broad, encompassing term that has the entire process of redemption in view, but more specifically the believer's sanctification, as the sacraments are for the "perfecting of the saints" (25.3). The divines attach saving efficacy to the means of grace, not just baptism. For example, the divines connect the Word to a person's regeneration, not baptism: "The Spirit of God makes the reading, but especially the preaching of the Word, an effectual means of enlightening, convincing, and humbling sinners…and establishing their hearts in holiness and comfort through faith unto salvation" (LC q. 155; cf. SC q. 89). In the same way, the Spirit uses the sacraments as He does the Word; though the Standards do not explicitly state it, they seem to conceive of the sacraments as the visible Word.

It seems difficult if not impossible to conclude that the Standards teach baptismal regeneration or anything approaching an *ex opere operato* view of the sacraments. This conclusion is especially evident in that the divines repeatedly explain that the sacraments are "signs and seals" of Christ and the benefits of the covenant of grace (LC qq. 165, 167; SC q. 94).

The confession, without naming the Roman Catholic view of sacramental efficacy, rejects baptismal regeneration when it states:

> The grace which is exhibited in or by the sacraments rightly used, is not conferred by any power in them; neither does the efficacy of a sacrament depend upon the piety or intention of him that does administer it: but upon the work of the Spirit, and the word of institution, which contains, together with a precept authorizing the use thereof, *a promise of benefit* to worthy receivers (27.3, emphasis added).

There are two points to note from this statement: the confession rejects Donatism—the efficacy of the sacrament depends on God, not man. The promise of God is central. Second, the sacraments are effectual only to "worthy receivers," namely, those who possess faith.

Beyond these matters, there are two other noteworthy things concerning the sacraments. The first is the divines' explanation of the nature of the sacramental union—the relationship between the sign and the thing signified. They explain that sometimes the names and effects of the one (the things signified) are attributed to the other (the sign) because of the sacramental union (27.2). The second, like that of other Reformed theologians of the past, is their explanation that the sacraments of the Old Testament, though different from those of the New Testament, signified and exhibited the same thing—the accidents were different but they were substantively the same, the substance being Christ (27.5; cf. 7.5)

On baptism

In chapter 28, the divines treat baptism, beginning with an important distinction that stands in contrast to Anabaptist views on the sacraments, but also represents a further refinement of the doctrine. The divines explain that baptism is "the solemn admission of the party baptized into the visible church" (28.1). This is an acknowledgment that whether adult or infant, there is no way to know whether the person is elect or whether an adult profession of faith is genuine. The divines therefore recognize that when a person is baptized, the rite admits him into the visible covenant community. Beyond this, the divines also acknowledge that baptism is a sign and seal of the covenant of grace, union with Christ, regeneration, the remission of sins, of the surrender to God, and walking in the newness of life (28.1).

The divines affirm the practice of infant baptism, stating, "Not only those that do actually profess faith in and obedience unto Christ, but also the infants of one, or both, believing parents are to be baptized" (28.4). The divines believed that because infants are born within the visible covenant community (i.e., born to at least one believing parent), they have a right to the sign of admission. If an infant is born outside the visible church, then such a one has to wait to make a valid profession of faith (LC q. 166; SC q. 95). There is a fuller statement of this theological principle in the Westminster Directory for Public Worship:

> That the promise is made to believers and their seed; and that the seed and posterity of the faithful, born within the church, have, by their birth, interest in the covenant, and right to the seal of it, and to the outward privileges of the church, under the gospel, no less than the children of Abraham in the time of the Old Testament; the covenant of grace, for substance, being the same; and the grace of God, and the consolation of believers, more plentiful than before: That the Son of God admitted little children into his presence, embracing and blessing them, saying, *For of such is the kingdom of God.*[7]

Two things demonstrate that the divines did not promote baptismal regeneration. First, in the following paragraph, they explain that though it is a great sin to contemn or to neglect baptism, grace and salvation are

---

7. Directory for Public Worship, in *Westminster Confession of Faith* (1646; Glasgow: Free Presbyterian Publications, 1995), 383. For a brief history of the Directory, see John H. Leith, *Introduction to the Reformed Tradition* (1977; Atlanta: John Knox, 1981), 190–92. For theological argumentation for the validity of infant baptism from a Westminster divine, see Samuel Rutherford, *The Covenant of Life Opened* (Edinburgh: 1655), 95–118.

not so inseparably joined to it that a person cannot be regenerated or saved without it. Likewise, they state that baptism does not mean that all who receive the rite are undoubtedly regenerated (28.5).

Second, the divines once again reject the Roman Catholic view of *ex opere operato* by explaining, "The efficacy of baptism is not tied to that moment of time wherein it is administered" (28.6). In other words, just because a person is baptized does not automatically mean he receives the grace annexed to it. A person might possibly receive it later in life, or perhaps not at all. The divines go on to explain: "By the right use of this ordinance, the grace promised is not only offered, but really exhibited, and conferred, by the Holy Ghost, to such (whether of age or infants) as that grace belongs unto, according to the counsel of God's own will, in his appointed time" (28.6). The divines wanted to ensure that God's sovereignty in salvation was maintained, and to be clear that God is not bound to a mechanical view of the sacraments, as they function in Roman Catholicism.

This is not to say, however, that the divines did not discuss and debate the way in which God's grace accompanies the sacrament of baptism. However, the extant records on the debates over baptismal efficacy are a bit sparse and even somewhat cryptic. For example, Jeremiah Whitaker (1599–1654) is recorded as saying: "That it does confer grace I do not find, but our divines do hold it.... When they oppose the Papists, they say it is more than a sign and seal.... Chamier says the grace that is signified is exhibited, so it is in the French Confession; it does *efficaciter donare*.... I conceive that it does not confer it *ex opere operato*."[8] Note that the ellipses are part of the original minutes—they are gaps in the record, not editorial elisions.[9]

There are several things to highlight in Whitaker's statement. First, he appeals to French Reformed theologian Daniel Chamier (1565–1621), who was trained under Theodore Beza at Geneva.[10] Second, he appeals to the French Confession (1559), specifically: "We believe, as has been said, that in the Lord's Supper, as well as in baptism, God gives us really and in fact that which he there sets forth to us; and that consequently with these

---

8. Alexander F. Mitchell and John Struthers, eds., *Minutes of the Sessions of the Westminster Assembly of Divines* (Edinburgh and London: William Blackwood and Sons, 1874), 174. For biographical information on Jeremiah Whitaker, see James Reid, *Memoirs of the Westminster Divines* (1811; Edinburgh: Banner of Truth, 1982), 2.216–446; William Barker, *Puritan Profiles: 54 Contemporaries of the Westminster Assembly* (1996; Fearn: Mentor, 1999), 136–40.

9. Wright, "Baptism at Westminster," 163–66.

10. Samuel MacCauly Jackson, *The New Schaff-Herzog Encyclopedia of Religious Knowledge* (New York: Funk and Wagnalls, 1909), 3.1.

signs is given the true possession and enjoyment of that which they present to us."[11] Also, Whitaker goes on to say, "From the union of the sign and the thing signified which is in the analogy,... and in *conjuncta exhibitione* as Ursin[us]...when we lawfully receive it."[12] Here Whitaker appeals to Zacharias Ursinus' commentary on the Heidelberg Catechism. Ursinus writes:

> The names and properties of the things signified are attributed to the signs; and, on the other hand, the names of the signs are attributed to the things signified, on account of their analogy, or on account of the signification of the things through the signs, and on account of the joint exhibition and reception of the things with the signs in their lawful use.[13]

So although the information is sparse, the minutes provide a small window by which the investigator can peer into the inner workings of the assembly to see that multiple streams of Reformed theology fed into the discussion on baptism.[14] One can only imagine how many other sources were cited and quoted, and fed into the final product. The divines did not appeal to one narrow strand of the tradition but drew upon the whole of it.

Returning to the subject of baptism and the grace it brings, the divines asked themselves how baptism can be of benefit to a person who cannot remember being baptized? The Directory for Worship states that God's grace in baptism "reaches to the whole course of our life." Therefore, those who have been baptized are "to look back to their baptism; to repent of their sins against their covenant with God; to stir up their faith; to improve and make right use of their baptism, and of the covenant sealed thereby between God and their souls."[15]

In addition, there is a noteworthy contribution to the development of the doctrine, particularly as it pertains to infant baptism. What about those infants who are baptized and then later apostatize from the visible church? According to the divines, baptism visibly unites infants to Christ and distinguishes them from the world; hence they, "By their baptism are bound to fight against the devil, the world, and the flesh...[for] they are Christians,

---

11. § 37, in Schaff, *Creeds*, 3.380–81.

12. Mitchell and Struthers, *Minutes*, 176.

13. Zacharias Ursinus, *The Commentary of Dr. Zacharias Ursinus on the Heidelberg Catechism* (1852; Phillipsburg, N.J.: P & R, n.d.), 355

14. For Ursinus' influence on the assembly, see R. Scott Clark and Joel Beeke, "Ursinus, Oxford, and the Westminster Divines," in *The Westminster Confession into the 21st Century*, vol. 2, ed. J. Ligon Duncan III (Fearn: Mentor, 2004), 1–32.

15. Directory for Public Worship, in *Westminster Confession*, 383.

and federally holy before baptism, and therefore are they to be baptized." To foster this commitment, the parents were consequently exhorted to raise their children in the knowledge of the Christian religion and nurture them in the fear and admonition of the Lord. At this point, the key element surfaces, as the Directory notes that the minister is also supposed to, "Let [the parent] know the danger of God's wrath to himself and child, if he be negligent."[16] In other words, it is implicit that not only will a child's baptism not be a sign of union with Christ but instead the opposite, namely, the ground for God to visit His wrath on both parent and child. This is something of a critical contribution, in that others, such as Calvin, said that baptism becomes a useless sign to the one who does not have faith, not the ground for God's wrath. However, we should not forget Ursinus's comments regarding the double-edged nature of the sacraments.[17]

In addition to these points, there are several liturgical observations concerning baptism. Baptism is to be administered to a person only once (28.7). Given that the divines believed that baptism is chiefly a sign and seal of the covenant of grace, baptism refers first and foremost to the promise of God, then secondarily it points to the believer's response to God's grace (LC q. 166). Stated simply, the promise does not depend on man, as it would in an Anabaptist soteriology, but on God. Concerning the mode of baptism, Robert Baillie (1602–1662), one of the Scottish advisors, comments in a letter, "At our sitting down this day, a great many of our brethren did complain of the great increase and insolencie, in diverse places, of the Antinomian and Anbaptisticall conventicles."[18] In spite of the concern, which was undoubtedly shared by others, the divines express a moderate degree of ambivalence regarding the proper mode of baptism: "Dipping of the person into the water is not necessary; but baptism is rightly administered by pouring, or sprinkling water upon the person" (28.3). This statement allows all three modes of baptism, though in a development beyond the positions of Thomas Aquinas, Martin Luther, Philip Melanchthon, Calvin, or Johannes Wollebius, the divines expressed a preference for sprinkling.[19] This conclusion is evident from the proof texts the divines cite, such as Hebrews

---

16. Directory for Public Worship, in *Westminster Confession*, 383.

17. Ursinus, *Commentary*, 355.

18. Robert Baillie, *The Letters and Journals of Robert Baillie*, ed. David Laing (Edinburgh: Robert Ogle, 1841), 2.215.

19. LW 35.29; Calvin, *Institutes*, 4.15.19.

9:10.[20] With regard to the preferred mode of sprinkling, further explanation comes from the Directory for Worship: "That the water, in baptism, represents and signifies both the blood of Christ.... That baptizing, or sprinkling and washing with water, signifies the cleansing from sin by the blood and for the merit of Christ."[21]

Even though different modes of baptism are mentioned, this small statement in the confession took some three days of theological discussion and debate to compose. John Lightfoot (1602–1675) comments in his personal journal, "We fell upon a large and long discourse, whether dipping were essential or used in the first institution, or in the Jews' custom."[22] The initial vote on the matter was twenty-five to twenty-four to exclude dipping (or immersion) from the Directory (though it should be noted that the debate was not over dipping versus the other modes, but whether dipping should be placed on the same level as sprinkling and pouring). The divines returned to the issue and later agreed to the statement now found in the Directory. Lightfoot comments: "But as for the dispute itself about dipping, it was thought fit and most safe to let it alone.... But this cost a great deal of time about the wording it."[23]

Lastly, the divines stipulate that only a minister of the gospel should administer baptism (28.2). The proof texts for this particular claim show that the divines held that Christ baptizes with the Spirit and fire (Matt. 3:11), and His apostles administer the visible sign of this outpouring of the Spirit. To this end, they cite the Great Commission (Matt. 28:19–20). The idea here is that Christ gave baptism to the church, not to individuals. Hence, Christ's ordained representatives stand in His stead to administer the visible sign of His outpouring of the Spirit.

---

20. For the original proof texts of the Westminster Standards see, *Westminster Confession*, *ad loc.*

21. Directory for Public Worship, in *Westminster Confession*, 382.

22. John Lightfoot, *The Journal of the Proceedings of The Assembly of Divines* (London: J. F. Dove, 1824), 299; cf. Wright, "Baptism at Westminster," 177–79.

23. Lightfoot, *Journal*, 301; see also Richard A. Muller and Rowland S. Ward, *Scripture and Worship: Biblical Interpretation & The Directory for Worship* (Phillipsburg, N.J.: P & R, 2007), 129–30.

FRANCIS TURRETIN

On the sacraments

Like many other theologians, Turretin began his treatment of the sacraments by tracing the etymology of the word. But when he described the term, he immediately and consistently connected the sacraments with the covenants. Turretin writes: "As God willed to enter into a covenant with the church...in order to apply to her the salvation purchased by Christ, so (such is his goodness) for the greater confirmation of faith, he has condescended to seal this covenant by sacraments as seals, that by them as badges he might distinguish and separate his people from the rest of the world."[24] Turretin affirmed a number of Reformed teachings, such as redemption through covenant, the sacraments as signs and seals, and the twofold nature of the sacraments, namely, that they are primarily representative of God's covenant promise and secondarily indicative of man's response.[25]

In his definition of the term, Turretin rehearsed various historic definitions, including Augustine's commonly employed statement that they are signs of sacred things and visible forms of invisible graces.[26] This is the path Calvin pursued, but Turretin adopted a more christologically focused definition. Rather than basing his definition in the classical history of the etymology of the term, he instead argued from the apostle Paul's statement in Romans 4:11, where Paul says that circumcision is "a sign and seal of the righteousness of faith." Based on this statement, Turretin writes: "Therefore, this torch throwing its light before us, we say: 'The sacraments are the signs and seals of the grace of God in Christ.' Or a little more explicitly: 'Sacred visible signs and seals divinely instituted to signify and seal to our consciences the promises of saving grace in Christ and in turn to testify our faith and piety and obedience towards God.'"[27] As seen also in the Westminster Standards, by this point in the development of the doctrine, Reformed theologians specifically identified the sacraments as signs of God's activity through Christ and the Spirit, not merely the created power of God (an infused habit).

Turretin, with scholastic precision, explained the way in which the sacraments operate, though he did not mention the Roman Catholic view. He

---

24. Francis Turretin, *Institutes of Elenctic Theology*, ed. James T. Dennison, Jr., trans. George Musgrave Giger (Phillipsburg, N.J.: P & R, 1992–97), 19.1.1.

25. Cf. Turretin, *Institutes*, 19.5.3, 15.

26. Turretin, *Institutes*, 19.1.8.

27. Turretin, *Institutes*, 19.1.9.

dissected the sacrament by explaining the relationship between the sign and the thing signified. Like other Reformed theologians, he rested on the formula of the sacramental union between the sign and the thing signified. Turretin specifies the nature of the union, asserting that it "is neither natural by bodily contact, nor local by contiguity, nor even spiritual by a spiritual energy (*energeian*) by which the signs are immediately made alive, or the power to regenerate or justify given to them; but is relative and sacramental, placed principally in three things—signification, sealing and exhibition."[28] Turretin used the hypostatic union of the two natures of Christ, divine and human, and the fact that, according to classical christological formulations, the two natures are not in any way mixed but are nevertheless joined together. In similar fashion, the sign and the thing signified are joined without being mixed or confounded.[29]

Turretin went on to define the four requirements of a sacrament: the visible element, the heavenly or spiritual thing to which the element points, the divine institution, and the stated and ordinary use by the church.[30] However, he amplified his explanation of the sacraments by stating that they are visible Words; the Word of God is audible, whereas the sacraments are visible. He stipulated, though, that there are differences between the audible and visible Words, in that the audible Word extends promiscuously to all, believer and unbeliever alike, whereas the sacraments pertain only to those who are covenanted with God. Furthermore, the audible Word offers the promises of God indiscriminately to all, but His visible Words confirm those promises singly to each one who partakes of them rightly.[31]

What happens to those who do not partake of the sacraments rightly? Turretin affirmed that although the sacraments are seals, their sealing function is not invalidated if hypocrites or unbelievers partake of them. The audible Word is not invalidated when preached and ignored by an unbeliever, and it is the same with the visible Word. Turretin stated that the sacraments seal nothing to hypocrites and unbelievers due to the lack of the necessary condition, faith. But the unbeliever or hypocrite who receives the sacraments without faith contracts a greater guilt.[32]

---

28. Turretin, *Institutes*, 19.1.12.
29. Turretin, *Institutes*, 19.1.13; cf. 19.4.3.
30. Turretin, *Institutes*, 19.1.16.
31. Turretin, *Institutes*, 19.2.6.
32. Turretin, *Institutes*, 19.5.11.

Turretin argued that the sacraments of the Old Testament (circumcision and Passover) and the New Testament (baptism and the Lord's Supper) are essentially the same (i.e. their essence versus their accidents). Turretin proves this by appealing to the apostle Paul (1 Cor. 10:1–4): "Paul ascribes to the ancients our baptism and Supper in their mode, not certainly with regard to the signs (which were diverse), but with regard to the thing signified because the clouds and the passage through the sea signified and sealed to them what baptism does to us; and the manna and the water from the rock, what the Supper does to us."[33] Turretin pointed out that the substance of the Old Testament sacraments was the same as those of the New Testament, namely, Christ. Building on this concept, Turretin explained that when Paul calls circumcision the sign and seal of the righteousness of faith, the righteousness of faith is common to all believers.[34] This means that circumcision was a seal of the forgiveness of sins and of salvation, and the same grace that wrought these things in Abraham is also promised in the sacraments of the New Testament to all of those who follow in the footsteps of faithful Abraham.[35] Turretin was careful to point out, however, that Old Testament sacraments did not foreshadow New Testament sacraments. In other words, circumcision did not foreshadow baptism; circumcision was not a type of baptism. Rather, circumcision was a type of Christ, who is the fulfillment of all types and the substance of all of the shadows of the Old Testament.[36] Though Turretin did not explicitly state it, the following is a logical conclusion from this construction: circumcision and the Passover are both types of Christ and sacraments, whereas baptism and the Lord's Supper are only sacraments.

On baptism

Turretin built on his doctrine of the sacraments and spelled out the details in his doctrine of baptism. Among the many aspects of the doctrine that Turretin treated were the internal matter, form, subjects, and end of baptism.

The internal matter of baptism (the thing signified) is union with Christ and the benefits of justification and regeneration, which come from a twofold washing—the washing with the blood of Christ to cleanse from sin and the washing with the Holy Spirit, who brings regeneration and

---

33. Turretin, *Institutes*, 19.9.5; cf. 19.9.15.
34. Turretin, *Institutes*, 19.5.5.
35. Turretin, *Institutes*, 19.9.8.
36. Turretin, *Institutes*, 19.9.12.

newness of life.[37] Turretin was careful, though, not to confuse the sign and the thing signified.[38]

The form of baptism consists of three things: the signification, the sealing and conferring of the internal matter by the external, and the thing sealed by the sign. In its signification, the water of baptism washes away the filthiness of the body; so the blood of Christ and the Holy Spirit wash away the filthiness of the soul. Turretin explained that in the past people were baptized by immersion, which signified both the death of the old man and the resurrection of the new. Additionally, for Turretin, baptism is a seal of the righteousness of faith, and finally the thing sealed is the promise of God. Turretin writes: "God really furnishes in the lawful use what is represented by baptism; not *ex opere operato*, but from the most firm truth of the promise, by which we become inwardly certain that what is done in the body by sprinkling of water is done in the soul spiritually to believers by the blood and Spirit of Christ."[39]

The proper subjects of baptism are only those who are covenanted with God, whether they are truly covenanted (the invisible church) or merely nominally covenanted (the visible church). The end of baptism is twofold. First, it is an aid to the faith of God's people, and second it is an aid to the church's public confession to the world. Turretin placed primary emphasis on the promises of God and the blessings that flow from union with Christ: forgiveness of sins, justification, and the regeneration of the Holy Spirit. At the same time, through baptism the people of God recognize their obligation to worship the true triune God, to love their neighbors, and to be united as the body of Christ, the church.[40]

Concerning the mode of baptism, Turretin, like many of his predecessors, was somewhat open. Turretin acknowledged that although immersion was the ordinary method in the church, it was not so universally practiced that sprinkling should be excluded. He presented several biblical examples to show the impracticality of immersion, such as the conversion of the three thousand believers at Pentecost (Acts 2:41), the administration of baptism within a house (Acts 16:27–33), or the administration of baptism in the ancient church to those who were bed-ridden. He also cited a number of passages to show that the term βαπτισμοὺς and the verb ἐβαπτίσθη refer

---

37. Turretin, *Institutes*, 19.11.13.
38. Cf. Turretin, *Institutes*, 19.5.13.
39. Turretin, *Institutes*., 19.11.14.
40. Turretin, *Institutes*, 19.11.16.

not only to immersion but also to sprinkling (Mark 7:4; Luke 11:38). To support his preference for sprinkling, Turretin appealed to 1 Peter 1:2 and Hebrews 10:22, which speak of the sprinkling and cleansing that come through the blood of Christ. Like Wollebius, Turretin argued that immersing infants in colder regions was dangerous. Additionally, because the baptism of adults often involved stripping naked, sprinkling was preferential for the sake of modesty. Lastly, Turretin expressed no preference as to whether baptism was single or threefold.[41]

On infant baptism

Concerning the baptism of infants, in many ways Turretin followed the well-worn paths established by his Reformed predecessors. He brought forth seven arguments in favor of the practice. Baptism should be administered to infants because:

1. Of the dominical command of the Great Commission. Turretin, like Zwingli before him (though he did not cite him), argued that the verb μαθητευειν does not mean "to teach" but "to make disciples," which is accomplished through baptism.

2. Of the covenant. Turretin believed that the seals of the covenant pertain to those to whom the covenant of God pertains. Arguing redemptive-historically, Turretin showed that the promise of the covenant pertained both to Abraham and to his seed after him (Gen. 17:7), as well as to the children of New Testament believers (Acts 2:39).

3. Of the analogy between circumcision and baptism (Col. 2:12).

4. Infants belong to the kingdom of heaven, according to the declaration of Christ (Matt. 19:13).

5. Children of believers are holy and therefore ought to be baptized (1 Cor. 7:14).

6. No impediment can be given as to why baptism should not be conferred upon infants.

7. The church fathers acknowledged the necessity and propriety of the practice.[42]

---

41. Turretin, *Institutes*, 19.11.11–12.
42. Turretin, *Institutes*, 19.20.3–11.

When Turretin was pressed, however, he retreated to the first two arguments, namely, the dominical command and the covenant of God. Baptism is therefore not administered because of *fides infantium* or on the basis of the seeds of faith.[43]

HERMAN WITSIUS

On the sacraments

In his *Economy of the Covenants*, Witsius begins by explaining that God confirms all of His covenants with man by some sacred symbol. Witsius states that these sacred symbols convey the certainty of the promises of God, as well as remind man of his covenant duty to God. These sacred symbols, writes Witsius, are called sacraments. Like Turretin, Witsius believed that the sacraments are the visible Word of God. He writes: "For, though nothing can be thought of that deserves more credit than the word of God, yet, where God adds signs and seals to his infallible promises, he gives a twofold foundation to our faith."[44] God gave the first sacraments to His people in the garden of Eden—the trees of life and knowledge, and the Sabbath.[45] In terms of the New Testament sacraments, Witsius gives the standard Protestant answer of baptism and the Lord's Supper: "These in short, are sufficient to signify and seal the fullness of grace we have in Christ."[46]

On baptism

Witsius explained that baptism generally signifies reception into the covenant of grace. Just as circumcision was the sign and seal of the Old Testament, so baptism is the sign of the New Testament, as the latter replaces the former.[47] Specifically, the water of baptism signifies both the blood and Spirit of Christ.[48] When Witsius specifically explained baptism, however, he made some valuable contributions.

Witsius focused on baptism by immersion and wrote that water has the power to drown and suffocate. He said that what is true of water is also

---

43. Turretin, *Institutes*, 19.20.18.

44. Herman Witsius, *Economy of the Covenants Between God and Man: Comprehending A Complete Body of Divinity*, trans. William Crookshank (1822; Phillipsburg, N.J.: P & R, 1990), 1.6.1.

45. Witsius, *Economy of the Covenants*, 1.6.2.

46. Witsius, *Economy of the Covenants*, 4.16.1.

47. Witsius, *Economy of the Covenants*, 4.16.18.

48. Witsius, *Economy of the Covenants*, 4.16.23.

true of the blood and Spirit of Christ, in that both mortify the old man. Witsius drew on Gregory of Nazianzus (ca. 330–379), who called baptism the "deluge of sin."[49] Witsius elaborates on the theme of baptism as drowning judgment and states that immersion in water represents the "tremendous abyss of divine justice" that Christ suffered.[50] As the person goes under the water and remains for a moment, it represents the burial of Christ, which was His lowest degree of humiliation, "when he was thought to be wholly cut off." Lastly, when the person rises out of the water, it represents the resurrection of Christ. This imagery, argues Witsius, comes from Romans 6:3–4.

In addition to this christologically cast theology of baptism, Witsius also made connections to eschatology. A number of the theologians and confessions surveyed thus far readily identify the baptism-resurrection connection vis-à-vis Romans 6:3–4 in terms of the *ordo salutis*, rising to walk in the newness of life. Witsius, however, expanded on this and made a connection to the *historia salutis*. Generally, Witsius explains, future blessings are signified by baptism: "For as in baptism, after we are immersed in water, we directly come out of it in safety: so in like manner, it shall be that though we may be pressed with afflictions in this life, yet we shall not be overwhelmed by them, but being at last delivered from them, shall be translated into everlasting joys." Witsius then drew a parallel between the Israelites who emerged out of their Red Sea baptism safely on land and believers who rise out of the miseries of life to stand on the sea of glass and sing the song of the Lamb.[51]

Witsius draws yet another connection to eschatology when he writes, "Moreover, as in baptism are set forth the death, burial and resurrection of Christ: but his resurrection is a pledge of our glorious resurrection: we may learn from our baptism, that after being buried, as it were in the water, we directly rise out of it, so at the last day, we shall be raised out of our graves, to eternal life." Witsius supports his point by appealing to Theodoret (ca. 393–ca. 460), the bishop of Cyrrhus, Syria: "It is an earnest of good things to come, a type of the future resurrection, a communion in the sufferings, and a participation of the resurrection of our Lord."[52] Witsius also appealed to Mark 16:16 to support his argument. These points appear to be a noteworthy contribution to the doctrine of baptism, as Witsius appealed to no

---

49. Witsius, *Economy of the Covenants*, 4.16.24.
50. Witsius, *Economy of the Covenants*, 4.16.26.
51. Witsius, *Economy of the Covenants*, 4.16.28.
52. Witsius, *Economy of the Covenants*, 4.16.29.

Reformed predecessors or contemporaries to make his case when copious references to other Reformed theologians appear elsewhere in his writings.

Given how much Witsius relied on the imagery of immersion, one might conclude that he therefore rejected other forms of baptism. This is not the case. Witsius admitted that immersion was the general practice among the church fathers, but he believed that aspersion or sprinkling could still capture the imagery of immersion. He writes: "For, the pouring out, or aspersion of the water, answers to the immersion into it, and perhaps it would be better, if it was so copious, as to run over the whole face, and as it were cover it: by which the emersion out of water would be answered by the dissipation of it."[53] He further argued that since the head represents the whole person, when a person receives baptism through sprinkling or pouring, the whole person may be accounted as having been immersed. Witsius also writes: "The communion in the thing signified should not be rated by the quantity of the external sign."[54]

On infant baptism

Witsius readily acknowledged that there is no express command in Scripture to practice infant baptism. Nevertheless, he states: "There are general commands, from which this special command is deduced by evident consequence."[55] Witsius relied on what the Westminster Confession calls a "good and necessary consequence." The confession states: "The whole counsel of God concerning all things necessary for his own glory, man's salvation, faith and life, is either expressly set down in Scripture, or by good and necessary consequence may be deduced from Scripture" (1:6).[56] Richard Muller explains the nature of the principle of a good and necessary consequence:

---

53. Witsius, *Economy of the Covenants*, 4.16.30.
54. Witsius, *Economy of the Covenants*, 4.16.30.
55. Witsius, *Economy of the Covenants*, 4.16.41.
56. For explanations by a Westminster divine, see George Gillespie, *Treatise of Miscellany Questions* (Edinburgh: Robert Ogle, and Oliver & Boyd, 1844), 100–103. It is interesting to note, once again to demonstrate the variegated streams of theological thought that flowed into the argumentation of the divines, the diverse body of authorities to which Gillespie points in his explanation of good and necessary consequence: John Cameron (1579–1625), professor of theology at the Academy of Saumur in France, Thomas Aquinas (1225–1274), the famous medieval Roman Catholic theologian, John Gerhard (1582–1637), the well-known Lutheran theologian, and rabbinic literature, including the Talmud (Gillespie, *Questions*, 100–102). To see the employment of the principle in the debates during the Westminster Assembly to prove the *jus divinum* of Presbyterian polity, worship on Sunday, and Christ's argument for

The issue is not how to balance truths of revelation and truths of reason in an argument in such a way that the truth of revelation determines the outcome of the argument—rather, the issue is the collation and comparison of biblical texts for the sake either of determining the meaning of one of them or of establishing a conclusion based on the collation and comparison itself. This interpretive technique does not import new concepts to the text but draws rational conclusions based entirely on a series of biblical texts. In short form, it is an exercise of the analogy of scripture, moving toward the clarification of the outlines of the analogy of faith.[57]

One might also add the comments of B. B. Warfield (1851–1921), who writes: "It is the Reformed contention…that the sense of Scripture is Scripture, and that men are bound by its whole sense in all its implications."[58]

While this hermeneutical practice was common among Reformed theologians, it seems that Witsius was one of the few to draw an explicit connection between it and the practice of infant baptism.[59] By way of contrast, some who rejected infant baptism, such as the Anabaptists, had no place for such a principle.[60] Even some who held Reformed convictions about soteriology attenuated their use of the principle.

---

the resurrection from the Old Testament, see Mitchell and Struthers, *Minutes*, 228, 231–32, 236–41.

57. Muller, *Reformed Dogmatics*, 2.499. For the specific principle as it comes through the Westminster Assembly, see Muller and Ward, *Scripture and Worship*, 35–36; C. J. Williams, "Good and Necessary Consequence in the Westminster Confession," in *The Faith Once Delivered: Essays in Honor of Dr. Wayne R. Spear*, ed. Anthony T. Selvaggio (Phillipsburg, N.J.: P & R, 2007), 171–90.

58. B. B. Warfield, "The Doctrine of Inspiration of the Westminster Divines," in *The Works of Benjamin B. Warfield*, eds. Ethelbert D. Warfield, et al. (1931; Grand Rapids: Baker, 1981), 6.226.

59. Mention of the principle appears in connection with infant baptism in James Ussher, *A Body of Divinity: Being the Sum and Substance of the Christian Religion*, ed. Michael Navarr (1648; Birmingham: Solid Ground Books, 2007), 378.

60. Worlds apart from Calvinistic (or Particular) Baptists are the Polish Anabaptists, who rejected the principle. They were followers of Faustus Socinus (1539–1604) and radical anti-Trinitarians. For example, the Racovian Catechism (1574) gives the following answer to the question of the propriety of infant baptism: "If you look at the ancient apostolic Church, and to the end for which this rite was instituted by the apostles, it does not pertain to infants; since we have in the Scriptures no command for, nor any example of, infant baptism, nor are they as yet capable, as the thing itself shows, of the Faith in Christ, which ought to precede this rite, and which men profess by this rite" (*The Racovian Catechism*, trans. Thomas Rees [1818; Indianapolis: Christian Educational Services, 1994], 3.5, 252). There is a connection between their rejection of the principle of good and necessary consequence, their rejection of infant baptism, and their anti-Trinitarianism. Unlike rationalist anti-Trinitarians, the

The mitigation is especially evident in the Second London Confession (1689), which was composed in the same year Witsius's *Economy of the Covenants* was published. The London Confession was essentially the Westminster Confession of Faith modified by Calvinistic Baptists. Among the modifications, they not only changed the chapter on baptism, but also modified the statement regarding "good and necessary consequence": "The whole counsel of God concerning all things necessary for his own glory, man's salvation, faith and life, is either expressly set down or necessarily contained in the Holy Scripture" (1.6).[61] This change highlights an important difference between Calvinistic Baptists and Reformed theologians. There-

---

Polish Anabaptists were biblical anti-Trinitarians, in that they did not believe that the Scriptures taught the doctrine. Concerning the doctrine of the Trinity, note the rejection of the principle: "How happens it, then, that Christians commonly maintain, that with the Father,—the Son and the Holy Spirit are persons in one and the same Deity? In this they lamentably err—deducing their arguments from passages of Scripture ill understood" (*Racovian Catechism*, 1.3, 34). Cf. Muller, *Reformed Dogmatics*, 2.497; Williams, "Good and Necessary Consequence," 173.

61. *The Baptist Confession of Faith of 1689* (Carlisle: Grace Baptist Church, n.d.); cf. Timothy George, "Baptists and the Westminster Confession," in Duncan, *The Westminster Confession into the 21ˢᵗ Century*, vol. 1, 153. Some contemporary commentators see no difference between Westminster and the Second London Confession: "The phrase 'or necessarily contained in the Holy Scripture' is equivalent to the phrase in the Westminster Confession it is intended to clarify: 'or by good and necessary consequence may be deduced from Scripture.' What may be by sound logic deduced from Scripture, that is to say, what is necessarily contained in it, has the authority of Scripture itself" (Samuel E. Waldron, *1689 Baptist Confession of Faith: A Modern Exposition* [1989; Darlington: Evangelical Press, 2005], 42–43). If this is the case, why did the framers of the Baptist Confession change the language? If they meant to affirm the principle of good and necessary consequence, why not simply repeat the phrase from the Westminster Confession? Waldron's explanation seems to restore what the framers of the Baptist Confession purposefully omitted. Fred Malone's analysis of the two confessions, on the other hand, is a bit more nuanced than that of Waldron: "The *Westminster Confession of Faith* 1:6 teaches that things may be 'deduced from Scripture' by 'good and necessary consequence' when trying to determine 'the whole counsel of God.' However, that which is 'expressly set down in Scripture' is specifically distinguished by the Westminster divines from good and necessary consequence. They are not the same things. The former is instituted revelation; the latter is human deduction from instituted revelation" (Fred A. Malone, *The Baptism of Disciples Alone: A Covenantal Argument for Credo Versus Paedobaptism* [2003; Cape Coral: Founders Press, 2007], 19). Malone then contrasts Westminster with the Baptist Confession: "It is interesting as a historical matter that the early Particular Baptists, who adopted the *Westminster Confession* as their own, with modifications, left out 'by good and necessary consequence' from the identical paragraph in the *London Baptist Confession*, substituting the phrase: 'or necessarily contained in Scripture' (*LBC* 1:6). Likely they did this in order to distinguish true good and necessary consequence, which should always be limited by the containment of Scripture, from the abuse of good and necessary consequence as logical inference alone, which is used by paedobaptists to establish

fore, "good and necessary consequence" is substantively present throughout the Reformed theological corpus on the doctrine of baptism, but it became explicit in Witsius's defense of infant baptism.

Beyond questions of hermeneutics, Witsius, like Turretin, presented a number of arguments for the propriety of infant baptism:[62]

1. God gave His unchanging covenant to Abraham and to those in covenant with Him. Circumcision was given as the sign of this covenant. Believers under the new Testament are the offspring of Abraham, and therefore they are the partakers in substance of the same gracious covenant. Not only were adults partakers with the Abrahamic covenant, but so were children. Hence, the sign of the covenant should not be denied to the children of New Testament believers.

2. The Lord commanded baptism in the Great Commission. There was no need to specifically mention infants because they were commonly included among the Jews. The apostles, then, would have naturally included infants under the command to baptize.

3. In Peter's Pentecost sermon, he extended the promise of salvation to those who believe and their children (Acts 2:38–39). Moreover, Christ admitted little children into His presence and said the kingdom of God belonged to them (Matt. 16:13–15).

4. It is unjust to preclude those who are partakers of the Holy Spirit. Citing Acts 10:47, Witsius argued that infants receive the Spirit, otherwise they could not be part of the kingdom of God, and why else would they be holy (1 Cor. 7:14)?

5. Those who belong to the church have a right to baptism.

6. Baptism takes the place of circumcision (Col. 2:11–12).

Based largely on these six arguments, Witsius believed the practice of infant baptism is warranted and necessary.

Witsius closed his argument with a series of pastoral and practical observations, which was only natural given that he was a pastor for some nineteen years in four congregations before he became a professor of theology.[63] Speaking of infant baptism, he said nothing could be a greater

---

infant baptism by instituting the subjects of a sacrament never contained in Scripture" (Malone, *Baptism of Disciples*, 20).

62. Witsius, *Economy of the Covenants*, 4.16.41–46.

63. Muller, *Reformed Dogmatics*, 49.

blessing than to be devoted by pious parents to the Supreme Being, and no one could be offended unless he was resolved to renounce entirely the name of Christ and all his hopes of eternal life.[64] On the other hand, Witsius stated that it should be a great delight for godly parents to present to God and to His Christ their dearest pledges to begin to enter the light and be consecrated in the water of the mystical font. This, according to Witsius, is the first step in seeing to the piety of their child. The baptism of an infant lays on the parents the most inviolable necessity to train their children carefully in the mysteries of the Christian religion, the practice of true piety, by instruction, admonition, and good example.[65]

Additionally, Witsius saw in infant baptism the outpouring of God's love, one that echoes throughout the life of the believer:

> Here certainly appears the extraordinary love of our God, in that as soon as we are born, and just as we come from our mother, he has commanded us to be solemnly brought from her bosom, as it were into his own arms, that he should bestow upon us, in the very cradle, the tokens of our dignity and future kingdom; that he should put that song in our mouth, "thou didst make me hope when I was upon my mother's breast: I was cast upon thee from the womb: thou art my God from my mother's belly" (Psa. 22:9–10) that, in a word, he should join us to himself in the most solemn covenant from our most tender years: the remembrance of which, as it is glorious and full of consolation to us, so in like manner it tends to promote Christian virtues, and the strictest holiness, through the whole course of our lives.[66]

Not only did Witsius see great pastoral and practical value in infant baptism, it was something, as in the Lutheran tradition, that echoed throughout the life of the believer. However, in Witsius's mind, far from being a license for antinomian behavior, infant baptism was a fountain of grace for obedience.

THE SECOND LONDON CONFESSION

During the 1630s and '40s, a number of Congregationalists and Baptists who had Calvinistic beliefs departed from the Church of England. In the wake of the Westminster Confession (1646) and the Savoy Declaration

---

64. Witsius, *Economy of the Covenants*, 4.16.48.
65.. Witsius, *Economy of the Covenants*, 4.16.49.
66. Witsius, *Economy of the Covenants*, 4.16.47.

(1658), the Particular Baptist pastors and theologians who left the Anglican Church wanted to create their own confession of faith so they would be able to declare their substantial doctrinal harmony with their Presbyterian and Congregational brothers. Hence, a circular letter was distributed to Particular (or Calvinistic) Baptist churches, in contrast to General (Arminian) Baptists, in England and Wales, asking each congregation to send representatives for a meeting in London in 1677. An initial confession was written, though no ministers signed it due to persecution by the government. When William and Mary assumed England's throne in 1689, they decreed the Act of Toleration. On the heels of this decree, the Particular Baptists published their confession with the names of the pastors and theologians who had written and affirmed it. The Baptist Confession of Faith (1689) is also known as the Second London Confession.[67]

On the ordinances

The confession repeats large portions of the Westminster Confession. However, there are key modifications, especially in the chapters on the sacraments and baptism. The first key change comes in the Baptist Confession's omission of the term *sacrament*. In the chapter titled "Of Baptism and the Lord's Supper," the document states, "Baptism and the Lord's supper are ordinances of positive and sovereign institution, appointed by the Lord Jesus, the only lawgiver, to be continued in his church to the end of the world" (28.1). The Baptists preferred the term *ordinance* to *sacrament*.[68] This was likely done to distance the confession from both Roman Catholic and Reformed views of the sacraments. In one sense, this change does not necessarily reflect a significant difference, since the Westminster Standards call the sacraments "ordinances" (WCF 28.5; SC q. 92). However, there are key omissions in the Baptist Confession that evidence a decided theological shift, one that emphasizes the discontinuities between the Old Testament and New Testament in contrast to the historic Reformed emphasis on the continuities.

A key to grasping the confession's different understanding of the relationship between the testaments comes in its chapter titled "Of God's Covenant," where the covenant of grace is discussed. The confession states: "This covenant is revealed in the gospel; first of all to Adam in the promise of salvation by the seed of the woman, and afterward by farther steps, until

---

67. *Baptist Confession of Faith*, 5; George, "Baptists and the Westminster Confession," 145–52.
68. George, "Baptists and the Westminster Confession," 152.

the full discovery thereof was completed in the New Testament" (7.3). Note that the full discovery of the covenant of grace was not made until the New Testament. This statement appears to place the fulcrum on the discontinuities between the testaments. By contrast, the Westminster divines place greater emphasis on the continuities when they write concerning the covenant of grace, "This covenant was differently administered in the time of the law, and in the time of the gospel: under the law it was administered by prophecies, sacrifices, circumcision, the paschal lamb, and other types and ordinances delivered to the people of the Jews, all foresignifying Christ to come" (WCF 7.5). Of particular interest is that the divines specifically identified circumcision as an administration of the covenant of grace, which therefore connects it to baptism. The Particular Baptists did not agree with this point and therefore deemphasized the continuity between the testaments.

These differences are significant, in that the Baptist Confession deemphasizes the *historia salutis* and the unfolding nature of typology, especially as it relates to the connections between circumcision and Christ. It seems as though the framers of the Baptist Confession were so interested in showing the discontinuity between the Old Testament and New Testament that they excised any reference to typology and severed the New Testament ordinances from the Old Testament.[69] By contrast, the Westminster divines wanted to show the continuity between the Old Testament and New Testament, and saw the ordinances (or sacraments) as signs and seals of the covenant of grace: "The sacraments of the old testament, in regard of the spiritual things thereby signified and exhibited, were, for substance, the same with those of the new" (WCF 27.5). The Baptist Confession's *ordo salutis* is somewhat naked, as it is not clothed by the whole of the *historia salutis*. The ordinances have been separated from the covenant and their redemptive-historical antecedents, circumcision and the Old Testament sacrificial meals. This trend is further highlighted by the fact that baptism is not seen as a sign and seal of God's covenant (WCF 28.1) but instead as a sign of the believer's fellowship with Christ (29.1). In the Second London Confession, there is a decided move in the direction of subjectivity and away from

---

69. This trend continues in contemporary explanations, as Waldron comments: "Baptism and the Lord's Supper are not a part of the law of nature. They did not exist in the Old Testament, but came into existence with the New Covenant" (*Modern Exposition*, 339). Are there no Old Testament antecedents to these New Testament sacraments in any sense?

the objective nature of the ordinances—the traditional Reformed theme of the sacraments as God's visible Word is weakened.

On baptism

As would be expected, the Baptist Confession removes all references to infant baptism. Instead, it defines baptism in the following manner: "Baptism is an ordinance of the New Testament, ordained by Jesus Christ, to be unto the party baptized, a sign of his fellowship with him in his death and resurrection; of his being engrafted into him; of remission of sins; and of his giving up unto God, through Jesus Christ, to live and walk in newness of life" (29.1). Given this definition, the following paragraph is a logical next step: "Those who do actually profess repentance towards God, faith in, and obedience to our Lord Jesus, are the only proper subjects of this ordinance" (29.2).

Another important point to note is that the Baptist Confession omits any reference to the idea that baptism is a means of grace. The Westminster Standards state that the sacraments are means of grace, even effectual means of salvation (WCF 27.3; LC q. 155). The Baptist Confession, however, mentions nothing of the sort in its chapters on the ordinances (28) and baptism (29). It is of interest, however, that the Baptist divines were willing to acknowledge that the Lord's Supper is a source of "spiritual nourishment and growth in" Christ (30.1). Granted, the exact terminology is not employed, but this statement seems very similar to the "means of grace" language of the Westminster Confession. Why is baptism not accorded the same role? Why is it not a source of spiritual nourishment? Perhaps a modified version of the old cliché best explains the Baptist view: they have thrown out the water in their effort to toss out the baby.[70]

Concerning the question of mode, the Baptist Confession makes a unique move, in that it outright rejects sprinkling and pouring: "Immersion, or dipping of the person in water, is necessary to the due administration of this ordinance" (29.4).[71] Given that the authors of the Baptist Confession

---

70. Not all seventeenth-century Particular Baptists eschewed a sacramental understanding of baptism. While the churches dropped it from their confession, individuals like Benjamin Keach (1640–1704) embraced baptism as a means of grace. See Brandon C. Jones, "Baptist Sacramental Theology: A Covenantal Framework for Believer Baptism," (Ph.D. Dissertation, Calvin Theological Seminary, 2010), 187–210.

71. George, "Baptists and the Westminster Confession," 152. Waldron writes: "Baptism literally means to immerse and figuratively means to overwhelm. Baptism points to our being completely and spiritually immersed into Christ and overwhelmed by his Spirit. It points to

began with the Westminster Confession, this statement seems to represent a direct rejection of the parallel statement: "Dipping of the person into the water is not necessary; but baptism is rightly administered by pouring, or sprinkling water upon the person" (WCF 28.3). The Westminster Confession, on the other hand, reflects the historic consensus of the Western church back to the *Didache*: flexibility in the mode of baptism, though arguably showing a preference for sprinkling or pouring. The Baptist Confession uniquely insists on immersion, something even the early Anabaptists did not demand.[72]

CONCLUSION

This chapter began with the Westminster Standards and then returned to the Continent to survey the views of Turretin and Witsius. The Baptist Confession also served as an excellent foil, as it is an example of a confession that has elements of a Reformed soteriology wedded to a Baptist view of the sacraments. These documents and scholars continued the trends that began in the Reformation, though there was a sharpening and honing of the theologies of the sacraments and baptism. Three key developments emerged.

First, especially with the theology of Witsius, a greater emphasis was placed on redemptive history. Reformed theologians have always related the sacraments and baptism to both testaments, but it seems as though such argumentation largely stood on a few limited texts, most notably Genesis 17. Witsius extended the redemptive-historical stance by incorporating imagery from the flood and the Red Sea crossing, and connected baptism not only to the believer's union with Christ but also to the promise of resurrection and eternal life.

Second, hermeneutical differences between Reformed and Particular Baptist positions emerged. The emphasis on the discontinuities between the testaments produced a distinct Baptist doctrine of the ordinances and baptism. In the Baptist Confession, baptism is not a sign and seal of the

---

the spiritual wealth and power we possess in Christ. Nothing less than immersion or such a pouring as literally overwhelms properly symbolizes this truth" (*Modern Exposition*, 358–59).

72. Hans Denck's *Confession Before the Nuremberg Council* (1525), Balthasar Hubmaier's *A Christian Catechism* (1526), and The Schleitheim Confession (1527) mention nothing regarding the mode of baptism (see Pelikan and Hotchkiss, *Creeds*, 663–703; Hughes Oliphant Old, *The Shaping of the Reformed Baptismal Rite in the Sixteenth Century* [Grand Rapids: Eerdmans, 1992], 93).

covenant of grace but a seal of the believer's fellowship with Christ. In many respects, this shows an incompatibility between historic Reformed expressions and the Baptist expression of the relationship between God's covenants and their respective signs. At least at a technical level, it seems more appropriate to call the Baptist Confession a Particular Baptist (or Calvinistic) confession rather than a Reformed confession. As a matter of historical theology, the Baptist Confession is thoroughly monergistic and therefore in harmony with other Reformed confessions and catechisms. But the Baptist Confession omits key features that cause it to fall short of the historic Reformed tradition.[73]

Third, the surveyed documents offer glimpses of the international character of the Reformed tradition, but especially in the area of the sacraments and baptism. The Westminster divines employed the Thirty-Nine Articles and the Irish Articles as source documents. Moreover, one of the divines appealed to the French Confession, as well as to the work of Zacharias Ursinus. The Westminster Standards represent the confluence of Irish, English, German, Swiss, and French Reformed theological streams that contributed to the codification of Reformed theology in general, and a Reformed statement on the sacraments and baptism in particular. The statements on the sacraments and baptism appear to incorporate trends from Zwingli, Calvin, and Ursinus, to mention a few.[74] There are also the patristic citations and quotations that Witsius drew upon. The Reformed theology of the sacraments and baptism evidences the pan-confessional nature of the Westminster Standards.

With the completion of this survey of High Orthodox Reformed theology on the sacraments and baptism, the study can now move forward to investigate contemporary expressions. While some of the contemporary expressions owe their origins to Reformation and post-Reformation theologies, some unique and diverse treatments of the subjects surface.

---

73. On the issue of defining the Reformed identity, see R. Scott Clark, *Recovering the Reformed Confession* (Phillipsburg, N.J.: P & R, 2008), 119–92; also see Richard A. Muller, "How Many Points?" *CTJ* 28 (1993): 425–33.

74. On the international character of the Reformed tradition, see Richard A. Muller, "John Calvin and Later Calvinism: The Identity of the Reformed Tradition," in *The Cambridge Companion to Reformation Theology*, eds. David Bagchi and David C. Steinmetz (Cambridge: Cambridge University Press, 2000), 130–49.

CHAPTER 7

Baptism in Modern Theology

In the modern period, there have been several divergent and interesting contributions to the doctrines of the sacraments and baptism.[1] A number of factors make several key theologians worthwhile figures for examination. All of them come from the typical sixteenth-century streams of thought, Reformed, Lutheran, and Roman Catholic. However, these theologians were certainly not beholden to their theological traditions. In one sense or another, each of them offered distinctive contributions. These contributions were not necessarily orthodox, but given the development and integration of biblical theology with systematic theology, there were a number of helpful insights.

The chapter therefore begins with the late eighteenth century and the father of modern theology, Friedrich Schleiermacher (1768–1834), then turns to Karl Barth (1886–1968), who was arguably the most influential theologian of the twentieth century. Both Schleiermacher and Barth came out of the Reformed tradition. From there, the chapter examines the thought of Karl Rahner (1904–1984) and Edward Schillebeeckx (1914–2009), two theologians who shaped the pronouncements of Vatican II (1962–1965). Lastly, the chapter surveys the Reformed theologian Jürgen Moltmann (1926–) and the Lutheran theologian Wolfhart Pannenberg (1928–).

FRIEDRICH SCHLEIERMACHER

Friedrich D. E. Schleiermacher, like all theologians to one degree or another, was a product of the theological milieu of his day. The period of High Orthodoxy had ended nearly one hundred years before his birth. The pietism of August Hermann Francke (1633–1727) and Philip Jacob Spener

---

1. Here the term *modern* is used in its historical sense to denote post-seventeenth century theology, not in its philosophical sense, which denotes a collection of beliefs embracing an Enlightenment-influenced epistemology.

(1635–1705) influenced the theology of the day through the university they had founded at Halle. Additionally, Enlightenment rationalism had infected biblical and theological studies, such as in the biblical theology of Johann P. Gabler (1753–1826). All of these streams of thought coalesced in the theology of Schleiermacher.

Schleiermacher was trained at the University of Halle and was influenced by the philosophy of Immanuel Kant (1724–1804).[2] In the wake of Kant's closing of the noumenal realm to theological inquiry, Schleiermacher constructed his theology entirely in the phenomenal realm.[3] Schleiermacher believed that theology could be constructed only on the basis of a proper understanding of religion. As Paul Tillich explains, for Schleiermacher, "Religion is not theoretical knowledge; it is not moral action; religion is feeling, feeling of absolute dependence." Schleiermacher therefore rejected historic orthodoxy, what he called supernaturalism, but also rejected Kant's program, which he believed was rationalistic.[4]

Instead, Schleiermacher cut a middle path for his theological program, one that centered on the believer's feeling of absolute dependence on God. Schleiermacher's anthropocentrism is evident in the following statement:

> Religion does not strive to bring those who believe and feel under a single belief and a single feeling. It strives, to be sure, to open the eyes of those who are not yet capable of intuiting the universe, for every one who sees is a new priest, a new mediator, a new mouthpiece; but for just this reason it avoids with aversion the barren uniformity that would again destroy the divine abundance.[5]

---

2. John W. Riggs, *Baptism in the Reformed Tradition: An Historical and Practical Theology* (Louisville: Westminster John Knox, 2002), 90; Johann P. Gabler, "An Oration on the Proper Distinction between Biblical and Dogmatic Theology and the Specific Objectives of Each," in *The Flowering of Old Testament Theology*, eds. Ben C. Ollenburger, Elmer A. Martens, and Gerhard F. Hasel (Winona Lake: Eisenbrauns, 1992), 489–502; August Hermann Francke, *A Guide to the Reading and Study of the Holy Scriptures* (Philadelphia: David Hogan, 1823); Philip Jacob Spener, *Pia Desideria*, trans. and ed. Theodore G. Tappert (Eugene, Ore.: Wipf & Stock, 2002); cf. Justo L. González, *A History of Christian Thought* (1975; Nashville: Abingdon, 1993), 302–304, 348.

3. On the noumenal-phenomenal distinction, see Robert E. Butts, "Noumenal/phenomenal," in *A Companion to Metaphysics*, eds. Jaegwon Kim and Ernest Sosa (Oxford: Blackwell, 1995), 365.

4. Paul Tillich, *A History of Christian Thought*, ed. Carl E. Braaten (1967–68; New York: Simon & Schuster, n.d.), 392; cf. Helmut W. Ziefle, *Dictionary of Modern Theological German*, 2nd ed. (Grand Rapids: Baker, 1992), q. v. *Gefül*, 102.

5. Friedrich Schleiermacher, *On Religion*, trans. Richard Crouter (Cambridge: Cambridge University Press, 1988), 108.

This anthropocentrism is palpable in his theological work, *The Christian Faith*, though its English title is misleading. The German title is *Glaubenslehre*, literally, "the doctrine of faith."[6] He purposely did not use the word *theology*, which is the study of God; rather, his work is a description of the Christian experience as it exists in the church.[7] As one can well imagine, this anthropocentrism had a great impact on Schleiermacher's theology in general and his theology of baptism in particular.

On the sacraments

Schleiermacher's doctrine of the sacraments appears in an appendix that follows his treatment of baptism and the Lord's Supper. What accounts for this odd organization in Schleiermacher's thought? Schleiermacher was well acquainted with the history of theology and the church's employment of the term *sacrament*. He acknowledged that Ulrich Zwingli defined the term as a soldier's oath to his commanding officer.[8] Schleiermacher was willing to use the term, but he nevertheless sought to eliminate it altogether: "Hence we may well wish even more unreservedly than Zwingli did that Church terminology had never adopted the word, and also that it might be found possible to dispense with it."[9] For this reason, Schleiermacher treated the concept of the sacraments in an appendix.

Schleiermacher argues that the ordinary procedure is to begin with the doctrine of the sacraments, what he calls the "so-called general notion," and then, under this genus, treat the two species, baptism and the Lord's Supper. However, he holds that this methodology confirms "the false idea that it is a strictly dogmatic conception expressive of something that is essential to Christianity."[10] Instead, Schleiermacher structures his doctrine of the church in such a way that he merely gives six invariable features of the church: Holy Scripture, the ministry of the Word, baptism, the Lord's Supper, the power of the keys, and prayer.[11] In this respect, baptism and the Lord's Supper are part

---

6. Friedrich Schleiermacher, *Der christliche Glaube nach den Grundsätzen der evangelischen Kirche. Glaubenslehre in 4 Bänden. Aus: Bibliothek theologischer Klassiker Bde 13–16* (Perthes: Gotha, 1889).

7. Tillich, *History*, 398–99; Riggs, *Baptism*, 92; Friedrich Schleiermacher, *The Christian Faith*, trans. H. R. Mackintosh and J. S. Stewart (1830; London: T & T Clark, 2006).

8. Cf. Ulrich Zwingli, *Of Baptism*, in *Zwingli and Bullinger*, LCC, ed., G. W. Bromiley (Philadelphia: Westminster, 1953), 131.

9. Schleiermacher, *Christian Faith*, 658.

10. Schleiermacher, *Christian Faith*, 658.

11. Schleiermacher, *Christian Faith*, 586–91.

of the features of the church, not because they are sacraments—or, in terms of historic Reformed theology, signs and seals of the covenant of grace—but because they are part of Christ's ministry to the church.[12] Schleiermacher explains the nature of baptism and the Lord's Supper:

> What is common to both, let the Church name them as it may, will always be this, that they are continued activities of Christ, enshrined in Church actions and bound up therewith in the closest way. By their instrumentality He exerts His priestly activity on individuals, and sustains and propagates that living fellowship between Him and us in virtue of which alone God sees individuals in Christ.[13]

There are some important points to note in Schleiermacher's construction. First, Schleiermacher understood that Christ uses baptism and the Lord's Supper instrumentally to exert His priestly activity on individuals. This is not to say that Schleiermacher held to an *ex opere operato* view of the rites. Second, the individualistic cast to his understanding of baptism and the Supper is manifest, in that these two rites are not for the church, but for Christ to act on the individual person. Third, as previously noted, there is no covenantal cast to his understanding of the rites.

This last feature is especially prominent in his explanation of the supposed connections between the New Testament rites and their antecedent Old Testament rites. Schleiermacher believed that circumcision and the Passover had no relation to one another. He states: "It is an entirely erroneous idea, for instance, that circumcision and the Passover had any particular relation to each other, as baptism and the Supper have. Circumcision as an Abrahamic institution had no other relation to the Passover than to other Mosaic institutions."[14] This statement shows the radical difference that existed between the various covenantal administrations, according to Schleiermacher. However, he also affirmed that the work of Christ was not represented in circumcision or Passover, which was the contention of historic Reformed theology.[15] For this reason, Schleiermacher states: "It is going much too far to assert that baptism took the place of circumcision and the Supper that of the Passover. Baptism was instituted quite independently of circumcision." He goes on to write, "A comparison of the

---

12. Schleiermacher, *Christian Faith*, 658.

13. Schleiermacher, *Christian Faith*, 659; cf. David P. Scaer, "Baptism and the Lord's Supper in the Life of the Church," *CTQ* 45.1 (1981): 53, n. 8.

14. Schleiermacher, *Christian Faith*, 660.

15. Cf. WCF 7.5.

two New Testament institutions with those of the Old Testament has the very definite result of bringing out with great clearness the real difference between the old covenant and the new."[16] Though Schleiermacher acknowledged the existence of the old and new covenants, he made no effort to connect baptism and the Lord's Supper to the idea of covenant.

On baptism

Schleiermacher begins his section on baptism with a definition of the rite: "Baptism as an action of the Church signifies simply the act of will by which the Church receives the individual into its fellowship; but inasmuch as the effectual promise of Christ rests upon it, it is at the same time the channel of the divine justifying activity, through which the individual is received into the living fellowship of Christ."[17] He goes on to stipulate that a person's reception into the church and his justification or regeneration must be one and the same act.[18] At first glance, this definition and stipulation might lead the reader to believe that Schleiermacher held to an *ex opere operato* view of baptism. However, Schleiermacher thought such a view was "monstrous."[19] He writes: "One can all too easily lapse unawares into the region of magic, if regeneration be brought into connection with our particular method of administering the sacrament of baptism."[20]

How, then, did Schleiermacher explain that a person is justified or regenerated at the same time he is received into the living fellowship of Christ? Schleiermacher held that in baptism one must distinguish between the action itself and the intention with which it is performed: the action is the external side of baptism, whereas the intention is internal. This means that the external action by itself cannot produce the desired effect, and the connection between the external and internal is mediated solely by the internal. Since the external relies on the internal, along with the external there must be the preaching of the Word, which is of great importance for both the baptizer and the one baptized. Preaching expresses the intention of the church and the catechumen by explaining the rite. This means that faith in the recipient is a prerequisite if baptism is truly to represent what

16. Schleiermacher, *Christian Faith*, 660.
17. Schleiermacher, *Christian Faith*, 619.
18. Schleiermacher, *Christian Faith*, 619–20.
19. Schleiermacher, *Christian Faith*, 626.
20. Schleiermacher, *Christian Faith*, 490.

is intended.[21] However, keep in mind that Schleiermacher understood faith very differently than it has been classically and historically defined in the Reformed tradition. For Schleiermacher, faith is not trusting in the life, death, and resurrection of Christ, but rather is *das Gefül*, the absolute feeling of dependence, or God consciousness.[22]

How does this all relate to Schleiermacher's idea that a person is both baptized and justified or regenerated in one act? Schleiermacher explains that baptism "effects salvation, but only along with citizenship in the Christian Church; that is to say, only in so far as it mediates reception into the fellowship." Schleiermacher elaborates:

> Faith as an inward state of the individual is the appropriation just described, but the influence of the appropriated perfection of Christ and the enjoyment of His appropriated blessedness become real only within the fellowship of believers; hence the man in whom faith develops also has the desire to enter the fellowship. In this sense baptism as a direct reception into the fellowship of believers is also named the seal of divine grace, because the real enjoyment of grace is thereby guaranteed.[23]

Unlike typical Reformed thought, which held that a person is justified the moment he believes, for Schleiermacher, a person is not justified until he is joined to the church.

Schleiermacher contended that his understanding of baptism navigated successfully between the Charybdis of Roman Catholicism and the Scylla of Anabaptism:

> And as our paragraph only asserts the efficacy of baptism in connection with divine grace in regeneration, and thus links up the act of the Church with what is going on in the individual soul, magical conceptions are very definitely barred out. But it distinctly ascribes a saving efficacy to baptism, as the conferring of Christian citizenship, and this is a rejection of the view according to which baptism is merely an external act.[24]

Schleiermacher formulated his doctrine in such a way that baptism became a part of the *ordo salutis*, as a person is not justified until he is

---

21. Schleiermacher, *Christian Faith*, 627–29.
22. Schleiermacher, *Christian Faith*, 22–24, 68–76; cf. WCF 14.2.
23. Schleiermacher, *Christian Faith*, 631.
24. Schleiermacher, *Christian Faith*, 632.

baptized and part of the church.[25] However, Schleiermacher did avoid an *ex opere operato* view of baptism, as the one baptized already possesses faith and needs to hear the Word preached prior to his baptism. While this construction is consistent, Schleiermacher did not interact with Scripture in any fashion to build his doctrine of baptism.

Schleiermacher agreed with Augustine that the validity of baptism does not depend on the state of the heart of the one who administers baptism. However, he stipulates that the same cannot be said regarding the saving efficacy of baptism: "If the person baptizing is not a pure organ of the Church in judging of the inward state of the person baptized, the saving virtue of baptism must be impaired in every case."[26] In this way, then, baptism for Schleiermacher hinged on the internal, the inward state, a person's faith.

On infant baptism

What did this mean for Schleiermacher's understanding of infant baptism? Schleiermacher rejected the idea, propagated by some in the English and German churches, that no conversion whatsoever is needed in the case of infants born within the church, since they are already members of the body of Christ and recipients of regeneration in baptism.[27] How, then, did Schleiermacher still promote the practice of infant baptism? Schleiermacher states: "Infant baptism is a complete Baptism only when the profession of faith which comes after further instruction is regarded as the act which consummates it."[28] This is not to say that Schleiermacher believed that the practice of infant baptism was of pure origins. Instead, he thought that it was taken from early church practice and that subsequent Protestant defenses of the rite merely defended tradition.[29] Schleiermacher also argues that there is an inconsistency in the practice: "If the children are already God's possession, they have no need of baptism in order to be thus offered to God and received by Him to grace; and conversely, if they need baptism for this, the justification of its being administered to them cannot lie in the fact that already they are God's possession."[30]

---

25. Riggs, *Baptism*, 92.
26. Schleiermacher, *Christian Faith*, 633.
27. Schleiermacher, *Christian Faith*, 488–89.
28. Schleiermacher, *Christian Faith*, 633.
29. Schleiermacher cites the Augsburg Confession, the Smalcald Articles, the French Confession, and the Belgic Confession (633–34); David P. Scaer, "Luther, Baptism, and the Church Today," *CTQ* 62.4 (1998): 249–50.
30. Schleiermacher, *Christian Faith*, 635.

In spite of the perceived inconsistencies, Schleiermacher was willing to allow the rite in the church. He assumed that if confirmation was held out as the goal of infant baptism, then it was permissible, and it was the church's negligence toward confirmation that led people either to attribute magical powers to baptism or to regard it as nothing more than an external rite.[31] Schleiermacher therefore rejected Anabaptist views of theology and believed that rebaptism was justly perceived as an offense. Concerning the importance of the link between infant baptism and confirmation, Schleiermacher writes:

> Hence our paragraph, by making confirmation a part of the adminis-
> tration of baptism, lays it as a duty on the Church to give confirmation
> very close attention, in order that, so far as the Church can secure it,
> the later rite may approve itself the true and worthy consummation
> of infant baptism. It is equally unjust when confirmation is torn away
> from this context and represented as a sacrament by itself. What-
> ever we ought to think otherwise of the importance and benefit of
> confirmation, to isolate it is to render infant baptism incomplete and
> ineffectual.[32]

Given Schleiermacher's construction, one might conclude that he believed that infant baptism, so long as it was not severed from confirmation, was an authoritative and binding practice on the church. After all, according to Schleiermacher, baptism is part of the ongoing ministry of Christ to the church. This, however, would be a premature conclusion.

Schleiermacher explained that it is only when infant baptism operates *ex opere operato* that it can confer a claim relating to eternal life or death. What, then, of the difference between those infants who are baptized but do not complete their "baptismal covenant" by confirmation because they die? Is not their fate the same as that of unbaptized infants who die? In other words, does not infant baptism become a meaningless external act if the infant or child dies before his confirmation? To this dilemma, Schleiermacher responds:

> It would therefore be a natural thing to leave it to each Evangelical
> household to decide whether it will present its children for baptism
> in the ordinary way or only when they make a personal profession of
> faith; and we ought to make it known that in regard to this point we
> cancel the sentence of condemnation passed on the Anabaptists, and

---

31. Riggs, *Baptism*, 93.
32. Schleiermacher, *Christian Faith*, 636–37.

that on our side we are prepared to enter into Church fellowship with the Baptists of today, if only they will not pronounce our infant baptism absolutely invalid, even when supplemented by confirmation. On this point it should easily be possible to reach an understanding.[33]

This quote reveals a pragmatic streak running between Schleiermacher's doctrine of infant baptism and his ecclesiology. Based on the idea that infant baptism is not a binding rite, as it falls on the individual household to decide whether to bring a child forward for infant baptism, it logically follows that the church is a place where both Baptists and paedobaptists can co-exist, so long as Baptists realize that infant baptism must be completed by confirmation. On this matter, some have opined that it was Schleiermacher who introduced the concept of infant dedication to Protestant liturgies.[34] Recall, though, that Balthasar Hübmaier also promoted infant dedication.[35]

Schleiermacher's position is entirely consistent within his own system of thought, in that baptism is not ultimately based on the Scriptures, as he brings not one scriptural passage to bear in his explanation of infant baptism, but is a practice of the church. Therefore, baptism is somewhat malleable and can be adapted to bring about greater cooperation and understanding in the broader church. Moreover, baptism is not part of God's covenantal dealings with His people, but is ultimately based on the person's decision, whether before or after his baptism, to join the fellowship of the church. In this case, it logically follows that individual households can make the decision to present or not to present their infant child(ren) for baptism. Infant baptism can also be incorporated in Schleiermacher's pietistic thought because in pietism, intention and feeling are key. If infant baptism generates a greater sense of *das Gefül* in the parents who bring the infant forward for baptism, then it is a good thing. Clearly, Schleiermacher did not fear striking out on his own and creating his own unique theology of baptism.

---

33. Schleiermacher, *Christian Faith*, 637–38.

34. Bryan D. Spinks, *Reformation and Modern Rituals and Theologies of Baptism: From Luther to Contemporary Practices* (Aldershot: Ashgate, 2006), 58.

35. See Hughes Oliphant Old, *The Shaping of the Reformed Baptismal Rite in the Sixteenth Century* (Grand Rapids: Eerdmans, 1992), 93.

KARL BARTH

Barth came out of the Reformed tradition, as noted above, though some might want to argue that he was not a Reformed theologian.[36] Can Barth be Reformed when he departed from traditional Reformed teaching at so many points?[37] While this question is beyond the scope of this study, it certainly helps frame the issue of Barth's view on baptism, as Barth made a significant departure from the Reformed tradition in his understanding of baptism at multiple levels, rejecting the common understandings of the sacraments, baptism, and infant baptism.

On baptism

Barth did not take the traditional approach of viewing baptism and the Lord's Supper as the two species of a genus of sacrament. Rather, Barth rejected the idea that baptism and the Lord's Supper are sacraments. This rejection of the concept of the sacraments, especially as it is related to baptism, was something that developed in Barth's theology.[38] When he wrote on baptism in his work *The Teaching of the Church Regarding Baptism* (1943), Barth considered himself in general agreement with the traditional Reformed doctrine of the sacraments, the idea that they are signs and seals of the covenant of grace.[39] However, his son Markus Barth's (1915–1994)

---

36. This section relies on the brief but helpful survey of Barth's view in Spinks, *Theologies of Baptism*, 139–42.

37. See Carl Trueman, "Calvin, Barth, and Reformed Theology: Historical Prolegomena," in *Calvin, Barth, and Reformed Theology*, eds. Neil B. MacDonald and Carl Trueman (Milton Keynes: Paternoster, 2008), 1–26, esp. 26.

38. On the development of Barth's doctrine of baptism, see Daniel Migliore, "Reforming the Theology and Practice of Baptism: The Challenge of Karl Barth," in *Toward the Future of Reformed Theology*, eds. David Willis and Michael Welker (Grand Rapids: Eerdmans, 1999), 494–511.

39. Karl Barth, *The Teaching of the Church Regarding Baptism* (1943; Eugene, Ore.: Wipf & Stock, 2006). Jay Collier has drawn my attention to the fact that though Barth initially accepted the Reformed doctrine of the sacraments, he always placed emphasis on the discontinuities between the testaments rather than on the continuities, as the Reformed tradition has historically done. For example, Barth leaned almost exclusively on the New Testament in his formulation of baptism (Barth, *Teaching of the Church*, 42). A second observation comes from Barth's lectures on the Heidelberg Catechism, where he writes: "The church is no longer Israel, and Israel was not yet the church, although it is true that the covenant of God has this double form. But this means that the argument for infant baptism from circumcision is not valid" (Karth Barth, *The Heidelberg Catechism for Today*, trans. Shirley C. Guthrie [Richmond: John Knox, 1964], 104).

Is Baptism a Sacrament? (1951) caused the elder Barth to change his mind.[40] Barth writes:

> When my son was studying the literature available at the time, he had to tell me kindly but firmly that "not one stone was left upon another" of my 1943 work. This has been more or less my own finding too. In face of the exegetical conclusions in my son's book, I have had to abandon the "sacramental" understanding of baptism, which I still maintained fundamentally in 1943, in so far as the reference is to the work of the candidates and the community which baptizes them.[41]

How, then, did Barth characterize baptism? Why did he reject the sacramental understanding of baptism and depart from the Reformed tradition?

Barth did not believe that baptism was a sacrament, namely, that it was chiefly a divine action. Rather, he viewed it as a human rite. Barth writes:

> A man's turning to faithfulness to God, and consequently to calling upon Him, is the work of this faithful God which, perfectly accomplished in the history of Jesus Christ, in virtue of the awakening, quickening and illuminating power of this history, becomes a new beginning of life at his baptism with the Holy Spirit. The first step of this life of faithfulness to God, the Christian life, is a man's baptism with water, which by his own decision is requested of the community and which is administered by the community, as the binding confession of his obedience, conversion and hope, made in prayer for God's grace, wherein he honors the freedom of this grace.[42]

In other words, baptism is not a sacrament but a rite that indicates what has already been accomplished by the work of God through the Spirit. It is a human work and an act of obedience. Therefore, there is a sharp distinction between baptism with the Holy Spirit and water baptism by the hand of man.[43] Barth explains: "Baptism is not a sacrament, its meaning, as indicated in the preliminary thesis, is to be sought in its character as a true and genuine human action which responds to the divine act and word."[44]

---

40. Markus Barth, *Die Taufe ein Sakrament? Ein Exegetischer Beitrag zum Gespräch über die Kirchliche Taufe* (Zürich: Evangelischer Verlag, 1951).

41. Barth, CD, IV.4, x.

42. Barth, CD, IV.4, 2.

43. Spinks, *Theologies of Baptism*, 140.

44. Barth, CD, IV.4, 128.

It should be no surprise, given Barth's rejection of baptism as a sacrament, that he considered himself to be a neo-Zwinglian.[45] Barth explained that Zwingli was basically correct to identify baptism as a sacrament, according to the "original" understanding of the Latin term *sacramentum*, namely, as an oath of allegiance. Barth describes Zwingli's view as, "Baptism is the sign of loyalty which marks all members of the covenant people," and then goes on to cite Zwingli's illustration of the white cross that Swiss confederates sewed on their clothing to commemorate the battle of Nähenfels.[46] Barth also points out that the Second Helvetic Confession (1566), written by Zwingli's successor, Heinrich Bullinger (1504–1575), was a marked departure from the first-generation Swiss Reformer's understanding of baptism and the sacraments in general:

> When we read what the *Confess. Helv. Post.* (published thirty-five years after his death) has to say both about the sacraments in general and baptism in particular, we should never suspect, if we did not already know, that its author Heinrich Bullinger was Zwingli's immediate successor. This work is wholly influenced by the dominant Reformed tradition of Calvin, so much so that in the doctrine of the Lord's Supper there is even a strange attempt at assimilation to the Roman Catholic doctrine of a change in the elements.[47]

---

45. Barth, CD, IV.4, 130.

46. Barth, CD, IV.4, 129–30; Cf. Zwingli, *Of Baptism*, 131. However, even Zwingli varied the way he defined the term: "When I call the body and blood of Christ a sacrament, I mean by sacrament what was first said of it, namely that which has been instituted by the unerring sure word of God" (idem, *Exposition and Basis of the Conclusions*, in *Huldrych Zwingli: Writings*, eds. E. J. Furcha and H. Wayne Pipken [Allison Park: Pickwick, 1984], 1.102). Barth, however, can also speak of *sacrament* in a different manner: "Revelation means the giving of signs. We can say quite simply that revelation means sacrament, i.e., the self-witness of God, the representation of His truth, and therefore of the truth in which He knows Himself, in the form of creaturely objectivity and therefore in a form which is adapted to our creaturely knowledge" (CD, II.1, 52). Given this use of the term *sacrament*, Barth then goes on to write: "As this first sacrament, the humanity of Jesus Christ is at the same time the basic reality and substance of the highest possibility of the creature as such" (CD, II.1, 54). Cf. James J. Buckley, "Christian Community, Baptism, and the Lord's Supper," in *The Cambridge Companion to Karl Barth*, ed. John Webster (Cambridge: Cambridge University Press, 2000), 201–202.

47. Barth, CD, IV.4, 128; cf. Second Helvetic Confession §§ 19–21, in *Creeds and Confessions of Faith in the Christian Tradition*, eds. Jaroslav Pelikan and Valerie Hotchkiss (New Haven: Yale University Press, 2003), 2.504–14.

Given Barth's rejection of the broader Reformed understanding of baptism, which he called the "dominant" understanding, naturally he also rejected the sacramental views of Roman Catholicism and Lutheranism.[48]

Instead, Barth was firmly convinced on exegetical grounds that baptism was not in any way a divine action:

> According to what the New Testament says concerning baptism, it is highly and even supremely probably that this Christian action is not to be understood as a divine work or word of grace which purifies man and renews him. It is not to be understood as a mystery or sacrament along the lines of the dominant theological tradition. According to the New Testament, man's cleansing and renewal take place in the history of Jesus Christ which culminates in His death, and they are mediated through the work of the Holy Spirit. The New Testament does not refer to any additional or accompanying history or mediation of salvation. It mentions no duplicate of this one divine act and word.[49]

Baptism in the hands of the church is therefore a human act of obedience, but it is based on the prior divine act of baptism with the Holy Spirit. Barth explained that the word *baptism* denotes an act of cleansing that is effected on a man, and that the chief biblical concept on which baptism rests is "baptism with the Holy Ghost" (Mark 1:8; 1 Cor. 12:13; John 1:33; Acts 1:5; 11:16; 19:2ff). This is, Barth claimed, in sharp contrast to the baptism with water that men give. Barth writes: "It is thus a baptism which only God Himself, or the Son of God sent by Him, the Messiah of Israel and Savior of the world, can accomplish, which can take place in this man only directly through Him." He therefore claims, "The power of the divine change in which the event of the foundation of the Christian life of specific men takes place is the power of their baptism with the Holy Ghost."[50] Barth therefore separated Spirit and water baptism because baptism by the Spirit does not take place either with, in, or through water. Man becomes a Christian in his human decision, in that he requests water baptism, though he does not become a Christian because of his human decision or through his water baptism. Barth based his conclusion on the distinction between the human work of John the Baptist, who baptized with water, and the divine work of Jesus, who baptized with the Holy Spirit.[51]

---

48. Barth, CD, IV.4, 105; cf. Spinks, *Theologies of Baptism*, 141.
49. Barth, CD, IV.4, 128.
50. Barth, CD, IV.4, 30.
51. Barth, CD, IV.4, 32–33.

The seeds of these theological conclusions were planted long before Barth penned the final, fragmentary installment of his *Church Dogmatics*. In 1943, he defined baptism as: "In essence the representation of a man's renewal through his participation by means of the power of the Holy Spirit in the death and resurrection of Jesus Christ, and therewith the representation of man's association with Christ, with the covenant of grace which is concluded and realized in Him, and with the fellowship of His Church."[52] Barth believed that when a person is united to Christ by his baptism with the Holy Spirit, which is set forth in baptism but not effected, that person is indeed reborn into the new life of the eschaton, the age to come.[53] Barth writes:

> One does no honor to baptism by interpreting it as if it were in its essence more than the representation of the sacred history (*Heilsgeschichte*) which comes to pass between God and man in Jesus Christ. It has its full honor precisely in being in fact the most living and expressive picture of that history: the visible sign of the invisible *nativitas spiritualis* at the entrance gate of the Church and at the beginning of every Christian life.[54]

On infant baptism

Given these conclusions and his definition of baptism, it is not surprising that Barth rejected infant baptism. Though Barth was arguing from the Reformed tradition, he plainly departed from it by linking baptism not to the administration of the covenant but to the faith of the believer, as in Anabaptist theology.[55] Given this key presupposition, Barth did not believe that the Reformed Church's baptismal theology had a mere chink in its argument but a gaping hole. He writes: "The baptismal practice found in use on the basis of the prevalent teaching is arbitrary and despotic. Neither by exegesis nor from the nature of the case can it be established that the baptized person can be a merely passive instrument (*Behandelter*)."[56] While Barth's characterization of infant baptism as "despotic" might not at first make sense, one of the reasons Barth likely described the rite in this manner was because it was the practice of the state church. When a child was born into the state church, he was automatically baptized. Barth was suspi-

---

52. Barth, *Teaching of the Church*, 9.
53. Barth, *Teaching of the Church*, 12.
54. Barth, *Teaching of the Church*, 15.
55. Spinks, *Theologies of Baptism*, 142.
56. Barth, *Teaching of the Church*, 41.

cious of the *volkskirche* in all its forms, especially in light of the historical
context and the relationship between the German state church and the
Nazi government.[57]

This is not to say, however, that Barth rejected infant baptism for politico-
theological reasons alone. Barth pointed out that every occurrence of
baptism in the New Testament was the indispensable response by a person who had come to faith. In the New Testament, Barth argued, no one
is brought to baptism but rather comes to baptism.[58] Beyond this, Barth
briefly interacted with some of the traditional exegetical arguments that
the Reformed tradition has brought forward in favor of infant baptism.
Barth contended that 1 Corinthians 7:14 deals with the broader kingdom
of Christ, but does not at all indicate that children are supposed to be baptized. Concerning Acts 2:39, he said the promise of salvation for "you and
your children" merely echoes the universality of the scope of the propaga-
tion of the gospel found in the Great Commission (Matt. 28:18–19) but
does not show that children should be baptized.

Barth did acknowledge that there is a parallel between circumcision
and baptism based on Colossians 2:11–12, but he placed the weight on
the discontinuity between the rites. Barth believed that circumcision was
tied to natural birth, the sign of election of the holy lineage of Israel, and
once the Messiah was born, circumcision had achieved its goal and lost its
meaning. Moreover, the succession of those who believed in the promise
of the Messiah was in no way identical with the succession of the race and
the circumcision of its male members. In a similar fashion, those called
into the church and the new covenant do not enter based on racial succession, but only through faith in Jesus and by the baptism of the Holy Spirit.
From the New Testament standpoint, argues Barth, "It is impossible to say
that 'everyone who is born of Christian parents is born into the Christian

---

57. Spinks, *Theologies of Baptism*, 138. Cf. Bengt Hägglund, *History of Theology* (1968;
St. Louis: Concordia, 2007), 398. The Barmen Declaration, for example, cites the errors of
the "German Christians" and the "Reich Church government" (*Barmen Declaration* [1934],
in Pelikan and Hotchkiss, *Creeds*, 3.504–508). One who opposed the German state church
alongside Barth but retained the practice of infant baptism was Dietrich Bonhoeffer (1906–
1945). Bonhoeffer argued that what was needed was exercising baptismal discipline, holding
parents and children accountable for the commitment made by submitting an infant to
baptism (Dietrich Bonhoeffer, "On the Question of Baptism," in *True Patriotism: Letters,
Lectures and Notes 1939–45*, ed. Edwin H. Robertson [1958–1972; New York: Harper and
Row, 1973], 143–64; cf. Glenn L. Borreson, "Bonhoeffer on Baptism: Discipline for the Sake
of the Gospel," *Word & World* 1/1 [2006], 20–31).

58. Barth, *Teaching of the Church*, 42.

Church (*Gemeinde*).'"[59] Based on this exegesis, Barth therefore concludes: "From the standpoint of a doctrine of baptism, infant-baptism can hardly be preserved without exegetical and practical artifices and sophisms—the proof to the contrary has yet to be supplied!"[60] This statement drew a series of responses over the next twenty years from the likes of Oscar Cullman (1902–1999) and Joachim Jeremias (1900–1979), and then a counter-response in support of Barth's position from Kurt Aland (1915–1994).[61]

Though Barth claimed to be a Reformed theologian, it is difficult to call his view of the sacraments and baptism "Reformed." He had no direct link between baptism and the covenant, as he rejected the concept of the sacraments. Baptism and the Lord's Supper are exclusively human acts in his view. What the Reformed tradition holds together by the concept of the sacramental union between the sign and the thing signified, Barth radically separated. Moreover, a staple of the Reformed view of the sacraments is that baptism is initiation into the visible church, yet Barth made no attempt to coordinate baptism to the doctrine of the church in this manner. He instead constructed it along Anabaptist lines: only those who have experienced the inner baptism of the Holy Spirit can receive baptism.

KARL RAHNER AND EDWARD SCHILLEBEECKX

Karl Rahner and Edward Schillebeeckx stand out as influential figures who warrant study. Both wrote on the sacraments, building on the Roman Catholic tradition. Rahner and Schillebeeckx did not represent the magisterium; nevertheless, the Roman Catholic Church incorporated some of their doctrinal views in subsequent official teaching. Perhaps it is helpful to begin not with the views of Rahner and Schillebeeckx, but rather where they see differences between Reformed and Roman Catholic theologies of the sacraments.

---

59. Barth, *Teaching of the Church*, 43–44; cf. CD, IV.4, 184–85.

60. Barth, *Teaching of the Church*, 49.

61. Spinks, *Theologies of Baptism*, 139; Joachim Jeremias, *Infant Baptism in the First Four Centuries* (1960; Eugene, Ore.: Wipf & Stock, 2004); Oscar Cullman, *Baptism in the New Testament* (London: SCM Press, 1961); Kurt Aland, *Did The Early Church Baptize Infants?* (1961; Eugene, Ore.: Wipf & Stock, 2004); Joachim Jeremias, *The Origins of Infant Baptism: A Further Study in Reply to Kurt Aland* (1966; Eugene, Ore.: Wipf & Stock, 2004).

On the Reformed view of the sacraments

Schillebeeckx explains that Protestant and Roman Catholic terminology is only superficially similar. What accounts for the difference? Schillebeeckx argues that it is the "peculiarly Protestant theology of the Covenant" that leads to a "spirituality that is entirely different." He writes that though Calvin spoke of the sacraments containing and really giving grace, there was nevertheless a world of difference between the Calvinist and Roman Catholic interpretations of the sacraments.[62] Schillebeeckx does note, though, that while Zwingli might be justly accused of holding the view that the sacraments are *signa nuda* (bare signs), Calvin and Protestants in general have reacted against this view.[63]

Schillebeeckx rightly holds that Protestants—and by this term he seems to have those of the Reformed church in view, as he states that Lutheran views are closer to the Roman Catholic understanding—believe that the sacraments derive their power from the promise of God, which is received by faith.[64] Schillebeeckx notes that this does not mean that Reformed theologians believe the sacramental economy is purely subjective, nor is this a denial of the objective reality of the sacraments. Nevertheless, he states that this understanding is very different from the Roman Catholic view. Schillebeeckx writes:

> In the Protestant view it is impossible to speak of an objectivity in grace and sacraments which would be extrinsic to faith. "Faith" here means not "the faith of the Church" in the Catholic sense, in which a believer enters personally (for without *this* faith we too can acknowledge no saving reality: "un au-delà de la pensée est impensable"; otherwise we should be agnostics), but *fides subjecti* or the faith of the individual. Without this contact in faith with God everything would be meaningless; the sacraments would signify nothing.[65]

In the broad strokes, Schillebeeckx correctly understands that, for classic Protestant theology, the efficacy of the sacraments hinges on the presence of faith. This is in contrast to the Roman Catholic view, which maintains that the sacraments function *ex opere operato*. Moreover, Schillebeeckx understands that Protestants, such as Calvin, coordinate the sacraments with the doctrine

---

62. Edward Schillebeeckx, *Christ the Sacrament of the Encounter with God* (New York: Sheed and Ward, 1963), 185.

63. Schillebeeckx, *Christ the Sacrament*, 186.

64. Schillebeeckx, *Christ the Sacrament*, 189.

65. Schillebeeckx, *Christ the Sacrament*, 188–89.

of the covenant. That Schillebeeckx notes these differences demonstrates that he is on a different trajectory from typical Protestant views; the same can be said of Rahner, whose views were very similar to those of Schillebeeckx.

To understand why Schillebeeckx rejects the Protestant understanding of the sacraments, one must return to the Council of Trent (1547). This council, specifically in the sixth session and the decrees on justification, presented doctrinal conclusions that are very different from those of the Protestant Reformation. Reformed theologians and confessions are explicit that in the sacraments a person receives not the power of God but Christ Himself. Calvin writes, "The sacraments have the same office as the Word of God: to offer and set forth Christ to us."[66] Zacharias Ursinus also explains that in the sacraments, "The thing signified is Christ, with all his benefits."[67] The Belgic Confession states that the truth of the sacraments is Jesus Christ.[68] Likewise, the Westminster Shorter Catechism states, "A sacrament is a holy ordinance instituted by Christ; wherein by sensible signs, Christ, and the benefits of the new covenant, are represented, sealed, and applied" (q. 92; cf. LC q. 162). The Reformed view is clear: the one who uses the sacraments receives the grace of God, but the term *grace* is interchangeable with *Christ*—the believer receives Christ.

The Council of Trent, on the other hand, distinguishes the grace of God from Christ. The sixth session of the council, concerning the recipients of the sacrament, reads, "In new birth, there is bestowed upon them, through the merit of his passion, the grace whereby they are made just."[69] The infusion of grace, specifically an infused habit, enables a person to progress in his justification. Based on this construction, Roman Catholic theologians speak of created and uncreated grace. *Gratia creata sed habitus creata* ("created grace or a created habit") is a divine gift infused into the soul of a person in such a way as to become part of the human nature. *Gratia creata* is also called "justifying grace" (*gratia iustificans*) or "sanctifying grace" (*gratia sanctificans*). Created grace is distinct from *gratia increata* (uncreated grace), which is the uncreated power of God (or the Holy Spirit) that brings *gratia*

---

66. John Calvin, *Institutes of the Christian Religion*, LCC, vols. 20–21, ed. John T. McNeill, trans. Ford Lewis Battles (Philadelphia: Westminster, 1960), 4.14.16.

67. Zacharias Ursinus, *The Commentary of Dr. Zacharias Ursinus on the Heidelberg Catechism* (1852; Phillipsburg, N.J.: P & R, n.d.), 342.

68. Belgic Confession, § 33, in Pelikan and Hotchkiss, *Creeds*, 2.405–57.

69. Council of Trent, Sixth sess., chap. 3, in Philip Schaff, *Creeds of Christendom* (1931; Grand Rapids: Baker, 1991), 2.90–91.

creata into existence.[70] This is not to say that Roman Catholic theologians speak with unanimity on created and uncreated grace, but created-uncreated grace distinction reveals what lies at the heart of the rejection by Roman Catholics, and by Schillebeeckx, of the Protestant view.[71]

On the sacraments

If Schillebeeckx bases his view of the sacraments on the idea of created and uncreated grace set forth by the Council of Trent, this explains why he states, "The man Jesus, as the personal visible realization of the divine grace of redemption, is *the* sacrament, the primordial sacrament, because this man, the Son of God himself, is intended by the Father to be in his humanity the only way to the actuality of redemption." Jesus is the sacrament and His saving activity is sacramental: "For a sacrament is a divine bestowal of salvation in an outwardly perceptible form which makes the bestowal manifest; a bestowal of salvation in historical visibility."[72] While Schillebeeckx does not state it or make reference to it, it appears that he relies on Augustine's aphoristic formulation that the sacraments are visible signs of invisible grace. In this case, Christ, through His incarnation, made visible the invisible grace of God, the application of the *gratia creata* to the recipient of the sacraments. This type of formulation is not restricted to Schillebeeckx, as it is also present in Rahner: "Christ in his historical existence is both reality and sign, *sacramentum* and *res sacramenti*, of the redemptive grace of God."[73] If Christ is the sacrament of God, then both Schillebeeckx and Rahner argue that Christology is the foundation for their theology of the sacraments.

Rahner argues that since Christ is the definitive sacramental Word of God, then the church, as Christ's body, is the "continuance, the contemporary presence, of that real, eschatologically triumphant and irrevocably established presence in the world."[74] Therefore, if a person desires salvation, he must be united to the church, as it is the only place of the presence of God's saving grace.[75] In this vein, Rahner argues that the church itself is a

---

70. Richard A. Muller, *Dictionary of Latin and Greek Theological Terms: Drawn Principally from Protestant Scholastic Theology* (Grand Rapids: Baker, 1985), 134, q. v. *habitus gratiae.*

71. See Karl Rahner, ed., *Encyclopedia of Theology: A Concise Sacramentum Mundi* (London: Burns & Oates, 2004), 584–98.

72. Schillebeeckx, *Christ the Sacrament*, 15.

73. Karl Rahner, *The Church and the Sacraments* (London: Burns and Oates, 1963), 15.

74. Rahner, *Church and Sacraments*, 18.

75. Rahner, *Church and Sacraments*, 21–22.

sacrament: "The Church in her visible form is herself an intrinsic symbol of the eschatologically triumphant grace of God; in that spatio-temporal visible form, this grace is made present."[76] Schillebeeckx likewise holds that Christ makes His presence actively visible and tangible through the sacraments, through the church. Christ, argues Schillebeeckx, continues to teach in the "sacramental Church which is the visible organ on earth of the living Lord."[77] Schillebeeckx elaborates:

> We know already that this sacramental body of the Lord is the Church. We called the sacraments the specific activity of this ecclesial reality and sign. Just as Christ through his risen body acts invisibly in the world, he acts visibly in and through his earthly body, the Church, in such a way that the sacraments are the personal saving acts of Christ realized as institutional acts in the Church.[78]

This sacramental construction is the underpinning for the broader understanding of the sacraments within Roman Catholic theology.

In classic Reformation theology, Christ specifically instituted the sacraments, baptism and the Lord's Supper. Rahner, however, explains, "The institution of a sacrament can (it is not necessarily implied that it must always) follow simply from the fact that Christ founded the Church with its sacramental nature." Given the sacramental nature of the church, the seven sacraments are part and parcel of the sacramental church.[79] To this end, Schillebeeckx explains: "The people of God is built upon sacrament and word; it is founded, that is to say, upon the historical manifestation of the divine saving reality which the word manifests as a reality given to us."[80] Then, according to Rahner, the sacraments are causes of God's grace.[81] Schillebeeckx can say that through the sacraments, "The Church itself now begins to bestow on other men the Spirit it has received directly from Christ."[82]

This general theology of the sacraments found its way into the doctrinal formulations of Vatican II. For example, *Lumen Gentium* states: "All those, who in faith look towards Jesus, the author of salvation and the source of unity and peace, God has gathered together and established as the church,

---

76. Rahner, *Church and Sacraments*, 39.
77. Schillebeeckx, *Christ the Sacrament*, 41–42.
78. Schillebeeckx, *Christ the Sacrament*, 59.
79. Rahner, *Church and Sacraments*, 41–42.
80. Schillebeeckx, *Christ the Sacrament*, 169.
81. Rahner, *Church and Sacraments*, 37–38.
82. Schillebeeckx, *Christ the Sacrament*, 120.

that it may be for each and everyone the visible sacrament of this saving unity."[83] The work of the Spirit, whom Christ sent, establishes the church "as the universal sacrament of salvation."[84]

On baptism

How does baptism fit within this general sacramental theology? Rahner held that baptism is a sacrament of initiation that also commits a person to the faith of the sacred community of the Lord. He writes, "The *protestatio fidei* is from the first not the enunciation of an individual and private view of the world, but the proclamation of acceptance of the Church's belief, adherence to a belief already there and manifestly exercised in the Church, is not only one effect in fact of baptism, but is itself a sacrament, a sign of the other effects of the grace of baptism."[85] Hence, Rahner maintained that baptism leads to membership in the church, the sacramental body of Christ. Rahner stipulated, however, that baptism is not primary, even though it is the sacrament of initiation. Instead, the Eucharist brings the real presence of the body of Christ and is the sacrifice of the new covenant, and thus the Eucharist is the source of all of the other sacraments.[86]

Schillebeeckx adds to these ideas by stating that through baptism people become children of the Father through the Spirit of sonship.[87] In contrast to Reformation theology, which argues that baptism is the sign and seal of the covenant of grace and of Christ and His benefits (chiefly union with Christ), Schillebeeckx argues that baptism brings about union with the Father: "Since baptism incorporates a person into the community of the Church, even if he lacks grace—union with the Father in the power of the Spirit of sonship—a baptized person is irrevocably a child of the Father, even though a 'lost son.'"[88] Baptism into the church gives a person his share in the service that the Son of God rendered to the Father through the invisible mission of the Spirit: "In baptism and in the person baptized, that which becomes visible, though in the power of the Spirit of Christ, is

---

83. *Lumen Gentium*, no. 9, in *Vatican Council II: Constitutions, Decrees, Declarations*, ed. Austin Flannery, O.P. (New York: Costello, 1995), 15.

84. *Lumen Gentium*, no. 48, in *Vatican Council II*, 72. Cf. Gustavo Gutiérrez, *A Theology of Liberation* (1971; New York: Orbis Books, 1988), 143–48, esp. 147.

85. Rahner, *Church and Sacraments*, 87–88.

86. Rahner, *Church and Sacraments*, 82.

87. Schillebeeckx, *Christ the Sacrament*, 162.

88. Schillebeeckx, *Christ the Sacrament*, 167.

the mystery of Passover; death to sin and life unto God in Christ Jesus."[89] In other words, the baptized person becomes sacramental, as he makes God's invisible grace visible to the world: "For a person who is baptized is truly incorporated into Christ's resurrection from the dead, through the character-given commission to make this ecclesial Easter mystery visible."[90] Through baptism, individuals are initiated and incorporated into the sacramental activity of the church. In this way, according to Rahner, "Through the baptismal character a human being shares in the priesthood of Christ." No matter if a person is a schismatic or a heretic, he always retains his relationship to the church because he has been baptized.[91]

On infant baptism

Like their predecessors, Rahner and Schillebeeckx both embraced infant baptism. However, Rahner moved in a direction to emphasize that infant baptism does not truly capture the victorious nature of God's grace. He explains:

> The infusion of grace at the baptism of an infant without such acceptance in faith and works, can be left out of account here. In the first place the Church cannot primarily consist of infants; the purely objective nature of their Christianity prevents their being typical Christians. Furthermore such a grace given solely through the sacrament without the intervention of personal decision as a supernatural habitus of the theological virtues is entirely intended for personal use by the recipient, and only in that way attains the full perfection of its nature, because grace is ultimately a sharing in the actual plentitude of God's life and all merely habitual grace is only rightly to be understood as the ontological presupposition of that life.[92]

This means that if the church is the historical sacrament of the victorious grace of God, the highest actualization of that grace is tangibly manifest in the life of an individual through his sanctification.

In this broader stream of thought, Schillebeeckx explains, "A sacrament is essentially realized for a particular individual."[93] If aimed at the individual, a sacrament can also "be seen as a reaching out in faith and love to take

---

89. Schillebeeckx, *Christ the Sacrament*, 162.

90. Schillebeeckx, *Christ the Sacrament*, 163.

91. Rahner, *Church and Sacraments*, 90. This is also the view of proponents of the so-called Federal Vision (see Douglas Wilson, *"Reformed" Is Not Enough: Recovering the Objectivity of the Covenant* [Moscow. Ida.: Canon Press, 2002], 13–20).

92. Rahner, *Church and Sacraments*, 77.

93. Schillebeeckx, *Christ the Sacrament*, 108.

hold of Christ's redemption."[94] Hence, a sacrament can be fully realized only if there is a positive response on the part of the recipient to the sacramental encounter with Christ, the response that manifests the recipient's desire for grace in the visibility of the ecclesial symbolic act.[95] Schillebeeckx applies this to his understanding of infant baptism and argues that it must be completed by confirmation.

Schillebeeckx makes an analogy between Christ and the baptized infant:

> Thus if confirmation is called the sacrament of Christian maturity, we must understand this not so much in the sense of human, biological or even psychological maturity, but rather as an aspect of saving history; just as Christ became Messiah to the full through his resurrection and exaltation by the Father's side and through his establishment as human sender of the Spirit, so too the baptized child of the Father becomes an adult Christian with his establishment in power through confirmation. From this it is clear that there can be no objection to giving the sacrament to infants and young children. For they will have within themselves the principle enabling them to act as children of God established in power when they develop psychologically.[96]

Keep in mind that Schillebeeckx's understanding of infant baptism is based on standard Roman Catholic dogma: in baptism, apart from faith, the recipient receives the infused created grace of God. This baptismal grace can be lost. Nevertheless, if a person perseveres and cooperates with the grace of God, he can grow and complete his baptism through confirmation, though even this does not assure a person of his salvation. To this end, Schillebeeckx writes: "From the moment a man is baptized, throughout the rest of his life, the character of baptism keeps exercising its infallible function, although other sacraments are needed to remove fresh obstacles that may arise and so to reconcile man with God again."[97] What other sacraments would be needed? The eucharist, confirmation, and reconciliation would undoubtedly top the list.

The sacramental theology of Rahner and Schillebeeckx is built on the foundation of the Council of Trent, particularly on ideas of created grace. In this respect, it is important to see that Roman Catholic theol-

---

94. Schillebeeckx, *Christ the Sacrament*, 134.
95. Schillebeeckx, *Christ the Sacrament*, 153.
96. Schillebeeckx, *Christ the Sacrament*, 165–66.
97. Schillebeeckx, *Christ the Sacrament*, 173.

ogy has an entirely different orbit than typical Protestant, and especially Reformed, theology. For Rahner and Schillebeeckx, the sacraments rotate on an ontological axis of transformation through created grace, whereas for historic Reformed theology, as Schillebeeckx points out, the sacraments rotate around the doctrines of Christ and covenant. Reformed theology has a covenantal view of grace, which is focused on Christ Himself, not created grace. This is especially evident in that Rahner and Schillebeeckx held to an *ex opere operato* view of baptism. However, it seems fair to say that both continued in the contemporary trend of highlighting the individual's experience, insofar as habitual grace finds its full expression only in an adult.

JÜRGEN MOLTMANN

Jürgen Moltmann is one of the better-known contemporary Reformed theologians. In many respects, Moltmann is quite conversant with both the history of doctrine and contemporary theology and philosophy. Nevertheless, as has been the trend in the contemporary period, while Moltmann is indebted to the Reformed tradition, he is not averse to departing from it. His departure from traditional Reformed theology is notable in his understanding of the sacraments, as well as his rejection of infant baptism.

On the sacraments

Like Schleiermacher, Moltmann critically engages the traditional understanding of the term *sacrament*. He is aware of the general concept of the term, namely, that the sacraments are means of grace.[98] However, Moltmann explains the developments that came through theologians such as Rahner and Barth, who defined Christ as the primal sacrament.[99] In light of these developments, Moltmann is aware that the use of the term has come into question, as is evident in the work of Schleiermacher, Otto Weber (1902–1966), and Pannenberg.[100] Along similar but not identical lines, Moltmann strives to interpret the two events of baptism and the Lord's Supper, which

---

98. Jürgen Moltmann, *The Church in the Power of the Spirit: A Contribution to Messianic Ecclesiology* (1975; Philadelphia: Fortress, 1993), 199.

99. Moltmann, *Church*, 200–201. Cf. Rahner, *Church and Sacraments*, 18; Barth, CD, II.1, 54.

100. Cf. Schleiermacher, *Christian Faith*, 657–60; Otto Weber, *Foundations of Dogmatics* (1955; Grand Rapids: Eerdmans, 1981), 2.592–94; Wolfhart Pannenberg, *Systematic Theology* (1993; Grand Rapids: Eerdmans, 1998), 3.336–69.

are constitutive for the church, according to what they have in common rather than seeing them as species of the broader genus of the sacraments. Moltmann places baptism and the Lord's Supper in the broader context of the "means of salvation" and "ministries" of the church so he can explain their reality and efficacy as comprehensively as possible.[101]

Based on this presupposition, Moltmann expounds the doctrine of the sacraments by tracing the history of the term. He acknowledges that the term does not occur in the New Testament but is the Latin translation of the Greek New Testament term μυστήριον ("mystery"). A mystery is a hidden secret of God that is subsequently revealed in the eschaton.[102] The revelation of divine mysteries finds its climax in the revelation of God in Christ, which is an eschatological event. Moltmann explains:

> Through the proclamation of Christ and the faith of Gentiles, the eschatological mystery of the summing up of the cosmos in Christ becomes manifest. The revelation of the eschatological divine secret (*apokalypsis*) takes place in veiled and hidden form, out of faith to faith, in the struggle between those who love God and the lords of the world; and it proclaims the coming glorification of believers and the consummation of God's decree of salvation.

In this way, Moltmann argues that the term *mystery* embraces Christology, because Christ is the supreme revelation of God; pneumatology, because the mystery is revealed through the Holy Spirit; ecclesiology, because the church is the locus of the revelation of God in Christ through the Spirit; and eschatology, because the revelation of the mystery coincides with the eschatological work of the Messiah and the Spirit.[103]

From this framework, Moltmann redefines baptism and the Lord's Supper not as sacraments but as emblematic revelations of Christ. Moltmann writes:

> In the eschatological gift of the Holy Spirit "word and sacrament," "ministries and charismata" become comprehensible as revelations of Christ and his future. As the emblematic revelations of Christ they are the messianic mediations of salvation. As glorifications of Christ they are actions of hope pointing towards the kingdom. In the framework of the trinitarian concept of the sacraments we therefore understand the proclamation, the "sacraments" and the charismata as the "signs

---

101. Moltmann, *Church*, 386–87.
102. Moltmann, *Church*, 202.
103. Moltmann, *Church*, 203–204.

and wonders" of the history of the Spirit who creates salvation and brings about new creation, and who through Christ unites us with the Father and glorifies him.[104]

Under the more expansive term of *mystery*, Moltmann includes the preaching of the Word, the "sacraments," baptism and the Lord's Supper, and the gifts of the Spirit. Keep in mind, however, that Moltmann still gives primacy to the preaching of the Word, as in traditional Reformed theology, which is evidenced by the fact that he places "proclamation" as the first "messianic mediation of salvation." He does this because "proclamation of the Word can take place without baptism and the Lord's supper; but the latter cannot take place without the proclamation of the Word."[105]

On baptism

With this understanding of the emblematic revelations (sacraments), Moltmann goes on to discuss the meaning and significance of baptism. He anchors the meaning of baptism in the eschatological understanding of baptism and the gospel of Christ.[106] What does Moltmann mean by this? The term *gospel* has been freighted by a didactic and doctrinal understanding. In other words, for many, the gospel is what a person must believe in order to be saved. However, Moltmann explains that the term originates not in the New Testament but in the so-called prophecy of deutero-Isaiah. The prophecy speaks of the last days (the eschaton), when God would lead His people on a final and last exodus. Before this would happen, the messenger would come to announce the rule of God and the liberation of His people. Moltmann writes:

> As he announces the rule of God and the liberation of man, and with them the eschatological era, his joyful message puts this era into effect and is, like the word of creation at the beginning, the word that creates the era of salvation. The new era begins for the world of the nations as well. The rule of Yahweh is proclaimed and the wonders of his liberation are praised among the Gentiles. The vision of the pilgrimage of the nations to Zion (Isa. 60:6) and the glorifying of Yahweh by the Gentiles shows the universality of hope in the "one who brings good tidings" in the last days.[107]

---

104. Moltmann, *Church*, 205–206.
105. Moltmann, *Church*, 200.
106. Moltmann, *Church*, 235.
107. Moltmann, *Church*, 216.

Observe how Moltmann sees the gospel as the proclamation of the eschaton, which centers on the work of Christ and the Spirit. This is the message that the gospel proclaims as mystery, as apocalyptic revelation.

When joined to Moltmann's concept of the "sacraments," this eschatological gospel creates the context that leads him to say that through baptism believers are publicly set within the fellowship of Christ. In this vein, he states that baptism is "a sign bound up with the gospel which is also the public sign of life of the Holy Spirit, who unites believers with Christ and brings about the new creation."[108] Baptism publicly sets the believer within the church. This means that baptism is the "sacrament of initiation and the door of grace," and believers are "accepted into the covenant of grace through baptism."[109] Moltmann further coordinates baptism with the work of the Holy Spirit by arguing that it is founded on Easter—as believers experience the Holy Spirit together with the proclamation of the gospel, they are baptized into the name of Christ, the Lord of the coming kingdom. Christian baptism is eschatology put into practice.[110] Moreover, baptism is also a call, in that through it the believer is called into the messianic community and is called to liberating creative service for the kingdom.[111]

While affirming these things, Moltmann carefully delineates the relationship between baptism and the *ordo salutis*. He stipulates, "The justification of the sinner and prevenient grace come about when a person believes, not directly at baptism."[112] This means that Moltmann rejects the Roman Catholic understanding of baptism. He writes:

> Baptism points to the liberation of man which took place once and for all in the death of Christ. At the same time it reveals the crucified Lord's claim to new life and anticipates in man the future of God's universal glory. In this context there can be no talk about the efficacy of baptism *ex opere operato*. Baptism is efficacious *ex verbo vocante*. Its word of promise is the word through which it calls. But the calling gospel is a call to faith, to the new obedience or righteousness, to freedom and to hope. It is hence perceived by faith and laid hold of in hope. It is a creative event, but it creates nothing without faith. In so

---

108. Moltmann, *Church*, 226.
109. Moltmann, *Church*, 227.
110. Moltmann, *Church*, 235.
111. Moltmann, *Church*, 238.
112. Moltmann, *Church*, 230.

far as faith is a call, baptism is necessary. But we cannot say that it is necessary for salvation.[113]

Moltmann therefore does not link baptism to the *ordo salutis*, but instead hinges his soteriology on the necessity of faith in the one who is baptized.

On infant baptism

Given what Moltmann has outlined thus far, he broadly falls within Protestantism on his understanding of baptism, but he does not fear departing from the Reformed tradition. This willingness is evident not only in his understanding of the "sacraments," but also in his rejection of infant baptism. Like Barth before him, Moltmann has reservations about infant baptism largely because of its associations with the state church of Germany and the broader idea of "Christendom." He states: "Infant baptism is without any doubt the basic pillar of the *corpus christianum*, the 'Christian society' which acknowledges—or at least does not reject—Christianity in the widest sense of the word as its tradition. Through baptism 'Christian society' regenerates itself in the bond that links one generation to another."[114] Moltmann therefore sees a need to separate the church from Christendom, which he sees as perpetuated by infant baptism. This is not to say, though, that Moltmann bases his rejection of infant baptism on dogmatic grounds alone. He also admits that children are not baptized apart from faith, as the parents who bring the children themselves have faith. Moltmann also evidences a fair familiarity with the historic biblical arguments in favor of the practice.[115]

Nevertheless, Moltmann explains, "The perpetual actualization of the New Testament continually calls this practice in question."[116] He instead argues that the way forward to a new and more authentic baptismal practice is to move away from infant baptism to adult baptism. By adult baptism, he refers to those who are called, confess their faith, and believe. He is in favor of allowing the time for a child's baptism to be decided by the parents, and believes baptism should not be forced on them by the church. In addition, he suggests that ministers should preach about baptism, not merely at a baptismal service, but even on other occasions so that people will better

---

113. Moltmann, *Church*, 240.
114. Moltmann, *Church*, 229.
115. Moltmann, *Church*, 230–32.
116. Moltmann, *Church*, 228.

understand the rite.[117] In this way, parents can carry out their messianic responsibility, as they are missionaries and evangelists to their children. However, Moltmann is quick to point out, "Children are not foundlings, so to speak, shut out from their parents' faith and condemned to find it for themselves."[118] To highlight this messianic function of the parents, Moltmann suggests that infant baptism should be replaced by infant dedication in the worship service as an "ordination" of the parents and the congregation for their messianic service to the children. Lastly, he suggests that confirmation classes, which ordinarily prepare a baptized child for admission to the Lord's Supper, should instead be directed toward baptism.[119]

Given these points, one might assume that Moltmann is a Baptist. While he leans in this direction, Moltmann himself sees some distinct differences between his rejection of infant baptism and Baptist theologies of the rite. Moltmann explains that Baptist theologies, what he calls "voluntary baptism," can lead to "inner emigration and resignation in the face of the 'wicked world.'" In other words, Moltmann sees voluntary baptism as leading to an individualistic view of the church, one in which the person withdraws from the world and folds in on himself. Instead of this inner emigration, Moltmann maintains that baptism liberates a person from his former familial, national, and societal bonds so that he can serve others in the missionary task of the church. In this way, "Baptism joins a fragmentary and incomplete human life with the fullness of life and the perfect glory of God."[120] The one who is baptized therefore becomes a part of the church, the community. Moltmann sees that this then leads to a democratization of the ministry of the church: "It must stop being a church of ministers functioning on behalf of laymen, and become a charismatic fellowship in which everyone recognizes his ministry and lays hold on his charisma. People then become 'subjects' within the church, losing their positions as objects of religious welfare." Moltmann warns, however, that the same individual inner emigration can occur at a corporate level and the community can become an introverted group in a "self-made ghetto." Moltmann finally distinguishes his view of baptism from Baptist theologies by stating, "A

---

117. Moltmann, *Church*, 240.
118. Moltmann, *Church*, 229.
119. Moltmann, *Church*, 240–41.
120. Moltmann, *Church*, 241.

liberal church may make adult baptism 'voluntary.' A church of liberation lives from baptism as liberating event. That is something different."[121]

Moltmann's understanding of the sacraments and specifically of baptism certainly evidences the overriding concern of eschatology. In many respects, this is a step in the right direction, as eschatology has often been left to the end of many Protestant theological systems. However, it also seems that this concern for eschatology pushes Moltmann in the direction of rejecting the traditional understanding of the sacraments and influences him to define them in terms of *mysteries*.

WOLFHART PANNENBERG

A similar pattern appears in the sacramental theology of Pannenberg, another Lutheran theologian. Like Moltmann, Pannenberg's theology of the sacraments is colored by his understanding of eschatology, as well as a willingness to depart from traditional Lutheran views. This does not mean, though, that Pannenberg is a carbon copy of Moltmann. Pannenberg has distinct views on the subjects under consideration.

On the sacraments

In similarity to Schleiermacher, Barth, and Moltmann, Pannenberg rejects the term *sacrament*, though unlike the former, he spends a great deal of space explaining why he does so. He writes, "Baptism and the Supper are significatory acts, 'signs of the nearness of God.'" Pannenberg argues that he rejects the word *sacrament* because the term μυστήριον does not fit the bill when one considers that in the New Testament "Jesus Christ is the quintessence of the mystery of God and his will."[122]

Like Schleiermacher, in a section that follows his exposition of baptism and the Lord's Supper, Pannenberg gives detailed reasons for his rejection of the term.[123] He explains that the traditional Reformation view that restricts the sacraments to things expressly instituted by Jesus withers in the wake of the findings of historico-critical exegesis. According to Pannenberg, as it currently stands, one can speak only of an express command for the Supper.[124] Pannenberg bases this conclusion on the evidence that Mark

---

121. Moltmann, *Church*, 242.
122. Pannenberg, *Systematic Theology*, 3.238.
123. Cf. Schleiermacher, *Christian Faith*, 657–60.
124. Pannenberg, *Systematic Theology*, 3.340.

16:16 is not found in the oldest Greek manuscripts and was likely added in the second century, long after Mark's Gospel was penned. He claims that this points only to the idea that the second-century church traced baptism back to the dominical command, not that it was actually part of Mark's Gospel. He also believes that Matthew 28:19 is a late addition to Matthew's Gospel, though he admits that Matthew traced baptism back to the command of Jesus. However, he is unsure whether Matthew merely gives a literary presentation or a genuine claim relating to the historical origins of baptism.[125] Based on this evidence, Pannenberg concludes, "As regards the special tradition in Matt. 28:19 it is hard to maintain, in face of the total witness of the New Testament, that the risen Lord instituted baptism as something the church must do."[126] He also writes, "We cannot find solid biblical support for the demand that a sacrament must have its origin in an act of institution by God in Jesus Christ, or in a *mandatum Dei*."[127]

A second reason Pannenberg gives for his rejection of the term is that the New Testament does not call baptism or the Lord's Supper μυστήριον.[128] He explains that Paul could speak in the plural of the "mysteries of God," of which he was a steward (1 Cor. 4:1), but he believes that it is anachronistic to see this as a reference to baptism and the Lord's Supper. Rather, the word *mysteries* refers to parts of God's historical plan, which is comprehensively summed up in Jesus Christ and has been proleptically revealed in Him. Pannenberg illustrates this point by appeal to 1 Corinthians 10:4 and argues that the mysteries were formerly revealed in types in the Old Testament, such as the rock Moses struck to give water to the people (Ex. 17:6) or the manna from heaven, which pointed not to the Lord's Supper but to Christ.[129] In his understanding of *mystery*, Pannenberg shows how marriage is identified as such by Paul (Eph. 5:32; cf. Gen. 2:24).

A third reason Pannenberg rejects the word *sacrament* is that the doctrine of the sacraments is based on the theology of Augustine, and Augustine was influenced too much by Platonism. According to Pannenberg, Augustine was inclined to believe that all things had a significatory function, or significance beyond themselves relative to God and His plan of salvation. In Augustine's Platonic worldview, argues Pannenberg, the visible world

---

125. Pannenberg, *Systematic Theology*, 3.276.
126. Pannenberg, *Systematic Theology*, 3.340.
127. Pannenberg, *Systematic Theology*, 3.368.
128. Pannenberg, *Systematic Theology*, 3.340.
129. Pannenberg, *Systematic Theology*, 3.346.

has a function of pointing and leading to the invisible reality of God. Given this pattern of thought, Augustine's view of the sacraments as visible signs of God's invisible grace therefore corrupted his understanding of baptism and the Lord's Supper.[130]

Beyond these reasons, Pannenberg believes it is much too restrictive to see the mystery of Christ only in the two actions of baptism and the Lord's Supper. He asks, "Or does it find comparable significatory manifestation in other acts or states of life in the church?" What other acts does Pannenberg have in mind? He suggests that Jesus is present in the actions of the church in works of mercy (Matt. 25:35–37), evangelization, or healings (Mark 11:4–5), which are signs of the presence of salvation characterizing the presence of Jesus.[131] Beyond this, Pannenberg also sees a "sacramental" quality to marriage, as marriage is a "sacrament" because it points to the relationship between Christ and the church.[132] For these reasons, then:

> If Jesus Christ himself is the quintessence of the divine mystery of salvation, individual parts of the divine plan could also come to be called mysteries: the temporary hardening of Israel for the sake of the Gentile mission, but also the typological prefiguring of the saving mystery of Christ and his church by the creation of humans in two sexes and finally, though only after biblical times, the presence of Christ to believers at the Lord's Supper and baptism.

Accordingly, Pannenberg calls baptism and the Lord's Supper "significatory acts," but this does not mean he completely dismisses the term *sacrament*. He concludes: "The best course for theology is to let the term 'sacrament' keep its many meanings. It should not insist on too narrow a usage."[133]

On baptism

From this framework, Pannenberg sets forth his doctrine of baptism. He believes that, according to the New Testament, "the event of regeneration of believers takes place in baptism."[134] Pannenberg explicitly relates the *ordo salutis* directly to baptism. He believes that both sides of the confessional divide, Protestant and Roman Catholic, have serious defects in

---

130. Pannenberg, *Systematic Theology*, 3.349; cf. Augustine, *City of God*, 10.5, in NPNF[1] 2.183.
131. Pannenberg, *Systematic Theology*, 3.355.
132. Pannenberg, *Systematic Theology*, 3.361–62.
133. Pannenberg, *Systematic Theology*, 3.364.
134. Pannenberg, *Systematic Theology*, 3.237.

their understanding of baptism and especially its relationship to justification. Pannenberg argues that Trent did not pay sufficient attention to the decisive significance of faith, while Protestants, specifically Martin Luther, did not pay enough attention to the relationship between baptism and justification.[135]

In opposition to these views, Pannenberg claims that one must examine Paul's vocabulary of justification alongside the New Testament accounts of the believer's participation in salvation, especially as it relates to regeneration and adoption. Pannenberg sees no reason to subordinate regeneration or adoption to justification. He therefore writes:

> We might do this best if we remember that each of them has a relation to baptism. In baptism there takes place our regeneration by the Holy Spirit. Baptism is the basis of the adoption of believers as God's children (Gal. 3:26–27; cf. John 1:12–13). Baptism relates to hope of the inheritance of eternal life (1 Pet. 1:3–4), which for Paul too, is part of belonging to God's family (Gal. 4:6–7; Rom. 8:17). The word of the righteousness of faith also relates to baptism (Gal 3:24–26; cf. Titus 3:7). Baptism is thus the common reference point for all these theological interpretations. The declaring righteous of those who are linked to Jesus Christ by baptism and faith has only a partial function in descriptions of the event, or its result, that is elsewhere called regeneration.[136]

For Pannenberg, baptism is part of the *ordo salutis*, though it is probably accurate to say that he holds a mediating position between Roman Catholic and Protestant views, as he emphasizes the importance of faith. Pannenberg stresses, "Baptism and faith belong together." He writes: "Faith fellowship with the destiny of the crucified and risen Lord (Phil. 3:9–11) is established by baptism. At the same time 'coming' to faith and its righteousness (Gal. 3:23–24) culminates in the event of baptism because baptism mediates participation in the filial relation of Jesus to the Father." Hence, baptism is the seal of faith.[137]

Beyond questions of the *ordo salutis*, baptism also is "an act that constitutes the new existence of Christians" as those who have been joined to the body of Christ. Baptism, argues Pannenberg, "is the basis of church membership." He writes that baptism is a church action and, "Whether it be given by ordained ministers or in exceptional cases by any Christian, those

---

135. Pannenberg, *Systematic Theology*, 3.234.
136. Pannenberg, *Systematic Theology*, 3.235.
137. Pannenberg, *Systematic Theology*, 3.257.

who administer baptism always give it in the name of the church as the comprehensive fellowship of all Christians that gains a new member by the act of baptism."[138] If baptism is the basis of church membership, baptism in the name of Jesus—or, by ancient church custom, in the name of the triune Lord—is an act of transfer. The one who is baptized is no longer his own but belongs to God (Rom. 6:10) or Christ (Rom. 7:4).

Thus, baptism must be understood as a seal (2 Cor. 1:22). This seal is "a distinguishing mark [that] will also assure the baptized of eschatological deliverance at the coming world judgment, a sign of their election and hope."[139] Believers are delivered from the world judgment because the recipients are united to Christ, buried with Him in the enacted sign of baptism. However, baptism also has significance not merely for future deliverance but for the present, in that there is a relation between baptism and the recipient's earthly life. "The story of the life of Jesus between his own baptism and death," writes Pannenberg, "is something that what is anticipated in the sign of baptism is to imitate. In terms of baptism the Christian life is a process of dying with Christ, and at the same time, by the Spirit, the new humanity, the resurrection life, is already at work in Christians (Rom. 6.9ff)."[140]

On infant baptism

Based on what Pannenberg has written on baptism, one might conclude that he would naturally be opposed to infant baptism. This is a premature conclusion. Pannenberg traces infant baptism through early church history all the way through Barth's criticism and rejection of the practice.[141] He argues that baptism is not merely a human act, but at its core is a divine action on the recipient. Pannenberg writes, "To be baptized in the name of God is to be baptized not by others but by God himself, so that even though others administer it, it is truly God's own work."[142] However, Pannenberg sets himself apart from Roman Catholicism and even to some extent from the later Lutheran tradition by stipulating that baptism does not bring salvation without faith. It always relates somehow to the faith of the baptized,

---

138. Pannenberg, *Systematic Theology*, 3.237.
139. Pannenberg, *Systematic Theology*, 3.239.
140. Pannenberg, *Systematic Theology*, 3.243.
141. Pannenberg, *Systematic Theology*, 3.257–60.
142. Pannenberg, *Systematic Theology*, 3.260–61.

but one's faith does not make baptism effectual—faith receives baptism. This is true even when faith and confession precede baptism.[143]

Pannenberg understands baptism as a divine gift, which means that its reception is not tied to a specific stage of human judgment or decision, and presupposes the absence of opposition. Pannenberg asks, Are adults really in a totally different situation from infants when it comes to vouching for the absolute certainty of their own profession of faith? Do adults bring more than a positive willingness?[144] Pannenberg therefore concludes: "In sum we may say that at the baptism of children, especially at the baptism of the children of Christian parents, will and judgment may not yet have developed, but we have to reckon with a positive readiness for unlimited trust whose real object, even if infants do not yet know it, is the true God who has revealed himself in the sending of Jesus."[145]

Once again, the overriding concern of eschatology is present in Pannenberg's understanding of the sacraments and baptism. This concern, like that of Moltmann, pushes Pannenberg in the direction of defining the sacraments as mysteries. In understanding the sacraments in this manner, he broadens the number of sacraments from two (baptism and the Lord's Supper) to include a number of the church's activities, even marriage. It appears that there is a significant convergence between contemporary Roman Catholic and Protestant theologies of baptism in Pannenberg.

CONCLUSION

In this survey of contemporary theologies of baptism, we have seen several notable trends. The first is the impact of pietism. A number of the theologians surveyed moved away from infant baptism. This is partially, though not completely, linked to the greater emphasis on personal experience. Infants, of course, are incapable of this experience, and therefore are not proper subjects of baptism. This is a decided departure from both the classic Protestant treatments, whether the Lutheran emphasis on the promise of God or the Reformed emphasis on the covenant signs and seals, both being reflective of divine action.

---

143. Pannenberg, *Systematic Theology*, 3.261.
144. Pannenberg, *Systematic Theology*, 3.262.
145. Pannenberg, *Systematic Theology*, 3.263.

A second trend is either the absence of Scripture or a low view of Scripture in the theological expositions of those surveyed. Most of those surveyed made little to no effort to interact with Scripture and instead set forth their views as dogma, which in one sense is understandable, given the influx of rationalism. When Pannenberg does bring Scripture to bear, it is often through the lens of historico-critical exegesis. In the case of Moltmann, it seems odd that he would ostensibly reject the practice of infant baptism because of the absence of New Testament precedent but then advocate the institution of another unbiblical practice in its place, infant dedication.

A third trend is the rejection of the term *sacrament*. This runs through all of the theologians surveyed. What unites them is the manner in which they defined the term, though this does not seem to be reflected in Schleiermacher's methodology. All except Schleiermacher defined the term in light of the Latin Vulgate's underlying Greek term, *mystery*. From there, they broadened the concept of the sacrament to include Christ, the church, and a host of the church's "activities." Yet such a methodology fails to account for the redemptive-historical character of the sacraments—in Reformed terms, the sacraments as signs and seals of the covenants. In other words, to define a sacrament as a mystery based on the Latin translation of Ephesians 5:32 fails to account for God's revelation of Christ in covenant.

These trends and developments, as well as the rest of the history of the doctrine of the sacraments and baptism, merit interaction and critique. However, this engagement should not begin with the positive construction of the document but with setting baptism in its redemptive-historical context. Baptism must be defined in terms of its historical and progressive unfolding through redemptive history; it must be traced from Genesis to Revelation. Setting the parameters of baptism in this manner not only will help one have a richer understanding of the rite, it will ground the positive construction not in a theological system but in divine revelation.

Summary of Part I

Part I surveyed the history of the doctrine of baptism. This survey revealed observations that inform what issues must be addressed in the positive construction of the doctrine.

Soteriology and the sacrament. What is the relationship between soteriology and baptism? On one end of the spectrum are the views of the ancient church, which ascribe regenerative powers to the water of baptism; these views are largely repeated and refined in the proclamations of the Council of Trent. On the other end of the spectrum are the views of Zwingli and the Anabaptists, who argued that baptism is merely a person's pledge-oath to God. In between lie the views of Luther and Calvin, who argued that baptism conveys grace, though that grace is hinged on the presence of faith.

Redemptive history and baptism. In the early periods of church history, theologians largely explicated doctrine vis-à-vis the individual and the *ordo salutis*, though at times Patristic and medieval theologians made connections to the *historia salutis*, either through typology, such as Tertullian's identification of the waters of Genesis 1:2 as a type of the waters of baptism, or medieval connections between circumcision and baptism. In the Reformation, however, the incidental connections to the Old Testament became more explicit as the Reformers explained and defended the doctrine of infant baptism as well as the unity of the church by drawing on the covenants and the signs thereof. The connections to redemptive history and particularly the administration of God's covenants, however, largely dropped out in the modern period with the theology of Schleiermacher and arguably in Barth, who identified baptism as exclusively a human action. Baptism was reconnected to redemptive history—especially with regard to eschatology—in the theology of Herman Witsius, but also in the constructions of Moltmann and Pannenberg. How does redemptive history factor into the construction of the doctrine? Should the doctrine begin with the New Testament or with the Old Testament at Genesis 1:2? Baptism must also be coordinated with the doctrine of the covenant.

Recipients. It appears that infant baptism was practiced in the earliest days of the church, though some objected, such as Tertullian. Infant baptism largely went unchecked until the Reformation and the writings of the Anabaptists. Since that time, the Anabaptists and General and Particular Baptists have rejected infant baptism as unbiblical, seeing it as a practice that the Reformers failed to reform. The question remains: Do Baptists have a legitimate objection?

Mode. Historically, there is a relative openness from a number of different periods in the church and from theologians from all of the various theological camps, Patristic, medieval, Reformation, and post-Reformation, Lutheran, early Anabaptist, and Reformed. All are in relative agreement regarding the propriety of a number of modes of baptism, immersion, pouring, or sprinkling, and single or threefold forms. The standout exception is the position of Particular Baptists and later Anabaptists, who argued that immersion is the only legitimate mode of baptism. A positive formulation of the doctrine must determine whether the common acceptance of all three modes is correct or whether the insistence on immersion-only baptism is more biblical.

PART II

Biblical-Theological Survey
of the Doctrine

Introduction to Part II

A historical study of baptism is an important way to begin the study of the doctrine. However, doctrine ultimately cannot rest on historical analysis alone. All doctrine stands or falls on its conformity to the biblical text. But at the same time, it has often been the case that theologians start their positive construction of the doctrine of baptism with the New Testament. They look at baptism as a historical phenomenon that arose in the New Testament with the ministry of John the Baptist. Therefore, they see no need to look to the Old Testament except for incidental connections. As stated in the introduction of this study, doctrine cannot be based on the New Testament alone but must be founded on the canon of Scripture. Theologians from across the spectrum have historically made the connection between baptism and Genesis 1:2, the Noahic flood, and the Red Sea crossing. As Geerhardus Vos has explained, the theologian must draw a line from Genesis to Revelation, tracing the progressively unfolding revelation of the doctrine through redemptive history. To this end, the study will trace the doctrine of baptism thematically: baptism as new creation, covenant judgment, and eschatological judgment. In this way, Part II will provide the major motifs required for the systematic-theological statement of the doctrine in Part III.

CHAPTER 8

Baptism as New Creation

The theme of new creation casts important biblical light on the doctrine of baptism. This chapter will begin, therefore, by briefly surveying the various suggestions for the origins of baptism. While it is popular to find the origins of baptism in inter-testamental Judaism or in the rituals of the Qumran community, this chapter argues that the waters of baptism are the waters of new creation. This means the origins of baptism lie in Genesis 1:2.

SUGGESTED ORIGINS OF BAPTISM

Over the years, theologians and New Testament scholars have sought to determine the origins and sources for the New Testament practice of water baptism. Two primary options have been offered: the practice was carried over from first-century Judaism, either Jewish proselyte baptism or Qumran cleansing rituals; or it originated in the Old Testament primarily, either in Levitical lustrations or in the Old Testament prophets. The literature on this subject is legion, so a brief survey will prove helpful.

Jewish proselyte baptism

There is evidence of the baptism of Gentile proselytes in rabbinic sources dating to the second century AD. The Mishnah states that the proselyte "immerses and eats his Passover offering in the evening." Subsequent to his immersion in water, the proselyte was supposed to be sprinkled with water on the third and seventh days after his circumcision and treated as if he had touched a corpse (Pesahim 8:8; cf. Num. 19:1–13). Scholars have explained that Jewish proselyte baptism was an initiation ceremony that symbolized a break with one's old life and a joyful acceptance of the new. It was an act of dedication to Israel's God, and it carried with it the idea of cleansing from sin.[1] Given these similarities between Jewish proselyte baptism and Christian baptism, some have argued that the former is a likely antecedent for the latter.

However, there are mitigating factors for such a conclusion. First, there are questions surrounding the rabbinic sources. The material from the Mishnah likely has a second century origin, well after the beginning of the Christian rite. Moreover, scholars holding to the New Perspective on Paul have argued that post-second temple rabbinic literature may not be the best source for determining Jewish theology of the first century in the wake of the destruction of the temple in AD 70.[2] Second, there is total silence concerning proselyte baptism in the Old Testament, the Apocrypha, the writings of Josephus (37–ca. 100) and Philo (20 BC–50 AD), and the New Testament. Given this absence, some suggest that Jewish proselyte baptism was a copy of the Christian rite, not vice versa.[3] Third, while there are some formal similarities between the two rites, there are significant points of difference. Baptized proselyte males still underwent circumcision, which was the decisive initiatory rite. Circumcision was viewed as key during the Maccabean period and this carried on into the New Testament period.[4] Additionally, Christian baptism includes the ideas of union with Christ (Rom. 6:1–4) and participation in the dawning eschaton (Gal. 6:15; 2 Cor. 5:17; cf. Isa. 65:17–25).[5] These two ideas are absent from Jewish proselyte baptism.

Qumran cleansing lustrations

The cleansing lustrations of the Dead Sea Scrolls community have also been suggested as an antecedent to Christian baptism. This connection has been put forth because John's baptism was marked by several characteristics also present in Qumran practices:

1. Alec Gilmore, "Jewish Antecedents," in *Christian Baptism: A Fresh Attempt to Understand the Rite in Terms of Scripture, History, and Theology*, ed. Alec Gilmore (Philadelphia: Judson Press, 1959), 68–70.

2. See, e.g., N. T. Wright, *The New Testament and the People of God* (Philadelphia: Fortress, 1992), 151–52.

3. See J. L. Garrett, *Systematic Theology: Biblical, Historical, and Evangelical* (Grand Rapids: Eerdmans, 1995), 2.509.

4. See Josephus, *Antiquities*, 13.257–58, 318–19, in *The Works of Josephus*, trans. William Whitson (Peabody: Hendrickson, 2005); Adela Yarbro Collins, *Cosmology and Eschatology in Jewish and Christian Apocalypticism* (Leiden: Brill, 2000), 227.

5. Garrett, *Systematic Theology*, 510; also G. R. Beasley-Murray, *Baptism in the New Testament* (1962; Carlisle: Paternoster, 1997), 30.

1. A water baptism.

2. Repentance and confession of sin.

3. An understanding that the repentance of the one baptized resulted in the forgiveness of sins.

4. A requirement that it be practiced by all Jewish people.

5. A requirement that it not be repeated.

6. An understanding that it was a precursor of the messianic baptism with Spirit and fire.[6]

Scholarship is divided about why John's baptism bore these characteristics and their origins. Some, such as G. R. Beasley-Murray, suggest that the Qumran community likely influenced John. Beasley-Murray rejects the idea that John's practice originated solely out of the Old Testament and instead suggests the alternative: "It would seem more plausible that John recognized in the newer use of lustrations among Jewish groups like the Essenes a means whereby the Old Testament predictions of cleansing in the last day, prior to the great Messianic purgation, should be fulfilled."[7] Even if the Qumran community influenced John, recent research has suggested that Qumran saw the origins of its lustration practices in the Old Testament.[8] In other words, Qumran baptismal practices likely did not appear *ex nihilo* but from the desire to see passages such as Ezekiel 13:1 and 36:25–26 fulfilled.

Even so, closer examination points away from the conclusion that John was influenced by the Essene community. For example, the Damascus Document shows that the Essenes would have considered the Jordan River an unsuitable place for ritual cleansing: "No-one should bathe in water which is dirty or which is less than the amount which covers a man. No one should purify a vessel in it" (10:11–12). While it was not impossible to use the Jordan for ritual cleansing, it was not ideal, since when one emerges from the river it is usually necessary to rinse off dirt and sediment. Additionally, the southern stretches of the Jordan that are accessible are often shallow and sluggish. There was no concern on John's part, though, for rit-

---

6. Garrett, *Systematic Theology*, 511–12.

7. Beasley-Murray, *Baptism*, 42–43; see also Charles H. H. Scobie, *John the Baptist: A Portrait Based Upon Biblical and Extra-Biblical Sources* (Minneapolis: Fortress, 1964), 102–10.

8. See, e.g., Casey Toews, "Moral Purification in 1QS," BBR 13/1 (2003): 71–96.

ual cleansing, but rather for confession of sin and repentance.[9] This seems to be the polar opposite from Qumran, as their ablutions did not include an initiatory baptism but seem to have been related to the Levitical washings related to ritual purity.[10] For these reasons, Morna Hooker concludes, "No real parallel to John's baptism has been discovered in contemporary Jewish practice."[11]

Old Testament Levitical and prophetic antecedents

If the Qumran community is an insufficient answer to the question of the origin of baptism, where did baptism originate? The simplest answer seems to be the Old Testament.

A number of places in the Old Testament mention washings that seem to be precursors to the New Testament practice of baptism in one way or another. The Pentateuch instructs Aaron and his sons to wash their hands and feet before entering the tabernacle (Ex. 30:17–21); the priests were supposed to wash before putting on their priestly garments (Lev. 13:6, 34); and there were required washings for those who were suspected of leprosy or who had a seminal or menstrual discharge (Lev. 15). Some, however, argue that such washings should not be considered antecedents to baptism because they merely involved ritual purification and were repeated multiple times. Nonetheless, key terminology is found in Numbers 19:18, where the one to be cleansed was to have water sprinkled on him by one holding a hyssop branch. These elements are repeated in David's plea for forgiveness: "Purge me with hyssop, and I shall be clean; wash me, and I shall be whiter than snow" (Ps. 51:7; cf. Isa. 1:16; Ezek. 36:25; Zech. 13:1).[12] In other words, ideally, the ritual cleansing of a person was supposed to reflect both his confession and the divine forgiveness of sin. The Levitical cleansing rituals are consequently an antecedent to baptism, but as with any theme carried from one testament to the next, there are continuities and discontinuities.[13] The continuities lie in the connection between water washing and the forgiveness of sins. The discontinuities lie in areas such as the repetitive

---

9. Colin Brown, "What Was John the Baptist Doing?" BBR 7 (1997): 41–42.

10. Collins, *Cosmology and Eschatology*, 223.

11. Morna D. Hooker, *The Gospel according to St. Mark*, BNTC (1991; Peabody, Mass.: Hendrickson, 1999), 39. See similar comments offered by Meredith G. Kline, *By Oath Consigned: A Reinterpretation of the Covenant Signs of Circumcision and Baptism* (Grand Rapids: Eerdmans, 1968), 54.

12. Garrett, *Systematic Theology*, 506.

13. Collins, *Cosmology and Eschatology*, 238.

nature of the lustrations, mixing water with the ashes of a heifer, and the method employed, sprinkling water with a hyssop branch.[14]

Also, there are the prophecies of the Old Testament, particularly those of Ezekiel, Isaiah, and Zechariah. When Ezekiel was in exile, he prophesied of a time when Israel would be restored to the land and cleansed of her sins. The prophet states: "I will sprinkle clean water on you, and you shall be clean; I will cleanse you from all your filthiness and from all your idols" (Ezek. 36:25). This language is evocative of the Levitical lustrations (e.g., Num. 19:18), particularly that of sprinkling water on Israel (cf. Ex. 24:6; Lev. 1:5, 11; 16:16, 19).[15] Likewise, Zechariah prophesies concerning the restoration of Israel: "In that day a fountain shall be opened for the house of David and for the inhabitants of Jerusalem, for sin and for uncleanness" (Zech. 13:1; cf. Lev. 12:2, 5; 2 Chron. 29:5; Ezra 9:11).[16] There are clear connections between the use of water and the cleansing of sin.

Note two things about passages such as these. First, the surrounding contexts indicate that both prophets were writing of the eschatological restoration of Israel. Second, water-cleansing imagery is often joined with the work of the Holy Spirit. This is certainly evident in Ezekiel, who states, "I will put My Spirit within you and cause you to walk in My statutes, and you will keep My judgments and do them" (36:27). Similar imagery appears in the prophet Isaiah, who likens the eschatological restoration of Israel to the rejuvenation of the desert with water: "I will pour water on him who is thirsty, and floods on the dry ground; I will pour My Spirit on your descendants, and My blessing on your offspring" (Isa. 44:3; cf. 12:3; 30:25; 32:3, 15; 33:21; 35:6; 41:18; 43:20; 51:3; 55:1; 66:12). The combination of water cleansing and the Spirit is key, and certainly points in the direction of several New Testament texts, such as those that speak of John's baptism and Pentecost (Matt 3:11; Mark 1:8; Luke 3:16; 24:49; Acts 1:4; 2:16, 38).[17]

---

14. See Gordon J. Wenham, *Numbers*, TOTC (Downers Grove, Ill.: InterVarsity, 1981), 145–47; Jacob Milgrom, *Numbers*, JPSTC (New York: Jewish Publication Society, 1990), 159–61.

15. See Daniel I. Block, *The Book of Ezekiel*, vol. 2, NICOT (Grand Rapids: Eerdmans, 1998), 354; Walther Zimmerli, *Ezekiel*, vol. 2 (Philadelphia: Fortress, 1983), 248–49.

16. See Meredith G. Kline, *Glory in our Midst: A Biblical-Theological Reading of Zechariah's Night Visions* (Overland Park, Kan.: Two Age Press, 2001), 111; cf. Thomas E. McComiskey, *Zechariah*, in *The Minor Prophets*, vol. 3, ed. Thomas E. McComiskey (Grand Rapids: Baker, 1998), 1218.

17. John N. Oswalt, *The Book of Isaiah*, vol. 2, NICOT (Grand Rapids: Eerdmans, 1998), 166–67; cf. John Goldingay, *The Message of Isaiah: A Literary-Theological Commentary* (Edinburgh: T & T Clark, 2005), 229–31.

These connections indicate strong ties between the prophetic witness of the Old Testament and New Testament baptism.

However, the question remains: In what way are they connected? A basic answer lies in the common denominators of water, the forgiveness of sins, and the outpouring and/or presence of the Holy Spirit. These elements are present in the Levitical lustrations, the prophetic witness, and New Testament baptism.

A greater underlying theme, however, unites all of these passages and practices—the broader theme of new creation, which comes about through water and Spirit. This thesis is substantiated by moving forward to survey the creation, the flood, the exodus Red Sea crossing, the prophetic witness, the baptism of Jesus, and key Pauline texts. In so doing, the unifying theme of baptism as new creation emerges quite clearly.

THE NEW TESTAMENT INTERPRETATION OF THE FLOOD

The New Testament's interpretation of the flood sets some important interpretive parameters for the broader biblical understanding of baptism. The apostle Peter establishes a redemptive-historical relationship between baptism and the flood when he writes that baptism is the antitype for the flood: "There is also an antitype which now saves us—baptism (not the removal of the filth of the flesh, but the answer of a good conscience toward God), through the resurrection of Jesus Christ" (1 Peter 3:21). Significantly, Peter calls baptism the antitype to the flood. As Leonhard Goppelt explains: "The manner in which baptism is the antitype of the Old Testament event is expressed by *antitypos*. This word is probably being used already as a technical term, since through Paul *typos* became in early Christianity an hermeneutical technical expression for Old Testament pre-representations of the eschatological event beginning with Christ (1 Cor. 10:6, 11; Rom. 5:14)."[18]

While the details must be explained, the broad observation is that the flood is a new creation or (re)creation event. This is evident in the events surrounding the flood and the language used in the flood narrative, which demonstrates that God was not merely judging the earth but re-creating it. For example, when God unleashed the deluge on the earth, He opened the fountains of the deep and the windows of heaven (Gen. 7:11). The flood

---

18. Leonhard Goppelt, *A Commentary on 1 Peter* (1978; Grand Rapids: Eerdmans, 1993), 266.

therefore was not merely a natural drenching of the earth by a torrential downpour. It most certainly did rain (Gen. 7:12), yet at the same time God released not only subterranean water sources but also the sea above the firmament, what the apostle John calls the sea of glass before the throne of God (Gen. 1:6–7; cf. Rev. 4:6).[19] In other words, God returned the creation to its chaotic state of Genesis 1:2a: "The earth was without form and void, and darkness was over the face of the deep." Recall, however, that when the watery chaos covered the earth, the Spirit hovered over the waters like a bird (Gen. 1:2b; cf. Deut. 32:11). In other words, the key elements of water and Spirit that were present in the initial creation were also present in the subsequent flood re-creation.

Stephen Dempster explains that Noah and his family were the beginnings of a new creation. He writes, "Following the flood, which is represented as a return to the pre-creation chaos of Genesis 1:2, a new creation occurs with the presence of the Spirit of God pushing back the primal waters (Gen. 8:1)."[20] Comparing the Hebrew terminology used in both passages cited by Dempster corroborates these connections. In Genesis 1:2, the רוח אלהים (the Spirit of God) hovers over the waters. Likewise, in Genesis 8:1, אלהים causes a רוח (wind) to drive the floodwaters back so that the new creation can emerge. While the translation of רוח in Genesis 8:1 is *wind*, not *Spirit*, the similarities between the two narratives are clear. Both place a רוח over the waters and the new creation emerges.

Further imagery connects the two events. When Noah tested the waters to see whether the flood had receded, he sent out several birds. Noah first sent several ravens, an unclean bird according to the Levitical code (Lev. 11:15), then a dove, the New Testament symbol of the Holy Spirit (Matt. 3:16; Mark 1:10; Luke 3:22; John 1:32). While the original audience might not have made the immediate connection between the dove and the Holy Spirit, there are nevertheless overlapping avian images in Genesis 1:2 and 8:8. The dove is a bird, and the Holy Spirit's creative activity is described in avian terms; the Holy Spirit hovered (רחף) over the creation just as God hovered over Israel during the exodus like an eagle that stirs up its nest (cf. Deut. 32:11–12). A formula clearly emerges from the correlation of these three passages, namely, 1 Peter 3:21, Genesis 1:2, and Genesis 7–8.

---

19. See Herman Gunkel, *Genesis*, Mercer Library of Biblical Studies (Macon, Ga.: Mercer University Press, 1997), 108.

20. Stephen G. Dempster, *Dominion and Dynasty: A Theology of the Hebrew Bible*, NSBT (Downers Grove, Ill.: InterVarsity, 2003), 73.

New creation comes about through water and Spirit, and thus Genesis 1:2 and chapters 7–8 are typical of the waters of baptism, which is the antitype according to Peter.

THE RED SEA CROSSING

The exodus Red Sea crossing provides further evidence that confirms this thesis.

The basic contours of the Red Sea crossing are known to most, but perhaps less well known is that Paul calls this event a baptism:

> Moreover, brethren, I do not want you to be unaware that all our fathers were under the cloud, all passed through the sea, all were baptized into Moses in the cloud and in the sea, all ate the same spiritual food, and all drank the same spiritual drink. For they drank of that spiritual Rock that followed them, and that Rock was Christ. (1 Cor. 10:1–4)

Though there is debate surrounding the exact nature of Paul's use of the term translated as "baptized," the same elements of the new creation-baptism construct appear here.[21] In fact, Gordon Fee notes that Paul "relates Israel's crossing of the Red Sea and their being sustained by manna and water from the rock in terms of Christian baptism and the eucharistic meal."[22] The parallel seems to be that in the same way the Christian life begins with baptism, so Israel's deliverance from Egypt began with a kind of "baptism." In the same way that believers are baptized into Christ as their Deliverer, so Israel was baptized into Moses as their deliverer. This is not to say, of course, that Israel had a mystical union with Moses as believers now have with Christ. There are differences between the type and the antitype, the shadow and the reality. Some details require elaboration so that the connections between the typical event and the antitypical reality are understood.

First, what does Paul mean when he says that the Israelites "were all under the cloud" and that they were "baptized into...the cloud"? What is the significance of the cloud? Two manifestations of God's divine presence accompanied Israel during the exodus—the glory cloud and the messen-

---

21. Cf. Beasley-Murray, *Baptism*, 181; also see Herman Witsius, *The Economy of the Covenants Between God and Man*, trans. William Crookshank (1822; Phillipsburg, N.J.: P & R, 1990), 4.16.28.

22. Gordon D. Fee, *The First Epistle to the Corinthians*, NICNT (Grand Rapids: Eerdmans, 1987), 443–44.

ger: "And the Angel [מלאך] of God, who went before the camp of Israel, moved and went behind them; and the pillar of cloud went from before them and stood behind them" (Ex. 14:19). It seems that the angel and the cloud shared in leading Israel in the wilderness (Ex. 23:20; 32:34; 40:36; Num. 20:16).[23] When the cloud led Israel during the night, it was a pillar of fire (Ex. 40:38). The glory cloud and the messenger (angel) of the Lord are both identified with the presence of God; the Lord would appear in the glory cloud in the tabernacle (Lev. 16:2) and the angel was in fact the Lord, as Joshua was allowed to worship Him in terms reminiscent of the Mosaic theophany on Horeb (cf. Ex. 3:1–5; Josh. 5:13–15). The Old Testament evidence, however, leads to the conclusion that the angel was the pre-incarnate Christ and the cloud was the Holy Spirit, or the second and third persons of the Trinity (cf. Jude 5).[24]

At this point, it is the glory cloud-Spirit connection that is of greater interest. Four passages of Scripture confirm this connection: Haggai 2:4–5, Isaiah 63:11–14, Nehemiah 9:19–20, and Deuteronomy 32:11. Haggai 2:4–5 validates the cloud-Spirit identity: "'Be strong, Zerubbabel,' says the Lord; 'and be strong, Joshua, son of Jehozadak, the high priest; and be strong, all you people of the land,' says the Lord, 'and work; for I am with you,' says the Lord of hosts. 'According to the word that I covenanted with you when you came out of Egypt, so My Spirit remains among you'[בתוככם ורוחי עמדת]." Here God's Spirit (רוח) is present at the exodus event. There is also the specific statement that the Spirit עמד (stood) in Israel's midst. This is interesting language, as the same term is used to describe the glory cloud's activity during the exodus: "The pillar of cloud went from before them and stood [ויעמד] behind them" (Ex. 14:19). Likewise, when the glory cloud descended on the tabernacle for the Lord to speak to Moses, the

---

23. Some interpreters argue that the messenger and the cloud were one and the same (see Umberto Cassuto, *A Commentary on the Book of Exodus* [1953; Jerusalem: Magnes Press, 1997], 166; cf. John I. Durham, *Exodus*, WBC, vol. 3 [Dallas: Word, 1987], 192–93).

24. There seems to be ample textual evidence for the reading, "Now I want to remind you, although you once fully knew it, that Jesus, who saved a people out of the land of Egypt...." It seems that the editors of the UBS Greek New Testament dismiss this reading on dogmatic rather than textual grounds: "Despite the weighty attestation supporting Ἰησοῦς (A B 33 81 322 323 424ᶜ 665 1241 1739 1881 2298 2344 vg copˢᵃ, ᵇᵒ eth Origen Cyril Jerome Bede; ὁ Ἰησοῦς 88 915), a majority of the Committee was of the opinion that the reading was difficult to the point of impossibility" (Bruce Metzger, *A Textual Commentary on the Greek New Testament* [Stuttgart: German Bible Society, 2002], 657). This seems to violate one of the cardinal rules of textual criticism, namely, that the *difficilior lectio* is to be preferred if it is well attested. Moreover, Paul had no problem placing Christ in the exodus narrative (1 Cor. 10:4, 9–10).

same language is used: "And it came to pass, when Moses entered the tabernacle, that the pillar of cloud descended and stood [עמוד] at the door of the tabernacle" (Ex. 33:9; cf. Num. 12:5; 14:14; Deut. 31:15).[25]

A similar pattern appears in Isaiah 63:11–12. The prophet writes: "Then he remembered the days of old, Moses and his people, saying: 'Where is He who brought them up out of the sea with the shepherd of His flock? Where is He who put His Holy Spirit within them, who led them by the right hand of Moses, with His glorious arm, dividing the water before them to make for Himself an everlasting name?" Within the broader context of the book of Isaiah, the prophet both rehearses Israel's past and looks to the eschaton, the ultimate restoration of the nation.[26] Isaiah returns to the exodus and, like Haggai, places the Holy Spirit at the Red Sea crossing. Note the connection between the leading of the Spirit and Israel's rest: "Who led them through the deep, as a horse in the wilderness, that they might not stumble? As a beast goes down into the valley, and the Spirit of the LORD causes him to rest, so You lead Your people, to make Yourself a glorious name" (Isa. 63:13–14). The glory cloud presence of the Lord led Israel (Ex. 40:36–38), but at the same time it was the Lord who would give them rest: "My Presence will go with you, and I will give you rest" (Ex. 33:14).[27] Isaiah identifies the glory cloud of the exodus as the Holy Spirit, the one who gives Israel rest.

The same imagery and events are invoked by Nehemiah, who states: "The pillar of the cloud did not depart from them by day, to lead them on the road; nor the pillar of fire by night, to show them light, and the way they should go. You also gave Your good Spirit to instruct them, and did not withhold Your manna from their mouth, and gave them water for their thirst" (9:19–20). Nehemiah associates the glory cloud presence of the Lord with the Holy Spirit.[28]

This connection is further substantiated by yet another passage that details the events surrounding the exodus. Deuteronomy 32:10–12 states: "He found him in a desert land and in the wasteland [ובתהו], a howling wilderness; He encircled him, He instructed him, He kept him as the

---

25. William N. Wilder, *Echoes of the Exodus Narrative in the Context and Background of Galatians 5.18*, Studies in Biblical Literature, no. 23 (New York: Peter Lang, 2001), 124–30.

26. See William J. Dumbrell, *The End of the Beginning: Revelation 21–22 and the Old Testament* (1985; Eugene, Ore.: Wipf & Stock, 2001), 18–19.

27. Wilder, *Echoes*, 130–38.

28. Wilder, *Echoes*, 138–48.

apple of His eye. As an eagle stirs up its nest, hovers [יְרַחֵף] over its young, spreading out its wings, taking them up, carrying them on its wings, so the LORD alone led him, and there was no foreign god with him." Here is a description of the Lord's care for Israel during the exodus and subsequent wilderness wanderings.[29] The only other occurrence of the verb רחף (hovers) is found in Genesis 1:2. Moreover, verse 10 says God found Israel in תהו, the same word used in the opening phrase of the creation account, ובהו תהו (without form, and void) (Gen. 1:2). In other words, the terminological connections between Genesis 1:2 and Deuteronomy 32:11 show that the same avian language that is used to describe the Spirit's activity in the creation is also used to describe God's leading of Israel in the wilderness.

Given all of these connections, Meredith Kline seems more than warranted when he writes:

> Isaiah 63, reflecting on Deuteronomy 32 (which depicts God's leading of Israel in terms of the Glory hovering over creation at the beginning), mentions the Angel of the Glory-Presence as the one who bore Israel (v. 9) and variously denotes the divine Presence as the Holy Spirit or Spirit of the Lord (vv. 10, 11, 14) or as his arm of Glory (v. 12, cf. v. 15). And the prophet attributes to the Glory-Spirit the guidance of Israel through the depths of the sea (v. 13; cf. Deut. 32:10; Gen. 1:2) on to the Sabbath-rest in the land of their inheritance: "The Spirit of the Lord brought him to rest" (v. 14; cf. Deut 12:9). In effect, the prophet says that in the exodus re-creation there was recapitulation of the role of the Glory-Spirit in creation from Genesis 1:2 to Genesis 2:2.[30]

This exegetical data verifies that when Paul says the Israelites were all baptized into the cloud, he was saying they were baptized into the Holy Spirit.

Israel's baptism into the cloud, and the Holy Spirit hovering over Israel like a bird and leading them out of the waters, is all suggestive of the initial creation as well as the flood re-creation. Even the descriptions of the parting of the Red Sea are evocative of the creation and flood re-creation: "The LORD caused the sea to go back by a strong east wind [בְּרוּחַ קָדִים] all that night, and made the sea into dry land, and the waters were divided"

---

29. Meredith G. Kline, *Treaty of the Great King: The Covenant Structure of Deuteronomy* (Grand Rapids: Eerdmans, 1963), 141.

30. Meredith G. Kline, *Images of the Spirit* (Eugene, Ore.: Wipf & Stock, 1998), 111–12. While the particulars of Kline's argument may differ, the overall interpretation connecting the glory cloud with the Holy Spirit goes as far back as Origen (185–ca. 254) (see *Homilies on Numbers*, 22, as cited in Beasley-Murray, *Baptism*, 183, n. 3).

(Ex. 14:21). Here, just as the רוח אלהים hovered over the waters of creation, and as the רוח caused the flood waters to recede, the Lord drove back the waters of the Red Sea with a רוח.

There are still other new creation elements in the exodus narrative. For example, God told Israel that the calendar would re-start with the exodus: "This month shall be your beginning of months; it shall be the first month of the year to you" (Ex. 12:2). With the re-starting of the calendar, the exodus represented a new beginning for Israel. Likewise, subsequent to the exodus there are significant parallels with the initial creation in God's instructions for the construction of the tabernacle. Scholars have noted the parallel between the seven days of creation (Gen. 1:1–2:3) and the seven speeches of God to Moses providing instructions for the building of the tabernacle. The seven speeches give explicit directions concerning the: materials (Ex. 25:1–9), ark (25:10–22), table (25:23–30), lampstand (25:31–40), tabernacle (26:1–37), bronze altar (27:1–8), courtyard (27:9–19).[31]

Gordon Wenham also notes that there are "parallels in phraseology between the conclusion of the creation account in 1:1–2:3 and the tabernacle building account in Exodus 25–40."[32] At the end of God's creative activity, He rested on the seventh day (Gen. 2:2–3). When God finished the seventh speech to Moses, He prescribed the Sabbath rest (Ex. 31:17), and when Moses finished constructing the tabernacle God's presence in the "the cloud rested above it, and the glory of the LORD filled the tabernacle" (Ex. 40:35).[33] God rested once the creation was finished in the garden-temple

31. Gordon J. Wenham, "Sanctuary Symbolism in the Garden of Eden Story," in *'I Studied Inscripturations from Before the Flood*,*'* eds. Richard S. Hess and David Toshio Tsumura (Winona Lake: Eisenbrauns, 1994), 403; David A. Dorsey, *The Literary Structure of the Old Testament: A Commentary on Genesis–Malachi* (Grand Rapids: Baker, 1999), 75; cf. Durham, *Exodus*, 473. Interestingly enough, Moshe Weinfeld notes that Moses had to wait six days at the foot of Sinai before climbing the mountain to receive the instructions for the tabernacle, which perhaps correspond to the six days of creation (Ex. 24:15ff; cf. Mark 9:2; Matt. 17:1). (Moshe Weinfeld, "Sabbath, Temple and the Enthronement of the Lord," in *Mélanges Bibliques et Orientaux en l'honneur de M. Henri Cazelles*, eds. A. Caquot et M. Delcor [Neukirchen: Verlang, 1981], 506).

32. Wenham, "Sanctuary Symbolism," 403; also Peter J. Kearney, "Creation and Liturgy: The P Redaction of Ex. 25–40," ZAW 89 (1977), 375–78; Joseph Blenkinsopp, *Prophecy and Canon* (Notre Dame: University of Notre Dame Press, 1977), 62; cf. Weinfeld, "Sabbath, Temple and the Enthronement," 502, n. 5.

33. Kearney, "Creation and Liturgy," 378; also Weinfeld, "Sabbath, Temple and the Enthronement," 501.

and likewise rested in the newly finished Holy of Holies in the wilderness tabernacle.

These are not new observations but have precedence in rabbinic interpretation. Rabbinic interpreters make the following connections between the construction of the tabernacle and the creation week:

> The expression, *eth the tabernacle* denotes that its importance was equal to that of the world, which is called "tent," even as the tabernacle is called "tent." How can this statement be supported? It is written, "In the beginning God created the heaven" (Gen. 1:1), and it is written, "Who stretches out the heaven like a curtain" (Psa. 104:2), while of the tabernacle it is written, "And you shall make curtains of goat's hair for a tent over the tabernacle" (Exo. 26:7). It is written in connection with the second day, "Let there be a firmament…and let it divide" (Gen. 1:6), and of the tabernacle it is written, "The veil shall divide unto you" (Exo. 26:33). Of the third day we read, "Let the waters under the heaven be gathered together" (Gen. 1:9), and of the tabernacle it is written, "You shall also make a laver of brass, and the base thereof of brass, whereat to wash" (Exo. 30:18). Of the fourth day, "Let there be lights in the firmament of the heaven" (Gen. 1:14), and of the tabernacle, "You shall make a candlestick of pure gold" (Exo. 25:31). Of the fifth, "Let fowl fly above the earth" (Gen. 1:20), and of the tabernacle, "The cherubim shall spread out their wings" (Exo. 25:20). On the sixth day man was created, and in connection with the tabernacle it says, "Bring near unto you Aaron your brother" (Exo. 28:1). Of the seventh day we have it written, "and the heaven and the earth were finished" (Gen. 2:1), and of the tabernacle, "Thus was finished all the work of the tabernacle" (Exo. 39:32). In connection with the creation of the world it is written, "And God blessed" (Gen. 2:3), and in connection with the tabernacle, "And Moses blessed them" (Exo. 39:43). On the seventh day God finished (Gen. 2:2), and in connection with the tabernacle, "It came to pass on the day that Moses had made an end." On the seventh day he hallowed it (Gen. 2:3), and in connection with the tabernacle he "sanctified it" (7:1). Thus we have explained the expression *eth the tabernacle* (*Mid Rabb* Num. 12:13).

In other words, the tabernacle, which was a temple, was a microcosmic reproduction of God's cosmic temple, the creation.[34] Josephus made these

---

34. G. K. Beale, *The Temple and the Church's Mission: A Biblical Theology of the Dwelling Place of God*, NSBT (Downers Grove. Ill.: InterVarsity, 2005), 31–38.

same connections, and explains that the tabernacle was "made in way of imitation and representation of the universe."[35]

The relationship between the creation and the tabernacle is evident in the following chart:

Day	Creation	Tabernacle
Day 1	Heavens are stretched out like a curtain (Ps. 104:2)	Tent (Ex. 26:7)
Day 2	Firmament (Gen. 1:2)	Temple veil (Ex. 26:33)
Day 3	Waters below	Temple laver or bronze sea (Ex. 30:18)
Day 4	Lights (Gen. 1:14)	Lampstand (Ex. 25:31)
Day 5	Birds (Gen. 1:20)	Winged cherubim (Ex. 25:20)
Day 6	Man (Gen. 1:28)	Aaron the high priest (Ex. 28:1)
Day 7	Cessation (Gen. 2:1) Blessing (Gen. 2:3) Completion (Gen. 2:2)	Cessation (Ex. 39:32) Mosaic blessing (Ex. 39:43) Completion (Ex. 39:43)

The tabernacle-creation parallels mean that, among other things, the events surrounding the exodus were considered to be a new creation of sorts.[36] The same may be said from some second-temple characterizations of the exodus as a new creation:

> For the whole creation in its nature was fashioned anew, complying with your commands, so that your children might be kept unharmed. The cloud was seen overshadowing the camp, and dry land emerging where water had stood before, an unhindered way out of the Red Sea, and a grassy plain out of the raging waves, where those protected by your hand passed through as one nation, after gazing on marvelous wonders (Wisd. Sol. 19:6–8).[37]

Recall that God called Israel His firstborn son (Ex. 4:22), and likewise, Adam was God's son (Luke 4:38); both were tied to creation or creation-

---

35. Josephus, *Antiquities*, 3.180.

36. Meredith G. Kline, *The Structure of Biblical Authority* (1989; Eugene, Ore.: Wipf & Stock, 1997), 88; also J. Luzarraga, *Las Tradiciones de La Nube en La Biblia y en el Judaismo Primitivo* (Rome: Biblical Institute Press, 1973), 245.

37. Translation from the New Revised Standard Version.

like events. All of these typical images find their fulfillment in the baptism of Christ, God's only begotten Son.[38]

THE BAPTISM OF CHRIST AND NEW CREATION

A dimension of the baptism of Christ that is unfamiliar to some is that it echoes many of the new creation themes from the Old Testament. However, the baptism of Christ must be understood against the backdrop of John the Baptist's activity at the Jordan River. Why was John baptizing at the Jordan? The answer comes from the Old Testament and the echoes of the baptism-new creation theme. This section therefore will begin by evaluating John the Baptist's actions and then proceed to examine Christ's own baptism.

John's actions at the Jordan

All four Gospels record the ministry of John the Baptist, which testifies to his importance as a transition figure, the last Old Testament prophet.[39] However, what was this prophet doing? Why was he encouraging Israelites to be baptized in the Jordan River? The answer to these questions comes from John's actions as well as from his words concerning his ministry. First, John appeared "baptizing in the wilderness and preaching a baptism of repentance for the remission of sins. Then all the land of Judea, and those from Jerusalem, went out to him and were all baptized by him in the Jordan River" (Mark 1:4–5). There are two issues that merit attention: the significance of the Jordan River and the repentance of sins. The geographical location of John's baptismal ministry is key. John could have chosen a number of places to perform his baptizing ministry, but he chose the Jordan, which was the gate to the Promised Land and the place where Israel re-enacted the Red Sea crossing.

When the feet of the Levites touched the waters of the Jordan, the waters stopped flowing and the Israelites crossed the river on dry ground (Josh. 3:11–17). Just as the Holy Spirit in the glory cloud led Israel through the Red Sea, the ark of the Lord led Israel through the Jordan on dry

---

38. See Kline, *Images of the Spirit*, 19; Luzarraga, *Las Tradiciones de la Nube*, 235. For adoption-exodus connections, see James M. Scott, *Adoption as Sons of God* (Tübingen: Mohr Siebeck, 1992), 121–48.

39. Kline, *By Oath Consigned*, 61; also James D. G. Dunn, *Baptism in the Holy Spirit* (Philadelphia: Westminster Press, 1970), 25.

ground to the Land of Promise. The connection between the two events is manifest in the word play in both narratives. The priests, for example, stood on dry ground (בחרבה) (Josh. 3:17), just as Moses turned the sea into dry land (לחרבה) (Ex. 14:21).[40] Likewise, the waters of the Jordan "stood still, and rose in a heap" (קמו נד אחד) (Josh. 3:16), just as the waters of the Red Sea "stood upright like a heap" (נצבו כמו נד) (Ex. 15:8; cf. Ps. 78:13).[41] Given these parallels between the Red Sea and Jordan River crossings, it seems that John's activity in the Jordan was connected not only to the idea of a cleansing ritual, but also to the redemptive-historical significance of the Jordan.

The connections between the Red Sea, the Jordan River, and John's activities have been previously observed by others. Geerhardus Vos (1862–1949) explains:

> Notwithstanding the preeminence thus ascribed to John, it is plain from the reason given for this preeminence that he was not so much a revealer of new truth as a recapitulator of the old. At the point where the old covenant is about to pass over into the new, John once more sums up in his ministry the entire message of all preceding revelation and thus becomes the connecting link between it and the fulfillment which was to follow.[42]

It appears that John was re-enacting Israel's post-exodus entry to the Promised Land. However, given Israel's sinfulness, he was calling the nation to repentance.[43] Israel needed to prepare for the second (or eschatological) exodus that would come by the ministry of Christ.

Evidently, John was preparing for this eschatological exodus because of his description of Christ's ministry. John told the people that he baptized only with water, but the One who was to come would baptize them with the Holy Spirit (Mark 1:8).[44] This statement, as well as John's overall activ-

---

40. See Richard S. Hess, *Joshua*, TOTC (Downers Grove, Ill.: InterVarsity, 1996), 105.

41. Marten H. Woudstra, *The Book of Joshua*, NICOT (Grand Rapids: Eerdmans, 1981), 86.

42. Geerhardus Vos, "The Ministry of John the Baptist," in *Redemptive History and Biblical Interpretation: The Shorter Writings of Geerhardus Vos*, ed. Richard B. Gaffin, Jr. (Phillipsburg, N.J.: P & R, 1980), 299.

43. Brown, "What Was John the Baptist Doing?" 44–47.

44. One should note that in the parallel passages from the other Gospels John says that Christ will baptize with Spirit and fire (Matt. 3:11; Luke 3:16). That John mentions *fire* is connected both to ideas of purification and judgment, subjects that will be explored in chapter 10.

ity, is reported on the heels of what some have called the thesis statement of the Gospel of Mark, namely, the quotation of Isaiah 40:3: "Prepare the way of the LORD; make straight in the desert a highway for our God" (cf. Matt. 3:3; Luke 3:4; John 1:23). God drove Israel into exile, but He promised in the book of Isaiah that they would return to the land in a second exodus, the exodus from Babylon. However, the ultimate goal of the typical second exodus was the final exodus led by the Anointed of the Lord. It was the Servant of the Lord on whom God would put His Spirit (Isa. 42:1; 61:1; Matt. 3:13–17; 12:18–21).[45] This Servant would lead Israel on the final exodus, and John explained that Christ would baptize with the Holy Spirit.

In the broader context of Isaiah 40–55, there is a close connection between the outpouring of the Spirit and the resulting new creation: "For I will pour water on him who is thirsty, and floods on the dry ground; I will pour My Spirit on your descendants, and My blessing on your offspring" (Isa. 44:3; cf. Gen. 49:25; Ezek. 34:26–27; Joel 2:14; Mal. 3:10–11). Here the dry and thirsty land receives the outpouring of water, which brings rejuvenation, and this imagery is tied to the outpouring of the Spirit. Concerning this verse, though, John Goldingay explains, "Yhwh's renewal of the people is an act of new creation."[46] This conclusion seems warranted, especially in light of Isaiah 44:2: "Thus says the LORD who made you and formed you from the womb [עשׂךָ וְיֹצֶרְךָ], who will help you." E. J. Young explains, "The expression Creator [יֹצֵר] used of God as the Creator of His people is found only in Isaiah, as also the parallels *Maker* and *Former*."[47] This language is used, for example, in the creation account of man (Gen. 2:7). All of this imagery comes with a kaleidoscope of ideas that ties together creation, exodus, new creation, and the eschatological outpouring of the Spirit.[48]

---

45. Kline, *Structure of Biblical Authority*, 181–95; also Rikki E. Watts, *Isaiah's New Exodus in Mark* (Grand Rapids: Baker, 1997), 53–122; J. Alec Motyer, *Isaiah*, TOTC (Downers Grove, Ill.: InterVarsity, 1999), 245; John D. W. Watts, *Isaiah*, vol. 2, WBC (Dallas: Word, 1987), 80–81.

46. Goldingay, *Isaiah*, 230.

47. E. J. Young, *The Book of Isaiah*, vol. 3 (1972; Grand Rapids: Eerdmans, 1997), 167.

48. For a broader treatment of this theme in Paul's famous fruits of the Spirit passage (Gal. 5:18–22), see G. K. Beale, "The Old Testament Background of Paul's Reference to 'the Fruit of the Spirit' in Gal 5:22," BBR 15/1 (2005): 1–38. Especially of note are the connections Beale draws between "fruit" and "Spirit" in Isaiah: "Some of the specific links between the 'Spirit' and 'fruit' in Isaiah, which are part of the new-creation theme, likely reflect the same original link at the first creation, where the 'Spirit' (*pneuma*, Gen 1:2) was the agent of the creation, including trees bearing 'fruit' (*karpos*, Gen. 1:11, 12, 29)" (10).

These observations are not new. J. Luzarraga, commenting on Isaiah 31:5, explains that this verse, as well as the others thus far surveyed, refer to:

> a "return," a second exodus, a new exodus, which…comes described with features taken from the first exodus, projecting upon an eschatological future, for the gifts that God has granted in the past are only a symbol of his provision in the future. As in the days past, so also in the ones to come, "Like birds hovering, so the LORD of hosts will protect Jerusalem; he will protect and deliver it; he will spare and rescue it." This text suggests the paschal liberation of the exodus from Egypt, when Israel was covered by the clouds of glory; comparing it with 1 Cor. 10:2, one can also see an allusion to the Spirit which hovered over the first creation.[49]

Therefore, John's baptism continued in this Old Testament vein and was typical of Christ's antitypical outpouring of the Spirit.[50] However, it is necessary to explore the baptism of Christ, in which this Old Testament imagery is fulfilled.

The baptism of Christ

The baptism of Christ is one of the key culminations of redemptive history, one of the critical events to which the surveyed Old Testament types point. When Christ came to John to be baptized, several things occurred: Christ rose from the water, the heavens were rent, the Spirit descended on Him in the form of a dove, and God declared that Jesus was His beloved Son. In all of these events, there are antitypical counterparts to a number of Old Testament types. The connections appear in Table 1.

There are numerous continuities between the Old Testament shadows and the New Testament realities, though there are some discontinuities as well. First, as in the Old Testament events, Jesus, representative of the coming new creation, emerged from the waters, just as there were emergences in the initial creation, the flood, and even the Old Testament exodus from Egypt.

---

49. Luzarraga, *Las Tradiciones de La Nube*, 234–35: "Isaías (31,5) nos habla de una 'vuelta', de un 2° Exodo, de un Nuevo Exodo, que…viene descrito con rasgos del Primero, proyectando en un futuro escatológico, pues los dones que Dios ha concedido en el pasado son solo un símbolo de su entrega en el futuro. Como en días pasados, tambié en el porvenir 'como pájaros voladores así rodeará defendiendo Yhwh de los Ejércitos sobre Jerusalén; defenderá para library y se extenderá para rescatar.' Este text sugiere la liberación *Pascual* a la salida de Egipto, cuando Israel fue cubierto por las nubes de la Gloria; comparándolo con 1 Cor 10,2 se puede descubrir también en él una alusion al Espíritu que revoloteaba en la primera creación."

50. Dunn, *Baptism*, 16.

TABLE 1. Old Testament Connections to Christ's Baptism

Element	Gen. 1–3 First Adam	Flood/Type	Exodus/Type	Second Adam/ Antitype
Water	"Darkness was over the face of the deep" (Gen. 1:2b).	"The waters prevailed on the earth" (Gen. 7:24).	"The LORD caused the sea to go back by a strong east wind [רוח]" (Ex. 14:21).	"When he had been baptized, Jesus came up, immediately from the water" (Matt. 3:16a).
Spirit	"The Spirit [רוח] of God was hovering" (Gen. 1:2c).	"God made a wind [רוח] to pass over the earth, and the waters subsided" (Gen. 8:1). "He also sent out from himself a dove, to see if the waters had receded from the face of the ground" (Gen. 8:8).	"He found [Israel] in a desert land.... As an eagle stirs up its nest, hovers over its young" (Deut. 32:10–11). "Then he remembered… Moses and his people. Where is He who brought them up out of the sea…who put His Holy Spirit within them?" (Isa. 63:11).	"The heavens were opened to Him, and He saw the Spirit of God descending like a dove" (Matt. 3:16b).
God's Son	"God created man in His own image" (Gen. 1:27).	"Noah was a just man, perfect in his generations. Noah walked with God" (Gen. 6:9).	"Israel is My son, My firstborn" (Ex. 4:22).	"This is My beloved Son, in whom I am well pleased" (Matt 3:17).
Baptism	Cf. Gen. 1:2; Gen. 7:24; 1 Peter 3:20–21a	"In the days of Noah…eight souls, were saved through water. There is also an antitype which now saves us—baptism" (1 Peter 3:20–21a).	"All passed through the sea, all were baptized into Moses in the cloud and in the sea" (1 Cor. 10:1–2).	"When he had been baptized, Jesus came up, immediately from the water" (Matt. 3:16a).

Second, just as Adam was called God's son, and so too Israel after him, God the Father declared definitively that Jesus was His beloved Son. The big difference, of course, between Adam, Israel, and Christ was that Jesus was an obedient Son, unlike His predecessors. Christ's submission to John's baptism, a baptism of repentance, was technically unnecessary because Christ was sinless, but He submitted to it in order to "fulfill all righteousness" (Matt. 3:15; cf. Mark 1:4–9; Isa. 63:7–64:8).[51] Moreover, in imagery evocative of the Old Testament exodus, immediately after Christ's baptism, the Holy Spirit led Him into the wilderness for a trial lasting forty days, which parallels Israel's forty-year wilderness wanderings.[52] Of course, once again the great difference is that Israel repeatedly failed in their testing, whereas Christ was faithful.

Third, there are important links not only to the Old Testament typical baptism events of the creation, flood, and exodus, but also to the prophecies of Isaiah and the outpouring of the Spirit. As the Holy Spirit hovered like a bird over the watery chaos of Genesis 1:2, as the dove was sent over the floodwaters by Noah, and as God hovered like an eagle over Israel at the exodus, so the Holy Spirit descended on Christ at His baptism.[53] The book of Isaiah also declares that there would come a time when God would rend the heavens: "Oh that you would rend the heavens! And that You would come down" (Isa. 64:1; 63:19 MT; cf. LXX; Matt. 3:16).[54] At the baptism of Jesus, God rent the heavens and poured His Holy Spirit on the Messiah, as Isaiah had prophesied that He would do: "The Spirit of the LORD shall rest upon Him, the Spirit of wisdom and understanding, the Spirit of counsel and might, the Spirit of knowledge and of the fear of the LORD" (Isa. 11:2; cf. 42:1). Jesus' anointing with the Holy Spirit was the mark of the beginning of the age of the Spirit, the eschatological jubilee, or what might be called the beginnings of the new heaven and earth, the new creation (Isa. 61–65).[55] There is an intimate connection between baptism, Spirit, and new creation.

---

51. John Paul Heil, "Jesus with the Wild Animals in Mark 1.13," *Catholic Biblical Quarterly* 68 (2006), 75.

52. D. A. Carson, *Matthew*, vol. 1, EBC (Grand Rapids: Zondervan, 1995), 112–15; Luzarraga, *Las Tradiciones de la Nube*, 241–42.

53. Cf. Dunn, *Baptism*, 27, n. 12; Luzarraga, *Las Tradiciones de la Nube*, 240; Geerhardus Vos, *Biblical Theology* (1948; Edinburgh: Banner of Truth, 1996), 322; David B. Capes, "Intertextual Echoes in the Matthean Baptismal Narrative," BBR 9 (1999): 47.

54. See Watts, *New Exodus*, 102–03; Dunn, *Baptism*, 26.

55. Dunn, *Baptism*, 24, 26; see also Donald A. Hagner, *Matthew 1–13*, WBC, vol. 33a (Dallas: Word, 1993), 57–58.

THE BAPTISM OF THE CHURCH AND NEW CREATION

These ideas come together not only in the baptism of Jesus, but also in the baptism of the church. The same type of imagery attends descriptions and statements surrounding baptism both at the corporate and individual levels in the New Testament. This section begins by looking at elements of Christ's discussion with Nicodemus and the curious statement that one must be born of water and Spirit to enter the kingdom of heaven, then surveys the events of Pentecost, the outpouring of the Spirit, and the subsequent baptism of the three thousand on that day.

Christ and Nicodemus

There is much to analyze in Christ's discourse with Nicodemus, but the following statement is of particular interest: "Most assuredly, I say to you, unless one is born of water and the Spirit, he cannot enter the kingdom of God" (John 3:5). Scholars have offered a number of explanations: (1) "water" refers to natural birth and "the Spirit" refers to spiritual birth; (2) water refers to baptism; (3) water refers to John's baptism; and (4) that Jesus is arguing against the purification rites of the Essenes.[56] The strongest option seems to be the second, namely, that this statement refers to baptism, though not merely to the ecclesiastical rite, but to the ideas that are represented in baptism. Several observations confirm this, especially keeping in mind the broader redemptive-historical backdrop surveyed thus far.

First, at crucial points in redemptive history, God has begotten sons through the activity of water and Spirit: Adam in the first creation, Noah and his family at the flood, and Israel, His firstborn son, at the exodus Red Sea crossing. We must add the water and Spirit baptism of Christ to this list, keeping in mind that the event is an economic begetting, not an ontological one. All of these events are characterized in one way or another as baptisms.

Second, water and Spirit are closely coordinated throughout the writings of the Old Testament prophets. God was to restore Israel through the outpouring of the Spirit (Joel 2:28), producing the fruit of blessing and righteousness (Isa. 32:15–20; 44:3; Ezek. 39:29). God was also going to cleanse Israel from its idolatry through the sprinkling of water and the giving of the Holy Spirit (Ezek. 11:19–20; 36:26–27). As explained above, the prophet Ezekiel displays the strongest connection between water and

---

56. For documentation and other views, see D. A. Carson, *The Gospel According to John*, Pillar New Testament Commentary (Grand Rapids: Eerdmans, 1991), 191–94.

Spirit, though it has an antecedent history in previous Old Testament revelation (cf. Num. 19:17–19; Ps. 51:9–10; Isa. 32:15; 44:3–5; 55:1–3; Jer. 2:13; 17:13; Joel 2:28–29; Zech. 14:8).[57]

In light of this data and the redemptive-historical backdrop, when Christ tells Nicodemus that one must be born of water and the Spirit, He is saying that a person must be part of the new creation in order to enter the kingdom of God. In this sense, to be born of water and the Spirit points to baptism, not that the waters of baptism accomplish the begetting, but that they point to the life-giving work of the Spirit, the power of the age to come, the One who applies the work of Christ to the individual and cleanses the sinner of his unrighteousness. In this way, then, one must be born of water and the Spirit.[58] This conclusion appears to be supported by Christ's words to Nicodemus, "That which is born of the flesh is flesh, and that which is born of the Spirit is spirit" (John 3:6).[59] This verse has the same flesh-Spirit antithesis found in Paul's writings, referring not to an ontological antithesis between the material and immaterial aspects of man, but to the redemptive-historical antithesis between the two major epochs of redemptive history.[60]

The outpouring of the Spirit at Pentecost

The outpouring of the Spirit at Pentecost provides a fuller picture of this water-Spirit-baptism connection.

In John the Baptist's description of his ministry, he specifically stated that it was a ministry of water baptism, but that Jesus would baptize with the Holy Spirit. In this way, John's ministry was typical of the antitypical ministry of Christ.

Hints pointing to the outpouring of the Spirit by Christ appear in two portions of the Gospels. In John's Gospel, Jesus did not personally perform water baptisms, but left this task to His disciples (John 4:1–2). Christ likely did not perform water baptisms because His was a greater task: to baptize with the Holy Spirit. In Christ's post-resurrection appearances, He alluded to His imminent outpouring of the Spirit.

---

57. Carson, *John*, 194–95.
58. Cf. Carson, *John*, 195.
59. Herman Ridderbos, *The Gospel of John: A Theological Commentary* (1987; Grand Rapids: Eerdmans, 1997), 128–29.
60. Geerhardus Vos, "The Eschatological Aspect of the Pauline Conception of the Spirit," in Gaffin, *Redemptive History and Biblical Interpretation*, 91–125.

One of these occasions was when He appeared to the disciples and presented Himself especially to Thomas: "And when He had said this, He breathed on them and said to them, 'Receive the Holy Spirit'" (John 20:22). There are a number of options for interpreting this event, but the strongest appears to be that Christ was symbolically pointing forward to the out-pouring of the Spirit on the church.[61] While Christ certainly promised that He would send the Spirit (John 14–16), the sending and outpouring of the Spirit was the fulfillment of the baptism of the Spirit of which John the Baptist spoke. Christ therefore breathed on His disciples, which evoked other pneumatic images from the Old Testament, to convey the idea that He would soon pour out the Holy Spirit and baptize the church, which was an act of new creation (cf. Gen 2:7; Ezek. 37:5–6).[62] In the immediate context of His breathing on the disciples, however, Christ also referred to the forgiveness of sins, a theme commonly found with the Levitical water lustration passages of the Old Testament (John 20:23).

At Pentecost, the church received the baptism of the Spirit, though there are perhaps elements of this event that are not often connected directly to baptism. The most obvious connection is that the events of Pentecost fulfill the Old Testament prophecy of Joel regarding the promised outpouring of the Spirit. Joel's prophecy does not stand alone but appears with the other Old Testament prophecies to the same effect. The outpouring of the Spirit was an eschatological event tied to the dawning of the kingdom of God and the ascension of Christ to His session at the right hand of the Father. This is especially evident in Peter's quotation and interpretive modifica-tion of the Joel prophecy. In the original prophecy, Joel states, "And it shall come to pass afterward that I will pour out my Spirit on all flesh" (Joel 2:28), but Peter says, "And it shall come to pass in the last days, says God, that I will pour out of My Spirit on all flesh" (Acts 2:17).[63] Peter places the fulfillment of the prophecy clearly in the ἐσχάταις ἡμέραις (last days). In other words, this is the long-awaited and promised eschatological baptism of the Spirit.

---

61. See Carson, *John*, 649–55; also Ridderbos, *John*, 643.

62. Morna Hooker, "John's Baptism: A Prophetic Sign," in *The Holy Spirit and Christian Origins: Essays in Honor of James D. G. Dunn*, eds. Graham N. Stanton, et al (Grand Rapids: Eerdmans, 2004), 39.

63. Richard N. Longenecker, *The Book of Acts*, EBC (Grand Rapids: Zondervan, 1995), 71; F. F. Bruce, *The Book of Acts*, NICNT (Grand Rapids: Eerdmans, 1988), 61.

Another feature of Pentecost is that Christ pours out the Spirit. Peter states: "This Jesus God has raised up, of which we are all witnesses. Therefore being exalted to the right hand of God, and having received from the Father the promise of the Holy Spirit, He [Christ] poured out this which you now see and hear" (Acts 2:32–33). Christ received the promise of the Holy Spirit. Some commentators, such as C. K. Barrett, argue that these verses refer to one of two possible events, either Christ's baptismal reception of the Spirit (Luke 3:22) or the empowering of the Spirit at His resurrection. Barrett opts for the latter, arguing that, in context, the allusion to Psalm 16 is decisive, in that on Christ's exaltation to the right hand of the Father He received the Spirit in order that He might give it away (cf. Phil. 2:9; Eph. 4:8).[64]

However, it seems that one need not pick between the baptism of Christ and His resurrection, for Christ's reception of the Spirit and His subsequent outpouring of the Spirit on the church can be seen as a unitary complex of events. As F. F. Bruce explains, "He who had earlier received the Spirit for the public discharge of his own earthly ministry had now received that same Spirit to impart to his representatives, in order that they might continue, and indeed share in, the ministry which he had begun."[65] In other words, God promised that He would anoint His servant with the Spirit, but He also promised that He would give His Son the Spirit to pour out on the church. In this way, then, through Christ's resurrection He became a πνεῦμα ζωοποιοῦν (life-giving spirit) (1 Cor. 15:45).[66] Christ poured out the promised Spirit on the church and baptized her.

This complex of events informing Pentecost should be seen in the light of the rich Old Testament background, not only the new creation-Spirit imagery but also the Levitical lustrations, as well as the words of John the Baptist, who prophesied that Christ would baptize with the Holy Spirit.[67] This means that Pentecost is the baptism in the Spirit.[68]

However, while this is a baptism of the Spirit, it is accompanied by water baptism. When the crowds ask what they must do to be saved, Peter responds: "Repent, and let every one of you be baptized in the name of Jesus

---

64. C. K. Barrett, *Acts*, vol. 1, ICC (Edinburgh: T & T Clark, 1994), 149–50.

65. Bruce, *Acts*, 67.

66. Geerhardus Vos, *The Pauline Eschatology* (1930; Phillipsburg, N.J.: P & R, 1994), 10, 184.

67. See Luzarraga, *Las Tradiciones de la Nube*, 236.

68. Dunn, *Baptism*, 40.

Christ for the remission of sins; and you shall receive the gift of the Holy Spirit" (Acts 2:38). Just as repentance was an element in John's baptism (Luke 3:3), it is also a regular part of New Testament baptism. Beyond this, those who place their faith in Christ belong to the Spirit-baptized community of the last days. In other words, those who have received the baptism of the Spirit of Christ receive water baptism and are marked as those belonging to the covenant community, the church.[69] As Bruce explains:

> Baptism in the Spirit is an inward work; baptism in water now becomes its external token. Baptism in water is thus given a richer significance than it formerly had, thanks to the saving work of Christ and the reception of the Spirit. The baptism of the Spirit which it was our Lord's prerogative to bestow was, strictly speaking, something that took place once for all on the day of Pentecost when he poured out the promised gift on his disciples and thus constituted them the people of God in the new age; baptism in water continued to be the visible sign by which those who believed the gospel, repented of their sins, and acknowledged Jesus as Lord were publicly incorporated into the Spirit-baptized fellowship of the new people of God.[70]

Those marked by water and Spirit baptism are therefore part of the eschatological humanity, the new creation, the new heaven and earth. As Paul says, if anyone is in Christ, he is new creation (2 Cor. 5:17).

PAUL AND BAPTISM AS NEW CREATION

There are other connections between baptism and new creation beyond the texts already surveyed. Within the Pauline corpus there are two significant texts that deal with baptism as new creation, Romans 6:1–4 and Titus 3:5. This section will survey these texts to demonstrate the connections between baptism and new creation.

Baptism and the newness of life

Students of Pauline theology are well aware of the apostle's famous statement concerning baptism in Romans 6:1–4, though it is specifically verses 3–4 that are of interest: "Or do you not know that as many of us as were baptized into Christ Jesus were baptized into His death? Therefore we were

---

69. Barrett, *Acts*, 154.
70. Bruce, *Acts*, 70.

buried with Him through baptism into death, that just as Christ was raised from the dead by the glory of the Father, even so we also should walk in newness of life." Verse 3 will be investigated in the following chapter when we examine baptism as eschatological judgment. For now, verse 4 is of particular interest, especially the connection that Paul draws between baptism and the newness of life. In verse 4, Paul makes a conclusion from verse 3: the believer's incorporation into Christ's death through baptism.[71] (Several exegetical questions surround these verses, but we will not cover them, as others have ably done so.[72])

In context, the believer's baptism, which is administered on the presumption of faith and the outpouring of the Spirit in adult converts, yields the result (ἵνα) of walking in the newness of life. As Douglas Moo explains, "'Newness of life' is a life empowered by the realities of the new age—including especially God's Spirit (Rom. 7:6)—and a life that should reflect the values of that new age."[73] While Paul does not use the explicit language of new creation, he nevertheless uses concepts and terms that are inextricably bound with it. Paul uses καινότης and καινός with reference to the new or eschatological age (cf. καινότης in Rom. 7:6 and καινός in 1 Cor. 11:25; 2 Cor. 3:6; 5:17; Gal. 6:15; Eph. 2:15; 4:24). The grammatical construction behind the phrase καινότητι ζωῆς (newness of life) could be a genitive of quality with the emphasis on the word *life* or an epexegetic genitive meaning "newness, that is, life," but καινότης most likely is an objective genitive—"the newness [the new age] that leads to, or confers, life."[74] In other words, baptism leads to the age to come, or the new heaven and earth, the new creation.

Washing of regeneration

Paul makes a similar point in his epistle to Titus, though at first glance the baptism-new creation connection might not be evident. Paul writes that God "saved us, through the washing of regeneration and renewing of the Holy Spirit, whom He poured out on us abundantly through Jesus Christ our Savior" (3:5–6). Paul has in view baptism and the outpouring of the Holy Spirit. Paul's use of the terms παλιγγενεσία (regeneration) and

---

71. Douglas Moo, *The Epistle to the Romans*, NICNT (Grand Rapids: Eerdmans, 1996), 361.

72. See Moo, *Romans*, 361–67.

73. Moo, *Romans*, 366.

74. Moo, *Romans*, 366, n. 71; cf. John Murray, *The Epistle to the Romans*, NICNT (1959–65; Grand Rapids: Eerdmans, 1968), 217.

ἀνακαίνωσις (renewal) are of particular relevance. Historically, some have interpreted παλιγγενεσία as a reference to the *ordo salutis*. John Calvin, for example, explains, "It is God's Spirit who regenerates us and makes us new creatures, but since His grace is invisible and hidden, a visible symbol of it is given to us in baptism."[75] More recently, others have made similar suggestions.[76] True, the work of the Holy Spirit in the application of redemption most certainly makes a person a new creature. However, it does not appear that these terms refer to the *ordo salutis* as much as to the new creation; the reference is primarily redemptive-historical.

While caution is necessary with the employment of extra-biblical sources to define biblical Greek terms, according to the Stoic use, such as in the writings of Philo, παλιγγενεσία referred to periodic restorations of the world. This is a kind of new creation, though obviously entrenched in the Stoic cyclical view of history, a view foreign to the Bible. However, this idea of new creation seems to be similar to the only other use of the term in the New Testament: "Assuredly I say to you, that in the regeneration [ἐν τῇ παλιγγενεσίᾳ], when the Son of Man sits on the throne of His glory, you who have followed Me will also sit on twelve thrones, judging the twelve tribes of Israel" (Matt. 19:28). Here Christ speaks of the eschaton, when the Son of Man will rule over the renewed creation, a statement entrenched in the Old Testament's linear view of history (cf. Gen. 1:28; Pss. 2, 8; Dan. 7).[77] Both Paul's and Matthew's use of the term has roots in the Old Testament expectation of the eschatological new creation. In this vein, Vos explains Matthew 19:28: "In this saying the word cannot be restricted to the more or less individualizing application of the resurrection; it covers the resurrection as a whole and even the renewal of the universe as is shown from the parallels in Mark and Luke which have as its equivalent descriptions the final state" (cf. Mark 10:29–30; Luke 3:20b–21; 22:29–30).[78]

---

75. John Calvin, *2 Corinthians and Timothy, Titus, & Philemon*, CNTC (1964; Grand Rapids: Eerdmans, 1996), 383.

76. See George W. Knight, *The Pastoral Epistles*, NIGTC (Grand Rapids: Eerdmans, 1992), 342.

77. J. Guhrt, *paliggenesia* in NIDNTT, 1.184; also J. N. D. Kelly, *The Pastoral Epistles*, BNTC (1960; Peabody, Mass.: Hendrickson, 1998), 252; G. K. Beale, "The New Testament and New Creation," in *Biblical Theology: Retrospect & Prospect*, ed. Scott J. Hafemann (Downers Grove, Ill.: InterVarsity, 2002), 169, n. 12; Hagner, *Matthew*, 2.565; Herman Bavinck, *Saved by Grace: The Holy Spirit's Work in Calling and Regeneration*, trans. Nelson D. Kloosterman, ed. J. Mark Beach (Grand Rapids: Reformation Heritage Books, 2008), 160.

78. Vos, *Pauline Eschatology*, 50. Vos also explains from extra-biblical literature that the term is synonymous with ἀποκατάστασις (Josephus, *Antiquities*, 9.3–9).

This conclusion also seems to be borne out by the use of the term in other second-temple contexts. For example, Josephus uses the term παλιγγενεσία interchangeably with the term ἀποκατάστασις (restoration). Josephus also uses these terms to describe the second exodus, the return from exile: "And all that Cyrus intended to do before him relating to the restoration [ἀποκαταστάσεως] of Jerusalem, Darius also ordained should be done accordingly.... So they betook themselves to drinking and eating, and for seven days they continued feasting, and kept a festival, for the rebuilding and restoration [παλιγγενεσίαν] of their country."[79] Coincidentally, when Clement of Rome (30–100) wrote to Corinth, he spoke of the flood re-creation in this way: "Noah, being found faithful, preached regeneration [παλιγγενεσίαν] to the world through his ministry."[80] Παλιγγενεσία as new creation seems to be a legitimate conclusion considering the other term Paul uses in Titus 3:5, ἀνακαίνωσις. The renewal of the Holy Spirit is connected to His eschatological work, and the one who receives baptism—the sacramental counterpart to the outpouring of the Holy Spirit and the acknowledgement of the presence of faith—becomes part of the new creation (2 Cor. 5:17).[81] Hence, even in the writings of Paul there is the intimate connection between baptism and new creation.

CONCLUSION

In this survey of pre-redemptive and redemptive history, there is a contiguous set of images that all point to the conclusion that the waters of baptism are the waters of new creation. The Spirit hovered like a bird over the creation's watery chaos. Noah released a dove over the receding floodwaters. The Spirit of God hovered over Israel in the void like a bird during the exodus Red Sea crossing. In all of these major pre-redemptive and redemptive-historical events, a new creation emerges from the waters under the superintendence of the Holy Spirit. These typical images, however, culminate in the descent of the Holy Spirit on Christ, the last Adam, who, subsequent to His earthly ministry, then baptized the church, and in so doing continued the dawn of the new heaven and earth at Pentecost. The waters of baptism are not in and

---

79. Josephus, *Antiquities* 11:63–66.
80. "The First Epistle of Clement," § 9, in ANF 1.7.
81. Kelly, *Pastoral Epistles*, 252; similarly, Knight, *Pastoral Epistles*, 344; Herman Ridderbos, *Paul: An Outline of His Theology* (Grand Rapids: Eerdmans, 1975), 213, 224.

of themselves magical. They are not the instrument that effects the church's birth and entry to the "already" of the eschaton, but rather point to Christ's outpouring of the Spirit on His people.

At this point, Part II of the study has focused only on the blessing aspects of baptism. There are, however, other ideas connected with baptism, namely, matters of judgment and wrath. To this end, the next chapter will explore the idea of baptism as covenant ordeal or covenantal judgment. When James and John ask Jesus for the privilege of sitting at His right and left in His kingdom, Jesus responds with a reference to baptism. Christ underwent baptism at the Jordan, but His statement to the Sons of Thunder is clearly future. Why does Christ invoke the language of baptism for His impending crucifixion? The answer lies in the idea of baptism as covenantal judgment.

CHAPTER 9

Baptism as Covenant Judgment

Over the years, much ink has been spilled to explain the doctrine of baptism, though one contextual element that has often been ignored is the doctrine of the covenant. Part I showed that in Anabaptist theology during the Reformation, Particular Baptist theology in the post-Reformation, and the formulations of Friedrich Schleiermacher in the modern period, theologians seldom mentioned the idea of covenant in connection with baptism or did so in a mitigated fashion in comparison with Reformed theology.[1]

Yet biblical scholars from different fields have noted the centrality of the covenant concept as the key to understanding the Bible. Walther Eichrodt, for example, explains: "The concept in which Israelite thought gave definitive expression to the binding of the people to God and by means of which they established firmly from the start the particularity of their knowledge of him was the covenant."[2] Likewise, N. T. Wright argues that the covenant is one of the main clues, usually neglected, for understanding Paul and his writings.[3] In one sense, these observations are not new, as the Reformed tradition has historically acknowledged the fundamental nature of the idea of covenant to a proper understanding of the Bible. This was especially evident in Part I in the survey of Reformation and post-Reformation understandings of baptism as the sign of the covenant. If any subject in the Bible must in some way relate to God's covenantal dealings with His people, it only makes sense that the connections between baptism and covenant must be explored.

---

1. More recently, see Stanley J. Grenz, *Theology for the Community of God* (Nashville: Broadman & Holman, 1994), 557–62; Millard J. Erickson, *Christian Theology* (Grand Rapids: Baker, 1985), 1100–1101.

2. Walther Eichrodt, *The Theology of the Old Testament*, vol. 1 (Philadelphia: Westminster, 1961), 36.

3. N. T. Wright, *The Climax of the Covenant: Christ and the Law in Pauline Theology* (Minneapolis: Fortress, 1991), xi.

To that end, a brief survey of some of the fundamental characteristics of Old Testament covenants is necessary. Of particular interest is the sign of the covenant, circumcision. Though there are some who contest the idea that circumcision is related to baptism, against the backdrop of the covenant-circumcision bond, the relationship between circumcision and baptism will become evident.

The purpose of this chapter is to prove that baptism, in addition to being connected to the idea of new creation, is also connected to the idea of covenant judgment. In other words, baptism is not exclusively representative of covenant blessing (or new creation), but also represents covenant sanction. Covenant judgment illuminates Christ's curious statement that His impending crucifixion was a baptism (Matt. 10:38–39; Luke 12:50). Covenant judgment also explains why Paul places circumcision and baptism in parallel when writing of the crucifixion of Christ (Col. 2:11–12). The chapter will first establish briefly the covenantal framework of the Old Testament. Second, it will examine circumcision as covenant judgment. Third, the chapter will explore the connections between baptism and circumcision. Fourth, it will examine baptism as covenant judgment.

GENERAL COVENANTAL FRAMEWORK OF THE OLD TESTAMENT

In the pages of the Pentateuch, the reader will find repeated reference to the idea of covenant. A generic definition of a ברית (covenant) is a treaty, alliance, contract, or agreement between two parties.[4] The similarities between the Hittite vassal treaties of the ancient Near East (2nd millennium BC) and the covenant in the book of Deuteronomy cast light on the nature of biblical covenants. There are typically six elements in Hittite vassal treaties:

1. A titular introduction of the treaty participants, such as the suzerain, or covenant lord, and his vassal, or servant.

2. A historical prologue rehearsing past relationships.

3. Stipulations to the treaty.

4. A clause requiring the treaty's regular reading and its preservation in a temple.

---

4. BDB, q.v. ברית, 136; HALOT, 1.157–59.

5. Blessings and sanctions (curses) for keeping or breaking the treaty.

6. A list of those who witness the treaty.

Some of these characteristics appear in a small excerpt from the Hittite treaty between Suppiluliumas and Aziras of Amurru: "These are the words of the Sun Suppiluliumas, the great king, the king of the Hatti land, the valiant, the favorite of the Storm-god. I, the Sun, made you my vassal. And if you, Aziras, 'protect' the king of the Hatti land, your master, the king of the Hatti land, your master, will 'protect' you in the same way."[5]

This is not to say that there is perfect consonance between the treaties of the ancient Near East and the Bible, Deuteronomy in particular.[6] Much of the content of the biblical covenants is unique, but there is nevertheless enough similarity between the ancient Near Eastern and Old Testament covenants that "the analogy of the treaties helps make the general point that Yahweh is Israel's suzerain and that the covenantal relationship demands for its preservation a certain commitment from the people."[7]

Two major types of covenants are found in the Old Testament: those between human parties and those between God and His people. There are several types of covenants between human parties:[8]

1. Friendship: such as David's covenant with Jonathan (1 Sam. 18:3; cf. 20:8).

2. Parity: between rulers or powerful individuals, such as Abraham's covenant with Abimelech (Gen. 21:27; cf. 26:28; 31:44; 1 Kings 5:12; 15:19; 2 Kings 11:4).

3. Suzerain and vassal: between a more powerful party that sets the terms and a weaker party, such as Joshua's treaty with the Gibeon-ites (Josh. 9:15; cf. 1 Sam. 11:1; Ezek. 17:13–18; Jer. 34:8).

4. Marriage: a permanent union between a man and woman (Mal. 2:14; cf. Ezek. 16:8).

The covenants between God and man are similar to suzerain-vassal agreements. In any covenant, God is clearly the more powerful party. Nevertheless, this does not mean that all of God's covenants with His people

---

5. ANE 2, 42.

6. Gordon J. McConville, *berit*, in NIDOTTE, 1.747. See also Delbert R. Hillers, *Treaty-Curses of the Old Testament Prophets* (Rome: Pontifical Biblical Institute, 1964), 2.

7. McConville, *berit*, 747.

8. McConville, *berit*, 748.

have the exact same form. Some covenants are clearly unilateral, wholly depending on God for their execution. Other covenants are bilateral in nature, requiring a response on the part of God's people.[9] Within the Bible, there are several major covenants between God and His people:

- **Adamic.** This is the covenant between God and Adam wherein, upon the condition of obedience to the commandment of God, Adam would have secured eternal life for himself and his offspring (cf. Gen. 2:16–17; 3:22; Lev. 18:5; Hos. 6:7; Rom. 5:12–20). The signs of this covenant were the trees of life and knowledge.

- **Noahic.** This is the covenant between God and Noah, but more broadly between God and the creation (Gen. 9:8–17). This covenant falls in the unilateral category, as it consists of God's promise. God also has an accompanying sign of the covenant, the rainbow (Gen. 9:13).

- **Abrahamic.** This is the covenant God made with Abraham (Gen. 15:18; 17:2), which includes Abraham's seed, land, and a continuing relationship with God. It has the ultimate goal of the blessing of the nations. Though emphasis lies on the unilateral administration of this covenant, the bilateral element is present in the expected response (Gen. 17:1, 9–14). This covenant also has a sign, circumcision (Gen. 17:9–14).

- **Mosaic.** This is the covenant between God and Israel on the occasion of their exodus from Egypt (Ex. 19–24). Once again, while there are clearly unilateral elements in this covenant, for only God could deliver Israel, there is a greater emphasis on the bilateral elements involved in keeping the covenant (Ex. 19:5). This covenant includes the Decalogue (Ex. 20:2–27), the book of the covenant containing additional covenant stipulations (Ex. 21–23), covenant ratification (Ex. 24:3–8), the covenant meal (Ex. 24:9–11), the construction of the tabernacle (Ex. 25–27), the consecration of the Aaronic priesthood (Ex. 28–29), and the ritual regulations of Leviticus. The most developed form of the Mosaic covenant appears in Deuteronomy, which bears

---

9. McConville, *b'rit*, 748–50. This is not to deny the sovereignty of God in His redemptive activities toward man. The bilateral aspects of a covenant do not admit synergism but recognize the importance of human responsibility. For a historical and theological treatment of these aspects of a covenant, see Richard A. Muller, *Dictionary of Latin and Greek Theological Terms: Drawn Principally from Scholastic Theology* (Grand Rapids: Baker, 1985), 120, 122, q. v. *foedus monopleuron* and *foedus dipleuron*; Lyle D. Bierma, "Federal Theology in the Sixteenth Century: Two Traditions?" *WTJ* 45 (1983), 304–21; cf. J. Wayne Baker, *Heinrich Bullinger and the Covenant: The Other Reformed Tradition* (Athens: Ohio University Press, 1980). There is also a balance between the uni- and bilateral elements in salvation in such confessional documents as the WCF (cf. §§ 3, 9).

strong similarities to Hittite vassal treaties.[10] This covenant builds on the Abrahamic covenant in that circumcision is still required by its male participants, but God gives the Israelites an additional sign of the covenant, the Sabbath (Ex. 31:13).

• **Davidic.** This is the promise of God to King David (2 Sam. 7:8–17). This covenant emphasizes the unilateral promise of God and contains no explicit conditions. It is described as a "covenant of salt" (2 Chron. 13:5), which conveys the idea of permanence (cf. Lev. 2:13; Num. 18:19). This covenant is rooted in the Mosaic and Abrahamic covenants.

While this list of covenants is not exhaustive, it gives a framework from which to examine circumcision as a sign of covenant judgment.[11]

CIRCUMCISION AS COVENANT JUDGMENT

Covenant and curse

Covenant curse is one of the realities to which the sign of circumcision points, but in what way is covenant linked to curse? When God made His covenant with Abraham, He instructed the patriarch to sever animals in half (Gen. 15:9–10). Later, after the sun had gone down, "Behold, a smoking fire pot and a flaming torch passed between these pieces" (Gen. 15:17). While the details are challenging, interpreters have identified the smoking fire pot and flaming torch with the presence of God (cf. Ex. 19:18; 20:5; 24:17; 34:5–7; Deut. 4:11, 24, 33).[12] Why did God pass between the severed animal halves? The answer comes from the parallels found in Hittite treaties.[13] The common practice was for the two parties making an agreement to walk between severed animal halves as an oath of self-malediction. If either party violated the terms of the covenant, the covenant-breaker would be severed in half, just as the animals had been severed. This is the sanction aspect of a covenant. Delbert Hillers explains, "The ancient treaty was basically an elaborate promise, and the function of the curses attached to the treaty was to make sure that the promise would be kept by invoking

---

10. Meredith G. Kline, *The Structure of Biblical Authority* (Eugene, Ore.: Wipf & Stock, 1989), 37.

11. For a more in-depth treatment of Old Testament covenants, see Michael Horton, *God of Promise: Introducing Covenant Theology* (Grand Rapids: Baker, 2006).

12. Bruce K. Waltke, *Genesis: A Commentary* (Grand Rapids: Zondervan, 2001), 244.

13. See Gordon J. Wenham, *Genesis*, vol. 1, WBC (Dallas: Word, 1987), 333.

the punishment of the gods on the defaulter."[14] In fact, it is from this practice of severing animals that the covenant initiation language of "cutting" (כרת) a covenant originates.[15]

Confirmation of this idea arises not only from the Hittite treaties of the ancient Near East, but from within the pages of the Old Testament.[16] The prophet Jeremiah states:

> And I will give the men that have transgressed my covenant, which have not performed the words of the covenant which they had made before me, when they cut the calf in twain, and passed between the parts thereof...into the hand of their enemies, and into the hand of them that seek their life: and their dead bodies shall be for meat unto the fowls of the heaven, and to the beasts of the earth (Jer. 34:18–20).[17]

This evidence shows that covenants typically have blessings and sanctions connected with them. In the case of the Abrahamic covenant, God walked through the severed animal halves alone, which meant that He took the self-maledictory oath. God alone would bear the curse for both His and Abraham's violations of the terms of the covenant. However, the curse of the covenant would fall on the covenant member who did not look to the promise of Yahweh by faith, as did Abraham (Gen. 15:6). This conclusion is evident from the sign of the covenant, namely, circumcision.

Circumcision and covenantal judgment

To explore the particulars of circumcision as a sign of the covenant, the first place to turn is God's command to Abraham that he circumcise himself and all of the males in his household. In the Genesis 17 covenant ratification, God tells Abraham, "You shall be circumcised in the flesh of your foreskins, and it shall be a sign of the covenant between Me and you" (Gen. 17:11).[18] In one sense, circumcision is a sign of covenant blessing, as it is connected to God's covenant promise to bless Abraham and make him a great nation (cf. Gen. 12:1–3; 13:14–16; 17:3–8). However, it is evident

---

14. Hillers, *Treaty-Curses*, 6; also Nahum Sarna, *Genesis*, JPSTC (New York: Jewish Publicaiton Society, 1989), 114–15.

15. Hillers, *Treaty-Curses*, 20.

16. For citations of ancient Near Eastern literature where one finds the severing of animals, see Hillers, *Treaty-Curses*, 19–20.

17. Hillers, *Treaty-Curses*, 25–26; Wenham, vol. 1, *Genesis*, 332; Waltke, *Genesis*, 244–45; cf. J. A. Thompson, *The Book of Jeremiah*, NICOT (Grand Rapids: Eerdmans, 1980), 612–13.

18. Gerhard Von Rad, *Genesis* (1961; Philadelphia: Westminster, 1972), 199; Waltke, *Genesis*, 259; Gordon J. Wenham, *Genesis*, vol. 2, WBC (Dallas: Word, 1994), 20.

from two further observations that judgment and sanction are connected to the covenant sign of circumcision as well. First, the rite in and of itself is bloody and painful; second, God declares, "And the uncircumcised male child, who is not circumcised in the flesh of his foreskin, that person shall be cut off from his people; he has broken My covenant" (Gen. 17:14). Even in the very giving of the sign, there are elements of blessing and curse associated with the rite.

Elements of covenant curse are manifest, considering that circumcision pointed either to the circumcision of the heart or to being cut off from the covenant community. In Jeremiah, for example, the prophet calls out to Israel, "Circumcise yourselves to the LORD, and take away the foreskins of your hearts" (Jer. 4:4). The removal of the foreskin, therefore, was supposed to point to the inward spiritual reality of the circumcision of the heart. As J. A. Thompson explains: "It was never intended as a mere outward sign, but as a witness to an inward reality, the surrender of the whole life to the sovereignty of Yahweh (Deut. 10:16; 30:6). It was not the removal of the loose foreskin that covered the extremity of the male organ that was significant, but the removal of the hard excrescence of the heart."[19] However, at the same time, if a newborn Israelite male was not circumcised, he was cut off from the covenant community. Likewise, if an Israelite male was guilty of any number of offenses against the law, he could find himself temporarily or permanently cut off from the covenant community. As Paul later writes, "For circumcision is indeed profitable if you keep the law; but if you are a breaker of the law, your circumcision has become uncircumcision" (Rom. 2:25). The relationship between the cutting of the covenant and the cutting away of the foreskin appears in the use of the same language. One "cut a covenant" (כרת ברית), and any uncircumcised male who was not circumcised was supposed to be cut off (ונכרתה) from the people; he was guilty of breaking the covenant, and therefore the covenant curse would fall on him (Gen. 17:14).[20] Either the foreskin was cut off, symbolic of one's effectual calling, or the person was cut off from the covenant community.

Circumcision and the exodus

The connections between circumcision and covenant judgment appear in several other Old Testament texts. Readers are often perplexed by the

19. Thompson, *Jeremiah*, 215.

20. Meredith G. Kline, *By Oath Consigned* (Grand Rapids: Eerdmans, 1968), 43.

rather peculiar incident early in the exodus narrative, when Yahweh came to kill Moses because he had not circumcised his son (Ex. 4:24–26). Zipporah, his wife, circumcised Moses' son, then touched Moses' feet with the severed foreskin, which averted the wrath of God and saved Moses' life. Admittedly, the details of this event are not crystal clear. Nevertheless, it seems that Moses had failed to circumcise his son as the Abrahamic covenant required.[21] The text does not state the specific reason why Moses had not done this. Umberto Cassuto suggests that it was because Zipporah and their son were not members of the covenant and Moses therefore assumed circumcision was not required.[22] Regardless of the reason, it appears that the blood of circumcision averted the wrath of God that otherwise would have fallen on Moses. Cassuto explains that when Moses' wife touched his feet with the blood, she was effectively saying, "Let the one take the place of the other." Cassuto goes on, "Just as the first-born son sometimes suffers on account of his father…so shall the shedding of a few drops of the blood of Moses' first-born son, which consecrates the infant to the service of the Lord, serve as an additional and decisive consecration of his father to the Lord's mission."[23]

A similar pattern unfolds in the Passover judgment-deliverance. In fact, it seems that the circumcision of Moses' son foreshadowed the coming Passover judgment-deliverance.[24] The Egyptian firstborn, who were not under the blood of the Passover lamb, fell under God's wrath, whereas the Israelite firstborn, who were under the blood, were redeemed from His wrath.[25] The link between these two outcomes seems likely given that the immediate context of the circumcision of Moses' son has to do with the Passover (Ex. 4:23, 24–26).[26] In this sense, the Passover is like the Abrahamic covenant ratification ceremony—either God bears the curse of the covenant or man does. Circumcision points to the substitute with the severing of the foreskin—or, in the case of the Passover, the sacrificial lamb—or the blood of the person is required.

---

21. Cf. e.g., J. Morgenstern, "'The Bloody Husband' (?) (Exod. 4:24–26) Once Again," *Hebrew Union College Annual* 34 (1963): 35–70; Geza Vermes, "Baptism and Jewish Exegesis: New Light From Ancient Sources," *NTS* 4 (1958): 308–19.

22. Umberto Cassuto, *A Commentary on the Book of Exodus* (1967; Jerusalem: Magnes, 1997), 60.

23. Cassuto, *Exodus*, 60.

24. Peter Enns, *Exodus*, NIVAC (Grand Rapids: Zondervan, 2000), 133–34.

25. Cassuto, *Exodus*, 60.

26. Kline, *By Oath Consigned*, 89, n. 11.

Circumcision and the conquest

A second and similar incident came on the eve of the Israelite entrance into the Promised Land. Before Israel entered the land, Joshua was instructed to circumcise Israel. The narrative states that the second generation had not been circumcised in the wilderness (Josh. 5:7). So Joshua did as he was told and circumcised all the men of Israel (Josh. 5:2–3). There are three important observations to make:

First, the first generation, all of whom were circumcised, died in the wilderness, and the text specifically states that they died "because they did not obey the voice of the LORD" (Josh. 5:6). The author of Hebrews also explains Israel's initial failure to enter the land: "For indeed the gospel was preached to us as well as to them; but the word which they heard did not profit them, not being mixed with faith in those who heard it" (Heb. 4:2). In other words, because they failed to look by faith to the promises of God, they suffered the curse of the covenant.

Second, Israel's circumcision was in preparation for the celebration of the Passover meal (Josh. 5:8–10). The circumcision-Passover combination recapitulates the pattern found in Exodus 4 and therefore evokes the same theme, namely, redemption and sanction-curse: for the substitute there is curse, symbolized by the severed foreskin and the sacrificial lamb, and redemption for the one who looks by faith to the substitute and is circumcised.[27] Moreover, circumcision was required to participate in the Passover (Ex. 12:48).

Third, as in Moses' encounter with the Lord in Exodus 4, the Israelites faced the pre-incarnate sword-wielding Christ (Josh. 5:13–14). Had Israel tried to proceed apart from their circumcision, the Lord would have turned the sword against them, just as the cherubim guarding the entrance of the garden-temple after the fall was prepared to do to Adam and Eve. Meredith Kline observes concerning this christophany, "It is as if the sword of the captain of the host of the Lord had been turned away from the uncircumcised nation by their cutting the covenant-allegiance oath anew through circumcision, and only then could be directed against the Canaanites to cut them off from the land" (cf. Josh. 5:13; Rom. 13:4; Rev. 19:15–16; Ezek. 28:10; 31:18; 32:10–13).[28] The narrative quietly insists that Israel's blessed

---

27. Marten H. Woudstra, *The Book of Joshua*, NICOT (Grand Rapids: Eerdmans, 1981), 102.

28. Kline, *By Oath Consigned*, 42–43, n. 11.

state in the land of promise could be secured only if a substitute suffered the curse of the covenant, which was represented in circumcision.

Circumcision and the second exodus

This brings a third observation that comes from the book of Isaiah. The prophet's oracles come from the context of the prophesied Babylonian exile. Within the broader scope of redemptive history, Israel, God's firstborn son (Ex. 4:22; Hos. 11:1), had been unruly and disobedient, and therefore had suffered the punishment of exile-death (Lev. 26:33–39; Deut. 21:18–21).[29] Israel had undergone a national circumcision; he had been cut off from the presence of God and was suffering the curse of the covenant for his disobedience (e.g., Ps. 37:9, 22). But even though Israel lay in exile-death, he would be raised from the dead (Ezek. 37). This restoration, however, would not occur with the wave of a wand, but would be accomplished by the Servant of Yahweh, the One who would die as a sacrifice and usher in the second exodus.

At the heart of the Suffering Servant passage in Isaiah 53, Yahweh says of Him, "He was cut off from the land of the living; for the transgressions of My people He was stricken" (Isa. 53:8). There is a parallel phrase in Jeremiah 11:19, where the more commonplace verb, one associated with circumcision and covenant, is used, namely, כרת. Here in Isaiah 53:8, though the rarer verb גזר is used, it conveys the same idea, namely, death and covenant curse (cf. Jer. 11:19, 21).[30] Read against the larger redemptive-historical backdrop, the statement in Isaiah and its parallel in Jeremiah convey the idea that the messianic Servant was to undergo the curse of the covenant; He would suffer not merely the symbolic rite in His own circumcision as an infant on the eighth day, but would be circumcised; He would be כרת. He would be cut off from the land of the living, which means not simply cut off from society or from the people, but in the currency of the foundational Old Testament revelation of the Pentateuch, He would undergo God's wrath. The Servant

---

29. Stephen G. Dempster, *Dominion and Dynasty: A Theology of the Hebrew Bible*, NSBT (Downers Grove, Ill.: InterVarsity, 2003), 172.

30. John Goldingay, *The Message of Isaiah 40–55* (Edinburgh: T & T Clark, 2005), 507. Commentators simply note the significance of the term גזר and explain it is associated with a violent death, which is a correct conclusion, but fail to read the statement against the broader redemptive-historical backdrop of covenant curse (cf. J. Alec Motyer, *Isaiah*, TOTC [Downers Grove, Ill.: InterVarsity, 1999], 336–37; John H. Oswalt, *The Book of Isaiah*, vol. 2 [Grand Rapids: Eerdmans, 1998], 395–96; cf. Kline, *By Oath Consigned*, 46).

would be cut off from the land, from the beneficent presence of Yahweh (cf. Isa. 38:11; Pss. 27:13; 142:5).

Circumcision and new creation

Before proceeding to the New Testament, we must note the important typological image that emerges, not from one particular text, but from the concatenated whole. Namely, those who are under the blood of the circumcised, the cut–off, firstborn Son, as with Moses and his son, are safe not only from the wrath of God and possess a circumcised heart, but also are participants in the coming new creation, an idea intimately connected with the second exodus (cf. Isa. 63–65). A connection between the new creation and circumcision appears in that male infants were circumcised on the eighth day (Gen. 17:12; Lev. 12:3). As Nahum Sarna explains, "The eighth day is particularly significant because the newborn has completed a seven-day unit of time corresponding to the process of creation" (cf. Ex. 22:29; Lev. 22:27).[31]

Wolfhart Pannenberg draws attention to the Jewish expectation of the completion of the seventh day of creation and the beginning of an "eighth day of creation, which as the first day of a new week corresponds to the first day of creation in its function as a new beginning."[32] Fourth Esdras, a non-canonical work of Jewish literature, states: "And after these years my son the Messiah shall die, and all who draw human breath. And the world shall be turned back to primeval silence for seven days, as it was at the first beginnings; so that no one shall be left. And after seven days the world, which is not yet awake, shall be roused, and that which is corruptible shall perish" (7:29–32). If the connection between the eighth day and the eschaton is sound, then those who either were not circumcised or were rebellious not only were cut off from the covenant and were under God's wrath, they also had no share in the new creation, the coming eschatological eighth day.

---

31. Sarna, *Genesis*, 125; Waltke, *Genesis*, 261.
32. Wolfhart Pannenberg, *Systematic Theology*, vol. 2 (1991; Grand Rapids: Eerdmans, 1994), 144–45.

CIRCUMCISION AND BAPTISM

The necessary groundwork from the Old Testament has been laid so that the chapter can cross over into the New Testament and see the connections between circumcision, covenant curse, and, more specifically, baptism as covenant judgment. In the New Testament, there are some peculiar statements that, read apart from the redemptive-historical background of the Old Testament, can be difficult to understand. The primary passage that should be explored in this regard is Colossians 2:11–12: "In Him you were also circumcised with the circumcision made without hands, by putting off the body of the sins of the flesh, by the circumcision of Christ, buried with Him in baptism, in which you also were raised with Him through faith in the working of God, who raised Him from the dead." This statement has drawn the attention of theologians and New Testament scholars for a host of reasons. In the broader scope of the survey thus far, these verses are the culmination of Old Testament covenant curse and circumcision concepts fulfilled in Christ. Significantly, Paul places these Old Testament ideas in parallel with the concept of baptism.

The circumcision of Christ

When Paul makes reference to the circumcision of Christ, what does he have in view? Is the reference to Christ's circumcision on the eighth day as an infant (Luke 2:21–24; cf. Gen 17:12)? Is this a genitive of possession denoting a circumcision that "belongs to Jesus" (NIV), in contrast to, for instance, the circumcision that belongs to Moses? Or does this refer to the circumcision that Christ underwent in His crucifixion? The best answer, especially given the redemptive-historical backdrop, is that Christ's crucifixion was a circumcision—He was cut off from the covenant community and the beneficent presence of God—He suffered the curse of the covenant.[33]

Christ was crucified "outside the camp" (Heb. 13:12–13). He was cut off from the land of the living. Christ "put off His body," not merely His foreskin but His life. The sword of judgment that sought the life of Moses, that fell on the Egyptian firstborn, and that would not let the uncircum-

---

33. Peter T. O'Brien, *Colossians, Philemon*, WBC, vol. 44 (Dallas: Word, 1982), 117; cf. F. F. Bruce, *The Epistles to the Colossians, to Philemon, and Ephesians*, NICNT (Grand Rapids: Eerdmans, 1984), 104; N. T. Wright, *Colossians & Philemon*, TNTC (Grand Rapids: Eerdmans, 1986), 106–107.

cised Israelites pass into the Promised Land was turned on Him.[34] Just as faithless Israel was cut off from the presence of God for his disobedience, the true and faithful Israel, Jesus, was cut off so that the exile under Satan, sin, and death would come to an end for God's people.

Up to this point, it may seem odd that a monograph dedicated to the subject of baptism has given so much space to the subject of circumcision. Nevertheless, the connections between circumcision and baptism as covenant judgment surface here in Colossians 2:11–12, particularly in how Paul parallels the two initiation rites.

Being buried with Christ in baptism

To be sure, there are commentators who do not see the parallel between baptism and circumcision.[35] These two verses are the location of a pitched battle between Baptists and paedobaptists. For the time, it is helpful to set aside the theological question of the proper recipients of baptism and look at the passage against the redemptive-historical backdrop to understand why Paul places circumcision and baptism in parallel. The underlying parallel is found not only in their identity as initiation rites, but also in understanding baptism as covenant judgment.

Notice what Paul says about each rite. He states: "In Him also you were circumcised with the circumcision made without hands" (v. 11a). Paul explains that through union with Christ believers undergo a circumcision—not a literal circumcision, as several passages in the Pauline corpus make abundantly clear, but a spiritual circumcision, the circumcision of the heart (cf. Rom. 2:28–29; Gal. 5:6; 6:15; Eph. 2:11; Phil. 3:3). What Old Testament Israel was unable to do through law keeping and the exhortations of Moses (Deut. 10:16), Christ has done through His life, death, resurrection, ascension, and consequent outpouring of the Spirit (Deut. 30:6). This is why Paul states that the believer undergoes a circumcision "made without hands," which is the work of the Spirit, who removes the foreskin of the heart, or, in terms of verse 11b, "putting off the body of the sins of the flesh." This work of the Spirit, the effectual calling and rebirth of a person, is accomplished, Paul writes, "by the circumcision of Christ" (v. 11c), which is a reference to Christ's crucifixion.

---

34. Kline, *By Oath Consigned*, 46.

35. See, e.g., Kurt Aland, *Did the Early Church Baptize Infants?* (1961; Eugene, Ore.: Wipf & Stock, 2004), 84; G. R. Beasley-Murray, *Baptism in the New Testament* (1962; Carlisle: Paternoster, 1997), 157–60.

The link between the suffering of Christ and the work of the Spirit is evident in another Pauline passage: "Christ has redeemed us from the curse of the law, having become a curse for us (for it is written, 'Cursed is everyone who hangs on a tree'), that the blessing of Abraham might come upon the Gentiles in Christ Jesus, that we might receive the promise of the Spirit through faith" (Gal. 3:13–14).[36] While the nomenclature is different, Paul's statement here has the same foundation, namely, that Christ underwent the curse of the covenant, hanging from a tree (Deut. 21:22–23) or being circumcised (being cut off), and the result was the outpouring of the Spirit, or the circumcision made without hands performed on the people of God (cf. 2 Sam. 21:10; Rev. 19:17–21).[37]

Paul goes on to write in Colossians 2:12: "…buried with Him in baptism, in which you also were raised with Him through faith in the working of God, who raised Him from the dead." Some commentators argue that there is a disjunction in this verse between the circumcision of which Paul writes in verse 11—which refers to the circumcision of the heart and Christ's crucifixion, not the Old Testament rite—and the baptism in which believers are buried with Christ. In other words, Paul has a non-literal referent in verse 11 and a literal referent in verse 12—spiritual circumcision and literal water baptism. Hence, some commentators do not see the connection between the two rites.[38]

However, such an interpretation seems to miss two things: (1) the relationship between the sign and the thing signified, whether in the Old Testament or New Testament; and (2) if both the believer and Christ undergo a circumcision in verse 11, it seems that the parallel Paul brings forward in verse 12 is that both the believer and Christ undergo a baptism. In both cases, the circumcision and the baptism, there are spiritual realities that stand behind the initiation rites. To state it another way, it seems to be overly fine exegesis to eliminate the signs from the things signified.[39] One should not have to choose between a reference to a rite or a work of the Spirit.

36. See James D. G. Dunn, *The Epistle to the Galatians*, BNTC (Peabody, Mass.: Hendrickson, 1993), 176–80.

37. Peter C. Craigie, *The Book of Deuteronomy*, NICOT (Grand Rapids: Eerdmans, 1976), 286; Meredith G. Kline, *Treaty of the Great King: The Covenant Structure of Deuteronomy* (Grand Rapids: Eerdmans, 1962), 109.

38. Beasley-Murray, *Baptism*, 157–58.

39. See, e.g., Thomas R. Schreiner, *Romans*, BECNT (Grand Rapids: Baker, 1998), 306–07.

The answer lies not in choosing between the sign and the thing signified but in explaining how the two properly relate. In other words, Paul can
have the literal rites of circumcision and baptism in view. However, both
rites point to the work of Christ and the Spirit (e.g., Rom. 2:25–29).[40]

Paul has the believer's water baptism in view, which is clear from his
statement in verse 12. This is not the only time Paul has used such imagery,
as it also occurs in Romans 6:3–4. Both there and in Colossians 2:12, Paul
has in mind the same foundational concepts that he set forth in Colossians 2:11, namely, the crucifixion of Christ and consequent work of the
Holy Spirit that terminates on the believer. In both passages, Paul makes
reference to a death-baptism connection both for the believer and Christ.
To be baptized into Christ is to be "baptized into His death" (Rom. 6:3)
and "buried with Him" (Col. 2:12). Some try to argue that Christ's burial
is in view here, but from the parallel in Romans it appears that Paul has in
mind the unitary complex of His crucifixion-death.[41] This relationship will
be further explored in the following section, but note that, for the believer,
baptism is not simply symbolic of new life but is also symbolic of death, of
judgment. The subject of baptism as covenant judgment must be explored
for a proper understanding of Colossians 2:12 and Romans 6:3–4.

BAPTISM AS COVENANT JUDGMENT

The Old Testament provides the necessary light that shows how baptism
is covenant judgment. Against this Old Testament background, not only
Colossians 2:12 and Romans 6:3–4, but also Christ's statement to James
and John regarding His forthcoming "baptism," make more sense: "Are you
able to drink the cup that I drink, and be baptized with the baptism that
I am baptized with?" (Mark 10:38b). There is also yet another statement
of Christ, "But I have a baptism to be baptized with, and how distressed
I am till it is accomplished!" (Luke 12:50). In the Gospels of Mark and
Luke, Christ's reference to baptism means His crucifixion and death. Why,
however, would Christ refer to His crucifixion in this manner? In what way
is it a baptism? Some argue that this is simply metaphorical language that

---

40. James D. G. Dunn, *Baptism in the Holy Spirit* (Philadelphia: Westminster, 1970), 146.
41. Cf. Beasley-Murray, *Baptism*, 133.

denotes being "overwhelmed." However, there seems to be a better answer that comes from the Old Testament.[42]

The previous chapter drew out the relationship between baptism and new creation, which is quite clear in 1 Peter 3:18–20, where the apostle identifies baptism as the antitype to the flood. Most certainly, the flood and baptism are the waters of new creation, but this is only half of the equation. Not only are the waters of the flood and baptism those of new creation, they are also the waters of judgment. Not all who passed through the waters of the flood were saved; in fact, only eight were saved through those waters. The rest of mankind perished. Ultimately, the presence and absence of faith in Christ determined whether the waters of the flood were waters of judgment or redemption. For these reasons, Geerhardus Vos comments: "First Peter 3:20ff compares the water of baptism with that of the flood. Both have an eschatological significance and are directed toward salvation. The water was an instrument of the world-judgment and separated godly and ungodly as it does in baptism."[43]

Everyone should agree that the flood was God's judgment on the earth. What might not be immediately evident is that it was a *covenantal* judgment. Some might reject this proposal because the term *covenant* first appears in Genesis 6:18, supposedly implying that the antecedent history had no covenantal activity. However, the language of Genesis 6:18 is that of covenant ratification, not covenant initiation. In other words, God ratifies an existing covenant with Noah—He re-administers the covenantal dominion mandate (Gen. 1:28; 6:18; 9:1–3). The concept of covenant does not appear *de novo* with Noah, but is already in place with the creation itself, hence making the flood a covenant judgment-deliverance.[44]

The same pattern unfolds in the exodus Red Sea crossing. Israel passed through the waters of the Red Sea, which Paul identifies as a baptism (1 Cor. 10:1–4). Once again, this is only one side of the coin, as two groups entered the sea but only one emerged. The Red Sea was a baptism-deliverance for Israel and a baptism-judgment for Pharaoh and his army. Recall the broader context of the exodus. This was a covenant-deliverance for Israel, in that God redeemed them because of His covenant with Abra-

---

42. E.g., William Hendrickson, *Luke*, NTC (Grand Rapids: Baker, 1996), 682.

43. Geerhardus Vos, *The Eschatology of the Old Testament* (Phillipsburg, N.J.: P & R, 2001), 82.

44. W. J. Dumbrell, *Covenant and Creation: A Theology of Old Testament Covenants* (1984; Carlisle: Paternoster, 2000), 11–26.

ham, Isaac, and Jacob (Ex. 2:24).[45] Conversely, if the Israelites were baptized into the cloud, the Holy Spirit, and for them it was a blessing, it stands to reason that the Egyptians also were baptized into the cloud, but for them it was a judgment.

These covenant baptism-judgments inform the New Testament passages that make reference to baptism. For instance, John the Baptist's ministry makes much more sense against this Old Testament backdrop, in that he was to prepare the way for the coming of the Lord. His ministry was a baptism ministry with water. Christ's ministry, however, was to be a baptism ministry of the Spirit. Hence, Christ was to baptize with "Spirit and fire" (Matt. 3:11; Luke 3:16). This is a subject that will be explored in the following chapter, namely, baptism as eschatological judgment. Nevertheless, note that Jesus submitted to John's baptism, which was a baptism of repentance, identifying Himself with sinful Israel, even though He was free from sin. His baptism, however, also pointed forward, not only to His own baptism with the Spirit, but also to His covenant-judgment, His baptism-crucifixion. Kline explains:

> As covenant Servant, Jesus submitted in symbol to the judgment of God of the covenant in the waters of baptism. But for Jesus, as the Lamb of God, to submit to the symbol of judgment was to offer himself up to the curse of the covenant. By his baptism Jesus was consecrating himself unto his sacrificial death in the judicial ordeal of the cross. Such an understanding of his baptism is reflected in Jesus' own reference to his coming passion as a baptism.[46]

Jesus' identification of His crucifixion as a baptism makes little to no sense by itself, but against the backdrop of the Old Testament, the bond between the two emerges.

Darrell Bock explains that the crucifixion as baptism depicts the "inundation of the waters of divine judgment."[47] Not only is this depiction based in the typical baptisms of the flood and Red Sea crossing, it is echoed throughout the Old Testament, where floodwaters are likened to judgment.[48] For example, the psalmist writes of deliverance in terms of being

---

45. Kline, *By Oath Consigned*, 55–56.
46. Kline, *By Oath Consigned*, 58–59.
47. Darrell L. Bock, *Luke*, vol. 1, BECNT (Grand Rapids: Baker, 1996), 1194; also E. Earle Ellis, *The Gospel of Luke*, NCBC (1966; Grand Rapids: Eerdmans, 1996), 183.
48. Cf. Morna Hooker, *The Gospel According to Saint Mark* (1999; Peabody, Mass.: Hendrickson, 1999), 247.

drawn from "many waters" (Ps. 18:16). Peter Craigie argues that this language is reminiscent of the Exodus and the Red Sea deliverance. Israel had been delivered through the sea and led out to the broad place (v. 19), the Promised Land that lay beyond the act of deliverance.[49] Similarly, the psalmist elsewhere describes his need for salvation in terms of being saved from floodwaters: "Save me, O God! For the waters have come up to my neck. I sink in deep mire, where there is no standing; I have come into deep waters, where the floods overflow me" (Ps. 69:1–2). Likewise, in Isaiah, floodwater language is used to describe God's judgment against the wicked (Isa. 8:7–8; 30:27–28).

Baptism as covenant judgment explains Paul's language in Colossians 2:12 and Romans 6:3–4. When Christ was crucified and underwent His baptism-judgment, He suffered the curse of the covenant on behalf of those who look to Him by faith. In so doing, the believer is united to Christ by faith, and Christ's baptism-judgment becomes the believer's baptism-judgment. At the same time, because Christ underwent the curse of the covenant even though He was righteous and innocent of violating the covenant, He was raised from the dead. He was publicly justified in His resurrection and declared righteous (Rom. 1:3–4; 1 Tim. 3:16). Since the believer receives the imputed righteousness of Christ in justification and the forgiveness of sins by the power of the Spirit, he is raised to walk in the newness of life. This judgment and resurrection is represented in the waters of baptism, which point to the baptism of the Holy Spirit, who brings judgment and new creation. However, only for those who look to Christ by faith alone is the water of baptism representative of redemption, purification, and new creation. For those who undergo the waters of baptism and never have faith in Christ, the waters of baptism are those of covenant-judgment.[50]

The combination of baptism-circumcision imagery, especially that of new creation on the eighth day, emerges at Pentecost. James Dunn explains: "What Jordan was to Jesus, Pentecost was to the disciples. As Jesus entered the new age and covenant by being baptized in the Spirit at Jordan, so the disciples followed him in like manner at Pentecost."[51] How do the baptism-new creation connections in the events of Pentecost relate to circumcision

---

49. Peter C. Craigie, *Psalms 1–50*, WBC (Dallas: Word, 1983), 174.

50. Cf. Morna Hooker, "John's Baptism: A Prophetic Sign," in *The Holy Spirit and Christian Origins: Essays in Honor of James D. G. Dunn*, eds. Graham N. Stanton, et al (Grand Rapids: Eerdmans, 2004), 24.

51. Dunn, *Baptism*, 40.

on the eighth day? Kline points out that the Christian first day, Sunday, is an eighth day, seven plus one. However, the seven plus one pattern is not new, but is found in the Old Testament. Not only is it present in circumcision, as previously observed, it also appears in the Feast of Booths. The seven days of offering are followed by an eighth day of holy gathering (Lev. 23:33–36), a solemn day of rest like the first day of the festival (Lev. 23:39), but an octave higher. This pattern continues at Pentecost, which occurs on a fiftieth day following forty-nine days, or seven multiplied by seven (Lev. 23:15–16). In this sense, the baptism of the church in the Spirit occurs on this "eighth day."[52]

CONCLUSION

Stepping back from what Paul states concerning circumcision and baptism in Colossians 2:11–12, it is evident why the apostle purposefully places the two rites in parallel. Table 2 elucidates the circumcision-baptism parallel.

Keep in mind that baptism has replaced circumcision. The fulfillment of circumcision is the person and work of Christ. The circumcision of Israelite males visibly preached that a future descendant would bring redemption; hence the circumcision of the male reproductive organ. The blood-substitute, the one who was to avert the wrath of God on behalf of God's people, the One who was to be cut off and circumcised from the land of the living, the long-promised seed of the woman, has come. He was cut off so that God's people would not be cut off and suffer covenant curse.

At the same time, the fact that circumcision has been fulfilled also means that the covenant Servant has come and, as promised, has begun to pour out the Spirit on the creation. Hence, God's people are no longer circumcised, they are baptized. This pneumatological outpouring is the fulfillment of God's covenant promises, but it is not exclusively a blessing. Rather, it is blessing for God's people—the outpouring of the Spirit brings new life, new creation, entrance into the eschaton. But for those who refuse to repent of their sin and rebellion, and continue their allegiance to the lord of this present evil age, the outpouring of the Spirit comes upon the creation like a flood. Like the waters of the Noahic deluge, the outpouring of the Spirit drowns the wicked in judgment. Without faith in Christ,

---

52. Meredith G. Kline, *God, Heaven, and Har Magedon: A Covenantal Tale of Cosmos and Telos* (Eugene, Ore.: Wipf & Stock, 2006), 197–98.

TABLE 2. Circumcision-Baptism Parallel

	Circumcision	Christ	Spirit	Baptism
Initiation rite	Administered to male converts or male infants born within the covenant (Gen. 17:11–13)	Circumcised on the eighth day (Luke 2:21)	Baptized in the Jordan (Mark 1:9–11; Matt. 3:13–17; 3:21–22; John 1:29–34)	Administered to male and female converts (Acts 2:37–38)
Covenant judgment	Uncircumcised males were guilty of breaking the covenant and hence cut off from the community (Gen. 17:14; cf. Gen. 15 Jer. 34:18–20).	Cut off from the land of the living (Isa. 53:8; Jer. 11:19); circumcised (Col. 2:11)	Baptized in His crucifixion (Luke 12:50; Mark 10:38)	Water baptism alone does not save but must ultimately point to "an appeal to God for a good conscience" (1 Peter 3:21)—that is, faith alone in Christ—or it becomes a sign of curse.
New creation	Infants circumcised on the eighth day (Gen. 17:12; Lev. 12:3)	Jesus is the eschatological Adam (1 Cor. 15:45)	Jesus begins His outpouring or baptizing of the church and creation with the Spirit (Matt. 3:11; Luke 3:16)	The church is baptized on the eschatological eighth day at Pentecost by Christ, which occurs in the last days (Lev. 23:33–39; 23:15–16; Joel 2:28; Acts 2).

baptism becomes "unbaptism," just as circumcision could become uncircumcision. In this way, then, both baptism and circumcision point to the same realities—covenant blessing and sanction.

Given this data, it makes perfect sense that Paul places circumcision and baptism in parallel in Colossians 2:11–12. Both rites point to the same realities, the work of Christ and the Spirit, but in different ways. Circumcision, the bloody covenant judgment, the work of Christ, would lead to the circumcision of the heart of God's people, the work of the Spirit. Likewise, the baptism-judgment of Christ would lead to the baptism of the Spirit, which would enable God's people to walk in the newness of life. Now that the work of Christ, that to which circumcision pointed, has been accomplished, circumcision is superseded by baptism, which points to the ongoing outpouring of the Spirit, the continued work of Christ. Both circumcision and baptism have covenant blessing and sanction connected to them.

If baptism is *covenant* judgment, that is, the curse that fell on Christ, this conclusion leads to the next subject, namely, baptism as *eschatological* judgment—the baptism with fire.

CHAPTER 10

Baptism as Eschatological Judgment

Part II has thus far explored two significant conceptual threads connected to baptism, new creation and covenant judgment. The waters of baptism are those of new creation, as those who emerge from them and believe in Jesus are inextricably joined to the last Adam and participate in the new heaven and earth. However, baptism is also a covenant judgment rite in that it either symbolizes the burial of the body of sin or the judgment that falls on the one who does not believe. In Christ's crucifixion, which Paul called a circumcision and Jesus called a baptism, the judgment aspect of baptism emerges. However, broader images beyond the individual's blessing or curse are associated with baptism. John the Baptist cried out to the crowds that the Messiah would baptize with Spirit and fire. Throughout the Bible, fire is associated with judgment. Further, John joined this judgment-language to the baptism of the Holy Spirit.

This chapter will explore the bond between baptism and eschatological judgment; it will explore, among other things, how this theme is related to the Old Testament flood judgment, a typical baptism. The overall thesis of this chapter is that the flood is the type and the Messiah's baptism of Spirit and fire is the antitype. Namely, just as God flooded the creation with water, bringing both judgment and deliverance, Jesus floods the creation with the Spirit, who brings the judgment of fire. To support the thesis, it is necessary first to review the connections between the ministry of the Messiah and His outpouring of the Spirit, but also the judgment that accompanies this baptism. Second, it is vital to review the relationship between water imagery and the work of the Holy Spirit.

THE BAPTISM OF FIRE

In the opening chapters of the Gospel of Matthew, John the Baptist speaks of the coming Messiah and the baptism that he will bring: "I indeed baptize you with water unto repentance, but He who is coming after me is mightier than I, whose sandals I am not worthy to carry. He will baptize you with the Holy Spirit and fire. His winnowing fan is in His hand, and He will thoroughly clean out His threshing floor, and gather His wheat into the barn; but He will burn up the chaff with unquenchable fire" (Matt. 3:11–12; Luke 3:16–17). Some believe that John was speaking of a twofold baptism, namely, the baptism of the Holy Spirit for the people of God and the separate judgment of fire for the wicked. However, both the baptism of the Holy Spirit and of fire are governed by one preposition: αὐτὸς ὑμᾶς βαπτίσει ἐν Πνεύματι Ἁγίῳ καὶ πυρί (Matt. 3:11). In addition to the governing preposition, the personal pronoun ὑμᾶς allows for no distinctions. There is therefore one baptism, which brings either blessing or curse, and this baptism is concomitant with the arrival of the Messiah and His kingdom.[1]

The fire of purification

The imagery of fire appears to have two connotations, depending on the purpose of the baptism. For the people of God, those whom He intends to bless, the baptism of the Spirit is a purifying and refining fire, one that purges the redeemed sinner of his impurities (cf. Zech. 13:9; Isa. 1:25; Mal. 3:2).[2] This is supported by a number of passages. For example, Peter's Pentecost sermon proclaims that Jesus poured out the Holy Spirit on the gathered church (Acts 2:33). That the people of God receive the fire of the Spirit as blessing is evident in that the disciples were "filled with the Holy Spirit" (Acts 2:4) and "divided tongues, as of fire,…sat upon each of them" (Acts 2:3). The image of tongues of flame is a clear indication of the presence of God, as is seen in the Old Testament connections between the presence of God and fire. Yahweh appeared as the burning bush (Ex 3:2–5), as the pillar of fire that guided Israel by night (Ex. 13:21), as the consuming fire on Mount Sinai (Ex. 24:17), and as the fire that hovered over the wilderness tabernacle (Ex. 40:38).[3] For the people of God, the fire-presence of the Spirit is one of blessing.

---

1. Donald A. Hagner, *Matthew 1–13*, WBC, vol. 33a (Dallas: Word, 1993), 52; see also Darrell L. Bock, *Luke*, BECNT (Grand Rapids: Baker, 1994), 1.322–23.

2. James D. G. Dunn, *Baptism in the Holy Spirit* (Philadelphia: Westminster, 1970), 12.

3. Richard Longenecker, *Acts*, EBC (Grand Rapids: Zondervan, 1995), 66.

One of the key Old Testament texts that brings forth the connection between Spirit, fire, and purification is Isaiah 4:4–5: "When the Lord has washed away the filth of the daughters of Zion, and purged the blood of Jerusalem from her midst, by the spirit of judgment and by the spirit of burning, then the LORD will create above every dwelling place of Mount Zion, and above her assemblies, a cloud and smoke by day and the shining of a flaming fire by night. For over all the glory there will be a covering." In the original context of this passage, the prophet was speaking to the people during the Assyrian invasions (ca. 740–700 BC) to tell them of the coming "day of the LORD" (Isa. 2:12), its effects (Isa. 2:17, 20), and its imminent arrival (Isa. 3:18; 4:1). Beginning with 4:2, the prophet turns his attention to the idea that the day of the Lord will bring holiness, life, cleansing, new creation, divine indwelling, and shelter. Isaiah begins by saying that on the day of the Lord the "Branch of the LORD" (the Messiah) will come and the earth will bring forth fruit (Isa. 4:2).[4] The mention of fruit invokes new creation imagery. Sin brought a curse on the earth, causing it to yield its goodness only sparsely (Gen. 3:17–19), but in the wake of the advent of the Messiah the earth will burst forth in fruitfulness (Rev. 21:3–5).[5]

Isaiah 4:3 says that those who are left in Zion and Jerusalem on the day of the Lord will be called "holy," which implies that the day will bring some sort of calamity. But God will preserve a remnant by His electing will, evident by the phrase "recorded among the living in Jerusalem." The filth of this remnant will be washed away and its bloodstains cleansed "by the spirit of judgment and by the spirit of burning" (Isa. 4:4). The use of the word רוח (spirit) could merely be a reference to a natural force under God's control, such as wind. However, given Isaiah's rich awareness of the Spirit of the Lord (cf. 30:1–2; 31:3; 63:10–14), especially in conjunction with messianic passages (11:2; 42:1; 59:21; 61:1), the more natural reading is that Isaiah is writing of the Holy Spirit. In other words, judgment and burning will come by the Holy Spirit.[6]

Isaiah 4:5 refers to the new creation, as the prophet says that the Lord will ברא (create), which is a word used of divine creative activity, such as in the initial creation (Gen. 1:1). What will the Lord create? He will create a dwelling for the remnant, and the prophet describes the dwelling in terms of the Spirit's exodus activity—a cloud by day and a pillar of fire by night.

4. J. Alec Motyer, *The Prophecy of Isaiah* (Downers Grove, Ill.: InterVarsity, 1993), 64.

5. J. Alec Motyer, *Isaiah*, TOTC (Downers Grove, Ill.: InterVarsity, 1999), 59.

6. Motyer, *Prophecy*, 66.

This dwelling will be a shelter, a canopy, a refuge, for God's people (cf. Isa. 43:1–3a).[7] Thus, there are clearly positive aspects of the baptism of fire.

The fire of wrath

The baptism of fire also has a negative side to it. John states that the Messiah will use the winnowing fork and separate the wheat from the chaff, then burn it with an unquenchable fire (Matt. 3:12). A number of passages in the Old Testament associate fire with the destruction of the wicked: "'For behold, the day is coming, burning like an oven, and all the proud, yes, all who do wickedly will be stubble. And the day which is coming shall burn them up,' says the LORD of hosts, 'That will leave them neither root nor branch'" (Mal. 4:1; cf. Isa. 31:9; Amos 7:4).[8] The prophet speaks of "the day [that] is coming," which undoubtedly refers to "the day of the LORD." Fire language used in connection with divine judgment and wrath appears in numerous other Old Testament passages (Gen. 19:24–28; Pss. 2:12; 89:47; Isa. 30:27; Jer. 4:4; 21:12; Amos 1:4, 7, 10, 12, 14; 2:2, 5). It is especially noteworthy that destruction by fire is a manifestation of covenant curse (Deut. 32:22).[9]

The use of fire imagery also surfaces in a number of places in the New Testament. For example, in a parallel to Matthew 3:11–12, Jesus speaks of division by fire: "I came to send fire on the earth, and how I wish it were already kindled! But I have a baptism to be baptized with, and how distressed I am till it is accomplished! Do you suppose that I came to give peace on earth? I tell you, not at all, but rather division" (Luke 12:49–51). Jesus not only mentions that He has come to cast fire on the earth (a reference to judgment), but He makes reference to His own baptism, which is an outpouring of judgment on Himself (cf. Job 9:31 LXX; Pss. 18:4, 16; 42:7; 69:1–2; Isa. 8:7–8; 30:27–38; Jonah 2:3–6).[10] In a similar passage, Jesus compares His return to the judgment of Sodom, when fire and sulfur rained down on the wicked city (Luke 17:29–30).[11] Another New Testament text speaks of the judgment of the world in fire: "But the heavens and the earth

---

7. Motyer, *Prophecy*, 66; also Meredith G. Kline, *By Oath Consigned: A Reinterpretation of the Covenant Signs of Circumcision and Baptism* (Grand Rapids: Eerdmans, 1968), 61, 68.

8. Dunn, *Baptism*, 12.

9. Douglas Stuart, *Malachi*, in *The Minor Prophets*, vol. 3, ed. Thomas E. McComiskey (Grand Rapids: Baker, 1998), 1386.

10. Bock, *Luke*, 2.1194.

11. Bock, *Luke*, 1.323.

which are now preserved by the same word, are reserved for fire until the day of judgment and perdition of ungodly men" (2 Peter 3:7; cf. vv. 10–13).

When John announces that the coming Messiah will baptize with Spirit and fire, he has a twofold effect in view: blessing for the people of God, as the fire purges, refines, and purifies; and cursing for the unbelieving world in the form of wrath and the fire of judgment. James Dunn has an excellent summary of these points:

> In short then, the baptism in the Spirit-and-fire was not to be something gentle and gracious, but something which burned and consumed, not something to be experienced by only Jew or only Gentile, only repentant and unrepentant, but by all. It was the fiery *pneuma* in which all must be immersed, as it were, and which like a smelting furnace would burn up all impurity. For the unrepentant, it would mean total destruction. For the repentant it would mean a refining and purging away of all evil and sin which would result in salvation and qualify to enjoy the blessings of the messianic kingdom. These were the sufferings which would bring in the messianic kingdom; it was through them that the repentant would be initiated into that kingdom.[12]

This baptism of fire comes with the messianic kingdom, which clearly places it in the eschatological realm, and thus this baptism is an eschatological judgment. The baptism of fire is a purification-judgment on the believer whose sin is cleansed, but it is a condemnation-judgment on the unbeliever who is unrepentant. This also means, as Dunn rightly notes, that baptism is universal.

At this point, the chapter turns to explore the universality of this fire-baptism. In a word, the Old Testament typical baptism-judgment (Noahic flood) foreshadows the messianic baptism-judgment (the outpouring of the Holy Spirit).

THE UNIVERSAL FIRE-BAPTISM FLOOD

Throughout the Scriptures, there are a number of important connections between the Holy Spirit and water. First, there are close connections between the outpouring of the Spirit and the waters of new creation, evident in such passages as Isaiah 44:3: "For I will pour water on him who is thirsty, and floods on the dry ground; I will pour My Spirit on your descendants, and

---

12. Dunn, *Baptism*, 13–14.

My blessing on your offspring." Second, these connections lead to the close identification of the Spirit with water imagery throughout the Scriptures. This is evident from a number of passages, especially those that center on the eschatological temple. Given the close identification between water and the Holy Spirit, the consequential link between the imagery of the Old Testament flood and the universal messianic outpouring of the Holy Spirit is manifest. The first point was explored in the previous chapter; therefore, this section focuses on the second, namely, the identification of water imagery with the Holy Spirit, which is seen in a number of passages in both testaments.

This connection appears in the eschatological city-temple in the book of Revelation. The apostle John describes the "river of the water of life" flowing from the throne of God and of the Lamb (Rev. 22:1). This passage has antecedents in the Old Testament, particularly in the prophets. For example, Zechariah says, "And in that day it shall be that living waters shall flow from Jerusalem" (14:8). Likewise, Joel 3:18 states, "A fountain shall flow from the house of the LORD."[13]

Psalm 46:4–5a has similar imagery: "There is a river whose streams shall make glad the city of God, the holy place of the tabernacle of the Most High. God is in the midst of her." Here the river that flows in the city of God is placed in parallel with the presence of God, who is in the midst of the city. In other words, there is a connection between the symbolic imagery of flowing water and the presence of God through the person and work of the Holy Spirit.

Ezekiel speaks of a time when God will sprinkle water on His people, when He will place His Spirit within them (36:25–27). Likewise, Jesus tells Nicodemus that one must be born of water and Spirit in order to see the kingdom of God (John 3:5). But perhaps the most telling statement comes when John reports a statement of Christ and then gives an interpretation:

> On the last day, that great day of the feast, Jesus stood and cried out, saying, "If anyone thirsts, let him come to Me and drink. He who believes in Me, as the Scripture has said, out of his heart will flow rivers of living water." But this He spoke concerning the Spirit, whom those believing in Him would receive; for the Holy Spirit was not yet given, because Jesus was not yet glorified (John 7:37–39).

---

13. G. K. Beale, *Revelation*, NIGTC (Grand Rapids: Eerdmans, 1999), 1103.

Though the statement and following interpretation are clear, it is nonetheless helpful to explore this passage in greater detail.

First, Jesus makes this statement at the conclusion of the Feast of Tabernacles, a celebration of Israel's wilderness wanderings that culminates in a water-drawing celebration that commemorates the provision of water in the wilderness (Num. 20:2–13). Christ's declaration at the conclusion of the feast is His way of announcing that He is the antitypical fulfillment of the Old Testament typical feast.[14] Second, Christ states, καθὼς εἶπεν ἡ γραφή (as the Scripture has said), which is equivalent to the statement γέγραπται (it is written), the phrase that introduces quotations from Scripture. The statement that Jesus makes, however, is neither a quotation nor an allusion to any one text. Nevertheless, given the close associations between water and Spirit, it seems that Christ's appeal is to this pair of ideas in the Old Testament.

One particular passage strikingly combines water imagery in conjunction with the messianic mission: "The Lord will guide you continually, and satisfy your soul in drought, and strengthen your bones; you shall be like a watered garden, and like a spring of water, whose waters do not fail" (Isa. 58:11). This statement comes in the context of the promised second-exodus, which invokes the Feast of Tabernacles, and also images of water-fertility. This statement fits within the overall matrix of the passages surveyed thus far, namely, the close association of water, Spirit, and the messianic mission (cf. Isa. 12:3; 44:3; 49:10; Ezek. 36:25–37; 47:1; Joel 3:18; Amos 9:11–15; Zech. 13:1).[15]

Third, and perhaps most important, is the interpretive comment the apostle makes, the symbolic identification of water with the Holy Spirit.[16] John links water and the Spirit, which further confirms that the imagery found in Revelation and in the Old Testament prophets primarily refers to the messianic Spirit baptism on the creation.

There are several important passages that show the universal nature of the outpouring of the Spirit. The Old Testament, particularly the prophet Ezekiel, reveals the eschatological temple through a vision of a perfect Solomonic temple (Ezek. 40–48). One of the key features of this temple vision is the presence of water flowing out from under the threshold (Ezek. 47:1).

---

14. D. A. Carson, *The Gospel According to John* (Grand Rapids: Eerdmans, 1991), 322–23.
15. Carson, *Gospel of John*, 326.
16. Beale, *Revelation*, 1104–1105.

In the verses that follow, the prophet is taken to the east gate to observe the water trickling out of the south side of the temple (v. 2). Then the prophet is taken one thousand cubits (about seventeen hundred feet) away from the temple, and the water is ankle-deep (v. 3). Next, the prophet is taken another one thousand cubits away from the temple, and the water measures waist-deep (v. 4). Going out yet another one thousand cubits, the water is so deep the prophet cannot pass and must swim in it (v. 5). In the verses that follow (vv. 6–12), the prophet is told that wherever the river flows, fruitfulness will ensue—in other words, the waters impart life.[17]

Ezekiel's vision comes from the matrix of divine revelation that begins in the garden-temple of Eden and the river that flows from it and ends with the city-temple of John's Apocalypse and the river of life.[18] If the symbolic relationship between water and the Spirit is correct, then the prophet's vision tells of a time when the Spirit shall flow from the eschatological temple of God and fill the earth. To put this in terms of previous Old Testament revelation, Ezekiel's vision shows that the waters gradually flood the earth. Ezekiel's vision speaks of the life-giving properties of the floodwaters, the positive aspect of the outpouring of the Spirit. The rest of Scripture shows that the converse is also true. The same flood of the Spirit will bring judgment and curse on the unrepentant, as well as destruction on the old creation.[19] Just as the Noahic flood brought judgment and new creation, so too the antitypical baptism-flood of the Spirit brings judgment and new creation.

The relationship between the Noahic flood and the Spirit-fire baptism is strongest in 2 Peter: "By the word of God the heavens were of old, and the earth standing out of water and in the water, by which the world that then existed perished, being flooded with water" (3:5–6). Peter uses the verb κατακλυσθεὶς (flooded), a hapaxlegomenon (it occurs only once in the New Testament). But the word is used in some of the literature of second-temple Judaism. For example, "When the earth was flooded [κατακλυζομένην] because of him, wisdom again saved it" (Wis. 10:4; NRSV). The term also appears in the LXX: "I will rain down on

---

17. See G. K. Beale, *The Temple and the Church's Mission: A Biblical Theology of the Dwelling Place of God* (Downers Grove, Ill.: InterVarsity, 2004), 335–64.

18. Daniel I. Block, *The Book of Ezekiel: Chapters 25–48* (Grand Rapids: Eerdmans, 1998), 696.

19. Geerhardus Vos, *The Eschatology of the Old Testament*, ed. James T. Dennison, Jr. (Phillipsburg, N.J.: P & R, 2001), 81.

him [κατακλύζοντι], on his troops, and on the many peoples who are with him, flooding rain, great hailstones, fire, and brimstone" (Ezek. 38:22). When Peter uses this term, he emphasizes that the first flood was by *water*, which he then contrasts with the second flood by *fire*: "But the heavens and the earth which are now preserved by the same word, are reserved for fire until the day of judgment and perdition of ungodly men" (2 Peter 3:7).[20]

The point of this parallel is that Peter envisages world history in three epochs divided by two great cataclysms: the world before the flood, the present world that will end in the eschatological judgment (v. 7), and the new world to come (v. 13). These three great periods are united by the floods of water and fire. Therefore, just as the creation emerged from beneath the floodwaters, so too a new creation will emerge from the fire judgment, the Spirit fire-baptism: "[Are we] looking for and hastening the coming of the day of God, because of which the heavens will be dissolved, being on fire, and the elements will melt with fervent heat? Nevertheless we, according to His promise, look for new heavens and a new earth in which righteousness dwells" (2 Peter 3:12–13).[21]

CONCLUSION

This chapter has chiefly explored the relationship between the Spirit and water images as well as the significance of the Noahic flood. In the flood, God judged the impenitent and redeemed the penitent through water. This event is typical of the eschatological ministry of the last Adam. It should be no surprise that Christ likens the time and conduct of those who will be found at His return to the days of Noah (Matt: 24:38–39).[22] Christ draws on the Noahic flood not merely to characterize the conduct of those who will be judged but also because the typical pattern of the Old Testament flood establishes the nature of the antitypical reality to which it points, namely, the eschatological outpouring of the Spirit. This Spirit-flood is therefore an act of eschatological judgment, one that separates the wheat from the chaff, brings an end to the old creation, and unleashes the new. Those who are united to the last Adam by faith alone through the work of

---

20. Vos, *Eschatology*, 82–83.
21. Richard J. Bauckham, *Jude, 2 Peter*, WBC, vol. 50 (Waco: Word, 1983), 299.
22. Vos, *Eschatology*, 82.

the Spirit have passed through the floodwaters of judgment in the baptism of Christ, His crucifixion. Those who are still united to the first Adam must pass through the floodwaters of judgment on their own. Unlike the Noahic flood, which brought temporal death and judgment, the antitypical flood of the Spirit brings eternal death and judgment.

Summary of Part II

Unlike the myopic constructions of baptism that narrowly focus on the New Testament and the lexical meaning of the word βαπτίζω, Part II has demonstrated the variegated imagery and ideas associated with the concept through the themes of baptism as new creation, covenant judgment, and eschatological judgment. Baptism is not an exclusive New Testament phenomenon, but emerges in the opening verses of the Bible. Any treatment of the doctrine that does not take the Old Testament origins of baptism into account has hardly scratched the surface regarding its redemptive-historical significance. This methodology surfaces as New Testament authors connect baptism with key Old Testament events such as the flood and the Red Sea crossing. Moreover, in recognizing the unfolding nature of redemptive history, the connections between baptism and circumcision as signs of the covenant become clearer. Circumcision gives way to baptism because the chosen Seed has been circumcised, cut off from the land of the living, and He has consequently poured out the Holy Spirit—He has baptized the church and the creation with the Spirit. As this picture unfolds, ideas of both covenant blessing and sanction accompany the Spirit-baptism of the church and creation.

This gathered evidence provides important data that must be included in a positive formulation of the doctrine of baptism. Part I showed that there are many who see baptism only as a blessing. This blessing-only understanding appears in Roman Catholic and Baptist views. There are those, such as John Calvin, who argued that baptism is of no benefit for the person who apostatizes. What, however, of the double-edged nature of baptism? Part I also showed a number of views that radically individualized baptism, such as those of the Anabaptists and the Second London Confession. However, it is clear that the baptisms of the Old Testament and New Testament are covenantal and corporate in nature. In other words, there are no individual, stand-alone baptisms. Rather, individuals stand in covenant with either the first or last Adam. Any doctrine of baptism must account for the covenant and the relationship to the corporate and universal baptism of the Spirit poured out on the creation and the church.

Beyond these observations, one thing is clear—the covenant signs of circumcision and baptism both point to the work of Christ and the Spirit. Circumcision pointed to the Messiah who would be cut off and to the cutting away of the foreskin of the heart; baptism points to Christ drowning in the waters of God's wrath and to the outpouring of the life-giving Spirit. Baptism does not save—Christ through the Spirit saves.

This gathered biblical-theological data is the necessary foundation for a positive systematic-theological construction of the doctrine of baptism. It is time to take the data of the straight line, the progressive unfolding of baptism through redemptive history from Genesis to Revelation, and use it to draw a circle to show how these gathered elements systematically cohere.

PART III

Systematic-Theological
Construction of the Doctrine

Introduction to Part III

In the previous two sections, this study explored the history of the doctrines of the sacraments and baptism, and looked at baptism through redemptive history from Genesis to Revelation. In the survey of the history of the doctrines of the sacraments and baptism, key questions were identified, such as the nature of the relationship between the sign and the thing signified. Part II began to answer this question by stating that the water of baptism does not possess magical powers but points to Christ's baptism of the church with the Holy Spirit.

However, at this point, there are many other questions that swirl about the investigation. Therefore, Part III will take the exegetical and biblical-theological data and organize it in such a way as to present a full-orbed doctrine of baptism. To this end, Part III will begin with the broader concepts related to baptism: the means of grace (chapter 11). A crucial but often-missing element in the discussion of the doctrine of baptism is grace. What is it? A biblical answer to this question has important ramifications for properly defining the relationship between soteriology and baptism. Is God's grace an infused created substance or is it God's personal action in Christ through the Spirit?

The study will then proceed in chapter 12 to discuss baptism as a sacrament. Historically, some, such as Friedrich Schleiermacher, have been critical of such a move. However, identifying baptism as a sacrament is not a capitulation to sacerdotalism, but grounds God's dealings with His people in His progressive self-revelation through Christ and covenant. This chapter will also take into account the all-important nature of the sacramental union.

Subsequently, chapter 13 will deal with baptism proper: the meaning, institution, baptismal formula, and mode. Defining these elements of baptism requires a firm foundation in the biblical-theological spadework from Part II; in other words, these points must be grounded in the canon of Scripture, not just the New Testament. Chapter 14 will then deal with the question of the proper recipients of baptism. To whom should baptism be administered? What role does the antecedent Old Testament revelation play in the discussion? How does the double-edged nature of baptism connect to matters of faith and unbelief in adults and infants?

Part III will conclude by addressing the difficult question of what constitutes a valid baptism (chapter 15). In other words, can Protestants accept Roman Catholic baptisms? Admittedly, this is a very challenging question to answer, but one that hinges on the question of whether baptism is defined by objective or subjective standards. If baptism is a sacrament, the visible revelation of God when accompanied by the Word, then it seems that God defines baptism, not man. People are baptized into the name of the triune God, not that of any man or denomination. If these things are true, then the objectivity of God's revelation in baptism has implications for the doctrine of the church.

CHAPTER 11

Baptism as a Means of Grace

The positive construction of the doctrine of baptism must begin with broad questions, such as whether baptism can be considered a means of grace. Historic Reformed teaching has generally answered in the affirmative. However, some from both within and without the Reformed community have rejected this idea.

This chapter will prove that baptism is indeed a means of grace. To accomplish this, we must first define the term *grace*, since not all confessional communities define it in the same manner. Second, with grace defined, the chapter will identify the means by which it is received. The Reformed church has historically identified two means of grace, Word and sacrament. Other communities and theologians have larger and more extensive lists of means. If a narrow, technical definition is used, one that makes the distinction between the objective revelation of God and its subjective reception and use, there can be only two objective means, Word and sacrament. As the chapter will show, God objectively communicates His grace through the means of divine revelation: the audible and visible Word. Third, the chapter will show that to acknowledge baptism as a means of grace does not entail sacerdotalism. Finally, the often-ignored but crucial connection between the means of grace and the doctrine of the covenant will be covered.

DIFFERING VIEWS

The term *grace* is often used in theological works, where its meaning is usually assumed with little definition or qualification. Wayne Grudem, for example, states, "All of the blessings we experience in this life are ultimately undeserved—they are all of *grace*."[1] He then discusses the various means

---

1. Wayne Grudem, *Systematic Theology: An Introduction to Biblical Doctrine* (Grand Rapids: Zondervan, 1994), 950.

of grace. Yet little specific exegetical attention is given to the term. Grace is simply described as life's blessings. Given this understanding, Grudem rejects the limitation of the means of grace to Word and sacraments, as in traditional Reformed theology, and instead argues that there are at least eleven means by which believers receive the blessing of the Holy Spirit:

1. The teaching of the Word
2. Baptism
3. The Lord's Supper
4. Prayer for one another
5. Worship
6. Church discipline
7. Giving
8. Spiritual gifts
9. Fellowship
10. Evangelism
11. Personal ministry to individuals.[2]

Grudem, therefore, has a very broad understanding of grace and, by extension, its means.

Others see no limitation on the means of grace. Brian McLaren, a representative of the Emergent Church movement, expresses his appreciation of Roman Catholicism because of its sacramental theology:

A sacrament is an object or practice that mediates the divine to humans. It carries something of God to us; it is a means of grace, and it conveys sacredness. I care little for arguments about how many sacraments there are (although I tend to prefer longer lists than shorter ones). What I really like about the sacramental nature of Catholicism is this: through learning that a few things can carry the sacred, we become open to the fact that all things (all good things, all created things) can ultimately carry the sacred: the kind smile of a Down's syndrome child, the bouncy jubilation of a puppy, the graceful arch of a dancer's back, the camera work in a fine film, good coffee, good wine, good friends, good conversation. Start with three sacraments—or seven—and pretty soon everything becomes potentially sacramental as, I believe, it should be.[3]

---

2. Grudem, *Systematic Theology*, 951.
3. Brian McLaren, *A Generous Orthodoxy* (Grand Rapids: Zondervan, 2004), 225–26.

In this understanding, quite literally anything can be a means of grace. While Grudem sees the means of grace as connected to the church, McLaren extends the means of grace even to the creation.

Others, such as Louis Berkhof (1873–1957), argue that the means of grace "are instruments, not of *common* but of, *special* grace, the grace that removes sin and renews the sinner in conformity with the image of God."[4] Berkhof qualifies his statement by distinguishing common (*gratia communis*) from special grace (*gratia paricularis sive specialis*), then links the means of grace not to the blessings of life in general, as with McLaren, but specifically to the transformation of the sinner.[5] Berkhof's view is also different from those espoused by the Roman Catholic Church.

Part I showed that Roman Catholic theology understands the grace of God in terms of an infused habit. According to the Roman Catholic Church, "The grace of Christ is the gratuitous gift that God makes to us of his own life, infused by the Holy Spirit into our soul to heal it of sin and to sanctify it. It is the *sanctifying* or *deifying grace* received in Baptism. It is in us the source of the work of sanctification." Note that grace is not the direct work of the Holy Spirit in the life of the believer, but an infused power: "Sanctifying grace is an habitual gift, a stable and supernatural disposition that perfects the soul itself to enable it to live with God, to act by his love."[6] According to the Roman Catholic Church, infused grace is a *habitual grace*, namely, "A divine gift infused into the soul in such a way as to become a part of human nature." A habit is a "disposition, capacity, or aptitude that does not belong to the natural capacities of man."[7] In baptism and the other six Roman Catholic sacraments, people receive this habitual grace.

The Roman Catholic view is very different from Reformation views, which the Council of Trent (1546) condemns: "If any says, that men are justified, either by the sole imputation of the justice of Christ, or by the sole remission of sins, to the exclusion of the grace and *the charity which is poured forth in their hearts by the Holy Ghost,* and is inherent in them; or even

---

4. Louis Berkhof, *Systematic Theology: New Combined Edition* (1932–38; Grand Rapids: Eerdmans, 1996), 605.

5. Richard A. Muller, *Dictionary of Latin and Greek Theological Terms: Drawn Principally from Protestant Scholastic Theology* (Grand Rapids: Baker, 1985), 130–31, q. v. *gratia communis, gratia particularis sive specialis.*

6. *Catechism of the Catholic Church* (Liguori. Mo.: Liguori Publications, 1994), 484.

7. Muller, *Dictionary*, 134–35, q. v. *habitus gratiae* and *habitus supernaturalis*. See also Alister E. McGrath, *Iustitia Dei: A History of the Christian Doctrine of Justification.* Third Edition (Cambridge: Cambridge University Press, 2005), 66–72.

that the grace whereby we are justified, is only the favor of God: let him be anathema."[8] For the Roman Catholic Church, people clearly may not deny the infusion of the habitual grace of God by the Holy Spirit, nor may they define the grace of God merely as His favor.

On the other side of the spectrum, some deny that the sacraments convey any grace whatsoever. Ulrich Zwingli saw the sacraments not as means of grace but as symbols of man's commitment and oath of loyalty to God. Zwingli writes, "I believe, yea, I know, that all the sacraments are so far from conferring grace that they do not even convey or distribute it."[9] Similarly, Anabaptists such as Balthasar Hübmaier believed that baptism was in no way a means of grace but merely "an outward and public testimony of the inner baptism in the Spirit."[10]

In the contemporary period, no less than during the Reformation, some deny that the sacraments are means of grace. Karl Barth agreed with Zwingli's definition of the term *sacrament* and saw baptism as a "sign of loyalty which marks all members of the covenant people."[11] Millard Erickson states, "The act of baptism conveys no direct spiritual benefit or blessing."[12] Stanley Grenz (1950–2005) also sees the sacraments as "acts of commitment" and "fitting vehicles for expressing our commitment to the Lord Jesus Christ," which broadly follows a Zwinglian or Barthian trajectory.[13]

Like those who see baptism as a means of grace but expand the means to every good thing in the creation, such as McLaren, others all but scuttle the sacraments and see them as irrelevant. Charles Ryrie (1925–) states that an ordinance "does not incorporate the idea of conveying grace but only the idea of a symbol."[14] Instead of an "actual baptism," which symbol-

---

8. Canons and Decrees of the Council of Trent, Canon 11, in Philip Schaff, *The Creeds of Christendom* (1931; Grand Rapids: Baker, 1990), 2.112–13.

9. Ulrich Zwingli, *Reckoning of the Faith*, in *Creeds and Confessions of Faith in the Christian Tradition*, eds. Jaroslav Pelikan and Valerie Hotchkiss (New Haven: Yale University Press, 2003), 2.260.

10. Balthasar Hübmaier, *Christian Catechism*, q. 35, in Pelikan and Hotchkiss, *Creeds*, 2.676–93.

11. Karl Barth, *Church Dogmatics*, eds. G. W. Bromiley and T. F. Torrance (Edinburgh: T & T Clark, 1969), IV.4, 129–30. Hereafter abbreviated as CD. Cf. Ulrich Zwingli, *Of Baptism*, in *Zwingli and Bullinger*, ed. G. W. Bromiley (Philadelphia: Westminster, 1953), 131.

12. Millard J. Erickson, *Christian Theology* (Grand Rapids: Baker, 1983–85), 1096.

13. Stanley J. Grenz, *Theology for the Community of God* (Nashville: Broadman & Holman, 1994), 676; cf. Barth, CD IV.4, 2.

14. Charles Ryrie, *Basic Theology: A Popular Systematic Guide to Understanding Biblical Truth* (1986; Chicago: Moody Press, 1999), 421.

izes "leaving the old life and entering the new," Ryrie suggests: "Why not erect a little closet on the church platform, have the candidate enter it in old clothes, change his clothes inside the closet, and then emerge in new clothes? Would that not illustrate the same truth as baptism does? And is it not a scriptural illustration (Col. 3:9–12)?" Ryrie therefore argues that the church should be flexible in its employment of the ordinances.[15]

Given these different views, it is necessary to define the term *grace* in order to establish the means by which it is communicated to the church.

DEFINING GRACE

To define a term, it is first necessary to distinguish biblical language from theological terminology. Theological terms are based on scriptural terms, but this does not mean that they always mean the same thing. This is evident, for example, in the use of the term *sanctify* or *sanctification*. In Reformed systematic theology, the term refers to the work of the Spirit throughout the life of the believer to conform him further to the image of Christ.[16] In Scripture, however, the term does not necessarily have the same meaning. When Paul writes to the Corinthians that they have been ἡγιασμένοις ἐν Χριστῷ Ἰησοῦ (sanctified in Christ Jesus) (1 Cor. 1:2), he does not have in mind the doctrine of sanctification; Paul uses a perfect participle that can hardly refer to the ongoing activity of the Spirit.[17] Instead, Paul means

---

15. Ryrie, *Basic Theology*, 403.

16. See Berkhof, *Systematic Theology*, 527–44.

17. John Murray (1898–1975) created the category of *definitive* sanctification because, as Murray writes: "It is a fact too frequently overlooked that in the New Testament the most characteristic terms that refer to sanctification are used, not of a process, but of a once-for-all definitive act" (John Murray, "Definitive Sanctification," in *Collected Writings of John Murray* [Edinburgh: Banner of Truth, 1977], 2.277). He argues, "It would be, therefore, a deflection from biblical patterns of language and conception to think of sanctification exclusively in terms of a progressive work" ("Definitive Sanctification," 2.278). This is a common pattern in Murray, as he also rejected the covenant of works on the same methodological grounds ("Adamic Administration," in *Writings*, 2.47–59). Yet such a methodology confuses biblical and theological terms and fails to recognize that while theological terms can echo biblical language, the concepts can be broader or narrower than the biblical terminology because, in the end, theological terminology does not merely repeat biblical terms but interprets them. Regarding some of the biblical sanctification terminology and its definitive nature, such passages are probably better categorized under the doctrine of justification, as the forensic declaration is the definitive act that sets apart the believer from his former sin-dominated existence into his new legal status in Christ. This is reflected in older Reformed works, which have no category of definitive sanctification.

that the Corinthians have been set apart in Christ Jesus. The confusion of biblical and theological terminology has been labeled "false assumptions about technical meaning."[18] Hence, this error must be avoided in the effort to define grace.

In the Old Testament, the term חֵן and its cognates are often translated by the LXX as χάρις and by the English terms *grace* or *favor*. This term is attributed not only to God, but also to conduct between people, such as Joseph, who "found favor" in Potiphar's sight (Gen. 39:4). Other examples include Boaz's care for Ruth (Ruth 2:13) and David's favor to Jonathan (1 Sam. 20:3). However, the term can also be used to describe God's conduct toward people, such as Noah, who found favor in the eyes of the Lord (Gen. 6:8–9). God can show His favor or grace to the righteous, but He also does so in the treatment of the unrepentant, such as His conduct toward Israel in the wilderness (Neh. 9:17, 31). Ultimately God's grace is grounded not in what people do, but in His own willingness to show it to them (Ex. 33:19; 34:6).[19] At least in a general sense, God's grace can be defined as His favor, though in the context of a fallen world it cannot be defined as His merited favor since no man can make such a claim against God. Neither can it be classified as His unmerited favor, since it is not merely undeserved. Rather, it must be defined as God's *demerited* favor, in that despite man's sinfulness God does not give to him what he has merited or earned, namely, God's justice, but rather His favor, His grace.

The same broad contours found in the Old Testament surface in the New Testament, in that God shows favor to all in a post-fall world; He makes the sun rise on both the evil and the good, and sends rain on both the just and the unjust (Matt. 5:45). Luke uses the term χάρις in its Old Testament sense, namely, as the expression of favor (Luke 1:30; 2:40).[20] The Pauline epistles have the bulk of the occurrences of the term: 100 out of 155 times.

Paul's use of the term has a distinctive christological, pneumatological, and eschatological cast that is rooted in the Old Testament. An example of the christological cast of grace comes from the prophet Zechariah: "And I will pour on the house of David and on the inhabitants of Jerusalem the

---

18. D. A. Carson, *Exegetical Fallacies* (1984; Grand Rapids: Baker, 1993), 45–48.

19. Terence E. Fretheim, "חנן," in NIDOTTE, 2.203–06; see also HALOT 1.334–35. Cf. John Piper, *The Justification of God: An Exegetical & Theological Study of Romans 9:1–23* (1983; Grand Rapids: Baker, 1993), 75–90.

20. H. H. Esser, "χάρις," NIDNTT, 2.118; also BDAG, 1079.

Spirit of grace and supplication; then they will look on Me whom they pierced. Yes, they will mourn for Him as one mourns for his only son, and grieve for Him as one grieves for a firstborn" (Zech. 12:10).[21] Zechariah prophesied of a time in the last days when God would pour out His grace on His people. This outpouring of grace would come through the work of Christ, which is evident in the mention of the one whom "they have pierced" (cf. Zech. 9:9; 11:4–14; 12:7, 10; 13:3; Dan. 7:13; Isa. 53; John 12:15; 19:37; Rev. 1:7).[22]

In the New Testament and especially the Pauline epistles, grace is not merely the favor of God. His grace is not a quality or abstract attribute. Neither does Paul conceive of grace as an abstract power that is infused into the believer to enable him to become holier. Rather, as Rudolf Bultmann (1884–1976) explains: "It is not a mode of dealing which God has decided henceforth to adopt, but is *a single deed* which takes effect for everyone who recognizes it as such and acknowledges it (in faith)—'grace' is *God's eschatological deed.*" Bultmann points out that this eschatological deed comes solely through the work of Christ.[23] Similarly, Herman Ridderbos (1909–2007) explains that God's grace is not a timeless attribute that is "discovered" by faith in the way of a consciousness of guilt and awareness of the insufficiency of one's own works. Rather, it consists in the redeeming activity of God; it is the grace that is revealed in the redemption in Christ.[24] The christological nature of God's grace is evident in Paul's words, "Grace to you and peace from God our Father and the Lord Jesus Christ" (2 Thess. 1:12).[25] God's grace does not come nakedly to sinners but in and through Christ. No one can approach God apart from the divine Mediator.

The connections between the grace of God and Christ are further manifest in other portions of Paul's writings. Romans 5 displays the Christ-centered aspect of God's grace: "But the free gift is not like the offense. For

21. Fretheim, "חנן," in NIDOTTE, 2.206.

22. Thomas McComiskey, *Zechariah*, in *The Minor Prophets*, 3 vols., ed. Thomas McComiskey (Grand Rapids: Baker, 1998), 3.1214–15; Eugene Merrill, *Haggai, Zechariah, Malachi: An Exegetical Commentary* (Chicago: Moody Press, 1994), 318–22; G. K. Beale and D. A. Carson, eds., *Commentary on the New Testament Use of the Old Testament* (Grand Rapids: Baker, 2007), 504–506, 1090–91.

23. Rudolf Bultmann, *Theology of the New Testament: Complete in One Volume* (New York: Charles Scribner's Sons, 1951–55), 1.288–89.

24. Herman Ridderbos, *Paul: An Outline of His Theology* (1975; Grand Rapids: Eerdmans, 1992), 183.

25. A. B. Luter, Jr., "Grace," in *Dictionary of Paul and His Letters*, eds. Gerald F. Hawthorne, Ralph P. Martin, and Daniel G. Reid (Downers Grove, Ill.: InterVarsity, 1993), 372.

if by the one man's offense many died, much more the grace of God and the gift by the grace of the one Man, Jesus Christ, abounded to many" (Rom. 5:15; cf. 2 Cor. 8:9; Gal. 2:21; Eph. 1:6–9). The free gift of grace comes in and through Jesus Christ. A similar statement appears in the third chapter, where Paul says that believers are "justified freely by His grace through the redemption that is in Christ Jesus" (Rom. 3:24).[26]

This grace of God is bound not only with the eschatological revelation of Christ but also with the work of the eschatological Spirit. In Romans 6:14, Paul explains that those who have been redeemed by Christ are no longer under the law but under grace. Paul has the two major epochs of redemptive history in view, not merely categories related to the *ordo salutis*. As redemptive-historical categories, law and grace cover both redemptive history and its relationship to the believer, the *ordo salutis* (cf. John 1:17; Rom. 1:3–4). Paul contrasts Christ as the head of the eschatological age with the present evil age brought on by Adam in two chief places: Romans 5 and 1 Corinthians 15 (cf. Gal. 1:4). Jesus and Adam represent the two major epochs in redemptive history, and the work of each is characteristic of each age: οὕτω καὶ γέγραπται, Ἐγένετο ὁ πρῶτος ἄνθρωπος Ἀδὰμ εἰς ψυξὴν ζῶσαν. ὁ ἔσχατος Ἀδὰμ εἰς πνεῦμα ζωοποιοῦν (And so it is written, "The first man Adam became a living being." The last Adam became a life-giving spirit) (1 Cor. 15:45).[27] Paul calls Christ a πνεῦμα ζωοποιοῦν, which indicates that Christ pours out the power of the eschaton, the Holy Spirit (cf. Acts 2:33; Heb. 6:4–5). The interconnected work of Christ and the Spirit proves that the term χάρις is also used as a correlative of God's Holy Spirit: "But if you are led by the Spirit, you are not under the law" (Gal. 5:18).[28] This statement parallels Romans 6:14: a person is either under law or grace (Spirit).

Given this exegetical data, some theological conclusions can be drawn. First, God's grace is chiefly revealed in Christ through the Holy Spirit. There is still room for the classic distinction between God's common and special grace; His common grace is His general favor toward man and

---

26. Bultmann, *Theology of the New Testament*, 1.290.

27. See Geerhardus Vos, "The Eschatological Aspect of the Pauline Conception of the Spirit," in *Redemptive History and Biblical Interpretation: The Shorter Writings of Geerhardus Vos*, ed. Richard B. Gaffin, Jr. (Phillipsburg, N.J.: P & R, 1980), 91–125.

28. Luter, "Grace," 373; cf. Bultmann, *Theology of the New Testament*, 1.290; James D. G. Dunn, *Jesus and the Spirit: A Study of the Religious and Charismatic Experience of Jesus and the First Christians as Reflected in the New Testament* (1975; Grand Rapids: Eerdmans, 1997), 202–205, esp. 203.

His special grace is that favor by which God redeems man from his fallen estate.[29] However, God's special grace is His favor in Christ that is applied directly by the Holy Spirit. This definition stands in stark contrast to Roman Catholic views, which characterize the grace of God in redemption as a *habitus gratiae* (a habit or disposition of grace). According to Roman Catholic teaching, the habitual grace of God is a *gratia creata* (created grace) in contrast to the *gratia increata* (uncreated grace) of the power of God.[30] For the Roman Catholic Church, God's grace in redemption is ontological—a created thing or power that transforms the sinner. Christ through the Holy Spirit gives this created grace—an impersonal, substantival power.

Paul's understanding of grace also stands in contrast to evangelical views such as those of Grudem, who describes grace only as God's favor. Instead, God's special grace is found in Christ and through the Holy Spirit; it is not an impersonal power or mere favor. Indeed, God's grace is the person of Christ Himself, who redeems fallen man through His life, death, resurrection, and ascension, then applies that work to the believer through the indwelling and transformative power of the Holy Spirit.[31] In the terminology of the *ordo salutis*, God's grace is the believer's union with Christ. As God brought forth the first creation through the agency of His Son and the Holy Spirit (cf. Gen. 1:2; John 1:3; Col. 1:16), so now through the God-man and the Holy Spirit He brings about the creation of the new heaven and earth. Grace is not an impersonal power that sanctifies and transforms the believer; Christ through the Holy Spirit brings about this transformation. Wolfhart Pannenberg makes the keen observation: "Grace is not a quality or power that is different from Jesus Christ and that is imparted to us; it is Jesus Christ himself."[32] In a word, grace is union with Christ.

This christological definition of grace is a fundamental truth that Reformed theology has historically grasped and expressed. The Westminster Shorter Catechism, for example, states: "A sacrament is a holy ordinance

---

29. Cf. Berkhof, *Systematic Theology*, 435–36; Francis Turretin, *Institutes of Elenctic Theology*, ed. James T. Dennison, trans. George Musgrave Giger (Phillipsburg, N.J.: P & R, 1992–97), 3.20.1–14; Geerhardus Vos, "The Scriptural Doctrine of the Love of God," in Gaffin, *Redemptive History*, 425–57.

30. Muller, *Dictionary*, 134, q. v. *habitus gratiae*. See also Thomas Aquinas, *Summa Theologica* (1948; Allen, TX: Christian Classics, 1981), IaIIae q. 110 art. 2; q. 113 art. 2.

31. Similarly, T. F. Torrance, *Theology in Reconciliation: Essays Towards Evangelical and Catholic Unity in East and West* (Grand Rapids: Eerdmans, 1975), 83.

32. Wolfhart Pannenberg, *Systematic Theology*, 3 vols., trans. G. W. Bromiley (Grand Rapids: Eerdmans, 1993), 3.202.

instituted by Christ; wherein by sensible signs, Christ, and the benefits of the new covenant, are represented, sealed, and applied to believers" (q. 92). The Heidelberg Catechism makes the same point: "Christ has instituted this external washing with water and by it has promised that I am as certainly washed with his blood and Spirit from the uncleanness of my soul and from all my sins, as I am washed externally with water which is used to remove the dirt from my body" (q. 69). The catechism goes on to ask, "Why does the Holy Spirit call baptism the water of rebirth and the washing away of sins?" It responds: "God does not speak in this way except for a strong reason. Not only does he teach us by baptism that just as the dirt of the body is taken away by water, so our sins are removed by the blood and Spirit of Christ" (q. 73). Recall from Part I that John Calvin argued that the sacraments have the same office as the Word—to herald Christ.[33] While the relationship between the sacrament and God's grace has yet to be defined, the Reformed tradition has understood the grace of God as His favor in Christ applied by the Holy Spirit.

In a nutshell, God's grace is not a thing but a person. This is an important conclusion that shows not only how God communicates His grace, but delimits that grace to Word and sacrament.

DEFINING THE MEANS

The definition of grace determines the means by which God communicates it to His people. Grudem, who defines God's grace only as His favor, seems to posit an expansive list that includes the different elements connected to life in the church. Grudem states, "The means of grace are any activities within the fellowship of the church that God uses to give more grace to Christians."[34] Based on this premise, Grudem argues that the Word and sacraments are means of grace along with Christian fellowship. If grace is only God's favor, then such a conclusion is warranted, though Grudem does place the teaching of the Word as the first and most important means.[35] If, however, God's grace is the person and work of Christ applied by the Holy Spirit, this sets the means on a different and more limited trajectory. This is especially the case vis-à-vis the views of McLaren, who basically eradicates

---

33. John Calvin, *Institutes of the Christian Religion*, LCC, vols. 20–21, ed. John T. McNeill, trans. Ford Lewis Battles (Philadelphia: Westminster, 1960), 4.14.17.

34. Grudem, *Systematic Theology*, 950.

35. Grudem, *Systematic Theology*, 953.

the difference between common and special grace by holding that anything in the creation can be a means.[36]

Since God's special grace is the person and work of Christ applied by the Holy Spirit, the means of grace must be anchored to the doctrine of revelation. Classic Reformed theology has acknowledged that the *principium cognoscendi externum* (external cognitive foundation) is divine revelation, both general and special. General revelation is in *res* (things) rather than in *verba* (words).[37] Special revelation, on the other hand, is primarily in *verba*. It is primarily in the Word, because God has also revealed Himself in theophanies and miracles, though even these revelations rely chiefly on the Word.[38] Ultimately, God's special revelation centers on the Word incarnate, the person of Jesus Christ. God does generally reveal Himself through nature (Rom. 1:18–20), but He has redemptively revealed Himself through His Son: "Whoever has seen me has seen the Father" (John 14.9). If God's grace is in Christ, and Jesus reveals the Father, then the means of grace must be inextricably bound to God's objective revelation in Christ.

The means by which God reveals Christ, and thereby His grace, centers principally on the Word of God. The book of Hebrews shows the link between revelation, christology, and eschatology: "God, who at various times and in various ways spoke in time past to the fathers by the prophets, has in these last days spoken to us by His Son" (Heb. 1:1–2a). God's Word is the only means by which He reveals His special grace, by which He reveals Christ in the last days.[39] This is a cardinal tenet of Reformed theology—people hear the gospel through the preaching of the Word and are

---

36. McLaren, *Generous Orthodoxy*, 225–26.

37. Berkhof, *Systematic Theology*, 128–29. See also Herman Bavinck, *Reformed Dogmatics*, 4 vols., ed. John Bolt, trans. John Vriend (Grand Rapids: Baker, 2003–08), 1.283–386.

38. Berkhof, *Systematic Theology*, 136–38.

39. Regarding the inextricable connection between christology and eschatology, see Geerhardus Vos, *The Pauline Eschatology* (1930; Phillipsburg, N.J.: P & R, 1994), 1–41. There are some who claim that the Holy Spirit does not restrict special revelation to the Scriptures. One finds this in the theology of Grudem, which would give a partial answer as to why he would see a more expansive list of the means of grace, since the believer is capable of uttering special revelation through the charismatic gifts (see Wayne A. Grudem, *The Gift of Prophecy in 1 Corinthians* [1982; Eugene, Ore.: Wipf & Stock, 1999]; cf. George W. Knight, III, *Prophecy in the New Testament* [Dallas: Presbyterian Heritage Publications, 1988]; Richard B. Gaffin, Jr., *Perspectives on Pentecost: New Testament Teaching on the Gifts of the Holy Spirit* [Phillipsburg, N.J.: P & R, 1979]). However, there are also those associated with the Emergent Church who claim that the Holy Spirit speaks through culture (John Franke, *The Character of Theology: An Introduction to Its Nature, Task, and Purpose. A Postconservative Evangelical Approach* [Grand Rapids: Baker, 2005], 141–42; cf. Franke's introduction to McLaren's *Generous Orthodoxy*,

in this way apprehended by Christ through the power of the Holy Spirit. Again, just as God spoke the creation into existence (Gen. 1:1; Heb. 11:3), so now He creates the new heaven and earth and calls into existence things that do not exist through His Word (cf. Rom. 4:17). In this manner, the Word of God is the chief means of grace. Through the reading or preaching of the Word, God sets forth the person and work of Christ, then applies them to the auditor by the power of the Holy Spirit.

In addition to the Word of God, there are the sacraments. Broadly considered, the sacraments are connected to the Word, being visible words. The sacraments' status as visible words is evident by their institution and practice. Concerning the Lord's Supper, for example, Christ identifies the bread as His body and the wine as His blood, and as such the supper invokes the remembrance of the crucifixion of Christ. Likewise, baptism invokes the remembrance of the crucifixion, as Jesus calls His crucifixion a baptism (Mark 10:39; Luke 12:50), but Paul also connects the death of Christ with baptism (Rom. 6:1–4). The death of Jesus is inherently and inextricably bound with the Word and the preaching of Christ crucified. Apart from the Word, the sacraments are empty symbols indistinguishable from any other washing or meal. The preaching of the Word with the explanation of the symbolism of the sacraments sets the washing with water and the meal of bread and wine apart as sacraments, as means of grace. To this end, Paul reminded the Corinthians that as they celebrated the sacrament of the Lord's Supper, they proclaimed the Lord's death (1 Cor. 11:26). Paul saw the Lord's Supper as a visible proclamation of the gospel.[40]

A number of Reformation theologians recognized baptism and the Lord's Supper as inherently connected to God's objective revelation. While both Martin Luther and Calvin were willing to agree generally with Augustine's definition of a sacrament as a visible form of an invisible grace, both saw the shortcomings of his definition and augmented it. Luther saw the sacraments as "promises which have signs attached to them," which evidenced his Word-centered view.[41] The same emphasis appears in the *Apology of the Augsburg Confession*, largely written by Philip Melanchthon. The *Apology* states:

9–14). While Franke's views should be distinguished from Grudem's, both either soften or, in Franke's case, eradicate the distinction between general and special revelation.

40. My thanks to Jay Collier for pointing me to this passage.

41. Martin Luther, *The Babylonian Captivity of the Church*, LW 36.124.

For just as the Word enters through the ear in order to strike the heart, so also the rite enters through the eye in order to move the heart. The word and the rite have the same effect. Augustine put it well when he said that the sacrament is a "visible word," because the rite is received by the eyes and is, as it were, a picture of the Word, signifying the same thing as the Word. Therefore both have the same effect.[42]

Calvin explains the sacraments in a similar fashion: "Just as men are known by their appearance and speech, so God utters His voice to us by the voice of the prophets, and in the Sacraments puts on, as it were, a visible form, from which He can be known according to our small capacity."[43] Hence, classic Reformation theology has recognized the revelatory nature of the sacraments; they are connected with God's objective revelation of His grace in Christ through the Holy Spirit. This means that the sacraments, baptism and the Lord's Supper, are means of grace along with the Word of God.

MEANS OF GRACE: WORD AND SACRAMENT

Why are the means of grace restricted to Word and sacrament? Some Reformed theologians, such as Charles Hodge (1797–1878), have included prayer as a means of grace. Hodge defines the means of grace as: "Those institutions which God has ordained to be the ordinary channels of grace, i.e., of the supernatural influences of the Holy Spirit, to the souls of men."[44] Hodge simply echoes the Westminster Standards: "The outward and ordinary means whereby Christ communicates to us the benefits of redemption are, his ordinances, especially the Word, sacraments, and prayer; all which are made effectual to the elect for salvation" (SC q. 88). Given Hodge's definition of the means of grace, prayer *should* be included.

In this vein, note how Paul explains that the believer receives the supernatural influences of the Holy Spirit in prayer: "Likewise the Spirit also helps in our weaknesses. For we do not know what we should pray for as we ought, but the Spirit Himself makes intercession for us with groanings which cannot be uttered" (Rom. 8:26). Hodge reflects something of Paul's

---

42. *Apology of the Augsburg Confession*, art. 13, in *The Book of Concord: The Confessions of the Evangelical Lutheran Church*, eds. Robert Kolb and Timothy J. Wengert (Minneapolis: Fortress, 2000), 219–20; cf. Augustine, *Tractates on John*, 80.3, on John 15:3, in NPNF[1] 7.344.

43. John Calvin, *John 1–10*, CNTC (1961; Grand Rapids: Eerdmans, 1995), 138.

44. Charles Hodge, *Systematic Theology* (rep; Grand Rapids: Eerdmans, 1993), 3.466.

statement when he describes prayer as the realm in which providence brings believers near to God, who is the source of all good. Prayer enables believers to "fellowship with Him [and] converse with Him, [and] calls into exercise all gracious affections, reverence, love, gratitude, submission, faith, joy, and devotion."[45] If the means of grace are the ordinary channels by which the people of God receive the supernatural influences of the Holy Spirit, then it also seems legitimate to include Grudem's expansive list: Word, sacraments, prayer for one another, worship, church discipline, giving, spiritual gifts, fellowship, evangelism, and personal ministry to individuals.[46] The gifts of the Spirit also evidence His supernatural influence.

Others have recognized the problem of including prayer as a means of grace. Berkhof, for example, writes:

> Faith, conversion, and prayer, are first of all fruits of the grace of God, though they may in turn become instrumental in strengthening the spiritual life. They are not objective ordinances, but subjective conditions for the possession and enjoyment of the blessings of the covenant. Consequently, it is better not to follow Hodge when he includes prayer.... Strictly speaking, only the Word and the sacraments can be regarded as means of grace, that is, as objective channels which Christ has instituted in the church, and to which He ordinarily binds Himself in the communication of His grace. Of course, these may never be dissociated from Christ, nor from the powerful operation of the Holy Spirit, nor from the Church which is the appointed organ for the distribution of the blessings of divine grace. They are in themselves quite ineffective and are productive of spiritual results only through the efficacious operation of the Holy Spirit.[47]

Berkhof argues that the means of grace are objective, that is, not dependent on man's subjective experience or reception. God's objective revelation is independent and true whether man accepts it or not. Both Word and sacrament are forms of divine revelation. Prayer, on the other hand, is not divine revelation. If grace is defined as the work of Christ applied through the Spirit, then the means of grace must be restricted to Word and sacrament. If, however, the means of grace are defined as the ordinary channels through which the supernatural influences of the Holy Spirit come to the believer, then prayer and other activities of the church may be included.

---

45. Hodge, *Systematic Theology*, 3.708.
46. Grudem, *Systematic Theology*, 951.
47. Berkhof, *Systematic Theology*, 604–05.

The answer to the potential antithesis between Hodge and Berkhof lies in understanding the range of meaning behind the concept of the means of grace. Hodge and Grudem represent the grace of God broadly defined as His favor, though Grudem has a more expansive list of means than Hodge. Berkhof's understanding of the means of grace is more strictly defined, namely, that they are objective ordinances, God's objective revelation in Christ. Hence, the two understandings of the means of grace are complimentary, not antithetical. In other words, the term *means of grace* can be defined broadly or narrowly and technically.

Historically in Reformed scholastic theology, *media gratia* (means of grace) was a technical term. The classification of the Word and sacraments as *media gratiae* does not intend to exclude the general operation of grace, but rather to indicate the function of both the Word and sacraments in the effectual call and sanctification of man as objective channels of special grace (*gratia specialis*). The Word and sacraments are thus essential both in the inception of salvation and in the believer's sanctification. The Word and sacraments are the sole officially ordained *objective* means of grace. God has promised His grace to faithful hearers of the Word and faithful participants in the sacraments, when the Word is rightly preached and the sacraments rightly administered.[48]

A close examination of the Westminster Standards reveals that they do not employ the *terminus technicus* of *media gratiae*, but instead describe the outward, ordinary means by which believers receive God's blessing and favor. The Larger Catechism asks, "What are the outward means whereby Christ communicates to us the benefits of his mediation?" (q. 154). The answer it gives is almost identical to the answer to question 88 of the Shorter Catechism: "The outward and ordinary means whereby Christ communicates the benefits of his mediation [redemption, q. 88], are all his ordinances; especially the Word, sacraments, and prayer; all which are made effectual to the elect for their salvation" (q. 154). The Word and sacraments are the objective means whereby God reveals Christ to His covenant people, but to cast the question in terms of Christ's mediation or redemption draws a broader circle. The Word and sacraments are objective, though they require subjective appropriation; likewise, prayer is subjective, though it has an objective element in that prayers are offered to Christ, who objectively

---

48. Muller, *Dictionary*, 187–88, q. v. *media gratiae*.

and truly exists. This is a difference in emphasis, as Word and sacrament are primarily objective, and prayer is primarily subjective.

Appealing to the way in which the Westminster Standards describe the Word, sacraments, and prayer substantiates that they do not employ the technical term *media gratiae*. Scripture is the revelation of God's will to His people, and the supreme judge of all controversies is "the Holy Spirit speaking in the Scripture" (WCF 1.1, 10). Sacraments are "holy signs and seals of the covenant of grace, immediately instituted by God, to represent Christ, and his benefits" (WCF 27.1). These things are objectively true of the Word and sacraments regardless of whether God's people acknowledge them as such or not. Prayer, on the other hand, "is an offering up of our desires unto God" (LC q. 178). There is a distinct difference between prayer and the Word and sacraments, though the divines place prayer in the context of worship (WCF 21.3–4), which indicates they have a broader goal in view than narrowly or technically defining the *media gratiae*.

This point can be further illustrated by examining several key statements in the Heidelberg Catechism. The catechism appears to reject prayer as a means of grace in the way that the Westminster Standards define it. Such a conclusion might be drawn from question 65 of the Heidelberg Catechism: "Since, then, faith alone makes us share in Christ and all his benefits, where does such faith originate? The Holy Spirit creates it in our hearts by the preaching of the holy gospel, and confirms it by the use of the holy sacraments." Yet this statement should be compared with what the Heidelberg Catechism says regarding prayer: "Why is prayer necessary for Christians? Because it is the chief part of the gratitude which God requires of us, and because God will give his grace and Holy Spirit only to those who sincerely beseech him in prayer without ceasing, and who thank him for these gifts" (q. 116). Clearly the catechism has a very high view of prayer and the blessing that accompanies it, and even allows that believers receive the grace of God through it. In fact, compared with the Westminster Larger Catechism, the Heidelberg Catechism appears to grant greater power to prayer (cf. HC 65, 116; LC 155, 161, 178–85).[49] But while there are some different emphases, there is no substantive difference between the

---

49. I am grateful to my colleague, David VanDrunen, for bringing these points to my attention.

English and Continental Reformed traditions on the Word and sacraments as the only objective means of grace.[50]

Part of the reason why theologians differ on the proper limit of the means of grace is a lack of terminological precision. Theologians often assume the meaning of *grace* and then cast a wide net without distinguishing between the objective and subjective categories.[51] This seems to be the case with Hodge and Grudem, though there is a total lack and even demonization of precision in McLaren.[52] Hence, it is preferable to recognize that the objective means of grace are Word and sacrament, as they are the means by which God reveals His grace, the person and work of Christ.

THE MEANS OF GRACE AND SACERDOTALISM

If Word and sacraments are the only objective means of grace, does this not legitimize the accusation that the Reformed church practices sacerdotalism, since only ordained ministers administer Word and sacrament?[53] The answer is no.

Generally speaking, sacerdotalism is the doctrine that teaches that only priests can administer the sacraments, which contain the grace of God and function *ex opere operato*. B. B. Warfield (1851–1921) offers a more specific description of sacerdotalism:

> Though salvation is declared to be wholly of God, who alone can save, it has been taught in a large portion of the Church…that God in working salvation does not operate upon the human soul directly but indirectly; that is to say, through instrumentalities which he has established as the means by which his saving grace is communicated to

---

50. See R. Scott Clark, *Recovering the Reformed Confession* (Phillipsburg, N.J.: P & R, 2008), 227–92.

51. Hence, *pace* Hodge (*Systematic Theology*, 3.466), prayer is not a *media gratiae* in the technical sense. However, *pace* Berkhof (*Systematic Theology*, 604–05), prayer is a means of grace in the broader, non-technical sense of the concept. One can find this same imprecision in others; see Francis R. Beattie, *The Presbyterian Standards* (rep.; Greenville, S.C.: Southern Presbyterian Press, 1997), 335–44; W. G. T. Shedd, *Dogmatic Theology* (Grand Rapids: Zondervan, 1969), 2.561–87; Johannes G. Vos, *The Westminster Larger Catechism: A Commentary*, ed. G. I. Williamson (Phillipsburg, N.J.: P & R, 2002), 433–35; Edmund P. Clowney, *The Church* (Downers Grove, Ill.: InterVarsity, 1995), 89–90. However, one should note that Shedd identifies prayer as a means of grace, but then in the subsequent pages only discusses Word and sacrament (Shedd, *Dogmatic Theology*, 2.562–87).

52. McLaren, *Generous Orthodoxy*, 155.

53. So Grudem, *Systematic Theology*, 950 n. 1.

men. As these instrumentalities are committed to human hands for their administration, a human factor is thus intruded between the saving grace of God and its effective operation in the souls of men; and this human factor indeed, is the determining factor in salvation.[54]

Warfield points out that the whole Protestant church, Lutheran and Reformed, Calvinistic and Arminian, raises a passionate protest against sacerdotalism. Against whom or what do they protest? Warfield identifies the target—the Roman Catholic Church.[55]

The Roman Catholic and Reformed views of the sacraments can be distinguished in that the former holds that the sacraments function *ex opere operato*. Moreover, the sacraments convey created or habitual grace whether or not faith is present in the recipient. By contrast, the historic Reformed position has always acknowledged that the efficacy of the sacraments depends not on the one who administers them—the human factor, as Warfield describes it—but ultimately on the work of the Holy Spirit. For example, the Larger Catechism explains that the sacraments become effectual means of salvation "only by the working of the Holy Ghost, and the blessing of Christ" (q. 161). Likewise, the Heidelberg Catechism states that the outward washing of water in baptism does not wash away sins, but "only the blood of Jesus Christ and the Holy Spirit cleanse us from all sins" (q. 72). In the Reformed understanding, God's grace in Christ comes through the Spirit, who comes directly on the recipient of the Word and sacrament. Stated succinctly, the Roman Catholic Church believes that grace is a thing doled out by priests, whereas the Reformed church believes grace is a person to whom a believer is sovereignly united by the Spirit. Only God through Christ and the Spirit orchestrates such a holy union. Man is incapable of such a miraculous feat. The Reformed view of the sacraments as means of grace is worlds apart, therefore, from the Roman Catholic view of sacramental efficacy.

The Reformed church restricts the administration of the means of grace to ordained ministers not out of sacerdotalism but because of the recognition of two key factors: the dominical command of the Great Commission and the sovereignty of the Spirit in the life of the church. The administration of Word and sacrament is grounded in the doctrine of the church, which is founded on the person and work of Christ but also empowered by

---

54. Benjamin B. Warfield, *The Plan of Salvation* (1915; Eugene, Ore.: Wipf & Stock, n. d.), 49–50.

55. Warfield, *Plan of Salvation*, 50.

the Holy Spirit. Christ gave the Great Commission (Matt. 28:18–19) not to individuals but to the church as a whole, which its ordained ministers represent—in technical language, the *ecclesia representiva* (the representative church).[56]

Some try to diminish the means of grace, such as McLaren, who sees everything as a means. Others try to democratize them, such as the contemporary Roman Catholic Church in the wake of Vatican II (1962–1965), which defined the church as the sacramental body and hence every person as a sacrament. Both trends ignore the nature of the work of the Spirit in the life of the church.[57] God through Christ and the Spirit has created certain offices within the church: "God has appointed these in the church: first apostles, second prophets, third teachers" (1 Cor. 12:28). These offices are filled by men who have been given the gifts of the Spirit to carry out the tasks of their offices: "And he gave some, apostles; and some, prophets; and some, evangelists; and some, pastors and teachers; for the perfecting of the saints, for the work of the ministry, for the edifying of the body of Christ" (Eph. 4:11–12, KJV). While no one part of the body of Christ is more important than any other (1 Cor. 12:20–27), the Spirit sovereignly dispenses His gifts. Thus, the ability to teach and preach is not a universal gift.

Ministers of the church, those to whom the Spirit gives the ability to teach and preach, administer the means of grace—the audible and visible words—Word and sacrament (1 Tim. 3:1–7; 5:17–18).[58] The sacrament is the visible Word and must always be accompanied by the preaching of the Word. Calvin writes, "For we ought to understand the word not as one whispered without meaning and without faith, a mere noise, like a magic incantation, which has the force to consecrate the element. Rather, it should, when preached, make us understand what the visible sign means." Moreover, Calvin insists, "The sacrament requires preaching to beget faith."[59] Apart

---

56. Muller, *Dictionary*, 100, q. v. *ecclesia representiva*.

57. McLaren, *Generous Orthodoxy*, 225–26; *Lumen Gentium*, nos. 9, 48, in *Vatican Council II: Constitutions, Decrees, Declarations*, ed. Austin Flannery, O. P. (New York: Costello Publishing Co., 1995), 15, 72; Gustavo Gutiérrez, *A Theology of Liberation* (1971; New York: Orbis Books, 1988), 143–48, esp. 147; Edward Schillebeeckx, *Christ the Sacrament of the Encounter with God* (New York: Sheed and Ward, 1963), 15, 59, 162–63; Karl Rahner, *The Church and the Sacraments* (London: Burns and Oates, 1963), 90.

58. See George W. Knight III, *The Pastoral Epistles*, NIGTC (Grand Rapids: Eerdmans, 1992), 152–66, 231–35.

59. Calvin, *Institutes*, 4.14.4.

from the preaching of the Word, Calvin explains, the sacraments have "no effect," are "pure corruptions," and are "empty and delusive signs."[60]

Calvin's statements echo the traditional formula that the Word can exist without the sacraments, but the sacraments cannot exist without the Word. As argued above, the sacraments are empty symbols apart from the Word of God. Many ancient cultures practiced circumcision, but it was only when God designated it as the sign of His covenant that it was given special meaning. The same principle applies with any covenantal sign, whether in the Old Testament or New Testament. There is therefore an inextricable bond between the Word and sacrament as revelation and the sovereign dispensation of the gifts of the Spirit. For these reasons, the Westminster Confession states, "Unto this catholic and visible church Christ has given the ministry, oracles, and ordinances of God, for the gathering and perfecting of the saints, in this life, to the end of the world: and does, by his own presence and Spirit, according to his promise, make them effectual thereunto" (25.3).

However, there is another element that has yet to be considered, namely, how the means of grace relate to the doctrine of the covenant. The doctrine of the covenant eliminates the claim that the Reformed church has a sacerdotal view of the sacraments.

THE MEANS OF GRACE AND THE COVENANT

The doctrine of the covenant seldom finds its way into the discussion of the means of grace in the broader church.[61] This subject will be explored in the next chapter in the examination of baptism as sacrament. Nevertheless, it is important to see that the means of grace are covenantal.

---

60. John Calvin, *A Harmony of the Gospels: Matthew, Mark & Luke*, CNTC (1963; Grand Rapids: Baker, 1995), 252; idem, *Isaiah 1–32*, CTS, vol. 7 (rep.; Grand Rapids: Baker, 1993), 212; idem, *Harmony of Exodus, Leviticus, Numbers, and Deuteronomy*, CTS, vol. 3 (rep.; Grand Rapids: Baker, 1993), 321.

61. See, e.g., Erickson, *Christian Theology*, 1089–1106; Grenz, *Theology*, 665–704; Wolfhart Pannenberg, *Systematic Theology* (Grand Rapids: Eerdmans, 1998), 3.237–83; Jürgen Moltmann, *The Church in the Power of the Spirit* (1977; Minneapolis: Fortress, 1993), 199–242; Donald G. Bloesch, *The Church: Sacraments, Worship, Ministry, Mission* (Downers Grove, Ill.: InterVarsity, 2002), 147–60; Daniel G. Akin, ed., *A Theology for the Church* (Nashville: Broadman & Holman, 2007), 783–89; Francis Pieper, *Christian Dogmatics* (St. Louis: Concordia, 1953), 3.104–219; J. T. Mueller, *Christian Dogmatics* (St. Louis: Concordia, 1955), 441–69; cf. Fred A. Malone, *The Baptism of Disciples Alone: A Covenantal Argument for Credo Versus Paedobaptism* (Cape Coral, Fla.: Founders Press, 2007).

The doctrine of the covenant cannot be written off merely as a peculiarity to Reformed theology.[62] Rather, covenant is all over Scripture and is key to a proper comprehension of both the Old Testament and New Testament.[63] To fail to acknowledge this fact produces a number of deviations in the construction of the doctrines of the means of grace, the sacraments, and baptism. God's grace comes in Christ through the Spirit to the believer, and the means by which man receives that grace is Word and sacrament. Hence, it must be acknowledged that Christ and the Spirit do not come to man in terms of a naked ontology or philosophical system of salvation, whether of the Gnostic or mystical sort, but rather through redemptive history in God's covenantal dealings with man.

Michael Horton explains the differences, for example, between a Roman Catholic and Reformed conception of the means of grace, especially highlighting the importance of covenant. Horton writes:

> For Thomas [Aquinas] grace is an infused substance—*a potency for overcoming estrangement*, [while] for the reformers grace is *the favorable event of meeting a stranger*. Although Lutheran and Reformed traditions affirm with Rome and Orthodoxy that the sacraments are means of grace, the deepest difference lies in quite different understandings of grace. For the Reformed, there is no such thing as a nature-grace problem, but only a sin-grace one. Consequently, their understanding of sacraments as means of grace is striving to overcome an ontological concept of grace and a causal understanding of the sacraments in favor of a covenantal, relational, promissory and proclamatory function that is thoroughly eschatological and therefore pneumatological.[64]

Horton's overall typology employs the two types of philosophies of religion defined by Paul Tillich: "ontological" and "cosmological" approaches, which Horton calls "overcoming estrangement" versus "meeting a stranger,"

---

62. So Schillebeeckx, *Christ the Sacrament*, 185. One finds a similar trend in the work of Veli-Matti Kärkkäinen, who develops his ecclesiological typology and labels Reformed ecclesiology as "church as covenant," which either reflects that the Reformed community alone has captured this important biblical tenet of redemption or that the doctrine of the covenant is peculiar to the Reformed church. It seems that the latter is intended, given his overall typology (Veli-Matti Kärkkäinen, *An Introduction to Ecclesiology: Ecumenical, Historical & Global Perspectives* [Downers Grove, Ill.: InterVarsity, 2002], 50).

63. See, e.g., Walther Eichrodt, *The Theology of the Old Testament*, vol. 1 (Philadelphia: Westminster, 1961), 36; N. T. Wright, *The Climax of the Covenant: Christ and the Law in Pauline Theology* (Minneapolis: Fortress, 1991), xi.

64. Michael Horton, *People and Place: A Covenant Eschatology* (Louisville: Westminster John Knox, 2008), 106–107.

to which he adds a third type, "a stranger we never meet."[65] Within this typology, he argues that the Roman Catholic response to the predicament of the fall is to rely on the infusion of grace to "overcome estrangement"— man is infused with habitual grace so he is equipped to scale the heights to heaven. On the other extreme are the views of Immanuel Kant (1724– 1804), who places God in the unknowable noumenal realm; hence, He is the "stranger we never meet."[66]

Reformed theology, on the other hand, offers the remedy to the predicament of the fall through "meeting a stranger"—God in Christ condescends to man to redeem him from his estrangement, his sin-fallen rebellious estate. The realm in which God condescends is the covenant. The covenant is the context where Christ and the Spirit are revealed through Word and sacrament. The covenant accounts for the necessity of the term *means* in means of grace, as covenant embraces both blessing and curse.

True, the sacraments are means of grace. However, because they are linked to the covenant and more broadly to divine revelation, they are not always means of grace but sometimes means of judgment.[67] The microcosm of the crucifixion shows that God's self-revelation in Christ is both a means of judgment and redemption. Two thieves were crucified with Him—one believed and was saved, but the other thief did not believe and was con-

---

65. Paul Tillich, "The Two Types of Philosophy of Religion," in *Theology of Culture* (New York: Oxford University Press, 1959), 10.

66. Michael S. Horton, *Lord and Servant: A Covenant Christology* (Louisville: Westminster John Knox, 2005), 3–21; idem, "Meeting a Stranger: A Covenantal Epistemology," *WTJ* (2004): 337–55.

67. While Reformed theologians have not always explored this aspect of the means of grace, Lutheran theologians have noted this dimension in Reformed theology as a corollary of the concept of particular grace. Muller explains that the Lutheran and Reformed orthodox employ the term *media gratiae* to refer to the Word and sacraments, but that the Lutherans often substitute a stronger term, *organa gratiae et salutis* (instruments of grace and salvation). Lutherans differ from the Reformed by rooting saving grace more completely in the Word and sacrament. The Reformed can speak of the non-reception of grace and the ineffectual calling of the external Word in the case of the non-elect or reprobate (Muller, *Dictionary*, 187–88). Pieper, a Lutheran theologian, for example, writes: "Because saving grace is particular, according to the teaching of the Calvinists, there are no means of grace for that part of mankind to which the grace of God and the merit of Christ do not extend. On the contrary, for these people the means of grace are intended as means of condemnation" (*Christian Dogmatics*, 3.118; cf. Mueller, *Christian Dogmatics*, 451). Pieper goes on to cite Calvin, *Institutes*, 3.24.8, as evidence of this point. This is not to say that the idea of the sacraments as means of judgment is completely absent from sixteenth-century Reformed theology (see Calvin, *Institutes*, 4.15.9, and Zacharias Ursinus, *Commentary on the Heidelberg Catechism*, trans. G. W. Williard, [1852; Phillipsburg, N.J.: P & R, n. d.], 360–61).

demned (Luke 23:39–43; cf. John 3:16–18). The same Jesus brought both redemption and judgment—He is both the cornerstone and the stone of offense and stumbling (Isa. 8:13–15; Rom. 9:33; 1 Peter 2:7–8).

God's revelation has always been double-edged. There are no neutral encounters with God. In the covenant with Adam, God revealed His command as well as the blessing and sanction—to eat from the tree of knowledge would bring death, but to obey the command would bring life (Gen. 2:17). In the Mosaic covenant, Israel was given the law and their tenure in the land, which was connected to the *historia salutis*, not the *ordo salutis*, and was conditioned by the same covenant blessings and sanctions—do this and live (Lev. 18:5), which implies that to disobey meant death (Deuteronomy 27–28). God's covenantal revelation has always come with both blessings and sanctions.

The double-edged nature of God's revelation is aptly captured in Paul's angst-filled statement that describes the apostolic role to bear the gospel of Christ: "For we are to God the fragrance of Christ among those who are being saved and among those who are perishing. To the one we are the aroma of death leading to death, and to the other the aroma of life leading to life. And who is sufficient for these things?" (2 Cor. 2:15–16). The author of Hebrews similarly states: "For the word of God is living and powerful, and sharper than any two-edged sword, piercing even to the division of soul and spirit, and of joints and marrow, and is a discerner of the thoughts and intents of the heart. And there is no creature hidden from His sight, but all things are naked and open to the eyes of Him to whom we must give account" (Heb. 4:12–13).

This blessing-sanction principle is true not only of God's revelation in Christ and the Word, but also of the sacraments. The sacraments are revelatory visible words and come through God's covenantal dealings with His people. The blessing-sanction principle is evident, for example, in the Lord's Supper. The supper is clearly a means of blessing and judgment, for Paul warned the Corinthians that some of them had died because they failed to recognize rightly the body of Christ (1 Cor. 11:27–30). Redemption and judgment are bound with baptism, as Part II of this study has shown. The same flood that delivered Noah and his family through a covenant brought judgment on the unbelieving world (cf. Gen. 6:17–18; 1 Peter 3:20–21). The Red Sea crossing that Paul calls a baptism was the covenantal deliverance of

Israel and judgment on Pharaoh's army (cf. Ex. 14; 1 Cor. 10:1–4).[68] Christ drowned in His crucifixion-baptism in the wrath of God (Luke 12:50); this crucifixion-baptism was also the curse of the covenant (Gal. 3:13; cf. Deut. 21:23). But the crucifixion-baptism of Christ is also the source of new creation and life (Rom. 6:1–4; Col. 2:11–14).

Despite this biblical evidence, some who claim fidelity to the Reformed tradition still see the sacraments more in Roman Catholic sacerdotal terms, rejecting the *means* in the means of grace: "Baptism is not, strictly, a 'means of grace,' a 'bottle containing the medicine of grace' or a 'channel' through which the fluid of grace flows. Rather baptism *is* a gift of God's grace, since through it He adopts us as sons. And the 'sonship' conferred by baptism is not 'external' to our basic identity but constitutive of it."[69] This statement is a caricature and does not accurately reflect the Reformed view. Nevertheless, those who reject the concept of the means of grace and see them as only bringing blessing fail to consider both the covenantal context in which Christ is revealed and the double-edged nature of revelation, whether the audible or visible Word.

The sacraments as means of grace are incomprehensible apart from covenant history. God revealed His audible and visible Word in the Old Testament. The visible words of the Old Testament, and hence means of grace and judgment, were the Passover, circumcision, sacrificial rites, and the like. These covenantal signs will be explored in the following chapter. For now, it is sufficient to note that the sacraments are *means* of grace, because apart from a Spirit-wrought faith, they become means of judgment.

CONCLUSION

This chapter has covered a broad spectrum of views, from those who see the sacraments as means of grace to those who reject them as such. There are also those who extend the means of grace far beyond Word and sacrament, not merely to other churchly activities but even into the creation and

---

68. Alexander Schmemann, *Of Water and the Spirit: A Liturgical Study of Baptism* (Crestwood: St. Vladimir's Seminary Press, 1974), 39–40.

69. Peter J. Leithart, *The Priesthood of the Plebs: A Theology of Baptism* (Eugene, Ore.: Wipf & Stock, 2003), 175; also similarly, Douglas Wilson, *"Reformed" Is Not Enough: Recovering the Objectivity of the Covenant* (Moscow, Idaho: Canon Press, 2002), 99–108; cf. Guy Prentiss Waters, *The Federal Vision and Covenant Theology: A Comparative Analysis* (Phillipsburg, N.J.: P & R, 2006), 168–210.

culture, thereby eradicating the distinctions between general and special revelation and common and special grace. Much of this confusion has ensued because of terminological imprecision, especially as it relates to the term *grace*. Grace is not a substance or an infused habit, but is generally the favor of God and especially His favor shown to sinful man in Christ through the Holy Spirit. God's grace is not a thing; it is a person. Word and sacrament are therefore the objective means by which God reveals Christ, and hence they are the means of grace. However, the means of grace come to God's people through the progressive unfolding of covenant history. Covenant is the realm in which God reveals Christ through Word and sacrament.

Consequently, baptism is most certainly a means of grace. At this point, it is necessary to examine in what way baptism is a sacrament.

CHAPTER 12

Baptism as a Sacrament

The previous chapter showed that baptism is a means of grace in that it is tied to the revelation of God in Christ. Just as the Word reveals God in Christ, the sacraments as visible words also reveal Him. However, while the previous chapter employed the term *sacrament*, it was left undefined for the sake of discussion. The Westminster Standards define the sacraments as "holy signs and seals of the covenant of grace" (WCF 27.1). But as Part I showed, there is a variety of definitions of the term, as well as outright rejection of it. Therefore, it is necessary not only to define the term but also to establish its propriety. First, this chapter will prove that the definition offered by the Westminster Confession is optimal by exploring and engaging challenges to the term. Second, the chapter will explore the relationship between the sacrament and that to which it points: the sacramental union.

DEFINING THE TERM

Critique of erroneous views

The term *sacrament* is still desirable and should therefore be employed. But this leaves the question of how it should be defined. To define the term, it is necessary to enter the realm of theological terminology. Just because a term does not occur in the Scriptures does not negate its viability. This is, of course, most evident with the term *Trinity*, which does not occur in the Scriptures but was developed to explain the biblical data concerning the way in which God is three in person and one in essence or substance.[1]

---

1. See Herman Bavinck, *Reformed Dogmatics*, 4 vols., ed. John Bolt, trans. John Vriend (Grand Rapids: Baker, 2003–2008), 4.472. For a classic Reformed statement on the Trinity, see WCF 2.3. For the history of the development of much of the trinitarian terminology as it came from Tertullian, see Robert Letham, *The Holy Trinity: In Scripture, History, Theology, and Worship* (Phillipsburg, N.J.: P & R, 2004), 97–101.

Accordingly, *sacrament* can be employed as a term. What theological substance should fill it?

Ultimately, all theological terms must be filled by exegetical data so that they reflect the truth of Scripture, not of a man-made system of thought. Thus, it is improper to define *sacrament* from its classical usage. Classically, a *sacramentum* was a loyalty oath of a soldier to his commanding officer, yet such a concept is a foreign imposition on the Scriptures. Such man-originated activity typically goes under the name of idolatry or will-worship. Granted, most acknowledge that man did not create these rites but that God instituted them, and therefore they are called ordinances. Christ ordained these rites for man to express his faith in Him. The sacraments certainly are expressions of faith when observed. But to see the sacraments exclusively as oath-pledges fails to account for the revelatory character of these rites.[2]

Those who want to replace the term, such as Wolfhart Pannenberg or Jürgen Moltmann, fail to acknowledge the nature of theological terminology. They are a bit biblicistic in their definitions of terms—if a term does not occur in Scripture, they reject it. Also, they base their rejection of *sacrament* on the faulty translation of the Greek term μυστήριον without taking into account how others, such as Martin Luther or John Calvin, or especially the subsequent Reformed tradition, nuanced and expanded the definition of the term.[3] Neither do they account for the important historical-contextual unfolding of the divine mysteries through God's covenants with His people—the sacred signs of the covenants. A similar observation applies to those who reject the term because of its supposed Roman Catholic overtones. Yes, *sacrament* is used by the Roman Catholic Church, but so are many other theological terms. Should Protestants jettison the terms *church*, *Scripture*, and *justification*? Roman Catholic theologians mean very different things by these terms than do their Protestant counterparts.[4] The use of a term should be accepted or rejected not merely on the basis of the term alone but on the basis of its definition.

2. Contra Karl Barth, *Church Dogmatics*, trans. G. W. Bromiley, ed. T. F. Torrance (Edinburgh: T & T Clark, 1969), IV.4:129–30.

3. Cf. Otto Weber, *Foundations of Dogmatics*, 2 vols., trans. Darrell L. Guder (1962; Grand Rapids: Eerdmans, 1983), 2.592.

4. Cf. WCF 11, esp. §1.

The need for precision

As we saw in the previous chapter, the sacraments must be understood within the context of the covenant. Divine revelation, Word and sacrament, comes through the historically unfolding plan of redemption. God gave the sacraments of baptism and the Lord's Supper as rites of the new covenant. The covenant is the context in which the covenant Lord sovereignly reveals the means of grace—in this case, the sacraments—and seeks a response from His covenant servants. Hence, contra Ulrich Zwingli and Karl Barth, the sacraments cannot be mere human pledges or oaths of loyalty.

Pannenberg, Moltmann, Rahner, and Schillebeeckx rightly define baptism and the Lord's Supper as mysteries, in that they reveal what was formerly hidden, namely, the person and work of Christ. However, they do not coordinate these mysteries with covenant history and the signs God instituted for His covenants. Instead, they begin with the concept of mystery and apply it to Christ and the church, then include other things in this category, such as acts of mercy, evangelism, healings, or even, in one case, marriage.[5] They do not account for the specific divine institution of certain mysteries as signs of the covenant.

The sacraments must be anchored in divine revelation; therefore, they are mysteries. But while all sacraments are mysteries, not all mysteries are sacraments.[6] Marriage, for example, is unquestionably a mystery (Eph. 5:32). But this does not mean that all who are married receive special grace. Marriage is a common-grace institution and part of the original creation; it is not redemptive. Special revelation identifies it as a mystery, but God has not ordained marriage to convey His saving favor (or grace).

The covenantal administration of divine revelation accounts for the specific means God has ordained through Christ as sacraments. Consequently, the definition offered by the Westminster Confession is optimal, as it defines the sacraments as holy signs and seals of the covenant of grace.

Holy signs of the covenant: blessing and sanction

The definition of the Westminster Confession accounts for the biblical data concerning baptism and the Lord's Supper. Baptism and the supper do not come to God's people apart from covenant history. This is especially evident

---

5. Wolfhart Pannenberg, *Systematic Theology*, 3 vols., trans. G. W. Bromiley (Grand Rapids: Eerdmans, 1998), 3.364.

6. So Johannes Wollebius, *Compendium Theologiae Christianae*, in *Reformed Dogmatics*, ed. John W. Beardslee (New York: Oxford University Press, 1965) 22.2.2, 120.

in the institution of the Lord's Supper, when Christ identifies His blood as that of the new covenant (Luke 22:20; cf. Jer. 31:31). To invoke the new covenant, one must understand the old covenant. Moreover, Christ institutes the supper employing the words *blood* and *covenant*, which hark back to the covenant ratification meal of Exodus 24.[7] This informs the reader that there is a relationship between the two covenant ratification meals and that they have a similar function.

Broadly speaking, the institution of the Lord's Supper fits God's general pattern of not only covenanting with His people but also giving specific visible signs with each covenantal administration. God made a covenant with Noah and the entire creation, promising never to destroy it by water again (Gen. 9:9–11), then established a visible sign of this covenant in the rainbow: "This is the sign of the covenant which I make between Me and you, and every living creature that is with you, for perpetual generations: I set My rainbow in the cloud, and it shall be for the sign of the covenant between Me and the earth" (Gen. 9:12–13). The rainbow was a visible reminder of God's covenant promise; it was a אוֹת or σημεῖον. But the rainbow is connected with the revelatory Word, the divine covenant promise; it points to both blessing and sanction. The blessing is the remembrance of God's promise to preserve the creation. The sanction is the remembrance of the flood-judgment against the earth. Scholars note that the rainbow is evocative of a bow and arrow. That is, God has hung His bow on the wall and no longer uses it to send arrows of wrath against mankind (Rev. 4:3).[8]

The sign of the Abrahamic covenant needs no introduction, as any reader vaguely familiar with the Old Testament knows that God gave to Abraham the sign of circumcision: "You shall be circumcised in the flesh of your foreskins, and it shall be a sign of the covenant between Me and you" (Gen. 17:11). There are both blessings and sanctions connected with this covenant sign. Circumcision, whether for the professing adult convert (Abraham) or for the one born within the covenant (Ishmael and Isaac), pointed to the inward reality of the Spirit's circumcision of the heart. Paul

---

7. See Meredith G. Kline, *God, Heaven and Har Magedon: A Covenantal Tale of Cosmos and Telos* (Eugene, Ore.: Wipf & Stock, 2006), 123–24; G. K. Beale and D. A. Carson, *Commentary on the New Testament Use of the Old Testament* (Grand Rapids: Baker, 2007), 229–32, 381–83, 736, 973–75.

8. So Josephus, *Antiquities*, 1.3.9, in *The Works of Josephus: Complete and Unabridged*, trans. William Whiston (1987; Peabody, Mass.: Hendrickson, 1999), 34; K. H. Rengstorf, *TDNT* 3.339–42; G. K. Beale, *The Book of Revelation*, NIGTC (Grand Rapids: Eerdmans, 1999), 321.

explains in his letter to Rome, "For he is not a Jew who is one outwardly, nor is circumcision that which is outward in the flesh; but he is a Jew who is one inwardly; and circumcision is that of the heart, in the Spirit, not in the letter" (Rom. 2:28–29a).[9] This is not a later Pauline interpolation of the meaning of the covenant sign but its original intent, as evidenced by the call of Moses to the Israelites to circumcise their hearts (Deut. 10:16). However, knowing that Israel was incapable of circumcising their hearts, Moses eventually told them that God would do it in the last days: "And the LORD your God will circumcise your heart and the heart of your descendants, to love the LORD your God with all your heart and with all your soul, that you may live" (Deut. 30:6; cf. Jer. 31:31–34; Ezek. 36:26).[10] Even intertestamental Judaism understood this in some respect.[11] God's circumcision of the heart is the blessing to which circumcision pointed.

Circumcision also had sanctions coupled to it, as the male who was not circumcised on the eighth day was cut off from the covenant community (Gen. 17:14). The circumcision of the Shechemites especially manifests the covenant sanctions connected with circumcision. Shechem saw Dinah, the daughter of Leah, and raped her (Gen. 34:2). To appease the anger of Dinah's brothers, Shechem's father suggested that the two families unite. The Shechemites received circumcision, the sign of the covenant, and then were put to death by Simeon and Levi (Gen. 34:25). Though Simeon and Levi undoubtedly used circumcision as way to weaken their enemies (Gen. 34:13), thereby gaining a tactical advantage, the Shechemites received the sign of the covenant apart from faith in the promised descendant to come (Gen. 12:7; Gal. 3:16; John 8:56). They therefore received the sign to their judgment (cf. Gen. 19; 34:25–29; Lev. 18:3; 20:23; Num. 25; 31:1–9).[12]

As we saw in Part II, circumcision points to covenant sanction, as is evident in Paul's identification of Christ's crucifixion as a circumcision (Col. 2:11). Beyond these observations, it is important to note how Paul characterizes the covenant sign of circumcision: "And he received the sign

---

9. Douglas Moo, *The Epistle to the Romans*, NICNT (Grand Rapids: Eerdmans, 1996), 173–74.

10. See Meredith G. Kline, *Treaty of the Great King: The Covenant Structure of Deuteronomy* (Grand Rapids: Eerdmans, 1963), 132–33; Werner E. Lemke, "Circumcision of the Heart: The Journal of a Biblical Metaphor," in *A God So Near: Essays on Old Testament Theology in Honor of Patrick D. Miller*, eds. Brent A. Strawn and Nancy R. Bowen (Winona: Eisenbrauns, 2003), 299–320.

11. See *Odes of Solomon* 11:2 and *Jubilees* 1:23.

12. Gordon J. Wenham, *Genesis 16–50*, WBC, vol. 2 (Dallas: Word, 1994), 316.

of circumcision, a seal of the righteousness of the faith which he had while still uncircumcised" (Rom. 4:11). Not only was circumcision a sign of the divine covenant, it was a seal of the righteousness Abraham had by faith. Circumcision was not only the sign instituted by the covenant Lord, it accounted for the response of the covenant servant.

God also instituted a sign of the Mosaic covenant: "Speak also to the children of Israel, saying: 'Surely My Sabbaths you shall keep, for it is a sign between Me and you throughout your generations, that you may know that I am the LORD who sanctifies you" (Ex. 31:13). The Sabbath was supposed to be a visual reminder of God's exodus-redemption of Israel from slavery in Egypt (cf. Ex. 20:8–11; Deut. 5:12–15). Some might question how a day of the week could be a visual sign. Cessation from labor in order to rest and worship was a visible sign that God was at work in the midst of Israel—He was giving Israel by grace a foretaste of the eschatological rest of the seventh day (cf. Gen. 2:3, Ex. 31:15; Heb. 4:1–11).[13]

As with other covenant signs, there are sanctions attached to the covenant sign of the Sabbath: "You shall keep the Sabbath, therefore, for it is holy to you. Everyone who profanes it shall surely be put to death; for whoever does any work on it, that person shall be cut off from among his people" (Ex. 31:14). Note the language of covenant curse: the cutting off of the Sabbath-breaker. The verse uses the niphal of כרת, which also appears in Genesis 17:14. כרת is covenant initiation language (Gen. 15:18; 31:44; Ex. 23:32). Recall that the use of the word כרת was associated with the ritual in which animals were cut in two, indicating the sanctions that were to fall on the participant who failed to keep the covenant (cf. Gen. 15:9–10, 18; Jer. 34:18–20).

This covenantal backdrop provides the necessary context to understand the nature of baptism and the Lord's Supper as signs and seals of the covenant of grace. Like other signs, God specifically instituted these rites, though in this case, He did so through Christ. The commands to repeat a meal in remembrance of Christ (Luke 22:29; 1 Cor. 11:24–25) and to baptize the nations (Matt. 28:19) manifest the divine institution.[14] Though

---

13. Geerhardus Vos, *The Teaching of the Epistle to the Hebrews* (Eugene, Ore.: Wipf & Stock, 1998), 66; Jon Laansma, *I Will Give you Rest* (Tübingen: Mohr Siebeck, 1997), 282–83, 352; A. T. Lincoln, "Sabbath, Rest, and Eschatology in the New Testament," in *From Sabbath to Lord's Day*, ed. D. A. Carson (Eugene, Ore.: Wipf & Stock, 1999), 208–209.

14. There are those, such as Pannenberg, who reject Matthew 28:18–19 on the grounds that it was a later addition to the Gospel of Matthew, along the same lines as the later additions to the ending of the Gospel of Mark. Therefore, on textual-critical grounds, he

the New Testament does not specifically identify baptism and the Lord's Supper as signs, they do not arrive on the scene divorced from the antecedent covenant history in which parallel Old Testament signs are so identified (e.g., Ex. 12:13; 1 Cor. 5:7; Gen. 17:11; Col. 2:11–12). God's covenantal dealings with man did not cease on the shores of the New Testament, but continued with accompanying divinely established signs.

There are many signs throughout the Scriptures, but while all sacraments are signs, not all signs are sacraments.[15] This point has been affirmed since the Middle Ages, such as in Peter Lombard's *Sentences*, but has been ignored by many contemporary theologians such as Moltmann and Pannenberg.[16] Hence, baptism and the Lord's Supper are sacred, holy, and set apart; hence, they are sacraments: sacred signs.[17]

Based on what Paul writes concerning the sign of circumcision, sacraments are also seals (Rom. 4:11). As Herman Bavinck explains, "Seals, after all, are distinguished from signs by the fact that they do not just bring the invisible matter to mind but also validate and confirm it."[18] Similarly, Calvin illustrates this point: "The seals which are attached to government documents and other public acts are nothing taken by themselves, for they would be attached in vain if the parchment had nothing written on it. Yet when added to the writing, they do not on that account fail to confirm and seal what is written."[19]

---

argues that there is no divine institution of baptism by Christ (*Systematic Theology*, 3.276–77). There is no evidence regarding Matthew 28:19 to support the claim that it was a later addition to the text of Matthew's Gospel (see Donald A. Hagner, *Matthew 14–28*, WBC, vol. 33b [Dallas: Word, 1995], 883; G. R. Beasley-Murray, *Baptism in the New Testament* [1962; Carlisle: Paternoster, 1997], 77–92).

15. Reformed theologians sometimes treat signs in general apart from the specific signs of the covenant, a practice that goes back to Augustine. On this point, see John Calvin, *Institutes of the Christian Religion*, LCC, vols. 20–21, ed. John T. McNeill, trans. Ford Lewis Battles (Philadelphia: Westminster, 1960), 4.14.18. Amandus Polanus, for example, explains that there are natural and given signs. A rainbow would be a natural sign that tells the observer that it has rained. A given sign does not occur naturally but is given by the appointment of God, such as circumcision as the sign of the Abrahamic covenant (see, e.g., Amandus Polanus, *The Substance of the Christian Religion* [London, 1595], 114; cf. Augustine, *On Christian Doctrine*, 2.1, in NPNF[1] 2.535–36; also Bavinck, *Reformed Dogmatics*, 4.476).

16. Petri Lombardi, *Sententiae in IV Libris Distinctae* (Grottaferrata: Collegii S. Bonaventurae ad Claras Aquas, 1981), 4.1.4.

17. So Calvin, *Institutes*, 4.14.13; also Leonard Riisen, *Compendium Theologiae*, 17.3, in Heinrich Heppe, *Reformed Dogmatics: Set Out and Illustrated from the Sources*, ed. Ernst Bizer, trans. G. T. Thomson (London: George Allen & Unwin Ltd., 1950), 591.

18. Bavinck, *Reformed Dogmatics*, 4.476.

19. Calvin, *Institutes*, 4.14.5.

Hence, the sacraments are sacred signs and seals of the covenant of grace. But as signs and seals of the covenant, they point to both blessing and sanction. The Lord's Supper can be a means of grace or judgment (1 Cor. 11:27–30). It points either to the eschatological marriage feast of the Lamb, where the righteous sup with the risen and ascended Christ, or to the feast where the wicked are themselves consumed by the vultures of the air, indicative of covenant curse (cf. Gen. 15:9–11, 18; Rev. 19:9, 21). Similarly, baptism is either the water that points to the blessings of the new creation or the sanctions of judgment. The difference between blessing and sanction is the presence or absence of a sovereignly given faith in Christ.

COVENANT AND SIGN

To identify the sacraments as signs and seals of the covenant of grace is to acknowledge the organic nature of the covenantal redemption found throughout the Scriptures. Too many theologians sever baptism and the Lord's Supper from the doctrine of the covenant and, in effect, suspend the practices in mid-air. Recognizing baptism and the Lord's Supper as signs and seals of the covenant of grace also binds them to the revelation of God in the mystery of Christ, and thereby acknowledges their revelatory character. Again, all sacraments are mysteries, but not all mysteries are sacraments. Connecting the sacraments with the covenant also binds them to eschatology, in that as the covenant unfolds, the signs and seals of the old covenant give way to the work of the eschatological Adam, who institutes new signs that point to Him.

Beyond this, there are two important observations to make concerning the sacraments as signs and seals of the new covenant. First, this construction is neither the hangover of Augustine's Neo-Platonism, the denigration of created matter, or of medieval theology. Dissecting Augustine's Neo-Platonic commitments and their influences on his theology is beyond the scope of this study, so it is sufficient to say that Augustine thought that sacraments as signs have a referent beyond them—they point to something else. Augustine's aphoristic statement, that the sacraments are visible signs of invisible grace, touched on a vital aspect of covenant theology, namely, that these signs point to the presently unseen incarnate Messiah and work of the Holy Spirit. Thus, though the relationship between the sign and the thing signified must be explained, Augustine discerned a general truth about the sacraments. Calvin and later Reformed theologians added needed qualifications. Sacraments are indeed God-given signs that point beyond themselves to Christ and the Spirit. Thus, the sacraments are bound not to Plato's two-world cosmology—one material and the other immaterial and superior—but to the New Testament's two-age model.[20]

Second, an inclination found in the Reformed tradition regarding the necessity of the sacraments should be revisited. Some theologians tend to characterize the sacraments as necessary due to man's weak embodied existence. Calvin, for example, writes:

> For God's truth is of itself firm and sure enough, and it cannot receive better confirmation from any other source than from itself. But as our faith is slight and feeble unless it be propped on all sides and sustained by every means, it trembles, wavers, totters, and at last gives way. Here our merciful Lord, according to his infinite kindness, so tempers himself to our capacity that, since we are creatures who always creep on the ground, cleave to the flesh, and do not think about or even conceive of anything spiritual, he condescends to lead us to himself even by these earthly elements, and to set before us in the flesh a mirror of spiritual blessings. For if we were incorporeal (as Chrysostom says), he would give us these very things naked and incorporeal. Now, because we have souls engrafted into bodies, he imparts spiritual things under visible ones.[21]

Why does Calvin argue that if man was incorporeal that God would give us truth incorporeally? Why does he characterize man as one who cleaves to the flesh and state that God must condescend by communicating spiritual truth in a corporeal form?

Berkhof exhibits a similar pattern: "The Word is adapted to the ear, and the sacraments to the eye. And since the eye is more sensuous than the ear, it may be said that God, by adding the sacraments to the Word, comes to the aid of sinful man."[22] Sight is characterized as "sensuous." Such a statement is problematic. If Berkhof means that the eyes are sensuous in that they seek gratification in aesthetic pleasure, then the same can be said of the ears—what fine art is to the eye, fine music is to the ear. Ears can seek what is sensuous. On the other hand, if he means that the eyes are sensual,

---

20. Michael S. Horton, *Covenant and Eschatology: The Divine Drama* (Louisville: Westminster John Knox, 2002), 20–46.

21. Calvin, *Institutes*, 4.14.3; cf. Belgic Confession, § 33.

22. Louis Berkhof, *Systematic Theology: New Combined Edition* (1938; Grand Rapids: Eerdmans, 1996), 616; see similar comments in Bavinck, *Reformed Dogmatics*, 4.489.

that they seek physical comfort or satisfaction, then cannot the Word comfort the ears?

Calvin and Berkhof's statements are wanting because they address the necessity of the sacraments simply because of the feebleness and sinfulness of man. Reformed theologians have long identified the covenants of works and grace as the theological rubrics under which to treat the works of the first and last Adams.[23] They have observed that the evidence that Adam was in covenant with God includes the presence of the sacramental trees of the garden-temple, the trees of life and knowledge.[24] Calvin did not formally acknowledge that Adam was in covenant with God, but he identified the tree of life as a sacrament, a natural thing to which God had enjoined the truth of His promise. In this case, the tree of life was a visible guarantee of immortality and hence a sacrament, a sign.[25] In Calvin's commentary on Genesis, he explains, "We know it to be by no means unusual that God should give to us the attestation of his grace by external symbols."[26]

Even in this pre-fall context, however, Calvin sees some sort of flaw in Adam: "But if Adam, hitherto innocent, and of an upright nature, had need of monitory signs to lead him to the knowledge of divine grace, how much more necessary are the signs now, in this great imbecility of our nature, since we have fallen from the true light?" Calvin further confuses matters by agreeing with the position of Augustine, who viewed the tree of life "as a figure of Christ," adding, "It could not indeed be otherwise a symbol of life, than by representing him in figure."[27] But to say that the tree of life points to Christ in a pre-fall world is to say that Adam needed a Mediator even before he fell. Calvin, in effect, says as much: "Wherefore, by this sign, Adam was admonished, that he could claim nothing for himself as if it were his own, in order that he might depend wholly upon the Son of God, and might not seek life anywhere but him." Calvin then draws an analogy to the believer: "Let us know, therefore, that when we have departed from

---

23. For standard expositions of the covenants of works and grace, see WCF 7; Berkhof, *Systematic Theology*, 211–18, 262–304; Bavinck, *Reformed Dogmatics*, 3.193–32.

24. On the garden as the archetypal earthly temple, see G. K. Beale, *The Temple and the Church's Mission: A Biblical Theology of the Dwelling Place of God*, NSBT (Downers Grove, Ill.: InterVarsity, 2004), 66–122; Gordon J. Wenham, "Sanctuary Symbolism in the Garden of Eden Story," in *I Studied Inscripturations from Before the Flood: Ancient Near Eastern Literary and Linguistic Approaches to Genesis 1–11*, eds. Richard S. Hess and David Toshio Tsumura (Winona: Eisenbrauns, 1994), 399–404.

25. Calvin, *Institutes*, 4.14.18.

26. John Calvin, *Genesis*, CTS, vol. 1 (rep.; Grand Rapids: Baker, 1991), 117.

27. Calvin, *Genesis*, 117.

Christ, nothing remains for us but death."[28] To place Adam's probation in the garden in a pre-fall world in parallel with sinful man's need for Christ compares apples to oranges. The Scriptures never make such a comparison. The Bible compares Adam to the last Adam, to Christ.

Calvin therefore saw a need for grace and visual symbols and signs because of man's weakness even in a sinless world. What explains Calvin's confusion? It is beyond the scope of this study to untangle Calvin's statements. Suffice it to say that, for Calvin, soteriology takes priority over eschatology.[29] This is a common pattern in much evangelical theology. It involves seeing eschatology only at the end of history and therefore as properly treated only at the end of the theological system.[30] However, this common prioritization should be reversed—eschatology should take priority over soteriology. In Adam's garden-temple probation, eschatological life was held out as the goal of his obedience. Adam looked forward to entering the eschatological rest of the seventh day upon the completion of his dominion labors. Hence, eschatology is the older strand and exists in pre-redemptive history prior to the intrusion of sin into the world, thereby bringing the necessity for soteriology. As Geerhardus Vos notes, "The eschatological is an older strand in revelation than the soteric."[31]

The tree of life therefore pointed not to Christ but to the eschatological hope of entering the seventh day, the eternal rest of God—of passing the probation in the garden-temple, demonstrating that Adam's righteousness had been tested and was now indefectible.[32] In a fallen world, through Christ, fallen man once again gains access to the tree of life (Rev. 2:7; 22:2, 14, 19).[33]

This conclusion has important implications for understanding the nature and necessity of sacraments. Sacraments are not instituted because

---

28. Calvin, *Genesis*, 117.

29. One finds similar trends in T. F. Torrance, *Theology in Reconciliation* (Eugene, Ore.: Wipf & Stock, 1996), 96–97; see also Donald M. Baillie, *The Theology of the Sacraments and Other Papers* (New York: Charles Scribner's Sons, 1957), 61–63.

30. Horton, *Covenant and Eschatology*, 5. Charles Ryrie, for example, states that eschatology is the study of last things, "those which are yet future from our viewpoint," which includes "the intermediate state, the resurrections, the Rapture of the church, the second advent of Christ, and the Millennium" (Charles Ryrie, *Basic Theology: A Popular Systematic Guide to Understanding Biblical Truth* [Wheaton: Victor Books, 1986], 439–40).

31. Geerhardus Vos, *Biblical Theology: Old and New Testaments* (1948; Edinburgh: Banner of Truth, 1996), 140.

32. Vos, *Biblical Theology*, 27–29.

33. See Beale, *Revelation*, 235.

of man's sinfulness, as demonstrated by the tree of life in the pre-fall world. Man was neither sinful nor sensuous there—he was righteous, having been created very good (Gen. 1:31). Neither did man need spiritual truth to be communicated in a visible or physical manner to accommodate his weakened material existence. Rather, the sacramental trees reflected both man's good created and physical existence and the concrete realities to which the signs pointed: the embodied eschatological state or the certainty of physical death (cf. Dan. 12:1–2).[34]

In other words, Word and sacrament are bound together because of man's very good, embodied, created, physical existence. Man is not a soul trapped in a body, as in Neo-Platonism.[35] The goodness of man's physical existence is reflected in Paul's holistic use of the terms *inner* and *outer* man to refer to man's immaterial and material aspects (2 Cor. 4:16). Both are a part of man, and both, material and immaterial, are very good. This is why man was originally created body and soul and why he will be redeemed body and soul through the resurrection of the dead (1 Corinthians 15). In a fallen world, the sacraments only amplify these truths that were audibly preached through the verbal prohibition against eating from the tree of knowledge and the issuance of the dominion mandate, and visibly preached through the trees of life and knowledge. Old Testament sacraments, such as the sacrifices, Passover lamb, and circumcision, pointed to the coming descendant, the real physical Seed of the woman, Seed of Abraham, and Seed of David. The Son of Man would come in the flesh, but only in the *likeness* of *sinful* flesh, as He was sinless, and He would redeem fallen man and secure the forfeited blessing of the eschatological rest for the people of God (Matt. 11:28; Heb. 4:1–11).[36]

In the wake of the eschatological Adam, baptism and the Lord's Supper are signs that indicate that the eschaton has begun. These signs visibly preach that Christ has accomplished His work, that He has been cut off from the land of the living God for the sake of His bride (Isa. 53:8) and that He has poured out the Holy Spirit, inaugurating the new heaven and earth. The sacraments indicate the "already" of the already/not yet continuum. They remind the believer that though Christ has come, at present

---

34. One should note in Daniel 12:1–2 that there is a double resurrection: the righteous receive glorified bodies, but the wicked are physically raised but are not glorified. The bodies of the wicked are physical, suited for eternal punishment, but not glorified.

35. Baillie, *Sacraments*, 62–63.

36. See Laansma, *I Will Give You Rest*, 359–66.

believers walk by faith and not by sight (2 Cor. 5:7). However, the fact that the sacraments are visible tells the church that one day faith will give way to sight when the dead in Christ are raised, clothed in immortality, given glorified bodies, and behold the face of God in the face of the incarnate God-man (cf. John 14:7–9; 1 John 3:2).[37]

The sacraments do comfort sinful man and strengthen his faith by giving him something to behold, taste, and feel (LC q. 162). The desire to know God through all of the senses is ultimately the goal of creation and redemption (cf. Gen. 3:8; Rev. 22:4). Therefore, the physical reality and goodness of both creation and redemption necessitate the sacraments in pre-redemptive and redemptive history, whether in the covenants of works or grace.

However, this still leaves the question of the exact relationship between the sign and the thing signified.

SACRAMENTAL UNION

Roman Catholic and Evangelical views

There are a number of views regarding the relationship between the sign and the thing signified, though there are three main categories. At one extreme, there is the Roman Catholic view, which equates the sign and the thing signified. The Roman Catholic Catechism states concerning baptism, "This sacrament is also called *'the washing of regeneration and renewal by the Holy Spirit,'* for it signifies and actually brings about the birth of water and the Spirit without which 'no one can enter the kingdom of God.'"[38] The sign and the thing signified are one and the same. This is an *ex opere operato* view of the sacrament—baptismal regeneration. This view also leads to the Roman Catholic belief in the real presence in the Lord's Supper.

Some Roman Catholic theologians, such as Schillebeeckx, even argue for a hypostatic union between the sign and the thing signified:

> Consider now that the man Jesus is not first a man and then God as well; he is God-man; not a mixture, but God existing *in* human form. In virtue of the Hypostatic Union we are confronted with a divine way of being man and a human way of being God. The man Jesus is the existence of God himself (the Son) according to and in the mode of

---

37. See David VanDrunen, "Iconoclasm, Incarnation, and Eschatology: Toward a Catholic Understanding of the Reformed Doctrine of the 'Second' Commandment," *IJST* 6 (2004): 130–47.

38. *Catechism of the Catholic Church* (Liguori, Mo.: Liguori Publications, 1994), § 1215.

humanity. For person and nature are never extrinsic elements separate from one another. The God-man is one person. Since the sacrifice of the Cross and all the mysteries of the life of Christ are personal acts of God, they are eternally actual and enduring. God the Son himself is therefore present in these human acts in a manner that transcends time.[39]

On the other side of the spectrum are those who, influenced by Zwingli's views, see the sacraments primarily as memorials. Millard Erickson, for example, argues: "The act of baptism conveys no direct spiritual benefit or blessing."[40] Barth equally sees a radical distinction between the sign (baptism) and the thing to which it points (the baptism of the Holy Spirit). He believes baptism is an act of obedience that merely represents what has been done by God through the Holy Spirit.[41]

Lutheran and Reformed churches hold positions between these two extremes.

Luther and Lutheranism

An argument can be made that there is a difference between Luther and later Lutherans on the relationship between the sign and the thing signified. Luther saw the efficacy of the sacrament not in the actual administration of the rite, as in Roman Catholicism, but in the promise of the Word of God. Moreover, in order for the promise to be of benefit, the recipient had to have faith: "A promise is useless unless it is received by faith. But the sacraments are the signs of the promises. Therefore, in their use faith needs to be present."[42] The sacrament of baptism was effective even for infants, though Luther did not adequately explain how this occurred. At times, he was willing to argue for *fides infantium* (infant faith), but in the end he simply retreated to the safe haven of the dominical command—infants are baptized because the Lord commands it.[43] So for Luther, Word and sacrament have the same efficacy—they effect what they promise, but only through faith and the working of the Holy Spirit.

---

39. Edward Schillebeeckx, *Christ the Sacrament of the Encounter with God* (New York: Sheed and Ward, 1963), 56–57.

40. Millard Erickson, *Christian Theology* (Grand Rapids: Baker, 1985), 1096.

41. Barth, CD IV.4: 128; idem, *The Teaching of the Church Regarding Baptism* (1943; Eugene, Ore.: Wipf & Stock, 2006), 9.

42. *Apology of the Augsburg Confession*, art. 13, in *The Book of Concord: The Confessions of the Evangelical Lutheran Church*, eds. Robert Kolb and Timothy J. Wengert (Minneapolis: Fortress, 2000), 221–22.

43. Large Catechism, Fourth part: Concerning Baptism, in *Book of Concord*, 464.

Later Lutheranism moved closer to the Roman Catholic position, embracing baptismal regeneration as it pertains to infants. Lutheran theologian Francis Pieper observes that some Lutherans speak in a Roman Catholic fashion of a communion with Christ, even of regeneration through baptism, without the simultaneous presence of faith for the forgiveness of sins.[44] Pieper explains the difference between paleo- and neo-Lutheranism: "According to the doctrine of Luther and our Lutheran Confessions, the remission of sins is the true 'chief thing' in Baptism, and for this reason they repudiate a saving effect of Baptism without faith on the part of the baptized." Pieper continues, "Many recent Lutherans, however, eliminate from Baptism both the remission of sins and faith, the means of receiving this remission. They teach that Baptism communicates psychic ('psychophysical') powers and gifts which the baptized do not receive with the hand of faith. This is the Romanizing element in their teaching."[45]

The Reformed understanding

Reformed theologians have always recognized the close relationship between the sign and the thing signified, and have done so without separating or confusing them. The Westminster Confession states: "There is, in every sacrament, a spiritual relation, or sacramental union, between the sign and the thing signified: whence it comes to pass, that the names and effects of the one are attributed to the other" (27.2). Here the confession picks up on biblical data that other confessional traditions have missed. Sometimes biblical language appears to equate the sign and the thing signified. For example, Christ gave the cup of the supper to His disciples and said, "This is My blood" (Matt. 26:28). Similarly, some interpreters see the identification of the sign and thing signified in Paul's statement to Titus: "Not by works of righteousness which we have done, but according to His mercy He saved us, through the washing of regeneration and renewing of the Holy Spirit" (3:5). And the apostle Peter says, "There is also an antitype which now saves us—baptism" (1 Peter 3:21a).

In one sense, this language is not new; there is a similar pattern in the Old Testament, where sacrificial rites were said to bring the forgiveness of sins. For example, on the Day of Atonement, the animal sacrifices were

---

44. Francis Pieper, *Christian Dogmatics* (St. Louis: Concordia, 1953), 3.265.
45. Pieper, *Christian Dogmatics*, 3.267; Bavinck, *Reformed Dogmatics*, 4.486; cf. Heinrich Schmid, *The Doctrinal Theology of the Evangelical Lutheran Church* (Philadelphia: Lutheran Publication Society, 1899), 546–47.

an atonement for sin (Lev. 16:34). But in the New Testament, there is the seemingly contradictory statement: "For it is not possible that the blood of bulls and goats could take away sins" (Heb. 10:4). This is not doublespeak, but is what exegetes have defined as a metonymy. A metonymy is "the use of one word (often an attribute) for another that it suggests, as the effect for the cause, the cause for the effect, the sign for the thing signified."[46] An example of a metonymy is Psalm 23:5a: "You prepare a table before me." Here the word *table* is a metonym for *food*. In this respect, biblical signs have never been an end unto themselves but have always pointed beyond themselves to the thing signified. Thus, the Old Testament sacraments, such as the sacrifices, had no saving efficacy but pointed to the person and work of Christ, the true sacrifice that brings the forgiveness of sins through faith by the working of the Holy Spirit. The sacraments of the New Testament function in the same manner. As argued in Part II, the water of baptism points to Christ's baptism of the church with the Spirit. Therefore, Christ through the Spirit saves, not the water. This conclusion is evident in the latter half of 1 Peter 3:21: "There is also an antitype which now saves us—baptism (not the removal of the filth of the flesh, but the answer of a good conscience toward God), through the resurrection of Jesus Christ." The "answer of a good conscience toward God" is God-given faith in the resurrected Christ. Calvin explains: "Neither ought our confidence to inhere in the sacraments, nor the glory of God be transferred to them. Rather, laying aside all things, both our faith and our confession ought to rise up to him who is the author of the sacraments and of all things."[47]

This relationship between the sign and the thing signified is impossible to maintain if, as with Roman Catholicism, the sacraments convey and infuse a *habitus gratiae* (a habit of grace). If, on the other hand, as in the previous chapter, Christ through the Holy Spirit is the grace of God, then contra Schillebeeckx, there is no hypostatic union between Christ and the sacraments. Rather, the sacraments as visible words function in the same manner as the invisible (audible) Word. No one argues that the preaching or reading of the Word automatically regenerates those who hear or read it. Otherwise, why not broadcast the Word of God through loudspeakers and automatically save anyone within earshot? On the other side of the spectrum, no one argues that the Word of God is of no spiritual benefit whatsoever

---

46. F. B. Huey, Jr. and Bruce Corley, *A Student's Dictionary for Biblical and Theological Studies* (Grand Rapids: Zondervan, 1983), 125–26, q. v. *metonymy*.

47. Calvin, *Institutes*, 4.14.12.

to the believer.[48] The Spirit makes the reading and preaching of the Word effectual unto salvation by grace through faith. In parallel fashion, the Spirit makes the Word-accompanied sacraments effectual means of salvation by grace alone through faith alone. The sacraments visibly preach the gospel. The content of Word and sacrament is completely identical. However, once again, the Word can stand alone, but the sacrament cannot. The sacrament is nothing without the Word.[49] To debunk an old cliché, a picture is not worth a thousand words. A picture is seldom worth much without words.

Peter Van Mastricht (1630–1706) explains the nature of the sacramental union between the sign and the thing signified: "The Reformed unanimously hold that there is no physical regenerating efficacy in baptism, but only a moral efficacy which consists in its being a sign and seal of regeneration." He further stipulates, however, "They also hold that the grace of regeneration is not confined to any sacrament, but yet believe that baptism is not a mere naked, useless sign, but a most efficacious sealing of the covenant of grace and of regeneration to those who receive it agreeably to its institution, and also to the elect infants of believers."[50] Along similar lines, Bavinck notes a parallel between the sacramental union and other concepts: "No one would call the connection existing between a word and the thing it signifies, between an image and the person it represents, between a pledge and that of which it is a pledge, a union. Yet the relationship that exists between the sign and the thing signified in the sacrament is of the same nature."[51]

The connection between the sign and the thing signified is therefore not physical, local, corporeal, or substantial, contra Schillebeeckx. Baptism and the Lord's Supper are not miracles, remedies, schemes, vehicles, channels, or physical causes of the thing signified. Rather, there is an ethical connection, one that is identical with that between Christ and the gospel and between the benefits of the covenant of grace and the Word through which they are known. In older theological terminology, the sacramental union is therefore a *unio relativa, significativa,* or *moralis* (a relative, sig-

---

48. Charles Hodge, *Systematic Theology*, 3 vols. (rep.; Grand Rapids: Eerdmans, 1993), 3.589.

49. Bavinck, *Reformed Dogmatics*, 4.468, 479; see also Weber, *Dogmatics*, 2.602.

50. Peter Van Mastricht, *A Treatise on Regeneration*, ed. Brandon Withrow (1699; Morgan, Pa.: Soli Deo Gloria, 2002), 51; cf. idem, *Theoretico-practica Theologia* (Utrecht: 1725), 7.3.8, as cited in Heppe, *Dogmatics*, 598.

51. Bavinck, *Reformed Dogmatics*, 4.481.

nificative, or moral union).[52] The classic Reformed understanding of the sacramental union best accounts for the biblical data and the relationship between baptism and redemption.

CONCLUSION

The covenantal context of the sacraments dictates that they are not merely human pledges or oaths. The sacraments do not bring regeneration automatically to the recipient. They do not convey or infuse created grace or habits. Neither Christ nor His church is a sacrament. The sacraments are signs and seals of the covenant of grace that point to Christ and the Holy Spirit and their respective works. They do not work faith, but instead reinforce it, as a wedding ring reinforces love.[53] They are visible words that function in the same manner as the invisible words of God. Just as the Word of God is double-edged, so too are the sacraments—they hold out covenant blessing and sanction. The difference between the reception of blessing or sanction depends on the presence or absence of faith in the recipient.

---

52. Heppe, *Dogmatics*, 598; cf. Richard A. Muller, *Dictionary of Latin and Greek Theological Terms: Drawn Principally from Protestant Scholastic Theology* (Grand Rapids: Baker, 1985), 316–17, q. v. *union sacramentalis, unio symbolica*.

53. Bavinck, *Reformed Dogmatics*, 4.489.

CHAPTER 13

Baptism Proper

The previous chapters explored baptism as a means of grace and as a sacrament, a sacred sign and seal of the covenant of grace. At this point in the study, it is necessary to continue to take the collected data from Part II and formulate the specifics of the doctrine of baptism. To that end, this chapter will examine the institution, formula, symbolism, and mode of baptism. Where and in what way was baptism instituted as a sacrament of the new covenant? Was it in the baptism of Christ or in the words of the Great Commission? What is the proper baptismal formula? The Great Commission tells the church to baptize into the name of the Father, Son, and Holy Spirit (Matt. 28:19), whereas a number of other passages in the New Testament speak of being baptized into the name of Christ alone. Does this mean there are two traditions or that there was a later liturgical development by the early church? Given all of the biblical-theological data that has been collected, as well as the material on baptism as a sacrament and means of grace, what is the symbolic significance of baptism? Lastly, what is the proper mode of baptism? Must baptism be administered by immersion only, or are there other legitimate modes of administration? This chapter will address these questions.

INSTITUTION

It is a common belief that, like the Lord's Supper, Christ instituted baptism not only by His divine command but also by His example when He was baptized.[1] John Calvin, for example, states, "We are assured that John's ministry was exactly the same as that afterward committed to the apos-

---

1. So Daniel L. Akin, ed., *A Theology for the Church* (Nashville: Broadman & Holman, 2007), 783.

tles."[2] While there are certainly similarities between Christ's baptism and that which the church practices, significant differences are also present. The contention of this chapter is that Christ instituted baptism in the Great Commission and not in His submission to John's baptism. The differences that emerge when the two baptisms are compared confirm this thesis.

First, note the redemptive-historical timeframe for John's ministry. John was the last of the great Old Testament prophets—he stood between the end of the old covenant and the beginning of the new (Matt. 11:13; Luke 16:16). As the last prophet of the Old Testament, he called the terminal generation to repentance. John's concern was not to summon the world at large but Israel—the people with whom Yahweh had entered a covenant at Sinai. His call for Israel's repentance was brought forward in his call to baptism. This baptism was not a perpetual rite for Israel but a special sign for that terminal generation. John's baptism epitomized the particular crisis in covenant history represented by John's mission as the messenger bearing the Lord's ultimatum.[3]

This leads to the second point, namely, John's ministry was preparatory for the ministry of Christ, and hence his baptism was preparatory, as well. John clearly saw a difference between his ministry and that of Christ: "I indeed baptize you with water unto repentance, but He who is coming after me...will baptize you with the Holy Spirit and fire" (Matt. 3:11). John's ministry was that of the messenger, Elijah, coming to prepare the way for the Lord (Isa. 40:3; Mal. 4:5; Matt. 3:3).[4] James Dunn explains:

> The purpose of John's baptism is to reveal Jesus to Israel, and presumably therefore it is only preparatory to the mission of Christ (1:31); the Christ's baptism will not be ἐν ὕδατι but ἐν Πνεύματι Ἁγίῳ (1:33). The implication is that John's water-baptism is only a shadow and symbol of the Christ's Spirit-baptism. The contrast between the two baptisms is the contrast between John and Jesus—the antithesis of preparation and fulfillment, of shadow and substance.[5]

---

2. John Calvin, *Institutes of the Christian Religion*, LCC, vols. 20–21, ed. John T. McNeill, trans. Ford Lewis Battles (Philadelphia: Westminster, 1960), 4.15.7.

3. Meredith G. Kline, *By Oath Consigned: A Reinterpretation of the Covenant Signs of Circumcision and Baptism* (Grand Rapids: Eerdmans, 1968), 31; also Herman Bavinck, *Saved by Grace: The Holy Spirit's Work in Calling and Regeneration*, trans. Nelson D. Kloosterman, ed. J. Mark Beach (Grand Rapids: Reformation Heritage Books, 2008), 115.

4. James D. G. Dunn, *Baptism in the Holy Spirit* (Philadelphia: Westminster, 1970), 13.

5. Dunn, *Baptism*, 19; cf. nearly identical comments by John Murray, *Christian Baptism* (Phillipsburg, N.J.: P & R, 1980), 2; G. C. Berkouwer, *The Sacraments*, trans. Hugo Bekker

The baptism of the new covenant, that which was commissioned and instituted by Christ, points to the outpouring of the Holy Spirit, something that had not yet happened in the days of John.[6] Hence, John's baptism was merely one of water.

Third, and finally, there is a distinct difference between the two baptisms in that John's baptism was one of repentance, whereas the baptism instituted by Jesus was to be administered in the name of the Trinity: Father, Son, and Holy Spirit. There is no textual support for Calvin's claim that John baptized "into the name of Christ."[7]

Based on these three points, the precise import and nature of baptism cannot be derived from John's baptism. The terms of the divine institution of the rite in the Great Commission explain the precise nature of the sacrament.[8] Christian baptism is therefore founded on the divine command, not the baptism of Christ.

FORMULA

Christ instituted baptism in the following words: "All authority has been given to Me in heaven and on earth. Go therefore and make disciples of all the nations, baptizing them in the name of the Father and of the Son and of the Holy Spirit" (Matt. 28:18–19). The first thing to note in this formula is that the risen Messiah institutes the rite of baptism on the ground of His authority. As Paul later explained, Jesus is the last Adam who came to take up the failed work of the first (Rom. 5:12–21; 1 Cor. 15:45–49). Christ is the eschatological Prophet, Priest, and King. The language of the imminence of the arrival of the kingdom is not found in the New Testament outside the Gospels, as imminence has given way to presence (cf. Matt. 3:2; 4:17; Mark 1:15; Luke 17:21).[9] Moreover, Jesus is the Messiah who rules over His kingdom, one marked by covenant—it is a covenanted kingdom. At the Lord's Supper, Christ not only identifies His body and blood as that which ratifies the new covenant (Matt. 26:28; Mark 14:24; Luke 22:20; 1 Cor. 11:25), He covenants with His disciples and gives to them the rights

---

(Grand Rapids: Eerdmans, 1969), 96–97; Herman Bavinck, *Reformed Dogmatics*, trans. John Vriend, ed. John Bolt (Grand Rapids: Baker, 2003–08), 4.501–502.

6. Berkouwer, *Sacraments*, 94.

7. Calvin, *Institutes*, 4.15.7; cf. Murray, *Christian Baptism*, 2.

8. Murray, *Christian Baptism*, 2.

9. See Herman Ridderbos, *The Coming of the Kingdom* (Phillipsburg, N.J.: P & R, 1962), 61–103.

and authority of the kingdom: κἀγὼ διατίθεμαι ὑμῖν, καθὼς διέθετό μοι ὁ πατήρ μου, βασιλείαν (And I bestow upon you a kingdom, just as My Father bestowed one upon Me) (Luke 22:29).[10]

The covenantal character of the institution of baptism surfaces in Christ's specific command to go and make disciples of πάντα τὰ ἔθνη (all the nations). This phrase has much Old Testament significance—it also characterizes the Abrahamic covenant: "In your seed all the nations [πάντα τὰ ἔθνη] of the earth shall be blessed" (Gen. 22:18; 12:3; 18:18). In a sense, Matthew comes full circle as he closes his Gospel with these words that are evocative of the manner in which he opened it, that is, identifying Jesus as the son of Abraham (Matt. 1:1).[11] These identifying marks, although subtle, show that baptism is situated within the context of the covenant history of God's people. However, baptism is specifically the sign of the new covenant.

Jesus said disciples were to be baptized "in the name of the Father and of the Son and of the Holy Spirit." What does it mean to be baptized εἰς τὸ ὄνομα (into or in the name)? This formula appears in other contexts; for example, Paul declares that the Israelites were εἰς τὸν Μωσῆν ἐβαπτίσαντο (baptized into Moses) (1 Cor. 10:2), but he rebukes the Corinthians and denies that they have been εἰς τὸ ὄνομα Παύλου ἐβαπτίσθητε (baptized into the name of Paul) (1 Cor. 1:13). This construction indicates that the person who is baptized into a name or person is baptized into a relationship.[12] Alternatively, "baptized into" is a way of expressing the idea that a person is "in union with" the person or name into which he has been baptized. To be "baptized into Moses" was to be bound to him in the covenant of which Moses was the mediator—it was to be a disciple of Moses. Paul, therefore, explained to the Corinthians that they were *not* baptized into his name, which would have meant that they had been baptized into discipleship of Paul rather than that of Jesus. To be baptized, therefore, into the name of the triune Lord, Father, Son, and Holy Spirit, is sacramentally to enter a relationship with the Lord by union with the Mediator of the new covenant, by which people are the beneficiaries of the blessings of redemption and submit to His covenant lordship.[13]

---

10. Meredith G. Kline, *Kingdom Prologue: Genesis Foundations for a Covenantal Worldview* (Overland Park, Kan.: Two Age Press, 2000), 139–40.

11. D. A. Carson, *Matthew*, EBC (Grand Rapids: Zondervan, 1995), 2.596.

12. Murray, *Christian Baptism*, 3.

13. Murray, *Christian Baptism*, 29–30; also Louis Berkhof, *Systematic Theology: New*

A related matter is the apparent difference between the divine institution found at the end of Matthew's Gospel and other occurrences in the New Testament where people were baptized "into the name of the Lord" (Acts 10:48). In a number of places in the New Testament, converts to Christianity were baptized εἰς Χριστὸν (into Christ) (Gal. 3:27; Rom. 6:3) or ἐβαπτίσθησαν εἰς τὸ ὄνομα τοῦ Κυρίου Ἰησοῦ (into the name of the Lord Jesus) (Acts 19:5). This apparent deviation from the Trinitarian formula in the Great Commission has led some, such as Wolfhart Pannenberg, to reject the divine institution found in Matthew's Gospel. Pannenberg contends that Christ did not divinely command the institution of baptism.[14] Others, such as D. A. Carson, argue that the Great Commission and other discourse narratives, such as the Sermon on the Mount (Matthew 5–7), are highly condensed and are not the *ipsissima verba* (very words) of Christ. Because of this condensed nature of the ascension narrative, the use of the triune name of God is not an exclusive formula.[15] Similarly, Louis Berkhof writes: "It is not necessary to assume that, when Jesus employed these words, He intended them as a formula to be used ever after. He merely used them as descriptive of the character of the baptism which He instituted, just as similar expressions serve to characterize other baptisms, Acts 19:3; 1 Cor. 1:13; 10:2; 12:13."[16] According to the aforementioned authors, it is legitimate to baptize a person into the name of the triune Lord or simply the name of Jesus.

While this conclusion is certainly possible, there is a better answer, both text-critically and theologically. Undoubtedly the discourses of Christ are accurate but nonetheless condensed versions of what He said. So Carson is correct; the Great Commission discourse does not represent the *ipsissima verba Christi*. However, the truth of this conclusion does not address the specific question of the baptismal formula. In other words, while Christ's ascension discourse was likely much longer than what is recorded in Matthew's Gospel (cf. Matt. 28:18–20; Acts 1:4–12), it is more than possible to argue that the specific formula itself represents the *ipsissima verba Christi*. How much more expansive could the baptismal formula have been before being condensed?

Combined Edition (1932–38; Grand Rapids: Eerdmans, 1996), 624–25.

14. Wolfhart Pannenberg, *Systematic Theology* (Grand Rapids: Eerdmans, 1991–98), 3.276, 340.

15. Carson, *Matthew*, 2.598.

16. Berkhof, *Systematic Theology*, 625.

If the baptismal formula is the *ipsissima verba Christi*, how does this formula harmonize with the occurrences of baptism into the name of Christ? The answer lies in the representative and mediatorial role of Christ in the economy of redemption. In a number of Old Testament passages, the prophets say that God Himself will redeem His people. For example: "whoever calls on the name of the LORD [יהוה] shall be saved" (Joel 2:32). The reference is clearly to Yahweh, but when Peter appeals to this text to explain the outpouring of the Spirit, he tells the angst-filled crowd, βαπτισθήτω ἕκαστος ὑμῶν ἐπὶ τῷ ὀνόματι Ἰησοῦ Χριστοῦ (be baptized in the name of Jesus Christ) (Acts 2:38). While the triune formula is not explicitly stated, it is materially present, in that God the Father sends the Son who pours out the Spirit. Moreover, the redemption-seeking crowd called on the name of the Lord, Yahweh, in the name of Jesus.

In Romans 10:13, Paul quotes Joel 2:32 (LXX 3:5) and shows that Christ reveals Yahweh. Douglas Moo explains, "In the Old Testament, of course, the one on whom people called for salvation was Yahweh; Paul reflects the high view of Christ common among the early church by identifying this one with Jesus Christ, the Lord."[17] In other words, in Joel the prophet tells the people to call upon Yahweh, but now Paul identifies Jesus as the one upon whom people must call. Jesus reveals Yahweh. To be baptized into the name of Christ is to be baptized into the name of the triune God. Thus, "baptized into the name of Christ" appears to be shorthand for the fuller triune formula. In other words, when Luke or Paul writes that a person was baptized into the name of Christ, these are not the *ipsissima verba* that were used in the actual baptism of the person but the shorthand formula.[18]

Beyond this conclusion, why is the triune baptismal formula important? The divine command and institution are alone sufficient to warrant the use of the baptismal formula, but there is another important theological point. The use of the Matthean baptismal formula harks back to the baptism of Christ in the Jordan, when the Father addressed Him as His Son in whom

---

17. Douglas J. Moo, *The Epistle to the Romans*, NICNT (Grand Rapids: Eerdmans, 1996), 660; cf. T. F. Torrance, et al., *The Biblical Doctrine of Baptism: A Study Document Issued by the Special Commission on Baptism in the Church of Scotland* (1958; Edinburgh: The St. Andrew Press, 1960), 21. See also the *Didache* (ca. early second century), which repeats the triune formula: "Now concerning baptism, baptize as follows: after you have reviewed all these things, baptize in the name of the Father and of the Son and of the Holy Spirit in running water" (7.1).

18. See Charles Hodge, *Systematic Theology*, 3 vols. (rep.; Grand Rapids: Eerdmans, 1993), 3.540.

He was well pleased and the Holy Spirit descended on Him in the form of a dove. Though the baptism of Jesus and Christian baptism are different, there is still substantial continuity. The waters of baptism represent the waters of new creation, and the Father's sending of the Son, the last Adam, inaugurates the new age. The last Adam pours out the life-giving Spirit and fills the earth with those who emerge from the water bearing His image, and hence the image and glory of the Father.[19] Believers are most certainly supposed to recall the baptism of Christ in connection with their own, as is evident in Christ's explanation of Pentecost just prior to His ascension (Acts 1:4–5). What was typified in John's baptismal ministry at the Jordan is now fulfilled through Christ and the outpouring of the Spirit.[20] Christians are supposed to realize that the realities that stand behind the sign and seal of baptism are the work of the triune Lord; hence, baptism is to be carried out in the triune name.

SYMBOLISM

In terms of the symbolism of baptism, two points should be explored, informed by the biblical-theological exposition in Part II: initiation into the covenant community (the church) and union with Christ.

Initiation into the covenant community

A cursory reading of the New Testament easily demonstrates that baptism is an initiatory rite, one that is administered to converts to Christianity. This fact is prominently displayed in the events at Pentecost: "Those who gladly received his word were baptized; and that day about three thousand souls were added to them" (Acts 2:41). The conversion of the Ethiopian eunuch manifests the same pattern; upon his profession of faith, he was immediately baptized by Philip (Acts 8:26–40). Baptism is administered to adult converts who profess faith in Christ. Because it is administered in the name of the triune Lord and occurs through the mediatorial office of Jesus, the one who is baptized is united to Christ—he joins the body of Christ, the church.[21]

Being united to Christ is not an isolated event for the individual, but is a rite enmeshed in the covenant. Christ is the covenant Mediator; therefore, to

---

19. Torrance, et al., *Doctrine of Baptism*, 21.
20. F. F. Bruce, *The Book of Acts*, NICNT (Grand Rapids: Eerdmans, 1988), 35.
21. Murray, *Christian Baptism*, 31.

be united to Christ is to be united to His body in a covenantal bond, namely, the covenant of grace. The one who is baptized does not exist in isolation but is part of the covenant community, the church. As Robert Jenson notes, "Baptism, first, lets the gospel be *unconditional* and, second, prevents the separation of faith from the community."[22] The gospel has been entrusted to the church, and as the audible Word is entrusted to men gifted by the Holy Spirit to preach, so too the visible Word of baptism has been placed in the hands of the minister. However, as P. T. Forsyth (1842–1941) explains, the minister "simply acts for the Church gathered around him." Forsyth continues: "He is its hand and voice. But he cannot feel that he is that if the Church be mainly absent. The hand is severed from the body. The voice is a thin, disembodied voice, a mere ventriloquism. Baptism is the Church's act, and, if the Church is not there, the act falls to the ground as a Sacrament."[23]

There is, then, a dynamic between the one who is baptized and the church that administers the baptism. The adult convert professes his faith as an individual. However, he does so as part of the community of those who have been called out of the world to be united to Christ. The unity of the covenant community is manifest in baptism (Gal. 3:27; Eph. 4:4–6). Its function is not solely the incorporation of the individual into the body of the church, the *corpus ecclesiae*, but in the establishment of this unity. It is wrongheaded and selfish for a person to ask, "What do I get out of baptism?" Of course the individual is involved, but by virtue of baptism the individual is destined for membership, for integration into a community. This means that the individual renounces his isolated existence and is joined to the body of Christ, the covenant community.[24]

There are two important points to note regarding baptism as a sign and seal of membership in the church or covenant community. First, baptism is a sign and seal of church membership, but it is "for the solemn admission of the party baptized into the *visible* church" (WCF 28.1, emphasis added).[25] Some fail to observe this important point. Millard Erickson, for example, states, "Baptism is, then, an act of faith and a testimony that one has been

---

22. Robert Jenson, *Visible Words: The Interpretation and Practice of Christian Sacraments* (Philadelphia: Fortress, 1978), 147.

23. P. T. Forsyth, *The Church and Sacraments* (1917; London: Independent Press Ltd., 1955), 184.

24. Otto Weber, *Foundations of Dogmatics*, 2 vols. (Grand Rapids: Eerdmans, 1983), 2.603.

25. Recall the development of the employment of this distinction by Zacharias Ursinus, Johannes Wollebius, and James Ussher from Part I, chapters 4–6.

united with Christ in his death and resurrection, that one has experienced spiritual circumcision."[26] While Erickson does not say so explicitly, his statement implies that only those who are members of the invisible church should be baptized. Others take what Erickson implies and make it explicit. Stephen Wellum writes of the transition from the old to the new covenant: "The change is found in the shift from a *mixed* community to that of a *regenerate* community with the crucial implication that under the new covenant, the covenant sign must only be applied to those who are in that covenant, namely, believers."[27] Such conclusions, however, are impossible to draw, as John Murray notes: "No man or organization of men is able infallibly to determine who are regenerate and who are not, who are true believers and who are not."[28]

Ministers and elders should always seek the purity of the church, but to say that the church is not a *mixed* body flies in the face of the biblical evidence. What of Simon Magus (Acts 8:9–25, esp. vv. 20–23), Hymenaeus and Alexander (1 Tim. 1:20), and those whom John described as "brothers" who commit a sin that leads to death, for whom one should not pray (1 John 5:16–17)? Some are visibly joined to Christ the vine but do not yield fruit, and therefore are cut off and thrown into the fire (John 15:1–10). The parable of the sower makes the same point. The seeds that were cast on the rocky soil grew, but the sun scorched them and, having no root, they withered away (Matt. 13:5–6). Christ explains the meaning of this portion of the parable: "But he who received the seed on stony places, this is he who hears the word and immediately receives it with joy; yet he has no root in himself, but endures only for a while. For when tribulation or persecution arises because of the word, immediately he stumbles" (Matt. 13:20–21).[29] This much seems clear—there are those who will profess faith in Christ and be baptized, but then apostatize under the pressures of trial or persecution. It was because of apostasy in the face of persecution that Augustine developed the distinction between the *visible* and *invisible* church.

Christ has inaugurated the eschaton and the new covenant. However, as long as the church is enmeshed in the overlap of the ages—the present

---

26. Millard J. Erickson, *Christian Theology* (Grand Rapids: Baker, 1985), 1101.

27. Stephen J. Wellum, "Baptism and the Relationship Between the Covenants," in *Believer's Baptism: Sign of the New Covenant*, eds. Thomas R. Schreiner and Shawn D. Wright (Nashville: Broadman & Holman, 2006), 138.

28. Murray, *Christian Baptism*, 31.

29. See Simon J. Kistemaker, *The Parables: Understanding the Stories Jesus Told* (Grand Rapids: Baker, 1980), 38–39.

evil age and the age to come—the church must be seen in terms of the already/not yet. The next chapter will explore this point in greater detail. Nevertheless, Augustine's explanation is helpful for the moment:

> We ought, therefore, to say that the rule is about the true and the mixed body of the Lord, or the true and the counterfeit, or some such name; because, not to speak of eternity, hypocrites cannot even now be said to be in Him, although they seem to be in His church. And hence this rule might be designated thus: Concerning *the mixed Church.*... The Church declares itself to be at present both; and this because the good fish and the bad are for the time mixed up in the one net.[30]

Hence, those who are baptized are admitted into the *visible* church. The visible church, the body of the baptized, does not correspond exactly to the number of the elect. Only God knows who is part of the invisible church. The baptism of those who permanently apostatize is not the sign of blessing and covenant membership, but of sanction and covenant judgment—a baptism of fire.

Second, baptism is a sign of church membership, but the church is a covenant community, not a voluntary association of people. Some theologians characterize the church as a voluntary association, seeing it as comprised only of those who voluntarily profess their faith in Christ. They stress that membership in the church is not coerced. This is true—no one can coerce a profession of faith. However, if the church is merely a voluntary association, there is no place for children who have yet to make a profession of faith. Dietrich Bonhoeffer explains that only a community (*Gemeinschaft*), not a society (*Gesellschaft*), can carry children. He elaborates:

> Baptism is a declaration of intent by the church-community to accept the child in order to prepare it for participation in the church-community in the future. Only a community, not a society, is able to carry children. It is possible to be born into a community, provided the parents guide the child's will; they decide what happens to the child. The child is thus sanctified by the parents' will (1 Cor. 7:14). Such a statement makes sense because a community by its nature is not merely organized for a specific purpose, but rather makes claim on one's entire attitude towards life. Baptism is the affirmation by the church-community to the child who is born into the community of

---

30. Augustine, *On Christian Doctrine*, 3.32.45, in NPNF[1] 2.569.

saints. This insight is an argument against the idea that the church is a voluntary association [*Verein*] or compulsory organization [*Anstalt*].[31]

More will be said about this in the following chapter, but for now it is essential to see that baptism admits the one who is baptized (infant or adult) into the visible church, the covenant community. It does not guarantee that a person is in the invisible church. To assume that baptism effects membership into the invisible church *ex opere operato* is to confuse the sign with the thing signified. It is to fail to recognize the covenantal nature of the church, as well as the already/not yet dynamic. As long as the church militant is on its pilgrimage through this present evil age, even as it is illuminated by the dawning of the age to come, the seed of the serpent will remain in the midst of the seed of the woman—the church will be a mixed body.

Within the realm of the covenant, God administers His signs and seals that bring both blessing and sanction. The difference between blessing and sanction is the presence or absence of faith in Christ in the one who is baptized. The blessing-sanction dynamic in the administration of the covenant sign of baptism is evident in the broad strokes of redemptive history. The Old Testament exodus narrative reveals a distinct typical pattern that finds its antitypical fulfillment in Christ and the church. Israel departed on the exodus from Egypt, where they were baptized in the Red Sea and then journeyed to the Promised Land for the consummation of their exodus redemption. The subsequent New Testament interpretation of these events is clear—the Red Sea baptism was a covenant blessing for believing Israel, but sanction and judgment for unbelieving Pharaoh and his army. However, there was an already/not yet tension at work even in this typical Old Testament baptism in that those who were baptized did not necessarily enter the Promised Land—even though they were, adult and infant alike, part of the visible covenant community. The author of Hebrews clearly states that what made the difference in the typical consummation of the exodus redemption was the presence or absence of faith: "For indeed the gospel was preached to us as well as to them; but the word which they heard did not profit them, not being mixed with faith in those who heard it" (Heb. 4:2).

The exodus-redemption events manifest the pattern of inauguration and consummation in that Israel's Red Sea baptism visibly separated the

---

31. Dietrich Bonhoeffer, *Sanctorum Communio: A Theological Study of the Sociology of the Church*, in *Dietrich Bonhoeffer Works*, vol. 1, ed. Clifford J. Green, trans. Reinhard Krauss and Nancy Lukens (Minneapolis: Fortress, 1998), 257–58, n. 395.

covenant community from the unbelieving Egyptians, but at the same time it pointed to Israel's need to follow the leading of Christ and the Spirit throughout their pilgrimage to its consummation by entry into the Promised Land (cf. Ex. 23:20; 32:34; 40:36; Lev. 16:2; Num. 20:16; Acts 2:1–4; 1 Cor. 10:1–4; Jude 5). This typical pattern is the play within the play, and so foreshadows what will occur in the eschaton with the antitypical Spirit-baptism of the church.

That these baptismal covenantal patterns continue in the New Testament is evident on a number of fronts. As the New Testament makes clear, the ministry of Christ is the second, or eschatological, exodus under the leadership of one greater than Moses. This is especially evident when Mark opens his narrative with the use of the term εὐαγγέλιον (gospel), a word connected not with the contemporary abstracted meaning of "historical account of the ministry of Jesus" but with the long-promised Isaianic second exodus: ἐπ' ὄρος ὑψηλὸν ἀνάβηθι ὁ εὐαγγελιζόμενος Σιων ὕψωσον τῇ ἰσχύι τὴν φωνήν σου ὁ εὐαγγελιζόμενος (LXX)![32] Luke characterizes Jesus' death as an exodus: καὶ ἰδού, ἄνδρες δύο συνελάλουν αὐτῷ, οἵτινες ἦσαν Μωσῆς καὶ Ἠλίας, οἳ ὀφθέντες ἐν δόξῃ ἔλεγον τὴν ἔξοδον αὐτοῦ (And behold, two men talked with Him, who were Moses and Elijah, who appeared in glory and spoke of His decease [exodus]) (Luke 9:30–31). This means that the salvation of the church is under the rubric of second exodus.

This conclusion explains Paul's appeal to the Red Sea crossing. The point of Paul's use of Israel's Red Sea baptism is that the Corinthians were to learn from the typical events of the Old Testament: ταῦτα δὲ τύποι ἡμῶν ἐγενήθησαν (1 Cor. 10:6).[33] Paul then segues to parenesis against idolatry and sexual immorality (1 Cor. 10:7–8) and concludes: "Nor let us tempt Christ, as some of them also tempted, and were destroyed by serpents" (1 Cor. 10:9). In this vein, Richard Hays notes, "Israel's story, as told

---

32. The translation from the Hebrew reads: "O Zion, You who bring good tidings, Get up into the high mountain; O Jerusalem, You who bring good tidings, Lift up your voice with strength, Lift it up, be not afraid; Say to the cities of Judah, 'Behold your God!'" (Isa. 40:9). See Jürgen Moltmann, *The Church and the Power of the Spirit* (1977; Minneapolis: Fortress, 1993), 216–17. On the second-exodus theme in Mark, see Rikki E. Watts, *Isaiah's New Exodus in Mark* (Grand Rapids: Baker, 2001); also G. K. Beale and D. A. Carson, eds., *Commentary on the New Testament Use of the Old Testament* (Grand Rapids: Baker, 2008), 111–20.

33. So Richard B. Hays, *Echoes of Scripture in the Letters of Paul* (New Haven: Yale University Press, 1989), 91; also Leonhard Goppelt, *Typos: The Typological Interpretation of the Old Testament in the New* (1939; Grand Rapids: Eerdmans, 1989), 146.

in Scripture, so comprehensively constitutes the symbolic universe of Paul's discourse that he can recall the elements of that story for himself and his readers with the sorts of subtle gestures that pass between members of an interpretive family."[34] So, then, how does Paul's use of the exodus narrative function in his epistle to Corinth? Again, Hays explains: "The Exodus quotation anchors the discourse at the point of its central concern (idolatry) and does so in a way that permits the poetic expansion of Paul's germinal metaphorical intuition into a metaphysical conceit, spanning the experiences of Israel and the church with multiple analogies."[35] In other words, the events of the Old Testament exodus were directed at the church in every age, but especially the church in the wake of the advent of Christ. Hence, this is Paul's point: as Israel was baptized and then judged for idolatry, those who are baptized into Christ must learn from this type and be careful not to fall into idolatry and judgment.

This is the whole point of the Hebrews 3–4 interpretation of the Old Testament exodus narrative—it is couched in terms of the typical first exodus under Moses and the antitypical second exodus under Christ:

> So we see that they could not enter in because of unbelief. Therefore, since a promise remains of entering His rest, let us fear lest any of you seem to have come short of it. For indeed the gospel was preached to us as well as to them; but the word which they heard did not profit them, not being mixed with faith in those who heard it.... Let us therefore be diligent to enter that rest, lest anyone fall according to the same example of disobedience (Heb. 3:19–4:2, 11).

As with Israel of old, therefore, baptism places a boundary and marks the covenant community off from the unbelieving world, but the community that is marked is the *visible* community. Just as with ancient Israel, faith and disbelief are the all-determining factors in whether baptism is received as covenant blessing or sanction.

This blessing-sanction model is true not only for adult converts but also for infants, as infant and adult alike were baptized in the Red Sea crossing. So also now infant and adult are baptized into the eschatological exodus—they are baptized into the Spirit. But both adult and infant enter the visible covenant community as it journeys to the New Jerusalem and the consummation of their exodus-redemption. The exodus narrative subtext in

---

34. Hays, *Echoes of Scripture*, 92.
35. Hays, *Echoes of Scripture*, 92–93.

1 Corinthians 10 therefore informs the nature of baptism. According to Paul, baptism (foreshadowed in Israel's Red Sea crossing) is not a miscellaneous cleansing rite or a general sign of initiation, but is that which brings God's people into the historical narrative of the eschatological exodus. The overarching narrative of the person and work of Christ and the redemption He brings was enacted typologically in Israel's history.[36] Baptism therefore must be coordinated not with election into the invisible church but with covenant, the context in which election is revealed.[37] Even then, election is ultimately and definitively revealed at the consummation, not during the present already/not yet.

With this important blessing-sanction dynamic in mind, the significance of baptism as union with Christ must be explored.

Union with Christ

As noted above, being baptized "into Christ" signifies union with Him. This union is in His death, burial, resurrection, and ascension.[38] Murray explains, "It is because believers are united to Christ in the efficacy of his death, in the power of his resurrection, and in the fellowship of his grace that they are one body."[39]

The connection between baptism and union with Christ is especially evident in Romans 6:3–11. Paul writes, "Or do you not know that as many of us as were baptized into Christ Jesus were baptized into His death?" (Rom. 6:3).

---

36. N. T. Wright, *Romans*, NIB, vol. 10 (Nashville: Abingdon, 2002), 534.

37. See Kline, *By Oath Consigned*, 79. There is no space here to elaborate this point at great length, but one must coordinate the doctrines of the church, visible and invisible, with election and perseverance of the saints. See Berkhof, *Systematic Theology*, 109–25, 545–51. This position is in contrast to those who reject the visible-invisible church distinction and argue that Christians genuinely do fall away and lose their salvation because they were not granted perseverance (see Douglas Wilson, *"Reformed" Is Not Enough: Recovering the Objectivity of the Covenant* [Moscow, Idaho: Canon, 2002], 123–60; idem, "The Church: Visible or Invisible," in *The Federal Vision*, eds. Steve Wilkins and Duane Garner [Monroe, La.: Athanasius, 2004], 263–70; Rich Lusk, "New Life and Apostasy: Hebrews 6:4–8 as Test Case," in *Federal Vision*, 271–90; cf. Guy Prentiss Waters, *The Federal Vision and Covenant Theology: A Comparative Analysis* [Phillipsburg, N.J.: P & R, 2006], 125–67; Wayne Grudem, "Perseverance of the Saints: A Case Study from Hebrews 6:4–6 and Other Warning Passages in Hebrews," in *The Grace of God and the Bondage of the Will*, eds. Thomas R. Schreiner and Bruce A. Ware [Grand Rapids: Baker, 1995], 1.133–82).

38. For standard expositions of the doctrine of union with Christ, see Lewis B. Smedes, *Union with Christ: A Biblical View of the New Life in Jesus Christ* (1970; Grand Rapids: Eerdmans, 1983); John Murray, *Redemption Accomplished and Applied* (Grand Rapids: Eerdmans, 1955), 161–73; Berkhof, *Systematic Theology*, 447–53.

39. Murray, *Christian Baptism*, 3.

Some believe that Paul uses βαπτίζω only in a metaphorical sense and does not have water baptism in view.[40] Dunn writes, "There is nothing in Paul to show that he intended to use the verb in an all-embracing sense—'baptized,' either as the inner reality effected in conjunction with or even by means of the human action, or as a description for the whole sacramental reality (there is some danger of reading the more sophisticated sacramental theology of later centuries into the language here)."[41] Dunn's warning is apropos. Nevertheless, if the sacraments are mysteries, and if they are accompanied by the divine revelation of the Word of God, it is unnecessary to choose between the baptism of the Spirit and water baptism. Given the sacramental union between the sign and the thing signified, Paul uses *baptism* not as a metaphor but as a metonymy. In systematic-theological terminology, the sacramental union is key. Water baptism points to the baptism of the Spirit. In this baptism, the believer receives the outpouring of the Spirit by which he is united to Christ in His death as well as His resurrection and ascension.[42] Remember, the written Word and the visible words (sacraments) preach the same message. This point deserves further elaboration.

There are many views of the exact relationship between water baptism and union with Christ as it relates specifically to Romans 6:3–4.[43] Nevertheless, Paul's understanding of the relationship between the two can be succinctly stated. Recall what Paul has written in the earlier portions of Romans—water baptism does not effect union with Christ. That Paul uses the preposition διὰ is no reason to think he has an *ex opere operato* view of baptism: συνετάφημεν οὖν αὐτῷ διὰ τοῦ βαπτίσματος εἰς τὸν θάνατον (Therefore we were buried with Him through baptism into death) (Rom. 6:4a). Paul has previously shown that circumcision was a sign and seal of the righteousness Abraham received by faith apart from works (Romans 3–4). As was argued in Part II, circumcision pointed to the same truth as baptism—the death of Christ and the cutting away or burial of the body of sin. Yet Abraham clearly was united to Christ by faith, not through his circumcision. His circumcision signified and sealed what the Spirit had accomplished through faith (Rom. 2:28–29). It would be a colossal contradiction to say that baptism is the instrumental cause of a person's union

---

40. Dunn, *Baptism*, 142–43; cf. similarly Murray, *Christian Baptism*, 28–29.

41. James D. G. Dunn, *Romans 1–8*, WBC (Dallas: Word, 1988), 311–12.

42. Moo, *Romans*, 359; also Thomas Schreiner, *Romans*, BECNT (Grand Rapids: Baker, 1998), 306–07.

43. For different views and relevant literature, see Moo, *Romans*, 359–67.

with Christ. Faith alone is the instrumental cause of union with Christ, and this faith is Spirit-wrought and sovereignly given (Eph. 2:8–9).

This means that while water baptism preaches union with Christ, the moment of its administration is not immediately tied to the realities that it signifies and seals. For the previously unbaptized adult convert, water baptism preaches union with Christ after his Spirit baptism. The Spirit baptism may have happened days, weeks, months, or even years before his water baptism. In similar fashion, infants receive water baptism before their Spirit baptism, though there are arguably exceptions to this rule (e.g., Luke 1:41). However, a person's water baptism continues to preach throughout his life, so that when he receives his Spirit baptism, the visible preaching of water baptism becomes a means of grace to him (WCF 28.6). This dynamic is no different than when adult converts to the faith of Israel received circumcision as a sign and seal of the covenant and the righteousness that they had by faith, but also administered that same sign and seal to male infants who had yet to make a profession of faith.

This particular point will be addressed at greater length in the subsequent chapter, but suffice it to say that both adult converts and infants born within the covenant are baptized into union with Christ. Keep in mind, once again, that both adult and infant are baptized into *visible* union with Christ (cf. John 15:1–10; WCF 28.1). For anyone (adult or infant) who later apostatizes, baptism becomes a means of judgment, not grace.

The sanction-element of baptism is especially evident in that, by the work of the Holy Spirit, the believer is united to Christ in His death and resurrection. This is not to say that he is mystically transported to Golgotha and then to the empty tomb. Rather, as Paul spells out (Rom. 5:12–21), Christ is the covenantal head, and His actions are representative for those who are united to Him. The believer therefore shares in the benefits of Christ's redemption through the baptism of the Spirit. Union with Christ is signified and sealed in baptism.[44]

This means that a person's baptism is tied to the theology of the cross—it is not connected to what Bonhoeffer called "cheap grace." Being baptized into the death of Christ means that a believer receives the forgiveness of sins. As is clear from the context of Romans 6:3–4, this means that through baptism the believer has died to sin with Christ. As Bonhoeffer famously

---

44. Herman Ridderbos, *Paul: An Outline of His Theology* (1975; Grand Rapids: Eerdmans, 1997), 408.

has written: "Cheap grace means grace as bargain-basement goods, cut-rate forgiveness, cut-rate comfort, cut-rate sacrament; grace as the church's inexhaustible pantry, from which it is doled out by careless hands without hesitation of limit. It is grace without a price, without costs."[45] By contrast, costly grace is the gospel that must be sought continually because it calls the church to discipleship in the way of the cross. Costly grace bids the world to follow Christ, condemns sin, and justifies the sinner. Above all else, grace is costly because it was expensive for God—it cost the life of His only begotten Son. The church was bought with a price, and nothing that is costly to God should be regarded as cheap by a believer. In the words of Bonhoeffer: "Thus, it is grace as living word, word of God, which God speaks as God pleases. It comes to us as a gracious call to follow Jesus; it comes as a forgiving word to the fearful spirit and the broken heart. Grace is costly, because it forces people under the yoke of following Jesus Christ; it is grace when Jesus says, 'My yoke is easy, and my burden is light.'"[46] If grace is an infused substance that cleanses man of sin and then enables him to overcome his estrangement with God, it is cheap. If a person falls into grievous sin, he can rely on penance to erase the stain. But if God's grace is Christ working through the Holy Spirit and is sacramentally received in baptism, uniting the recipient to Christ's death, a person knows that he has been bought with a price and that to engage in grievous sin would be at odds with his identity, his union with Christ. He has been baptized into the death of Christ.

Some have called infant baptism "cheap grace."[47] While infant baptism will be covered in detail in the following chapter, it too should be coordinated with the theology of the cross. In some ecclesiastical contexts, infant baptism has become an empty ritual. Forsyth laments how, in his own day, many in the church regarded baptism not as a sacrament, not as the visible Word preaching union with the crucified Christ, but as a "mere act of interesting dedication." He decries the notion that in the baptism of an infant, the parents or the child are the primary focus instead of the "Word of life and cleansing enacted by the Lord through His Church." Forsyth writes,

---

45. Dietrich Bonhoeffer, *Discipleship*, in *Dietrich Bonhoeffer Works*, vol. 4, ed. Geoffrey B. Kelly and John D. Godsey, trans. Barbara Green and Reinhard Kraus (Minneapolis: Fortress, 2003), 43.

46. Bonhoeffer, *Discipleship*, 45.

47. So Donald G. Bloesch, *The Church: Sacraments, Worship, Ministry, Mission* (Downers Grove, Ill.: InterVarsity, 2002), 159.

"This is only one of several current indications how the cult of the child in the Church may destroy the worship of the Gospel; how natural religion drives out spiritual, and especially evangelical."[48] In this respect, there are not two baptisms—one for adults and another for infants, one that unites the recipient to the death of Christ and the way of the cross, and another that brings him or her merely into the forgiveness of sins or cleansing. For adults and infants alike, baptism is inseparable from the death of Christ, for both adult and infant baptism signify and seal union with Christ.

The theology of the cross, not the theology of glory, must mark the doctrine of baptism as it relates to union with Christ. To say that in baptism a person receives an infusion of a created grace is to look beyond the cross—such is the theology of glory. As Martin Luther wrote in his famous Heidelberg Disputation, "That person deserves to be called a theologian, however, who comprehends the visible and manifest things of God through suffering and the cross." Gerhard Forde (1927–2005), reflecting on this thesis, writes:

> God refuses to be seen in any other way, both for our protection and to put down the theologian of glory in us. Theologians of the cross are therefore those whose eyes have been turned away from the quest for glory by the cross, who have eyes only for what is visible, what is actually there to be seen of God, the suffering and despised crucified Jesus. It was the pagan Pilate who said it: *Ecce Homo!* Behold the man! Faulty eyesight is to be corrected by the cross.[49]

In this vein, according to Paul, baptism visibly preaches to the recipient: "What shall we say then? Shall we continue in sin that grace may abound? Certainly not! How shall we who died to sin live any longer in it? Or do you not know that as many of us as were baptized into Christ Jesus were baptized into His death" (Rom. 6:1–3)? Baptism preaches the crucifixion of our old man, our old existence in Adam (Rom. 6:6). This means that the baptized adult and infant alike are committed to the way of the cross, the way of discipleship—they are both visibly inseparable from Christ.

While the historic Reformed faith has always affirmed the necessity that there be at least one parent who professes faith in order for an infant to be baptized, just because a person professes his faith in Christ does not

---

48 Forsyth, *Church and Sacraments*, 171–72.

49. Gerhard O. Forde, *On Being a Theologian of the Cross: Reflections on Luther's Heidelberg Disputation, 1518* (Grand Rapids: Eerdmans, 1997), 77–79.

automatically mean that his child should be baptized. Baptism is wrong, not when it is applied to children, but when it is separated from the other means of grace—from the nurture of the church and especially from the preaching of the gospel. Infant baptism is wrong when it is divorced from union with Christ—the way of the cross. Baptism should not be administered where there is no prospect of Christian nurture. Baptism and the gospel must go hand in hand, and must continue to be conjoined throughout the life of the one who is baptized, infant, child, or adult.[50] If there is no commitment from the parent(s) to raise the child in the way of the cross, in the fear and admonition of the Lord, then the church practices idolatry and turns the baptism of the child into a mere dedication or saccharine ceremony.[51] However, the same may be said of an adult baptism. Bonhoeffer explains, "There is always a threat that infant baptism will detach baptism from faith, just as there is always a threat that adult baptism will destroy the grace of baptism which is grounded solely in Christ's word."[52]

When the church administers baptism, it must continually keep the theology of the cross and the recipient's sacramental relation to Christ in His death at the fore. This means that for all baptismal recipients, the church must be willing, in love, to exercise church discipline, even upon children who are baptized and live in a way contrary to the way of the cross of Christ. Bonhoeffer argues, "The Christian community of today requires an authentic evangelical baptismal discipline rather than the abolition of infant baptism."[53] Bonhoeffer's point is not new; recall from Part I that William Ames coordinated baptism with church discipline.[54]

---

50. Forsyth, *Church and Sacraments*, 223.

51. Such was one of the elements behind the so-called "half-way covenant," whereby Solomon Stoddard (1643–1729), grandfather of Jonathan Edwards (1703–58), allowed the infants of unbelievers to be baptized if they so desired. On the half-way covenant, see John H. Gerstner, *The Rational Biblical Theology of Jonathan Edwards* (Orlando, Fla.: Ligonier Ministries, 1993), 3.434–35, 440, 451, 454–56, 462; Perry Miller, "The Half-Way Covenant," *The New England Quarterly* 6/4 (1933): 676–715.

52. Dietrich Bonhoeffer, "On the Question of Baptism," in *True Patriotism: Letters, Lectures and Notes 1935–45*, in *The Collected Works of Dietrich Bonhoeffer*, vol. 3, ed., Edwin H. Robertson, trans. Edwin H. Robertson and John Bowden (London: Harper and Row, 1973), 159.

53. Bonhoeffer, "On the Question of Baptism," 163; cf. Glenn L. Borreson, "Bonhoeffer on Baptism: Discipline for the Sake of the Gospel," *Word & World* 1/1 (1981): 20–31.

54. William Ames, *The Marrow of Theology*, trans. John Dykstra Eusden (1968; Grand Rapids: Baker, 1997), locus 37.

Shamefully, this baptism-discipleship connection has not always been embraced in the Reformed tradition. Lewis Schenck (1898–1985) documents that when the Northern and Southern Presbyterian churches were seeking to unite, the union hinged on their agreed revision of the Presbyterian Book of Discipline. In the South, James H. Thornwell (1812–1862) believed that children should not be subject to judicial discipline because they were not full members of the church. Thornwell was opposed by Charles Hodge (1797–1878) in the North, as well as by Robert L. Dabney (1820–1898) in the South. Hodge and Dabney argued that baptized children were members of the church and therefore subject to discipline.[55]

---

55. See Lewis Bevens Schenck, *The Presbyterian Doctrine of Children in the Covenant: An Historical Study of the Significance of Infant Baptism in the Presbyterian Church* (1940; Phillipsburg, N.J.: P & R, 2003), xiii, 81–103. The proposed change to the Book of Discipline is recorded by Robert Lewis Dabney: "The Revised Discipline proposes to change the propositions which here assert that all baptized persons 'are members of the church,' are 'subject to its government and discipline,' and when adult 'bound to perform all the duties of church members,' in the following respects. For the first proposition it substitutes the words: 'are under its government and training.' At the end of the paragraph it proposes to add the following: 'Only those, however, who have made profession of faith in Christ are proper subjects of judicial prosecution'" (R. L. Dabney, "The Changes Proposed in our Book of Discipline" *The Southern Presbyterian Review* 12/1 [1859]: 44). What is surprising about the arguments brought forward by James Henley Thornwell is that he all but adopts a Baptist understanding of the doctrine of the church: "The idea of the Church, according to the reformed conception, is the complete realization of the decree of election. It is the whole body of the elect considered as united to Christ their head" (J. H. Thornwell, "A Few More Words on the Revised Book of Discipline," *The Southern Presbyterian Review* 13/1 [1861]: 15). Thornwell goes so far as to write: "The visible Church is, accordingly, the society or congregation of those who profess the true religion" (Thornwell, "A Few More Words," 16). However, this statement contradicts the Westminster Confession: "The visible church…consists of all those throughout the world that profess the true religion; and of their children" (WCF 25.2). Thornwell's error is in his equating the decree of election with the visible church and failing to coordinate the doctrine of the covenant with election as well as the signs and seals of the covenant, in this case baptism. One must recall that the fundamental error of the Baptist position is in failing to recognize that the administration of the covenant is broader than election. This point did not go by unnoticed, as both Charles Hodge and Dabney pointed out that Thornwell's position was Baptist (see Charles Hodge, "The General Assembly of 1859," *The Biblical Repertory and Princeton Review* 31/3 [1859]: 598–99; Dabney, "The Changes Proposed," 49–50). Though the revisions were eventually passed, later denominations that came from what was eventually the Presbyterian Church in the United States (PCUS), the Orthodox Presbyterian Church (OPC) and the Presbyterian Church in America (PCA), returned to the classic Reformed position. The OPC *Book of Church Order* states: "All members of the church, both communicants and those who are members by virtue of baptism only, are under the care of the church, and subject to ecclesiastical discipline including administrative and judicial discipline" (*The Book of Church Order of the Orthodox Presbyterian Church* [Willow Grove, Pa.: The Committee on Christian Education of the OPC, 2005], 87). Likewise, the PCA *Book*

Either infants are baptized into the death of Christ or they are not. If they are, then they are baptized into the way of the cross, and hence are subject as members of the body of Christ to church discipline. In a word, Thornwell was a Baptist in Presbyterian clothing.

There is, however, another side of baptism as it relates to the recipient's union with Christ. Baptism is connected not only with the theology of the cross but with eschatology. Paul states that one who has been baptized has been united to Christ in His death, but also has been united to Him in His resurrection (Rom. 6:4). Just as the old man is crucified, so our new man is raised to walk in the newness of life through the last Adam's outpouring of the eschatological Spirit: "But now we have been delivered from the law, having died to what we were held by, so that we should serve in the newness of the Spirit and not in the oldness of the letter" (Rom. 7:6; cf. 1 Cor. 15:45).[56] The believer's death, burial, and resurrection with Christ transfers him from the old age to the new, from the age of the fallen kingdom of Adam to the age of the kingdom of the last Adam. The transition from the old age to the new, however, while applied to people at their conversion, was accomplished through the crucifixion and resurrection of Christ in the first century. Paul refers to a redemptive-historical union that has as its locus both the cross and resurrection of Christ—where the eschatological intrusion of the new creation took place historically. A conversion occurs when this intrusion of the eschaton becomes applicable to an individual. More briefly and technically stated, the *ordo salutis* must always be grounded in the *historia salutis*.[57]

The intrusion of the eschaton through the resurrection of Christ is also visibly preached in baptism. The minister is the herald of the gospel, the clarion of the eschaton, the one who proclaims the outpouring of the eschatological Spirit in both audible and visible Word. The creation emerged from the waters that covered the earth through the Word of God and the superintendence of the רוח אלהים (the Spirit of God) (Gen. 1:1–10). The

---

of Church Order states, "All baptized persons, being members of the Church are subject to its discipline and entitled to the benefits thereof" (*The Book of Church Order of the Presbyterian Church of America*, Sixth Edition [Lawerenceville, GA: The Office of the Stated Clerk of the Presbyterian Church of America, 2009], 27–2; see also Morton H. Smith, *Commentary on the Book of Church Order of the PCA* [Taylors, S.C.: Southern Presbyterian Press, 2000], 278).

56. See Geerhardus Vos, "The Eschatological Aspect of the Pauline Conception of the Spirit," in *Redemptive History and Biblical Interpretation: The Shorter Writings of Geerhardus Vos*, ed. Richard B. Gaffin, Jr. (Phillipsburg, N.J.: P & R, 1980), 91–125.

57. Moo, *Romans*, 365; cf. Dunn, *Romans*, 313; Schreiner, *Romans*, 311.

creation emerged from beneath the Noahic deluges as a רוח blew over the earth and a dove flew looking for dry land (Gen. 8:1–11). Israel, God's son, emerged from its Red Sea baptism as a רוח blew the waters back and Israel emerged on dry land (Ex. 14:21). These Old Testament typical patterns of creation through water and Spirit all point to the antitypical new creation. Jesus, God's only begotten Son, emerged from the waters and the אלהים רוח descended upon Him (Mark 1:1–11; Matt. 3:1–17; Luke 3:21–22).

So, too, those who believe in Jesus have the message of the gospel of the new creation signified and sealed in baptism—they are those who are born of water and Spirit (John 3:5). This means that in recognizing the connection between baptism and union with Christ, especially as it relates to the resurrection and the newness of life, baptism is as much a visible portrait of the work of Christ as it is of the Holy Spirit, the power of the age to come (Heb. 6:4–5). Weber explains that while baptism is certainly christocentric, "Its reality and its effects are pneumatic. In the Spirit, he is the Present One, and in the pneumatic-charismatic work his past is present and his present in turn is opened toward his coming. Pneumatic reality is the reality of the age of salvation; it is the presence of the One who is Coming and the Coming of the One who is present all at once."[58]

The church, therefore, wields the Spirit-empowered "new-creating Word" not only in its preaching but also in the sacraments.[59] This means that in the administration of baptism, the church cannot play the role of spectator. Every baptism is a renewed baptism for every person in the church as they witness the visible Word of the eschatological gospel in the water and hear it in the preaching of the Word.[60] The church, not merely the individual who is baptized, receives the grace of God through the audible and visible preaching of the gospel in Word and sacrament. In this way, not only do believers individually benefit from their union with Christ, but all believers in the church recognize that they are in union with one another.[61] As the Westminster Confession states:

> All saints, that are united to Jesus Christ their Head, by his Spirit, and by faith, have fellowship with him in his grace, sufferings, death, resurrection, and glory: and, being united to one another in love, they have communion in each other's gifts and graces, and are obliged to

---

58. Weber, *Dogmatics*, 2.601.
59. Forsyth, *Church and Sacraments*, 132.
60. Forsyth, *Church and Sacraments*, 181–82.
61. Bavinck, *Reformed Dogmatics*, 4.521.

the performance of such duties, public and private, as do conduce to their mutual good, both in the inward and outward man (26.1).

Baptism, therefore, for both infant and adult, binds the church together as the visible body of Christ. When one is baptized, all are baptized.[62]

MODE

Lines of division are often drawn along denominational boundaries when it comes to the mode of baptism. Baptists largely practice immersion, whereas Presbyterians, Dutch Reformed, Methodists, Episcopalians, and Roman Catholics baptize by pouring or sprinkling. Historically, the matter has usually been considered one of *adiaphora*. As surveyed in Part I, the *Didache*, Thomas Aquinas, Luther, Calvin, Francis Turretin, Wollebius, Witsius, and the Westminster Confession (28.3), to name a few, held that there was a great degree of flexibility concerning the mode.[63] Immersion-only views developed among later Anabaptist theologians, but Particular Baptists apparently were the first to incorporate the exclusivity of immersion in a confessional document—the First London Confession (1644); immersion was also identified as the only legitimate mode in the subsequent Second London Confession (1689). The insistence on immersion-only baptism was an unprecedented move in the history of the doctrine.[64] In contrast to the Westminster Confession, the Baptist Confession states: "Immersion, or dipping of the person in water, is necessary to the due administration of this ordinance" (29.4).[65] On the other hand, some presently insist on the

---

62. So James Ussher, *A Body of Divinity: Being the Sum and Substance of the Christian Religion*, ed. Michael Navarr (Birmingham: Solid Ground Christian Books, 2007), 377.

63. See, e.g., Thomas Aquinas, *Summa Theologiae* (Allen: Christian Classics, 1948), IIIaq. 66, art 7; Martin Luther, LW 35.29; cf. Jonathan Trigg, *Baptism in the Theology of Martin Luther* (Leiden: Brill, 2001), 93, n. 142; Calvin, *Institutes*, 4.15.19; Francis Turretin, *Institutes of Elenctic Theology*, ed. James T. Dennsion, trans. George Musgrave Giger (Phillipsburg, N.J.: P & R, 1992–97), 19.11.11; Johannes Wollebius, *Compendium Theologiae Christianae*, in *Reformed Dogmatics*, ed. and trans. John W. Beardslee, III (New York: Oxford University Press, 1965), 23.1–9; Herman Witsius, *Economy of the Covenants Between God and Man: Comprehending A Complete Body of Divinity*, trans. William Crookshank (1822; Phillipsburg, N.J.: P & R, 1990), 4.16.30.

64. Hans Denck's *Confession Before the Nuremberg Council* (1525), Balthasar Hubmaier's *A Christian Catechism* (1526), and The Schleitheim Confession (1527) mention nothing regarding the mode of baptism (see *Creeds and Confessions of Faith in the Christian Tradition*, eds. Jaroslav Pelikan and Valerie Hotchkiss [New Haven: Yale University Press, 2003], 663–703). For the First London Confession (1644), see idem, *Creeds and Confessions*, 59.

65. *The Baptist Confession of Faith of 1689* (Carlisle: Grace Baptist Church, n.d.);

exclusivity of pouring or sprinkling. Robert Reymond insists: "The fact is that there is not a single recorded instance of a baptism in the entire New Testament where immersion followed by emersion is the mode of baptism. The Baptist practice of baptism by immersion is simply based upon faulty exegesis of Scripture."[66]

So the question stands, what mode or modes are acceptable? The answer cannot hinge on the opinions of theologians alone, but must rest on the exegesis of Scripture.

Some, primarily from the Baptist tradition, try to base their case for the exclusive validity of baptism by immersion largely on two points: (1) the meaning of the term βαπτίζω, and (2) the grammar involved in New Testament accounts of baptism: ὅτε δὲ ἀνέβησαν ἐκ τοῦ ὕδατος (Now when they came up out of the water) (Acts 8:39).

Erickson argues that the dominant meaning of the term βαπτίζω is "to dip or to plunge under water."[67] Others argue that the Greek text specifies that Jesus came ἐκ (out of) the water, not that He came away from it, which would be expressed by the Greek preposition ἀπό.[68]

There are two problems with this line of argumentation. First, Erickson defines βαπτίζω by appeal to a lexicon. Methodologically, terms should not be defined merely by lexical material isolated from a biblical context. For example, John told the crowds that he baptized with water but that Jesus would baptize with the Holy Spirit and fire (Matt 3:11; Luke 3:16). Later, when the ascended Christ baptized the church at Pentecost with the Holy Spirit, baptism was not connected with immersion but with pouring: "Therefore being exalted to the right hand of God, and having received from the Father the promise of the Holy Spirit, He [Jesus] poured out this which you now see and hear" (Acts 2:33). Peter's explanation alludes to Joel 2:28 and the promised outpouring or baptism of the Spirit.[69] Βαπτίζω cannot be defined merely by appealing to a lexicon, but must be defined by

---

Timothy George, "Baptists and the Westminster Confession," in *The Westminster Confession into the 21st Century*, vol. 1, ed. J. Ligon Duncan (Fearn: Mentor, 2003), 152; Fred A. Malone, *The Baptism of Disciples Alone: A Covenantal Argument for Credobaptism Versus Paedobaptism* (Cape Coral, Fla.: Founders Press, 2007), xix.

66. Robert Reymond, *A New Systematic Theology of the Christian Faith*, Second Edition (Nashville: Thomas Nelson, 1998), 935, emphasis removed.

67. Erickson, *Christian Theology*, 1104.

68. Wayne Grudem, *Systematic Theology* (Grand Rapids: Zondervan, 1994), 967.

69. Beale and Carson, *Commentary*, 542.

its contextual use in the New Testament and against the backdrop of its use in the Old Testament.

Second, it is not grammatically possible to hinge the mode of baptism on the use of the preposition ἐκ. Certainly ἐκ can denote emersion out of the water following immersion into it. But notice how Luke uses the preposition ἐκ in the baptism of the Ethiopian eunuch: ὅτε δὲ ἀνέβησαν ἐκ τοῦ ὕδατος (Now when they came up out of the water) (Acts 8:39). Baptist theologians focus on the preposition and ignore the verb. The use of the third person plural verb ἀναβαίνω unmistakably shows that *both* Philip and the eunuch came up out of the water. If ἐκ means that the eunuch was immersed, as Grudem has argued, then the same must be said of Philip. Does this mean immersion-only advocates believe that both the one who is baptized and the one who performs the baptism must be immersed? The answer is obviously no. Grudem tries to argue that both Philip and the eunuch descended into the water so that only the eunuch would be immersed. Why else would they both go into the water? But can one split prepositional hairs so finely, concluding that ἐκ means the eunuch was immersed and Philip merely stood in the water? Whether Jesus or the eunuch was immersed cannot be determined from the scriptural narratives. It is certainly a possibility that the eunuch was immersed. However, this approach tries to squeeze too much out of a preposition rather than look-ing at the broader scope of redemptive history. A lone preposition should not decide the mode of baptism when the Scriptures have so much to say on the topic. It seems that all too many miss the forest for the trees when it comes to the mode of baptism.

In the canon of Scripture, all three modes of baptism appear: immer-sion, pouring, and sprinkling.[70] For example, Peter calls the flood a type of baptism (1 Peter 3:21). Noah and his family were saved through this baptism, but the unbelieving world was immersed in the baptism-judg-ment of God. Similarly, Paul calls the Red Sea crossing a baptism (1 Cor. 10:1–2): Israel was saved through that baptism, but the Egyptian army was immersed in the baptism-judgment. To this, one could also add Jonah's immersion in the waters of the sea—a miry grave (Jonah 1:7–16).[71] Scrip-ture unfolds a rich biblical-theological tapestry that provides the backdrop to understand why Christ called His crucifixion a baptism (Luke 12:50).

---

70. Cf. Malone, *Baptism of Disciples Alone*, 209, 219.
71. See Grudem, *Systematic Theology*, 968, n. 7.

He was immersed in the flood of His Father's wrath. With this information, it is evident why Paul writes that believers are buried with Christ in
His death (Rom. 6:3). The connection between burial and baptism does
not seem to be so much an analogy between death and burial in the earth
(something first-century Jews did not practice, as they buried their dead
above ground in caves; cf. Genesis 23; e.g., Mark 15:46), but rather between
death and being immersed in the waters of judgment.

In fact, scholars argue that Psalm 69:1–2 is one of the passages that
stand behind Jesus' application of baptism to His crucifixion: "Save me,
O God! For the waters have come up to my neck. I sink in deep mire,
where there is no standing; I have come into deep waters, where the floods
overflow me" (cf. Pss. 18:4, 16; 42:7; Isa. 8:7–8; 30:27–28; Jonah 2:3–6).[72]
Based on this broader redemptive-historical picture, baptism by immersion
surely portrays in an eloquent way the great wrath of God. By comparison, a few moistened fingertips, effecting that which is generously called a
"sprinkling," must appear to many Baptists to fall short of the crisis of being
buried with Christ in death.[73] Baptism by immersion is therefore certainly
biblically appropriate, but this does not mean that baptism should be exclusively administered in this mode.

As observed in Part II, there is a close connection between water, Spirit,
and new creation. Baptism is as much connected with the work of Christ as
it is the work of the Spirit. The baptism of the Spirit is promised through
pouring in the Old Testament: "For I will pour water on him who is thirsty,
and floods on the dry ground; I will pour My Spirit on your descendants, and
My blessing on your offspring" (Isa. 44:3). Likewise, the prophet Ezekiel says:
"'And I will not hide My face from them anymore; for I shall have poured
out My Spirit on the house of Israel,' says the Lord GOD" (39:29). There are
similar references scattered in the Old Testament (Prov. 1:23; Joel 2:28–29;
Zech. 12:10). At Pentecost, Christ poured out the Spirit on the church (Acts
2:33). Therefore, the mode of pouring is certainly biblically warranted.[74]

---

72. Beale and Carson, *Commentary*, 332.

73. Kline, *By Oath Consigned*, 83.

74. See I. Howard Marshall, "The Meaning of the Verb 'To Baptize,'" *EQ* 45/3 (1973):
130–40; idem, "The Meaning of the Verb 'To Baptize,'" in *Dimensions of Baptism: Biblical
and Theological Studies*, JSNT, Sup 234, eds. Stanley Porter and Anthony R. Cross (Sheffield:
Sheffield Academic Press, 2003): 8–24; see also the older work of James W. Dale, *Judaic
Baptism*. ΒΑΠΤΙΖΩ: *An Inquiry Into the Meaning of the Word as Determined by the Usage of
Jewish and Patristic Writers* (1869; Phillipsburg, N.J.: P & R, 1991); idem, *Johannic Baptism*.
ΒΑΠΤΙΖΩ: *An Inquiry Into the Meaning of the Word as Determined by the Usage of the*

The mode of sprinkling, however, also commends itself and finds varied testimony in the Old Testament. The cleansing rituals of the Old Testament, such as the consecration rites of the Levitical priests, involved the sprinkling of water (Num. 8:5–22, esp. v. 7). David's cry to the Lord that He cleanse him, that the Lord purge him with hyssop and wash him that he might be whiter than snow (Ps. 51:7), is based on the Old Testament cleansing ritual. When a person came into contact with a dead body, he was to be taken outside the camp, and one who was clean was to dip a hyssop branch in water in which had been mixed the ashes of a heifer, a sacrificial animal of atonement, and sprinkle the water on the dwelling, furnishings, and person of the one who was unclean (Num. 19:18–20). This imagery informs the well-known passage from Ezekiel: "Then I will sprinkle clean water on you, and you shall be clean; I will cleanse you from all your filthiness and from all your idols" (Ezek. 36:25; cf. Ex. 24:8; Lev. 8:30; Heb. 9:19–21; 11:28; 12:24). Within the context of this verse, the prophet also speaks of the giving of the Spirit (Ezek. 36:27), the agent of purification and sanctification. In other words, sprinkling is equally valid alongside immersion and pouring.

How can all three modes adequately capture the intended signification of baptism? How can sprinkling, which focuses on forgiveness, convey the idea of new birth or new creation? How can pouring, which focuses on the Spirit and new creation, capture adequately the imagery connected with judgment, such as with the flood or Red Sea crossing? The signification is provided not so much by the mode of baptism as by the necessary accompanying preaching of the Word. The gospel proclaims Christ crucified, the forgiveness of sins, and the blessings of the Spirit and the new creation. As Jürgen Moltmann explains:

> Before the coming rule of God the one eschatological messenger of joy appears, proclaiming the royal rule of God and the final liberation of his people. As he announces the rule of God and the liberation of man, and with them the eschatological era, his joyful message puts this era into effect and is, like the word of creation at the beginning, the word that creates the era of salvation. The new era begins for the world of the nations as well. The rule of Yahweh is proclaimed and the wonders of his liberation are praised among the Gentiles. The vision

---

Holy Scriptures (1898; Phillipsburg, N.J.: P & R, 1993); idem, *Christic Baptism and Patristic Baptism. ΒΑΠΤΙΖΩ: An Inquiry Into the Meaning of the Word as Determined by the Usage of the Holy Scriptures and Patristic Writings* (1874; Phillipsburg, N.J.: P & R, 1995).

of the pilgrimage of the nations to Zion (Isa 60:6) and the glorifying of Yahweh by the Gentiles shows the universality of hope in the "one who brings good tidings" in the last days.[75]

The proclamation of Isaiah's good news and the coming of the new creation through the Spirit is brought about through the Suffering Servant (Isa. 53). His sacrifice liberates God's people from their bondage and sets them free from their sin. Hence, the weight of the significance of baptism hinges not on the mode but on the preaching of the Word. Recall that the Word can exist apart from the sacrament, but the sacrament cannot exist apart from the Word.[76] No matter the mode of baptism, the preaching of the gospel must accompany the administration of the rite, as well as an explanation of what baptism means. Hence, the conclusion of the *Leiden Synopsis* (1625) seems prudent and biblically warranted: "Whether baptism must be in a single or threefold dipping has always been considered indifferent in the Christian Church. Similarly whether immersion or aspersion is to be used, since no express command of the former is extant and examples of sprinkling as well as of dipping may be gathered in the Scriptures."[77]

SUMMARY AND CONCLUSION

This chapter has surveyed the institution, formula, symbolism, and mode of baptism. Christ instituted baptism in His Great Commission as the sign and seal of the covenant of grace. It is to be administered in the name of the triune Lord, as it is the Father who sends the Mediator, His only begotten Son, to redeem a people for Himself, and to sanctify them and apply the work of redemption through the outpouring of the Holy Spirit. To be baptized into the name of Christ, then, signifies union with Him and to His body, and the shared benefits of His redemption. The Westminster Confession succinctly states these conclusions:

---

75. Moltmann, *The Church*, 216.

76. So Moltmann, *The Church*, 200; also, e.g., Bavinck, *Reformed Dogmatics*, 4.479; Calvin, *Institutes*, 4.14.4.

77. *Leiden Synopsis* 44.19, as cited in Heinrich Heppe, *Reformed Dogmatics: Set Out and Illustrated from the Sources*, ed. Ernst Bizer, trans. G. T. Thomson (London: George Allen & Unwin Ltd, 1950), 614. Cf. G. W. Bromiley, "Baptism in the Reformed Confessions and Cathechisms," in *Baptism, the New Testament, and the Church*, eds. Stanley Porter and Anthony R. Cross (Sheffield: Sheffield Academic Press, 1999): 408.

Baptism is a sacrament of the new testament, ordained by Jesus Christ, not only for the solemn admission of the party baptized into the visible church; but also, to be unto him a sign and seal of the covenant of grace, of his engrafting into Christ, of regeneration, of remission of sins, and of his giving up unto God, through Jesus Christ, to walk in newness of life. Which sacrament is, by Christ's own appointment, to be continued in his church until the end of the world (28.1).

Immersion, pouring, and sprinkling all find precedent in the tapestry of redemptive history. But this chapter has assumed a point that is likely accepted by some but rejected by others, namely, the inclusion of infants as proper recipients of baptism. It is to the subject of the proper recipients of baptism, and especially that of the propriety of infant baptism, that the next chapter will turn.

CHAPTER 14

Baptism and Its Recipients

All denominations practice believer's baptism—the baptism of adults who make a profession of faith. Debate focuses on the practice of baptizing infants or small children who have not made a profession of faith.

The Roman Catholic Church supports the practice of infant baptism from both Scripture and church tradition: "The practice of infant Baptism is an immemorial tradition of the Church. There is explicit testimony to this practice from the second century on, and it is quite possible that, from the beginning of the apostolic preaching, when whole 'households' received baptism, infants may also have been baptized."[1] For those denominations that rightly place a premium on *sola Scriptura* as the source for theology, the Roman Catholic appeal to church tradition is unacceptable.

However, those who appeal to Scripture alone in their arguments *against* infant baptism often build their case solely from the New Testament.[2] In response to Karl Barth's rejection of infant baptism, Pierre-Charles Marcel (1918–2006) notes that Barth cited only one text from the Old Testament, and so states: "On this particular question, on the sacraments, or every other question which has anything to do with baptism, the Old Testament counts for nothing, it does not even exist!"[3] Perhaps the exclusive appeal to the New Testament, at least in the American context, is due to the influence of dispensationalism, which sees the Old Testament as largely irrelevant for the New Testament church, since the church is a different entity from Old

---

1. *Catechism of the Catholic Church* (Liguori, Mo.: Liguori Publications, 1994), § 1252, 319.

2. So Kurt Aland, *Did the Early Church Baptize Infants?* (1961; Eugene, Ore.: Wipf & Stock, 2004), 112–13; Stanley Grenz, *Theology for the Community of God* (Nashville: Broadman & Holman, 1994), 686; Millard J. Erickson, *Christian Theology* (Grand Rapids: Baker, 1985), 1103–1104.

3. Pierre-Charles Marcel, *The Biblical Doctrine of Infant Baptism: Sacrament of the Covenant of Grace* (1953; London: James Clarke & Co., 2002), 16.

Testament Israel.[4] Whatever reasons lie behind the exclusion of the Old Testament, such a methodology is inherently myopic, cutting off half of the Bible. It is essential to build doctrine on the canon of Scripture, a necessity that has been pressed with the recent flowering of the formal discipline of biblical theology. Individual texts must be placed within the context of the scope of redemptive history.[5] Part II of this study demonstrated that baptism is present in the Old Testament and, by contrast, circumcision is present in the New Testament. The apostles Peter and Paul place baptism at the Noahic flood (1 Peter 3:21) and the Red Sea crossing (1 Cor. 10:1–4). Likewise, Paul calls Christ's crucifixion a circumcision (Col. 2:11). Redemptive history accounts for and informs the investigator of the meaning of the rite. Baptism does not emerge *de novo* in the New Testament with John's appropriation or adaptation of a Qumran or contemporary Jewish ritual, but in the opening chapter of the Bible.

Biblical theology is therefore a necessary tool for unpacking the meaning of baptism, not only generally, but especially as it relates to the question of infant baptism. Baptism must be explained in a canonical fashion, not by appealing only to the New Testament, but to the whole of Scripture. At the same time, it is necessary to account for the context in which revelation about baptism comes to the church. As Geerhardus Vos has emphasized, "God has not revealed himself in a school, but in a covenant; and the covenant as a communion of life is all-comprehensive, embracing the conditions and interests of those contracting it."[6] It is especially important to recognize the connection between baptism and covenant, as well as the antecedents of baptism in the covenant history.[7]

---

4. See Charles Ryrie, *Dispensationalism Today* (1965; Chicago: Moody Press, 1970), 48–64, 132–55.

5. In terms of classic Reformed theology, the canonical approach is what the Westminster divines called a "good and necessary consequence," which relies on the *analogia Scripturae* (WCF 1.6, 9). See also Herman Bavinck, *Reformed Dogmatics*, ed. John Bolt, trans. John Vriend (Grand Rapids: Baker, 2003–2008), 4.526. Baptists, even some Particular Baptists, have expressed unease over this hermeneutical principle (see *The Baptist Confession of Faith of 1689*, 1.6; also Shawn D. Wright, "Baptism and the Logic of Reformed Paedobaptists," in *Believer's Baptism: Sign of the New Covenant in Christ*, eds. Thomas R. Schreiner and Shawn D. Wright [Nashville: Broadman & Holman, 2006], 254–55).

6. Geerhardus Vos, "The Idea of Biblical Theology as a Science and as a Theological Discipline," in *Redemptive History and Biblical Interpretation: The Shorter Writings of Geerhardus Vos*, ed. Richard B. Gaffin, Jr. (Phillipsburg, N.J.: P & R, 1980), 10.

7. G. C. Berkouwer, *The Sacraments* (Grand Rapids: Eerdmans, 1969), 164.

For these reasons, this chapter will first survey the propriety of infant baptism by an exploration of circumcision in the Old Testament. Circumcision is not merely a physical, national, ceremonial rite; rather, like baptism, it has a spiritual aspect and is a sign of the gospel. Second, the chapter will explore the corporate nature of all baptisms in both the Old and New Testaments. Third, the chapter will explore the relationship between the church and the already/not yet dynamic as it pertains to the question of baptism. This is essential because those who argue against infant baptism attempt to prove that the church, unlike Old Testament Israel, is not supposed to be a mixed community but rather a regenerate one. Therefore, only those who profess their faith are supposed to be baptized. Fourth, this chapter will address the subject of the administrative ground of baptism. The ground is not, as many believe, a profession of faith, but rather God's covenant promise. Fifth, and lastly, the chapter will show why infant baptism does not lead to the unbiblical practice of paedocommunion.

CIRCUMCISION AS A SIGN OF THE GOSPEL

In a book written on a semi-popular level for ministers, Baptist pastor-theologian John Piper cordially argues against the practice of infant baptism. He succinctly states one of the common misconceptions about circumcision in the Old Testament and its difference with baptism in the New Testament:

> The new thing, since Jesus has come, is that the covenant people of God are no longer a political, ethnic nation, but a body of believers. John the Baptist inaugurated this change and introduced the new sign of baptism. By calling all *Jews* to repent and be baptized, John declared powerfully and offensively that physical descent does not make one part of God's family and that circumcision, which signifies a physical relationship, will now be replaced by baptism, which signifies a spiritual relationship.[8]

The common assumption is that circumcision was tied to the Israelite theocracy and was administered to the physical descendants of Abraham, but with the dissolution of the theocracy, a new spiritual order was inaugurated. Hence, baptism is now to be administered only to those who are born

8. John Piper, *Brothers, We Are Not Professionals: A Plea to Pastors for Radical Ministry* (Nashville: Broadman & Holman, 2002), 134.

of the Spirit. This misreading, however, fails to see two important points: (1) circumcision signifies a spiritual relationship; and (2) circumcision signifies a physical relationship, but not in the manner that Piper explains.

Part II proved that circumcision and baptism are related in that they both point to the person and work of Christ.[9] Circumcision as the sign of the covenant looked forward to the Seed who was to come, who was to be cut off from the land of the living, and who was to suffer the curse of the covenant on behalf of God's people. Hence, males were circumcised because they collectively pointed to the male Seed who would redeem God's people. In this sense, circumcision certainly signified a physical relationship, but not the one Piper posits. He sets forth a physical relationship between a father and his male son who is born within the theocracy and therefore receives circumcision to identify him as a citizen of Israel. This import is certainly present, as circumcision separated Israelite from Gentile. However, and perhaps more significant, the physical relationship denoted was also between the men of Israel and the Messiah.[10] Collectively, the males of Israel, God's son (Ex. 4:22), pointed to Jesus, God's only begotten Son.

In his antitypical baptism with the descent of the Spirit in avian form, as well as in His Spirit-led forty days of wilderness temptation, Jesus recapitulated Israel's Red Sea baptism and wandering in the wilderness for forty years. But where Old Testament Israel failed, Jesus succeeded. Hans LaRondelle explains, "In the light of a more detailed study of the linguis-

---

9. Bavinck, *Reformed Dogmatics*, 4.499. Some disagree with the connection between circumcision and baptism as argued by paedobaptists. For example, Kurt Aland writes: "Where pagans were involved it may be feasible to follow Jeremias and say that baptism is the 'ritual which replaced circumcision.' But what about the Jew, who has already been circumcised and then becomes baptized? This example alone, to say nothing of the women, is enough to show that in Col. 2:11 Paul did not have in mind the setting aside of circumcision by baptism" (Aland, *Did the Early Church Baptize Infants?* 84). Aland's point is that it would seemingly be redundant for Jews to receive two signs of the same covenant, unless, of course, baptism was of an entirely different order and therefore necessary. But Aland fails to see the signs of circumcision and baptism in the scope of redemptive history. The Jews received both signs, not as a redundancy, but as the progressive unfolding of the mystery of the gospel in the visible revelation in the covenant signs. They received circumcision to point to the Seed of the woman who was to come and be cut off, and they received baptism as the sign that the Messiah had poured out the Holy Spirit on the church. Those few who lived during the transition from the Old Testament to the New Testament, who lived through the dawning of the eschaton, received both signs. Those who live in the inaugurated eschaton, since Christ has already come, receive only the sign of the new covenant, baptism (see Berkouwer, *Sacraments*, 165, 168; Bavinck, *Reformed Dogmatics*, 4.527).

10. Contra Timothy George, "The Reformed Doctrine of Believer's Baptism," *Interp* 47 (1993): 250.

tic and theological context of Deuteronomy 8, which several scholars have undertaken, it becomes clear that Jesus saw Himself in typological terms as the new Israel."[11] Simply stated, Jesus embodies the Israel of God. This certainly shows that circumcision was not merely physical in nature, but pointed to the person and work of Christ. Circumcision was therefore not primarily a sign of family, racial, or national identity. Any such connection was secondary. The primary and essential significance of circumcision was that it was the sign and seal of the highest and richest spiritual blessings God would bestow on His people in the Messiah.[12]

Circumcision was also connected to the work of the Spirit; this is evident in the ratification of the Mosaic covenant. Moses exhorted the people, "Therefore circumcise the foreskin of your heart, and be stiff-necked no longer" (Deut. 10:16). Israel as the descendants of Abraham was supposed to be circumcised, but the outward mark alone was insufficient; the inward reality of the circumcised heart was ultimately necessary. Meredith Kline explains, "Genuine devotion can flow only from a heart that has experienced the reality of that qualification which was symbolized in the initiatory sign of the covenant."[13] Yet can man circumcise his own heart? Who is the agent of the circumcision of the heart but the Spirit of God? The circumcision of the heart points to a person's effectual calling, which is evident in Paul's explanation of the rite: "But he is a Jew who is one inwardly; and circumcision is that of the heart, in the Spirit, not in the letter" (Rom. 2:29). Paul's explanation of circumcision is not a reorientation or redefinition of the rite, but is merely the logical extension of the Old Testament law and the prophets.[14]

The Israelites' inability to circumcise their hearts is evident from the broader context of Deuteronomy. Moses eventually tells the people: "And the LORD your God will circumcise your heart and the heart of your descendants, to love the LORD your God with all your heart and with all your soul, that you may live" (Deut. 30:6). The imperatives of Deuteronomy 6:4 and 10:16

---

11. Hans K. LaRondelle, *The Israel of God in Prophecy: Principles of Interpretation* (Berrien Springs, Mich.: Andrews University Press, 1983), 64–65.

12. John Murray, *Christian Baptism* (Phillipsburg, N.J.: P & R, 1980), 45; see also Charles Hodge, *Systematic Theology* (rep.; Grand Rapids: Eerdmans, 1993), 3.554; contra Stephen J. Wellum, "Baptism and the Relationship Between the Covenants," in Schreiner and Wright, *Believer's Baptism*, 155–57.

13. Meredith G. Kline, *Treaty of the Great King: The Covenant Structure of Deuteronomy* (Grand Rapids: Eerdmans, 1963), 77.

14. Patrick D. Miller, *Deuteronomy* (Louisville: John Knox, 1990), 126.

become promises, which are brought about by Christ and the Spirit through the new covenant (cf. Jer. 31:31–34; 32:36–41; Ezek. 11:19–20; 36:22–38).[15]

More will be said about the relationship between the Mosaic covenant, the new covenant, and the New Testament church. Suffice it to say for now that there are certainly differences between the old and new covenants, but one cannot say that the Holy Spirit was not operative in the old covenant. The only agent of effectual calling that the Bible knows is the Holy Spirit.[16] Therefore, circumcision pointed to the work of the Holy Spirit. Is there a salvific reality that involves the work of Christ and the Spirit other than the gospel? Quite simply, no.

This connection between circumcision and the gospel is perhaps one of the lesser-appreciated but nonetheless crucial points in the whole question of the propriety of infant baptism. It seems that there is a common belief that circumcision was connected with the Mosaic covenant, as this covenant was constitutive of Israel's existence as a nation. Circumcision marked off Jews from Gentiles; therefore, circumcision was a national and ethnic boundary marker, according to some.[17] Circumcision undoubtedly was connected with the Torah (that is, the Pentateuch), but even the New Testament qualifies this: "Moses therefore gave you circumcision (not that it is from Moses, but from the fathers)" (John 7:22). Jesus qualifies His statement by saying that though it is part of the Torah and therefore from Moses, circumcision actually came from the patriarchs (cf. Ex. 12:44; Lev. 12:3; Gen. 17:10–14). Circumcision therefore was connected first and foremost with the Abrahamic covenant. Circumcision was older than the Mosaic covenant; it was older than the theocracy.

Of what significance is this? Simply put, the apostle Paul identifies the Abrahamic covenant as the gospel: "And the Scripture, foreseeing that God would justify the Gentiles by faith, preached the gospel to Abraham beforehand, saying, 'In you all the nations shall be blessed'" (Gal. 3:8). God

---

15. Kline, *Treaty*, 132–33.

16. In reading some Baptist works, one is left with the impression that if the argument were followed to its logical conclusion, the conclusion would be that there were no believers in the Old Testament. Fred Malone writes, "By standard hermeneutics of typology, the type of circumcision (entrance into the Abrahamic covenant) is fulfilled in its antitype, regeneration (entrance into the effectual New Covenant)" (Fred A. Malone, *The Baptism of Disciples Alone: A Covenantal Argument for Credobaptism Versus Paedobaptism* [Cape Coral, Fla.: Founders Press, 2007], 116). Malone's argument implies that few if any were regenerated in the Old Testament because regeneration is only typified in the Old Testament, not present.

17. So, e.g., James D. G. Dunn, *Jesus, Paul, and the Law: Studies in Mark and Galatians* (Louisville: Westminster John Knox, 1990), 183–241.

later gave to Abraham the "covenant of circumcision" (Acts 7:8), which Paul calls the sign and seal of the righteousness that Abraham had by faith (Rom. 4:11). When Stephen calls the Abrahamic covenant a διαθήκην περιτομῆς (covenant of circumcision), he means that circumcision characterizes the gospel promise given to Abraham.[18] Stephen does not identify two different covenants of circumcision. In the divine administration of circumcision, God clearly states that it is a sign of the covenant (Gen. 17:1). Given what Paul says concerning the Abrahamic covenant, this means that circumcision is a sign and seal of the gospel. This is not to say that circumcision revealed the gospel as clearly as does baptism, as baptism is given in the wake of the revelation of Christ. Nevertheless, the same realities were connected to circumcision as to baptism.

Some try to argue that circumcision was significantly different because it did not symbolize union with Christ, as does baptism.[19] If the gospel is progressively revealed with greater clarity, however, then it is sound to say that circumcision symbolized union with Christ. To be baptized into the name of the triune Lord signifies being baptized into a relationship with Him, specifically, into visible union with Christ. Circumcision signified the same thing, though with less clarity. It was the sign of the covenant between God, Abraham, and his offspring (Gen. 17:11). God was the God of Abraham and his offspring (cf. Gen. 17:7; Ex. 19:5–6; Deut. 7:6; 14:2; Jer. 31:33). John Murray explains: "In a word it is union and communion with Jehovah, the God of Israel. It was this blessing circumcision signified and sealed."[20] That Israel was in union with Yahweh is evident from other portions of the Old Testament that characterize Israel's relationship with God as a marriage (e.g., cf. Deut. 24:1–4; Jer. 3:1–9). This relationship was not unmediated, as it was ultimately grounded in the mediatorial work of Christ (Heb. 9:15), which was typified in the priesthood as well as the sacrificial system.

Baptism is connected with the forgiveness of sins, and the same was true of circumcision. This is evident in the circumcision of the heart, which pointed to the effectual call of the Holy Spirit and the forgiveness and cleansing that the Spirit brings. Recall, however, that Paul identifies circumcision as the sign and seal of the righteousness that Abraham had by faith (Rom. 4:11), clearly echoing Genesis 17:11. Some argue that Abra-

---

18. Darrell L. Bock, *Acts*, BECNT (Grand Rapids: Baker, 2007), 285.
19. Wellum, "Relationship Between the Covenants," 158.
20. Murray, *Christian Baptism*, 47.

ham's circumcision was a sign and seal of the righteousness of faith for Abraham alone. For instance, Thomas Schreiner states, "The text does not teach that circumcision in general is a seal."[21] However, Schreiner's point cannot be sustained in the face of the following two points.

First, why does Paul call Abraham's circumcision a sign and seal of righteousness? Is he merely interested in addressing questions related to Abraham's salvation alone? Paul certainly addresses questions surrounding salvation as he addresses the relationship between Abraham's justification (Gen. 15:6) and the administration of circumcision (Gen. 17:1–14). But to say that Paul is concerned with this question alone is to abstract Abraham's redemption from the context of the covenant God made with Abraham. Circumcision was not a sign and seal for Abraham alone; it was not a private rite but was the sign of the covenant. Paul says that Abraham was "the father of circumcision to those who not only *are* of the circumcision, but who also walk in the steps of the faith" that Abraham possessed (Rom. 4:12). Who are the circumcised but adult and infant males? Moreover, the righteousness that Abraham received was not privately his alone—he received it by faith alone in the covenant promise, which ultimately came through Christ. Given the covenantal context, circumcision was a sign and seal of justification by faith alone for any Old Testament saint who trusted in the promise, not Abraham alone.[22]

Second, Paul's whole point in expounding the relationship between circumcision and justification is not only to explain the nature of redemption but to show that Abraham was the model New Testament believer. In this sense, what was written about Abraham and his justification by faith alone was written for others, the covenant community of the New Testament (Rom. 4:23–24). Otto Weber explains: "Romans 4:11 shows that for Paul the circumcision of an Israelite received its power and significance from the 'promise' (Rom. 4:13), out of which the circumcision of Abraham became for him the 'sign' and 'seal' of the righteousness of faith. Abraham was not a believer just for himself, but he is the 'father of us all' (Rom. 4:16)."[23]

---

21. Thomas R. Schreiner, "Baptism in the Epistles: An Initiation Rite for Believers," in Schreiner and Wright, *Believer's Baptism*, 86–87; also Malone, *Baptism of Disciples Alone*, 112.

22. Murray, *Christian Baptism*, 47–48; Meredith G. Kline, *By Oath Consigned: A Reinterpretation of the Covenant Signs of Circumcision and Baptism* (Grand Rapids: Eerdmans, 1968), 47; Geerhardus Vos, *Biblical Theology: Old and New Testaments* (1948; Edinburgh: Banner of Truth, 1996), 90.

23. Otto Weber, *Foundations of Dogmatics* (Grand Rapids: Eerdmans, 1983), 2.612.

All of the following elements bear on the question of infant baptism, for circumcision pointed to the work of Christ and the Spirit, and signified the blessings of the covenant: circumcision of the heart, forgiveness of sins, justification by faith alone, and union with God through the covenant Mediator. That circumcision meant all of these things and was applied to Abraham as an adult convert makes sense. However, circumcision was administered not only to adult converts such as Abraham but also to male infants. Male infants received the sign of the covenant, the sign of justification by faith alone, before they were capable of making a profession of faith. Abraham received believers' circumcision and his male offspring received infant circumcision. Or, as Geoffrey Bromiley states, "[The] first baptisms in the New Testament are parallel to the first circumcision or circumcisions in the Old Testament."[24] This means that to administer the sign of the covenant to those who have not made a profession of faith is not foreign to the Scriptures.

There are still details that need to be explored, as critics are likely to point out that not only Abraham's male offspring but also his servants received the sign of circumcision (Gen. 17:12). This points in the possible direction that adult males were given the sign apart from a profession of faith. Critics of infant baptism therefore argue that this is evidence that baptism cannot be applied to anyone apart from a profession of faith. Critics contend that the organizing principle of the Old Testament was ethnic identity and not faith in the messianic covenant promise. By contrast, the organizing principle of the New Testament church is faith in Christ. They say that the circumcision of slaves is evidence of this ethnic principle and therefore counter-evidence against the practice of infant baptism. This requires examination of the second subject of this chapter, namely, the corporate nature of baptism.

THE CORPORATE NATURE OF BAPTISM

The covenant signs of circumcision and baptism contain a corporate dimension. To acknowledge this corporate factor runs against the grain of today's individualism, but it certainly reflects threads found in the Scriptures. Individuals are saved by faith in Jesus, but they are saved as members of the

---

24. Geoffrey W. Bromiley, *Children of Promise: The Case for Baptizing Infants* (Eugene, Ore.: Wipf & Stock, 1998), 21.

covenant community, the church. This is true for the church in both the Old and New Testaments. However, there are elements of the Abrahamic covenant and circumcision that raise questions for the New Testament church. Particularly, how does the household formula found in the Old Testament relate to the household formula found in the New Testament? Abraham was instructed to circumcise his household, which included his slaves. Yet such a practice is seemingly out of accord with the practice of baptism, since baptism is administered to individuals who make a profession of faith and, as argued thus far, to their children. How is this apparent discrepancy reconciled? The answer comes in acknowledging both the corporate nature of baptism as well as the progression of the *historia salutis*.

The first thing to note is that, in one sense, there is not a single individual baptism recorded in the Scriptures.[25] Rather, all baptisms in the Scriptures are corporate in nature. True enough, individuals are baptized, but always as part of a larger corporate baptism. This pattern is evident in the Noahic flood-baptism. Noah and his household, his entire family, were corporately saved through the flood-baptism (Gen. 7:1; Heb. 11:7).[26] This is an important principle, namely, the whole *household* was saved. God dealt with family units, not isolated individuals. This familial principle surfaces in a number of places in the Old Testament, including the families of Abraham (Gen. 17:12–13), Jacob (Gen. 34:30), and Esau (Gen. 36:6). One of the key points associated with the use of this term is that, as the head of the household goes, so goes the family. This was true of Joshua, who declared that both he and his house would serve the Lord (Josh. 24:15), but also extended even to Rahab in the preservation of her father's household from the destruction of Jericho (Josh. 6:25).

But just because God dealt with households, even in the Old Testament, did not automatically guarantee a person's salvation. This is certainly evident with Esau, who was a circumcised member of Isaac's household, but was nevertheless excluded from the blessings of the covenant (Rom. 9:13; Heb. 12:16). The household principle could also function in the opposite direction and bring suffering and covenant sanction on a family, as is evident in the judgment against Korah and his household (Num. 16:32) or the similar fate of Achan and his household, including his sons and

---

25. Contra Malone, who argues that there is "a new individualistic element in the New Covenant administration that was not as patent in the Old Testament covenants of promise (Ephesians 2:12)" (*Baptism of Disciples Alone*, 72).

26. Bromiley, *Children of Promise*, 16.

daughters (Josh. 7:22–26). While God can and does deal with individuals, He more often deals with familial units in a representative fashion, which echoes the corporate nature of redemption. G. C. Berkouwer notes how the Reformers understood this point: "The Reformers saw, in the Old as well as in the New Covenant, that God did not isolate man from the contexts of his earthly life, but went out toward him in the line of families. Therein was realized the mystery of the salvation of the Lord from generation to generation."[27]

The corporate pattern continued in the exodus. Israel was corporately saved in the Red Sea baptism as a nation, having been founded on the Passover-deliverance of households, which included men, women, and children. Israelite infants were baptized in the Red Sea and into the Holy Spirit, revealed in the cloud (Ex. 12:3–4).[28]

This same corporate pattern appears, at least nominally, in the New Testament. A number of households were saved and baptized: the household of Lydia at Philippi (Acts 16:15); that of the Philippian jailer (Acts 16:33); that of Crispus (Acts 18:8); the household of Stephanas (1 Cor. 1:16); and that of Onesiphorus (2 Tim. 1:16, 4:19). While there is disagreement as to how to interpret the use of the term *household* in the New Testament, this much is certain—the baptism of individuals is part of Christ's once-for-all

---

27. Berkouwer, *Sacraments*, 172; similarly Herman Bavinck, *Saved by Grace: The Holy Spirit's Work in Calling and Regeneration*, trans. Nelson D. Kloosterman, ed. J. Mark Beach (Grand Rapids: Reformation Heritage Books, 2008), 76.

28. Joachim Jeremias, *The Origins of Infant Baptism: A Further Study in Reply to Kurt Aland* (1962; Eugene, Ore.: Wipf & Stock, 2004), 32; William N. Wilder, *Echoes of the Exodus Narrative in the Context and Background of Galatians 5:18* (New York: Peter Lang, 2001), 100; Oscar Cullman, *Baptism in the New Testament* (Philadelphia: Westminster Press, 1950), 45. Contra G. R. Beasley-Murray, who argues that Paul's point in 1 Corinthians 10:1–4 is only to use Old Testament stories to make an ethical point (G. R. Beasley-Murray, *Baptism in the New Testament* [1962; Carlisle: Paternoster, 1997], 181–85). As James Scott notes, "It is no accident that in Gal. 3:26–27 those who are 'sons of God' (υἱοὶ Θεοῦ) by faith in Christ Jesus have been 'baptized into Christ' (εἰς Χριστὸν ἐβαπτίσθητε), and that, as Gal. 4:4–5 goes on to say, the Son was sent to redeem them that they might receive the adoption as sons of God. For the role of the Son in redemption and baptism of the sons is similar to that of Moses!" Scott then goes on to cite Cyril of Alexandria (ca. 378–ca. 444): "Therefore, the people who should attain to adoption (υἱοθεσίαν) by faith in Christ, were prefigured in it [sc. The people of Israel] as in shadow.., (and) all things about us were in them typologically (*typikōs*). Thus we say that Israel was typologically (τυπικος) called to adoption (υἱοθεσίαν) through the mediator Moses (cf. Gal. 4:1–2; Rom. 9:4). Therefore, they 'were baptized into' him too, as Paul says, 'in the cloud and in the sea' (1 Cor. 10:2)" (James M. Scott, *Adoption as Sons of God: An Exegetical Investigation into the Background of HUIOTHESIA in the New Testament* [Tübingen: Mohr Siebeck, 1992], 166).

baptism of the church at Pentecost by the Holy Spirit, a corporate baptism (cf. Matt. 3:11; Acts 2:33).

Baptists argue that when a household was baptized in the New Testament, only those capable of making a profession of faith were present.[29] On the other hand, paedobaptists argue that given the use of the term *household* in the Old Testament, children were not necessarily present, but certainly could have been.[30] The New Testament's unqualified use of the household principle lends greater credence to the paedobaptist position, namely, given its use in the Old Testament, a household allows for the presence of children or infants. Noah's household, for example, included his adult sons. Abraham's household, on the other hand, included infants. In fact, the Old Testament makes specific mention of infants and children as members of households (Gen. 18:19; 36:6; 46:27; cf. vv. 5–7; 47:12; 1 Sam. 22:15–19; Jer. 38:17–23). By contrast, the Old Testament specifies when children or infants are excluded (Gen. 50:8; 1 Sam. 1:21–22).[31] To argue that every single mention of the household formula in the New Testament excludes infants goes against the grain of Scripture.[32] However, the key point is not the speculative question of whether infants and children were absent or present, but rather that in the New Testament the household principle is still operative. The principle is operative without qualification, and the fact that the Old Testament does at times exclude children from the household formula, but no such exclusion appears in New Testament occurrences, points in the direction of continuity, not discontinuity as Baptists maintain.

Further evidence of this conclusion comes from Paul's epistles. Paul writes that an elder must manage his household well, "having his children in submission with all reverence" (1 Tim. 3:4). Paul cannot have in mind adults—rather, he writes of those under the authority of their parents, ostensibly young children. The broader context of Paul's letter to Ephesus reveals the apostle addressing the household of God through what Martin Luther called a *Haustafel*, or rules for the household.[33] Paul addresses husbands, wives, children, slaves, and masters (Eph. 5:22–6:9), continuing the pattern found in the Old Testament.

---

29. See Aland, *Did the Early Church Baptize Infants?* 87–94.

30. See Beasley-Murray, *Baptism*, 312–20.

31. Jeremias, *Origins of Infant Baptism*, 20–22.

32. Jeremias, *Origins of Infant Baptism*, 17, 21.

33. Peter T. O'Brien, *The Letter to the Ephesians*, PNTC (Grand Rapids: Eerdmans, 1999), 405.

Against the redemptive-historical background of the whole of Scripture, the household baptisms of the New Testament make sense. If there were children, even nursing infants, or slaves present, they too would have been baptized. The children would have been baptized because they were to be included as children of the covenant, as in the Old Testament. The slaves would have been baptized providing they too would have made professions of faith. More will be said about the baptism of slaves below.

The household principle lies behind Paul's counsel in 1 Corinthians 7:12–16. Paul can say that both the unbelieving spouse and the children, because of the one believing spouse, are holy. In what way are they holy? *Holy* ($\H{\alpha}\gamma\iota o\varsigma$) is a cultic term.[34] This is evident as Paul contrasts *holy* with the term *unclean* ($\mathring{\alpha}\kappa\mathring{\alpha}\theta\alpha\rho\tau o\varsigma$).[35] In the canonical use of these terms, Gentile nations were unclean and Israel was holy (cf. Ex. 19:6; Lev. 18:24; Acts 10:28). Anyone or anything unclean was not allowed within the camp, the covenant community (e.g., Lev. 13:46). The Israelite cult and covenant community were essentially the same. In other words, to be holy was to be in the covenant, but to be unclean was to be outside the covenant. The holy and unclean categories cannot be divorced from the concept of covenant. To do so is to abstract them from redemptive history, thus loosing their historical anchor. The words become mere adjectives to describe independent individuals rather than terms that describe individuals within the covenant (or households) and indeed the church as the covenant community vis-à-vis the unbelieving world.[36] Soteric holiness is therefore covenantal. However, in the Old Testament, Israel was holy and the Gentile nations were unclean. In the New Testament, it is the church (both Jew and Gentile) that is holy and the unbelieving world that is unclean.

The question then arises, in what way are the unbelieving spouse and children covenantally holy? The main thrust of Paul's argument is to show that the unbelieving, and hence "Gentile," spouse (cf. 1 Peter 2:12) does not profane the marriage. Rather, the believing spouse brings the sanctity of the covenant into the marriage.[37] The marriage is considered a "Christian marriage" even if only one spouse is a believer (cf. Rom. 11:16).[38] In

---

34. See BDAG, 10–11.

35. See BDAG, 34; cf. Vos, *Biblical Theology*, 173.

36. So Anthony C. Thiselton, *The First Epistle to the Corinthians*, NIGTC (Grand Rapids: Eerdmans, 2000), 530

37. Colin Brown, "Holy," in NIDNTT, 2.230.

38. Bavinck, *Reformed Dogmatics*, 4.529; Gordon D. Fee, *The First Epistle to the Corinthians*, NICNT (Grand Rapids: Eerdmans, 1987), 299–302. One should note that

the language of the Old Testament, the unbelieving spouse is like the for-
eigner or sojourner in the land (e.g. Ex. 22:21). But whereas the sojourner
would come to dwell in the land in the midst of the covenant community,
God brings the covenant community to the unbelieving spouse through
the believing spouse. In the same way in which the temple sanctified the
gold connected with it (Matt. 23:17, 19), the believing spouse sanctifies the
unbelieving spouse.[39]

This sanctity, however, is not connected to the individual but to the covenant, which encompasses more than the individual. The believing spouse
casts the light of the new covenant, the gospel of Christ, on the unbelieving
spouse through his or her conduct and, in some cases, is God's instrument
by which the unbelieving spouse is saved (1 Cor. 7:16). But while the unbelieving spouse might be sanctified, this does not automatically entitle the
person to the sign of the covenant, because as an adult, he or she must make
a profession of faith, as would be the case for slaves within a household.
This is evident in that Paul instructs the believing spouse to remain married
to the unbelieving spouse if he or she is willing to do so (1 Cor. 7:12–13).
Peter gives similar instructions to Christian wives whose husbands do not
obey the Word of God (1 Peter 3:1–2). Baptism cannot be coerced on one
who refuses to believe.

The children of the believing spouse are treated differently.[40] They are
covenantally holy and therefore receive the sign of the covenant, circumcision in the Old Testament and baptism in the New Testament.[41] Children

---

Paul's argument here is parallel with the Jewish understanding of the children of proselytes,
who were considered full covenant members of Israel subject even to covenant sanctions.
We read in Ketubot 4.3: "The convert whose daughter converted with her, and she [the
daughter] committed an act of fornication [when she was a betrothed girl]—lo, this one
is put to death through strangling.... If her conception was not in a state of sanctity but
her parturition was in a state of sanctity, lo, this one is put to death with stoning.... If her
conception and parturition were in a state of sanctity, lo, she is equivalent to an Israelite girl
for every purpose." Likewise, we read in Yebamot 11.2: "The convert whose sons converted
with her—they [the sons] neither perform the rite of *halisah* [consanguinity] nor enter into
levirate marriage, even if the conception of the first was not in a state of sanctity and the birth
was in a state of sanctity, and the second was conceived and born in a state of sanctity. And
so is the law in the case of a slave girl whose sons converted with her" (*The Mishnah: A New
Translation*, ed. and trans. Jacob Neusner [New Haven: Yale University Press, 1988]).

39. Charles Hodge, *1 & 2 Corinthians* (1857; Edinburgh: Banner of Truth, 1994), 116.

40. See T. F. Torrance, et al., *The Biblical Doctrine of Baptism: A Study Document Issued by
the Special Commission on Baptism in the Church of Scotland* (1958; Edinburgh: The St. Andrew
Press, 1960), 53.

41. Contra Aland, *Did the Early Church Baptize Infants?* 81.

have not yet rejected the covenant, and Christian parents have the responsibility to raise them "in the training and admonition of the Lord" (Eph. 6:4). What else can this mean but to raise them in the covenant, the place where the covenant Lord exercises His authority and where His people serve Him?[42] Paul clearly teaches that children are not treated like an unbelieving spouse. If children are not to receive baptism, as Baptists maintain, then why are they not treated the same as the unbelieving spouse? How can they be raised in the covenantal discipline and revelation of the Lord? There is no isolated, individualistic avenue to God, only that of covenant. But keep in mind the all-important point—the administration of the covenant is broader than election; the visible covenant community is not synonymous with the elect of God.

THE CHURCH AND THE ALREADY/NOT YET

Baptists object to this interpretation of the household formula because they argue that with the inauguration of the new covenant, God no longer deals with family units as He did in the Old Testament, but now deals with individuals—only those who make a profession of faith. This objection requires an explanation of the relationship between the New Testament church and the already/not yet dynamic.

Many theologians recognize that the church exists in the overlap of the ages, the overlap between the present evil age and the inaugurated age to come. This means that until the consummation, the church will always be a mixed body. The divine institution of church discipline (Matthew 18; 1 Corinthians 5) is evidence that some will fall under discipline for their disobedience but be restored, while others will fall away never to return, showing they were never part of the invisible church. How does baptism relate to this dynamic? It must not be forgotten that divine revelation has a double edge—it can bring blessing or sanction. The same must be said of God's visible revelation in the sacraments. Baptism undoubtedly is administered to both adults and infants for whom it is a means of grace, but it also is administered to those for whom it is a means of judgment. Unbelievers

---

42. Interestingly enough, Karl Barth acknowledges that children are to be raised in the discipline and instruction of the Lord (ἐν παιδείᾳ καὶ νουθεσίᾳ κυρίου), but then demurs from extending to them baptism (Karl Barth, *Church Dogmatics* [Edinburgh: T & T Clark, 1936–1969], IV.4.185. Hereafter cited as CD).

drowned in the Noahic flood-baptism and the Red Sea crossing-baptism.[43] The double-edged nature of baptism must be kept in mind as this section continues to consider New Testament household baptisms.

The baptism of entire households in the early church is beyond dispute. The Philippian jailer asked what he had to do to be saved, to which Paul responded: "Believe on the Lord Jesus Christ, and you will be saved, you and your household" (Acts 16:31). The Lukan narrative then states that his whole household believed and "he and all his family were baptized" (Acts 16:33–34). Other portions of the New Testament, however, indicate that there were also situations in which only portions of households were saved. Paul, for example, addresses the question of what a believer should do if he or she is married to an unbeliever (1 Cor. 7:12–16). There is no indication that the unbelieving spouse should be baptized. Likewise, in Paul's correspondence to Philemon, the head of a house church and brother in Christ (vv. 1–2), there is no indication that his slave Onesimus was baptized prior to his conversion in prison. In this respect, there is a degree of discontinuity between the Old Testament practice of household circumcision and household baptisms. Where does the line of discontinuity lie?

Baptist theologians argue that the line of discontinuity lies along the profession of faith—only those who profess their faith in Christ can be baptized, which would therefore exclude unbelieving spouses, unbelieving slaves, and children incapable of making a profession of faith. They argue that this practice reflects the promises of the new covenant that all of God's people will know Him (Jer. 31:31–34; Heb. 8:6–13); hence, the church is not a mixed community of believer and unbeliever, as it was in the Old Testament. Paedobaptist theologians, on the other hand, argue that unbelieving spouses and slaves would not be baptized, but that children are the legitimate recipients of baptism. Which position best accounts for all of the biblical data?

The paedobaptist position is the best response for the following reasons. To be sure, Baptist theologians are correct that the church is the new covenant community and that the new covenant has been fulfilled with the first advent of Christ. However, in terms of the already/not yet dynamic, the new covenant promises of Jeremiah have been inaugurated but not consummated.[44] The author of Hebrews clearly indicates that Christ has

---

43. See Kline, *By Oath Consigned*, 57.

44. See Richard L. Pratt, "Infant Baptism in the New Covenant," in *The Case for Covenantal Infant Baptism*, ed. Gregg Strawbridge (Phillipsburg, N.J.: P & R, 2003), 156–200.

inaugurated the new covenant. This is evident when he writes: ὅθεν οὐδ ἡ πρώτη χωρὶς αἵματος ἐγκεκαίνισται (Therefore not even the first covenant was dedicated without blood) (Heb. 9:18), indicating that the new covenant has been inaugurated by Christ, not that it has been completely fulfilled (cf. Heb. 2:6–8; 4:3, 9).[45] The writer uses the procedures of the Day of Atonement (Leviticus 16) to illustrate this point. On the Day of Atonement, the high priest would enter the Holy of Holies and the nation would collectively hold its breath, waiting for him to emerge. The priest's safe return from the Holy of Holies signaled that the sacrifice had been accepted and that atonement had been made for Israel's sins of that year. The author uses this pattern to show that Christ has yet to emerge from the heavenly Holy of Holies: "So Christ was offered once to bear the sins of many. To those who eagerly wait for Him He will appear a second time, apart from sin, for salvation" (Heb. 9:28).[46] Here, then, is the already/not yet dynamic regarding Christ's mediatorial work as the High Priest of the new covenant.

The already/not yet dynamic is also present in the original prophecy from Jeremiah. The prophet states: "I will put My law in their minds, and write it on their hearts; and I will be their God, and they shall be My people" (Jer. 31:33). This most certainly happens when the Lord, through the work of Christ and by the agency of the Holy Spirit, circumcises the heart. God writes His law upon the heart of the one who is baptized in the Spirit by Christ. However, this does not mean that everyone who makes a verbal profession of faith has been baptized in the Holy Spirit. The Scriptures clearly speak of false teachers, even those who promote a false gospel (Gal. 1:8–9). Moreover, some elements in the prophecy have not yet been fulfilled, even in the wake of the first advent of Christ: "No more shall every man teach his neighbor, and every man his brother, saying, 'Know the LORD,' for they all shall know Me, from the least of them to the greatest of them, says the LORD. For I will forgive their iniquity, and their sin I will remember no more" (Jer. 31:34). As long as the church evangelizes, those within the church must teach their neighbors and brothers.

Kline explains the already/not yet dynamic as it pertains to the new covenant when he writes: "It is in accordance with this still only semi-eschatological state of affairs that the administration of the new Covenant is

---

45. William L. Lane, *Hebrews 9–13*, WBC (Dallas: Word, 1991), 244.
46. See Lane, *Hebrews 9–13*, 249–51.

presently characterized by dual sanctions, having, in particular, anathemas to pronounce and excommunications to execute."[47] At the consummation, no longer will each one teach his neighbor or brother, as the church triumphant (*ecclesia triumphans*) will know the Lord. The fact that the church is now awaiting the consummation does not in any way mean that the covenant of grace can be broken—Jeremiah clearly says that the new covenant is eternal. However, there is an important distinction to raise, namely, the visible and invisible church. Those who fall away in permanent apostasy were never part of the invisible church—neither were they elect nor part of the covenant of grace. If the church is a completely regenerate body, as some Particular Baptists maintain, then why does the author of Hebrews warn against apostasy? Apostates are the plants without root that wither away. To be in the covenant of grace is to be united to Christ. Recall Justin Martyr's statement: Christ is the new covenant.[48] Those who are elect and joined to Christ will persevere to the end, to the consummation, and will never fall away.[49]

Some still reject such conclusions because they say this approach fails to see the newness of the new covenant, as the prophecy clearly states: "Behold, the days are coming, says the LORD, when I will make a *new* covenant with the house of Israel and with the house of Judah—not according to the covenant that I made with their fathers in the day that I took them by the hand to lead them out of the land of Egypt, My covenant which they broke, though I was a husband to them, says the LORD" (Jer. 31:31–32, emphasis added). Some argue that the old covenant was a mixed community, whereas the new

---

47. Kline, *By Oath Consigned*, 76–77; cf. Neville Clark, "Initiation and Eschatology," in *Baptism, the New Testament, and the Church. Historical and Contemporary Studies in Honor of R. E. O. White*. JSNT, Sup 171, eds. Stanley Porter and Anthony R. Cross (Sheffield: Sheffield Academic Press, 1999), 347.

48. Justin Martyr, *Dialogue with Trypho*, chap. 51, in ANF 1.221.

49. On the doctrine of the perseverance of the saints, see Louis Berkhof, *Systematic Theology: New Combined Edition* (1932–1938; Grand Rapids: Eerdmans, 1996), 109–25, 545–51; Wayne Grudem, "Perseverance of the Saints: A Case Study from Hebrews 6:4–6 and Other Warning Passages in Hebrews," in *The Grace of God and The Bondage of the Will*, eds. Thomas R. Schreiner and Bruce A. Ware [Grand Rapids: Baker, 1995], 1.133–82). It is interesting to note that according to Jeremias, the early church understood Hebrews 6:4, and particularly the term *enlightened* (φωτίζω), as a reference to baptism. Hence, one could gloss Hebrews 6:4 in the following manner: "For it is impossible to restore again to repentance those who have once been baptized, who have tasted the heavenly gift, and have shared in the Holy Spirit" (see Jeremias, *Origins of Infant Baptism*, 84; idem, *Infant Baptism in the First Four Centuries* [London: SCM Press, 1960], 30; also Rudolf Schnackenburg, *Baptism in the Thought of St. Paul* [New York: Herder and Herder, 1964], 56).

covenant is a regenerate community and therefore not mixed. Therefore, the new covenant does not include children as did the old covenant.

To make such arguments fails to take note of the finer details of this prophecy. First, the contrast is not between the new covenant and the Abrahamic covenant, but between the new and old covenant (the Mosaic covenant).[50] Verse 32 clearly states that the new covenant would not be like the covenant that God made with the fathers when He brought them out of Egypt. Jeremiah has the Mosaic covenant specifically in view, not the Abrahamic covenant.[51] Second, even within the context of the promise of the new covenant, God still holds out the promise to believers and their children: "They shall be My people, and I will be their God; then I will give them one heart and one way, that they may fear Me forever, for the good of them and their children after them. And I will make an everlasting covenant with them, that I will not turn away from doing them good; but I will put My fear in their hearts so that they will not depart from Me" (Jer. 32:38–40). The promise to include children in the covenant does not fade away with the expiration of the Mosaic covenant.

---

50. This is a point that some miss. They believe the contrast is between the new covenant (read New Testament) and the old covenant (read Old Testament) (Wellum, "Relationship Between the Covenants," 143–44). For a similar misreading of the Jeremiah text, see Samuel E. Waldron and Richard C. Barcellos, *A Reformed Baptist Manifesto: The Covenant Constitution of the Church* (Palmdale: Reformed Baptist Academic Press, 2004), 65–79; also Malone, *Baptism of Disciples Alone*, 73, 81.

51. This is something that Malone consistently misses (*Baptism of Disciples Alone*, 52–53, 70, 72). Malone does not give attention to the different nature of the Abrahamic and Mosaic covenants, but simply lumps them together. Even the administration of each covenant signals that they are different: God promises to Abraham that He will bless him and make his name great. By contrast, God conditions Israel's presence in the land on their obedience. In broad technical terms, the difference between the two covenants is one of a royal grant versus a suzerainty treaty (see Michael Horton, *God of Promise: Introducing Covenant Theology* [Grand Rapids: Baker, 2007], 33–34). Paul in Galatians especially highlights the differences between the two when he characterizes the covenants as the slave and freewoman. The Mosaic covenant is Hagar and the Abrahamic covenant is Sarah. Paul casts out the slave woman (read Mosaic covenant) and concludes: "So then, brethren, we are not children of the bondwoman but of the free [read Abrahamic covenant]" (Gal. 4:22–31). Interestingly enough, Malone does not deal at all with this key passage from Galatians in his book (*Baptism of Disciples Alone*, 317). As further evidence, when Malone quotes the promise of the new covenant, he excises a key phrase: "Behold, days are coming,' declares the Lord, 'when I will make a new covenant with the house of Israel and with the house of Judah.... [*sic*] I will put My law within them'" (*Baptism of Disciples Alone*, 73). Malone excises vv. 32–33, but it is specifically v. 32 that is key. God says that the new covenant will not be "'like the covenant that I made with their fathers on the day when I took them by the hand to bring them out of the land of Egypt, my covenant that they broke.'" Malone excises the specific reference to the Mosaic covenant.

This means that the new covenant is organically connected to the Abrahamic covenant and that the Mosaic covenant expires. The Abrahamic covenant, which Paul calls the gospel, had circumcision as its covenant sign, one administered to adults and infants. Consequently, in the wake of the outpouring of the Spirit, the sign of baptism is administered to adult converts and to their children, as they are the sons of Abraham, heirs of the Abrahamic covenant.

Regarding the baptism of the Holy Spirit, recall that Joel prophesied of a time when God would pour out His spirit on "all flesh," both young and old, male and female, and even slaves (Joel 2:28–29). In this context, Joel's use of the phrase כל בשר (all flesh) does not refer to mankind in general (cf. Gen. 9:15).[52] Rather, it refers to Israel alone, which is explained in context as Israel's sons, daughters, slaves, young, and old.[53] In the broader context of Joel, when he calls for the gathering of the people, he calls for the consecration of the קהל, the ἐκκλησία, the church. The church in Joel's day included the elders, children, and even nursing infants (Joel 2:16). Hence, the children of believers receive the sign that the Holy Spirit has been poured out collectively on the church, the community of the sons of Abraham, the beneficiaries of the new covenant work of Christ.

However, the church as the new covenant community is still enmeshed in the overlap of the ages—it is a mixed community. Not all who are baptized are automatically saved, whether adult or infant. Nevertheless, the sign of the covenant is to be administered to professing adults and their children.

THE ADMINISTRATIVE GROUND

In one sense, ultimately the whole debate over the question of infant baptism rests on the administrative ground of the rite. Baptists contend that a profession of faith is the administrative ground for baptism; only those who make a profession of faith receive the rite. They base this argument on what they see in the New Testament narratives that recount the baptisms of converts to the Christian faith. However, this argument rests on only half of the canon and fails once again to account for the doctrine of the covenant. A Zwinglian conception of the sacraments and baptism is incompatible

---

52. See William R. Domeris, אלך, in NIDOTTE, 2.657.

53. Raymond B. Dillard, *Joel*, in *The Minor Prophets*, ed. Thomas E. McComiskey (Grand Rapids: Baker, 1992), 1.295.

with the teaching of Scripture. What does baptism mean? What does God declare through baptism? God has given not only the covenant but also its accompanying signs, circumcision and baptism. He reveals Himself through Christ, but also in Word and sacrament, invisible and visible revelation. Circumcision and baptism are not a stage created by God only for man to profess his fidelity. The sacraments are the opposite—they are the revelatory stage (when accompanied by the Word) by which God heralds His covenant promises and trumpets the gospel of His Son.

Abraham was supposed to administer the sign of God's covenant promise to his male offspring (Gen. 17:10). Peter echoes this command in his sermon at Pentecost. When the angst-filled crowd asked what they could do to be saved, Peter replied: "Repent, and let every one of you be baptized in the name of Jesus Christ for the remission of sins; and you shall receive the gift of the Holy Spirit. For the promise is to you and to your children, and to all who are afar off, as many as the Lord our God will call" (Acts 2:38–39). To what promise does Peter refer? The promise is undoubtedly weighted on the whole of redemptive history: the *protoevangelium* (Gen. 3:15); God's promise to Abraham (Gen. 12:1–3; 15; 17:1–14); and his promise to David (1 Sam. 7:14). However, Peter also mentions the gift of the Holy Spirit, which invokes the fulfillment of Joel's prophecy (2:28–29) and is certainly connected to the promise of the new covenant, which included the promise to children (Jer. 31:31; 32:39; Isa. 32:15; 44:3; Ezek. 11:19; 36:26–27; 37:14).[54] Peter echoes Joel's prophecy that God would pour out His Spirit on Israel's sons and daughters, both young and old (Joel 2:28), but also His promise that He would be the God of Abraham and of his generations to come (cf. Gen. 9:9; 13:15; 17:7; Gal. 3:16, 29; Pss. 18:50; 89:34–37; 132:11–12).[55]

When Peter adds that the promise is also for those who are "far off,"[56] he employs a phrase from Isaiah 57:19: "'Peace, peace to him who is far off

---

54. Bock, *Acts*, 144–45.

55. Simon J. Kistemaker, *Acts*, NTC (Grand Rapids: Baker, 1990), 107; F. F. Bruce, *The Book of Acts*, NICNT (Grand Rapids: Eerdmans, 1988), 71; G. K. Beale and D. A. Carson, eds., *Commentary on the New Testament Use of the Old Testament* (Grand Rapids: Baker, 2007), 543.

56. Barth argues that when Peter refers to "children" and those who are "far off," the combined effect of these words is to imply that it is the descendants of those present, their children, who will make their own professions of faith in due time: "At the right time and place their children and those who are afar off will come to receive and grasp it as they have done; they will thus repent and have themselves baptized" (Barth, CD, IV.4.184). In other words, the "far off" is not geographical but temporal—it refers to future generations. Barth's

and to him who is near," says the Lord, 'and I will heal him.'" When Paul cites this same passage (Eph. 2:13–17), he has in mind the inclusion of the Gentiles into Israel, which is also Peter's likely meaning.

Peter concludes by saying, "as many as the Lord our God will call," which comes from Joel 2:32 and stresses God's gracious initiative in the proclamation of salvation and its universal scope.[57] The new covenant is more expansive than the Mosaic covenant in terms of its scope and blessing. The Mosaic covenant was made specifically with Israel. By contrast, the Abrahamic covenant had a global scope, as its blessings were for πάντα τὰ ἔθνη τῆς γῆς (all the nations of the earth), which was repeated by Christ in the Great Commission, the commission of the new covenant (cf. Gen. 22:18 LXX; Matt. 28:19).

Peter's proclamation would have made complete sense to a Jewish audience, which would have been familiar with the covenant history of Israel. Israel included infant offspring in the promise of salvation. The visible form of that promise was the administration of circumcision. Now, Peter says, especially in light of the outpouring of the Spirit on sons and daughters, infants are to continue to receive the visible form of that promise in baptism (cf. Acts 16:14–15). The inclusion of infants had been the practice of the covenant community for nearly two thousand years (cf. Deut. 29:9–13). As Charles Hodge notes, "The visible Church has always consisted of those who professed the true religion, together with their children."[58] For there to have been a change in this covenantal practice without so much as a syllable of explanation would not have gone over well with first-century Jews. There would have been an outcry. The absence of such an outcry, as well as the absence of a counter-indicative command, points in the direction that the inclusion of male infants continued as it had since the Abrahamic covenant.[59]

---

conclusions, while possible, fail to account for the Old Testament background of these words (Isa. 57:19). Moreover, the term μακράν (far off) is consistently used in the LXX and New Testament to indicate geographical (or spatial), not temporal, distance. In Acts, the term is used for the geographic regions of the Gentiles (e.g. Acts 22:21) (see Richard N. Longenecker, *Acts*, EBC [Grand Rapids: Zondervan, 1995], 81; cf. BDAG, 162).

57. Beale and Carson, *Commentary*, 543; cf. Bock, *Acts*, 144–45.

58. Hodge, *Systematic Theology*, 3.574.

59. Along similar lines, Bromiley writes: "From the church's very beginning women have been admitted to the Lord's table on equal terms with men. But no explicit text for this can be found" (*Children of Promise*, 3).

Furthermore, the fact that women such as Lydia (Acts 16:14–15) received the sign of the covenant demonstrates that the new covenant blessings are more expansive than anything found in the Old Testament—the covenant sign is extended to female adults and infants. Baptists argue that the sign is restricted to believers. But now that women receive the sign, there is an expansion, not a contraction of the administration of the covenant sign. In the absence of any explicit prohibition against the inclusion of male infants, it is necessary to conclude that female infants are also now included as recipients of the covenant sign.

Peter closes by saying that God will save as many as He calls, but the administration of the covenant sign to anyone, adult or infant, is not an automatic guarantee of salvation. The revelatory nature of the sign, and therefore its double edge, must not be forgotten. Baptism preaches both blessing and sanction, as did circumcision. Both Ishmael and Isaac received the sign, as did Esau and Jacob. Ishmael and Esau received it as a sign of covenant judgment, as there was no accompanying Spirit-wrought circumcision of the heart, whereas Isaac and Jacob received it as a sign of covenant blessing (cf. Gen. 17:15–27; Mal. 1:2–3; Rom. 9:10–16; Heb. 11:20; 12:15–17). The gospel and its sign, whether in the Old Testament and the Abrahamic covenant or in the New Testament, is always double-edged (2 Cor. 2:16–17).[60]

This means that the administrative ground for the sign of the covenant is the covenant promise of God.[61] For this reason, the sign is to be administered to adult converts and to the children of believers. The ground is not a profession of faith, as Baptist theologians argue. On the other hand, neither is the ground presumptive regeneration, whether in the case of adults or infants, as some in the Reformed tradition have argued.[62] The administra-

---

60. Kline, *By Oath Consigned*, 90.

61. Murray, *Christian Baptism*, 54; Robert L. Reymond, *A New Systematic Theology of the Christian Faith*, Second Edition (Nashville: Thomas Nelson, 1998), 938; Herman Hoeksema, *Reformed Dogmatics* (1966; Grand Rapids: Reformed Free Publishing Association, 1985), 698–99; Bavinck, *Saved By Grace*, 76; Francis Turretin, *Institutes of Elenctic Theology*, ed. James T. Dennison, trans. George Musgrave Giger (Phillipsburg, N.J.: P & R, 1992–1997), 19.20.3–11.

62. Murray, *Christian Baptism*, 71; Bavinck, *Reformed Dogmatics*, 4.525, 531; idem, *Saved by Grace*, 78–94; Berkouwer, *Sacraments*, 183–84. The idea of basing baptism for both adults and especially infants on the presumption of a person's regeneration has a distinguished pedigree, but nevertheless is incorrect. Those who have advocated it include Heinrich Bullinger (in the First Helvetic Confession, 1536), Peter Martyr Vermigli, Amandus Polanus, Theodore Beza, Charles Hodge, B. B. Warfield, Abraham Kuyper, and Lewis Schenck (see

tion of the covenant is grounded not on an individual profession of faith but on the covenant. Stated another way, the promise of redemption, or the covenant, is grounded in redemption accomplished, the person and work of Christ as it is progressively unfolded in covenant history, not on the application of redemption. To ground the application of the sign of the covenant on a profession of faith shifts the soteric center of gravity away from God to man—it is to say, "I am saved because I have believed." Instead, one must always say, "I am saved because God has saved me" (e.g., Gal. 4:9). Such a statement is not to minimize the faith of the one who is saved. Rather, it is to acknowledge that the covenant Lord has first condescended to His people—the sign of the covenant belongs to Him first and foremost. Baptism is the sign of *His* covenant promise.[63] When received by faith, baptism is secondarily a sign of the response of the covenant servant.

Adult and infant baptism presents to the church an important and central element of the work of God in the gospel. The very helplessness of infants highlights the truth that God saves His people. Man cannot initiate, achieve, supplement, complement, or complete His own redemption. To attempt to do so is to marginalize the supreme place of Christ in man's redemption. If the temptation in adult baptism is to overemphasize an individual's faith in Jesus, then the temptation in infant baptism is to devalue the importance of faith and thereby destroy the evangelistic message of the news of God's saving action.[64] Adult and infant baptism maintain this necessary balance.

---

the following literature for pro, con, and analysis of the arguments: First Helvetic Conf., art. 21; Charles Hodge, "The Church Membership of Infants," *Biblical Repertory and Princeton Review* 58/2 (1858): 347–89, esp. 376–77; B. B. Warfield, "The Polemics of Infant Baptism," in *Studies in Theology* [1932; Grand Rapids: Baker, 1981], 390; Lewis Bevens Schenck, *The Presbyterian Doctrine of Children in the Covenant: An Historical Study of the Significance of Infant Baptism in the Presbyterian Church* [1940; Phillipsburg, N.J.: P & R, 2003], 104–47, esp. 118, 130–31, 136–37; Bavinck, *Reformed Dogmatics*, 4.511; Reymond, *Systematic Theology*, 946, nn. 69–71; Geerhardus Vos, "The Doctrine of the Covenant in Reformed Theology," in *Redemptive History and Biblical Interpretation: The Shorter Writings of Geerhardus Vos*, ed. Richard B. Gaffin, Jr., [Phillipsburg, N.J.: P & R, 1980], 263–67). John Calvin, although cited in favor of this practice, waffles on the subject and seems to land on the divine institution as the ground of baptism (cf. John Calvin, *Institutes of the Christian Religion*, LCC, vols. 20–21, ed. John T. McNeill, trans. Ford Lewis Battles [Philadelphia: Westminster, 1960], 4.16.5–6; 4.16.9, 20). In this connection, see also Robert S. Rayburn, "The Presbyterian Doctrines of Covenant Children, Covenant Nurture, and Covenant Succession," *Presbyterion* 22/2 (1996): 76–112, esp. 109–12.

63. Bromiley, *Children of Promise*, 79.
64. Bromiley, *Children of Promise*, 64.

It also appears that balance was an implication of Paul's appeal to Israel's Red Sea baptism. All of Israel was baptized into the Holy Spirit, the sea, and Moses. Ironically, it was the professing baptized adult believers who were barred from the land and condemned to die in exile. By contrast, the younger Israelites, including the baptized children and infants, possessed the faith to enter the Land of Promise (cf. Heb. 3:16–19; 4:2). If Paul applies this typical baptism to the eschatological new covenant church, then his warning means that the church still needs the balance represented in adult and infant baptism: God saves His people. Geerhardus Vos summarizes this necessary balance by making reference to the image of the church as mother:

> Reformed theology has certainly realized that the church has two sides, and that besides being the assembly of believers and the revelation of the body of Christ, she must also be the means by which new believers are added. But it has not separated these two sides; rather it has kept them in organic connection. Just because the promises of God have been given to the assembly of believers, in its entirety, including their seed, this assembly is also a mother who conceives sons and daughters and is made to rejoice in her children by the Lord. The name "mother" signifies this truly Reformed point of view in distinction from other terms such as "institution of salvation."[65]

This means that the holy children of believers are to receive the sign of the covenant. They are to be baptized, called to faith and repentance, and instructed in the fear and admonition of the Lord.

THE ILLEGITIMACY OF PAEDOCOMMUNION

Just because infants are baptized and are members of the church does not mean that they are automatically entitled to participate in the Lord's Supper.[66] Paedocommunion is the teaching that affirms that a profession of faith is not necessary to partake of the Lord's Supper, but that once a person is initiated into the church through baptism, he is entitled to all of the rights of membership, including participation in the supper. Just as children were admitted to all of Israel's sacrificial feast-meals, it is argued,

65. Vos, "Doctrine of the Covenant," 262–63.
66. Contra Malone, *Baptism of Disciples Alone*, 23.

children in the New Testament should be admitted to the supper.[67] As with any movement, there are right and left wings. Among those who advocate paedocommunion, some believe that infants should partake of the supper through intinction, that is, parents dipping the bread into wine and placing the elements in the mouths of the infants. On the other side of the spectrum, others believe that children who show an interest in the supper should be allowed to partake of it apart from a profession of faith. Proponents of paedocommunion will undoubtedly find this brief response insufficient, but the following points demonstrate the illegitimacy of the practice.

First, proponents of paedocommunion argue that there are parallels between circumcision and baptism and between the Passover and the Lord's Supper. The assumption is that just as children are circumcised in the Old Testament and baptized in the New Testament, the same pattern exists with the Passover and the Lord's Supper. Such a conclusion does not adequately account for the explicit instructions regarding the administration of the Passover meal. At the institution of the meal, God told the people through Moses: "And it shall be, when your children say to you, 'What do you mean by this service?' that you shall say, 'It is the Passover sacrifice of the LORD, who passed over the houses of the children of Israel in Egypt when He struck the Egyptians and delivered our households'" (Ex. 12:26–27). This statement shows that children who were capable of inquiry and comprehension partook of the meal. There is a parallel in Paul's instructions to those who partake of the supper—they are supposed to discern the Lord's body, the significance of the bread and the cup, and examine themselves (1 Cor. 11:23–29). In this connection, Murray writes: "Children of such age and intelligence are in a different category from infants. Paedobaptists do not refuse to admit to the Lord's Table children of sufficient age and understanding to know the meaning of the Lord's Supper."[68] Advocates of paedocommunion therefore misread the nature of the administration of the Passover.

However, there is a more fundamental question regarding the proper Old Testament backdrop for the Lord's Supper. Did Christ celebrate the Passover in the Lord's Supper, or was the Passover the occasion for the

---

67. See Peter Leithart, "A Response to '1 Corinthians 11:17–34: The Lord's Supper,'" in *The Auburn Avenue Theology: Pros & Cons*, ed. E. Calvin Beisner (Ft. Lauderdale, Fla.: Knox Theological Seminary, 2004), 297–304; idem, *The Priesthood of the Plebs: A Theology of Baptism* (Eugene, Ore.: Wipf & Stock, 2003), 146–53; cf. Guy Prentiss Waters, *The Federal Vision and Covenant Theology: A Comparative Analysis* (Phillipsburg, N.J.: P & R, 2006), 287–92.

68. Murray, *Christian Baptism*, 74.

inaugural Lord's Supper? While there is certainly a connection between the Passover and the Lord's Supper, the more specific background passage is Exodus 24 and the ratification of the covenant. The Passover was not an end in itself, but pointed to the covenantal goal of Exodus 24, worshipping and fellowshiping in God's presence.[69] What commends this connection is the appearance of the phrase דם הברית / τὸ αἷμα τῆς διαθήκης (the blood of the covenant) (Ex. 24:8). This precise phrase occurs only once in the Old Testament (cf. Zech. 9:11) and four times in the New Testament (Matt. 26:28; Mark 14:24; Heb. 9:20; 10:29). In the Exodus covenant ratification, only Moses, Aaron, the priests, and the elders ascended Sinai to eat the covenant ratification meal in the presence of God unharmed—in other words, professing adults alone (Ex. 24:9–11). Similarly, in the covenant ratification meal of the New Testament, only Christ and His disciples participated. This raises the all-important but often missed distinction between baptism as covenant *initiation* and the Lord's Supper as covenant *ratification*. More will be said about this below.

Second, Christ gives the specific instruction that participants in the Lord's Supper are supposed to partake of it in remembrance of Him: "This do, as often as you drink it, in remembrance of Me" (1 Cor. 11:24–25). In order to recognize the body of Christ, one must comprehend and grasp by faith the significance of the life, death, resurrection, and ascension of Jesus. Such a remembrance demonstrates the difference between baptism and the Lord's Supper. In baptism, the recipient, either an infant or an adult, passively receives the rite as another baptizes him. In the Lord's Supper, on the other hand, there is the requirement of active participation—self-examination and recognition of the body of Christ.[70] This self-examination is the aforementioned covenant ratification. As Calvin writes, "By baptism they are admitted into Christ's flock, and the symbol of their adoption suffices them until as adults they are able to bear solid food. Therefore, we should wait for the time of examination, which God expressly requires in the Sacred Supper."[71] Advocates of paedocommunion err in thinking that baptism and the Lord's Supper function in precisely the same manner and therefore have the same participants.

Third, and lastly, is the relationship between the supper and redemptive history. Baptism is a sacrament of initiation, of entry to the visible

69. Beale and Carson, *Commentary*, 229–32.
70. Torrance, et al., *Doctrine of Baptism*, 54.
71. Calvin, *Institutes*, 4.16.31.

covenant community. By contrast, the supper is a sacrament that looks to covenant ratification and to the consummation. In the types of the Old Testament, Israel was baptized in the Red Sea, and then Moses, Aaron, his sons, and the seventy elders climbed Sinai and ate a covenant ratification meal in the presence of God unharmed (Ex. 24:1–11). In the broader narrative, the exodus baptism gave way to dwelling in the presence of God and consuming the covenant meal in His presence at the tabernacle and later the temple in the Land of Promise. Christ institutes the supper in anticipation of the consummation of the kingdom (Matt. 26:29; Mark 14:25; Luke 22:18). The sacramental presence of Christ in the supper focuses the church's attention on the last day and the consummation.[72]

However, the supper not only focuses the attention of the church on the last day, but serves as an anticipation of the final judgment. In remembering Christ and rightly recognizing His body in the supper, the recipient's self-examination is not merely an introspective gaze at the soul to see whether he has committed sin that he has not yet repented of. Rather, the Lord's Supper is an anticipatory parousia of Christ, and the self-examination is a form of judgment by which the communicant asks whether he looks by faith to Christ, the One who has borne his condemnation on his behalf. Baptism represents an anticipation of the final judgment, as those who receive the rite are sacramentally united to the representative man, the last Adam, in His death and resurrection. The divine condemnation on sin has fallen on Christ, who bore the wrath of God on behalf of His bride. But between baptism and the final judgment there is the lamentable but unavoidable fact that professing baptized Christians sin. Hence, the Lord's Supper is the anticipatory final judgment and parousia that strengthens the promise of judgment and justification that is sacramentally proclaimed in baptism.[73]

Given this emphasis on initiation and consummation in baptism and the Lord's Supper respectively, the supper therefore requires self-examination. First Corinthians 11:27–34 instructs the church regarding the imminent parousia of Christ, when He will celebrate the marriage supper of the Lamb with His bride. However, in light of the relationship between initiation and consummation, the supper is celebrated in the interval between baptism and the final judgment. The Christian is therefore supposed to

---

72. Geoffrey Wainwright, *Eucharist and Eschatology* (Akron, Ohio: OSL Publications, 2002), 103; also G. K. Beale, "The New Testament and New Creation," in *Biblical Theology: Retrospect & Prospect*, ed. Scott J. Hafemann (Downers Grove, Ill.: InterVarsity, 2002), 170.

73. Wainwright, *Eucharist and Eschatology*, 100–01.

test himself (1 Cor. 11:28) and show enough discrimination about himself (v. 31) to know that he is a sinner saved by Christ. The participant confesses his sin and looks to Christ by faith in the present, so that he will not eat and drink judgment upon himself. The verb κρίμα usually indicates a guilty verdict (v. 29; cf. v. 34). The believer performs this self-judgment so that he is not finally pronounced guilty of the Lord's death and thus does not share in the world's condemnation (v. 32). At every celebration of the Lord's Supper, the Christian is supposed to ratify and renew his baptismal acceptance of the divine condemnation on sin. In other words, the Lord's Supper is a proleptic final judgment and marriage supper of the Lamb—a miniature anticipation of the return of Christ and the great wedding feast.[74]

This is why Paul explains that the supper calls for self-examination: it preaches the return of Christ, the final judgment, and the consummation of all things. The supper beckons the church to seek shelter in the ark of His life, death, resurrection, and ascension by faith in anticipation of the ever-rising flood-judgment of the Spirit on the earth—the baptism of fire. The supper proclaims that not all those who are visibly covenanted with Christ will sup with Him at the eschatological marriage feast of the Lamb. The invitation goes out and many are invited. But those who come can stay only if they wear proper wedding attire—the robe of the righteousness of the last Adam. Paedocommunion does not account for the relationship between the Lord's Supper and eschatology.

Advocates of paedocommunion therefore fail to deal adequately with these three points: the nature of the Passover and the more likely background of the exodus covenant ratification meal; the differences between baptism and the supper (covenant initiation vs. ratification); and the coordination of the supper with eschatology. Some may cry foul and claim that these points negate what has been argued concerning infant baptism. This is not the case. Baptism is a means of grace only by the work of the Spirit through faith. The Bible clearly shows that the administration of the initiatory rite, whether circumcision or baptism, can precede a profession of faith. However, the Bible is equally clear that a profession of faith is necessary for the Lord's Supper. The difference between the two sacraments ultimately lies in the distinction between the passive initiation into the covenant and the active participation in the consummation and purification of the covenant community.

---

74. Wainwright, *Eucharist and Eschatology*, 103.

CONCLUSION AND SUMMARY

This chapter has surveyed the proper recipients of baptism and has concluded, first, that circumcision was a sacrament of the gospel—the sign and seal of the righteousness that comes by faith alone, justification. It was also the sign and seal of union with Yahweh through the mediatorial work of the Seed who was to come and be cut off for the sake of His people. Second, all baptisms in Scripture are corporate, and this is manifest in the baptism of households. Third, the corporate baptism of the church must be related to the already/not yet dynamic of redemptive history. Concomitant with the overlap of the ages is the necessity to recognize that the sacrament of baptism is not exclusively a means of grace; it is also a means of covenant sanction. Fourth, the administration of baptism hinges not upon a profession of faith or presumptive regeneration of an infant, but upon the covenant promise of God. Fifth, the fact that the church baptizes its children does not lead to paedocommunion.

Ultimately, the case for infant baptism stands or falls on the canon of Scripture—the whole of the Bible. Unless the church constructs her doctrine, including baptism, on the entire witness of Scripture, she fails to reflect faithfully the teaching of her covenant Lord. If the above analysis is correct, then Hodge accurately describes the consequences of eschewing the teaching of Scripture: "To be unbaptized is a grievous injury and reproach; one which no parent can innocently entail upon his children. The neglect of baptism, which implies a want of appreciation of the ordinance, is one of the crying sins of this generation."[75] It seems that Hodge's words, written in the mid-nineteenth century, are equally applicable in the present day, not only in the broader church but even within the Reformed community. How many do not understand why the church baptizes its members? How many bring their children to receive baptism for the sake of tradition or for emotional or sentimental reasons, thus turning baptism into a rite of the cult of the child? How many abandon infant baptism out of embarrassment or instead participate in a man-made ceremony of infant dedication of which the Scriptures say nothing?[76]

---

75. Hodge, *Systematic Theology*, 3.579.

76. So George, "The Reformed Doctrine of Believer's Baptism," 252; Derek Tidball, "A Baptist Perspective on David Wright, *What Has Infant Baptism Done to Baptism? An Enquiry at the end of Christendom*," *EQ* 78/2 (2006): 159. See also Friedrich Schleiermacher, *The Christian Faith* (1830; London: T & T Clark, 1990), 637–38.

The church must embrace the canonical understanding of the signs of the covenant and administer those signs on the ground of the divine promise. The divine promise cannot be apprehended by man, but must apprehend him as God sends His grace, Jesus Christ, who pours out the Holy Spirit, who gathers the bride of Christ through Word and sacrament. Whether an adult or infant receives the covenant sign, when one looks at the water and hears the Word, it becomes an effectual means of salvation through faith. How can an infant benefit if he has no faith? A believer remembers the promises of the Scriptures that he has heard or read, and receives the full benefit of that promise. Likewise, the one who received the sign as an infant receives the full benefit of baptism when he is regenerated, savingly believes, and matures in Christ. He does so as he hears the gospel preached in the Word and sees it visibly proclaimed in the baptism of others, all in the knowledge that he too was baptized in his infancy. If a person believes in the promises that were signed and sealed to him in baptism, it is a means of grace for him. Baptism therefore benefits infants and adults through a Spirit-wrought faith.[77] As with Luther and Calvin, the church must recognize that baptism for adult and infant echoes throughout the life of the believer until faith gives way to sight.[78]

---

77. Hodge, *Systematic Theology*, 3.590.

78. See Calvin, *Institutes*, 4.15.11; Martin Luther, LW 36.69; Herman Witsius, *Economy of the Covenants Between God and Man*, trans. William Crookshank (1822; Phillipsburg, N.J.: P & R, 1991), 4.16.47; James Ussher, *A Body of Divinity: Being the Sum and Substance of the Christian Religion*, ed. Michael Navarr (1648; Birmingham: Solid Ground Books, 2007), 380; *Directory for Public Worship* in *Westminster Confession of Faith* (1646; Glasgow: Free Presbyterian Publications, 1995), 383.

CHAPTER 15

Baptism and Ecclesiology

In the face of the challenge of Anabaptist theologians, Reformed churches have had to deal with the thorny question of whether Roman Catholic baptisms are valid. Given the data surveyed in Part I, some might conclude that the Reformers rejected Roman Catholic baptisms. However, while the Reformers generally took great issue with the Roman Catholic theology of baptism, they nonetheless accepted Roman Catholic baptisms. The Anabaptists took the opposite view; they believed that the Roman Catholic Church's theology invalidated its administration of baptism, and therefore people coming from Roman Catholic to Protestant churches needed to be rebaptized—or, as the Anabaptists put it, be baptized properly for the first time.[1] Beyond these sixteenth-century debates, there were disputes in the nineteenth-century American Presbyterian church. Charles Hodge took the position that Roman Catholic baptism was valid, while J. H. Thornwell took the opposing view.

The question of what constitutes a valid baptism does not arise only along Catholic-Protestant lines; it is sometimes an issue within Protestantism. For example, some Baptist churches reject not only Roman Catholic but Presbyterian baptisms. They reject baptisms that were performed on infants, seeing infant baptism as illegitimate and unbiblical, and some reject any baptism that was not performed by immersion.[2] Particular Baptists, for

---

1. Justo L. González, *A History of Christian Thought*, vol. 3 (1975; Nashville: Abingdon, 1993), 89; Hughes Oliphant Old, *The Shaping of the Reformed Baptismal Rite in the Sixteenth Century* (Grand Rapids: Eerdmans, 1992), 77; William R. Estep, *The Anabaptist Story: An Introduction to Sixteenth-Century Anabaptism* (1963; Grand Rapids: Eerdmans, 1996), 201–36.

2. See J. L. Garrett, *Systematic Theology: Biblical, Historical, & Evangelical*, vol. 2 (Grand Rapids: 1995), 529–33.

example, have historically argued that immersion "is necessary to the due administration" of baptism.[3]

The question can also be framed from a Presbyterian perspective. Some reject Roman Catholic baptism because of the theology that stands behind its administration of the rite. Based on this presupposition, it seems necessary to reject other forms of baptism, as well. Particular Baptists have a correct understanding of the relationship between the sovereignty of God and salvation. What, however, of those Baptists or evangelicals who believe that salvation comes to all men through God's prevenient grace, which hinges man's salvation solely on his decision?[4] In such contexts, baptism is viewed not as the covenant sign of God but as the oath-pledge of the believer.[5] Does this improper view of salvation and the nature of baptism therefore invalidate the rite, requiring rebaptism? This chapter will address these questions.

The chapter will proceed along the following lines. First, it will survey the theological arguments of the sixteenth-century Reformation and its codified theology, as represented in its confessions. Second, the chapter will survey the debate between Hodge and Thornwell. Third, the chapter will set forth an argument for what constitutes a valid baptism and demonstrate that both Roman Catholic and evangelical baptisms can be valid.[6] The question of what constitutes a true baptism hinges on who ultimately administers it. Is baptism administered by man or by God Himself? It also hinges on the question of whether baptism is objectively or subjectively defined. Does God define it through His self-revelation in Christ and cov-

---

3. *The Baptist Confession of Faith 1689* (Carlisle: Grace Baptist Church, n.d.), 29.4.

4. See, e.g., Roger E. Olson, *Arminian Theology: Myths and Realities* (Downers Grove, Ill.: InterVarsity, 2006), 158–78.

5. So Karl Barth, *Church Dogmatics* IV.4, 2, eds. G. W. Bromiley and T. F. Torrance (1969; Edinburgh: T & T Clark, 2000), 128. Hereafter cited as CD.

6. Note that the term *evangelical* is somewhat theologically ambiguous, as it can encompass a broad scope of doctrinal beliefs ranging from conservative Reformed to liberal Open Theism. Moreover, unlike confessional denominations, such as the Roman Catholic Church and various Reformed, Lutheran, and Anglican bodies, there are few defining confessional documents that set forth evangelical belief, though some groups, such as the Alliance of Confessing Evangelicals, have attempted to do so (see *Cambridge Declaration* in *Creeds and Confessions of Faith in the Christian Tradition*, eds. Jaroslav Pelikan and Valerie Hotchkiss [New Haven: Yale University Press, 2003], 3.861–66; cf. D. G. Hart, *Deconstructing Evangelicalism: Conservative Protestantism in the Age of Billy Graham* [Grand Rapids: Baker, 2004], *passim*, esp. 131–52).

enant through the Word, or is it defined by those bodies or individuals who administer it?

IN THE REFORMATION AND POST-REFORMATION

During the Reformation, both Lutheran and Reformed theologians often faced two- and three-front battles, depending on the theological issue. In the debates over the Lord's Supper, for example, Lutheran and Reformed theologians faced off against one another, but they were united in their opposition to the Roman Catholic Church (RCC). On the doctrine of baptism, the Reformed faced two key opponents—on the one side was the RCC and on the other were the Anabaptists.[7] The positions of these camps were covered in Part I. However, a brief review of what key theologians have said regarding Roman Catholic baptism is certainly helpful, as this particular aspect of the history of the doctrine was not covered in depth in Part I.

Historically, the question of the nature and legitimacy of a baptism has hinged on the earlier debates between Augustine (354–430) and the Donatists.[8] Augustine came to the conclusion that baptism did not depend on the worthiness of the minister who administered the rite, but ultimately on God, the One who instituted it and whose promise stood behind it. John Calvin basically agreed with Augustine's position: "Among men, if a letter is sent, provided the handwriting and seal are sufficiently recognized, it makes no difference who or of what sort the carrier is. In like manner, it ought to be enough for us to recognize the hand and seal of our Lord in his sacraments, whatever carrier may bring them."[9] Calvin was essentially repeating Augustine's argument against the Donatists.

Calvin's position was based on the nature of baptism itself. He believed that it is ultimately God who initiates people into the church through bap-

---

7. For his polemical treatises against these various groups, see John Calvin, *Selected Works of John Calvin: Tracts and Letters*, eds. Henry Beveridge and Jules Bonnet (1851; Grand Rapids: Baker, 1983).

8. For Augustine's anti-Donatist writings, see NPNF[1] 4.369–652; cf. B. B. Price, *Medieval Thought: An Introduction* (Oxford: Blackwell, 1996), 38–40; Jaroslav Pelikan, *The Christian Tradition: A History of the Development of Doctrine* (Chicago: University of Chicago Press, 1971), 1.307–13; Bengt Hägglund, *History of Theology*, trans. Gene J. Lund (St. Louis: Concordia, 2007), 124–32; Alister E. McGrath, *Historical Theology: An Introduction to the History of Christian Thought* (Oxford: Blackwell, 1998), 77–79; Peter Brown, *Augustine of Hippo* (Berkley, Calif.: University of California Press, 1969), 212–25.

9. John Calvin, *Institutes of the Christian Religion*, vols. 20–21, LCC, ed. John T. McNeill, trans. Ford Lewis Battles (Philadelphia: Westminster, 1960), 4.15.16.

tism, not into one particular fellowship of believers but into the one catholic (universal) church. This, Calvin argues, is reflected in the baptismal formula; a person is baptized into the name of the Father, Son, and Holy Spirit, not the RCC: "Ignorant or even contemptuous as those who baptized us were of God and all piety, they did not baptize us into the fellowship of either their ignorance or sacrilege, but into faith in Jesus Christ, because it was not their own name but God's that they invoked, and they baptized us into no other name."[10] To support his argument further, Calvin appeals to the practice of the Old Testament, pointing out there were undoubtedly apostate priests who circumcised many an Israelite, yet the circumcisions they administered were not therefore invalidated.

Calvin also brought an argument against his Anabaptist critics. The Anabaptists argued that baptism was supposed to be celebrated within the assemblies of the godly—in other words, those with correct theology.[11] In contrast, Calvin believed that God's truth in baptism was not totally extinguished even by the RCC: "For when we teach what ought to be done in order that baptism may be pure and free of all defilement, we do not abolish God's ordinance, however idolaters may corrupt it."[12] Note that Calvin basically identifies the RCC as an assembly of idolaters. He has no problem characterizing the RCC in the most negative terms. However, in spite of this, he did not see baptisms administered by the RCC as invalid.

This same tension appears in the French Reformed Confession (1559/71), or *Confession de foi*. While Calvin was not its sole author or source, scholars believe he played a key role in its formulation, and it reflects his teachings.[13] The French Confession includes a clear rejection of the RCC based on the standard three-point checklist of the Reformation regarding the marks of the church: the right preaching of the Word, the proper administration of the sacraments, and church discipline.[14] The confession states that the true church is "according to the word of God…the company

---

10. Calvin, *Institutes*, 4.15.16.

11. See, e.g., Menno Simons, *On the Ban: Questions and Answers*, in George Hunston Williams, ed., *Spiritual and Anabaptist Writers*, LCC, vol. 25 (Philadelphia: Westminster, 1957), 261–71.

12. Calvin, *Institutes*, 4.15.16.

13. Pelikan and Hotchkiss, *Creeds*, 2.372.

14. On the three marks of the church, see Heinrich Heppe, *Reformed Dogmatics: Set Out and Illustrated from the Sources*, ed. Ernst Bizer, trans. G. T. Thomson (London: George Allen & Unwin Ltd, 1950), 669–70; Louis Berkhof, *Systematic Theology: New Combined Edition* (1932–1938; Grand Rapids: Eerdmans, 1996), 576–78; Herman Bavinck, *Reformed Dogmatics* (Grand Rapids: Baker, 2003–2008), 4.307–16.

of the faithful who agree to follow his word, and the pure religion which it teaches."[15] By contrast, it states that the pure Word of God is banished from the RCC, and that its sacraments are corrupted, debased, falsified, or destroyed, being little more than superstitions and idolatries. All who take part in these acts therefore separate themselves from the body of Christ, according to the confession. The characterization of the RCC is clear—it is not part of the true church and is an apostate body. However, the same article continues by stating: "Nevertheless, as some trace of the church is left in the papacy, and the virtue and substance of baptism remain, and as the efficacy of baptism does not depend upon the person who administers it, we confess that those baptized in it do not need a second baptism. But, on account of its corruptions, we cannot present children to be baptized in it without incurring pollution."[16] From these statements, it is clear that while the confession regards the RCC as an apostate body, there are elements of truth still within its fellowship. The confession argues, therefore, that one can come out of the RCC with a valid baptism, but cannot go back to the RCC and have one's children baptized in it. There is a one-way door by which people may exit the RCC with a valid baptism but may not return to obtain one.

Calvin and the French Confession were not unique in this conclusion, which was common among other Reformed theologians and also among Lutherans.[17] Martin Luther strongly rejected the arguments of the Anabaptists. In his *Concerning Rebaptism* (1528), Luther took aim against the Anabaptist argument that Roman Catholic theology invalidates RCC baptism.[18] He employed a fine distinction here, as did Calvin and the French Confession. Luther had no problem identifying the pope as the Antichrist, but he distinguished between the pope and the one catholic church. Like Calvin, Luther believed that it was necessary to distinguish between the false and true elements within the apostate RCC. Luther, Calvin, and the French Confession all believed that there were not multiple churches but

15. French Confession, § 27, in Pelikan and Hotchkiss, *Creeds*, 3.382.
16. French Confession, § 28, in Pelikan and Hotchkiss, *Creeds*, 3.382–83.
17. See Belgic Confession, art. 34; Second Helvetic Confession, 18.21, 19.2–3, 11–12; Augsburg Confession, art. 9; *Apology of the Augsburg Confession*, arts. 8–9 (see Pelikan and Hotchkiss, *Creeds*, 2.504–05; 510; 422–23; and *The Book of Concord: The Confessions of the Evangelical Lutheran Church*, eds. Robert Kolb and Timothy J. Wengert [Minneapolis: Fortress, 2000], 42–43, 179, 183). Also see Heinrich Schmid, *The Doctrinal Theology of the Evangelical Lutheran Church* (Philadelphia: Lutheran Publication Society, 1899), 545.
18. Martin Luther, *Concerning Rebaptism* (1528), LW 40.233.

rather one holy catholic church. Luther, Calvin, and other first and second generation Reformers, such as Ulrich Zwingli, did not see themselves as schismatics, sectarians, or founders of new churches of their own, but as reformers of the one true church. The Reformation was precisely that, a *reform* movement. In this light, the Reformers recognized that elements of truth remained in the RCC.

This same trend continued in the theology of the post-Reformation period. The Westminster Standards are among the most prominent post-Reformation doctrinal statements, giving a detailed exposition of the Reformed faith not only in confessional but in catechetical form. The standards set forth the three marks of the church: the right preaching of the Word, the proper administration of the sacraments, and church discipline (WCF 25.4; 30.1–4). They identify the visible church in this way: "The visible church…consists of all those throughout the world that profess the true religion; and of their children: and is the kingdom of the Lord Jesus Christ, the house and family of God, out of which there is no ordinary possibility of salvation" (WCF 25.2; cf. LC 62). In the light of this understanding of the church, the confession remarks that some churches have so degenerated from bearing the three marks that they are not churches of Christ but "synagogues of Satan" (WCF 25.5).[19]

The Westminster Standards are often oblique in their disagreement with the RCC, but in an unusually direct statement the confession says: "There is no other head of the Church, but the Lord Jesus Christ; nor can the Pope of Rome, in any sense, be head thereof; but is that Antichrist, that man of sin, and the son of perdition, that exalts himself, in the Church, against Christ and all that is called God" (WCF 25.6). Here the divines identify the pope as the Antichrist based on 2 Thessalonians 2:3–4, 8–9.[20] The Westminster divines did not in any way believe that the RCC was a true church, but arguably, given their statements concerning the pope, believed that it was a synagogue of Satan.

This did not mean, however, that they believed Roman Catholic baptisms were invalid. The confession says much regarding Roman Catholic

---

19. The use of this scriptural phrase (Rev. 2:9) was not original to the WCF but has precedence as early as 1536 in the Geneva Confession, which is ascribed to the pen of Calvin (see art. 18 in Pelikan and Hotchkiss, *Creeds*, 2.217), though the exact phrase is "synagogues of the devil."

20. Cf. *Westminster Confession of Faith* (1646; Glasgow: Free Presbyterian Publications, 1995); *The Confession of Faith and Catechisms of the Orthodox Presbyterian Church with Proof Texts* (Willow Grove, Pa.: Committee on Christian Education of the OPC, 2005).

baptisms by what it does not say. The absence of any statement condemning Roman Catholic baptisms is evidence of the divines' view concerning their validity. The confession has nothing in its chapter on baptism that comes close to what it states in its chapter on the church regarding the pope. Rather, the confession says only that the outward element of baptism is water; that dipping is not necessary, but the water can be rightly administered through pouring or sprinkling; and that baptism must be done in the triune name of God by a minister lawfully called (WCF 28.2–3). In a refutation of Anabaptism and its tenet that a person coming out of Roman Catholicism must be rebaptized, the confession states, "The sacrament of baptism is but once to be administered unto any person" (WCF 28.7). This understanding of baptism is supported by a reaffirmation of Augustine's arguments against the Donatists: "Neither does the efficacy of a sacrament depend upon the piety or intention of him that does administer it: but upon the work of the Spirit, and the word of institution, which contains, together with a precept authorizing the use thereof, a promise of benefit to worthy receivers" (WCF 27.3).[21] The substance of the confession's argument is the same as the statements of the sixteenth-century Reformers: a Roman Catholic baptism is not automatically invalid despite the fact that the RCC is a false church.

On the Continent some twenty-five years later, another well-known Reformed theologian came to similar conclusions. Francis Turretin engaged this question with his usual clarity and razor-sharp intellect. Turretin approached the question of whether the validity of a sacrament hinges on the intention of the minister who administers it. He framed the question in this way in response to the Council of Trent's (session 7, canon 11) insistence that the minister must perform a sacrament according to the theological understanding of the church. Among other points, Turretin argues:

> The relation of the sacrament is the same as the preached word, since each is the instrument of God and the former indeed the visible word and the later the audible. And yet the efficacy of the preached word does not depend upon the intention of the minister, but upon the virtue attending the word itself. Hence Paul shows that it makes little difference whether the gospel is preached from the mind or from contention (Phil. 1:16–17).

---

21. Cf. A. A. Hodge, *The Confession of Faith: A Handbook of Christian Doctrine Expounding the Westminster Confession* (rep.; London: Banner of Truth, 1958), 332–34; Robert Shaw, *An Exposition of the Westminster Confession of Faith* (1845; Fearn: Christian Focus, 1998), 341.

Turretin's point was that the validity of the Word and sacrament depend not on the one who administers them but on the Holy Spirit, God Himself.[22]

Turretin brought another important point to bear. He argued that if the efficacy of the sacrament depends on the one who administers it, then it depends not on the principal agent, God, but on the intention of the inferior cause, the minister. This would make the truth of God void, and is contrary to Paul's teaching (Rom. 3:3).[23] In his argument, Turretin relied on Augustine's argumentation against the Donatists. Turretin approvingly quotes Augustine's *On Baptism*: "The truth of the sacraments does not depend upon the morals, faith and qualities of the minister, but on the institution of God; whatever the exterior minister may be, still God is the interior worker. A bad minister does not injure where the good Lord is. The sacraments are completed not by the faith of the user or of the one administering, but by the words of their author."[24]

This is not to say, however, that Turretin therefore had a lax view concerning the administration of the sacraments. Turretin believed that just because a father uttered the words "I wash you in the name of God the Father, Son, and Holy Spirit" while he was bathing his son did not mean a true baptism had been performed. Rather, he argued that such an action was not a true sacrament. He did so not because proper intention was lacking, but because the institution of Christ was not observed. An ordained minister must perform the sacrament with solemnity and due reverence, and administer it in a public assembly.[25]

This general argumentation and understanding of the nature and efficacy of the sacraments led Turretin to his conclusions regarding the validity of baptisms performed by the RCC. Turretin was abundantly clear that the RCC is not a true church because it does not bear two of the marks of the church, the pure preaching and profession of the Word and the lawful administration and use of the sacraments.[26] The RCC impinges on the one true foundation of the church, Christ. Turretin believed the RCC to be heretical, idolatrous, opposed to the certainty of salvation, opposed to piety and good morals, tyrannical, led by the Antichrist, and Babylon the

---

22. Francis Turretin, *Institutes of Elenctic Theology*, ed. James T. Dennison, Jr., trans. George Musgrave Giger (Phillipsburg, N.J.: P & R, 1992–97), 19.7.6.

23. Turretin, *Institutes*, 19.7.8.

24. Turretin, *Institutes*, 19.7.11; also Augustine, *On Baptism*, NPNF[1] 4.512–13.

25. Turretin, *Institutes*, 19.7.12.

26. Turretin, *Institutes*, 18.12.1–29.

great whore.[27] In other words, like the Reformers, he pulled no punches regarding the corrupt nature of the RCC. Yet like Lutheran and Reformed theologians, he recognizes that there is still some truth in her midst: "It is one thing to retain something of the true church; another to be the true church simply; as it is one thing for the body to have some sound parts, another for the body to be sound simply." He goes on to illustrate this point from the Old Testament and church history: "The Pharisaic church retained something of the true church in the time of Christ, nor yet on that account was she a true church. The same is the judgment concerning the Arian, Donatist and other factions whose baptism and ordinations the Catholics never repeated."[28]

What elements of truth did Turretin believe remained in the RCC? Turretin explained that the Apostles' Creed, the Lord's Prayer, and the Ten Commandments were elements of truth that remained. To hold to these things with a proper faith is one thing; however, to hold to them nominally is another. He believed the RCC held them in the latter rather than the former manner.[29] He carefully qualifies his statement by writing: "If some of our divines have said that the fundamentals remain in the papacy, they did not on that account think that the Roman church is a true church in which salvation can be obtained—the contrary of which they maintained with so much zeal, urging secession from her as a thing of the highest necessity for salvation."[30]

Nevertheless, Turretin follows Luther and Calvin in acknowledging the validity of Roman Catholic baptisms:

> The verity of baptism proves indeed that truth of a church with regard to Christianity in general, in opposition to assemblies of unbelievers; but not with regard to Christianity pure and purged from the errors of heretics. For true baptism can be found among heretics who are not the true church; as true circumcision and sacrifices to the one God were consecrated in the church of the ten tribes, which was not on that account a true church.[31]

Turretin, therefore, was able to distinguish between the correct form of the sacrament—that it was administered by a minister, in the triune name

---

27. Turretin, *Institutes*, 18.14.1–23.
28. Turretin, *Institutes*, 18.14.24.
29. Turretin, *Institutes*, 18.14.25.
30. Turretin, *Institutes*, 18.14.26.
31. Turretin, *Institutes*, 18.14.27.

of God, and with water—from its apostate context. He did not endorse the Roman Catholic theology behind baptism. He saw that God, not man, ultimately defines baptism's meaning. Moreover, he could distinguish between an element of truth within an apostate church and the false doctrine.

IN NINETEENTH-CENTURY PRESBYTERIANISM

This brief survey suggests that the Reformed response to the question of the validity of Roman Catholic baptisms has been uniform. This, however, would be a hasty conclusion. In the nineteenth-century, Hodge and Thornwell debated this very issue, the former affirming the Reformation view and the latter denying it. The debate occurred during the General Assembly of 1845. In a reversal of the trend among the historic Reformed churches to accept Roman Catholic baptisms, the General Assembly, led by Thornwell, voted 169 to 8 that Roman Catholic baptisms were invalid.[32] This outcome elicited a response from Hodge in his coverage of the assembly in the *Princeton Review*; Thornwell replied to Hodge in *The Southern Presbyterian Review*; then Hodge penned a subsequent rejoinder.[33]

In his response, Thornwell repeated arguments that he made on the floor during the General Assembly. Thornwell summarizes his argument: "In the General Assembly it was maintained by those who denied the validity of Popish baptism that the ordinance itself was so corrupted in its constituent elements—its matter and its form—that it could not be treated as the institution of Christ."[34] Thornwell had two pillars in his argument: the teaching of Scripture and the union between matter and form. On the first point, Thornwell argued that the rite must conform to the definition of baptism set forth in Scripture.[35] On the second pillar, Thornwell appeals to philosophy: "According to Aristotle it is the *forms* impressed upon the first matter which enable us to discriminate betwixt different substances." Since the intention of the one who administers baptism "is part of the *essence* of baptism, it is consequently an error of arrangement to make it different

---

32. Charles Hodge, "The General Assembly of 1845," *PR* 17/3 (1845): 444.

33. J. H. Thornwell, "The Validity of the Baptism of the Church of Rome," in *The Collected Writings of James Henley Thornwell*, vol. 3, eds. John B. Adger and John L. Girardeau (Edinburgh: Banner of Truth, 1986), 283–412; Charles Hodge, "Is the Church of Rome a Part of the Visible Church?" *PR* 18/2 (1846): 320–44.

34. Thornwell, "Baptism of Rome," 283–84.

35. Thornwell, "Baptism of Rome," 284.

from the form."[36] While this point may or may not be true, it ran contrary to the historical understanding of the nature of the sacraments going back to the days of Augustine and the Donatist controversy.

Going into particulars, Thornwell asks: "Do her priests wash with *water* in the *name of the Trinity*, with the *professed design of complying with the command of Christ*, and are *they themselves* to be regarded as *lawful ministers of the Word?*"[37] On the first item of this question, Thornwell answered that the RCC does not baptize with water. Thornwell pointed to the Roman Catholic practice of mixing the baptismal water with oil, or "holy chrism."[38] Thornwell references the *Catechism of the Council of Trent* to demonstrate that the RCC does not baptize with pure water: "But it should be noted that while in case of necessity simple water unmixed with any other ingredient is sufficient for the matter of this Sacrament, yet when Baptism is administered in public with solemn ceremonies the Catholic Church, guided by Apostolic tradition, has uniformly observed the practice of adding holy chrism which, as is clear, more fully signifies the effect of baptism."[39] Thornwell believed that this mixture corrupted the symbolism of baptism. He argues that water drawn from natural sources often contains other elements, but nevertheless "men still *wash* with it." On the other hand, "a water which cannot be used in *washing* is not suitable matter for baptism, as *oil* evidently impairs its cleansing properties." Water's ability to cleanse represents the "purifying influence of regeneration and the renewing of the Holy Ghost."[40]

Thornwell also argued that the RCC had corrupted the form of baptism, which hinges on the relationship between baptism and the appointment of Christ.[41] In particular, it is not merely the invocation of the name of the Trinity that constitutes the form, but also the doctrine that stands behind the use of the name. Thornwell stated that there must be reference to the economy of grace and recognition of the essential features and fundamental doctrines of the gospel. Without such doctrines informing baptism, the "ordinances are worthless and duties are bondage."[42] This argument was unique in the history of Reformed doctrine, in that Thornwell said that

36. Thornwell, "Baptism of Rome," 285.
37. Thornwell, "Baptism of Rome," 286.
38. Thornwell, "Baptism of Rome," 288.
39. *The Catechism of the Council of Trent*, trans. John A. McHugh and Charles J. Callan (Rockford, Ill.: Tan Books, 1982), 166.
40. Thornwell, "Baptism of Rome," 291.
41. Thornwell, "Baptism of Rome," 295.
42. Thornwell, "Baptism of Rome," 296–97.

not merely the form of baptism but also the doctrine behind it must be sound. Like his Reformed predecessors, Thornwell saw the Roman Catholic soteriology and doctrine of the sacraments as erroneous. But unlike his Reformed predecessors, he argued that RCC doctrine therefore corrupted its sacraments.

In the past, Reformed theologians typically had appealed to Augustine's principle from the Donatist controversy, namely, that the intention of the minister does not affect the administration of the sacrament. Thornwell, however, modified this and instead argued, "The *creed* of the Church, not the intentions of individuals, must be our standard of judgment."[43] In other words, Thornwell paid no attention to the individual who administered baptism, but instead looked to the theology of the church in which the baptism was performed. According to his view, not only does the Roman Catholic condemnation of *sola fide* invalidate its sacraments, so does its teaching regarding sacramental efficacy, namely, *ex opere operato*.

It would seem that since Thornwell argued that the creed of the RCC nullified its baptism, he must have had similar problems with the theology of other Protestant churches outside the Reformed community. Yet this was not so: "The argument, therefore, as urged against Rome, does not apply with equal force to the strictly Lutheran and the English churches, unless it can be shown that these communions embrace the principle that the sacraments confer, *ex opere operato*, the grace which they signify."[44] The Roman Catholic view of sacramental efficacy, then, seems to have been the line in the sand for Thornwell between the validity and invalidity of a church's baptism.

Thornwell spent the vast majority of his response to Hodge, well over half, explaining the errors of Rome's understanding of justification and sanctification, which in many respects is something of a red herring, since no Reformed theologian has ever argued that the Roman Catholic understanding of these doctrines is correct. The more relevant—and unanswered—question centers on ecclesiology.

Thornwell was convinced that he and the General Assembly were correct when they reversed course against some three hundred years of Reformed theology: "It was on the ground of *heresy, fatal, damnable heresy*, that Rome was declared to be apostate and her ordinances pronounced

---

43. Thornwell, "Baptism of Rome," 328.
44. Thornwell, "Baptism of Rome," 323.

invalid."[45] However, Thornwell and the Assembly went against the historic Reformed tradition without any interaction with Luther, Calvin, Turretin, or the Reformed confessions on this specific point.

Hodge was one of a very small minority who opposed the position of Thornwell and the General Assembly. Hodge was stunned: "What stern necessity has induced the Assembly to pronounce Calvin, Luther, and all the men of that generation, as well as thousands who with no other than Romish baptism have since been received into the Protestant churches, to have lived and died unbaptized?"[46] This is certainly an important question. If Thornwell was correct, then only were there thousands during the Reformation who were never rebaptized, but even before then, stretching back to Augustine or beyond, there had been no legitimate baptism in the church for well over one thousand years.

Nevertheless, Hodge does not pin the whole of his argument on this point, but focuses on the definition of baptism: "It is a sacrament, wherein the washing of water, in the name of the Father, the Son, and the Holy Ghost, does signify and seal our engrafting into Christ, and partaking of the covenant of grace, and our engagements to be the Lord's."[47] Hodge took his definition from the Shorter Catechism (q. 94) and used it to argue that the RCC meets the minimum requirements. He also invoked the Augustinian principle of the Donatist controversy: "The validity of baptism depends upon the appointment of God, and not upon the character or faith of the administrator; and therefore, any baptism which is administered according to His appointment, the church has felt constrained to admit to be baptism." Hodge argued that the baptismal doctrine of the Westminster Standards is the precise doctrine of the ancient church, in that it captures the three essential elements of a baptism: the matter, form, and intention. The matter is baptism with water; the form is washing in the name of the Trinity; and the intention is not the Roman Catholic notion of the administering priest's doctrine, but the divinely designed intention of the act.[48]

Hodge recognized that the RCC used water in the administration of baptism. He also observed that the form prescribed by the Council of Trent is accurate and identical to that of the Westminster Standards: *"Ego te baptizo in nominee Patris, et Filii, et Spiritus Sancti"* (I baptize you in the name

---

45. Thornwell, "Baptism of Rome," 343.
46. Hodge, "General Assembly," 444.
47. Hodge, "General Assembly," 445.
48. Hodge, "General Assembly," 447–47, 449.

of the Father, and the Son, and the Holy Spirit). Hodge then went on to cite Roman Catholic authorities to support the claim that the RCC believed that baptism is a sensible sign of spiritual blessings, instituted by Christ, and has a promise of grace.[49] Beyond these basic points, Hodge brought forward other arguments. To answer the charge that Roman Catholic ministers invalidated baptism because they were not duly ordained, he cited the common Protestant opinion: An ordained minister is a man appointed to perform the holy functions of teaching and administering the sacraments in any community of professing Christians.[50] He writes: "We maintain that as the Romish priests are appointed and recognized as presbyters in a community professing to believe the scriptures, the early creeds, and the decisions of the first four general councils, they are ordained ministers." For these reasons, Hodge concludes: "Consequently baptism administered by them is valid. It has accordingly been received as valid by all Protestant churches from the Reformation to the present day."[51]

Hodge also responded to the general argument that the RCC is not a true church and therefore her sacraments are invalid by taking issue with the nature of the definition of a church. According to Hodge, the critics were declaring that any community not in complete and total conformity to the definition of a pure church was no church at all. He said that such an application of the definition of a Christian would require a person to be perfected before he could be considered a true Christian.[52] Hodge believed, therefore, that a church could bear the label of a church if it held, at minimum, to a number of key doctrines. Hodge then spells out the doctrines that he believed the RCC held that qualified it to be called a church:

> They retain the doctrine of the Incarnation, which we know from the infallible word of God, is a life-giving doctrine. They retain the whole doctrine of the Trinity. They teach the doctrine of atonement far more fully and accurately than multitudes of professedly orthodox Protestants. They hold a much higher doctrine as to the necessity of divine influence, than prevails among many whom we recognize as Christians. They believe in the forgiveness of sins, the resurrection of the body, and in eternal life and judgment. These doctrines are in their

---

49. Hodge, "General Assembly," 450.
50. Hodge, "General Assembly," 454–55.
51. Hodge, "General Assembly," 457–58.
52. Hodge, "General Assembly," 462.

creeds, and however they may be perverted and overlaid, still as general propositions they are affirmed.[53]

Like his Reformed predecessors, Hodge was willing to admit that the RCC was, in some sense, still a church.[54] Like Calvin, he argued that there were two ways in which Old Testament Israel could be classified.[55] If Israel were classified according to the character of her rulers and the mass of the people, or from their authoritative declarations and acts, she clearly was apostate and idolatrous. If, however, she were classified according to the relation she still had with God and the elements of truth she professed, she was still a church. The prophets addressed her as such, and the administration of circumcision was still regarded as the sign and seal of God's covenant with her.

In addition to this Old Testament argument, which resembled Calvin's, Hodge also appealed to Turretin, who argued that the RCC could not be called a true church without qualification. Turretin, as surveyed above, argued that the RCC may be viewed either in reference to the profession of Christianity and the evangelical truths that it retains or in reference to its subjection to the papacy, with all its corruptions. Based on these qualifications, Hodge agreed with Turretin's conclusion that the RCC is a church in respect to its external form of its preaching and administration of the sacraments, and its adherence to Christian and evangelical doctrines, such as the Trinity, Christ the Mediator, and Jesus' incarnation, death, and resurrection.[56]

In his rejoinder to Thornwell, he further distinguished the nature by which the RCC can be considered a church. Hodge observes Turretin's two ways of looking at the RCC: "Under the one she is a church, i.e., a body in which the people of God still are; which retains the word of God and the preaching of it, though corrupted, and the sacraments, especially baptism." On the other hand, "As a papal body, she is not a church, i.e., her popery and all her corruptions are anti-Christian and apostate. She is not therefore a *true* church, for a *true* church is free from heresy, from superstition, from oppressive regimen, from corruption of manners, and from doubt of diffidence."[57]

---

53. Hodge, "General Assembly," 463–64.
54. Hodge, "General Assembly," 465.
55. Cf. Calvin, *Institutes*, 4.2.10–12.
56. Hodge, "General Assembly," 466–67; also idem, "Visible Church," 325.
57. Hodge, "Visible Church," 325.

Hodge even went a step further, one that would perhaps make many contemporary Presbyterians uneasy. He admitted that the RCC had grievously apostatized from the faith, held to a host of false doctrines, and had corrupt, superstitious, and even idolatrous worship. Nevertheless, he still concludes: "As a society she still retains the profession of saving doctrines, and as in point of fact, by those doctrines men are born unto God and nurtured for heaven, we dare not deny that she is still a part of the visible church."[58] This statement is not without its qualifications, for Hodge relied on Turretin's nuanced distinctions.

Based on this argumentation, Hodge concluded that baptism is not the ordinance of one particular church, but rather of the church universal, that every person who professes saving faith is a member of the church, and therefore that baptism administered by the RCC is valid. Hodge writes: "It is baptism administered by a member of the visible church, having public authority in that church, which is all that can be said of baptism administered by the Archbishop of Canterbury, or by the moderator of our Assembly."[59] The uniqueness of the conclusion of the General Assembly of 1845 was not lost on Hodge, as he closes his argument by noting: "For in protesting against the decision of 169 members of the Assembly, we can hide ourselves in the crowd of 169 millions of faithful men, who since the Reformation, have maintained the opposite and more catholic doctrine."[60]

POSITIVE CONSTRUCTION

In the argument for the validity of Roman Catholic baptisms, it is important to keep in mind the previously surveyed history. The historic majority report of the Reformed tradition has been to accept Roman Catholic baptisms. However, doctrine should not be built on tradition. Rather, all doctrine should be constructed from the Scriptures, though it should be informed by the historical development of doctrine. Therefore, the answer to this question should be based on several key points: (1) the objectivity of baptism; (2) the catholicity of the church; and (3) the constituent elements of a true baptism. It should also be noted that the following argument is not a defense of the RCC but of the objectivity of baptism as God's visible revelation.

---

58. Hodge, "Visible Church," 341.
59. Hodge, "General Assembly," 469.
60. Hodge, "General Assembly," 470.

In the debate over this question, especially in the exchange between Hodge and Thornwell, one important issue has been the question of what defines a baptism. Previous chapters have established that a sacrament is the objective revelation of God—visible revelation in contrast to invisible (or audible) revelation. God speaks audibly in Word and visibly in sacrament. A number of theologians throughout the ages have attested this point, though perhaps its significance has been forgotten at present.[61] Thornwell is among those who have affirmed this point. Of the sacraments, Thornwell explains: "They are a double preaching of the same Gospel, and confirm the Word just as an additional witness establishes a fact. They are, in short, *visible promises*, which we cannot contemplate in their true character without an increased conviction of the truth and faithfulness of God."[62] However, he did not expand the principle of the objectivity of baptism in the rest of his argument.

Since baptism, like the Word, has an objective character, it cannot be defined by man or any institutional church. God defines baptism through the revelation of Christ in the Word. God gave circumcision to Abraham, not vice versa, and denominated it as the "sign of the covenant" (Gen. 17:11). To what covenant does the narrative refer? It refers to the Abrahamic covenant, again, a covenant that God initiated with Abraham and by which He promised to make him a great nation and to bless all of the families of the earth through him (Gen. 12:2–3; 15:1–21). Circumcision symbolized the cutting off of the Seed to come, the One who would suffer on behalf of God's people (cf. Gen. 17:14; Rom. 2:25; Isa. 53:8; Jer. 11:19, 21; Col. 2:11–12; Heb. 13:12–13). Moreover, it symbolized the cutting away of the foreskin of the heart—the Spirit's effectual calling of the believer (cf. Deut. 10:16; 30:6; Rom. 2:25–29). The same is true of baptism, in that it points to the crucifixion of Christ and His baptism in the wrath of God, but also to the death, burial, and resurrection of the believer unto new life (Luke 12:50; Rom. 6:1–4). These elements are objectively a part of baptism. Whether the one baptized or the one who baptizes recognizes these things does not change the objective character of baptism.

---

61. So, e.g., Augustine, *Tractates on John* 80.3, in NPNF[1] 7.344; Luther, *The Babylonian Captivity of the Church*, LW 36.124; Philip Melanchthon, *Apology of the Augsburg Confession*, art. 13, in *Book of Concord*, 219–20; John Calvin, *Genesis*, CTS, vol. 1 (rep.; Grand Rapids: Baker, 1993), 451.

62. Thornwell, "Baptism of Rome," 300–301.

It is perhaps helpful to see the parallel between the audible and visible Word. When an ordained minister opens the Bible and reads the Word, whether he is Roman Catholic, Baptist, Methodist, or Presbyterian, the objective character of what is read does not change. No matter what doctrinal falsehood may accompany the reading of the Word of God, such as the ornate and often idolatrous liturgy of the RCC, the Word of God is still the Word of God. If it is argued, however, that when a Roman Catholic minister reads the Word it is no longer God's Word, then the authority of the Word of God does not rest in the Word and the sovereign Spirit, but subjectively in the minister who reads it or in his church. Such a construction is at odds with Scripture's self-authenticating authority and its God-breathed character, and has more in common with a Barthian conception of divine revelation.[63] While there are still some details that must be explained, suffice it for now to say that if baptism, when accompanied by the Word of God, is objective divine revelation, then like the Word, baptism is not defined by the one who administers it but by the Scriptures, by God Himself.

This is a conclusion with which portions of the evangelical community would undoubtedly disagree, especially those that align themselves with a Zwinglian understanding of the sacraments. If the sacraments are oath-pledges of a believer, then they are primarily—and for some, exclusively—subjective in nature. If baptism is an oath-pledge of a believer, then the one who makes such an oath must understand what he is saying, as it is his confession that fills the rite with meaning. More broadly, if the church defines the significance of baptism, it is no wonder that many Baptist churches will not accept a baptism unless it is done by immersion. Sprinkling and pouring, according to some Baptist theologians, do not represent a true baptism, even though such modes are clearly found in the Scriptures (Num. 8:5–22, esp. v. 7; 19:18–20; Isa. 44:3; Ezek. 36:25; 39:29; Joel 2:28–29; Zech. 12:10; Heb. 9:19–21; 11:28; 12:24).[64] If the church or individual defines baptism, then in order for a baptism to be valid, it must conform to those definitions. Hence, the first pillar for recognizing the validity of Roman Catholic baptisms is the objectivity of the sacraments as God's visible revelation.

---

63. See Barth, CD I.1.198–227; cf. Berkhof, *Systematic Theology*, 133–69; Bavinck, *Reformed Dogmatics*, 1.323–448; Edward J. Young, *The God-Breathed Scripture* (Willow Grove, Pa.: Committee for the Historian, 2007).

64. So the Baptist Confession of 1689, 29.3; Abstract of Principles, art. 15; and Baptist Faith and Message, art. 13, in Pelikan and Hotchkiss, *Creeds*, 3.319, 441.

A second point to consider is the catholicity of the church. Though there are literally thousands of denominations with differing doctrinal commitments, they are all part of one catholic church in some sense. The Scriptures are clear that there is one body of Christ (Rom. 12:4–5; 1 Cor. 10:17; 12:12; Eph. 4:4). This is not to say that all institutions that bear the title *church* are a part of the visible church. The Westminster divines, for example, define the visible church in the following manner: "The visible church, which is also catholic or universal under the gospel (not confined to one nation, as before under the law), consists of all those throughout the world that profess the true religion; and of their children: and is the kingdom of the Lord Jesus Christ, the house and family of God, out of which there is no ordinary possibility of salvation" (WCF 25.2).[65] This definition is stated somewhat abstractly, as the divines define the visible church as those who profess the true religion. However, what church is absolutely perfect and pure in its proclamation of the gospel? The divines were well aware of this problem and therefore qualify their definition with the following: "The purest churches under heaven are subject both to mixture and error; and some have so degenerated, as to become no churches of Christ, but synagogues of Satan" (WCF 25.5).

To support these statements, the divines appeal to a number of Scripture passages. For example, to show that there is one catholic church, the Westminster Standards appeal to 1 Corinthians 12:12–13: "For as the body is one and has many members, but all the members of that one body, being many, are one body, so also is Christ. For by one Spirit we were all baptized into one body—whether Jews or Greeks, whether slaves or free—and have all been made to drink into one Spirit." Paul clearly states that there is one body, one church. At the same time, individuals can be separated from the visible church, which is why the standards appeal to Romans 11:18–22. In fact, both individuals and groups of individuals organized as churches can be broken off. In the letters to the seven churches, for example, the apostle John makes reference to the Jews who are a "synagogue of Satan" (Rev. 2:9; 3:9).[66] A group of Jews was claiming to be the true קְהַל יהוה, the ἐκκλησία

---

65. On the visible and invisible church, see Heppe, *Reformed Dogmatics*, 664–69; Berkhof, *Systematic Theology*, 565–67; Bavinck, *Reformed Dogmatics*, 4.301–07. Contra Douglas Wilson, *"Reformed" Is Not Enough: Recovering the Objectivity of the Covenant* (Moscow, Idaho: Canon, 2002), 69–88.

66. The original 1646 WCF appeals to Rev. 2 and 3, whereas some modern editions, such as the OPC WCF, do not (*ad loc.*).

κυρίου (Mic. 2:5), the true church of the Lord, claiming to worship the one true God, but failing to worship Him as He has been revealed in Christ. They failed to profess the true religion and were therefore outside of the visible church. In contrast to the synagogue of Satan, the church of Smyrna was therefore visibly the true Israel.[67] This means that the visible church extends to those who profess the true religion.

It is here that the distinctions that Hodge, Turretin, and Calvin employ are helpful. Where the boundaries of the visible church lie depends on how the church is defined. If the visible church is defined in terms of the various formal institutions that claim to worship the one true God, then some churches fall outside the bounds because they clearly do not institutionally (or formally) profess the one true religion. The RCC is an example. However, whatever denominational boundaries people might establish to protect themselves from others, in the end there is only one body, one catholic church. This means that if the visible church is defined materially, in terms of the individuals who profess the true religion (which is the thrust of WCF 25.2), then the visible church extends across denominational boundaries. The visible church then materially extends into institutions, such as the RCC, that formally are not a part of the visible church. In other words, the visible church qua those who profess the true religion is within the RCC, but the RCC is not itself formally part of the visible church.

The divines define the invisible church as "the catholic or universal church, which is invisible, [and] consists of the whole number of the elect, that have been, are, or shall be gathered into one, under Christ the Head thereof; and is the spouse, the body, the fullness of him that fills all in all" (WCF 25.1). If there are genuine believers in the RCC, by what means have they been effectually called? The only way to be saved is by faith alone in Christ alone by God's grace alone, and the Holy Spirit effects this salvation through the use of the Word of God. However, does God draw people to Himself within the RCC only through the audible Word? Does He not do so through the visible Word, the "double preaching" of the gospel, to borrow Thornwell's expression? If the sacraments derive their meaning and benefit from the individual or institution that administers them, then baptism is what each church says it is. For those who reject Roman Catholic baptisms, God can only use the Word to effectually call sinners in contexts

---

67. G. K. Beale, *The Book of Revelation*, NIGTC (Grand Rapids: Eerdmans, 1997), 241–42.

such as the RCC (though some might say it is impossible for God to effectually call anyone through the RCC). However, if the sacraments derive their meaning and benefit from God through His objective revelation, then God can effectually call sinners even through the clouded, apostate ministry of the RCC. For those people who are converted under the ministry of the RCC, it is not the voice of the apostate church that they hear, and hence its erroneous theology of baptism. Rather, they hear the voice of Christ speaking in the Scriptures, and it is the Scriptures that define what baptism means. Consequently, God uses both the audible and visible Word to draw sinners to Himself even in the RCC.

Do such believers have an obligation to leave the RCC? That is another question entirely.[68] Christians should most certainly leave apostate churches. However, the specific issue at hand is whether God can act through irregular means such as a Roman Catholic baptism. Yes, He can act through irregular means if He so chooses. But do not forget the double-edged nature of the sacraments. While some in the RCC can receive the Word and sacrament to their blessing, many others undoubtedly receive them to their judgment.

This brings us to the third and final matter, namely, the elements that constitute a true baptism. Baptism is defined objectively by God's Word, but improper administration can compromise the objectivity of the sacrament. Once again the parallel between the audible and visible Word is helpful. When a minister reads the objective Word of God, he can omit words, add his own words to the text, or perhaps stutter to such a degree that the Word becomes unintelligible. In such a case, the defect lies not with the Word of God because, in the end, it has not been read. The same can be said of baptism. What elements therefore, at minimum, constitute a baptism?

Historically, baptism has been defined in terms of its matter and form. A baptism must be done with water.[69] The amount of the water is a mat-

---

68. For a historical treatment of this question in Calvin's theology, see Carlos M. N. Eire, *War Against the Idols: The Reformation of Worship from Erasmus to Calvin* (Cambridge: Cambridge University Press, 1990), 234–75.

69. Regarding Thornwell's objection to the use of oil in baptismal water—which, in his mind, invalidated the rite—a number of Reformed confessions have rejected such a practice, but have not stated that the use of oil invalidates a baptism (see Scots Confession, 22; Second Helvetic Confession, 20; and the Irish Articles, 91, in Pelikan and Hotchkiss, *Creeds*, 2.401–02, 509–10, 566; also Geoffrey Bromiley, "Baptism in the Reformed Confessions and Catechisms," in *Baptism, The New Testament, and the Church: Historical and Contemporary Studies in Honor of R. E. O. White*, JSNT, Sup 171 [Sheffield: Sheffield Academic Press, 1999], 408).

ter of adiaphora, which means immersion, pouring, and sprinkling all are acceptable and biblical. This answers the question concerning the matter of baptism. When it comes to the form, a minister must perform the baptism in the name of the triune Lord, saying, "I baptize you in the name of the Father, the Son, and the Holy Spirit," in accordance with the divine institution of Christ (Matt. 28:18–19). Were a minister to use another liquid or fail to recite the baptismal formula, the sacrament would be invalid. In such circumstances, if the error is caught, a baptism has not occurred.

However, what if a person receives an invalid baptism and the error is never noticed? In such cases, it is imperative to remember that baptism is not ultimately for the lone individual. The individual who receives an improper baptism still benefits from the sacrament when he sees others receive the visible Word in baptism. In the ecclesial context, the sacraments are not for the individual alone, but for the individual as a part of the corporate body, the church. Therefore, with every baptism the church collectively is baptized anew as one of its members individually receives baptism. Through the double preaching of the Word, the church is reminded of Christ's outpouring of the Spirit on the church. Moreover, like the repeated preaching of the gospel or reading of the Word, as others are baptized the visible Word continues to proclaim the gospel to the eyes long after the individual has received his own baptism. Baptism does not hinge on *ex opere operato* but *ex verbo vocante* (by the spoken word).[70] Churches should always seek to preserve the integrity of the administration of baptism, but all is not lost if for some reason a minister falters.[71]

It seems that these basic points (the use of water, the words of institution, and an ordained minister) at a minimum constitute a valid baptism. But such a statement undoubtedly raises questions: How can a minister of an apostate church perform a valid baptism? Does not his personal and corporate apostasy nullify the sacrament?

---

70. Jürgen Moltmann, *The Church in the Power of the Spirit* (Minneapolis: Fortress, 1993), 240.

71. I write this because a colleague (who shall remain nameless to protect the guilty!) once performed a baptism in the name of "the Father and the Son," but failed to mention the Spirit. He sent the family and their child to their seats, only to have one of his elders whisper in his ear what had just happened. Chagrined, he called the couple with their child back to the front of the church and explained that what the congregation had just witnessed was not a valid baptism. He then baptized the child in the triune name of God. Had the elder—or anyone else—not caught the error, the child still would have benefited from the sacrament through the baptism of others—the continued visible preaching of the Word—in spite of his own defective baptism.

While answering such questions could undoubtedly fill a large tome, it seems that a point should be pressed: Who validates a baptism—man or God? If it is man, then by no means would a baptism performed by a representative of an apostate church be valid. T. F. Torrance makes a helpful observation: "It was surely this anthropocentric tendency that opened up the way for the rise of Donatism."[72] However, if God defines baptism, then there is another answer. A Roman Catholic minister is a representative of an apostate church, but it helps to recognize that Protestant theologians, though they disagree with and condemn Roman Catholic apostasy, nevertheless still call the RCC a church. This is not to say that it is a manifestation of the visible church, but rather that there are still some elements of truth within the RCC. As Turretin argued, it is one thing to say that the whole body is sound, and entirely another to say that there are some sound organs.

Some still object to such a conclusion and ask whether baptisms performed by Mormon "ministers" are valid. A Mormon "baptism" is invalid given that the Mormon cult cannot in any sense be denominated a church. Mormons reject the doctrine of the Trinity, the deity of Christ, and the doctrine of salvation among many others, and have added much to the teaching of Scripture through the self-proclaimed revelation of their founder, Joseph Smith (1805–1844). They in effect reject the doctrine of the divine inspiration, inerrancy, and infallibility of Scripture. In this case, the Mormons are not like the person who reads the Bible and omits and adds words. Rather, they are reading an entirely different book and only giving lip service to the Bible. Thus, Mormon water rituals are not baptisms.

There are circumstances when a genuine group of believers might, on the spur of the moment, decide to administer baptism to a new convert. This is often the case on mission trips or perhaps in the context of personal evangelism, when well-intending but nevertheless misguided believers baptize a friend in a swimming pool. Why is such a baptism invalid? Baptism is God's visible revelation and has been given to the church, not the individual. Through the work of Christ and the outpouring of the Spirit on the church, God has gifted certain men as ordained ministers to propagate His revelation—to preach and teach the Word, whether visible or invisible (Eph. 4:11–12; 1 Tim. 3:1–7; 4:14; 5:22). Therefore, for an un-ordained person to administer baptism fails to account for the teaching of the Word

---

72. T. F. Torrance, *Theology in Reconciliation: Essays Towards Evangelical and Catholic Unity in East and West* (Grand Rapids: Eerdmans, 1975), 97.

in the administration of the sacrament. Moreover, such "baptisms" manifest a failure to recognize that the sacrament is not the property of the individual but the corporate body of Christ. The administration of baptism by a duly ordained minister means that he baptizes as the hands and voice of the church, not merely a few individuals.[73] There are no individual baptisms—all individuals are baptized as part of the one corporate body of Christ.

There will undoubtedly be some within the church who will read these conclusions and nonetheless side with Thornwell, declaring that a Roman Catholic baptism is no baptism at all. However, such a position creates more problems than it solves. Recall that Thornwell drew the line of demarcation at *ex opere operato*. Thornwell writes, "From the foregoing discussion it will be seen that Rome vitiates the *form* of the sacraments by inculcating the dogma that they produce their effects *ex opere operato*." When it comes to other churches' baptisms, Thornwell clarifies: "The argument, therefore, as urged against Rome, does not apply with equal force to the strictly Lutheran and the English churches, unless it can be shown that these communions embrace the principle that the sacraments confer *ex opere operato*, the grace which they signify."[74]

Thornwell never states why an *ex opere operato* view of the sacraments alone is the demarcation line for a valid baptism. However, he bases his argument not on the Scriptures but on Aristotle. At this point, his theology devolves into philosophy. Recall Thornwell's statement regarding the inseparability of the form and substance of baptism: "According to Aristotle it is the *forms* impressed upon the first matter which enable us to discriminate betwixt different substances." He goes on to say that the intention of the one who administers baptism "is part of the *essence* of baptism, it is consequently an error of arrangement to make it different from the form."[75] While such things may be so according to Aristotelian philosophy, they do not appear to be true according to Scripture. For example, recall Turretin's appeal to Paul, who knew that some proclaimed Christ with sinful intentions (Phil. 1:16–17). Intention can be separated from the message that is proclaimed. In Thornwell's terms, form and substance are not inextricably linked in every case.

---

73. P. T. Forsyth, *The Church and Sacraments* (1917; London: Independent Press Ltd., 1955), 184; Otto Weber, *Foundations of Dogmatics* (Grand Rapids: Eerdmans, 1983), 2.603.

74. Thornwell, "Baptism of Rome," 323.

75. Thornwell, "Baptism of Rome," 285.

Thornwell's principle—that baptism must be validated by the theology of the administering body—taken to its logical conclusion significantly narrows the scope of a true baptism. On this principle, Zwinglian baptisms are unacceptable. It seems that the vast majority of the church understands baptism in a Zwinglian fashion, yet such an understanding fails to account for what God says in baptism.[76] Heinrich Bullinger, by contrast, the chief author of the Second Helvetic Confession, explains: "The author of all sacraments is not any man but God alone. Men cannot institute sacraments. For they pertain to the worship of God, and it is not for man to appoint and prescribe a worship of God, but to accept and preserve the one he has received from God."[77]

While it is understandable to reject the Roman Catholic view because it confuses the sign with the thing signified, why would it be acceptable to say that a baptismal theology that strips the rite bare of God's grace is valid? Is it not an equally objectionable error to attribute too much grace as to attribute no grace at all to baptism? All of God's covenant signs are means of grace. Hence, why would Thornwell, or those who hold a position like his, accept Zwinglian baptisms, or indeed any baptisms that are less than that which reflects a proper theology of baptism? If Thornwell's position is carried out to its logical conclusion, churches, sessions, and consistories would be required to examine a person not only for a credible profession of faith but also for a credible theology of baptism. Those coming from a Roman Catholic background could automatically be ruled as candidates for rebaptism. However, what about Anglican baptisms? What about Baptist baptisms? What about baptisms that have been performed by non-denominational churches with no stated theology of baptism? To fail to acknowledge the objective character of baptism and its basic requirements opens Pandora's box and, however well-intended, moves the authority of baptism away from God, His authoritative revelation, and His covenant to man and the shifting sands of his subjective understanding and his created institutions.

For some churches, this is no dilemma at all, as they have made their own theological understandings of the rite the measure of what constitutes

---

76. See, e.g., the Baptist Confession of 1689, 29.3; Abstract of Principles, art. 15, in Pelikan and Hotchkiss, *Creeds*, 3.319; Baptist Faith and Message, art. 13, in Pelikan and Hotchkiss, *Creeds*, 3.441; and Baptist Faith and Message, art. 7, at www.sbc.net/bfm/default.asp.

77. Second Helvetic Confession, 19.2, in Pelikan and Hotchkiss, *Creeds*, 2.505. Broadly speaking, Bullinger's point falls under what the Reformed tradition has called the regulative principle (see WCF 21.1). Namely, it is God who prescribes worship according to His Word, not man according to his desires.

a valid baptism. Baptist churches refuse to admit baptisms done by pouring or sprinkling, and given their commitment to exclusive believer's baptism, they of course reject baptisms that have been performed on infants, whether those done by the RCC or conservative Reformed churches.[78] This practice is perfectly consistent with their theology of baptism, as they believe it is merely man's oath-pledge to God and that infants are incapable of making such an oath. However, while it may be consistent with their theology, it is entirely another question as to whether it is consistent with the Scriptures.

In the end, to accept a Roman Catholic baptism is not to cave to the pressures of ecumenism at the expense of the truth, nor is it to give legitimacy to an apostate church. Rather, it is to recognize the objectivity of baptism as God's authoritative covenantal revelation. The church must recognize that baptism is first and foremost God's covenant sign and that it points ultimately to the work of the triune Lord, not the efforts of man.

SUMMARY AND CONCLUSION

The sixteenth-century Reformers were not soft on their Roman Catholic adversaries by accepting their baptisms. Some might think that they simply did not want to grant an ounce of legitimacy to Anabaptist doctrine and instead sided with the RCC. True, theologians must scrutinize the reasons why they adopt a theological position. Regrettably, sometimes the Scriptures do not mold doctrine, but the exigencies of the day have greater sway. However, in this particular case, the Reformers stood not merely on Augustinian anti-Donatist tradition but also on the objective character of baptism. They understood that a person is baptized into the name of the one triune God, not into any one particular church, such as the RCC. For this reason, they denounced the RCC as a synagogue of Satan and the pope as the Antichrist, but nevertheless recognized that there were still flickering lights of truth piercing the dark clouds of doctrinal obscurity in the RCC—the light of the revelation of God in Word and sacrament.

What is troubling about the debate between Thornwell and Hodge at the General Assembly of 1845 was the relative speed with which the historic practice of the Reformed church was abandoned and turned on its head. No one should continue tradition for the sake of tradition, fearful of

---

78. There are and have been exceptions to this practice (see Garrett, *Systematic Theology*, 2.532).

sacrificing sacred cows at the altar of truth. Nevertheless, dispensing with the collective wisdom of the Reformation and post-Reformation without engaging it did not set a helpful precedent for future generations. What might seem objectionable and unthinkable might actually be founded on solid principles and scriptural truth. Sometimes truth can sound stranger than fiction. This is especially so at present, when theological subjectivity has only increased its intensity and the objectivity of God's revelation in Word and sacrament seems all but lost in a sea of relativity, even within the walls of the visible church and within the Reformed church.

Nevertheless, regardless of whether man chooses to recognize and accept the objectivity of God's revelation, God's Word is always God's Word. Churches of all denominations need to recognize who stands behind and ultimately administers baptism—God does not stutter. If this is so, then it seems that a limited form of ecumenical cooperation might be fostered as churches begin to receive members who have been baptized in other denominations, not because they have given in to the pressures of compromise, but because they recognize the objectivity of baptism and the authority of God's Word, both visible and invisible. This is not to say that there might not be challenging cases in the effort to determine whether a person has received a valid baptism. Nonetheless, in this debate there are clear choices: either the one who administers baptism defines it or God does so through His Word; either the minister and the church stand behind baptism or God and His promises do; either a person is baptized into one denomination or into the triune name of God—the one catholic church. To acknowledge the validity of a Roman Catholic baptism is, therefore, to acknowledge the objectivity of God's revelation in Word and sacrament. Given the alternative, this is the preferable choice.

Summary of Part III

Part III has offered a positive systematic-theological construction of the doctrine of baptism by first identifying baptism as a means of grace. Baptism is a means of grace because God's grace, His redemptive favor, is found in Christ. God objectively reveals Himself in Christ through Word and sacrament, the audible and visible revelation of God. However, there are no neutral encounters with God and His revelation. Baptism is therefore either a means of grace or judgment. The difference between grace and judgment is the absence or presence of faith in Christ.

Second, baptism is a sacrament, a sacred sign and seal of the covenant of grace. While many theologians think the term *sacrament* is antiquated and misguided, or that it is too closely associated with the sacerdotal views of the Roman Catholic Church, properly defined, it is an important and necessary term. It grounds baptism in God's covenantal administration to His people. The term recognizes that God has used numerous signs throughout redemptive history, but that He has ordained and instituted specific things as sacred signs and seals of His covenant. This is an important element, as it reminds the church that God institutes these signs, not man. However, it is always important to keep the nature of the sacramental union in mind, that is, the relationship between the sign and the thing signified. The Roman Catholic Church and much of the Lutheran Church confuses the sign and the thing signified. Those from a Zwinglian perspective radically separate the sign and the thing signified. The Reformed church has historically recognized that the sign and thing signified are distinct but not separate.

Third, as a doctrine, Christ instituted baptism in the Great Commission, not His own baptism. A proper baptism employs water and the baptismal formula, "I baptize you in the name of the Father, Son, and Holy Spirit." This formula sacramentally unites the one baptized to Christ. Through the double preaching of the Word in baptism, a person is united to Christ in

His life, death, and resurrection. Christ was plunged beneath the wrath of God in His crucifixion-baptism, circumcised from the benevolent presence of His heavenly Father. But Christ was also raised from the dead and inaugurated the new heaven and new earth, as He is the cornerstone of the centerpiece of the new creation, the eschatological temple. Therefore, those who look to Christ by faith, adult or infant, have this message of the gospel of Christ visibly preached in Word and sacrament through their baptism. In this respect, all who are baptized are sacramentally united to the crucified and risen Messiah, which means they are His disciples. Baptism must be irrefragably joined to the theology of the cross and the cost of discipleship. Regarding the mode, as was shown in Part II, all three (immersion, pouring, and sprinkling) are biblical. The meaning of baptism does not hinge on the amount of water used in the rite, but how the Word of God objectively defines it.

Fourth, the recipients of baptism are adults who make a profession of faith and their children. This is a much-debated point, but those who reject infant baptism typically construct their doctrine almost exclusively on the New Testament. Those Baptists who do appeal to the Old Testament typically misunderstand the nature of the Old Testament covenants such that they sweep away God's antecedent dealings with His people. Any theology of baptism must be founded on both testaments and grounded in God's covenantal dealings with His people. Applying the sign of the covenant to infants apart from a profession of faith is not foreign to the Scriptures. God commanded that male infants receive the sign of the covenant in the Old Testament, and in the absence of a counter-indicative command, as well as the continued unqualified use of the household formula in the New Testament, not only do women now receive the covenant sign, but so do female infants.

If baptism is an attestation of a person's profession of faith, his oath-pledge to God, then infants must be excluded. However, if baptism is first and foremost God's sign of the covenant, the sacrament that preaches that, in the wake of His crucifixion-circumcision, Christ has baptized the covenant community (the church) in Spirit and fire, then all of those who are part of the visible church receive baptism, old and young, male and female. This is not to say that all who are baptized are saved. The administration of the covenant is broader than election. Because the church lives in the overlap of the ages, the already/not yet, there will be those who are initiated into the covenant through baptism but who later fail to repent and believe the gospel and ultimately apostatize. For those who permanently apostatize, their baptism is still a sign of the covenant—but it is no longer one of blessing but of covenant sanction. The baptism of infants also does not lead to the unbiblical practice of paedocommunion. Critics of infant baptism, as well as proponents of paedocommunion, fail to distinguish the difference between covenant initiation and ratification. They also fail to coordinate the Lord's Supper with eschatology, in that the Supper is an anticipatory parousia and final judgment in the present. Only those who can rightly recognize the body and blood of Christ can examine themselves, ratify the covenant, and renew their commitment to Christ.

Fifth, and lastly, Part III covered the important question of the validity of Roman Catholic baptisms. The chapter argued for the validity of Roman Catholic baptisms on the ground of the objectivity of God's divine revelation in Word and sacrament. While the relationship between baptism and ecclesiology is certainly a challenging one, at the same time people must recognize the scriptural teaching that there is one church and one baptism. People are not baptized into the name of any one church, but into the name of the one true triune God. God defines His covenant signs, not man. God stands behind His promises, not man. God ultimately administers baptism, not man.

Conclusion

This study began by pointing out that all Christian denominations practice the rite of baptism, but that even though the administration may look the same, there are often radically different theologies standing behind the practice. The historical survey in Part I evidenced the wide range of views stretching from the post-apostolic church to the present day, showing theological chaos that demanded a fresh reexamination of the doctrine. Part I also established many of the questions for the subsequent positive construction of the doctrine.

However, this study offered an important but sometimes neglected step in the construction of the doctrine, a necessary biblical-theological survey of the Scriptures. Part II traced the doctrine of baptism from Genesis to Revelation to show that baptism does not appear *de novo* in the New Testament but, as Tertullian once observed, it first appears in Genesis 1:2. Moreover, Part II showed that baptism, or any doctrine for that matter, must take into account two fundamental theological points: Christ and covenant. God does not nakedly reveal Himself as a divine being, but reveals Himself definitively in His Son—to know Jesus is to know the Father. Moreover, as Geerhardus Vos has noted, God has not revealed Himself in a school but in covenant. God has never approached man apart from a covenant. This important canonical exegetical data showed that baptism is God's objective revelation as the visible Word. Hence, God's Word (audible and visible) brings either covenant blessing or sanction.

Part III took the exegetical data from Part II and moved forward to offer a positive construction of the doctrine and validate what the Westminster Confession says about baptism: "Baptism is a sacrament of the new testament, ordained by Jesus Christ, not only for the solemn admission of the party baptized into the visible church; but also, to be unto him a sign and seal of the covenant of grace, of his engrafting into Christ, of regeneration, of remission of sins, and of his giving up unto God, through Jesus Christ, to walk in the newness of life" (WCF 28.1). This study has not sought merely to defend entrenched tradition, but has instead shown exegetically and theologically that the Westminster divines accurately reflect Scripture's teaching on baptism.

Besides these chief points, there are two observations to be made regarding baptism. First, if anything, this study has shown that one's soteriology says a lot about his doctrine of baptism. If we want to understand what a person or church believes about salvation, we have only to ask what they believe about the sacraments. For the Roman Catholic Church, the sacraments save. God infuses His created grace, habits, and virtues substantially into the sacraments, which are then administered by the priests of the church. If a person wants to grow in grace, he needs more of God's infused grace, and so he needs the sacraments. According to the greater portion of the evangelical church, the sacraments are personal oath-pledges—the believer has secured his salvation by his personal commitment, and it is his obedience that will keep him in. At worst, the sacraments are superfluous. Who needs ministers, sacraments, or churches when a person can directly commune with God? However, if a person asks someone in a Reformed church what he believes about the sacraments, ideally the response would be that they reveal Christ, and it is Christ through God's covenant who has saved him. God reveals Himself in Christ through Word and sacrament, and therefore, like the preaching of the Word, the church needs the regular administration of the sacraments because they visibly preach Christ's gospel.

Second, the church must recognize that God reveals His extraordinary grace in Christ through the most ordinary and even foolish means: Word and sacrament. Hopefully this study has made a step in the direction of a better understanding of baptism. God not only preaches through the audible Word, but also through the visible Word. God proclaims through Word and water, and applies it by the sovereign work of His Holy Spirit. God announces through Word and water that the Seed of the woman, Abraham, and David has come and has been cut off from the land of the living in His bloody crucifixion-circumcision. He also pronounces through Word and water that His Son has now baptized not only the church but the entire creation in the Holy Spirit, a baptism of Spirit and fire. For those who look to Christ by faith, this baptism of Spirit and fire is one of cleansing, purification, and new creation. For those who refuse to believe, the baptism of Spirit and fire is one of condemnation and judgment. As the Noahic generation drowned in the waters of judgment, so unbelievers will drown in the flood-baptism of Spirit and fire.

The church, however, never offers the double preaching of the Word in the hope of judgment, but of redemption, deliverance, and salvation. Therefore, as the corporate body of Christ preaches through Word and water, the universal hope should be that those who are baptized will be united to Christ and sacramentally enter the new heaven and earth. For this reason, Word, water, and Spirit preach a message of hope and redemption.

Bibliography

Akin, Daniel G., editor. *A Theology for the Church*. Nashville: Broadman & Holman, 2007.

Aland, Kurt. *Did the Early Church Baptize Infants?* 1961; Eugene, Ore.: Wipf & Stock, 2004.

Althaus, Paul. *The Theology of Martin Luther*. Philadelphia: Fortress, 1966.

Ames, William. *The Marrow of Theology*. Translated by John Dykstra Eusden. 1968; Grand Rapids: Baker, 1997.

Aquinas, Thomas. *Summa Theologica*. Allen, Texas: Christian Classics, 1948.

Augustine. *Against Julian*. In *Fathers of the Church*. Volume 35. Translated by Michael Schumacher. Washington: Catholic University Press of America, 1957.

Bagchi, David and David C. Steinmetz, editors. *The Cambridge Companion to Reformation Theology*. Cambridge: Cambridge University Press, 2000.

Baillie, Donald M. *The Theology of the Sacraments and Other Papers*. New York: Charles Scribner's Sons, 1957.

Baillie, Robert. *The Letters and Journals of Robert Baillie*. 2 volumes. Edited by David Laing. Edinburgh: Robert Ogle, 1841.

Bainton, Roland. *Here I Stand: A Life of Martin Luther*. Nashville: Abingdon, 1978.

Baker, J. Wayne. *Heinrich Bullinger and the Covenant: The Other Reformed Tradition*. Athens, Ohio: Ohio University Press, 1980.

The Baptist Confession of Faith of 1689. Carlisle: Grace Baptist Church, n.d.

Barker, William. *Puritan Profiles: 54 Contemporaries of the Westminster Assembly*. 1996; Fearn: Mentor, 1999.

Barth, Karl. *Church Dogmatics*. 14 volumes. Edited by G. W. Bromiley and T. F. Torrance. Edinburgh: T & T Clark, 1936–69.

_____ . *The Teaching of the Church Regarding Baptism*. 1943; Eugene, Ore.: Wipf & Stock, 2006.

Barth, Markus. *Die Taufe Ein Sakrament? Ein Exegetischer Beitrag zum Gespräch über Die Kirchliche Taufe*. Zürich: Evangelischer Verlag, 1951.

Barrett, C. K. *Acts*. 2 volumes. International Critical Commentary. Edinburgh: T & T Clark, 1994.

Bateman IV, Herbert W., editor. *Three Central Issues in Contemporary Dispensationalism: A Comparison of Traditional and Progressive Views*. Grand Rapids: Kregel, 1999.

Bauckham, Richard J. *Jude, 2 Peter*. Word Biblical Commentary. Volume 50. Waco: Word Books, 1983.

Bavinck, Herman. *Reformed Dogmatics*. 4 volumes. Edited by John Bolt. Translated by John Vriend. Grand Rapids: Baker, 2003–2008.

_____ . *Saved by Grace: The Holy Spirit's Work in Calling and Regeneration*. Translated by Nelson D. Kloosterman. Edited by J. Mark Beach. Grand Rapids: Reformation Heritage, 2008.

Beale, G. K. and D. A. Carson, editors. *Commentary on the New Testament Use of the Old Testament*. Grand Rapids: Baker, 2007.

Beale, G. K. *The Book of Revelation*. New International Greek Testament Commentary. Grand Rapids: Eerdmans, 1999.

_____ . "The Old Testament Background of Paul's Reference to 'the Fruit of the Spirit' in Gal. 5:18–22." *Bulletin of Biblical Research* 15/1 (2005): 1–38.

_____ . *The Temple and the Church's Mission: A Biblical Theology of the Dwelling Place of God*. New Studies in Biblical Theology. Downers Grove, Ill.: InterVarsity, 2005.

Beardslee, III, John W., editor and translator. *Reformed Dogmatics: A Library of Protestant Thought*. New York: Oxford University Press, 1965.

Beasley-Murray, G. R. *Baptism in the New Testament*. 1962; Carlisle: Paternoster, 1997.

Beattie, Francis R. *The Presbyterian Standards*. Reprint; Greenville: Southern Presbyterian Press, 1997.

Beckwith, Roger. *Return to Rome: Confessions of an Evangelical Catholic*. Grand Rapids: Baker, 2009.

Beisner, E. Calvin, editor. *The Auburn Avenue Theology Pros and Cons: Debating the Federal Vision*. Ft. Lauderdale, Fla.: Knox Theological Seminary, 2004.

Berkhof, Louis. *Systematic Theology: New Combined Edition*. 1932–1938; Grand Rapids: Eerdmans, 1996.

Berkouwer, G. C. *The Sacraments*. Translated by Hugo Bekker. Grand Rapids: Eerdmans, 1969.

Beza, Theodore. *The Christian Faith*. Translated by James Clark. 1558; Sussex: Focus Christian Ministries Trust, 1992.

Bierma, Lyle D. "Federal Theology in the Sixteenth Century: Two Traditions?" *Westminster Theological Journal* 45 (1983): 304–21.

_____ . *German Calvinism in the Confessional Age: The Covenant Theology of Caspar Olevianus*. Grand Rapids: Baker, 1996.

_____ . *The Doctrine of the Sacraments in the Heidelberg Catechism: Melanchthonian, Calvinist, or Zwinglian*. Studies in Reformed Theology and History. Number 4. Princeton: Princeton Theological Seminary, 1999.

Bierma, Lyle D., et al., editors. *An Introduction to the Heidelberg Catechism: Sources, History, and Theology*. Grand Rapids: Baker, 2005.

Blenkinsopp, Joseph. *Prophecy and Canon*. Notre Dame, Ind.: University of Notre Dame Press, 1977.

Block, Daniel I. *The Book of Ezekiel*. 2 volumes. New International Commentary on the Old Testament. Grand Rapids: Eerdmans, 1998.

Bloesch, Donald G. *The Church: Sacraments, Worship, Ministry, Mission*. Downers Grove, Ill.: InterVarsity, 2002.

Bloom, Harold. *The American Religion*. 1994; New York: Chu Hartley, 2006.

Bock, Darrell L. *Acts*. Baker Exegetical Commentary on the New Testament. Grand Rapids: Baker, 2007.

_____ . *Luke*. 2 volumes. Baker Exegetical Commentary on the New Testament. Grand Rapids: Baker, 1996.

Bockmuehl, Markus. *Seeing the Word: Refocusing New Testament Study*. Grand Rapids: Baker, 2006.

Bonaventure. *The Works of Bonaventure: Breviloquium*. Volume 2. Edited by Jose de Vinck. Paterson, N.J.: St. Anthony Guild Press, 1963.

Bonhoeffer, Dietrich. *Discipleship. Dietrich Bonhoeffer Works*. Volume 4. Edited by Geoffrey B. Kelly and John D. Godsey. Translated by Barbara Green and Reinhard Krauss. Minneapolis: Fortress, 2003.

_____ . *Sanctorum Communio: A Theological Study of the Sociology of the Church. Dietrich Bonhoeffer Works*. Volume 1. Edited by Clifford J. Green. Translated by Reinhard Krauss and Nancy Lukens. Minneapolis: Fortress, 1998.

_____ . *True Patriotism: Letters, Lectures and Notes 1939–45*. Volume 3. Edited by Edwin H. Robertson. 1958–1972; New York: Harper and Row, 1973.

The Book of Church Order of the Orthodox Presbyterian Church. Willow Grove, Pa.: The Committee on Christian Education of the OPC, 2005.

Bornkamm, Heinrich. *Luther and the Old Testament*. Philadelphia: Fortress, 1969.

Borreson, Glenn. "Bonhoeffer on Baptism: Discipline for the Sake of the Gospel." *Word and World* 1/1 (2006): 20–31.

Bromiley, G. W. *Children of Promise: The Case for Baptizing Infants*. Eugene, Ore.: Wipf & Stock, 1998.

_____ , editor. *Zwingli and Bullinger*. Philadelphia: Westminster, 1953.

Brown, Colin, editor. *New International Dictionary of New Testament Theology*. 4 volumes. Grand Rapids: Zondervan, 1986.

_____ . "What Was John the Baptist Doing?" *Bulletin for Biblical Research* 7 (1997): 37–50.

Brown, Francis, et al. *The New Brown-Driver-Briggs-Gensenius Hebrew and English Lexicon*. Peabody, Mass.: Hendrickson, 1979.

Bruce, F. F. *The Book of Acts*. New International Commentary on the New Testament. Grand Rapids: Eerdmans, 1988.

_____ . *The Epistles to the Colossians, to Philemon, and to the Ephesians*. New International Commentary on the New Testament. Grand Rapids: Eerdmans, 1984.

Bultmann, Rudolf. *Theology of the New Testament: Complete in One Volume*. New York: Charles Scribner's Sons, 1951–1955.

Calvin, John. *Calvin's Commentaries*. Calvin Translation Society. 22 volumes. Reprint; Grand Rapids: Baker, 1993.

_____ . *Calvin's New Testament Commentaries*. 12 volumes. Edited by T. F. Torrance and J. B. Torrance. 1961–1965; Grand Rapids: Eerdmans, 1995.

_____ . *Institutes of the Christian Religion*. Library of Christian Classics. Volumes 20–21. Edited by John T. McNeill. Translated by Ford Lewis Battles. Philadelphia: Westminster, 1960.

_____ . *Institutes of the Christian Religion: 1536 Edition*. Translated by Ford Lewis Battles. 1975; Grand Rapids: Eerdmans, 1995.

_____ . *John Calvin's Sermons on Timothy and Titus*. 1579; Edinburgh: Banner of Truth, 1983.

_____ . *The Bondage and Liberation of the Will: A Defense of the Orthodox Doctrine of Human Choice Against Pighius*. Edited by A. N. S. Davies. Translated by G. I. Davies. Grand Rapids: Baker, 1996.

_____ . *Selected Works of John Calvin: Tracts and Letters*. 7 volumes. Edited by Henry Beveridge and Jules Bonnet. Translated by Henry Beveridge. 1849; Grand Rapids: Baker, 1983.

Capes, David B. "Intertextual Echoes in the Matthean Baptismal Narrative." *Bulletin of Biblical Research* 9 (1999): 37–49.

Cassuto, Umberto. *A Commentary on the Book of Exodus*. 1953; Jerusalem: Magnes Press, 1997.

Catechism of the Catholic Church. Ligouri, Mo.: Ligouri Publications, 1994.

The Catechism of the Council of Trent: Ordered by the Council of Trent. Edited by St. Charles Borromeo. 1566; Rockford: Tan Books and Publishers, 1982.

Caquot, A. and M. Delcor, editors. *Mélanges Bibliques et Orientaux en l'honneur de M. Henri Cazelles*. Neukirchen: Verglang, 1981.

Carson, D. A. *Exegetical Fallacies*. 1984; Grand Rapids: Baker, 1993.

_____ , editor. *From Sabbath to Lord's Day*. Eugene, Ore.: Wipf & Stock, 1999.

_____ . *Matthew*. 2 volumes. Expositor's Bible Commentary. Grand Rapids: Zondervan, 1995.

_____ . *The Gospel According to John*. Pillar New Testament Commentary. Grand Rapids: Eerdmans, 1991.

Childs, Brevard. *Biblical Theology of the Old and New Testaments: Theological Reflections on the Christian Bible*. Minneapolis: Fortress, 1992.

Chemnitz, Martin. *Loci Theologici*. 2 volumes. Translated by J. A. O. Preus. St. Louis: Concordia, 1989.

Clark, R. Scott. *Caspar Olevian and the Substance of the Covenant: The Double Benefit of Christ*. Edinburgh: Rutherford House, 2005.

_____ . "Iustitia Imputata Christi: Alien or Proper to Luther's Doctrine of Justification?" *Concordia Theological Quarterly* 70 (2006): 269–310.

_____ . *Recovering the Reformed Confession*. Phillipsburg, N.J.: P & R, 2008.

Collins, Adela Yarbro. *Cosmology and Eschatology in Jewish and Christian Apocalypticism*. Leiden: Brill, 2000.

The Confession of Faith and Catechisms of the Orthodox Presbyterian Church with Proof Texts. Willow Grove, Pa.: Committee on Christian Education of the OPC, 2005.

Coniaris, Anthony M. *Introducing the Orthodox Church*. Minneapolis: Light and Life, 1982.

Craigie, Peter C. *The Book of Deuteronomy*. New International Commentary on the Old Testament. Grand Rapids: Eerdmans, 1976.

_____ . *Psalms 1–50*. Word Biblical Commentary. Dallas: Word, 1983.

Cullmann, Oscar. *Baptism in the New Testament*. London: SCM Press, 1961.

Dabney, R. L. "The Changes Proposed in our Book of Discipline." *The Southern Presbyterian Review* 12/1 (1859): 36–82.

Danker, Frederick William, editor. *A Greek Lexicon of the New Testament and Other Early Christian Literature*. Third Edition. 1957; Chicago: University of Chicago Press, 2000.

Dempster, Stephen G. *Dominion and Dynasty: A Theology of the Hebrew Bible*. New Studies in Biblical Theology. Downers Grove, Ill.: InterVarsity, 2003.

Dorsey, David A. *The Literary Structure of the Old Testament: A Commentary on Genesis–Malachi*. Grand Rapids: Baker, 1999.

Dumbrell, William J. *Covenant and Creation: A Theology of Old Testament Covenants*. 1984; Carlisle: Paternoster, 2000.

_____ . *The End of the Beginning: Revelation 21–22 and the Old Testament.* 1985; Eugene, Ore.: Wipf & Stock, 2001.

Dunn, James D. G. *Baptism in the Holy Spirit.* Philadelphia: Westminster Press, 1970.

_____ . *Jesus, Paul, and the Law: Studies in Mark and Galatians.* Louisville: Westminster John Knox, 1990.

_____ . *Jesus and the Spirit: A Study of the Religious and Charismatic Experience of Jesus and the First Christians as Reflected in the New Testament.* 1975; Grand Rapids: Eerdmans, 1997.

_____ . *The Epistle to the Galatians.* Black's New Testament Commentary. Peabody, Mass.: Hendrickson, 1993.

Duncan, J. Ligon, editor. *The Westminster Confession into the 21st Century.* 3 volumes. Fearn: Mentor, 2003.

Durham, John I. *Exodus.* Word Biblical Commentary. Volume 3. Dallas: Word, 1987.

Eichrodt, Walther. *Theology of the Old Testament.* 2 volumes. Translated by J. A. Baker. Louisville: Westminster John Knox, 1961.

Eire, Carlos M. N. *War Against the Idols: The Reformation of Worship from Erasmus to Calvin.* Cambridge: Cambridge University Press, 1990.

Ellis, E. Earle. *The Gospel of Luke.* New Century Bible Commentary. 1966; Grand Rapids: Eerdmans, 1996.

Enns, Peter. *Exodus.* New International Version Application Commentary. Grand Rapids: Zondervan, 2000.

Erickson, Millard J. *Christian Theology.* Grand Rapids: Baker, 1985.

Estep. William R. *The Anabaptist Story: An Introduction to Sixteenth-Century Anabaptism.* 1963; Grand Rapids: Eerdmans, 1996.

Evans, Craig A., editor. *From Prophecy to Testament: The Function of the Old Testament in the New.* Peabody, Mass.: Hendrickson, 2004.

Fee, Gordon D. *The First Epistle to the Corinthians.* New International Commentary on the New Testament. Grand Rapids: Eerdmans, 1987.

Flannery, Austin, O. P., editor. *Vatican Council II: Constitutions, Decrees, Declarations.* New York: Costello Publishing Co., 1995.

Forde, Gerhard O. *On Being a Theologian of the Cross: Reflections on Luther's Heidelberg Disputation, 1518.* Grand Rapids: Eerdmans, 1997.

Forsyth, P. T. *The Church and Sacraments*. 1917; London: Independent Press, Ltd., 1955.

France, R. T. *The Gospel of Mark*. New International Greek Testament Commentary. Grand Rapids: Eerdmans, 2002.

Francke, August Hermann. *A Guide to Reading and Study of the Holy Scriptures*. Philadelphia: David Hogan, 1823.

Franke, John. *The Character of Theology: An Introduction to Its Nature, Task, and Purpose. A Post-Conservative Evangelical Approach*. Grand Rapids: Baker, 2005.

Furcha, E. J. and H. Wayne Pipkin, editors. *Prophet, Pastor, Protestant: The Work of Huldrych Zwingli After Five Hundred Years*. Allison Park, Pa.: Pickwick, 1984.

Gabler, Johann P. "An Oration on the Proper Distinction Between Biblical and Dogmatic Theology and the Specific Objectives of Each." In *The Flowering Old Testament Theology*. Edited by Ben C. Ollenburger, Elmer A. Martens, and Gerhard F. Hasel. Winona Lake: Eisenbrauns, 1992.

Gaffin, Jr., Richard B. *Perspectives On Pentecost: New Testament Teaching on the Gifts of the Holy Spirit*. Phillipsburg, N.J.: P & R, 1979.

_____ . *Resurrection and Redemption: A Study in Paul's Soteriology*. Phillipsburg, N.J.: P & R, 1987.

Ganoczy, Alexandre. *The Young Calvin*. Philadelphia: Westminster, 1987.

Garrett, J. L. *Systematic Theology: Biblical, Historical, and Evangelical*. 2 volumes. Grand Rapids: Eerdmans, 1995.

George, Timothy. "The Reformed Doctrine of Believer's Baptism." *Interpretation* 47 (1993): 242–54.

Gerrish, B. A. *Grace and Gratitude: The Eucharistic Theology of John Calvin*. Edinburgh: T & T Clark, 1993.

Gerstner, John H. *The Rational Biblical Theology of Jonathan Edwards*. 3 volumes. Orlando, Fla.: Ligonier Ministries, 1993.

Gillespie, George. *Treatise of Miscellany Questions*. Edinburgh: Robert Ogle, and Oliver & Boyd, 1844.

Gilmore, Alec, editor. *Christian Baptism: A Fresh Attempt to Understand the Rite in Terms of Scripture, History, and Theology*. Philadelphia: Judson Press, 1959.

Goldingay, John. *The Message of Isaiah: A Literary-Theological Commentary.* Edinburgh: T & T Clark, 2005.

González, Justo. *A History of Christian Thought.* 3 volumes. Nashville: Abingdon, 1987.

Gootjes, Nicolaas. *The Belgic Confession: Its History and Sources.* Grand Rapids: Baker, 2007.

Goppelt, Leonhard. *A Commentary on 1 Peter.* 1978; Grand Rapids: Eerdmans, 1993.

_____ . *Typos: The Typological Interpretation of the Old Testament in the New.* 1939; Grand Rapids: Eerdmans, 1982.

Graves, Frank Pierrepont. *Peter Ramus and the Education Reformation of the Sixteenth Century.* New York: MacMillan, 1912.

Grenz, Stanley. *Theology for the Community of God.* Nashville: Broadman & Holman, 1994.

Grislis, Egil. "Calvin's Doctrine of Baptism." *Church History* 31 (1962): 45–65.

Grudem, Wayne. *Systematic Theology: An Introduction to Biblical Doctrine.* Grand Rapids: Zondervan, 1994.

_____ . *The Gift of Prophecy in 1 Corinthians.* 1982; Eugene, Ore.: Wipf & Stock, 1999.

_____ . "Perseverance of the Saints: A Case Study from Hebrews 6:4–6 and Other Warning Passages in Hebrews." In *The Grace of God and the Bondage of the Will.* Edited by Thomas R. Schreiner and Bruce A. Ware. 2 volumes. Grand Rapids: Baker, 1995.

Gunkel, Herman. *Genesis.* Macon, Ga.: Mercer University Press, 1997.

Gutiérrez, Gustavo. *A Theology of Liberations.* 1971; New York: Orbis Books, 1988.

Haffemann, Scott J., editor. *Biblical Theology: Retrospect & Prospect.* Downers Grove, Ill.: InterVarsity, 2002.

Hägglund, Bengt. *History of Theology.* 1968; St. Louis: Concordia, 2007.

Hagner, Donald A. *Matthew 1–13.* Word Biblical Commentary. Volume 33. Dallas: Word Books, 1993.

Hahn, Scott W. "The Authority of Mystery: The Biblical Theology of Benedict XVI." *Letter & Spirit* 2 (2006): 97–140.

Hall, Thor. "The Possibilities of Erasmian Influence on Denck and Hübmaier in Their Views on Freedom of the Will." *Mennonite Quarterly Review* 35 (1961): 149–70.

Hampson, Daphne. *Christian Contradictions: The Structures of Lutheran and Catholic Thought*. Cambridge: Cambridge University Press, 2001.

Harder, Leeland, editor. *The Sources of Swiss Anabaptism: The Grebel Letters and Related Documents*. Scottdale, Pa.: Herald Press, 1985.

Hart, D. G. *Deconstructing Evangelicalism: Conservative Protestantism in the Age of Billy Graham*. Grand Rapids: Baker, 2004.

Hawthorne, Gerald F., Ralph P. Martin, and Daniel G. Reid, editors. *Dictionary of Paul and His Letters*. Downers Grove, Ill.: InterVarsity, 1993.

Hays, Richard B. *Echoes of Scripture in the Letters of Paul*. New Haven: Yale University Press, 1989.

Heil, John Paul. "Jesus with the Wild Animals in Mark 1:13." *Catholic Biblical Quarterly* 68 (2006): 63–78.

Hendrickson, William. *Luke*. New Testament Commentary. Grand Rapids: Baker, 1996.

Heppe, Heinrich. *Reformed Dogmatics: Set Out and Illustrated from the Sources*. Edited by Ernst Bizer. Translated by G. T. Thomson. London: George Allen & Unwin Ltd., 1950.

Hess, Richard S. *Joshua*. Tyndale Old Testament Commentary. Downers Grove, Ill.: InterVarsity, 1996.

Hess, Richard S. and David Toshio Tsumura, editors. *"I Studied Inscripturations from Before the Flood."* Winona Lake: Eisenbrauns, 1994.

Hillers, Delbert R. *Treaty-Curses of the Old Testament Prophets*. Rome: Pontifical Biblical Institute, 1964.

Hippolytus. *The Treatise on the Apostolic Tradition of St. Hippolytus of Rome, Bishop and Martyr*. London: Alban Press, 1992.

Hodge, A. A. *The Confession of Faith: A Handbook of Christian Doctrine Expounding the Westminster Confession*. Reprint; London: Banner of Truth, 1958.

Hodge, Charles. *1 & 2 Corinthians*. 1857; Edinburgh: Banner of Truth, 1994.

_____ . "Is the Church of Rome a Part of the Visible Church?" *The Biblical Repertory and Princeton Review* 18/2 (1846): 320–44.

_____ . *Systematic Theology*. 3 volumes. Reprint; Grand Rapids: Eerdmans, 1993.

_____ . "The General Assembly of 1845." *The Biblical Repertory and Princeton Review* 17/3 (1845): 428–71.

_____ . "The General Assembly of 1859." *The Biblical Repertory and Princeton Review* 31/3 (1859): 538–618.

Hoeksema, Herman. *Reformed Dogmatics*. 1966; Grand Rapids: Reformed Free Publishing Association, 1985.

Hooker, Morna. *The Gospel According to St. Mark*. Black's New Testament Commentary. 1991; Peabody, Mass.: Hendrickson, 1999.

Horton, Michael S. *God of Promise: Introducing Covenant Theology*. Grand Rapids: Baker, 2006.

_____ . *Lord and Servant: A Covenant Christology*. Louisville: Westminster John Knox, 2005.

_____ . "Meeting a Stranger: A Covenantal Epistemology." *Westminster Theological Journal* 66.2 (2004): 259–73.

Huey, F. B. and Bruce Corley, *A Student's Dictionary for Biblical and Theological Studies*. Grand Rapids: Academie Books, 1983.

Jackson, Samuel MacCauly, editor. *The New Schaff-Herzog Encyclopedia of Religious Knowledge*. New York: Funk and Wagnalls, 1909.

Jenson, Robert. *Visible Word: The Interpretation and Practice of Christian Sacraments*. Philadelphia: Fortress, 1978.

Jeremias, Joachim. *Infant Baptism in the First Four Centuries*. 1960; Eugene, Ore.: Wipf & Stock, 2004.

_____ . *The Origins of Infant Baptism: A Further Study in Reply to Kurt Aland*. 1926; Eugene, Ore.: Wipf & Stock, 2004.

Jewett, Paul K. *Infant Baptism and the Covenant of Grace*. Grand Rapids: Eerdmans, 1978.

Josephus. *The Works of Josephus: Complete and Unabridged*. Translated by William Whitson. 1987; Peabody, Mass.: Hendrickson, 1999.

Kärkkäinen, Veli-Matti, *An Introduction to Ecclesiology: Ecumenical, Historical & Global Perspectives*. Downers Grove, Ill.: InterVarsity, 2002.

Kelley, J. N. D. *Early Christian Doctrines*. San Francisco: Harper Collins, 1978.

_____ . *The Pastoral Epistles*. Black's New Testament Commentary. 1960; Peabody, Mass.: Hendrickson, 1998.

Kearney, Peter J. "Creation and Liturgy: The P Redaction of Ex 25–40." *Zeitschrift für die Alttestamentliche Wissenschaft* 89 (1977): 375–87.

Kim, Jaegwon and Ernest Sosa, editors. *A Companion to Metaphysics*. Oxford: Blackwell, 1995.

Kistemaker, Simon J. *Acts*. New Testament Commentary. Grand Rapids: Baker, 1990.

Kistemaker, Simon J. *The Parables: Understanding the Stories Jesus Told*. Grand Rapids: Baker, 1980.

Kline, Meredith G. *By Oath Consigned: A Reinterpretation of the Covenant Signs of Circumcision and Baptism*. Grand Rapids: Eerdmans, 1968.

_____ . *Glory in Our Midst: A Biblical-Theological Reading of Zechariah's Night Visions*. Overland Park, Kan.: Two Age Press, 2001.

_____ . *God, Heaven, and Har Magedon: A Covenantal Tale of Cosmos and Telos*. Eugene, Ore.: Wipf & Stock, 2006.

_____ . *Images of the Spirit*. Eugene, Ore.: Wipf & Stock, 1998.

_____ . *Kingdom Prologue: Genesis Foundations for a Covenantal Worldview*. Overland Park, Kan.: Two Age Press, 2000.

_____ . *The Structure of Biblical Authority*. 1989; Eugene, Ore.: Wipf & Stock, 1997.

_____ . *Treaty of the Great King: The Covenant Structure of Deuteronomy*. Grand Rapids: Eerdmans, 1963.

Knight, III, George W. *Prophecy in the New Testament*. Dallas: Presbyterian Heritage Publications, 1988.

_____ . *The Pastoral Epistles*. New International Greek Testament Commentary. Grand Rapids: Eerdmans, 1992.

Koehler, Ludwig and Walter Baumgartner. *The Hebrew and Aramaic Lexicon of the Old Testament*. 2 volumes. Translated and edited by M. E. J. Richardson. Leiden: Brill, 2001.

Kolb, Robert. *Martin Luther as Prophet, Teacher, and Hero: Images of the Reformer, 1520–1620*. Grand Rapids: Baker, 1999.

Kolb, Robert and Timothy J. Wengert, editors. *The Book of Concord: The Confessions of the Evangelical Lutheran Church*. Minneapolis: Fortress, 2000.

Laansma, Jon. *I Will Give You Rest*. Wissenschaftlische Untersuchungen zum Neuen Testament. Tübingen: Mohr Siebeck, 1997.

Lane, William L. *Hebrews 9–13*. Word Biblical Commentary. Dallas: Word Books, 1991.

LaRondelle, Hans K. *The Israel of God in Prophecy: Principles of Interpretation*. Berrien Springs, Mich.: Andrews University Press, 1983.

Leith, John H. *Introduction to the Reformed Tradition*. 1977; Atlanta: John Knox Press, 1981.

Leithart, Peter J. *The Priesthood of the Plebs: A Theology of Baptism*. Eugene, Ore.: Wipf & Stock, 2003.

Letham, Robert. "Amandus Polanus: A Neglected Theologian?" *Sixteenth Century Journal* 21/3 (1990): 463–76.

_____ . *The Holy Trinity: In Scripture, History, Theology, and Worship*. Phillipsburg, N.J.: P & R, 2004.

Lightfoot, John. *The Journal of the Proceedings of the Assembly of Divines*. London: J. F. Dove, 1824.

Lohse, Bernhard. *Martin Luther's Theology: Its Historical and Systematic Development*. Minneapolis: Fortress, 1999.

Lombardi, Petri. *Sententiae in IV Libris Distinctae*. 2 volumes. Grottaferrata: Collegii S. Bonaventurae ad Claras Aquas, 1981.

Longenecker, Richard N. *The Book of Acts*. Expositor's Bible Commentary. Grand Rapids: Zondervan, 1995.

Luzarraga, J. *Las Tradiciones de La Nube en Law Biblia y en el Judaismo Primitivo*. Rome: Biblical Institute Press, 1972.

Machen, J. Gresham. *What Is Faith?* 1937; Edinburgh: Banner of Truth, 1991.

Malone, Fred A. *The Baptism of Disciples Alone: A Covenantal Argument for Credobaptism Versus Paedobaptism*. 2003; Cape Coral, Fla.: Founders Press, 2007.

Marcel, Pierre-Charles. *The Biblical Doctrine of Infant Baptism: Sacrament of the Covenant of Grace*. 1953; London: James Clarke & Co., 2002.

Marshall, I. Howard. "The Meaning of the Verb 'to Baptize.'" *Evangelical Quarterly* 45/3 (1973): 130–40.

Melanchthon, Philip. *Common Places (1521)*. Library of Christian Classics. Philadelphia: Westminster, 1969.

_____ . *Loci Communes (1543)*. Translated by J. A. O. Preus. St. Louis: Concordia Publishing House, 1992.

Metzger, Bruce. *A Textual Commentary on the Greek New Testament*. Stuttgart: German Bible Society, 2002.

McComiskey, Thomas E., editor. *The Minor Prophets*. 3 volumes. Grand Rapids: Baker, 1998.

McDonald, Neil B. and Carl Trueman, editors. *Calvin, Barth, and Reformed Theology*. Milton Keynes: Paternoster, 2008.

McLaren, Brian. *A Generous Orthodoxy*. Grand Rapids: Zondervan, 2004.

McGrath, Alister E. *Historical Theology: An Introduction to the History of Christian Thought*. Oxford: Blackwell, 1998.

_____ . *Reformation Thought: An Introduction*. 1988; Grand Rapids: Baker, 1993.

Milgrom, Jacob. *Numbers*. Jewish Publication Society Torah Commentary. New York: Jewish Publication Society, 1990.

Miller, Patrick D. *Deuteronomy*. Louisville: John Knox, 1990.

Miller, Perry. "The Half-Way Covenant." *The New England Quarterly* 6/4 (1933): 676–715.

Mitchell, Alexander F. and John Struthers, editors. *Minutes of the Sessions of the Westminster Assembly of Divines*. Edinburgh and London: William Blackwood and Sons, 1874.

Moltmann, Jürgen. *The Church in the Power of the Spirit: A Contribution to Messianic Ecclesiology*. 1975; Philadelphia: Fortress, 1993.

Moo, Douglas J. *The Epistle to the Romans*. New International Commentary on the New Testament. Grand Rapids: Eerdmans, 1996.

Morgenstern, J. "'The Bloody Husband' (?) (Exod. 4:24–26) Once Again." *Hebrew Union College Annual* 34 (1963): 35–70.

Motyer, J. Alec. *Isaiah*. Tyndale Old Testament Commentary. Downers Grove, Ill.: InterVarsity, 1999.

_____ . *The Prophecy of Isaiah*. Downers Grove, Ill.: InterVarsity, 1993.

Moyise, Steve. *The Old Testament in the New*. London: T & T Clark, 2001.

Mueller, J. T. *Christian Dogmatics*. St. Louis: Concordia, 1955.

Muller, Richard A. *After Calvin: Studies in the Development of a Theological Tradition.* Oxford: Oxford University Press, 2003.

_____ . *Dictionary of Latin and Greek Theological Terms: Drawn Principally from Protestant Scholastic Theology.* Grand Rapids: Baker, 1985.

_____ . "How Many Points?" *Calvin Theological Journal* 28 (1993): 425–33.

_____ . *Post-Reformation Reformed Dogmatics: Prolegomena to Theology.* Volume 1. Grand Rapids: Baker, 1987.

_____ . *Post-Reformation Reformed Dogmatics.* 4 volumes. Grand Rapids: Baker, 2003.

Muller, Richard A. and Rowland S. Ward. *Scripture and Worship: Biblical Interpretation & the Directory for Worship.* Phillipsburg, N.J.: P & R, 2007.

Mullins, E. Y. *The Axioms of Religion.* Edited by Timothy and Denise George. 1908; Nashville: Broadman & Holman, 1997.

Murray, John. *Christian Baptism.* Phillipsburg, N.J.: P & R, 1980.

_____ . *Collected Writings of John Murray.* 4 volumes. Edinburgh: Banner of Truth, 1977.

_____ . *Redemption Accomplished and Applied.* Grand Rapids: Eerdmans, 1955.

_____ . *The Covenant of Grace: A Biblico-Theological Study.* Phillipsburg, N.J.: P & R, 1987.

_____ . *The Epistle to the Romans.* New International Commentary on the New Testament. 1959–1965; Grand Rapids: Eerdmans, 1968.

Neusner, Jacob, editor and translator. *The Mishnah: A New Translation.* New Haven: Yale University Press, 1988.

Niesel, Wilhelm. *The Theology of Calvin.* 1956; Cambridge: James Clarke, 2002.

O'Brien, Peter T. *Colossians, Philemon.* Word Biblical Commentary. Volume 44. Dallas: Word, 1982.

Old, Hughes Oliphant. *The Shaping of the Reformed Baptismal Rite in the Sixteenth Century.* Grand Rapids: Eerdmans, 1992.

Olson, Roger E. *Arminian Theology: Myths and Realities.* Downers Grove, Ill.: InterVarsity, 2006.

Ong, Walter J. *Ramus, Method, and the Decay of Dialogue: From the Art of Discourse to the Art of Reason.* Cambridge: Harvard University Press, 1958.

Origen. *Homilies on Leviticus: 1–16.* Translated by Gary Wayne Barkley. Washington: Catholic University Press of America, 1990.

_____ . *Homilies on Luke: Fragments on Luke.* Translated by Joseph T. Lienhard. Washington: Catholic University Press of America, 1996.

Oswalt, John N. *The Book of Isaiah.* 2 volumes. New International Commentary on the Old Testament. Grand Rapids: Eerdmans, 1998.

Pannenberg, Wolfhart. *Systematic Theology.* 3 volumes. 1993; Grand Rapids: Eerdmans, 1998.

Pelikan, Jaroslav and Valerie Hotchkiss, editors. *Creeds and Confessions of Faith in the Christian Tradition.* 3 volumes. New Haven: Yale University Press, 2003.

Pelikan, Jaroslav. *The Christian Tradition: A History of the Development of Doctrine.* 5 volumes. Chicago: University of Chicago Press, 1971.

Pieper, Francis. *Christian Dogmatics.* 4 volumes. St. Louis: Concordia, 1953.

Piper, John. *Brothers, We Are Not Professionals: A Plea to Pastors for Radical Ministry.* Nashville: Broadman & Holman, 2002.

_____ . *The Justification of God: An Exegetical & Theological Study of Romans 9:1–23.* 1983; Grand Rapids: Baker, 1993.

Pipkin, H. Wayne and John H. Yoder, editors and translators. *Balthasar Hübmaier.* Scottdale, Pa.: Herald Press, 1989.

Pipkin, H. Wayne. "The Baptismal Theology of Balthasar Hübmaier." *Mennonite Quarterly Review* 65 (1991): 34–53.

Price, B. B. *Medieval Thought: An Introduction.* Oxford: Blackwell, 1996.

Pritchard, James B. *Ancient Near East.* 2 volumes. Princeton University Press, 1978.

Polanus, Amandus. *The Substance of Christian Religion, Soundly Set Forth in Two Books.* London: 1595.

Porter, Stanley and Anthony R. Cross, editors. *Dimensions of Baptism: Biblical and Theological Studies. Journal for the Study of the New Testament Supplement* 234. Sheffield: Sheffield Academic Press, 2003.

_____ , editors. *Baptism, the New Testament, and the Church. Historical and Contemporary Studies in Honor of R. E. O. White. Journal for the Study of the New Testament Supplement 171.* Sheffield: Sheffield Academic Press, 1999.

The Racovian Catechism. Translated by Thomas Rees. 1818; Indianapolis: Christian Educational Services, 1994.

Rahner, Karl, editor. *Encyclopedia of Theology: A Concise Sacramentum Mundi.* London: Burns & Oates, 2004.

_____ . *The Church and the Sacraments.* London: Burns & Oates, 1963.

Raitt, Jill. "Three Inter-Related Principles in Calvin's Unique Doctrine of Infant Baptism." *Sixteenth Century Journal* 11/1 (1980): 51–61.

Ramus, Peter. *The Logike.* 1574; Leeds: The Scholars Press, 1966.

Rayburn, Robert S. "The Presbyterian Doctrines of Covenant Children, Covenant Nurture, and Covenant Succession." *Presbyterion* 22/2 (1996): 76–112.

Reid, James. *Memoirs of the Westminster Divines.* 2 volumes. 1811; Edinburgh: Banner of Truth, 1982.

Reymond, Robert. *A New Systematic Theology of the Christian Faith.* Second Edition. Nashville: Thomas Nelson, 1998[2].

Ridderbos, Herman. *Paul: An Outline of His Theology.* Grand Rapids: Eerdmans, 1975.

_____ . *The Coming of the Kingdom.* Phillipsburg, N.J.: P & R, 1962.

_____ . *The Gospel of John: A Theological-Commentary.* 1987; Grand Rapids: Eerdmans, 1997.

Riggs, John W. *Baptism in the Reformation Tradition: An Historical and Practical Theology.* Louisville: Westminster John Knox, 2002.

Rupp, Gordon, editor. *Luther and Erasmus on Free Will and Salvation.* Library of Christian Classics. Volume 17. Philadelphia: Westminster, 1957.

Rutherford, Samuel. *The Covenant of Life Opened.* Edinburgh, 1655.

Ryrie, Charles. *Basic Theology: A Popular Systematic Guide to Understanding Biblical Truth.* Wheaton, Ill.: Victor Books, 1986.

_____ . *Dispensationalism Today.* Chicago: Moody Press, 1970.

Sarna, Nahum. *Genesis*. Jewish Publication Society Torah Commentary. New York: Jewish Publication Society, 1989.

Scaer, David P. "Baptism and the Lord's Supper in the Life of the Church." *Concordia Theological Quarterly* 45/1 (1981): 37–57.

————— . "Luther, Baptism, and the Church Today." *Concordia Theological Quarterly* 52/4 (1998): 247–68.

Schaff, Philip, editor. *The Creeds of Christendom*. 3 volumes. 1931; Grand Rapids: Baker, 1990.

Schenck, Lewis Bevens. *The Presbyterian Doctrine of Children in the Covenant: An Historical Study of the Significance of Infant Baptism in the Presbyterian Church*. 1940; Phillipsburg, N.J.: P & R, 2003.

Schmemann, Alexander. *Of Water and the Spirit: A Liturgical Study of Baptism*. Crestwood: St. Vladimir's Seminary Press, 1974.

Schillebeeckx, Edward. *Christ the Sacrament of the Encounter with God*. New York: Sheed and Ward, 1963.

Schleiermacher, Friedrich. *On Religion*. Translated by Richard Crouter. Cambridge: Cambridge University Press, 1988.

————— . *The Christian Faith*. London: T & T Clark, 1999.

Schmid, Heinrich. *The Doctrinal Theology of the Evangelical Lutheran Church*. Philadelphia: Lutheran Publication Society, 1899.

Schnackenberg, Rudolf. *Baptism in the Thought of St. Paul*. New York: Herder and Herder, 1964.

Schreiner, Thomas R. *Romans*. Baker Exegetical Commentary on the New Testament. Grand Rapids: Baker, 1998.

Schreiner, Thomas R. and Shawn D. Wright, editors. *Believer's Baptism: Sign of the New Covenant in Christ*. Nashville: Broadman & Holman, 2006.

Scobie, Charles H. H. *John the Baptist: A Portrait Based Upon Biblical and Extra-Biblical Sources*. Minneapolis: Fortress, 1964.

Scott, James M. *Adoption as Sons of God: An Exegetical Investigation into the Background of HUIOTHESIA in the New Testament*. Wissenschaftlische Untersuchungen zum Neuen Testament. Tübingen: Mohr Siebeck, 1992.

Selvaggio, Anthony T., editor. *The Faith Once Delivered: Essays in Honor of Dr. Wayne R. Spear*. Phillipsburg, N.J.: P & R, 2007.

Shaw, Robert. *An Exposition of the Westminster Confession of Faith*. 1845; Fearn: Christian Focus, 1998.

Shedd, W. G. T. *Dogmatic Theology*. 3 volumes. Grand Rapids: Zondervan, 1969.

Smedes, Louis B. *Union with Christ: A Biblical View of the New Life in Jesus Christ*. 1970; Grand Rapids: Eerdmans, 1983.

Smith, Morton. *Commentary on the Book of Church Order of the PCA*. Taylors, S.C.: Southern Presbyterian Press, 2000.

Spener, Philip Jacob. *Pia Desideria*. Translated and edited by Theodore G. Tappert. Eugene, Ore.: Wipf & Stock, 2002.

Spinks, Bryan. *Early and Medieval Rituals and Theologies of Baptism: From the New Testament to the Council of Trent*. Aldershot: Ashgate, 2006.

_____ . *Reformation and Modern Rituals and Theologies of Baptism: From Luther to Contemporary Practices*. Aldershot: Ashgate, 2006.

Stanton, Graham N. et al., editors. *The Holy Spirit and Christian Origins: Essays in Honor of James D. G. Dunn*. Grand Rapids: Eerdmans, 2004.

Steinmetz, David C. *Luther in Context*. Grand Rapids: Baker, 1995.

_____ . *Reformers in the Wings*. 1971; Grand Rapids: Baker, 1981.

_____ . "Scholasticism and Radical Reform: Nominalist Motifs in the Theology of Balthasar Hübmaier." *Mennonite Quarterly Review* 35 (1961): 149–70.

Stephens, W. P. *The Theology of Huldrych Zwingli*. Oxford: Clarendon Press, 1986.

Strawbridge, Gregg, editor. *The Case for Covenantal Infant Baptism*. Phillipsburg, N.J.: P & R, 2003.

Strawn, Brent A. and Nancy R. Bowen, editors. *A God So Near: Essays on Old Testament Theology in Honor of Patrick D. Miller*. Winona: Eisenbrauns, 2003.

Thiselton, Anthony C. *The First Epistle to the Corinthians*. New International Greek Testament Commentary. Grand Rapids: Eerdmans, 2000.

Thompson, J. A. *The Book of Jeremiah*. New International Commentary on the Old Testament. Grand Rapids: Eerdmans, 1980.

Thornwell, J. H. "A Few More Words on the Revised Book of Discipline." *The Southern Presbyterian Review* 13/1 (1861): 1–38.

_____ . *The Collected Writings of James Henley Thornwell*. Volume 3. Edited by John B. Adger and John L. Girardeau. Edinburgh: Banner of Truth, 1986.

Tillich, Paul. *A History of Christian Thought: From Its Hellenistic Origins to Existentialism*. New York: Simon & Schuster, 1968.

_____ . *The Protestant Era*. Chicago: University of Chicago Press, 1948.

_____ . "The Two Types of Philosophy of Religion," in *Theology of Culture*. New York: Oxford University Press, 1959.

Toews, Casey. "Moral Purification in 1 QS." *Bulletin for Biblical Research* 13/1 (2003): 71–96.

Torrance, T. F. et al. *The Biblical Doctrine of Baptism: A Study Document Issued by the Special Commission on Baptism of the Church of Scotland*. Edinburgh: St. Andrew Press, 1960.

Torrance, T. F. *Theology in Reconciliation: Essays Towards Evangelical and Catholic Unity in East and West*. Grand Rapids: Eerdmans, 1975.

Tranvik, Mark D. "Luther on Baptism." *Lutheran Quarterly*. 13/1 (1999): 75–90.

Trigg, Jonathan D. *Baptism in the Theology of Martin Luther*. Leiden: Brill, 2001.

Trueman, Carl R. "Is the Finnish Line a New Beginning? A Critical Assessment of the Reading of Luther Offered by the Helsinki Circle." *Westminster Theological Journal* 65/2 (2003): 231–44.

Turretin, Francis. *Institutes of Elenctic Theology*. 3 volumes. Edited by James T. Dennison. Translated by George Musgrave Giger. Phillipsburg, N.J.: P & R, 1992–97.

Ursinus, Zacharias. *The Commentary of Dr. Zacharias Ursinus on the Heidelberg Catechism*. 1852; Phillipsburg, N.J.: P & R, n.d.

Ussher, James. *A Body of Divinity: Being the Sum and Substance of the Christian Religion*. Edited by Michael Navarr. 1648; Birmingham, Ala.: Solid Ground Books, 2007.

_____ . *The Whole Works of the Most Rev. James Ussher*. 17 volumes. Dublin: Hodges and Smith, 1847–64.

VanDrunen, David. "Iconoclasm, Incarnation, and Eschatology: Toward a Catholic Understanding of the Reformed Doctrine of the 'Second'

Commandment." *International Journal of Systematic Theology* 6 (2004): 130–47.

VanGemeren, Willem A., editor. *New International Dictionary of Old Testament Theology and Exegesis.* 5 volumes. Grand Rapids: Zondervan, 1997.

Van Mastricht, Peter. *A Treatise on Regeneration.* Edited by Brandon Withrow. 1699; Morgan, Pa.: Soli Deo Gloria, 2002.

Vermes, Geza. "Baptism and Jewish Exegesis: New Light from Ancient Sources." *New Testament Studies* 4 (1958): 308–19.

Von Balthasar, Hans Urs. *Theo-Drama: Theological Dramatic Theory.* 5 volumes. San Francisco: Ignatius Press, 1988.

Von Rad, Gerhard. *Genesis.* 1961; Philadelphia: Westminster, 1972.

_____ . *Old Testament Theology.* 2 volumes. Translated by D. M. G. Stalker. Louisville: Westminster John Knox, 1960–65.

Vos, Geerhardus. *Biblical Theology.* 1948; Edinburgh: Banner of Truth, 1996.

_____ . *Redemptive History and Biblical Interpretation: The Shorter Writings of Geerhardus Vos.* Edited by Richard B. Gaffin, Jr. Phillipsburg, N.J.: P & R, 1980.

_____ . *The Eschatology of the Old Testament.* Phillipsburg, N.J.: P & R, 2001.

_____ . *The Pauline Eschatology.* 1930; Phillipsburg, N.J.: P & R, 1994.

_____ . *The Teaching of the Epistle to the Hebrews.* Eugene, Ore.: Wipf & Stock, 1998.

Vos, Johannes G. *The Westminster Larger Catechism: A Commentary.* Edited by G. I. Williamson. Phillipsburg, N.J.: P & R, 2002.

Wainwright, Geoffrey. *Eucharist and Eschatology.* Akron, Ohio: OSL Publications, 2002.

Waldron, Samuel E. *1689 Baptist Confession of Faith: A Modern Exposition.* 1989; Darlington: Evangelical Press, 2005.

Waldron, Samuel E. and Richard C. Barcellos. *A Reformed Baptist Manifesto: The Covenant Constitution of the Church.* Palmdale: Reformed Baptist Academic Press, 2004.

Wallace, Ronald S. *Calvin's Doctrine of the Word and Sacrament.* Edinburgh: Scottish Academic Press, 1995.

Waltke, Bruce K. *Genesis: A Commentary*. Grand Rapids: Zondervan, 2001.

Warfield, B. B. *The Plan of Salvation*. 1915; Eugene, Ore.: Wipf & Stock, n.d.

_____ . *The Works of Benjamin B. Warfield*. 10 volumes. Edited by Ethelbert D. Warfield, et al. 1931; Grand Rapids: Baer, 1981.

Waters, Guy Prentiss. *The Federal Vision and Covenant Theology: A Comparative Analysis*. Phillipsburg, N.J.: P & R, 2006.

Watson, Francis. *Text and Truth: Redefining Biblical Theology*. Grand Rapids: Eerdmans, 1997.

Watts, John D. W. *Isaiah*. 2 volumes. Word Biblical Commentary. Dallas: Word, 1987.

Watts, Rikki E. *Isaiah's New Exodus in Mark*. Grand Rapids: Baker, 1997.

Webster, John, editor. *The Cambridge Companion to Karl Barth*. Cambridge: Cambridge University Press, 2000.

Weber, Otto. *Foundations of Dogmatics*. 2 volumes. Grand Rapids: Eerdmans, 1981.

Wendel, François. *Calvin: Origins and Development of His Religious Thought*. 1950; Grand Rapids: Baker, 1997.

Wengert, Timothy J., editor. *Harvesting Martin Luther's Reflections on Theology, Ethics, and the Church*. Grand Rapids: Eerdmans, 2004.

Wenham, Gordon. *Genesis*. 2 volumes. Word Biblical Commentary. Dallas: Word, 1987.

_____ . *Numbers*. Tyndale Old Testament Commentary. Downers Grove, Ill.: InterVarsity, 1981.

Westminster Confession of Faith. 1646; Glasgow: Free Presbyterian Publications, 1995.

Wilder, William N. *Echoes of the Exodus Narrative in the Context and Background of Galatians 5:18*. Studies in Biblical Literature. Number 23. New York: Peter Lang, 2001.

Wilkins, Steve and Duane Garner, editors. *The Federal Vision*. Monroe, La.: Athanasius Press, 2004.

Williams, George Hunston, editor. *Spiritual and Anabaptist Writers*. Library of Christian Classics. Volume 25. Philadelphia: Westminster, 1957.

Wilson, Douglas. *"Reformed" Is Not Enough: Recovering the Objectivity of the Covenant.* Moscow, Idaho: Canon, 2002.

Witsius, Herman. *Economy of the Covenants Between God and Man: Comprehending a Complete Body of Divinity.* 2 volumes. Translated by William Crookshank. 1822; Phillipsburg, N.J.: P & R, 1990.

Woudstra, Marten H. *The Book of Joshua.* New International Commentary on the Old Testament. Grand Rapids: Eerdmans, 1981.

Wright, David F. *What Has Infant Baptism Done to Baptism? An Enquiry at the End of Christendom.* Milton Keynes: Paternoster, 2005.

Wright, N. T. *Colossians & Philemon.* Tyndale New Testament Commentary. Grand Rapids: Eerdmans, 1986.

_____ . *Romans.* New Interpreter's Bible. Volume 10. Nashville: Abingdon: 2002.

_____ . *The Climax of the Covenant: Christ and the Law in Pauline Theology.* Minneapolis: Fortress, 1991.

_____ . *The New Testament and the People of God.* Philadelphia: Fortress, 1992.

Young, E. J. *The Book of Isaiah.* 3 volumes. New International Commentary on the Old Testament. 1972; Grand Rapids: Eerdmans, 1997.

_____ . *The God-Breathed Scripture.* Willow Grove, Pa.: Committee for the Historian, 2007.

Ziefle, Helmut W. *Dictionary of Modern Theological German.* Second Edition. Grand Rapids, Baker, 1992.

Zimmerli, Walthre. *Ezekiel.* 2 volumes. Philadelphia: Fortress, 1983.

Zwingli, Huldrych. *Huldrych Zwingli: Writings.* 2 volumes. Edited by E. J. Furcha and H. Wayne Pipkin. Allison Park, Pa.: Pickwick, 1984.

Scripture Index

Subject Index

infused grace, 39, 139, 267–68, 289
initiation, in covenant community, 314–21
inner baptism, 67–69, 70–71, 72, 171
institution, of baptism, 308–10
instrument, baptism as, 122–26, 130, 131
internal act, of baptism, 160
invalid baptism, 389
invisible church, 114, 318, 321
invisible grace, 130, 174, 187, 276, 297
inward washing, 98, 101, 110
Irish Articles, 105, 120–27, 131–32, 155, 388n69
Isaac, 90, 359
Isaiah, 208, 218, 237
Ishmael, 359
Israel
　cleansing of, 219
　as firstborn son, 212, 219
　restoration of, 203, 208, 237

Jacob, 359
Jenson, Robert, 315
Jeremias, Joachim, 171, 354
Jesus Christ
　baptism of, 31, 216–18, 219, 308–309, 313–14
　burial and resurrection of, 145, 224, 240–42, 328
　as covenant mediator, 314–15
　crucifixion as baptism, 229, 242–44, 249, 276, 288, 332, 396
　crucifixion as circumcision, 237, 239–41, 246, 249, 338
　as new Israel, 340–41
　as primal sacrament, 179
　reception and outpouring of Spirit, 222–23, 226, 227
　resurrection of, 328
　as substance of sacraments, 82, 141

wilderness trial of, 218
Jewett, Paul, ix
Jewish proselyte baptism, 199–200
Joel, 221, 313
John the Baptist, 7–8, 92, 168, 200–202, 213–16, 219, 220–21, 244, 249, 253, 308–10
Jonah, immersion in waters of sea, 332
Jordan River, 201, 213–14
Joseph, 270
Josephus, 200, 211–12, 226
Joshua, 346
judgment, 144–45, 252–53, 401. *See also* covenant judgment; eschatological judgment
justification, 109, 119, 132, 188
　Calvin on, 90
　Denck on, 68
　Roman Catholic church on, 34, 36, 38, 379
　Zwingli on, 60–61
Justin Martyr, 5, 17–18, 20, 24, 25, 354

Kant, Immanuel, 3, 157, 286
Kärkkäinen, Veli-Matti, 285n62
kingdom of God, 310–11
Kline, Meredith, 209, 236, 244, 246, 341, 353–54
Korah, and household, 346
Kuyper, Abraham, 359n62

LaRondelle, Hans, 340–41
last Adam, 226, 249, 257, 260, 272, 299–300, 301, 310, 314, 328, 364, 365
law and grace, 272
Leiden Synopsis, 335
leprosy, 202
Levitical washings, 202–203
liberation, baptism as, 185
Lightfoot, John, 138

About the Author

Dr. J. V. Fesko is a minister in the Orthodox Presbyterian Church, and is also academic dean and associate professor of systematic theology at Westminster Seminary California. He was ordained as a church planter in 1998 and was installed as a pastor in 2003, thus serving in pastoral ministry for over ten years. He has also taught systematic theology for Reformed Theological Seminary for over eight years as a part-time professor. His present research interests include the integration of biblical and systematic theology, soteriology, ecclesiology, and sixteenth- and seventeenth-century Reformed theology. Dr. Fesko and his wife, Anneke, have two sons and reside in Escondido.